President and Publisher
Ira Shapiro

Vice President Sales and Marketing
Marie-Christine Matter

Vice President Operations
Wendl Kornfeld

Production Director
Karen M. Bochow

Marketing Director
Ann Middlebrook

Marketing
Promotion/New Projects Manager
Stephanie Whitney
Marketing Coordinator
Lisa Wilker
Book Sales Coordinator
Cynthia Breneman

Advertising Sales
Sales Representatives:
John Bergstrom
Kate Hoffman
Ellen Kasemeier
Barbara Preminger
Joe Safferson
Wendy Saunders
Dave Tabler

Administration
Controller
Joel Kopel
Executive Assistant
Connie Grunwald
Accounting Assistant
Susan Su
Administrative Assistant
Paula Cohen

Published by:
American Showcase, Inc.
724 Fifth Avenue, 10th Floor
New York, New York 10019-4182
(212) 245-0981
FAX: (212) 265-2247
Telex: 880356 AMSHOW P

American Photography
Showcase 13
ISBN 0-931144-63-9
ISSN 0278-8314

Cover Credits:
Front Cover Photography:
Franco Accornero
Lead Page Photography:
Stephen Green-Armytage

Production
Production Manager
Chuck Rosenow
Production Administrators:
Diane Cerafici
Tracy Russek
Traffic Coordinator
Stokes Hagg

Grey Pages
Distribution Manager
Scott Holden

Special Thanks to:
Ron Canagata
Amie Cooper
Julia Curry
Michael Joseph
Kyla Kanz
Fiona L'Estrange
Tina McKenna
Annie Newhall
Melissa Roldan
Joe Scala
Carol Schultz
Adam Seifer
Courtney Shapiro
Sandra Sierra
John Towey
Henrietta Valor

U.S. Book Trade Distribution:
Watson-Guptill Publications
1515 Broadway
New York, New York 10036
(212) 764-7300

For Sales outside the U.S.:
Rotovision S.A.
9 Route Suisse
1295 Mies, Switzerland
Telephone 022-735-3055
Telex 419246 ROVI

Book and Package Design:
Michael Peters Group

Mechanical Production:
American Showcase, Inc.

Typesetting:
**Ultra Typographic
Services, Inc.**

Color Separation, Printing and
Binding:
Dai Nippon Printing Co., LTD.

**We're especially grateful to
Julia Martin Morris
for her ten years of
contribution to the growth
and success of
American Showcase.**

AMERICAN SHOWCASE

C O N T E N T S

TR
690.4
.A4
1990
no.13

V I E W P O I N T S

G R A P H I C   A R T S
O R G A N I Z A T I O N S

I N D E X

G R E Y   P A G E S

M O S H E
KATVAN
4 0   W   1 7   S T
NEW YORK CITY
212 • 242 • 4895

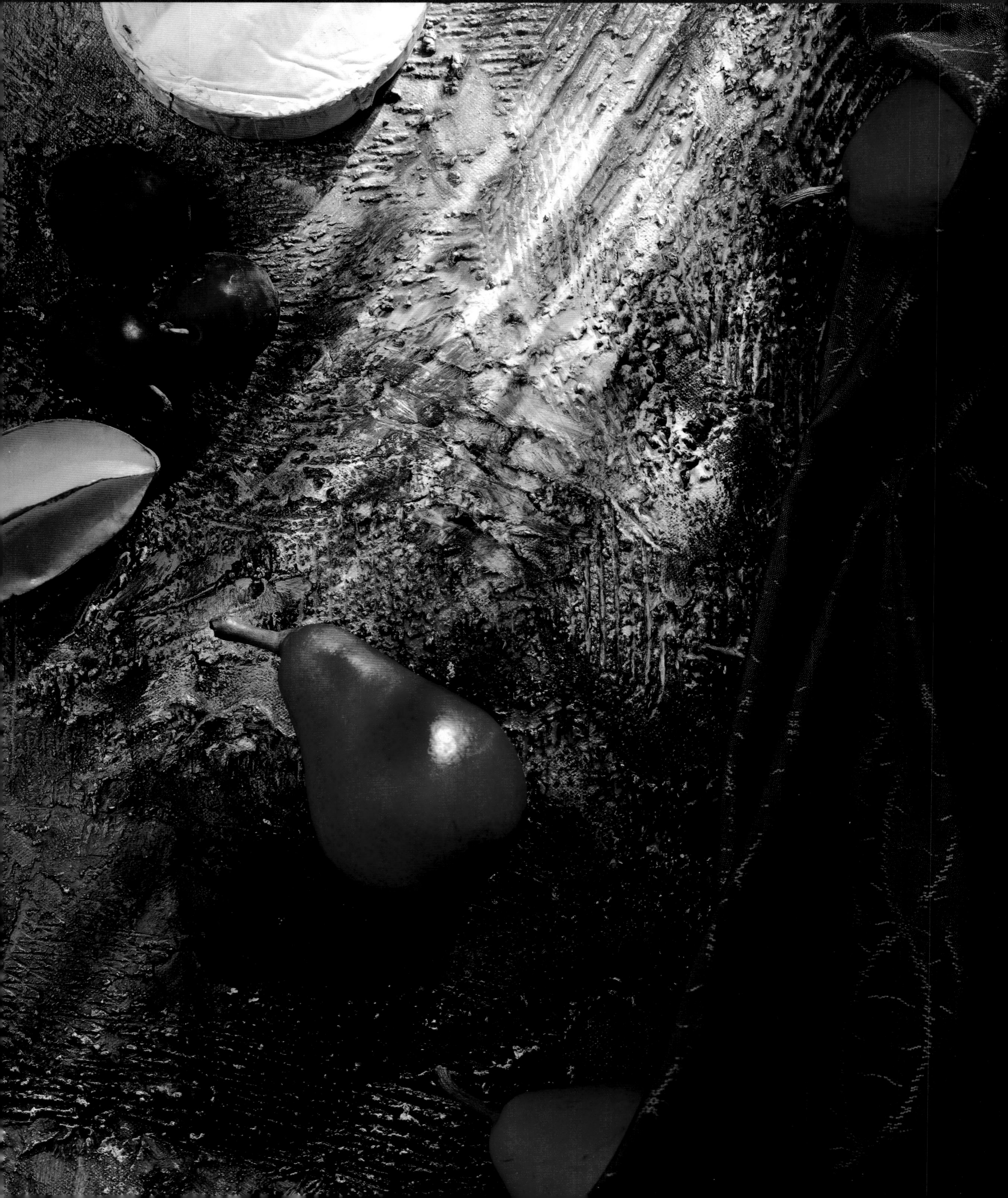

245 West 29TH Street, New York, NY 10001

MORELLO

Joe Morello
Photography
40 West 28 St.
NYC 10001
212/684/2340

INTRODUCING
THE TECHNICS CAR CD PLAYER.
FOR THOSE DRIVEN BY PERFECTION.

Technics creates a programmable car CD player with a built-in digital AM/FM stereo tuner.

Now enjoy the musical perfection of the compact disc from behind the wheel. It's Technics combination compact disc player and stereo tuner—CQ-DP5.

First, the CD player. With random access programming. To play any selection in any order. With a fine-focus single-beam laser system (FF1). So strong and accurate it "reads" digital information through most fingerprints, scratches and even imperfections in the disc itself. With a shock-absorbing, 4-wire suspension system to help ensure a flawless musical performance no matter where the road may lead.

Then, unlike some car CD players, Technics adds a built-in, high-performance AM/FM stereo tuner. With seek and scan. 12 FM and 6 AM presets for instant recall. And more.

If you're driven by perfection, make your next stop Technics.

Technics
The science of sound

If you're moving,
here are some thoughts on packing.

Sad is the salad never seasoned with Bertol

Pitiful is the pasta never prepared with Bertolli.

JOHN
PAUL
ENDRESS
Incorporated

254 West 31st Street
New York City, New York 10001
(212) 736-7800

Represented by
BRUCE LEVIN (212) 832-4053

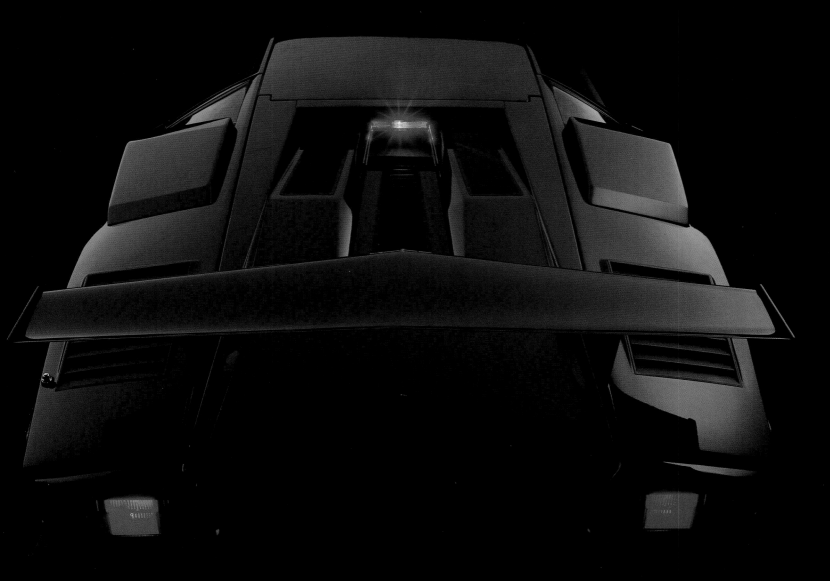

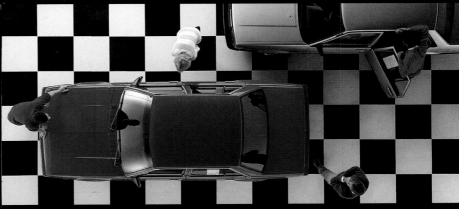

JOHN PAUL ENDRESS
Incorporated

254 West 31st Street
New York City, New York 10001
(212) 736-7800

Represented by
BRUCE LEVIN (212) 832-4053

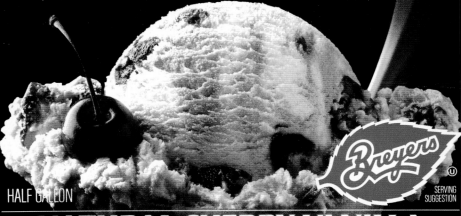
Pioppo

NYC

FARBERWARE

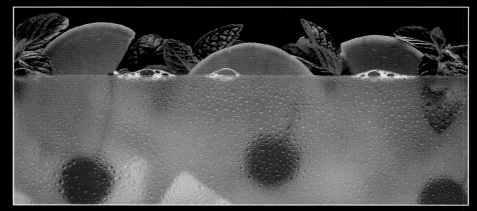

STAN WAN
PHOTOGRAPHY

310 EAST 46th STREET • NEW YORK, NY 10017

212 674 0068

FRANCO

FRANCO
ACCORNERO
6 2 0
BROADWAY
NEW YORK,
N.Y. 10012

B O Y D · H A G E N

P H O T O G R A P H Y

448 WEST 37th STREET NEW YORK, NY 10018 212 244-2436

24

Clients Include:
Carbone Smolan Associates, J. Walter Thompson,
The New York Times, Munsingwear, Bell Laboratories,
HDM Advertising, TIME, Fortune, Rolling Stone,
Honeywell, BBD&O, N.W. Ayer, Shiseido Cosmetics,
Alternatives, 3M, Mazda, AT&T, Citicorp, L'Oréal,
Sloan Kettering Institute, Guthrie Theater,
Columbia Business School, Control Data,
New York Magazine, Doyle Dane Bernbach

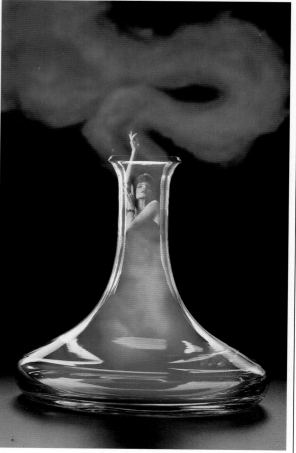

MYRON JAY
Dorf
ILLUSIONIST

Don't limit your imagination.

Illusions by Myron Jay Dorf let you express the inexpressible.

**205 West 19th Street
New York, New York 10011
(212) 255-2020**

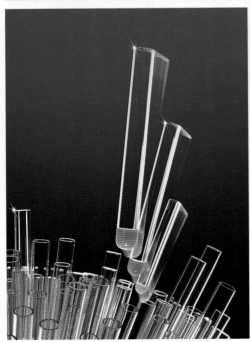

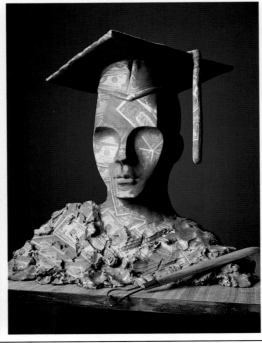

J. Paul Simeone Photographer

116 West Baltimore Pike
Media, Pennsylvania 19063
215-566-7197

FAX 1-215-566-0179

Sample portfolio sent upon request.

J. PAUL SIMEONE
PHOTOGRAPHER
215·566·7197

J. Paul Simeone Photographer

116 West Baltimore Pike
Media, Pennsylvania 19063
215-566-7197

FAX 1-215-566-0179

Sample portfolio sent upon request.

J. PAUL SIMEONE
PHOTOGRAPHER
215 · 566 · 7197

TULLY
roger

Clients include:

Bristol-Myers

First Boston

American Express Co.

Continental Insurance

Hitachi, N.A.

New York Telephone

Roger Tully, Inc.
344 West 38th Street
New York, NY 10018
212.947.3961
FAX 212.643.0976

Advertising &
Corporate Photography
Stock Available

Union Camp

Merrill Lynch

Oppenheimer

Tandum Computers

American Airlines

Grand Marnier

WOLFGANG PHOTOGRAPHER FREITHOF

38 Greene Street New York, NY (212) 996-6380

WOLFGANG FREITHOF

PHOTOGRAPHER

38 Greene Street   New York, NY   (212) 996-6380

YOU CAN
THIS

Vietnamese orphans wait for help. Photograph taken at North Fort Lewis, Washington, in 1975 by Guy Powers.   Portfolios upon request.

CHANGE PICTURE.

In Vietnam one out of two orphaned children die from lack of food, love and knowledge. The Vietnamese people are desperately seeking help — not for themselves, but for their children.

I adopted the last child out of Vietnam from the 1975 airlift in addition to three Korean children. Now my oldest son Michael and I are going to Vietnam to shoot stills and make a documentary film to raise money for Vietnamese children because hospitals, child care, an adoption program, medical supplies, food, clothing, equipment and education are in such desparate need.

I adopted Michael in 1972 when he was 4½ years old. Now at age 21, he has taken on the task of helping other children in need. In celebration of this, and to continue my own help, I will donate 10% of all my photo fees generated from this ad to Love The Children, an organization dedicated to helping these Vietnamese children.

Sincerely,

Guy Powers

Guy Powers

RICK YOUNG

212-929-5701   27 WEST 20TH STREET, NY 10011   FAX 929-5303

Partial List of Clients

Baccarat
Cerelene
De Francesco & DeLuca, Inc.
Burlington Industries
Fortunoff
General Foods
Colgate-Palmolive
H.J. Delaney Adv.
Dorritie & Lyons, Inc.
Laurence, Charles & Free, Inc.
Twentieth Century Fox
Dollar Dry Dock
Amtoy
American Greeting Company
Hasbro
John Wannamaker
Arthur Brown & Bros., Inc.
Simon & Schuster
Warren Kramer Adv.
Jean Patou
Johnson & Johnson
Napier Jewelery
Service Merchandise
Coopers & Lybrand
Triton Advertising
Bloomingdales
Peters Chocolate
Columbia Diamonds

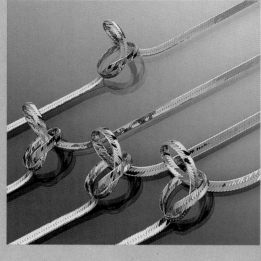

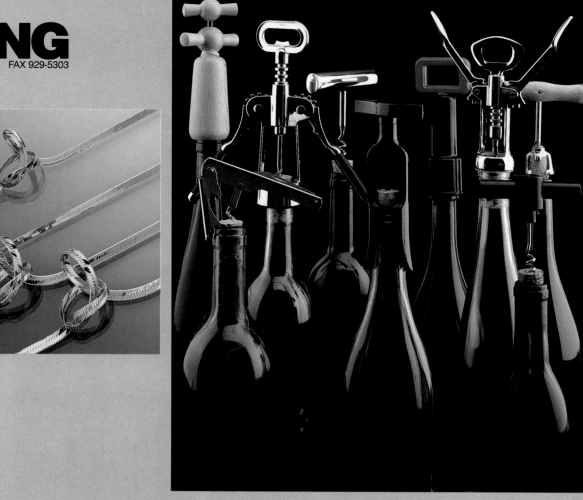

RICK YOUNG

212-929-5701   27 WEST 20TH STREET, NY 10011   FAX 929-5303

Photo for Design Partners Inc.

Creative Director - George McCathern

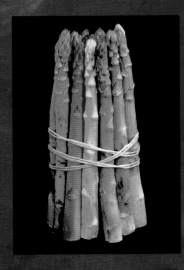

Michael Furman

115 Arch Street
Philadelphia, Pennsylvania 19106
(215) 925-4233
Fax (215) 925-6108

Represented by Victoria Satterthwaite

Michael Furman
115 Arch Street
Philadelphia, Pennsylvania 19106
(215) 925-4233
Fax (215) 925-6108

Represented by Victoria Satterthwaite

FORD/O&M

BARROW

SCOTT BARROW. Represented by RANDY COLE. 914-265-4242

NORFOLK SOUTHERN RAILROAD/JWT

JEEP EAGLE/CHRYSLER

When you want your work to have a strong individual style.

LINDA BOHM

L.D. BOHM STUDIOS, INC.
7 PARK STREET
MONTCLAIR, NJ 07042

201 746-3434
212 349-5650
FAX 201 746-4905

See Black Book '90 for more.

L.D. BOHM STUDIOS, INC.
7 PARK STREET
MONTCLAIR, NJ 07042

201 746-3434
212 349-5650
FAX 201 746-4905

Linda Bohm

43

MORT ENGEL STUDIO INC. 260 5TH AVENUE • NEW YORK, N.Y. 10001 • 212 889-8466

LASZLO STERN PHOTOGRAPHY
CLOSEUP · MACRO · MICRO

57 west 19th · new york · 10011 · 212 · 691 · 7696

SHONNA VALESKA

140 EAST 28 STREET NEW YORK NY 10016 (212) 683-4448

BAKER VAIL PHOTOGRAPHY INC.

111 WEST 24TH STREET · NYC

(212) 463-7560

JOSEPH
BERGER

121 MADISON AVE N.Y. 10016
212 685 7191

CONTACT: NANCY SLOME
212 685 8185

FELLERMAN

STAN FELLERMAN 152 WEST 25TH STREET, NEW YORK, NY 10001 **(212)-243-0027**

ROBERT GRANT
P H O T O G R A P H Y

(212) 925 1121
62 GREENE STREET
NEW YORK, N.Y. 10012

FAX 431 5280

AGENT
ELLEN CULLOM
(212) 777 1749

SEE ALSO
AMERICAN SHOWCASE
VOLUME 11–PAGE 99
VOLUME 12–PAGE 47

JIM DOUGLASS
PHOTOGROUP, INC.
5161 RIVER ROAD, 2A
WASHINGTON, DC 20816
TEL 301.652.1303

Would you trust your car to a guy who's been through 19 Volvos, 4 Cadillacs, 3 Mercedes, and 26 rent-a-cars in just one year?

One of Europe's most dependable cars only lasts an average of six months.

At Hertz, we're always replacing our cars with new ones. In fact, we replace them so often, the average age of a Hertz car in Europe is less than six months.

That's why when you rent with Hertz Affordable Europe, you can be sure that we've done everything we can to give you a good car.

You can also be certain that we've done all we can to give you a dependable one. Because before we rent one of our cars, it goes through 19 checkpoints for safety and comfort. If it fails even one, it's not rented.

Of course, when you rent from us, you also get to take advantage of all the special services that make Hertz Affordable Europe such a great value for vacation travelers. Like unlimited mileage and our 24-hour Emergency Road Service.

Plus, we have over 1300 locations throughout Europe, each with an English-speaking staff.

So call your travel agent or Hertz at 1-800-654-3001. Because at Hertz, we don't just give you a car to drive. We give you a car to trust.

*REG. U.S. PAT. OFF © HERTZ SYSTEM INC. 1989

Hertz rents Fords and other fine cars.

Hertz

Affordable Europe

©Kevin Gregory

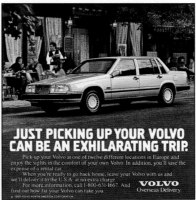

JUST PICKING UP YOUR VOLVO CAN BE AN EXHILARATING TRIP.

Pick up your Volvo at one of twelve different locations in Europe and enjoy the sights in the comfort of your own Volvo. In addition, you'll save the expense of a rental car.

When you're ready to go back home, leave your Volvo with us and we'll deliver it to the U.S.A. at no extra charge.

For more information, call 1-800-631-1667. And find out how far your Volvo can take you.

© 1989 VOLVO NORTH AMERICA CORPORATION

VOLVO
Overseas Delivery

ENJOY THE FRUITS OF YOUR LABOR LONGER.

The Volvo 760

The Volvo 760 is that rare automobile that not only gives you the instant satisfaction of driving one of the finest luxury cars now being built. But also the long-term satisfaction of knowing that, like all Volvos, it will continue to reward you long into the future.

And considering all the amenities the 760 has to offer, that's comforting news.

From its Multi-link independent rear suspension and anti-lock braking to its automatic climate control and

six-speaker stereo system, the 760 is designed to give you a most refined ride.

Better still, the 760 is priced considerably less than many comparable European sedans. Which means it's the ideal car for those who have both an appreciation for the finer things in life. As well as an appreciation for what the finer things in life cost.

So spend more time enjoying the benefits of your success. Spend it in the Volvo 760.

VOLVO
A car you can believe in.

SEE YOUR DEALER TO BUY OR LEASE THE VOLVO 760 TODAY.

Although your vacation time is limited, your mileage isn't.

Starting September 1, get great low rates and unlimited mileage on all Affordable and Super Affordable Weekly rates.

When you plan your Fall vacation, call Hertz and reduce your traveling expenses. Just rent a car at these low weekly rates and the mileage is unlimited.

And we'll guarantee availability of the Aerostar Mini-Van through December 31 if you guarantee the reservation with a major credit card.

Call your travel agent or Hertz at 1-800-654-3031.

For your information. These rates are available at participating locations and may not be available at all places at all times. Be sure that your reservations are made 1 day in advance for Escorts and 3 days in advance for Lincolns and Mini-Vans. If your Aerostar Mini-Van reservation is cancelled less than 24 hours before the rental date, or if the vehicle is not picked up on the rental date, a cancellation fee of $50 will be charged to your credit card. Our minimum rental age is 25 years old. You must keep the car for 5 days including a Saturday night, except in Hawaii. Your car must be returned to the renting location. All cars are subject to availability. Taxes and optional items extra.

Escort or similar size subcompact	
Florida	$89 a week
Reno Denver Salt Lake City Phoenix Hawaii single island rate	$99 a week
San Francisco Los Angeles Las Vegas	$119 a week

Rates start September 1. Limited availability. Optional LDW $10.95 a day or less, $8.95 a day in California.

Aerostar Mini-Van Guarantee Program	
Florida subject to availability	$209 a week
Other participating locations	$229 a week

Rates start September 1. Limited availability. Optional LDW $12.95 a day or less.

Lincoln Continental or Town Car	
Florida Denver Phoenix	$229 a week
Other participating locations	$259 a week

Rates start September 1. Limited availability. Optional LDW $12.95 a day or less.

Hertz rents Fords and other fine cars.

Hertz

Kevin Gregory
237 W. 26th St., NY, NY 10001
(212) 807-9859

■

Contact
Alison Korman
(212) 633-8407

53

See great plays with the American Express Card.

Eggstraordinary!

LORENZ FERICH

516 East
78 Street
(Suite 2D)
New York
NY 10021
(212) 517 • 6838

**PHOTOGRAPHER /
DIRECTOR**
specializing in
"night-life"
photography
with a unique
point of view

stock photography
available

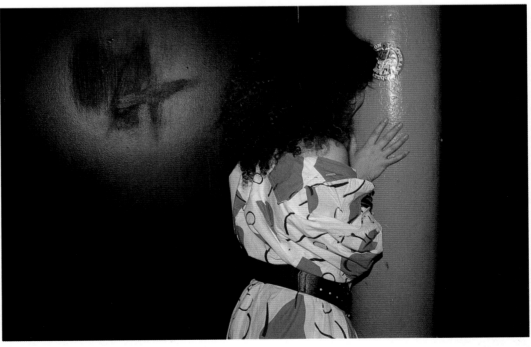

BILL FREDERICKS

ANDY WASHNIK STUDIO

145 WOODLAND AVE · WESTWOOD, NJ 07675
201·664·0441

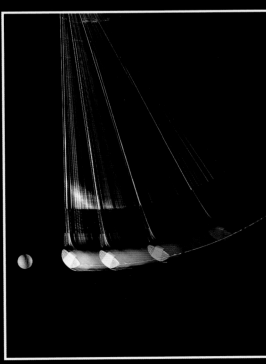

Andris · Hendrickson
Photography
314 North 13th Street
Philadelphia, Pennsylvania 19107
(215) 925-2630
(215) 925-2653 FAX

Andris · Hendrickson
Photography
314 North 13th Street
Philadelphia, Pennsylvania 19107
(215) 925-2630
(215) 925-2653 FAX

Jerry Anton
(212) 633-9880
FAX: (212) 691-1685
In the Midwest:
(312) 606-0633

Representing:
Aaron Rezny
119 West 23rd Street
New York, New York 10011
(212) 691-1894

REZNY

Jerry Anton
(212) 633-9880
FAX: (212) 691-1685
In the Midwest:
(312) 606-0633

Representing:
Chris Vincent
119 West 23rd Street
New York, New York 10011
(212) 691-1894
In association with Aaron Rezny, Inc.

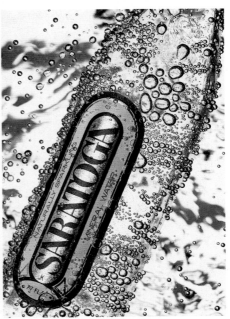

VINCENT

Bill Ashe
534 West 35th Street
New York, New York 10001
(212) 695-6473
FAX: (212) 695-9286

My specialties are automobiles, still life, large productions, advertising, corporate and editorial which I photograph on location and in my mid-town studio. The studio facility is 6000 sq. feet, column free and accommodates trucks and cars through a 16' x 22' door.

Fifteen years of award winning photography for clients like Bulgari, Toshiba, Bristol Myers, Shell Oil, G.E., American Express, Schering, DeBeers, Oscar de la Renta, N.Y. Times, Times Mirror, Sony, Audio Magazine, General Motors, Ford, Car Stereo Review, Purina Mills, Mitsui, American Cyanamid, Peerless, CBS, Newsweek, Hearst Corp., Range Rover of N.A., Dept. of Defense...

© 1990 Bill Ashe

Bill Ashe
534 West 35th Street
New York, New York 10001
(212) 695-6473

Photography in my studio and on location.

Quality stock photographs available.

WHERE ADVERTISING COMES FROM

This is probably going to sound familiar.

The account team and the client hammer out a strategy.

The account team gives the strategy to creative to do creative.

They give it to media to do a media plan.

And later they give it to research to test it and see if it worked. (I told you it was going to sound familiar).

That's how most advertising agencies work. And it works pretty well.

So why change it?

At Della Femina, McNamee WCRS, Boston I think we've stumbled onto something that works better. It's called "The Brand Team" and it's pretty much based on the premise that if two heads are better than one, then eight heads are better than two.

No, it's not a committee, it's a team. And it works like this:

For every major project people are assigned from creative, account services, media, research and production (The Brand Team). Everyone is involved right from the beginning. Everyone is thinking about the project from their own discipline. And believe me, a good idea (not necessarily an ad but an advertising idea) is as likely to come from media as it is from creative or production. After a few meetings there's a wonderful camaraderie among the players. Everyone's on track. Everyone feels ownership. And I think the creative product benefits from it.

Production is on line ahead of time thinking about ways of getting it done. The marketing people are setting up the client as to where we're going so nobody's blindsided. And let's face it, when you run in a pack, some of you are going to get through. The Brand Team will help sell creative.

The advertising agency business brings together the most diverse groups of people I know. And if you can get everyone talking the same line, it's very powerful.

The creative product is better for it and with all that support you've definitely got a better chance of selling it.

Ron Lawner
Creative Director
Della Femina, McNamee WCRS, Inc.
Boston, Massachusetts

Rick Barrick
12 East 18th Street
New York, New York 10003
(212) 741-2304

Specializing in problem solving in photoillustration...for clients like Iberian Airlines, Mid-Lantic Bank, Equitable Life

Insurance, Citibank, Young & Rubicam, McGraw-Hill, Murdoch Publications, Fairchild Publications, Great Scot

Advertising, William Esty, MasterCard, AT&T, American Express and more.

**Wendy Barrows
Photography**
205 East 22 Street
New York, New York 10010
(212) 685-0799

See my work in American Showcase
vols. 8-13.

MOHAN MURJANI, CHAIRMAN, MURJANI INTERNATIONAL

**Wendy Barrows
Photography**
205 East 22 Street
New York, New York 10010
(212) 685-0799

Lane Berkwit
262 Fifth Avenue
New York, New York 10001
(212) 889-5911

Represented By:
John Henry
(212) 686-6883

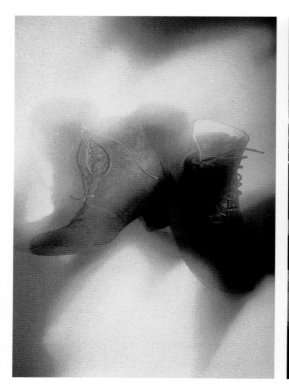

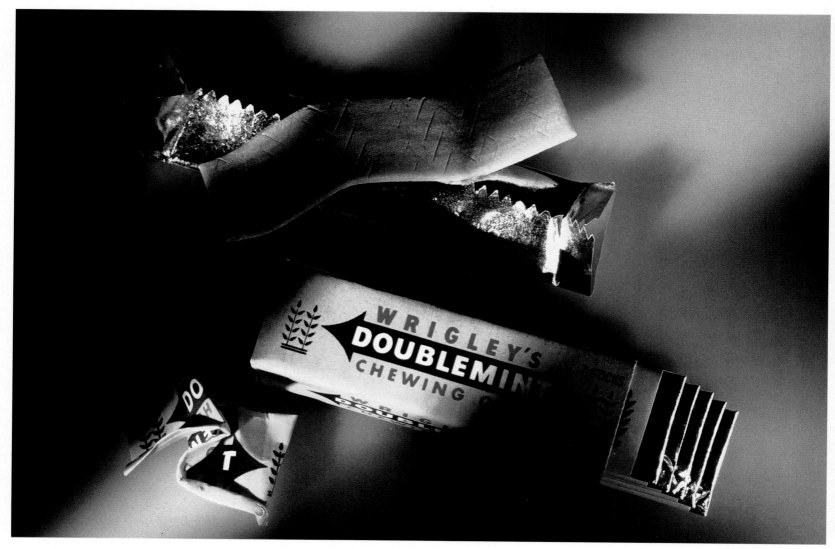

Bill Bernstein
38 Greene Street
New York, New York 10013
(212) 334-3982

Advertising, Entertainment, Music, Editorial.

Portfolio available upon request. Stock photography available through Outline.

WARREN WOLF

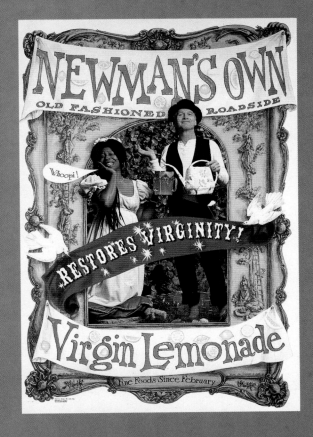

BERNARD TSCHUMI

SPALDING GRAY

DAVID COPPERFIELD

Barry Blackman
150 Fifth Avenue
Suite #220
New York, New York 10011-4311
(212) 627-9777

Special effects photography and computerized image manipulation.

An Art Director's dream. A photographic image so perfect, it doesn't need retouching; and so unique, it had to be created on a computer.
Barry Blackman is the only photographer in the country to combine his talent and experience with the cutting edge capabilities of the Super

High Resolution Creator 2600 computer. Barry Blackman - you come in with an idea and go out with a finished transparency.

After all, he wrote the book on special effects.

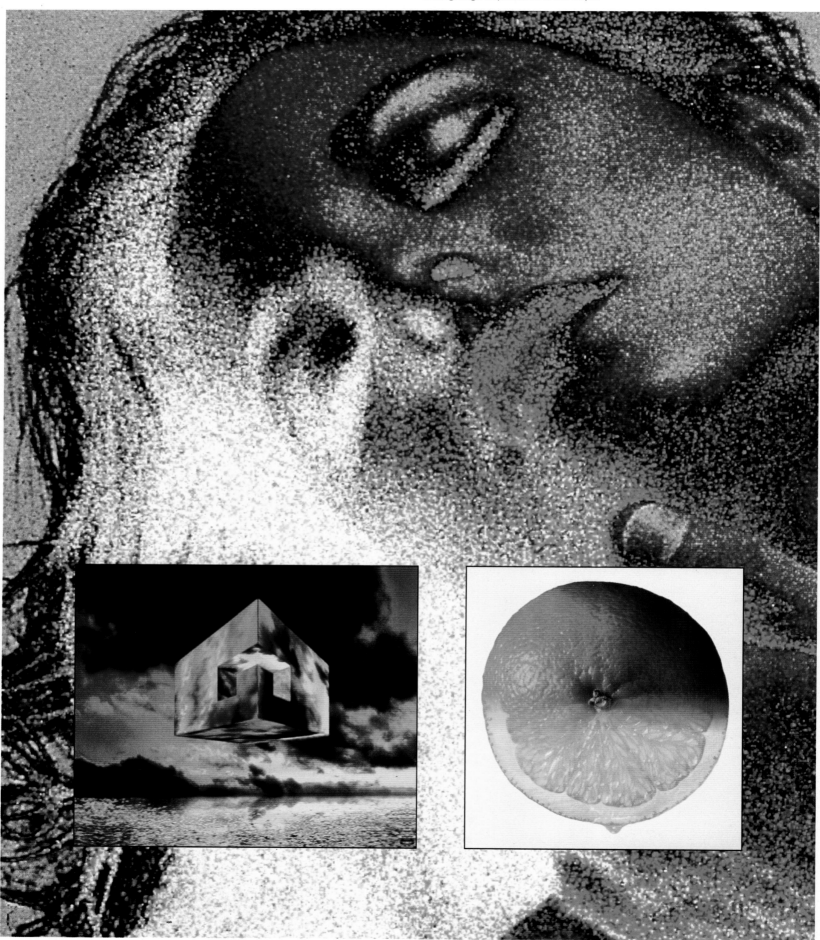

Barry Blackman
150 Fifth Avenue
Suite #220
New York, New York 10011-4311
(212) 627-9777

Clients Include:
AT&T
IBM
Polaroid
Xerox
AMF Voit
TWA
Federal Express

Sony
Colgate
General Electric
Citibank
Reynolds Metals
Pepsi Cola
Marriott, Hilton, Hyatt Hotels
Continental Telephone

Fairchild Industries
London Fog
Owens Corning
Amtrak
Export A & Bright Cigarettes
Life, Newsweek & Parents Magazines
National Geographic, Smithsonian
Avon, Dell & Bantam Books

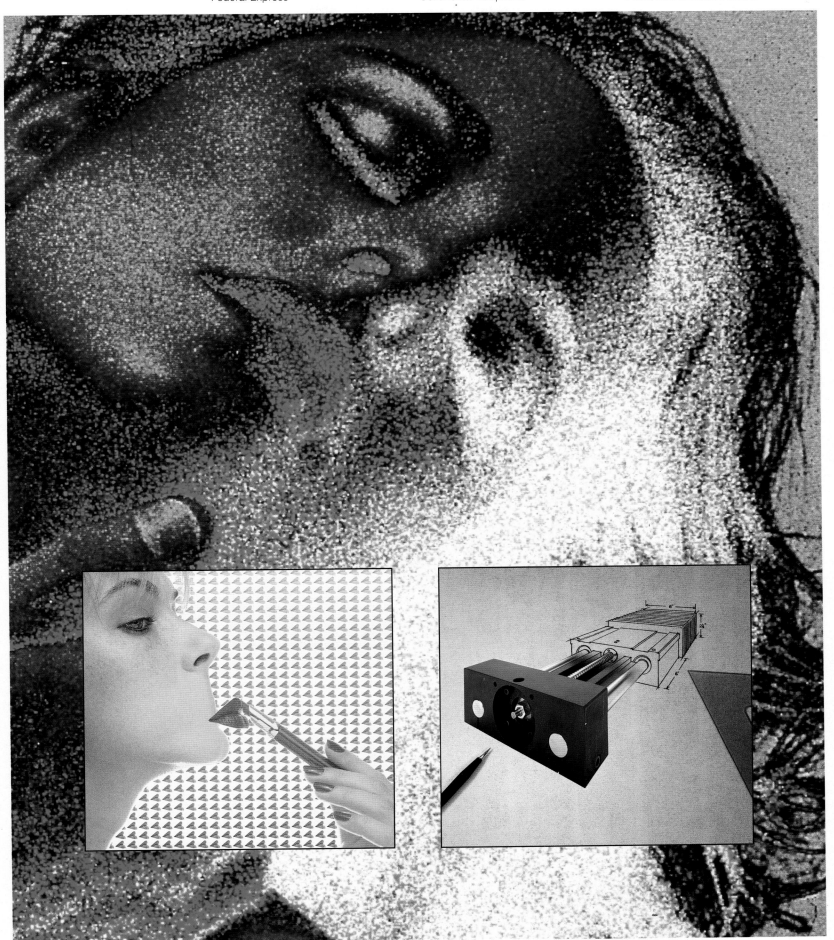

Joseph Boisseau
3250 Hering Avenue, Suite 1
North Bronx, New York 10469
(212) 519-8672
(212) 359-2509

Architectural Models, Interiors and
Exteriors. Advertising Brochures and
Communications, Executive Portraiture
and Annual Reports. International
Location Assignments Excepted.

Also view work in American Showcase
vol. 12, page 59.
Portfolio available, please make request
on Company Letterhead.

Bruno Photography, Inc.   Represented by Holly Kaplan
43 Crosby Street
New York, New York 10012
(212) 925-2929

J&B on the rocks.

ROY, GRACE, GRACE & ROTHSCHILD

Not all men dream of castles.

LESTER FELDMAN, DDB NEEDHAM

How Can Other Reconditioners Catch Our Performance When They're Not Even On The Right Track?

DOUG MALOTT, HAWLEY MARTIN PARTNERS

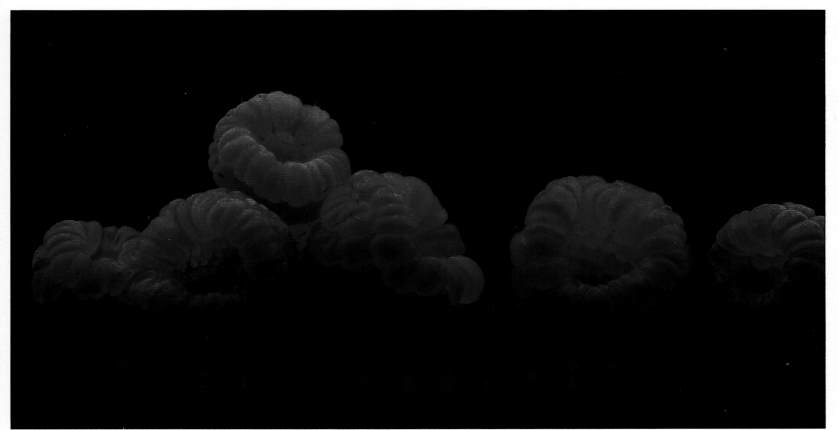

**Robert Buchanan
Photography**
56 Lafayette Avenue
White Plains, New York 10603
(914) 592-1204 • (212) 627-8558

"Photography demands technique and
artistry. Robert Buchanan brings your
most treasured ideas to light to enhance
the concept of visual communication.
As a fine commercial photographer, his
sensitivity to details and commitment to
follow-through has created a lasting
relationship with clients."

Clients: A&W, General Foods, Nestlé,
Texaco, Chesebrough, Pepperidge
Farms, New Zealand Lamb, Xerox,
Boarshead, TCBY, SOLOBaker.

Awards: N.Y. Art Directors Club, DESI,
ART Direction....

Robert Buchanan
PHOTOGRAPHY

914/592-1204
212/627-8558

Vincent Colabella
(212) 949-7456

Casey Cronin
115 Wooster Street
New York, New York 10012

Represented by:
Betsy Pearce
(212) 219-9674

Phoebe Dunn
20 Silvermine Road
New Canaan, Connecticut 06840
(203) 966-9791

Phoebe Dunn is internationally recognized for capturing the magic world of babies and children with imagination, sensitivity and versatility. Experience in advertising, magazine illustrations, packages, annual reports, promotional materials, calendars.
Hasselblad transparencies available through the studio in Connecticut or Al Forsyth at DPI. (212) 627-4060.
© Phoebe Dunn, 1990
Clients include: Reader's Digest, P&G, Chesebrough-Ponds, General Foods, J&J, Eli Lilly, Parents, Random House, Univar, Merrill-Lynch, Hallmark, Kodak, 3M, Argus, Aetna Life, Ciba-Geigy.

ASMP

Bill Farrell
343 East 30th Street
New York, New York 10016
(212) 683-1425

Rep: Ursula Kreis
(212) 562-8931
FAX: (212) 562-7959

Bill Farrell likes people - and people respond well to him in front of the camera. Bill's sensitive lighting makes his images look natural and spontaneous.

Bill Farrell

Allan Finkelman
118 East 28 Street
New York, New York 10016
(212) 889-5489
(212) 684-3487
FAX: (212) 889-6210

Carl Flatow
20 East 30th Street
New York, New York 10016
(212) 683-8688

You have a great photographic concept but you only wish it were possible. With my knowledge of the latest photographic and image generating technology, I can grant your wishes.

Bob Forrest
273 Fifth Avenue
New York, New York 10016
(212) 288-4458

Specialist in high-tech still life, complex
multiple-image special effects,
post-production image manipulation,
posterization, solarization, strobe-zoom
and staccato-zoom effects.
All images below were produced
in-camera, and are unretouched.

Additional work can be seen in:
Showcase 9, 10, 11, 12.

SCHOLASTIC, INC.

PANASONIC

BMW 750IL

VIDEO MAGAZINE

©1990 BOB FORREST

FIBER INDUSTRIES

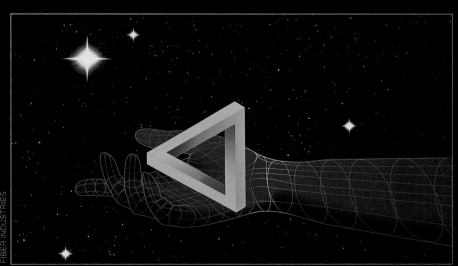

FORREST
BOB FORREST   273 FIFTH AVENUE, NEW YORK CITY   212/288-4458

Al Francekevich
73 Fifth Avenue
New York, New York 10003
(212) 691-7456
FAX: (212) 727-9617

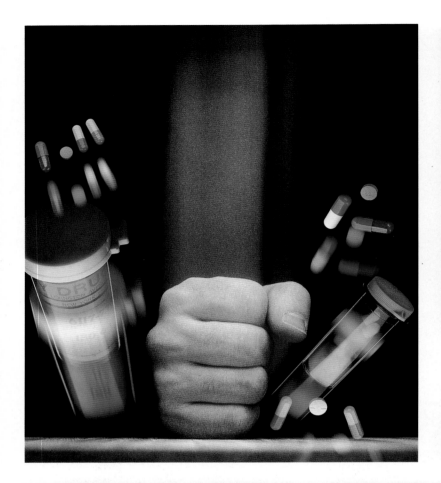

Al Francekevich
73 Fifth Avenue
New York, New York 10003
(212) 691-7456
FAX: (212) 727-9617

Mitchell Funk
500 East 77th Street
New York, New York 10162
(212) 988-2886

Large stock file available

Mitchell Funk
500 East 77th Street
New York, New York 10162
(212) 988-2886

Large stock file available

THE A TO Z OF STARTING AN ADVERTISING AGENCY

If you want to learn how to start an advertising agency from scratch, opening up without any clients, you must learn how to cope with your emotions and that means running the gamut of emotions from A to Z.

A is for Anticipation
It's a great feeling. The anticipation of starting an agency from scratch, only working with the people and the clients you truly want. The anticipation of doing only great work. The anticipation of becoming famous.

B is for Bravado
You've got to have plenty of this to make cold calls every day, to deal with the stalling, the "we'll ring you back" routine but they don't, the no's, the maybe's, the "call again in three months," the silences, the endless waiting for replies. Bravo bravado!

C is for Confidence
The confidence of starting up, knowing that so much advertising is so infernally dull and boring that, given the chance, you can do so much better, with innovative, exciting, breakthrough ideas. At this stage, you have the confidence that your advertising will be more noticed, more motivating and more memorable than anything else around.

D is for Disappointment
The days, the weeks, even the months of disappointments, waiting for your first major account to put the agency on its feet. Continually waiting for people to call you back. And so the waiting takes your daring to disappointment on to dejection and sometimes to despair.

E is for Excitement
Through all the calling and the waiting, there is always the excitement of the unknown, the excitement of suddenly having a prospect to present to, then the excitement of preparing totally new campaign ideas and the excitement of the chance to pitch for an account. Only then does excitement come close to exhilaration.

F is for Fear
The fear that, after all the hard work and the long hours, you might just never make it. The fear of failure is the worst fear of all. And you must do your best to turn this into a self-motivator, driving yourself with the willpower to keep saying you will succeed.

G is for Gungho
This is the spirit of battle that carries you through the ups and downs of every week. Whenever things are looking bleak, you have to use this gungho feeling to convince yourself you're going to make it.

H is for Hope
You live on it every day. Hoping prospects will call you back. Hoping for a meeting. Hoping for the chance to present your work and show how good you are. Hoping, above all, the prospect liked you and loved your work enough to actually want to pay you money.

I is for Independence
That inner feeling that got you started. The independent feeling of having no one else to tell you what to do. The quietly confident feeling of knowing your future is in your own hands. From here on, it's up to you.

continued on page 90

Tony Generico
130 West 25th Street
New York, New York 10001
(212) 627-9755
FAX: (212) 727-2856

Clients Include: AT&T, R.J. Reynolds,
Chase Manhattan, CBS, Guerlain,
Lancome, Western Union,
Encyclopaedia Britannica,
McGraw Hill, Hasbro, Coleco,
The Conde Nast Publications.

Stephen Green-Armytage
171 West 57th. Street
New York, New York 10019
(212) 247-6314

Member APA and ASMP

Stephen Green-Armytage
171 West 57th. Street
New York, New York 10019
(212) 247-6314

Advertising:
Levi, Camel, Winston, Rolex, Hancock, E.F. Hutton, Sperry, Nestlé, Kodak, AT&T, IBM, Georgia Power.

Corporate:
Olin, A & P, Weyerhaeuser, Champion

Paper, ABC T.V., AT&T, Baybanks, Medserv, Occidental, IBM, G + W.

Hotels:
Kauai Westin, Mauna Kea, Princess Hotels in Bermuda, Bahamas and Acapulco, The Plaza, Mallihouhana.

Editiorial:
Life, Sports Illustrated, Fortune, Smithsonian, GEO, Travel and Leisure, Good Housekeeping.

Member APA and ASMP

VIEWPOINTS

continued from page 86

J is for Jealousy
The sheer jealousy you feel from seeing other agencies win business with work you know you could do better than. Or worse, the jealousy of seeing agencies pitch accounts you weren't given the chance to compete for, simply because you are a start-up and don't have their resources. Isn't talent more important, you ask?

K is for Knowing
Knowing how good you are. Knowing how good you can be. Knowing that you have the talent to do great work, even if the chances to prove it are few and far between. When the future looks barren, knowing yourself is often all you have to fall back on.

L is for Laughter
Mistakes. Comments. Criticism. You have to laugh. This is the laughter and fun you know is missing from so many bigger agencies today. The laughter of working in a small friendly group. The laughter of enjoying being out on your own. It's this laughter that keeps lifting you up and cheering you on.

M is for Melancholy
The melancholy mood that comes through when calls to prospects don't get returned. The mood that strikes late at night when you realize getting started is a lot tougher than you thought. This is the mood you constantly have to shake yourself out of.

N is for Nervousness
The nervous feeling of watching the money flow away with nothing coming in. The nervous feeling you always get before meeting any prospect. The nervous feeling before every presentation. Console yourself, this is what keeps the adrenalin flowing.

O is for Optimism
The optimism of believing in yourself, your partners, their talent and their work. The optimism of believing something good is just around the corner. The optimism of believing every prospect you talk to is your next client.

P is for Pessimism
The pessimism of finding out you haven't persuaded the prospect to become a client. Not yet. The pessimism of listening to excuses and wondering how much of the blame to put on yourself. The pessimism you pick up from your bank manager who keeps reminding you the cost of starting up was more than you expected.

Q is for Queasiness
The queasiness of never being sure how prospects react to your presentations and your work. The queasiness of wondering how long you can last without a major account. The queasiness of uncertainty.

R is for Resolution
The resolution to maintain your standards. The resolution not to take on tiny projects for hardly any money. The resolution not to roll over when a potential client makes suggestions that undermine your big idea. This is the resolve to be the agency you set out to be.

continued on page 98

René Gregg
New York City
(800) 441-1996 New York
(314) 361-1963 St. Louis
(407) 239-8928 Florida

92

George Haling
(212) 736-6822

Ronald G. Harris
119 West 22nd Street
New York, New York 10011
(212) 255-2330

Represented by Hyla Crane

Ronald G. Harris
119 West 22nd Street
New York, New York 10011
(212) 255-2330

Represented by Hyla Crane

Haruo
37 West 20th Street
New York, New York 10011
(212) 505-8800

Additional work may be seen in
American Showcase Vol. 9, 10, 11 & 12

John Henry
(212) 686-6883

Represents
Lois Greenfield

SHARE THE FEELING 「共感」はサンスイからのメッセージです。

SANSUI

踊らせる、力。

SANSUI ARTS

音楽は、ヒトだけにさずけられた快楽だから。もっと楽しく、楽しみたい。マニア
チックにスペックをうんぬんしたり、お子様ランチの機能に惑わされているうち
は、人間、修行がまだまだです。生きていることを楽しむひとつのカタチとして
オーディオがあるのだから。そこに、わたしたちの心を踊らせてくれる"力"を
求めたい。SANSUI ARTS。それは軽やかな芸術品。そして美しい技術作。
モスビンテージ。サンスイによる、オーディオの新しいカタチがここにあります。

AU-X1111 MOS VINTAGE
MASTER INTEGRATED AMPLIFIER

山水電気株式会社

Photographed by Lois Greenfield

DICK & JANE

continued from page 90

S is for Sanity

The sanity you need to carry you through the surprises. The sanity to deal with a trillion trivial details of paperwork you never realized had to be done. The sanity you need to keep filling in forms and paying out bills when all you want to do is create great advertising.

T is for Thrills

The thrill of getting prospects to see you. The thrill of getting projects that bring in money. The thrill of creating your own campaigns from nothing. And the biggest thrill of all is getting your first real client to sign a contract.

U is for Understanding

You have to understand that your friends, however close, never seem to be able to do you favors. You have to understand that however urgent returning calls and having meetings are to you, they are low priorities for everyone else. You also have to understand that all the people who wish you well expect someone else to do something about it.

V is for Vulnerability

As a start-up operation, you become vulnerable to wild goose chases, vulnerable to any rumors of "inside" tips of clients who might be unhappy or about to move, vulnerable to doing a lot of research and preparing presentations for people who feel just giving you an hour or two of their time is enough in itself.

W is for Weariness

The weariness of long hours doing several jobs way into the night to make presentation deadlines without all the troops you used to have working for you when you were in a large agency. Wearing several hats every day takes its toll.

X is for Xenophobia

The fear of anything foreign. A new agency thrives on change, creating new ideas to persuade people to change their attitudes, their behavior, their brands. Unfortunately, a lot of the prospects you talk to have a fear of anything foreign, a fear of anything different, a fear of change. Coping with the xenophobia of your prospects is a task in itself.

Y is for Yelling

You need this emotional release. Yelling at suppliers to bring their charges down. Yelling at machines that go wrong. Yelling at each other because you've no one else to yell at. Yelling for things to go right when you feel they're going wrong is your ultimate right.

Z is for Zaniness

The zany feeling you have wondering why you gave up a good highly paid job in a big comfortable agency to be crazy enough to want to start your own agency in the toughest, most competitive, most cutthroat era the advertising business has faced. But it's advertising. You love it. And you knew it was going to be zany. Only not this zany.

Dennis Barham
Managing Partner
Dennis Barham & Partners
New York, New York

Paul Hyman Productions
(212) 255-1532
FAX: (212) 874-5365

Impact Studios, Ltd.
Scott Nibauer / Peter Lien
(800) 726-3988

IMPACT STUDIOS, LTD.

Photography

1084 N. Delaware Ave.

Phila Pa 19125

2 1 5 4 2 6 3 9 8 8

FAX 4 2 6 6 0 6 7

IMPACT

IMPACT STUDIOS, LTD.

Photography

1084 N. Delaware Ave.

Phila Pa 19125

215 426 3988

FAX 426 6067

Spencer Jones
23 Leonard Street
New York, New York 10013-2918
(212) 941-8165
FAX: (212) 941-1699

Stock photography available through
Bruce Coleman Inc., New York
and Mega Press, Japan.

Partial Client List: Atari, Bridal Guide
Magazine, Carnegie Hall, Chemical
Bank, Citibank, Cotton Incorporated,
Equitable Insurance, Food & Wines
of France, Gevalia Coffee, Letts of
London, Libby's, Metropolitan Life
Insurance, National Wildlife Federation,
Popular Mechanics Magazine.

SPENCER JONES
PHOTOGRAPHY

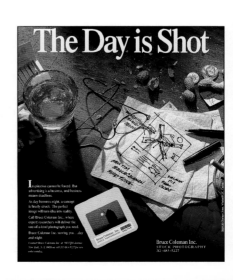

The Day is Shot

Steven Jones
120 West 25th Street
New York, New York 10001
(212) 929-3641

Available for Assignment and Stock
Requests.

STEVEN JONES

George Kamper Productions Ltd.
15 West 24th Street
New York, New York 10010
(212) 627-7171
FAX: (716) 454-4737

Rep.: Ursula Kreis
(212) 562-8931
FAX: (212) 562-7959

In the studio or on location, George Kamper succeeds in eliciting the right emotions from people of all ages: the professional model or the "real person".

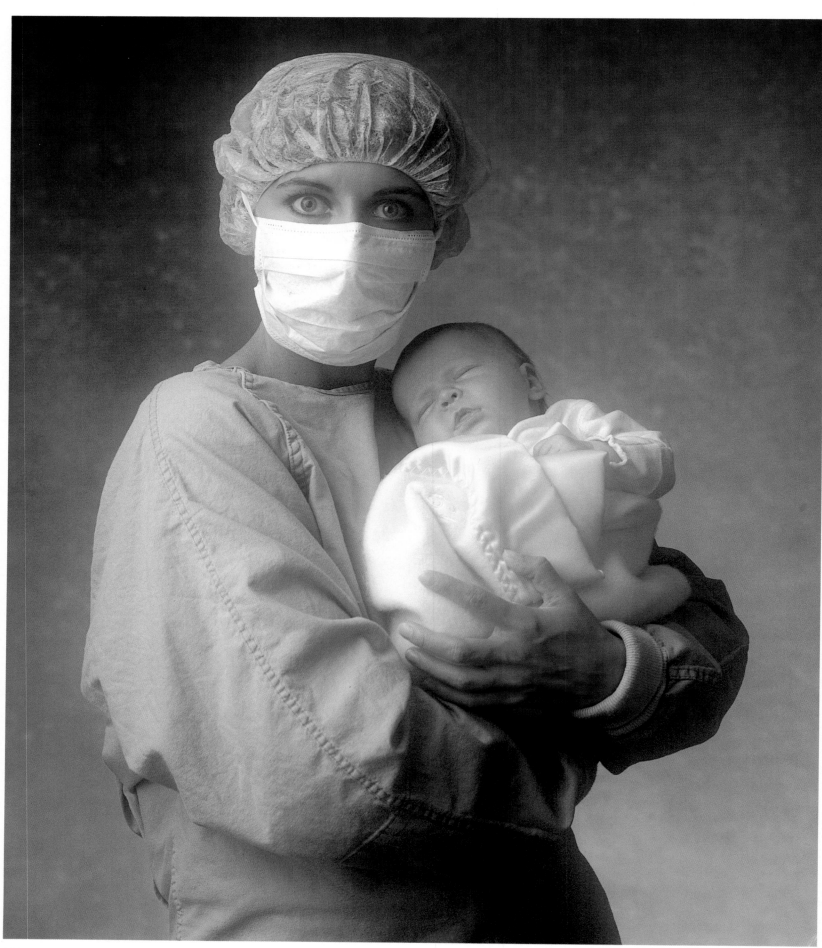

**George Kamper
Productions Ltd.**
15 West 24th Street
New York, New York 10010
(212) 627-7171
FAX: (716) 454-4737

Rep.: Ursula Kreis
(212) 562-8931
FAX: (212) 562-7959

Frank LaBua Photography
37 North Mountain Avenue
Montclair, New Jersey 07042
(201) 783-6318

New York City
(212) 967-7576

Advertising
Corporate
Editorial

Frank LaBua

Location

Frank LaBua Photography
37 North Mountain Avenue
Montclair, New Jersey 07042
(201) 783-6318

New York City
(212) 967-7576

Assignments
Fine Art Prints
Stock Images

Frank LaBua

Photography

Don Landwehrle

9 Hother Lane
Bay Shore, New York 11706
(516) 665-8221 Phone & FAX

Special effects photography shot in the studio and on location.
Exciting imagery for advertising, corporate and editorial.
Additional images can be seen in American Showcase #8, #9, #10, and #12.

Call for Don's portfolio and see for yourself that anything is possible.

Stock images available through The Image Bank (212) 529-6700.

Whitney Lane
109 Somerstown Road
Ossining, New York
(914) 762-5335

Represented by:
Betsy Heisey
(914) 762-5335

I specialize in photography for
Advertising and Corporate
Communications.

Not all my clients see things the same
way: Chemical, CUC, Duracell, Frank B.
Hall, Holly Farms, Wyeth-Ayerst,
Reader's Digest, and...My studio (part
of a 200-year-old farmhouse) is located
in Westchester, only a short distance
from New York City. Unique locations
are everywhere. You deserve

photography as strong as your ideas.
Call for samples or telephone your
layouts to us via "FAX". Also see:
Corporate Showcase 3, 4, 5, 6, 7;
American Showcase 7, 12, ASMP 6, 7.
Studio and location work done by
assignment, or stock: The Image Bank.
ASMP/APA. Photos © Whitney Lane.

WHITNEY LANE

READER'S DIGEST INTERNATIONAL

YOUTH DIRECT: USA (HOW MANY MORE CHILDREN MUST WE LOSE, BEFORE WE STOP DENYING THAT DRUGS KILL?)

Michel Legrand
152 West 25th Street
New York, New York 10001
(212) 807-9754

Clients include:
Wamsutta
Bloomingdale's
The Bibb Company
By Design
McCall Pattern Company
Vignelli Associates

Norman Graphic Arts
Macy's
Perfect Fit Industries
Doubleday & Company
Van Heusen
The New York Times

© 1990 Michel Legrand

Michel Legrand

Represented by: Valerie Baker   and   David Delp
(212) 807-7113   (212) 315-5907

Thomas Leighton
321 East 43rd Street
New York, New York 10017
(212) 370-1835 (office)
(212) 714-2880 (service)

Architectural, interior, and structural
photography

Clients include: Merrill Lynch, Morgan
Stanley, E.F. Hutton, Salomon Brothers,
Bear Stearns, Prudential Bache, Chase,
The Morgan Bank, Shearson Lehman,
New York Life, IBM, Subaru, Honeywell,
Digital Corp., W.R. Grace, General
Electric, Wurlitzer, Toys R Us, Texaco,
Ford, Houghton-Miflin, Real Estate
Board of New York, JMB Realty.

ALASKA

Alaska Artists Guild
PO Box 101888
Anchorage, AK 99510
(907) 277-1962

ARIZONA

Arizona Artist Guild
8912 North Fourth Street
Phoenix, AZ 85020
(602) 944-9713

CALIFORNIA

Advertising Club of Los Angeles
3600 Wilshire Boulevard, Suite 432
Los Angeles, CA 90010
(213) 382-1228

APA Los Angeles, Inc.
7201 Melrose Avenue
Los Angeles, CA 90046
(213) 935-7283

Art Directors and Artists Club
2791 24th Street
Sacramento, CA 95818
(916) 731-7532

Book Club of California
312 Sutter Street, Suite 510
San Francisco, CA 94108
(415) 781-7532

Los Angeles Advertising Women
5000 Van Nuys Boulevard, Suite 400
Sherman Oaks, CA 91403
(818) 995-7338

San Francisco Art Directors Club
2757 16th Street, Box 277
San Francisco, CA 94103
(415) 387-4040

Society of Illustrators of Los Angeles
5000 Van Nuys Boulevard, Suite 400
Sherman Oaks, CA 91403
(818) 784-0588

Society of Motion Pictures & TV Art Directors
14724 Ventura Boulevard, Penthouse #4
Sherman Oaks, CA 91403
(818) 905-0599

Visual Artists Association
5364 Venice Boulevard
Los Angeles, CA 90019
(213) 933-7199

Western Art Directors Club
PO Box 996
Palo Alto, CA 94302
(415) 321-4196

Women's Graphic Center
The Woman's Building
1727 North Spring Street
Los Angeles, CA 90012
(213) 222-5101

COLORADO

Art Directors Club of Denver
1900 Grant Street, Suite 1130
Denver, CO 80203
(303) 830-7888

International Design Conference in Aspen
1000 North 3rd
Aspen, CO 81612
(303) 925-2257

CONNECTICUT

Connecticut Art Directors Club
PO Box 639
Avon, CT 06001
(203) 651-0886

DISTRICT OF COLUMBIA

American Advertising Federation
1400 K Street NW, Suite 1000
Washington, DC 20005
(202) 898-0089

American Institute of Architects
1735 New York Avenue, NW
Washington, DC 20006
(202) 626-7300

Art Directors Club of Washington, DC
1015 20th Street NW, Suite M100
Washington, DC 20036
(202) 955-5775

NEA: Design Arts Program
1100 Pennsylvania Avenue, NW
Washington, DC 20506
(202) 682-5437

GEORGIA

Art Directors Club of Atlanta
125 Bennett Street, NW
Atlanta, GA 30309
(404) 352-8726

Atlanta Art Papers, Inc.
PO Box 77348
Atlanta, GA 30357
(404) 588-1837

Creative Arts Guild
PO Box 375
Dalton, GA 30722
(404) 278-0168

Graphic Artists Guild
PO Box 8178
Atlanta, GA 30306
(404) 473-8620

continued on page 118

Jook Leung
Photography
35 South Van Brunt Street
Englewood, New Jersey 07631
(212) 254-8334 Studio
(201) 894-5881
FAX: (201) 894-5882

Additional work can be seen in:
American Showcase:
Volume 12, page 105
Volume 11, page 118
Volume 9, page 97
Volume 8, pages 110, 111
Volume 7, page 118
Volume 6, page 88

Volume 5, page 111
Volume 4, page 130

Corporate Showcase:
Volume 4, page 89
Volume 3, page 91
Volume 2, page 36
Volume 1, page 52

Allan Luftig
873 Broadway
New York, New York 10003
(212) 533-4113
FAX: (212) 979-8672

Allan Luftig
873 Broadway
New York, New York 10003
(212) 533-4113
FAX: (212) 979-8672

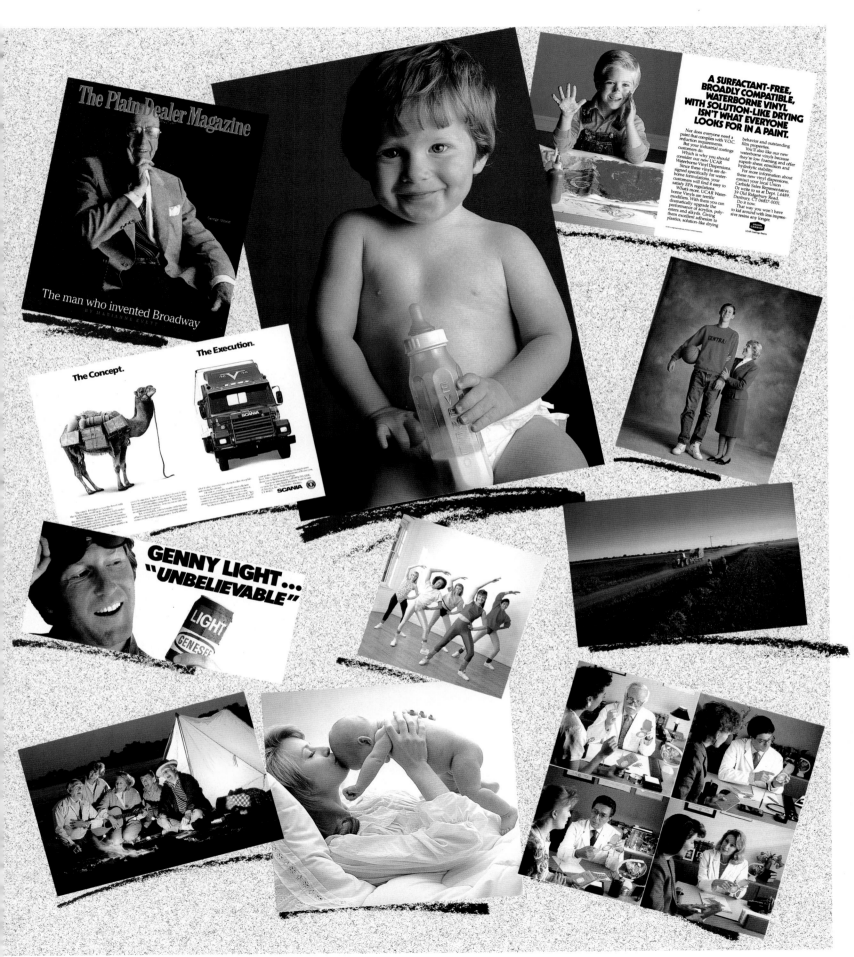

Lee Marshall
201 West 89th Street
New York, New York 10024
(212) 799-9717

Joseph Meacham
601 North Third Street
Philadelphia, Pennsylvania 19123
(215) 925-8122

Represented by
Robert Rotella
(215) 968-3696
FAX: (215) 968-8828

Clients:
Arnold Foods
Campbell Soup Company
Delacre Chocolates
Durkee French
Franco American
Hershey
Mrs. Paul's

Nabisco Foods
Pepperidge Farm
Quaker Oats Company
Swanson Foods
Vlasic Foods
Weaver Chicken
Whitman Chocolates

continued from page 112

ILLINOIS

Artists Guild of Chicago
410 North Michigan Avenue
Lower Level
Chicago, IL 60611
(312) 951-8252

Chicago Society of Artists, Inc.
1142 West Morse Avenue
Chicago, IL 60626
(312) 764-6119

Institute of Business Designers
341 Merchandise Mart
Chicago, IL 60654
(312) 467-1950

Society of Typographic Arts
233 East Ontario Street, Suite 500
Chicago, IL 60611
(312) 787-2018

Women in Design
2 North Riverside Plaza, Suite 2400
Chicago, IL 60606
(312) 648-1874

INDIANA

Advertising Club of Indianapolis
3833 North Meridian
Suite 305 B
Indianapolis, IN 46208
(317) 631-2000

IOWA

Art Guild of Burlington
Arts for Living Center
PO Box 5
Burlington, IA 52601
(319) 754-8069

KENTUCKY

Davidson County Art Guild
224 South Main Street
Lexington, KY 27292
(704) 249-2742

MASSACHUSETTS

Boston Visual Artists Union
77 North Washington Street, 3rd Floor
Boston, MA 02114
(617) 227-3076

Creative Club of Boston
155 Massachusetts Avenue
Boston, MA 02115
(617) 536-8999

Center for Design of Industrial Schedules
221 Longwood Avenue
Boston, MA 02115
(617) 734-2163

Graphic Artists Guild
PO Box 1454-GMF
Boston, MA 02205
(617) 451-5362

Guild of Boston Artists
162 Newbury Street
Boston, MA 02116
(617) 536-7660

Society of Environmental Graphics Designers
47 Third Street
Cambridge, MA 02141
(617) 577-8225

MICHIGAN

Creative Advertising Club of Detroit
c/o Josephine LaLonde
30400 Van Dyke
Warren, MI 48093

Michigan Guild of Artists and Artisans
118 North Fourth Avenue
Ann Arbor, MI 48104
(313) 662-3382

MINNESOTA

Advertising Federation of Minnesota
4248 Park Glen Road
Minneapolis, MN 55416
(612) 929-1445

MISSOURI

Advertising Center of Greater St. Louis
440 Mansion House Center
St. Louis, MO 63102
(314) 231-4185

Advertising Club of Kansas City
1 Ward Parkway Center, Suite 102
Kansas City, MO 64112
(816) 753-4088

Kansas City Art Directors Club
Westport Station
PO Box 10022
Kansas City, MO 64111
(816) 561-4301

NEW JERSEY

Federated Art Associations of New Jersey, Inc.
PO Box 2195
Westfield, NJ 07090
(201) 232-7623

Point-of-Purchase Advertising Institute
66 North Van Brunt Street
Englewood, NJ 07631
(201) 894-8899

NEW YORK

The Advertising Club of New York
155 East 55th Street
New York, NY 10022
(212) 935-8080

continued on page 126

Abraham Menashe
Humanistic Photography
306 East 5th Street
New York, New York 10003
(212) 254-2754
FAX: (212) 505-6857

Photography that affirms life and the pursuit for excellence. Highlighting the human factor by focusing on people and their vital spirit.

Worldwide location photography.

Stock: Adoption • AIDS • Autism • Birth • Children • Counseling • Drug Rehabilitation • Foster Grandparents • Geriatric Nursing • Handicapped • Homeless • Homosexuals • Hospice • Laying On Of Hands • Learning

Disabled • Medical • Nursing • Operating Room • Prayer • Prisoners • Prostitutes • Religions • Senior Citizens • Therapeutic Touch • Volunteers • Wholistic Health • And more.

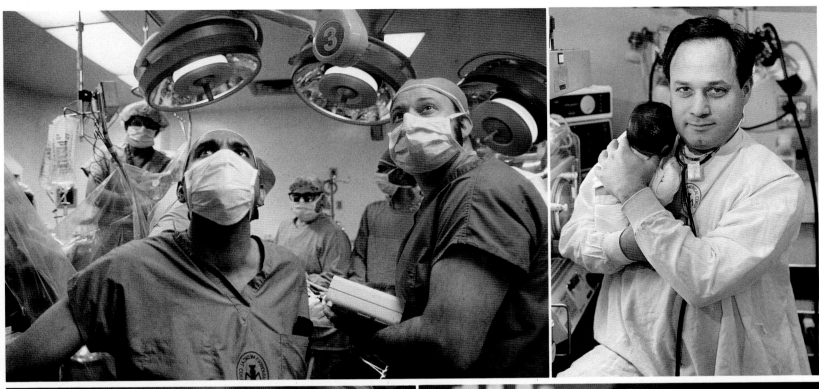

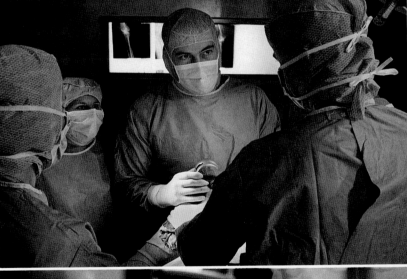

Donald L. Miller
295 Central Park West
New York, New York 10024
(212) 496-2830

Specializing in C.E.O.'s, Chairmen,
Presidents, Directors, and top
management.

Donald L. Miller
295 Central Park West
New York, New York 10024
(212) 496-2830

Specializing in C.E.O.'s, Chairmen,
Presidents, Directors, and top
management.

Dan Nelken Studio, Inc.
43 West 27th Street
New York, New York 10001

Represented by:
Adele Q. Brown
(212) 532-7471

People Photography
Black/White and Color
Studio and Location
Advertising, Corporate and Editorial

Refer to American Showcase 10-12 and
Corporate Showcase 8 to view more
of our work.

Stock available.

© Dan Nelken 1990

DAN NELKEN STUDIO INC

Dan Nelken Studio, Inc.
43 West 27th Street
New York, New York 10001

Represented by:
Adele Q. Brown
(212) 532-7471

People Photography
Black/White and Color
Studio and Location
Advertising, Corporate and Editorial

Refer to American Showcase 10-12 and
Corporate Showcase 8 to view more
of our work.

Stock available.

© Dan Nelken 1990

DAN NELKEN STUDIO INC

Nancy Palubniak
144 West 27th Street
New York, New York 10001
(212) 645-2838

Joe Peoples
11 West 20th Street
New York, New York 10011
(212) 633-0026

For additional work please see
American Showcase Photography
Volumes 11 & 12.

continued from page 118

The Advertising Council, Inc.
825 Third Avenue
New York, NY 10022
(212) 758-0400

APA
Advertising Photographers of America, Inc.
27 West 20th Street, Room 601
New York, NY 10011
(212) 807-0399

Advertising Production Club of N.Y.
60 East 42nd Street, Suite 1130
New York, NY 10165
(212) 983-6042

Advertising Typographers Association of America, Inc.
Two Penn Plaza, Suite 1070
New York, NY 10121
(212) 629-3232

Advertising Women of New York Foundation, Inc.
153 East 57th Street
New York, NY 10022
(212) 593-1950

A.A.A.A.
American Association of Advertising Agencies
666 Third Avenue
New York, NY 10017
(212) 682-2500

American Booksellers Association, Inc.
137 West 25th Street
New York, NY 10001
(212) 463-8450

American Council for the Arts
1285 Avenue of the Americas
Third Floor
New York, NY 10019
(212) 245-4510

The American Institute of Graphic Arts
1059 Third Avenue, 3rd Floor
New York, NY 10021
(212) 752-0813

American Society of Interior Designers
National Headquarters
1430 Broadway
New York, NY 10018
(212) 944-9220

New York Chapter
200 Lexington Avenue
New York, NY 10016
(212) 685-3480

American Society of Magazine Photographers, Inc.
419 Park Avenue South, #1407
New York, NY 10016
(212) 889-9144

Art Directors Club of New York
250 Park Avenue South
New York, NY 10003
(212) 674-0500

Association of American Publishers
220 East 23rd Street
New York, NY 10010
(212) 689-8920

Association of the Graphic Arts
5 Penn Plaza
New York, NY 10001
(212) 279-2100

The Children's Book Council, Inc.
PO Box 709
New York, NY 10276
(212) 254-2666

CLIO
336 East 59th Street
New York, NY 10022
(212) 593-1900

Foundation for the Community of Artists
280 Broadway, Suite 412
New York, NY 10007
(212) 227-3770

Graphic Artists Guild
11 West 20th Street
New York, NY 10011
(212) 463-7730

Guild of Book Workers
521 Fifth Avenue
New York, NY 10175
(212) 757-6454

Institute of Outdoor Advertising
342 Madison Avenue
New York, NY 10173
(212) 986-5920

International Advertising Association, Inc.
342 Madison Avenue, Suite 2000
New York, NY 10173
(212) 557-1133

The One Club
3 West 18th Street
New York, NY 10011
(212) 255-7070

The Public Relations Society of America, Inc.
33 Irving Place
New York, NY 10003
(212) 995-2230

Society of American Graphic Artists
32 Union Square, Room 1214
New York, NY 10003
(212) 260-5706

Society of Illustrators
128 East 63rd Street
New York, NY 10021
(212) 838-2560

Society of Photographers and Artists Representatives
1123 Broadway
New York, NY 10010
(212) 924-6023

continued on page 138

Clayton J. Price
205 West 19 Street
New York, New York 10011
(212) 929-7721

Conceptual Photographs
Assignment and Stock

Additional work can be seen in
American Showcase
Volumes 9, 10, 11 & 12,
and New York Gold Volumes 1, 2 & 3.
All photographs ©1989 Clayton J. Price.

Clayton J. Price
205 West 19 Street
New York, New York 10011
(212) 929-7721`

Conceptual Photographs
Assignment and Stock

Additional work can be seen in
American Showcase
Volumes 9, 10, 11 & 12,
and New York Gold Volumes 1, 2 & 3.

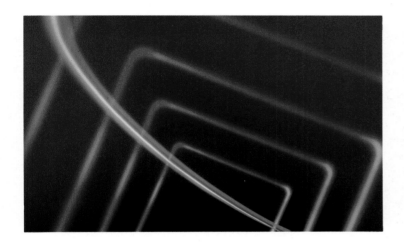

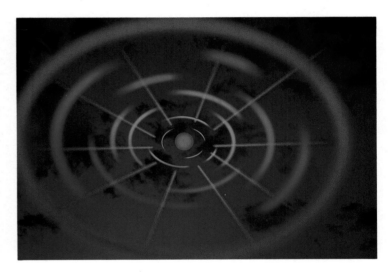

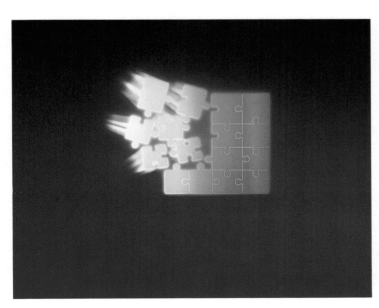

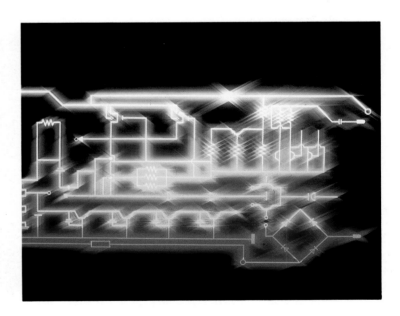

Jack Reznicki
568 Broadway
New York, New York 10012
(212) 925-0771
FAX: (212) 219-8176

Represented by:
Elyse Weissberg
(212) 406-2566

Jack Reznicki
568 Broadway
New York, New York 10012
(212) 925-0771
FAX: (212) 219-8176

Represented by:
Elyse Weissberg
(212) 406-2566

Rĕz·nick·i
S T U D I O

Jon Riley
12 East 37th Street
New York, New York 10016
(212) 532-8326
FAX: (212) 532-8594

Jon Riley
12 East 37th Street
New York, New York 10016
(212) 532-8326
FAX: (212) 532-8594

Roy Silverstein
(212) 941-7497
FAX Available

Advertising, Corporate and Editorial
Photography

Ken Skalski
866 Broadway
New York, New York 10003
(212) 777-6207

Member APA

KEN SKALSKI · PHOTOGRAPHY   866 BROADWAY N.Y. N.Y. 10003   212·777·6207

Don Spiro
(201) 729-6535
(212) 484-9753
FAX available

Location Photography

Advertising, Corporate and Editorial

Don Spiro
(201) 729-6535
(212) 484-9753
FAX available

continued from page 126

Society of Publication Designers
60 East 42nd Street, Suite 1130
New York, NY 10165
(212) 983-8585

Television Bureau of Advertising
477 Madison Avenue
New York, NY 10022
(212) 486-1111

Type Directors Club of New York
60 East 42nd Street, Suite 1130
New York, NY 10165
(212) 983-6042

U.S. Trademark Association
6 East 45th Street
New York, NY 10017
(212) 986-5880

Volunteer Lawyers for the Arts
1285 Avenue of the Americas
New York, NY 10019
(212) 977-9270

Women in the Arts
325 Spring Street, Room 200
New York, NY 10013
(212) 691-0988

O H I O

Advertising Club of Cincinnati
PO Box 43252
Cincinnati, OH 45243
(513) 575-9331

Cleveland Society of Communicating Arts
Maggie Moore
PO Box 14759
Cleveland, OH 44114
(216) 621-5139

Columbus Society of Communicating Arts
c/o Orby Kelly
1900 Crown Park Court
Columbus, OH 43220
(614) 761-9405

Design Collective
D.F. Cooke
131 North High Street
Columbus, OH 43215
(614) 464-2883

P E N N S Y L V A N I A

Art Directors Club of Philadelphia
2017 Walnut Street
Philadelphia, PA 19103
(215) 569-3650

T E X A S

Advertising Club of Fort Worth
1801 Oak Knoll
Colleyville, TX 76034
(817) 283-3615

Art Directors Club of Houston
PO Box 271137
Houston, TX 77277
(713) 661-7267

Dallas Society of Visual Communications
3530 High Mesa Drive
Dallas, TX 75234
(214) 241-2017

Print Production Association of Dallas/Fort Worth
PO Box 160605
Irving, TX 75016

V I R G I N I A

Industrial Designers Society of America
Walker Road, Suite 1142-E
Great Falls, VA 22066
(703) 759-0100

National Association of Schools of Art and Design
11250 Roger Bacon Drive
Reston, VA 22090
(703) 437-0700

Tidewater Society of Communicating Arts
PO Box 153
Norfolk, VA 23501

W A S H I N G T O N

Allied Arts of Seattle, Inc.
107 South Main Street
Seattle, WA 98104
(206) 624-0432

Seattle Ad Federation
c/o Margaret Oliver
PO Box 4159
Seattle, WA 98104
(206) 623-8307

Seattle Design Association
PO Box 1097
Main Office Station
Seattle, WA 98111
(206) 285-6725

Society of Professional Graphic Artists
c/o Steve Chin, President
85 South Washington Street, Suite 204
Seattle, WA 98104

W I S C O N S I N

Coalition of Women's Art Organizations
123 East Beutel Road
Port Washington, WI 53074
(414) 284-4458

Illustrators & Designers of Milwaukee
c/o IDM
5600 West Brown Deer Road
Browndeer, WI 53223
(414) 355-1405

Milwaukee Advertising Club
231 West Wisconsin Avenue
Milwaukee, WI 53203
(414) 271-7351

Jeanne Strongin
61 Irving Place, 5d
New York City, New York 10003
(212) 473-3718

For additional samples see: American
Showcase #12, pgs 132, 133.

Corporate Reports/CONTEL

Oprah Winfrey

PORTRAITS

strongin

JEANNE STRONGIN 212·473·3718

139

Michel Tcherevkoff
873 Broadway
New York, New York 10003
(212) 228-0540

1. Magna AD: Ward Graham
2. Hewlett Packard AD: Joe Gallo & Rex Gee
3. ARRS AD: Anthony Cosintino
4. Panasonic AD: Michel Tcherevkoff
5. Dolisos AD: Charles Barral
6. Prescriptives AD: Jim Gager
7. Pepsi AD: Laura Otani
8. AD: Michel Tcherevkoff

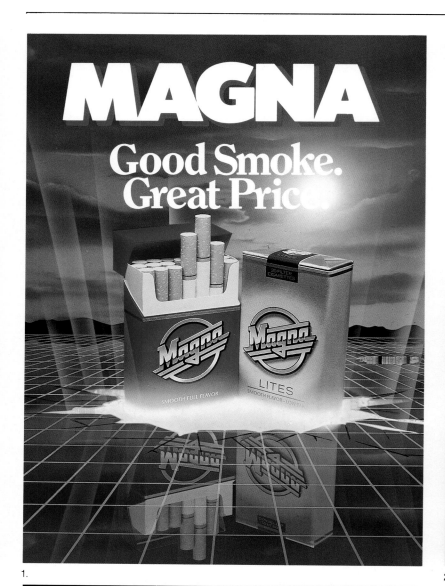

1.

2.

3.

4.

5.

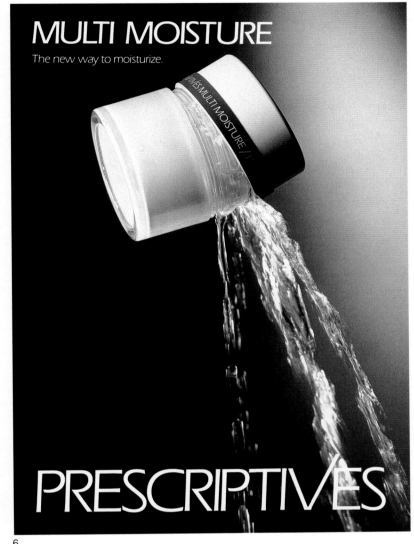

6.

7.

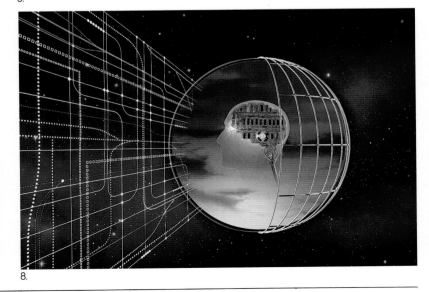

8.

HOW TO SELL BREAK-THROUGH ADVERTISING

The only way to sell breakthrough advertising is by doing breakthrough work. If that's all the client ever sees throughout your myriad of presentations, eventually they'll buy something good.

But, when the fresh ideas stop coming on a campaign as a result of many rejections, beg off. Press the creative director to put someone else on the account. This happens all the time, and it's better to move onto something new. We've all gotten burned out after dozens of layouts and storyboards. I generally threaten to quit and, depending on your seniority, this strategy can work.

A case comes to mind of a recent retail account I was assigned to (the client shall remain nameless). I found out after a year that there's a limit to how many ways I can say, BUY ONE. GET ONE FREE. After accusing the account team of turning me into a hack, I was politely excused from that particular piece of business.

Breakthrough work doesn't always require a breakthrough strategy, but it helps. The more you know about what you're advertising, the more focused you will be. That's why creative people should not let terms like 'demographics' and 'user friendly' frighten them. The information is there to assist you. If you already know it, at least pretend you're listening when the account team debriefs the client.

I spent a year studying acting in New York early in my career, not because I wanted to be an actor, but because doesn't every profession require you to be a salesman?

So, you've got a good strategy. The client hasn't seen any work yet, so they still like you. Now the time comes to conceive. Personally, I do my best not to pick up a copy of CA, The One Show Book, or the D & AD Annual for inspiration until at least the second day. It's a bad habit we all get into, and can often spurn ideas that resemble previously traversed territory. Where can you look for inspiration outside of your head?

• Books (not about advertising). These are always a good place to start. I spend at least a day, early in the development of a campaign, in the best bookstore I can find. I pore through all kinds of subjects until the owner pressures me to start buying. Then I charge them to the project.

• Movies. The video rental store is a whole new kind of research library. Rental fees also apply to the project.

• Magazines (preferably those where you don't understand the language). Look at photographs, type design, anything that stretches the boundaries of conventional advertising layouts. Personally, if I see Garamond typeface one more time, condensed or otherwise, I think I'll scream.

• Your mother. Don't be afraid to bounce ideas off anyone willing to listen. In my case, it generally ends up being my mother, rather than another art director. I figure she's the consumer.

• Copywriters. Something else I'm open to is letting the writer art direct while I write. Who ever remembers who came up with which idea? In the long run it's irrelevant, because everyone ends up taking the credit anyway.

So, now you've come up with a campaign that's going to win a gold pencil in The One Show. How do you sell it? At Chiat/Day/Mojo, it's more difficult to get the idea out of the agency than it is to sell it to the client. Is it the best ad it can be? Now you can open up CA, The One Show, or D & AD and compare notes.

When the day comes to present your campaign to the client, it is important that you show at least three great ideas. If you've only got one after two weeks' work, then run with it. But remember, if you project to the client that they're going to think you've gone too far, they will.

No matter how off the wall your concept may be, keep referring to its relevance to the research. That helps. Also, make sure the layouts and storyboards are rough. If you can, draw them yourself. If not, find a storyboard artist and try to teach him or her how not to draw...the looser the better. I often swipe photos in frames to help the client visualize the concept.

continued on page 146

Togashi
36 West 20 Street
New York, New York 10011
(212) 929-2290
FAX: (212) 463-9073
Tokyo: 03-586-1620

Represented by
Eileen C. Togashi
(212) 420-0206

Client List:
Abrams Publishers • American Express AT & T • Buddy L Toys • Bulgari Jewellers • Burlington Mills • Chase Manhattan Bank • CPC/Best Foods • Elle Magazine • HBO • iittala Crystal • Jaz Watch • Kirin Beer • Lever

Bros/Promise Margarine • Marantz Electronics • National Car Rental • New York Magazine • Paddington Corp./Amaretto de Saronno Liqueur • Purina • Salon de Metro Jewellers • Tourneau Corner • US Magazine • Wella Corp./Expertisse Shampoo

David A. Wagner
568 Broadway, Suite 103
New York, New York 10012
(212) 925-5149
FAX: (212) 219-9629

Computer Manipulated Photography
via Graphics Paintbox and others.
Tradtionally Assembled Photography.
Plain Old Photography.

Send us a FAX and we'll send you a bid.

All images on this page
© 1989 David A. Wagner

David A. Wagner
568 Broadway, Suite 103
New York, New York 10012
(212) 925-5149
FAX: (212) 219-9629

Computer Manipulated Photography
via Graphics Paintbox and others.
Traditionally Assembled Photography.
Plain Old Photography.

Send us a FAX and we'll send you a bid.

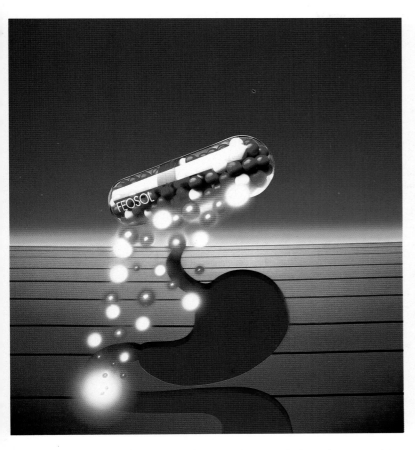

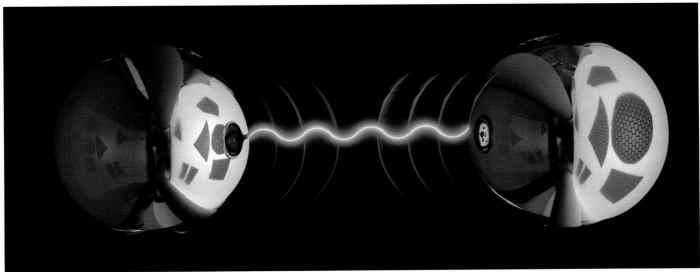

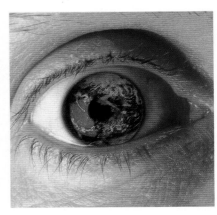

continued from page 142

The same goes for TV. If your idea requires moving images and you can swipe those from movies, TV, MTV, wherever, do it. Assemble a video storyboard, lay down some music—anything to get your idea across.

If the client is still having difficulty, ask if you can expose some consumers to the concept. They rarely say no to this suggestion—how can they? I find the consumer is usually much smarter than the client when it comes to taking chances.

You've sold the idea! Now you have to execute it. Look to hire photographers and illustrators outside their given area of expertise. Some of my best fashion work has been done by photojournalists or still life photographers. Keep an open mind.

All of this is about challenging yourself and the medium of advertising. Because if it's not fresh, if we've seen it before, if you know you're going to hate it when it's done—why bother?

Michael Smith
Art Director
Chiat/Day/Mojo Inc. Advertising
Venice, California

Bonnie West
156 Fifth Avenue
New York, New York 10010
(212) 929-3338
FAX: (212) 929-0388

Portraiture at its best.

Shown here:
"Danger" for E.P. Dutton;
Mickie Spillane for E.P. Dutton;
Ad for Brooklyn Union Gas.

All photographs © Bonnie West 1989

*Bonnie**West***
Photographer

Walter Wick
560 Broadway
New York, New York 10012
(212) 966-8770
FAX: (212) 941-7597

Superbly crafted conceptual
photography available as stock
or by assignment.

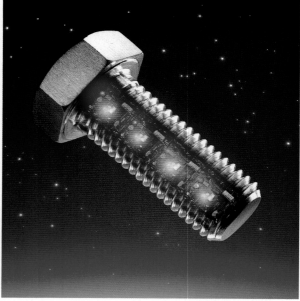

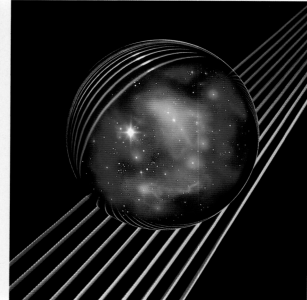

Walter Wick
560 Broadway
New York, New York 10012
(212) 966-8770
FAX: (212) 941-7597

Superbly crafted conceptual
photography available as stock
or by assignment.

"THANKS TO LOU DORFSMAN FOR MAKING US AT CBS NEWS LOOK GOOD ON PAPER, ON THE TUBE, IN SO MANY WAYS, FOR SO MANY YEARS."

Mike Wallace
CBS News/60 Minutes

"CBS has a corporate commitment to excellence in design, but Lou Dorfsman is the one whose genius has translated that commitment into reality. Deservedly, he has become a legend in the annals of commercial design. He combines a lively creative flair with an innate, sure sense of style and superb taste. Lou is a man of great warmth, humor and kindness. He is also a total per- fectionist. The special 'CBS style' that he has created reflects to a large extent what I like to think of as the company personality. I am very proud of the way he has defined CBS visually. I doubt anyone else could have done it as well.''

*William S. Paley
Founder Chairman
CBS Inc.*

...fsman is not just a ...e is a thinker who ...ms and has ...s. He bears a ...esponsi-

"Lou is the ultimate in graphic design; his work is a reflection of his profound intellect, intuition and elegance."

**David Levy
Executive Dean and Chief
Administrative Officer
Parsons School of Design**

"Everything Lou Dorfsman has touched was made better for his efforts. Whether it was a television studio set, a matchbook cover, a book, a booklet, a paper cup, a cafeteria wall, an annual report, an annual meeting, Lou has done it with taste and style and integrity."

Dr. Frank Stanton
President Emeritus CBS

"I DID NOT GO TO ART SCHOOL. MUCH OF WHAT I LEARNED ABOUT THIS CRAFT I LEARNED BY STUDYING DORFSMAN. I WAS AMAZED TO DISCOVER HOW GREATLY I AM INDEBTED TO HIS EXAMPLE."

Dick Hess
Designer

"QUITE SIMPLY THE BEST CORPORATE DESIGNER IN THE WORLD."

*Milton Glaser
Designer*

"The CBS image has been helped more by Lou than anyone else."

Fred Friendly
Former President CBS News

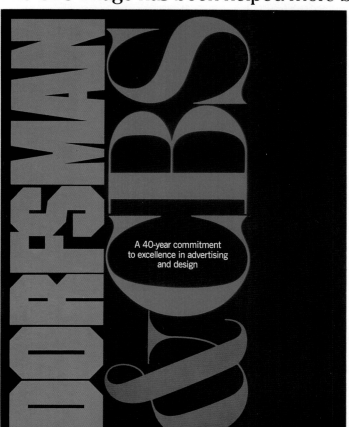

DORFSMAN & CBS

A 40-year commitment to excellence in advertising and design

"Anyone who's any good in the business keeps watching him to see what he's coming up with. He's done the most elegant design work in the world consistently over the years. And this isn't atelier stuff, but right on the firing lines at CBS."

**George Lois Chairman
Lois Pitts Gershon PON/GGK**

"I consider him one of the truly extraordinary talents in the field, one of the true luminaries in communications."

Saul Bass
Designer

Need we say more?

Yes, only that it is a 40-year retrospective of one of the greatest graphic designers of our time. Clothbound, 216 pages. Designed by Dick Hess.

Send for your copy of DORFSMAN & CBS at $49.95. Postage and handling are FREE within the U.S. and Canada. To order, call 212-245-0981 and charge to your AMEX, Visa or MasterCard. Or send your check or money order to:

American Showcase-Dept. T.
724 Fifth Ave., NY, NY 10019

NORTHEAST

Bruno Joachim Photography
326 A St, Boston, MA 02210 (617) 451-6156
FAX (617) 451-0265

Bruno

THAYER

MARK THAYER PHOTOGRAPHY

25 DRYDOCK AVENUE

BOSTON, MASSACHUSETTS

617·542·9532

JOHN RIZZO PHOTOGRAPHY
146 Halstead Street
Rochester, New York 14610
716•288•1102

ADVERTISING • CORPORATE • EDITORIAL

SIMMONS

SIMMONS

Specializing in location photography for Advertising, Annual Reports, Corporations and Industry. Clients include: Acushnet, Adage, Alpha Industries, American Airlines, Amtrak, Analog Devices, Apollo Computer, Avon, Bank of Boston, Bank of New England, Boise-Cascade, Bose Corp., The Boston Company, Bozell Jacobs Kenyon & Eckhardt, CBS, Citibank, Codex, Commercial Union Assurance, Conde Naste Publications, Data General, Deere & Company, Dexter Hysol, Digital Equipment Corp., EG&G, Fairchild, Ferrofluidics, Fidelity, Foote Cone & Belding, Forbes Magazine, GCA, General Electric, General Foods, Gillette, Goodyear, W.R. Grace, Graylock Industries, Grumman Aerospace, HHCC, Holt Rinehart & Winston, Horticulture, IBM, HBM-Creamer, Kimberly-Clark, John Hancock, McGraw-Hill, Mobay, Moore Business Forms, Nashua Corp., New England Electric, Pfizer Inc., Pitney-Bowes, Polaroid, Prentice-Hall, Prime Computer, Putnam Funds, Rockwell International, St. Regis, Scott Paper, Schorr and Howard Co., Sheraton Corp., Sonat Inc., State Street Bank & Trust, Syncor, Sun Co., Teradyne, TWA, 3M, J. Walter Thompson, Time Magazine, Time-Life Books, Touch of Class Catalog, Touche-Ross, Unionmutual, Warner Communications, S.D. Warren, Westinghouse, Young & Rubicam.

ERIK LEIGH SIMMONS
60 K Street
Boston, Massachusetts 02127
(617) 268-4650
Represented by Meara
(617) 268-7895

GARY MIRANDO PHOTOGRAPHY

27 CLEVELAND STREET
VALHALLA NY 10595

PHOTOGRAPHY

(914) 997-6588
FAX (914) 428-2953

HORNICK/RIVLIN STUDIO, Nº 25 DRYDOCK AVENUE, BOSTON, TEL 617.482.8614

SHAFFER-SMITH PHOTOGRAPHY 203.236.4080

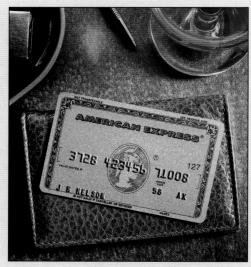

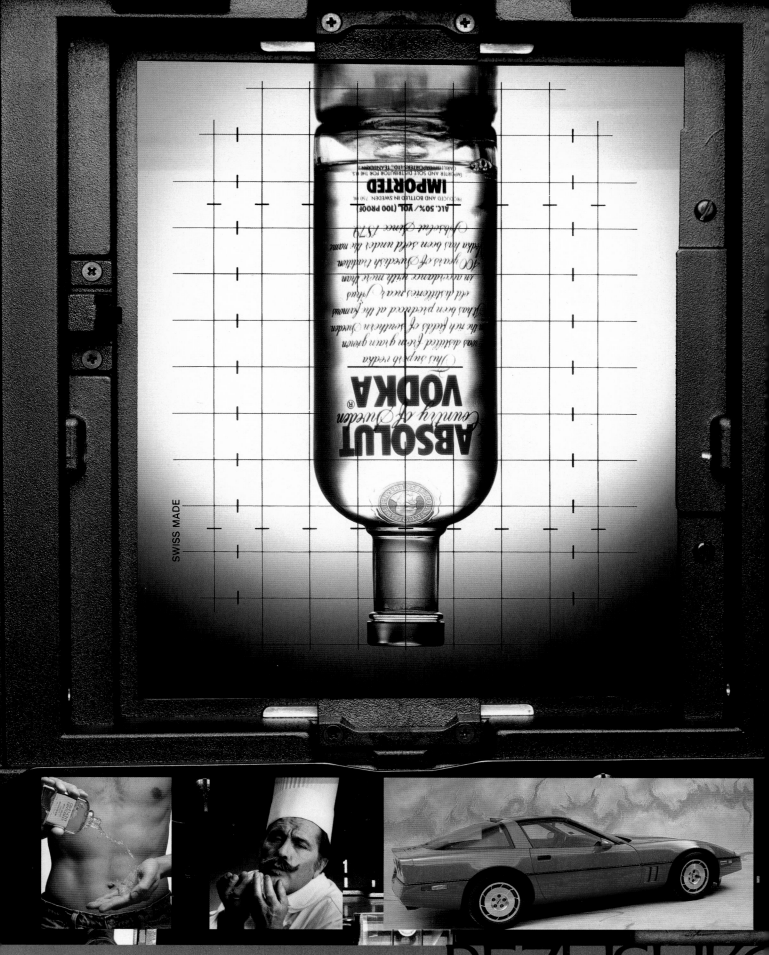

b and George Bezushko
1 Irving Street
adelphia, PA 19107

215-735-7771
Represented by Vivienne Plant
FAX: 215-735-7795

BEZUSHKO

John J. Payne

43 Brookfield Place
Pleasantville, New York 10570
(914) 747-1282

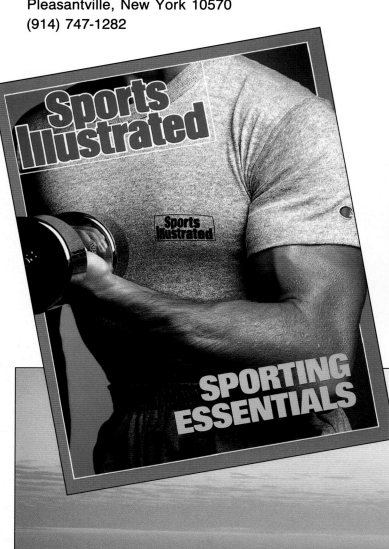

A Good Appearance Is Only Half The Story.

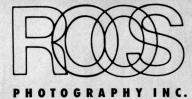

The other half is Warren Roos behind the camera. It's not enough to take good pictures. What it takes is someone who can listen.

MAINE
207-773-3771

ROOS
PHOTOGRAPHY INC.

Someone who knows when to stay within the limits or when to bust out. Now that that's been said, let's go to film.

NEW YORK
212-563-1012

Paul Avis
(603) 627-2659
FAX: (603) 627-4854

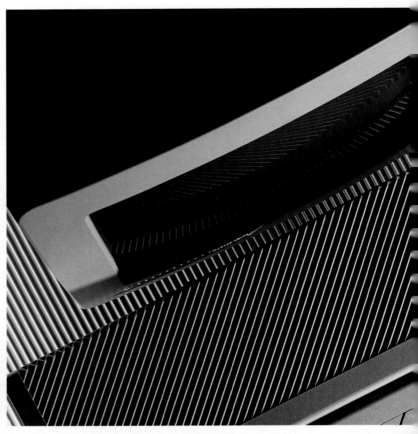

For additional samples
see the 1989 and 1990 Black Book,
Mini Portfolio available upon request.

Contact Jane 603/627-2659

Fax 603/627-4854

Paul Avis Photographer, Inc.

Blackfan Studio
286 Meetinghouse Road
New Hope, Pennsylvania 18938
(215) 862-3503

Philip Isaiah Katz-Photographer
Jacqueline Katz-Stylist

Blackfan Studio
286 Meetinghouse Road
New Hope, Pennsylvania 18938
(215) 862-3503

Philip Isaiah Katz-Photographer
Jacqueline Katz-Stylist

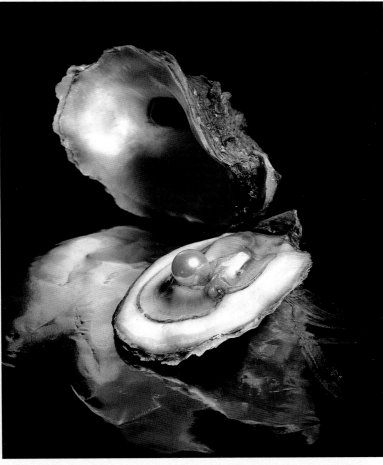

Visual Thinking

methods for making images memorable

Henry Wolf

Creation by design, not accident.

Outstanding visual images rarely just happen. They are the result of careful premeditation, planning and design.

This new book by Henry Wolf, one of today's foremost photographers and art directors, examines the many creative methods he employs—from use of strange perspective to settings in improbable places to unexpected combinations.

Here are 17 chapters of techniques for translating words into photographic images that will be more com-pelling, more unique and therefore more memorable.

Any visual communicator will find inspiration in these pages.

Clothbound with hundreds of full-color photographs, as well as reproductions of many classic works of art that have been an influence on them.

184 pages. $45.00. Released in October 1988. Order now! American Showcase, 724 Fifth Avenue, New York, New York 10019, (212) 245-0981.

John Burke
60 K Street
Boston, Massachusetts 02127
(617) 269-6677
FAX: (617) 269-0713

Francis   *Francis again*   *Francis too*

client - Susan Bristol   *client - Fisher Hill*   *client - Soft Spots*

C. Fatta Studio
Carol Fatta
25 Dry Dock Avenue
Boston, Massachusetts 02210
(617) 423-6638

Clients include:
American Express
Della Femina McNamee/WCRS
DDB/Needham
Maytag
Westinghouse

Specializing in:
Annual Reports
Portraits
Editorial
Advertising

To view more work:
American Showcase 12, 11, 10
Corporate Showcase 9, 8
Adweek's Portfolio 1989, 1988, 1987
Call for the portfolio.

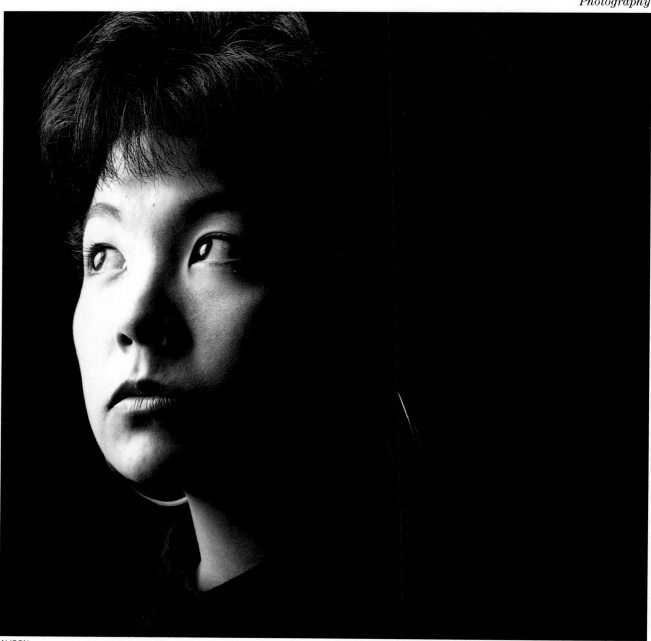

ALISON

ROBERT MANNING, AMERICAN EXPRESS
CAMPAIGN

LARRY O'BRIEN, DOREMUS ADVERTISING

AUDUBON SOCIETY, DELLA FEMINA MCNAMEE

C. Fatta Studio
Carol Fatta
25 Dry Dock Avenue
Boston, Massachusetts 02210
(617) 423-6638

Clients include:
Allendale Insurance
GTE/Sylvania
Leo Burnett Company
Sheraton Corporation
Wunderman Worldwide

Specializing in:
Annual Reports
Portraits
Editorial
Advertising

To view more work:
American Showcase 12, 11, 10
Corporate Showcase 9, 8
Adweek's Portfolio 1989, 1988, 1987
Call for the portfolio.

JUKE BOX KIDS, CONSUMERS WATER ANNUAL

INC. MAGAZINE

CHET COLLIER, AMERICAN EXPRESS CAMPAIGN

NEW ENGLAND CRITICAL CARE ANNUAL

Morocco Flowers
Morocco Flowers Photo Illustration
520 Harrison Avenue
Boston, Massachusetts 02118
(617) 426-3692

Other samples of work can be found in
American Showcase vol. 12, 1989 and
Adweek Portfolios, 1988.

Peter Gallo
Photography
1238 Callowhill Street
Philadelphia, Pennsylvania 19123
(215) 925-5230
FAX: (215) 440-9752
(800) 331-7770

H/O Photographers, Inc.
John S. Sheldon
John Sherman
197 Main Street, PO Box 548
Hartford, Vermont 05047
(802) 295-6321
FAX: (802) 295-6324

Photography for advertising, industry,
and corporate communications

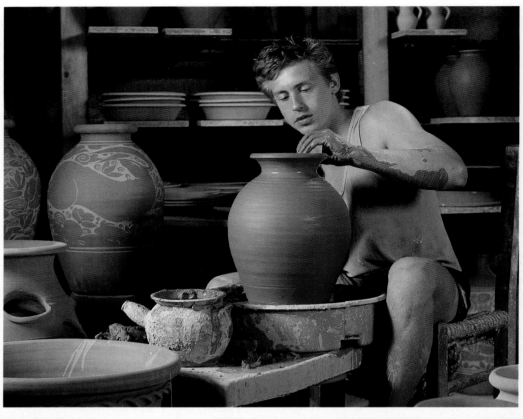

Lou Jones
22 Randolph Street
Boston, Massachusetts 02118
(617) 426-6335
(212) 463-8971

International representation by
Thé Image Bank

Specializing in location, photo/illustration
& corporate advertising

Clients include:
Chase Manhattan
Fidelity Investments
Teledyne
Amtrak

Raytheon
Otis
Alpha
New York Times
New Balance

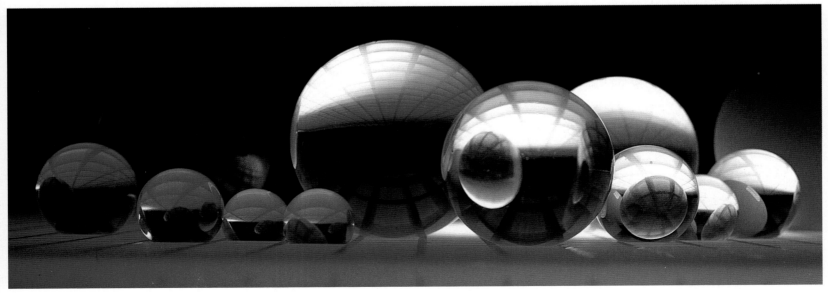

**Barney Leonard
Photography**
518 Putnam Road
Merion, Pennsylvania 19066
(215) 664-2525

Corporate and Industrial Location
Photography for Annual Reports,
Corporate Publications and Multi-Image
Presentations. Packaged for travel -
Barney is a commercial instrument
rated pilot and aircraft owner.

**Barney Leonard
Photography**
518 Putnam Road
Merion, Pennsylvania 19066
(215) 664-2525

Corporate and Industrial Location
Photography for Annual Reports,
Corporate Publications and Multi-Image
Presentations. Packaged for travel -
Barney is a commercial instrument
rated pilot and aircraft owner.

VISUAL THINKING

Is it so important in this age of nuclear threat, AIDS, terrorism and polyester shirts that magazine covers, building entrances, corporate logos, lipstick ads or abstract collages be beautiful?

Was it important that Haydn played beautifully at Prince Esterházy's musical soirées for 80 people? That Dürer signed his etchings in much more elegant lettering than is available from all of today's computer typesetting marvels? That Stradivari treated the wood of the violins he built for a handful of clients in Cremona in a way that hasn't been duplicated in four centuries?

Yes. The answer is <u>yes</u>, it is important. It is the small monuments, the details that are the milestones of civilization; they accumulate to make history. Sometimes I feel that we are near the entrance to a tunnel leading into a long night, and we must leave marks before the darkness. This is not the first time that mankind has been at such an impasse; the armless Venuses of Greece and the murals of Pompeii have survived the long night that followed the golden age of Rome. And then the cathedrals started to rise; Gutenberg's movable type made it possible to disseminate ideas. Suddenly art was everywhere—in Florence and Venice and in Germany, in Holland, in Austria and Spain. Henry VIII remains with us because of Holbein's portrait, as do Vivaldi and Bach because of a few ink marks on some pieces of paper which, when piled up on the floor, would not even reach as high as a man's head.

Some works of art are by nature unrecordable. The cook at the Court of Louis XIV may have prepared culinary masterpieces of which we have no knowledge. Casanova's lovemaking may still be unsurpassable or it may simply be a legend, an early press agent's fabrication. Molière's actors could have been great or cornier than Rodney Dangerfield. It is the words, the plays themselves that survive undiminished. Certainly more people heard Mozart's music by watching the film <u>Amadeus</u> than during his lifetime and all the years thereafter.

With imagery there is a legacy. It was Jorge Luis Borges who said: "Painters after death become books—not a bad incarnation." We can look back at our few thousand years of history because they are made up of these landmarks. Paintings, buildings, sculptures, novels, photographs, sonatas, and, yes, dresses, door handles, posters and watch faces become guideposts in looking back. The taillight of a 1932 Packard evokes the USA in the thirties as much as a Fitzgerald novel does.

Enormous quantity and high quality have seldom gone hand in hand. There will be more imagery produced and reproduced in this one year than in all of history before World War II. Even though we now have infinitely more imagery, it is hardly better. Our mania for preserving, xeroxing, microfilming, videotaping hasn't raised our standards of excellence, and mediocrity may yet overwhelm us by its sheer volume. More than ever, more than in the times of Pericles, Rembrandt or Whistler, it is important to create worthwhile words, music and images. History will examine our era, and we must leave a decent report card.

From **Visual Thinking: Methods for Making Images Memorable**
© 1988 by Henry Wolf
Published by American Showcase, Inc.

Phil Matt

Box 10406
Rochester, New York 14610
(716) 461-5977
Studio:
1237 East Main Street
Rochester, New York 14609

Phil specializes in corporate, editorial, and advertising location photography. His sense of design and wide experience in working with people of diverse backgrounds have been recognized by many major national and international publications and Business Week 1000 firms. See our ads in

American Showcase 8, 9, 10, 11, 12 and in Corporate Showcase 7 and 8.

Stock available directly and through:

Gamma/Liaison (New York and Paris)
Tony Stone Associates (London)
Photographic Resources (St. Louis)

Member: ASMP

All Photographs © Phil Matt.

Some clients:

American Airlines
American Diabetes
    Association
Barron's
Black Enterprise
Business Week
Business Month
Cahners Publishing
CFO
Changing Times
Columbia Records
Connoisseur
Cornell University
Corning Glass
Datamation
Eastman Kodak
Eastman School of
    Music
Entre' Computer
Essence
Euromoney
Farm Journal

Federal Express
Financial World
First
Forbes
Fortune
Gannett Foundation
GEO
Grolier's
High Technology
I.B.M.
Inc.
Industry Week
Information Week
Maclean's
MacWeek
Monsanto
National Law Journal
Newsweek
New Choices
N.Y. Stock Exchange
The New York Times
Nutri/System

Nynex
Ogilvy & Mather
PC Week
Pillsbury
Price Waterhouse
Redbook
Rochester Philharmonic
    Orchestra
Silver Burdett
Ken Silvia Design
Simon Graduate School of
    Business Administration
13-30 Corporation
Time
Travel & Holiday
U.P.I.
USA Today
U.S. Information Agency
U.S. Kids
U.S. News & World Report
Venture
Xerox

D.W. Mellor
1020 Mount Pleasant Road
Bryn Mawr, Pennsylvania 19010
(Philadelphia)
(215) 527-9040

Specializing in executive portraiture

Please refer to American Showcase
volumes 7, 8, 9, 10, 11, and 12

NOLAN D. ARCHIBALD
CHAIRMAN, PRESIDENT AND CHIEF EXECUTIVE OFFICER/BLACK AND DECKER
COOK AND SHANOSKY ASSOCIATES, INC.

D.W. Mellor
1020 Mount Pleasant Road
Bryn Mawr, Pennsylvania 19010
(Philadelphia)
(215) 527-9040

Specializing in executive portraiture

Please refer to American Showcase
volumes 7, 8, 9, 10, 11, and 12.

RICHARD M. FURLAUD
CHAIRMAN AND CHIEF EXECUTIVE OFFICER/SQUIBB CORPORATION
COOK AND SHANOSKY ASSOCIATES, INC.

**David Revette
Photography**
111 Sunset Avenue
Syracuse, New York 13208
(315) 422-1558
FAX: (315) 422-1555

REVETTE

OMNI
Communications

Latorra
Advertising

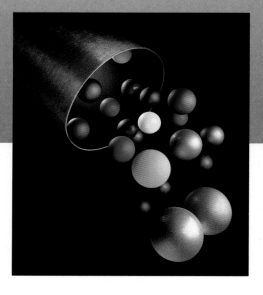

Lamson
Corporation

Syracuse
Lacrosse

Susan Robins
124 North 3rd Street
Philadelphia, Pennsylvania 19106
(215) 238-9988
FAX: (215) 625-2675

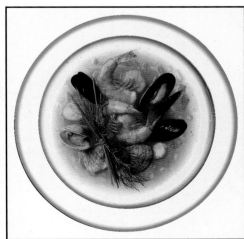

Eric Roth
337 Summer Street
Boston, Massachusetts 02210
(617) 338-5358

Portraiture on location or in the studio
for advertising, editorial, corporate, and
personal use.

JULIA CHILD

Eric Roth
337 Summer Street
Boston, Massachusetts 02210
(617) 338-5358

Portraiture on location or in the studio
for advertising, editorial, corporate, and
personal use.

SHERRI PEACOCK, BOSTON BALLET

Russell Schleipman
298A Columbus Avenue
Boston, Massachusetts 02116
(617) 267-1677

AMCA International, AT&T, Bank of New England, Bausch & Lomb, Centocor, Chelsea Industries, Citizen's Bank, Courier Corp., Cullinet, Digital Equipment Corp., Dunkin' Donuts, Ernst & Whinney, First NH Banks, Forbes Magazine, Fortune Magazine, Helix Technology Corp., Integrated Genetics, Life Magazine, Mobil Solar, Money Magazine, New England Electric, Neworld Bank, Omni Flow, Outside Magazine, Pitney Bowes, Polaroid Corp., Raytheon Corp., Repligen Corp., Rockresorts Inc., Sail Magazine, Shawmut Bank, Tech Ops.

Walt Seng
810 Penn Avenue
Suite 400
Pittsburgh, Pennsylvania 15222
(412) 391-6780
FAX: (412) 391-7675

Partial list of clients include:
Roffler, Sorbie, Framesi, Bayer USA,
Mobay, Taster's Choice, H.J. Heinz,
PPG, Pittsburgh National Bank, Digital
Equipment, Westinghouse, Alcoa, Lean
Cuisine.

Portfolio on request

Member ASMP

© 1989, Walt Seng

SENG

The Army is There

In Time of Need

The Salvation Army
Allegheny County
1988 Annual Report

Walt Seng Photography

810 Penn Avenue, Suite 400
Pittsburgh, Pennsylvania 15222
(412) 391-6780

Steve Sharp
153 North Third Street
Philadelphia, Pennsylvania 19106
(215) 925-2890
FAX: 925-0575

Represented in New York by:
Jack Petrie
(212) 301-5196

Yamil R. Sued/
Photographics

425 Fairfield Avenue
Building #4
Stamford, Connecticut 06902
(203) 324-0234

Advertising and editorial photography, studio or location. Specializing in product still-life, fashion and beauty. Extensive stock photography file available. Portfolio available for review upon request.

Clients Include:
AGFA Compugraphic, Anderson & Lembke, Bull's Head Printers, Berema Inc., Comp-u-card Int., Conair Corp., DCA, Dow Chemical, Helo Sauna & Fitness, Hyers Smith, Hill Holliday Connors & Cosmopulos, James River Corp., Landis & Gyr, Marquardt &

Roche, Mimer, Oce Copiers, Phillips, Plus Development Corp., Primo Lighting, Westvaco Paper.

Member ASMP APA.

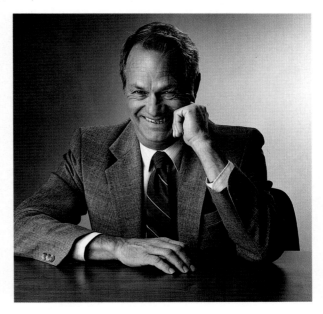

191

Breakthrough Advertising!

ARCHIVE, the magazine of international advertising that will pierce, challenge, shatter and break through your creative thinking.

Send $43.97 for a full year (six issues) of the most innovative print and TV ad campaigns being done anywhere in this world. Or call (212) 245-0981 for even faster service.

Lürzer's Int'l
ARCHIVE
Ads, TV and Posters world-wide

ARCHIVE Magazine, 724 Fifth Avenue, New York, NY 10019

MID ATLANTIC

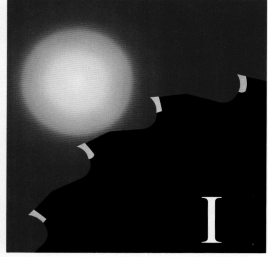

I
M
A
G
I
N
E

Imagine a photographer who *prefers* to tackle the difficult assignments.

Imagine a photographer who can translate your most complex project into a photograph that *works*.

Imagine a photographer who delivers everything you wanted on *one* piece of film.

Imagine your next job. Then call *Jim Noble*.

NOBLE

Noble Inc. 2313 Maryland Ave., Baltimore
301-235-5235   FAX 301-235-5258

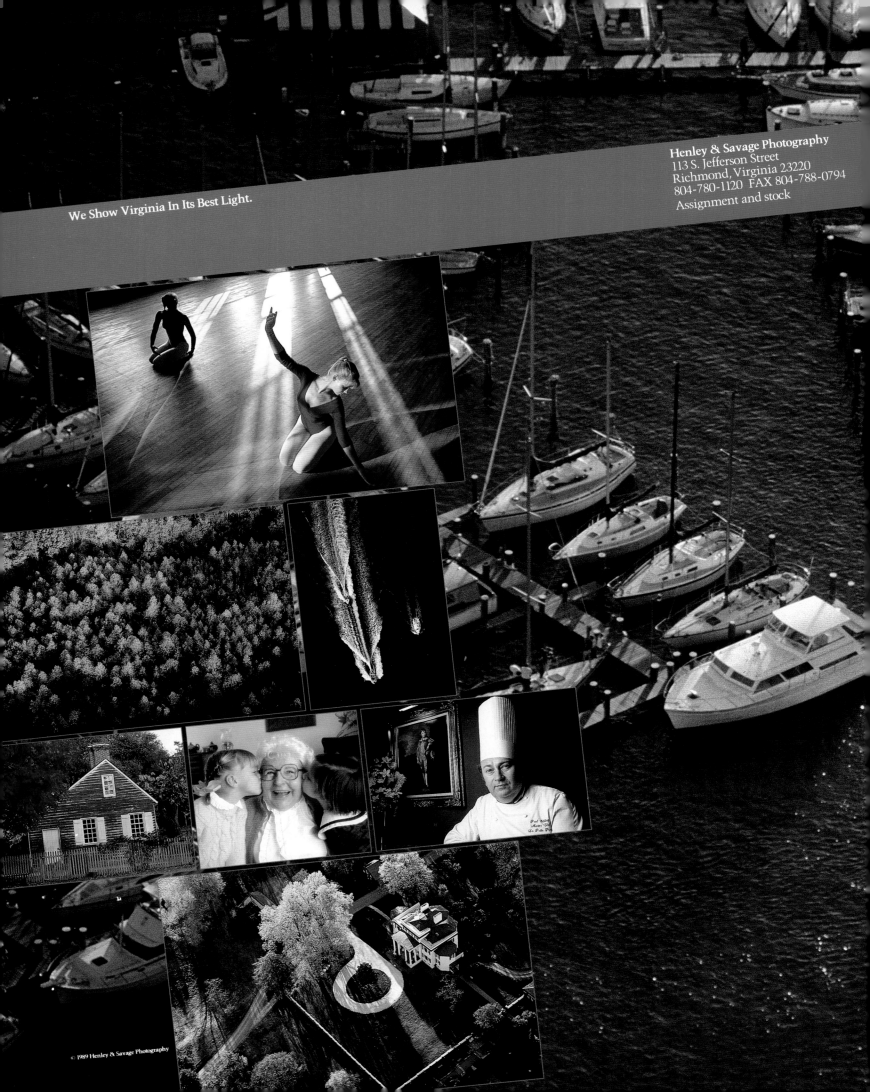

STEPHANIE LAWRENCE

Elegant

Bold

Intriguing

Always

Cameron Davidson

202.328.3344

PHOTOGRAPHY AGELOPAS

Michael Agelopas Photography

2510 North Charles Street
Baltimore, Maryland 21218

Phone: 301.235.2823
Fax: 301.235.7557

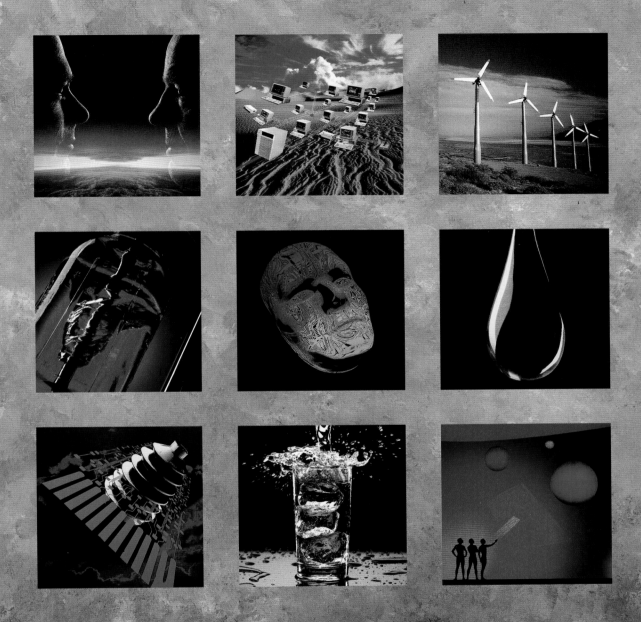

DEAN

FLOYD DEAN INC.   302·655·7193

Cosby Bowyer, Inc.
209 North Foushee Street
Richmond, Virginia 23220
(804) 643-1100
FAX: (804) 644-2226

Operating out of one of the most beautiful and functional photography studios on the eastern seaboard, Herbert Cosby and Sonny Bowyer consistently produce top-notch studio and location work.

The 10,000 sq. ft. facility includes an in-house E-6 lab, a large cyc with overlooking balcony in the main shooting area and a sophisticated kitchen/shooting space that food stylists love to work in.

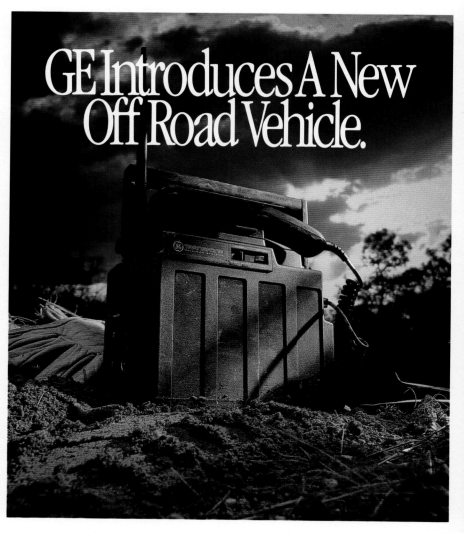

Mark Daniels
8413 Piney Branch Road
Silver Spring, Maryland 20901
(301) 587-1727
FAX service available

Photography in the Washington DC area

Howard Davis
Howard Davis Studios
19 East 21st Street
Baltimore, Maryland 21218
(301) 625-3838
FAX: (301) 625-3839

Specializing in America at work, product illustration and still life. On location or in the studio. Advertising, Editorial, and Corporate assignments accepted.

Clients Include: Alliance Wall, Amtrack, Bechtel, Black & Decker, Conrail, Control Data, Jaguar, Jockey, Johns Hopkins, Manor Hill Foods, Maserati, McCormick, Microwise, Preston, Ramada Inns, USF&G, Wang, Yamaha.

For additional samples see American Showcase 5, 6 and ASMP Silver Book 1, 2, 4, 5 & 7.

Stock available.

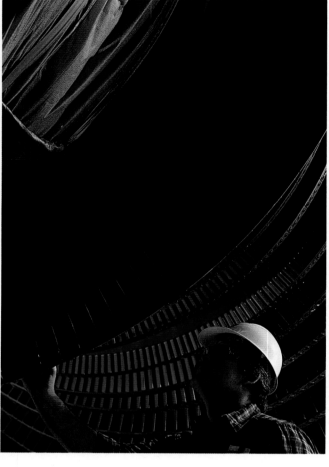

Catherine Karnow
1707 Columbia Road NW #518
Washington DC 20009
(202) 332-5656

Represented by
Woodfin Camp.
New York (212) 481-6900

Location photography:
Advertising, people,
travel, stock.

Photographs on this page taken
in Scotland for Seagram, Inc.

K A R N O W

Greg Pease
Greg Pease & Associates, Inc.
23 East 22nd Street
Baltimore, Maryland 21218
(301) 332-0583
FAX: (301) 332-1797

Stock photography available
Studio Manager: Kelly Baumgartner

Also see: American Showcase
4 through 12
Corporate Showcase 1, 4 through 8

Photo: Inc. Magazine

Greg Pease
Greg Pease & Associates, Inc.
23 East 22nd Street
Baltimore, Maryland 21218
(301) 332-0583
FAX: (301) 332-1797

Stock photography available
Studio Manager: Kelly Baumgartner

Also see American Showcase 4
through 12
Corporate Showcase 1, 4 through 8

Photos:
1. JCB, Inc.
2. Lasting Paint
3. The Johns Hopkins University
   School of Medicine

1.

2.

3.

DERAILING THE MOMMY TRACK

All right, I'll admit it. I know all the words to the reggae hit "Do the Rubber Duckie" from "Sesame Street." And according to Felice Schwartz of Catalyst, the fact that the last video I saw was "Big Bird's Party Games" probably means that it's curtains for my career. The Mommy Track. If it had been written by a man, no one would have published it. The tragic part is, that even if I don't take her assumptions seriously, a lot of people do. The most damaging part of Schwartz's statement that women who have children should stay on less ambitious and less stressful career paths is that it serves to reinforce all of the old stereotypes about women—that they can never really make it in business, that they are inferior because they bear children, that they belong in the kitchen.

Her other rather misguided assumption is that middle management is less stressful than upper management and therefore a better position to be in to raise children. Who is she kidding? Middle management is being between a rock and a hard place. It has always proven to be more stressful than upper or lower management. If anything, when you reach the ranks of upper management you generally have more income, more vacation, more control or influence over meetings and trips—in general, more.

Look around. Advertising is filled with examples of women who made it to the top while they were raising children. If Schwartz's opinions had been around then, we might have missed all the contributions that these women have made to our business.

A recent study shows the 1950s to be an aberration in this country's history. For the last hundred years, whether it was in the fields or in the factories, women have worked. It was only after WWII that women stayed home. The Fifties are dead. But obviously, a number of people still cling to that mythology.

The Mommy Track? Shouldn't it be called the Mommy and the Daddy Track?

These days, no new father is (or wants to be) immune to night feedings or teething pains at three in the morning. I have men reporting to me who often have to leave early or come in late due to child-care arrangements or pediatric appointments—men who would prefer not to travel excessively because of their family responsibilities. It is not that difficult to work around their schedules, any more than it is when any employee has personal issues to resolve. And I certainly don't view them as being less able to perform their jobs because of their family obligations.

Most of the men I know who have small children are much more involved in the care of their children than their fathers were, or even than they themselves were the first time around. There are three men on our board of directors who have young babies and are involved in their care. Does that mean they can't function in top form?

And that's the point. The issues we are all facing with regard to work and the family affect all of us, not just women. If you believed in Schwartz's philosophy, you would promote men without children over men with children. What a wonderful world that would be. Thank heavens the world is changing. And as global competition grows more intense, we can't afford to lose any talent. Men or women, mothers or fathers, and, as the work force grows old, grandmothers or grandfathers. Typecasting and generalizations about some members of the work force are going to limit all of us.

Don't look now, Felice Schwartz, but the world is changing even more than you imagined. The Mommy Track, my foot. Thanks to you, some mommies may get sacked.

And in case you missed the season's last episode of "Sesame Street," ask any guy. He'll tell you that Maria had a baby—and it was a girl!

Jeanne Chinard
SVP/Executive Creative Director
N.W. Ayer Incorporated
New York, New York

Ron Solomon
PO Box 237
Glyndon, Maryland 21071
(301) 833-5678

Member ASMP

Steve Uzzell
1419 Trap Road
Vienna, Virginia 22182
(703) 938-6868

Steve Uzzell
1419 Trap Road
Vienna, Virginia 22182
(703) 938-6868

Terry Wild
The Terry Wild Studio
RD#3 Box 68
Morgan Valley Road
Williamsport, Pennsylvania 17701
(717) 745-3257

On Assignment:
Real People/Real Situations
Editorial, Corporate, Industrial

For Stock Images Call:
Victoria Neely/Picture Editor
The Terry Wild Studio
(717) 745-3257
or
Design Photographers International
(212) 627-4060

"PEARS AND URN"

SUPERNATURAL STILL LIFE

"OFFERING"

SUPERNATURAL STILL LIFE

M I L L E R

(305) 667-5765/Fax: (305) 667-0892

Rick McQuiston/Weiden & Kennedy

The official suit of The 1987 Summer Games.

Tom Saputo/Honda Motorcycles

Grant Richards/The Richards Group

black & white

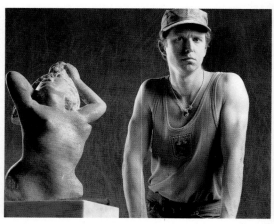

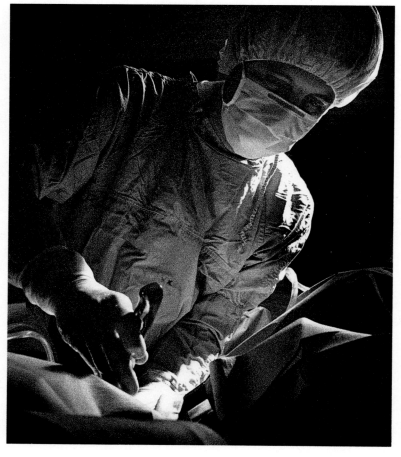

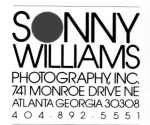

& in color

JIMI STRATTON
p h o t o g r a p h y
FAX.876.9511
404.876.1876

BACH TO BANJOS

904 A   Norwalk St.   Greensboro   North Carolina   27407   919-299-1400   FAX 919-292-8070

ANTHONY BARRERAS

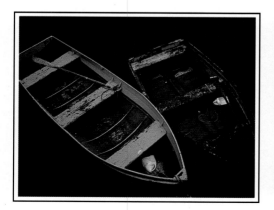

1231-C BOOTH STREET ATLANTA, GEORGIA 30318 (404) 352-0511

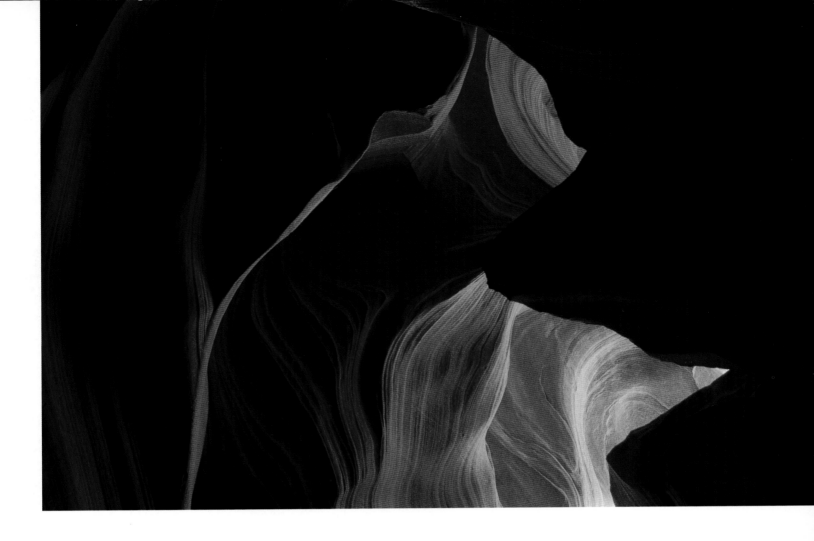

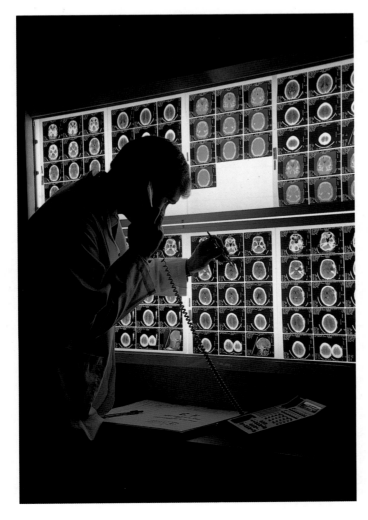

223

MICHAEL HARRISON PHOTOGRAPHY

1124 SOUTH MINT STREET STUDIO A

CHARLOTTE, NORTH CAROLINA 28203

704 334 8008 FAX 334 2312

STEVE KNIGHT

1212 E. 10th ST.

CHARLOTTE, NC 28204

704-334-5115

KNIGHT

SEIFRIED
photography

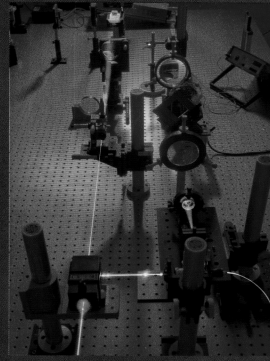

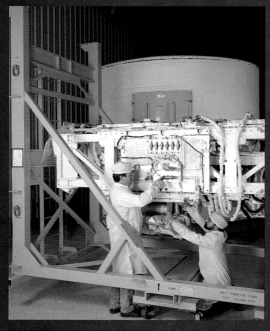

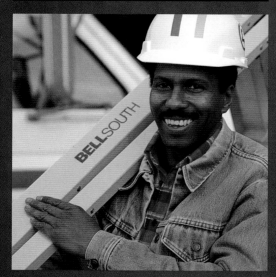

©1989 Roger Ball Photography

Roger Ball

PHOTOGRAPHY

1402-A WINNIFRED STREET • CHARLOTTE, NC 28203 • 704-335-0479

STOCK AVAILABLE
Also
please see
Volumes 8, 9, 10 & 12

ASMP

P.O. Box 1371
Columbus, Georgia 31902
404/323-5703

Advertising
Annual Reports
Corporate/Industrial
Architectural
Editorial
Location/Studio

Stock Images Available

Additional work can be seen
in American Showcase
Volume 12.

I. Wilson Baker

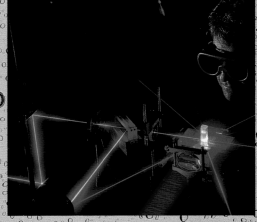

I. Wilson Baker

P.O. Box 20995
Charleston
South Carolina 29413
(803) 577-0828

• advertising
• corporate/industrial
• resort

Member ASMP

CHARLES BROOKS
800 LUTTRELL · KNOXVILLE, TN
615 · 525 · 4501
STOCK AVAILABLE

Dick Dickinson
1781 Independence Boulevard
Number One
Sarasota, Florida 34234
(813) 355-7688
(800) 229-7688
FAX #: (813) 355-4104

E.P. Productions
Commercial Photography
Erich S. Allen
602 Riverside Avenue
Kingsport, Tennessee 37660
(615) 246-7262

Erich S. Allen • 602 Riverside Ave. • Kingsport, TN. 37660 • 615-246-7262

Ken Glaser & Associates
5270 Annunciation Street
New Orleans, Louisiana 70115
(504) 895-7170

I produced this image for The Schering Corporation's 1989 Afrin Poster Calendar. Art direction and design are by Tim Campbell.

My specialty is location photography for advertising, architectural, corporate and editorial. Stock available.

Clients include: Shell Oil Company, Dean Witter Reynolds, Suntory International, Ocean Spray Cranberry, Tulane Medical Center, AT&T and USF&G.

See American Showcase Volumes 10, 11 and 12 or call for our book.

FEAR AND LOATHING ON THE AIRLINE TRAIL

I awoke one Friday morning to the telephone blaring at 5 a.m.

"Hey, Phil. Sorry to wake you, but could you come in early today? We've got a crunch job on a full page newspaper ad."

I told the production coordinator that I'd get there as quickly as I could.

The agency I was working for was one of the larger Houston advertising firms. I'd been there just about a year and I'd been in the business just about a year.

A client of ours had to get an ad into the weekend Atlanta paper. We had all the materials, but had to make a noontime flight to get the ad counter-to-counter to beat the deadline. One hitch: the copy was still getting the final run-through in the client's legal department. As time dragged on, we decided to typeset the copy that we did have and I'd knife the changes as required.

"When will the typesetter have the copy output?"

"About 10:30. Maybe 11:00."

"When am I supposed to paste this thing together and get it to the airport? The flight is at noon."

The Intercontinental Airport in Houston is a terrific airport, don't get me wrong. Well, at least it's not O'Hare. But everyone in Houston is at least 45 minutes away from the airport. It doesn't matter where you live in town. I've got one friend who's a scant six miles away and it still takes him 45 minutes.

We decided that I'd get the ad together as best as possible, blue line everything else on the board, and paste up the ad on the airplane. Not just fly-by-night advertising, but production-by-flight advertising. A new service for the agency repetoire. I taped the keyline securely to a lap board, affixed a t-square down the side to keep things square, and took along a large triangle to do my type alignment. Remember, this was a full page newspaper ad, so you can imagine what the mess looked like.

Racing down to the typesetter, I grabbed the copy and a duplicate for making corrections as soon as it came out of the soup and passed through the wax. I think I broke every speed limit in Texas to get to the airport 24 miles away. Yes, it took me 45 minutes. Getting there, I found no parking spots around the terminal. I mean none. My flight was departing in minutes. I shot into an opening under an entry ramp that had just about four inches of clearance above my car. I bet myself that it wouldn't be here when I got back, but I couldn't worry about that now. I bolted for the gate.

I made the plane just as they were preparing to close the door. Stowing the board and type for take-off, I relaxed in the first First Class seat I'd ever been in. I'd argued that if I was to have enough room to put together an ad in flight, I'd have to go First Class. Once up to altitude, I pulled out the board and feverishly worked on cramming the reams of copy into the ad. The gentleman in the seat next to me was concerned as to what I was doing, especially since it was to the exclusion of food, drink, and all the other trappings of First Class.

"I've got to get this ad together for an afternoon deadline at the paper", I told him without so much as a glance up.

He ordered the second of four Bloody Marys that he would have on that two hour flight.

The ad was done ten minutes before touchdown in Atlanta. Once down, I rushed out of the airport and grabbed the first available cab. We got to the newspaper five minutes before deadline. My contact came down to meet me at the front desk.

"How was the flight?"

"Fine. I've got the ad here. Can I get to a phone to call to see if there are any corrections or revisions?" I asked.

"Would you like something to drink?"

continued on page 240

David Guggenheim
167 Mangum Street
Atlanta, Georgia 30313
(404) 577-4676
FAX: (404) 875-9733

Represented by Alexander/Pollard
(404) 875-1363 Atlanta, GA
(813) 725-4438 Tampa Bay, FL

**Henderson/Muir
Photography**
6005 Chapel Hill Road
Raleigh, North Carolina 27607
(919) 851-0458 • FAX: (919) 851-9787

HENDER

onMuir

continued from page 236

Something was definitely up. There was no newspaper person on earth this laid back without a reason. I finally convinced him to get me to a phone. Calling back to the agency, I found out the client's lawyers had decided that there were some legal questions remaining on the copy and that the ad had been killed for now. I sat back and looked at the clock. It was 5:20 p.m. and I was in the process of missing my return flight to Houston.

Thanking the contact for his help and sending the ad over to the client's Atlanta office by messenger, I made one more call—this time, to an old college buddy who lived in town. I told him that there was a dinner and some Cuervo Tequila that needed attention if he weren't tied up.

That was ten years ago. Today, I could have leisurely arranged the entire ad on my Mac, easily inserted copy changes or revisions, then modemed the ad to the Atlanta paper without the fear and loathing on the airline trail theatrics. Technology is such a wonderful thing, but it would have killed this story as surely as our client killed the ad.

At least my car was still where I left it when I got back to the airport. All in all, that's probably the most amazing thing about this entire tale.

Phil Watkins III
Associate Creative Director
Carmichael Lynch
Kansas City, Missouri

Neil Isgett Photography
4303-D South Boulevard
PO Box 9347
Charlotte, North Carolina 28299
(704) 376-7172

Advertising
Annual Reports
Corporate/Industrial
Illustration

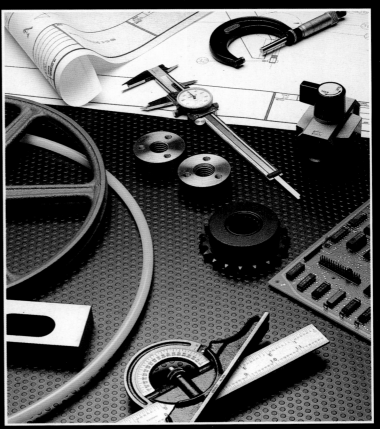

Neil Isgett (704) 376-7172

Peter Langonē
Studio/Peter Langonē Inc.
516 Northeast 13th Street
Fort Lauderdale, Florida 33304
(305) 467-0654
FAX: (305) 522-2562

Complete production services available: stylists, location finders, hair and make-up artists, model/castings, transportation and lab facilities.

For additional work see American Showcase volumes 8, 9, 10, 11 & 12. Stock photography available see INSTOCK. (305) 527-4111.

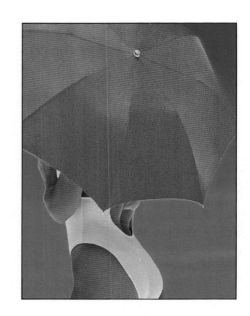

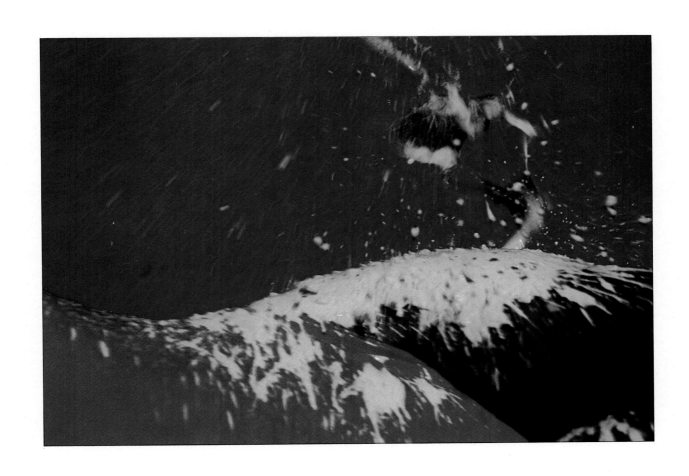

Peter Langonē

(305) 467-0654

Debra Lex Photography
PO Box 56-1974
Miami, Florida 33256
(305) 667-0961
FAX: (305) 856-0467

People & Locations:
• Advertising
• Corporate
• Travel
• Editorial

Clients include:
Federal Express, Bell South, E.F. Hutton,
AT&T, Pepsi-Cola, Wellcraft, Exxon,
General Electric, Xerox, Astro-Lab,
IDS/American Express.

Life, People, Smithsonian, Air & Space,
Time, The Yacht, Boat International,
A Day In the Life of America, Stern,
Bunte, Business Week, Rolling Stone,
TV Guide.

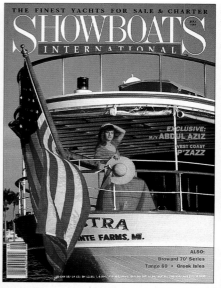

Lowery Photo/Graphics, Inc.
409 Spears Avenue
Chattanooga, Tennessee 37405
(615) 265-4311

When photography or illustration is not enough, try putting them together. With this total image control our only limitations are your imagination.

David Luttrell
1500 Highland Drive
Knoxville, Tennessee 37918
(615) 588-5775
(615) 584-4813

Specializing in studio and location photography. Portfolio and stock are available upon request. For more work see Corporate Showcase #4 and American Showcase #11, 12.

A partial client list includes: Aramco World Magazine, Cahners Publications, Country Journal, DeRoyal Industries, Dollywood, Fogelman Properties, Fort Sanders Medical Center, Healthknit, Heil Trucks, Jeffrey Chain, Krisland Group, Newsweek, Park West Hospital, Perceptics Corp., Publish Magazine, Publishing Corporation of America, Red Food, Scott-Forseman, Sports Illustrated For Kids, Southern Magazine, TEC, TeleRobotics, Tellico Village, Texas Instruments, Toyota USA, USA Today, White Lily Foods and Whittle Communications.

Tom McCarthy
8960 Southwest 114th Street
Miami, Florida 33176
(800) 344-2149
(305) 233-1703
FAX: (305) 235-9368

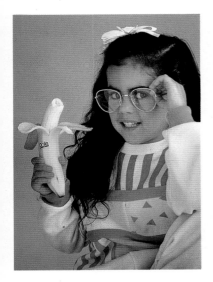

© Tom McCarthy 1989

**Tom McCarthy is in New York
and Miami.
Stock available.**

Clients:
Agfa, Bahamas, Blue Cross/Blue Shield,
Burger King, Coca Cola, Dole,
Eastern Airlines, IBM, Kodak, Lipton,
Mazola, Mead/Johnson, Mexico Tourism,
Nikon, Pillsbury, Polaroid, Royal Caribbean,
Salem, Seagrams, Sears

Tom McCarthy

Allen Mims
107 Madison Avenue
Memphis, Tennessee 38103
(901) 527-4040

Allen Mims
107 Madison Avenue
Memphis, Tennessee 38103
(901) 527-4040

John Petrey
Photographic Illustrator
670 Clay Street/PO Box 2401
Winter Park, (Orlando) Florida 32790
(407) 645-1718

Studio and location photography for advertising, corporate and editorial clients.

Please refer to American Showcase 11 and 12 for more of my work.

Portfolio available upon request.

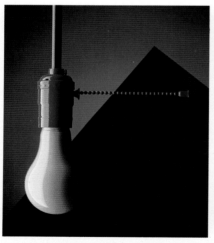

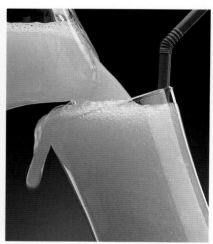

Tom Raymond
2608 West Market
Johnson City, Tennessee 37604
(615) 928-2700

Studio and Location

For additional work see American Showcase 11, 12 and Corporate Showcase 6.

INOVÉ COMMUNICATIONS, SAM BARNETT, A.D.

FIRST TENNESSEE BANK

JACKIE TORRENCE, STORYTELLER

ASMP

ARCATA BOOK GROUP

Bob Schatz
112 Second Avenue North
Nashville, Tennessee 37201
(615) 254-7197 Studio
(615) 943-4222 Mobile

Partial list of clients:
Hospital Corporation of America,
Nissan, Trane Corp., Chardon Rubber
Co., Provident Insurance, Ametek,
Sovran Bank, Third National Bank, and
Acme Boot Co.

Stock available.

Michael Terranova
1135 Cadiz Street
New Orleans, Louisiana 70115
(504) 899-7328

Additional work can be seen in:
Showcase 12, page 232

Arthur Tilley
Photographer
Atlanta, Georgia
(404) 371-8086

"Improve your people skills" For fifteen years I've enjoyed photographing people, mostly on location, for a wide range of clients.

To obtain a list of available stock, a portfolio, bid or reference, call Leslie or me. Thanks, Arthur.

Clients I've shot for: Arvida, CocaCola, Federal Express, Hilton, Hitachi, IBM, KinderCare, Merrill Lynch, Omni Hotels, Quaker Foods, Rubbermaid, Sheraton, Stouffers & Westin Hotels, Valvoline.

A R T H U R

T I L L E Y

Doug Van de Zande
307 West Martin Street
Raleigh, North Carolina 27601
(919) 832-2499

Location and studio photography
35 mm, 2 1/4, 4x5, and 8xl0
Please call or write for more samples or
to get on my mailing list.
"197 million square miles of studio
space"

Van Dezande
Photography
Circa 1900

Mexico

North Carolina

Yugoslavia

Louisiana

VandeZande
PHOTOGRAPHY

Circa 1990

A CULTURAL REVOLUTION

Literacy rates, measured among high school graduates in the United States and in Europe are falling, and politicians and public figures from Barbara Bush to Prince Charles decry the decline in educational standards. While this can't be a good thing to happen, is it really as surprising and depressing as people make out? Are our children really becoming less able to understand the language of the world around them? Or is it that one kind of literacy is being replaced by another? Is traditional written literacy being replaced by visual literacy?

If that supposition were true, then we would need to change the whole way we view other cultures. Civilization is conventionally measured through language. We compare the sophistication of Latin or Greek with the simple oral traditions of African tribes, and we conclude that the Romans and Greeks with their complex, subtle, precise and vivid languages were more advanced. In our own country our basic standards for education are grounded in linguistic ability.

We have always admired "Art" as the decorative element in civilization. But while it has always been held in high esteem it has also been held at arm's length. Art is the sort of thing one enjoys in other peoples' countries when on vacation. It's one of life's luxuries, to be indulged pre-school and post-retirement. Over the centuries and across the globe, families have breathed sighs of relief when the errant son gives up his idea of becoming an artist and opts for a steady job as an air traffic controller or taxidermist or photographer's agent.

But maybe times are changing. Maybe today's school leaves us no less able to understand and communicate than its predecessors. Perhaps it is our measurement of communicative skills that has become lopsided. In my view we are poised on the cusp of a cultural revolution; the shift from a civilization dominated by words to a civilization dominated by pictures.

This has all happened in the last forty years and it has been driven by technology. The invention of the "unblinking eye" is of greater significance than Caxton's invention of the printing press in the fourteenth century. Within a staggeringly short period of time, the TV and its never-ending stream of visual impressions has penetrated the vast majority of homes in the developed world. Today's children spend more time each year in front of the screen than they do in school. This time spent exercising and developing the muscles in the right half of the brain is not wasted. Research work sponsored by advertising agencies testifies to the enormous scope of the mind to absorb, assimilate and recall images and the increased fluency in visual literacy exhibited by children of the TV age. A child of ten takes out more from a 15 second TV commercial than his grandparents would take from a two minute one.

In the future, when historians make comparisons between different societies, they will be assessing visual literacy rather than written literacy as a measure of the sophistication of each culture. It's the work of today's photographers and illustrators that will be their barometer.

Michael Davies
Client Services Director
Michael Peters Group
New York, New York

Christian Verlent
PO Box 530805
Miami, Florida 33153
(305) 751-3385

People on location.
Advertising, Editorial, Travel.
Fluent French.
ASMP Member

Stock available through
Southern Stock Photos
(305) 486-7117
(305) 949-5191

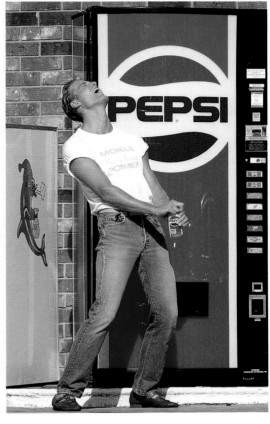

Mark Weinkle
(919) 383-8449
FAX: (919) 382-8188

Mark Weinkle
(919) 383-8449
FAX: (919) 382-8188

Woodbury & Associates
6801 North West 9th Avenue
Fort Lauderdale, Florida 33309
(305) 977-9000 • FAX: (305) 977-7045

Extensive stock available

• Advertising, Annual Reports. Corporate & Industrial
• Studio/Location • Inhouse Color & BW Labs
• See American Showcase 12
• Client List and portfolio available on request.
© Woodbury & Associates 1990

John Zillioux
663 Woodcrest Road
Miami, Florida 33149
(305) 361-0368

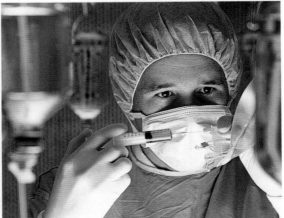

WHO WAS HERB LUBALIN?

THE FACE BEHIND THE FACES.

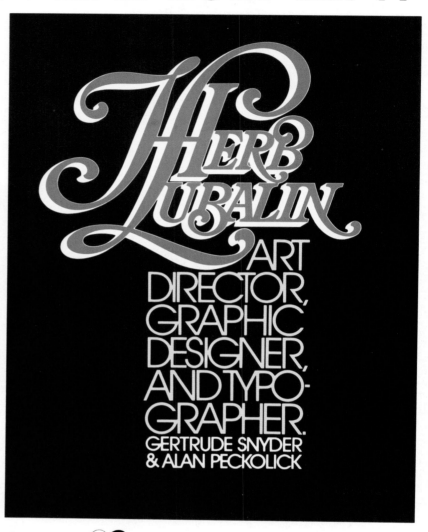

He was a skinny, colorblind, left-handed artist, known to friends and colleagues as a deafeningly silent man. But through his typography-based and editorial designs, he created bold new forms for communication and changed the demensions of advertising and graphics. **Herb Lubalin** is the definitive book about the typographic impresario and design master of our time. It is illustrated with more than 360 extraordinary examples of Lubalin's award-winning work, including: ■ Logos and Letterheads ■ Editorial and Book Design ■ Packaging ■ Advertising and Sales Promotion ■ Annual Reports ■ Best of U&lc, and more.

Now in paperback. 184 pages, Color throughout, 9"x 11 7/8". Paperback: $25.00.

Send for your copy of **Herb Lubalin** today. Pay $25.00 plus $3.00 for postage and handling within the US and Canada. To order, call **(212) 245-0981** and charge your AMEX, Visa or Mastercard. Or send a check or money order to:
AMERICAN SHOWCASE, INC.
724 Fifth Avenue,
New York, NY 10019

·AL TEUFEN·

JOEL CONISON
PHOTOGRAPHY
3201 EASTERN
CINCINNATI, OHIO 45226
513 241-1887
FAX

Michael L. Abramson
3312 West Belle Plaine
Chicago, Illinois 60618
(312) 267-9189

Advertising
Corporate
Editorial

Periodicals include: Business Week,
Forbes, Fortune, Money, Newsweek,
Time.

Sequence of photographs:
1. Allen F. Jacobson, CEO 3M
2. Miles, Inc.
3. Deere & Co.
4. Frederick Rentschler, CEO Beatrice
Company
5. Harvey Kapnick, CEO Chicago
Pacific

David K. Atkinson
The Atkinson Image
14 North Newstead
St. Louis, Missouri 63108
(314) 535-6484

Food styling by Joni
of The Atkinson Image

THE
ATKINSON
IMAGE

14 North Newstead
St. Louis, MO 63108
314-535-6484

DUBRO CATERING

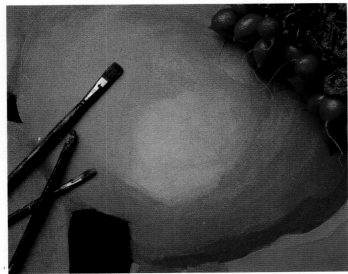

BUSCH CREATIVE SERVICES

ANHEUSER-BUSCH, INC. P.P.G.

Bob Campbell
722 Prestige Street
Joliet, Illinois 60435
(815) 725-1862

Campbell

Lucky Curtis
1540 N. North Park Avenue
Chicago, Illinois 60610
(312) 787-4422

Represented by:
Gigante Moore
(312) 819-1400

LUCKY CURTIS PHOTOGRAPHY INC. / 1540 N. NORTH PARK AVE. / CHICAGO, IL 60610
REPRESENTED BY GIGANTE MOORE / 312-787-4422

ART DIRECTION: WHAT IT BE

Whenever friends and process servers visit my swell cubicle with a view of an office with a view, they invariably ask me "Ken, which way is the men's room?" Unless of course they're women who, being the naturally more astute of the sexes, usually ask "Ken, what's it like being an art director?" I like to tell them it's just like in the movies. This doesn't work, however, because there are no movies about art directors.

So I guess the old "movie" analogy is actually a pretty crummy way to explain what I do. The point is that mine may seem a glamorous profession only because nobody knows a damn thing about it. Let's face it, it sounds cool to "direct" something as long as it isn't traffic. And any use of the work "ART" really makes people stand up and take notice, a response similar to that triggered in large dogs by the sound of a can opener.

But what, after all, is it we do? We breathe any and all kinds of noxious fumes one can propel via fluorcarbons, usually in areas about as well ventilated as a pizza oven. We labor for hours over ponderous tomes of talent searching for just the perfect style of illustration to match the task at hand, even though the client wouldn't know Fuchs from Blechman, except to recognize both as familiar throat-clearing noises. We take eager young fledglings under our protective wings, nurturing, guiding, and teaching the ungrateful wretches with the patience of Job—even after they inadvertently tossed a month's worth of mechanicals into a passing dumpster because they had to move them quickly to get at $28,000.00 worth of artwork on which they just dumped a fresh pot of coffee.

We spend 72 hours in a frigid photo studio the size of an airplane hangar shooting 12 juggling fools, 11 llamas lleaping, 10 scantily clad dancers, 9 tables full of quickly decomposing waxed and prepped food stuffs, 8 unhappy models because they're only doing this until they get an opportunity to star in a feature film, 7 make-up and wardrobe and hair professionals and food stylists at 80 bucks per 1/8 of a mile (or each minute not in motion), 6 high school marching bands, 5 golden arches worth of cold food, 4 angry clients, 3 foreign sports cars, 2 french contortionists, and a photographer who's out of his tree.

But enough about the perks. If you think that you, too, would like a rewarding career as an Art Director, take the following test at home and see how you score:

AN ART DIRECTOR IS PRIMARILY RESPONSIBLE FOR:
(a) Coordinating the visual and conceptual efforts of a unified team of talented individuals in an effort to produce effective, provocative communication
(b) Helping copywriters maintain their sense of superiority
(c) Directing anybody named Art, Arthur or Arturo

I THINK I'D MAKE A DARN FINE ART DIRECTOR BECAUSE:
(a) I'm gifted with rare insight into the human drama that is mankind, and seek to share that vision through the modern wonder of advertising
(b) I'd like to get some free product samples
(c) It's a great way to meet babes

I BELIEVE ADVERTISING TO BE THE QUINTESSENTIAL CREATIVE ENVIRONMENT—MORESO EVEN THAN FILM, TELEVISION OR THEATRE—BECAUSE:
(a) It's the only medium that is designed for and reaches the masses, as truly meaningful art is meant to do
(b) I've been thrown out of every film set, TV studio and public theatre I've ever tried to visit, probably because of my unruly appearance and the unpleasant odor I exude
(c) What's "quintessential"?

Score one point for every answer "c". Subtract 2 points for every answer "a". Divide your total by the square root of Pi, take 2 aspirin, drink plenty of fluids and if pain and nagging doubts persist, see your doctor.

Better yet, why not just forget the whole thing and pursue a fulfilling career in the fast food industry? Flexible hours, earn while you learn. For more information write in care of this publication.

Ken Pisani
Senior Art Director
Doubleday and Co., Inc.
Garden City, New York

Rick Dieringer
19 West Court Street
Cincinnati, Ohio 45202
(513) 621-2544

Location and studio photography for advertising, corporate, industrial and architectural clients.

A partial list of clients includes: Chevron Oil, Miller Brewing, Motorola, Honeywell, Conrail, Formica Corp., Roadway Express, Litton Industries, Satellite Healthcare Systems, Campbell-Hausfeld, Prudential, American Olean Tile Inc., Sub-Zero Corp., Inc. Magazine,

Dainichiseika Color & Chemicals Inc., CTL Aerospace, Concept USA.

Additional work can be seen in Corporate Showcase 4, 6, 7, 8
© 1989 Rick Dieringer

Image Studios
David Wallace
1100 South Lynndale Drive
Appleton, Wisconsin 54914

For representation contact
Jim Weiland
(414) 738-4080
FAX: (414) 738-4089

PROFILE

Image Studios
Will Croff
1100 South Lynndale Drive
Appleton, Wisconsin 54914

For representation contact
Jim Weiland
(414) 738-4080
FAX: (414) 738-4089

IMAGE
S T U D I O S

P R O F I L E

Image Studios
Glen Hartjes
1100 South Lynndale Drive
Appleton, Wisconsin 54914

For representation contact
Jim Weiland
(414) 738-4080
FAX: (414) 738-4089

IMAGE
STUDIOS

PROFILE

Image Studios
John Luke
1100 South Lynndale Drive
Appleton, Wisconsin 54914

For representation contact
Jim Weiland
(414) 738-4080
FAX: (414) 738-4089

PROFILE

P R O F I L E

Image Studios
Charles A. Blackburn
1100 South Lynndale Drive
Appleton, Wisconsin 54914

For representation contact
 Jim Weiland
(414) 738-4080
FAX: (414) 738-4089

IMAGE
S T U D I O S

P R O F I L E

Doug McKay
512 South Hanley
Box 55
St. Louis, Missouri 63105
(314) 863-7167

Location work...it's what I want. Be it a fast-paced corporate headquarters, a noisy industrial plant or the serenity of an isolated outdoor location, it's what excites me. That excitement drives my photography and makes my images work for my clients. I work for many Fortune 500 and industry leading corporations including: Citicorp, Transamerica, Mallinckrodt Chemical, Southwestern Bell, Monsanto, A.G. Edwards & Sons, General Motors, Emerson Electric, Wang, Anheuser-Busch, Sverdrup Corporation, AT&T, Ralston-Purina, Maritz, Eveready, Carlin, Hunter and Mastercard International.

**Dan Moustakas
Photography**
1255 Rankin
Troy, Michigan (Detroit) 48084
(313) 589-0100

Advertising illustration, people, still life
on location or studio.

All special effects produced in camera.

Studio rental available.

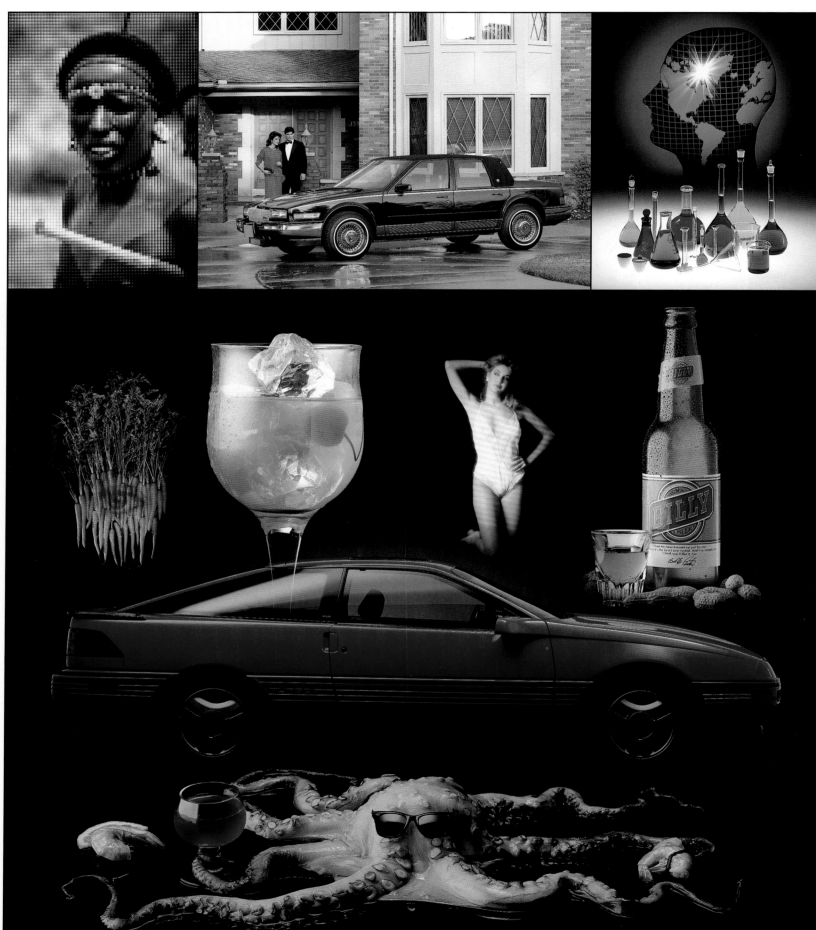

Eric W. Perry
Charles Schridde Photography Inc.
600 Ajax Drive
Madison Heights (Detroit),
Michigan 48071
(313) 589-0111

Paul Poplis Photography
3599 Refugee Road, Building B
Columbus, Ohio 43232
(614) 231-2942
FAX: (614) 231-1698

For beautifully lit, well composed photography that is shot in a studio with video image monitoring, a complete kitchen, a large prop collection, a portfolio you will appreciate and a client list you will recognize...Call Paul.

For additional images please see:
Creative Black Book 84 85, 86, 87, 88, 89.
Work Book 90.

Extensive food stock photography available.

Harry J. Przekop, Jr.
950 West Lake Street
Chicago, Illinois 60607
(312) 829-8201
FAX: (312) 829-6324

Represented by Ellen Harmon

Saks Photography, Inc.
Steve Keltsch
9257 Castlegate Drive
Indianapolis, Indiana 46256
(317) 849-7723
FAX: (317) 849-7885

Represented by Ann Keltsch; portfolio available upon request.

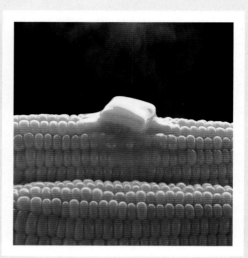

steve keltsch

284

Saks Photography, Inc.
John David Fleck
9257 Castlegate Drive
Indianapolis, Indiana 46256
(317) 849-7723
FAX: (317) 849-7885

john fleck

IS RETAIL BAD FOR YOUR IMAGE?

Stop me if this has ever happened to you. You try to convince a marketing director or ad manager who has already closed off the list of agencies to include your agency. "You're not the type of agency we're looking for..." he says. You respond, "we do alot of retail-type advertising...aren't you interested in selling your products?" His response, "of course, but we need to build our image and frankly you're not an image agency."

My true story was for a pitch to the folks who invented Teddy Ruxpin, the talking teddy bear. They also created Laser Tag, the "bang, you're dead! toy" of the eighties using infrared light shot from pistols. Worlds of Wonder was the name of the company and their next venture was into the world of inter-active video. I couldn't convince the senior marketing people that despite selling hamburgers for McDonald's, cars for Toyota, or Ralphs groceries or tickets to amusement parks like Knott's Berry Farm or Marine World Africa USA, that Davis, Ball & Colombatto (formerly DJMC) could also sell, or more importantly, attract purchasers for their new inter-active video. It seems our heavy mix of retail-type clients suggested to the folks at WOW that we couldn't sell their products as well as a packaged goods or brand-type agency. What happened? Well, they hired the other type of agency and like all the rest of the products from WOW, they folded. Belly-up! Their stock when last reported traded at something like .17 cents a share, if that, down from $33.00.

Should they have demanded a little more from their advertising? Like the objective to sell their products? I believe so. And so should most clients. For our entire history we've been labeled as a retail agency, like the term suggests we don't care about good creative or that all we debate over in creative meetings is logo size and how big the prices should be.

In fact, we do argue about those things but only after we agree that the concept is both original and zap-proof.

That it will momentarily paralyze the viewers' forefingers preventing that ultimate form of criticism, zapping, from happening.

But, we also work the concept over and over to assure ourselves that it sells the product with such appeal and conviction that viewers become consumers and respond not within weeks, but hours. Agencies that steep themselves with retail clients and grow, have to come to think in terms of minutes, hours and days versus weeks, months and years. Our clients' businesses demand advertising that gets their business moving immediately; not long-term or over time. Sure those are nice residual effects of the advertising, but clients usually worry about today's sales or this weekend's numbers versus that proverbial five year plan. After all, most clients are just as worried about losing their jobs for lack of performance as agencies are about losing the account, for the same reason.

Retail is not an ugly word if you're in the business to sell something. Nor does it have to imply ugly looking ads or commercials. At DBC, the two co-exist quite nicely...to such an extent that we proudly point to our Clio winning retail approach for Borateem Bleach, or our international homerun in creating the "Mac Tonight" campaign for McDonald's, and more. Combining an intrusive creative approach with a hard-selling, "buy it today" approach has helped us dramatically, and of course, more to the point—our clients. If we're accused of creating advertising that makes people buy things, terrific. So before you rule out certain client possibilities because you're worried that their retail needs will limit your creative potential and hurt your image or reel, don't!

There's plenty of creativity in making cash registers ring.

Brad A. Ball
President
Davis, Ball & Colombatto Advertising
Los Angeles, California

Charles Schridde Photography, Inc.

600 Ajax Drive
Madison Heights (Detroit),
Michigan 48071
(313) 589-0111

One Charlie Schridde
is worth a thousand words.

Unfortunately we haven't got room for a thousand words. So we can only give highlights of the Charlie Schridde Legend. His childhood abduction by a crazed film salesman. His lifelong fear of sanity. His successful fight to have his name changed (to Schridde). And above all, his great eye (it's four inches across).

But his pictures say it all. See? They speak of light and mood and tight deadlines. They speak of everything from movie stars to sexy cars. And they whisper TRUTH. Listen. Closely. There!

Take a look at the car your kid will be driving in the year 2000.

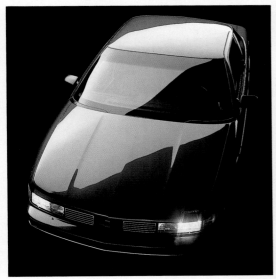

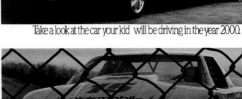

Feeding time at the zoo.

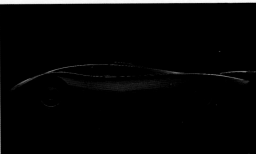

Richard Hamilton Smith
(612) 645-5070
FAX: (612) 645-8263

Agents:
Mary Atols
John Hoffman
(312) 222-0504
FAX: (312) 222-0503

NY Agent:
Susan Miller
(212) 905-8400

For Stock Call:
Jan Bliss (612) 645-5070
FAX: (612) 645-8263

Richard Hamilton Smith
(612) 645-5070
FAX: (612) 645-8263

Agents:
Mary Atols
John Hoffman
(312) 222-0504
FAX: (312) 222-0503

NY Agent:
Susan Miller
(212) 905-8400

For Stock Call:
Jan Bliss (612) 645-5070
FAX: (612) 645-8263

MAY WE SUGGEST
THE CONDENSED VERSION?

To find the best corporate photographers and illustrators in America, you could wade through a sea of zippered portfolios, holding transparencies up to the light as printed samples spill out on the floor around you.

Or you could buy Corporate Showcase 8.

Inside this one creative sourcebook, you'll find 290 professional photographers and illustrators. Artists with styles appropriate to every type of corporate communication. And unlike those bulky books you have to call in, Corporate Showcase 8 fits neatly on your desk for quick and easy reference.

So buy the condensed version. $35.00 (paperback) including postage and handling. The only thing you'll miss is the mess.

Corporate Showcase by American Showcase. 724 Fifth Avenue, New York, New York 10019 **212-245-0981**.

T E R R Y   V I N E   P H O T O G R A P H Y

5455 DASHWOOD, SUITE 200 · HOUSTON, TEXAS 77401 · (713) 664-2920

ON LOCATION

LIKE LIGHT WITH CHARACTER. I LIKE ROADSIDE DINERS

WHERE YOU CAN GET HOMEMADE CHERRY PIE FOR BREAKFAST.

AND THERE ARE AT LEAST THREE TRUCKS PARKED OUTSIDE.

ON LOCATION

602·277·7701

BOX 10397

PHOENIX, AZ 85064

ASSIGNMENT AND STOCK

© KENT KNUDSON 1990

MATTHEW SAVINS   101 HOWELL ST.   DALLAS, TEXAS 75207   214.651.7516

S A V I N S

ART REP INC

Linda Smith
3525 Mockingbird Lane
Dallas, Texas 75205.2225
214.521.5156
Fax 214.520.6366

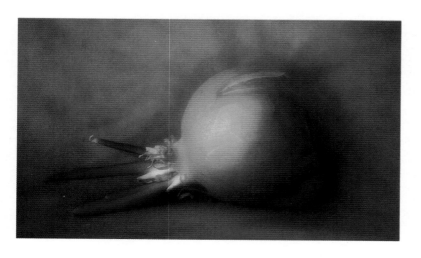

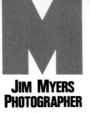

M

JIM MYERS
PHOTOGRAPHER

165 Cole Street   Dallas, Texas 75207   (214) 698-0500   Represented by Barbara Boster

BEN
BRITT
Photography

Represented by
Berry Hawkins 214-327-7889

1345 Chemical
Dallas, Texas 75207
214-634-9846

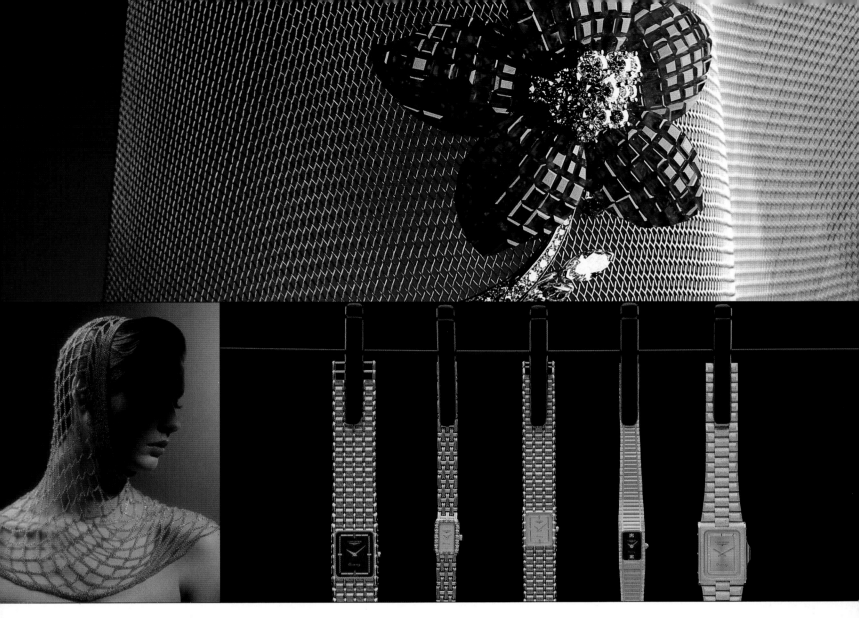

K E N T K I R K L E Y

4906 DON DRIVE DALLAS, TEXAS 75247 214 688-1841 FAX 214 688-1844

REPRESENTED BY ART REP INC. 214 521-5156 FAX 214 520-6366

© Kent Kirkley 1990

David Schmidt

David has travelled the back roads and high roads of Arizona and the Southwest, so he knows exactly where to find the right canyon, mountain, desert, lake, golf course, or resort setting.

Investigate the possibilities, just thumb through David Schmidt's portfolio and see photographs that will cause second glances and inspire spontaneous human reaction.

Please call David in Phoenix at 602-258-2592 or Marla Matson Represents at 602-252-5072. We'll make the arrangements and send you a free "paid vacation" package, then you can start packing.

ANDY VRACIN  PHOTOGRAPHY

4906 Don Drive
Dallas, Texas 75247
214-688-1841

Represented By
Art Rep Inc.
214-521-5156

© Andy Vracin 1990

Dennis Murphy

101 Howell, Dallas, Texas 75207, 214-651-7516, Fax 214-748-0856. Call Katie.

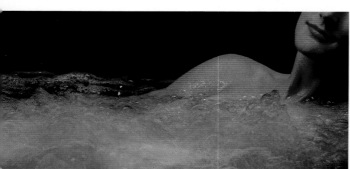

Joe Abraham
11944 Hempstead Road, Suite C
Houston, Texas 77092
(713) 460-4948
FAX: (713) 460-9553

Represented by: Lee Ann Langbehn

Various techniques to suit your needs in Color, BW and Hand-tinted Coloration.

Advertising, editorial, people, corporate and industrial on location or in our full service studio.

Clients include: American Capital, Compaq, Compri Hotels, Computer Graphics World Magazine, Conoco, Dupont, Financial Planning Magazine, Geosource, Good Housekeeping, Houston Lighting & Power, Kellogg, Macy's, Moore Industries, Oshman's, Palais Royal, Penn Well Publishing, Riviana Foods, Sakowitz, 7-Up, Shell Oil, Stop & Go, Sysco, The Robb Report, Uncle Ben's, Union Carbide, United Technologies, U.S. Homes, West Agro Chemical and Wilsonart.

© 1989 Joe Abraham

abraham

Creative Connections
Berry Hawkins
(214) 327-7889

matt BOWMAN

Photostration™
Combining photography
with illustration for a creative
solution to unique problems.

1345 Chemical, Dallas, Texas 75207 • (214) 637-0211

matt BOWMAN

Represented by
Berry Hawkins
214•327•7889

1345 Chemical, Dallas, Texas 75207 • (214) 637-0211

WHY OGILVY MATTERED

On May 15, a blob called WPP Group PLC devoured Ogilvy & Mather, original knight-errant of advertising enlightenment, in a hostile takeover. As the agency he founded in 1948 surrenders its sovereignty, mull 20 reasons why David Ogilvy and his works will live long after the tycoon who bought his name is forgotten.

1. David Ogilvy single-handedly savaged advertising's hoary by-the-cretins, for-the-cretins formulas. "The consumer is not a moron," he thundered. "She is your wife." Result: advertising discourse elevated forever.

2. Ogilvy made advertising a respectable craft for the literate. His best ads read as if written by E.B. White on speed. Sample O&M copy alumni: Don DeLillo, Edmund Morris.

3. "The more you tell," Ogilvy postulated, "the more you sell." Caramba! His fact-packed, nugget-studded long copy broke all rules. And most readership records.

4. Ogilvy, he of the Churchillian ego, built his career and his agency on humility. The humility of placing subjective opinion and "gut feeling" second to impartial consumer research.
Forcefully applied, this transformed advertising from so much voodoo into a new religion: relentless rationalism.

5. Ogilvy quantified his findings on what worked and didn't work to unzip the buyer's money belt into a cranky catechism of dos and don'ts. Samples:

• Always caption illustrations: people read captions more than body copy.

• Never set body text in sans-serif type. It tires the eye and diminishes readership.

• Always put coupons in the lower right-hand corner. They're easiest to cut out that way.
Ogilvy's rules torpedoed the entrenched and self-serving conceit—prevalent among many of those who created them—that ads were 99 percent divine inspiration and 1 percent methodical cerebration.

No wonder the vast majority of creative advertising types, who had owed their three-hour lunches to said conceit, never forgave him.

Down With Smarm

6. Ogilvy's pithy, head-on, no-nonsense style ("Should every corporation buy its president a Rolls-Royce?") suddenly made most other advertising seem as sincere as a mortician's handshake.
This hastened the disappearance of unctuousness and smarm from America's ad-biz lexicon.
The decline of Western civilization—arrested.

7. Ogilvy worshiped good taste but never succumbed to the fatal delusion that advertising is art.
He assumed clients used it as a money-making tool. Perhaps because he did ditto.

8. Spared the endless and sterile Art-vs.-Commerce debates that consume six of every eight hours in the average agency creative department, O&M merrily harnessed itself to the single-mindedly mercantile end of selling stuff.
O&M sold so much stuff that it became one of the top-ten agencies worldwide, with billings in the billions.
By the end of the '70s, meanwhile, most of O&M's post-war Art-over-Commerce contemporaries had vanished as advertising entities. Along with their shelves full of Clios.

continued on page 310

Jay Brousseau
Photographer
2608 Irving Boulevard
Dallas, Texas 75207
(214) 638-1248
FAX: (214) 638-1249

Represented by:
Elizabeth Simpson
(214) 761-0001

Location and studio photography for advertising, corporate and editorial clients.

You can see more of our work in Corporate Showcase 4, 5, and 6. Stock available.

Jim Caldwell
101 West Drew
Houston, Texas 77006
(713) 527-9121

Corporate/commercial/advertising/travel
photography
On location or in our 3000 sq. ft. studio.
Stock available direct.
For more examples of my work, please
consult American Showcase Volumes 8,
9, 10, 11 & 12 and Corporate Showcase
Volumes 4, 6 & 7. Or...call for a packet

of samples rushed directly to you.
Partial listing of clients includes:
Austin Industries, Coca-Cola Foods,
Columbia Artists, Coldwell Banker,
Compaq, Continental Can, Exxon USA,
Houghton Mifflin Publishers, Humana
Hospitals, Kentucky Fried Chicken,
Kingdom of Saudi Arabia, McCann

Erickson, Ogilvy & Mather, Owens-
Corning, Pitney Bowes, Prudential
Insurance, Southwestern Bell, Texas
Children's Hospital, Texas Heart
Institute, Unisys Corp., Warner Amex
Communications...and the list goes on.

Jim Caldwell
101 West Drew
Houston, Texas 77006
(713) 527-9121

Corporate/commercial/advertising/travel photography

On location from the Middle East to our own backyard.

Please call for samples or for stock listings:
The stock file emphasizes North America (including Alaska, Canada and Mexico), and also contains Egypt, Saudi Arabia, and the U.S.S.R.

Subject areas range from architecture to computers to industry to people and places...and more!

Photographs © 1989 Jim Caldwell

SAKKARA, EGYPT

BAYTOWN, TEXAS

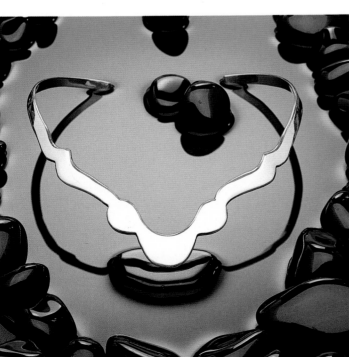

continued from page 306

9. Neurotics and drunks abounded at O&M as in all creative enterprises—but interesting neurotics and drunks.

By prizing intellectual curiosity over flash, Ogilvy attracted the intellectually curious. And repelled artistes, prima donnas, and auteurs.

Most agencies function like adolescent encounter groups. O&M did not.

Sleazeballs Need Not Apply

10. Ogilvy foreswore the adman's ancient self-protective carapace of cynicism. His respect for the client, the product, the consumer, and the vocation of selling was absolute.

This ennobled the agency and its work.

Years later, Ogilvy graduates don't say ad. They say advertisement.

True Story

Ogilvy encounters one of his copywriters igniting a fresh cigar.

"Why aren't you smoking our client's cigar?" he demands.

"Because our client's cigar tastes like rope," retorts the copywriter.

Two weeks hence, he is an ex-O&M copywriter.

Browbeating the Babbitts

11. Ogilvy used his eminence as a bully pulpit from which to scold his brethren. Advertising's Babbitts tended to trade Rotarian homilies. Ogilvy liked to remind them that the public trusted used car salesmen more than admen. Ad infinitum.

12. This Great Man was visible to even his lowliest minions. O&M employees worked not for some corporate blob but for David Ogilvy. He called them "partners."

No cubicle was safe from impromptu Ogilvy visits. These stimulated as much as they terrified.

They also exhausted. "Do you know how many Americans say grace before every meal?" "Why should you write any differently to the rich?" "Do you think using big words makes you look smart?"

Ogilvy did not converse. He interrogated.

The Rewards of Monomania

13. Advertising was not the compromise career for Ogilvy that it is for many. He was an advertising monomaniac. His focus never blurred. His intensity never flagged. And his agency never slept.

Ogilvy taught himself to write brilliantly—the better to sell, period. The idea of writing as art or personal expression was to him anathema. He was hurt and baffled by copywriters who pined to be novelists. Why would they want to squander their talents on literature?

14. Ogilvy was allergic to equivocation. Emphatic certitude was his sole mode.

This certitude became O&M's certitude. In an industry notorious for belief systems as firm as custard, Ogilvy & Mather stood for something. And against almost as much. Against nepotism. Against bullying clients. Against jingles. Against silliness in advertising: "People don't buy from clowns."

15. Ogilvy's 1962 <u>Confessions of an Advertising Man</u> was the only inside book about advertising capable of keeping the lay reader awake. It was a bible of advertising common sense. After 27 years and god knows how many shifts in advertising styles and practice, it still is.

continued on page 318

Dick Clintsman
C Studio
3001 Quebec Street
Suite 102
Dallas, Texas 75247
(214) 630-1531
FAX: (214) 630-1532

People. Situation. Lifestyle.
Advertising. Design. Editorial.

Worldwide location photography.
Full-service studio.

Clients include: American Airlines;
Bailey, Banks & Biddle; Greyhound;
Olivetti; Texas Instruments; Northern
Telecom; Pepsi USA; Frito-Lay; Mobil;
Phillips 66; Pizza Hut; Burger King;
Southland Corporation; American
Express.

EDS
Photography Services
4718 Iberia
Dallas, Texas 75207
(214) 631-1157
Steve McAlister

Represented by:
Tom Tingdale
(214) 631-1157

People. Places. Things. Big things. Little things. Things you can't normally see with the naked eye. You know, things like service, commitment, dedication, pride, happiness, seriousness, professionalism.

Corporate/Industrial, Annual Reports, Advertising, Architecture, Location, Studio, People, Aerial. Stock available.

312

EDS
Photography Services
4718 Iberia
Dallas, Texas 75207
(214) 790-5075
Gary Jenkins

Represented by:
Tom Tingdale
(214) 631-1157

People. Places. Things. Big things. Little things. Things you can't normally see with the naked eye. You know; things like service, commitment, dedication, pride, happiness, seriousness, professionalism.

Corporate/Industrial, Annual Reports, Advertising, Architecture, Location, Studio, People, Aerial. Stock available.

Linda Enger Photography
915 South 52nd Street, Suite 5
Tempe, Arizona 85281
(602) 966-5776

Compelling photo paintings for use in advertising, corporate communications, editorial, and corporate interior art.

Linda combines her photographic "staged spontaneity" with various painting techniques to create unforgettable images.

Portfolio samples and stock photography available upon request. See also CA Photo Annual 1987.

EXPRESSED ENGER

Gary Faye Photography

2421 Bartlett
Houston, Texas 77098
(713) 529-9548

One of the best things about the photography we do is that it brings together many of our favorite things - and that covers a lot of ground, from studio sets to location, from people to places & things, from light that's found to light that's made. The common thread is they all can be fun.

A partial list of clients includes: Continental Airlines, Chemical Bank, Crocker Bank, Gerald D. Hines Interests, Title USA, Arco, Shell, Texaco, Exxon, Houston Symphony, Texas Monthly Magazine, Memorial Hospital Systems.

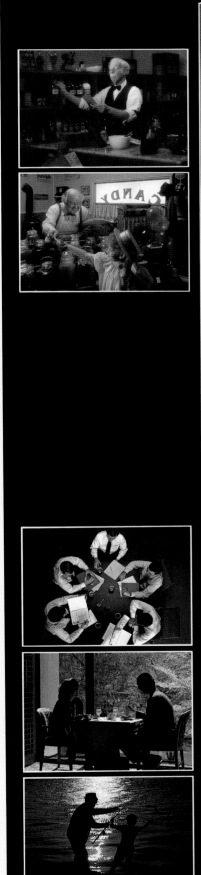

Mark Green
2406 Taft Street
Houston, Texas 77006
(713) 523-6146
FAX: (713) 523-6145
TELEX: 4997187 GREEN UI

Location photography for Corporate
Communications, Advertising, and
Editorial clients nationwide, including
Polaroid Corporation, 3M Company,
Brown & Root Incorporated, Continental
Airlines, Kool Cigarettes and HCA
Hospitals.

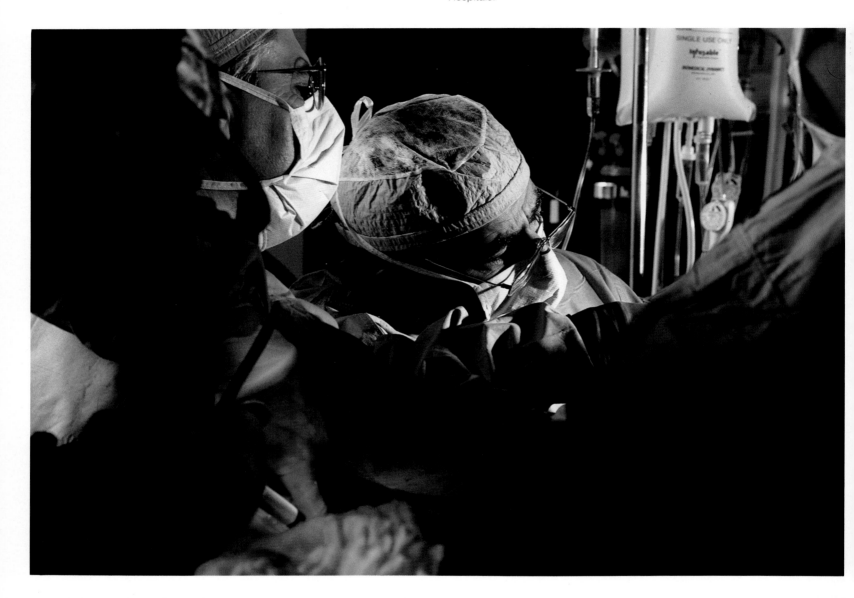

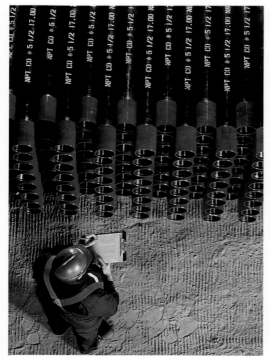

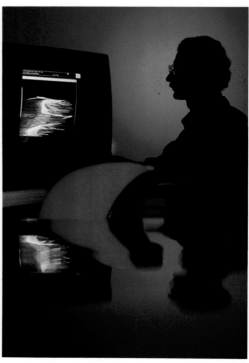

**Zigy Kaluzny
Photographer**
4700 Strass Drive
Austin, Texas 78731
(512) 452-4463

Annual reports, corporate and editorial
photography on location worldwide.
Member ASMP.

Stock available.

See: AS 7, 10; ASMP 4, 5.

Rapports annuels, photographie
d'entreprise, de presse et d'edition, en
exterieurs et dans le monde entier.
Membre ASMP

Phototheque a disposition.

Voir AS 7, 10; ASMP 4, 5.

Jahresberichte, Industrie- Redaktions-
und Pressefotografie, weltweite
Aussenaufnahmen.
ASMP Mitglied.

Archiv-Fotos erhältlich.

Siehe: AS 7, 10; ASMP 4, 5.

continued from page 310

What British Accent?

16. Ogilvy introduced a welcome note of upper-class British civility into American advertising—but checked the Britishisms at the door. Perhaps he knew the colonial mind. More likely he knew condescension doesn't sell.

17. Being put in your place by Ogilvy was often more edifying than being praised by your mom.
The device of choice was a withering mix of sarcasm, name-dropping, historical quotation, odd facts, and research statistics, compressed into three or four lines, max, on a 3-by-5-inch (Memo From D.O.). Victims saved them. The agency recently published a small book of them. Hagiography? No, entertainment.

18. Ogilvy's hatred of muddy thinking, bombast, and bad writing had salutary effects on more than his ads. He judged interoffice correspondence as a Marine sergeant judges a footlocker.

Upside: The pith level of routine interoffice correspondence at O&M was close to that of the ads.

Downside: Having to read any other agency's interoffice correspondence causes hives.

19. Ogilvy-trained advertising people have infiltrated the bloodstream of the industry over the years—as agency chairmen, presidents, and creative bigwigs.

20. Ogilvy the legendarily vain, petulant, spoiled, incessantly demanding tyrant, who never said thanks if he could avoid it, created an agency culture of singular esprit and pride and durability.
O&M publishes a fat quarterly newsletter—for ex-O&M employees.
Or will until the minute WPP Group PLC calculates how much money not publishing it will save.

Bruce McCall
Vice Chairman/Chief Creative Officer
McCaffrey and McCall, Inc.
New York, New York

This article originally appeared in the June 14, 1989 issue of 7 Days.

Bryan Kuntz Photography
7700 Renwick, Suite 5-A
Houston, Texas 77081
(713) 667-4200

Markow Southwest Inc.
Paul Markow
2222 East McDowell Road
Phoenix, Arizona 85006
(602) 273-7985

Represented in Phoenix by Marjorie Rosenman at (602) 273-7985 or use our FAX by calling (602) 273-0928

Paul Markow Shoots for Print. Photomatics and stock on location. Anywhere.

His clients include America West Airlines, Anheuser-Busch, Armstrong Tires, Audi, Best Western International, Chiat/Day, Citicorp, Coca-Cola, Dial Corporation, Federal Express, General Foods, Greyhound, Harley-Davidson, Honeywell, ITT, Lowe Marshchalk, Miller Brewing, NAPA, Ogilvy & Mather, Porsche, Procter & Gamble, Saatchi & Saatchi DFS, Southwest Forest, Stetson and United Airlines.

MARKOW

Call for our new
portfolio. Also see
our Black Book pages
from 1984-1989.

Robert Maxham
223 Howard
San Antonio, Texas 78212
(512) 223-6000
FAX: (512) 223-6192

Studio and location photography.
Specializing in advertising, annual
reports, fashion, catalogs, editorial,
and whatever it takes to communicate.

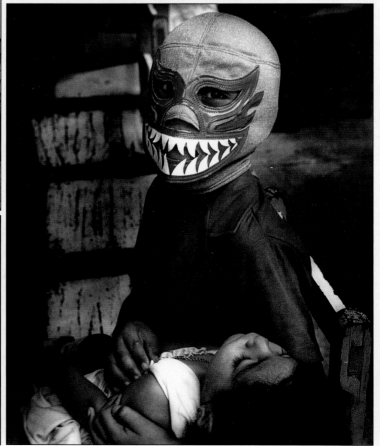

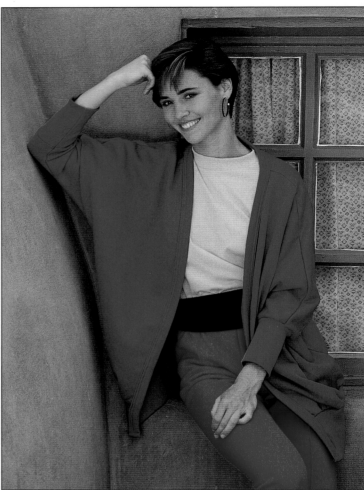

Dale O'Dell

2040 Bissonnet
Houston, Texas 77005
(713) 521-2611

Location photography, optical and computer photo-illustration for advertising, corporate/industrial and editorial.

For additional work see:
Communication Arts photography annuals: 1985, 1987, 1988, 1989.

Stock available through Comstock.

Jim Olvera
235 Yorktown Street
Dallas, Texas 75208
(214) 760-0025
FAX: (214) 748-1463

I shoot color photographs for a wide variety of discriminating clients, including Woody Pirtle, Young & Rubicam, and J. Walter Thompson.

Jim Olvera
235 Yorktown Street
Dallas, Texas 75208
(214) 760-0025
FAX: (214) 748-1463

In addition to color, I shoot black and white. In either case, it takes more than one exposure to get beautiful results. But to me, and to my clients, the effort isn't wasted.

John Parrish
1218 Manufacturing
Dallas, Texas 75207
(214) 742-9457

Represented by:
Elizabeth Simpson
(214) 943-9355

John Parrish
1218 Manufacturing
Dallas, Texas 75207
(214) 742-9457

Represented by:
Elizabeth Simpson
(214) 943-9355

Joe Robbins
7700 Renwick, Suite 5A
Houston, Texas 77081
(713) 667-5050
FAX: (713) 667-3600

Advertising
Corporate

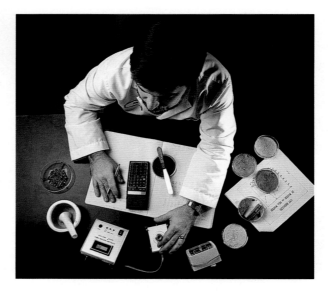

Joseph Savant
4756 Algiers Street
Dallas, Texas 75207
(214) 951-0111

See our ads in Corporate Showcase 3 &
4 and American Showcases 8, 9, 10,
11 & 12. Portfolio available upon
request.

Michael Schneps
7700 Renwick, Suite 5A
Houston, Texas 77081
(713) 668-4600 or (713) 520-8224

For additional work please see
Showcase volumes 8, 9, 10, 11 & 12,
A.R. volumes 1 & 2, CA Photography
Annuals 1985, '87 & '89, and

The 65th and 66th Art Directors Club of
New York Annuals.
Stock available through The Image
Bank.

マイク・シネプスは日本に18年間滞在し
ました。彼は日本語を流暢に話し、仕事
の関係もあり日本全国を旅行しました。
日本そして日本人を良く理解した説得力
のある彼のフォトグラフィック・イメージ
は日本人の顧客の皆様に充分に御満足い
ただけるでしょう。

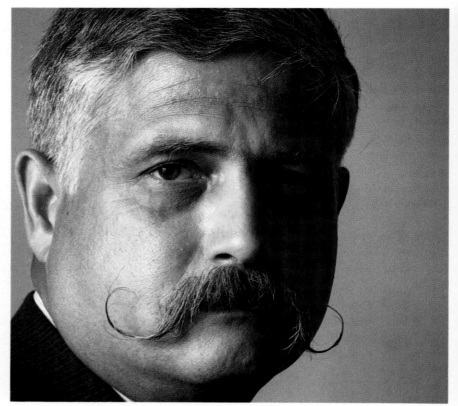

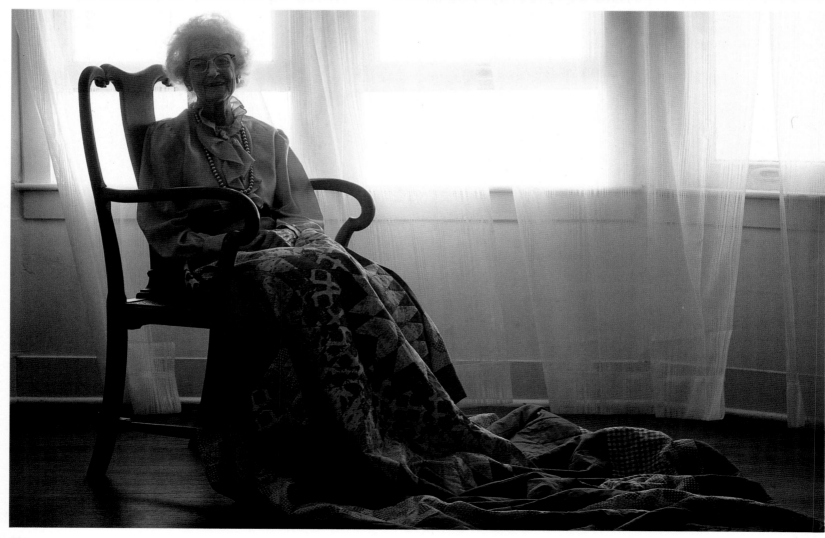

Frank Simon
Represented by:
Photo Group
(602) 381-1332
(602) 381-1406 FAX
(602) 279-4635 studio

Micheal Simpson
1415 Slocum Street, #105
Dallas, Texas 75207
(214) 761-0000

Represented by:
Elizabeth Simpson
(214) 761-0001
The New York Portfolio
(214) 989-8588

For additional work please refer to:
Corporate Showcase Volumes: 4, 5, 6, 7 & 8

Stock Photography Available Through FPG International, New York or contact the Studio.

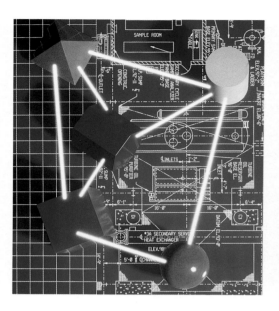

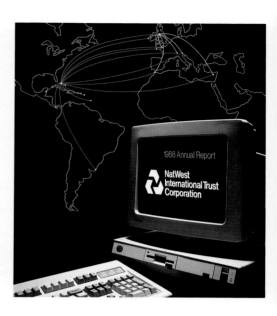

Micheal Simpson
1415 Slocum Street, #105
Dallas, Texas 75207
(214) 761-0000

Represented by:
Elizabeth Simpson
(214) 761-0001
The New York Portfolio
(214) 989-8588

For additional work please refer to:
Corporate Showcase Volumes: 4, 5, 6, 7 & 8

Stock Photography Available Through FPG International, New York or contact the Studio.

Hans Staartjes
34 Lana Lane
Houston, Texas 77027
(713) 621-8503

FOCUS
NOT
GUARANTEED

STAARTJES

Bob Werre Photography
2437 Bartlett Street
Houston, Texas 77098
(713) 529-4841

"Fantastic lighting...precise techniques...nice guy..."

BOB WERRE PHOTOGRAPHY

335

Keith Wood Photography, Inc.
1308 Conant
Dallas, Texas 75207
(214) 634-7344

There must be a fine balance between pure creativity and pure business...for neither can exist without the other. Photographer, Keith Wood walks delicately in that balance. A dull Australia mine can be represented with the humor of its workers. An unattractive "Oil Patch" setting can be represented (saved) with proper visual design. It's a matter of experience and excitement in finding solutions. More importantly, it's a matter of the reliability that maintains professional balance in his work. He is dedicated to the viewers of his images.

Freeport-McMoRan/Mineral Recovery • Diamond Shamrock/Oil & Gas• Motorola Corporation • Dresser Industries • Schlumberger Inc. • Tyler Corporation • Maxus Energy • Texas Industries • First Mississippi Gold • Kimberly Clark • Swearington/ Commercial Real Estate • Surgikos/Medical

Butch

Adams

Photography

1414

South

700

West

Salt

Lake

City

Utah

84104

801-973-0939

"Perfume"

DAVID HOLT

Photography/an alternative view

1624 Cotner Avenue, Los Angeles, California 90025

(213) 478-1188

"Angela"

DAVID HOLT

Photography/an alternative view

1624 Cotner Avenue, Los Angeles, California 90025

(213) 478-1188

MARC SOLOMON

BOX 480574 • L.A., CA. 90048 • (213) 935-1771

MARC SOLOMON • BOX 480574 • L.A., CA. 90048 • (213) 935-1771

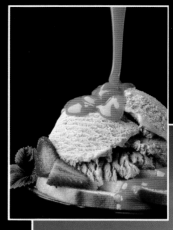

deGENNARO ASSOCIATES

902 SOUTH NORTON AVE., LOS ANGELES, CALIFORNIA 90019
(213) 935-5179 FAX (213) 935-9120

NAKASHIMA, TSCHOEGL & ASSOCIATES, INC.

600 Moulton Avenue · Studio 101A · Los Angeles, California 90031 · 213/226-0506 · 415/421-1406

Les Nakashima · Chris Tschoegl · Mike Narciso

Marketing: Patricia Deacon · Chris Tschoegl

NAKASHIMA, TSCHOEGL & ASSOCIATES, INC.

600 Moulton Avenue · Studio 101A · Los Angeles, California 90031 · 213/226-0506 · 415/421-1406

Hyatt Grand Champions

Century Plaza

Century Plaza

Dana Point Resort

Las Vegas Hilton

Les Nakashima · Chris Tschoegl · Mike Narciso

Marketing: Patricia Deacon · Chris Tschoegl

Baja Adventures

John Wayne Airport

DW and Associates

EliotCrowley
PHOTOGRAPHER

Baja Adventures

3221 BENDA PLACE

HOLLYWOOD, CA 90068

213 • 851 • 5110

Brent Whitfield Studio   Los Angeles   213·624·75 11

Nissan . Bausch & Lomb . Carnation . Princess Cruise Lines . Contadina . Neutrogena . Vivitar . Winchells . Libbys . Hills Bros .
Chiat Day . Gumpertz Bently Fried . Kaiser McEuen . J. Walter Thompson . McCann Erickson . Spear Young & Hollander

Burke/Triolo

Los Angeles
Studio (213)687-4730   Fax (213)687-3226

NOLTONSTUDIO
107 N.W. FIFTH AVENUE
PORTLAND, OREGON 97209
(503) 228-0844
FAX: 228-0857

SHOWN: AT WINDMERE RANCH,
OREGON, FOR SMOKECRAFT.
IN THE UTAH CANYONLANDS FOR
ALL CONDITIONS GEAR.
NOT SHOWN: THE REST OF MY BOOK.
SO CALL.

GARY NOLTON

Also see
American Showcases #8, #9, #10, #12
Corporate Showcase #4, #8

TOM TRAVIS
PHOTOGRAPHY

1219 SOUTH PEARL STREET, DENVER, COLORADO 80210

© 1989

LOCATION

Advertising

Corporate

Editorial

STUDIO

ROBERT G. EARNEST

Orange County

California

714 259 9190

714 498 6488

PHOTOGRAPHY

People you can believe

Harmel

PHOTOGRAPHER

Mark Harmel

Los Angeles

213 659-1633

ROBERT ADLER

☐ 33 ELLERT STREET ☐
SAN FRANCISCO, CA 94110
☐ 415-695-2867 ☐

Client: The Portman, San Francisco

Client: *Friends* Magazine/
Aegis Publishing

Client: Georgia Durante, Performance Two

Client: Chevrolet Motor Division

Client: Chevrolet Motor Division

819½ NORTH FAIRFAX AVENUE

LOS ANGELES, CA 90046

213/655-7287

FAX: 658-7464

KAZ KURISU PHOTOGRAPHY

neil b. nissing
PHOTOG
213 • 849 • 1811

American Honda
Argus Publications
Automobile Quarterly
Auto Trend Graphics
Circle Track Magazine
Franklin Mint
General Motors
Liesure Publications
Motor Trend Magazine
Sears
Suzuki Motor Corp.
Winston Tire Co.

Steve Welsh Photography, Inc.
1121 Grove St.
Boise, Idaho 83702

208-336-5541

Member A.S.M.P.

Welsh

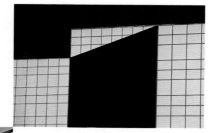

Clients

Boise Cascade
Ore-Ida
Weight Watchers
Morrison-Knudsen
Trus Joist Corp.
Penn West Ltd.
Hewlett-Packard
Micron Technology
Key Bank
West One Bank
Swix Sport

ZIMMERMAN

Dick Zimmerman Studio 8743 W. Washington Blvd. LA, CA 90230 (213) 204-2911

AMERICAN SHOWCASE

VOLUME 13

THIS BOOK WAS PRINTED BOUND AND SEPARATED BY

DAI NIPPON SINCE VOLUME 3

DAI NIPPON PRINTING CO., LTD.

New York
Düsseldorf
Hong Kong
San Francisco

INTERNATIONAL OPERATIONS
1-1, Ichigaya-Kagacho 1-chome, Shinjuku-ku,
Tokyo, 162 Japan. Telephone: 03-266-3340
Telex: J22737   DNPRINT   TOKYO

London
Sydney
Jakarta
Singapore
Los Angeles

Ron Starr, architectural and interior photographer specializing in location work both nationally and internationally.

PARTIAL CLIENT LIST
Dean, Witter, Reynolds
Hellmuth, Obata, Kassabaum Inc.
Hemmeter Corp.
Marquis Assoc.
Media 5
Skidmore, Owings, & Merrill
Time-Life Inc.

SELECTED PUBLICATIONS
Architectural Record
Architecture
Designer's West
Garden Design
Interior Design
Restaurant & Hotel Design

Russell Abraham
60 Federal Street, Suite 303
San Francisco, California 94107
(415) 896-6400
FAX: (415) 896-6402

In Los Angeles:
(213) 381-3798

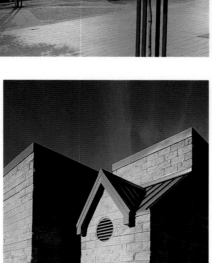

Russell Abraham
60 Federal Street, Suite 303
San Francisco, California 94107
(415) 896-6400
FAX: (415) 896-6402

In Los Angeles:
(213) 381-3798

Craig Buchanan
1026 Folsom Street
San Francisco, California 94103
(415) 861-5566

Location Work
Specialities: Interiors, Architecture,
Aerials, Direction of Talent, Complex
Lighting Situations

For more, see American Showcase
Volumes 5, 7, 8, 11 & 12

Jim Cambon
Denver, Colorado
(303) 221-4545

Our "implied motion" techniques leave details clear, colors bright and effects stunning.
First generation transparencies in 4x5 or 8x10, ready for separation.

You can imagine what we could do for your next project.
Or you can call.

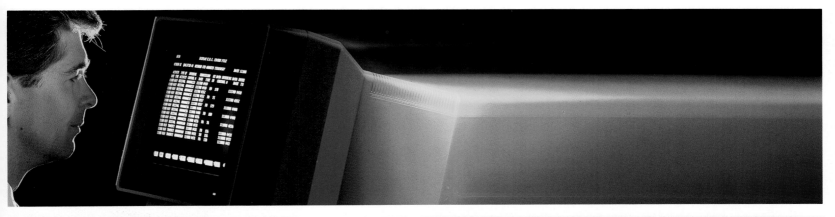

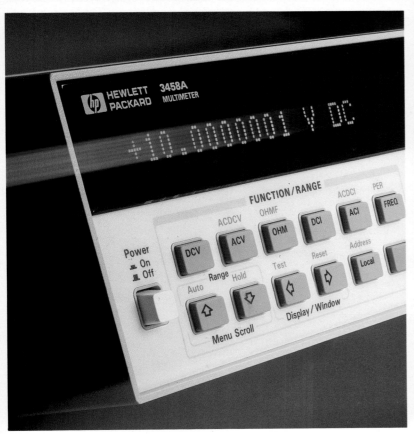

Charles Daniels
905 North Cole Avenue
Studio 2120
Hollywood, California 90038
(213) 461-8659

Advertising, Editorial, Industrial, Aerials, Real Estate, Furniture.

Clients include: M. J. Brock & Sons Inc., Ebasco, E & L Technologies, Gensler & Associates, Gruen & Associates, J G Enterprises, Kaiser-McCuen

Advertising, JW Marriott Hotel Group, Mitsubishi Electric, Morphosis, POD Landscape Architecture, RD Olson Construction, St. Jame's Club Hotel, Steinmann Grayson Smylie, Turner Construction Co., Universal Studios, Unocal Oil Co., Westinghouse.

Charles Daniels
905 North Cole Avenue
Studio 2120
Hollywood, California 90038
(213) 461-8659

Advertising, Editorial, Industrial, Aerials, Real Estate, Furniture.

Publications include: Architecture, Casa Vogue, City Network, Designers West, H G Home and Garden, Interior Design,

L. A. Style, Metropolitan Home, Self, American Vogue.

Brochures: E & L Technologies, Gruen & Associates, J G Enterprises, Marina City Club, St. Jame's Club.

Vernon W. Durke
San Francisco Studio:
842 Folsom, #128
San Francisco, California 94107
(415) 648-1262
Houston Studio:
5250 Gulfton, Suite 4A
Houston, Texas 77081

Represented in Houston by
DiOrio Associates,
(713) 960-0393

Locale Color

Western glow, Southern sunsets or
Cape light. When Durke works with
you - so does the locale.

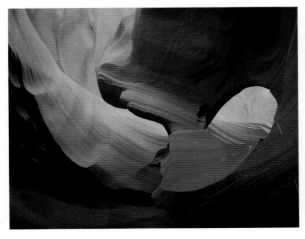

Steve Firebaugh
6750 55th Avenue South
Seattle, Washington 98118
(206) 721-5151

Specializing in location photography
worldwide.

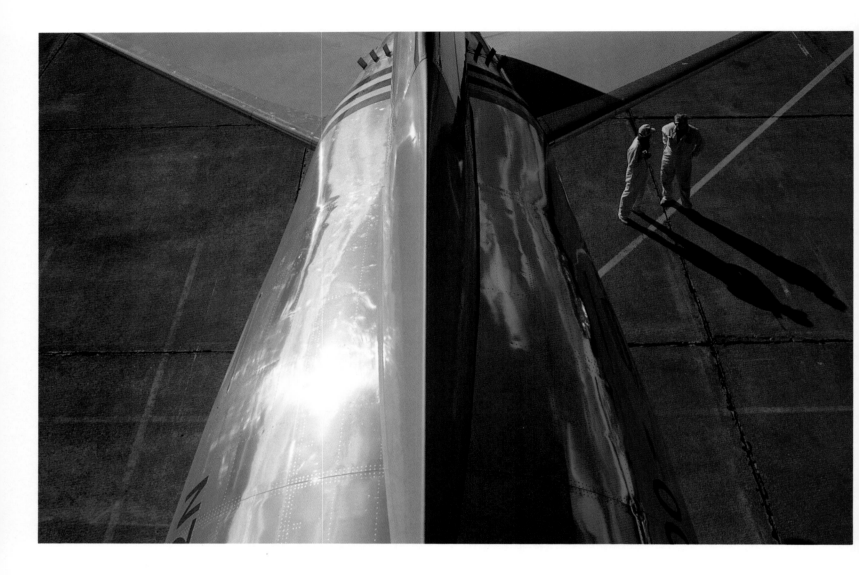

Steve Firebaugh
6750 55th Avenue South
Seattle, Washington 98118
(206) 721-5151

Specializing in location photography
worldwide.

Charly Franklin
3352 20th Street
San Francisco, California 94110
(415) 824-4000

Additional images may be seen in
American Showcase volumes 10 and 11

PHOTO METRO MAGAZINE

EXCELAN

SUN MICROSYSTEMS

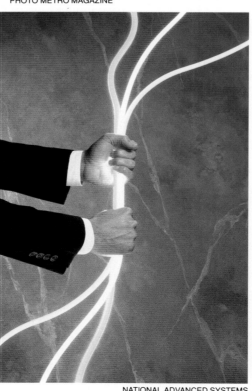

NATIONAL ADVANCED SYSTEMS

SIMPSON PAPER COMPANY

Michael Fritz Photography

PO Box 4386
San Diego, California 92104
(619) 281-3297

Raymond Gendreau
300 2nd Avenue West
Seattle, Washington 98119
(206) 285-1999

1989 Clients Include:
American Airlines
Alaska Air Magazine
Chempro Inc.

Frito-Lay
Ms. Magazine
N.W. Natural Gas
Pacific Northwest Magazine

Success Magazine
Voluntary Hospitals of America
Washington Magazine
Washington M...

CEO'S PNW MAGAZINE

WASHINGTON MAGAZINE

FLORIDA GULF COAST

RAYMOND GENDREAU PHOTOGRAPHY RAYMOND GENDREAU PHOTOGRAPHY RAYMOND GENDREAU

DOMAIN MAGAZINE

TURGEON-RAINE JEWELLERS

R A Y M O N D
G E N D R E A U

Raymond Gendreau
300 2nd Avenue West
Seattle, Washington 98119
(206) 285-1999

Represented by:
Santee Lehmen Dabney Inc.
(206) 467-1616

In Dallas:
Elizabeth Simpson
(214) 943-9355

Stock available:
Allstock
(206) 282-8116

More work can be seen in Corporate
Showcase 5, 6, and 7.

CHEMPRO, INC.

PHOTO   GENDREAU

PORT OF SEATTLE

Stephen Harvey
7801 West Beverly Boulevard
Los Angeles, California 90036
(213) 934-5817
FAX: (213) 934-5116

Represented by
Nick Barton

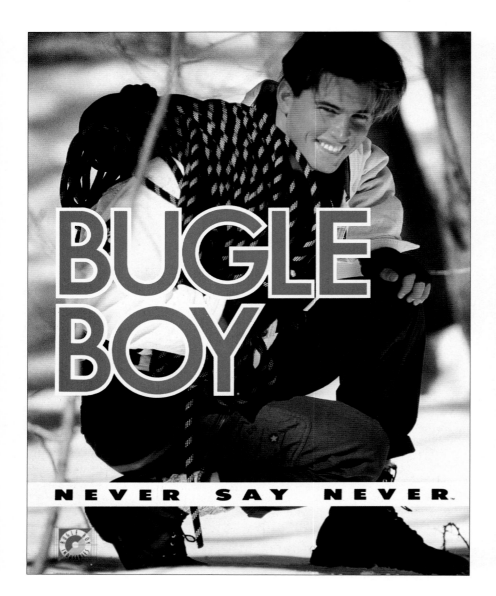

Larry Keenan
421 Bryant Street
San Francisco, California 94107
(415) 495-6474
FAX # upon request

Photo-realism for advertising, annual reports, corporate/industrial, conceptual, special effects and computer graphics photography. International assignments, numerous awards.

Clients: Advanced Micro Devices, Amdahl, Ampex, Apple Computers, Bank of America, Bechtel, Bell & Howell, Broderbund, Clorox, Del Monte, Electronic Arts, Fuji Photo Film,

Genentech, Hewlett-Packard, Intel, Levi-Strauss, Microsoft, Omni Magazine, Pacific Bell, Spectra-Physics, Tandem Computers.

Photographs are not retouched.

John P. Kelly
Box 1550
140 Homestead
Basalt, Colorado 81621
(303) 927-4197

Kent Miles Photography

465 Ninth Avenue
Salt Lake City, Utah 84103
(801) 364-5755

Evocative images in Black and White
and in Color.
Assignment and Stock photography on
location, emphasizing people and
portraiture, travel, scenic, performance
and documentary subjects. Extensive
experience shooting for multi-media
productions.

For Color samples see our page in the
Stock section of this volume. Also see
American Showcase 12 and Corporate
Showcase 6, 7, 8.
Portfolios and client list available on
request.
Member ASMP.

Photos: I-80N, Eastbound, Idaho;
Father and Son, Bangor State Fair,
Maine;
Rodeo Cowboy, Ute Stampede, Utah;
Prairie after a storm, Western Nebraska.

© 1988, Kent Miles.

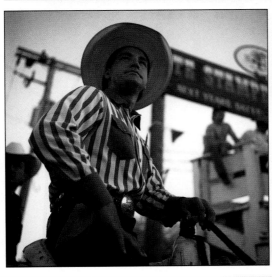 

DMiller
Dennis Miller
1467 12th Street, #C
Manhattan Beach, California 90266
(213) 546-3205

Location
Corporate
Industrial
Stock
"Shooting Corporate America!"

Shooting Corporate America!

Rosanne Olson
(206) 633-3775

Represented by:
Santee Lehmen Dabney Inc.
(206) 467-1616

Stock with Allstock
1-800-248-8116
FAX: (206) 286-8502

Black & white and hand-tinted portfolios
also available.
See American Showcase Volume 12 for
examples.

**Michael Peck
Photography**
2046 Arapahoe Street
Denver, Colorado 80205
(303) 296-9427

Photographs as unique as the people themselves.

Please refer to Corporate Showcase 8.

Burton Pritzker
San Francisco
(415) 626-3471

Babcock & Brown, Bank of America, California First Bank, Capital Guaranty, Chevron, Dep, Compact Video, Lockheed, Maxtor, Priam, Stanford University, Tandem Computers, Transamerica, Doug Akagi, Lawrence Bender, Besser Joseph Partners, James Cross, Pentagram, Robert Miles Runyan, Sibley/Peteet, Sidjakov Berman & Gomez, Sussman/Prejza, Goodby, Berlin & Silverstein, Ogilvy & Mather, J. Walter Thompson.

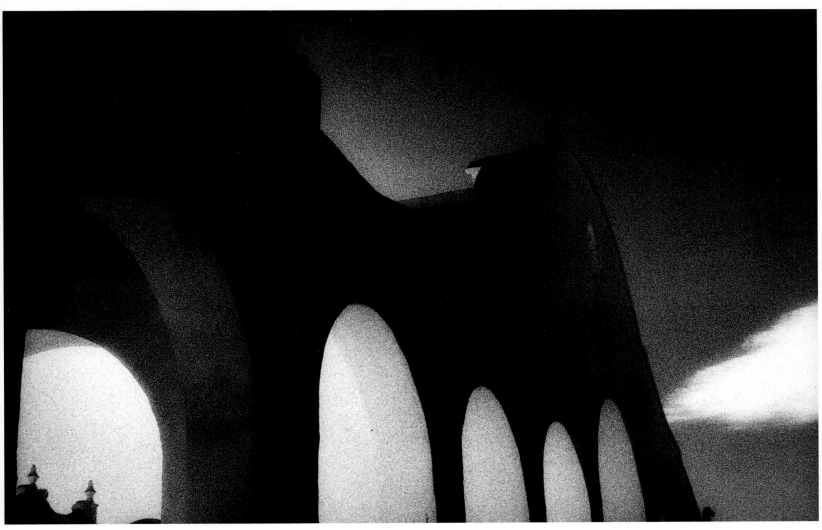

David Quinney Jr.
Photographic Illustration
423 East Broadway
Salt Lake City, Utah 84111
(801) 363-0434

Studio & location capabilities. Specializing in advertising and corporate/industrial visual communication.

Clients include: Aldus Corp., American Barrick Resources, Axonix, Chevron, Coldwell Banker, Control Data, Cover Pools, Cura Financial, DOD Electronics, Evans & Sutherland, Hilton Hotel, IOMEGA, Jackson Hole, Jetway Systems, Mountain Fuel, Rockford Fosgate, USA Weekend, Unimobil Systems, UNISYS, United States Film Festival, WordPerfect Corporation.

STUDIO
Q

**Marshal Safron
Studios, Inc.**
1041 North McCadden Place
Los Angeles, California 90038
(213) 461-5676

Specializing in hotels, furniture,
architecture, interiors, and related
products on location and in the
studio. Work has appeared in all
related national consumer and trade
publications.

Additional work can be seen in
American Showcase Volumes 9,
10, 11 & 12.

**Marshal Safron
Studios, Inc.**
1041 North McCadden Place
Los Angeles, California 90038
(213) 461-5676

**Marshal Safron
Studios, Inc.**
1041 North McCadden Place
Los Angeles, California 90038
(213) 461-5676

Mark Sokol
6518 Wilkinson Avenue
North Hollywood, California 91606
(818) 506-4910
FAX: (818) 506-6580

Represented by:
Randy Pate & Assoc, Inc.
(818) 985-8181
FAX: (818) 995-4566

1. Tyco Industries Inc. / Huerta Design Associates
2. Mazda / Desalvo & Diehl Communications*
3. Promotional / Mark Sokol
4. Space Labs Inc. / Baxter, Gurian & Mazzei, Inc.
* Truck Photos / Doug Taub

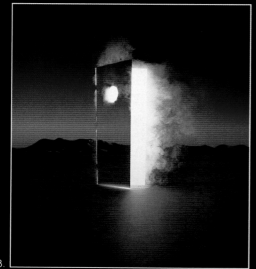

MARK SOKOL PHOTOGRAPHY

(818) 506-4910 • FAX (818) 506-6580

Represented by Randy Pate & Assoc. Inc.

(818) 985-8181 • FAX (818) 995-4566

Mark Sokol
6518 Wilkinson Avenue
North Hollywood, California 91606
(818) 506-4910
FAX: (818) 506-6580

Represented by:
Randy Pate & Assoc, Inc.
(818) 985-8181
FAX: (818) 995-4566

5. Pasha Records / Hugh Syme Design
6. Fox Hills Video / Mark Matsuno
   Design Inc.
7. Walt Disney Studios / Penguin Art &
   Design
8. Universal Studios Inc.
9. Warner Bros. Inc. / TLR & Associates

5.

6.

7.

8.

9.

Tom Till

PO Box 337
Moab, Utah 84532
(801) 259-5327

My stock file celebrates the natural beauty of America. I specialize in 4x5 and 8x10 landscapes and closeups, and in 6x7 and 35mm aerials from stock or by assignment. We send submissions for any editorial needs promptly upon request.

Look for my books published by Westcliffe Publishers: Colorado: Images from Above, Utah: Magnificent Wilderness, and my collaboration with John McPhee, published by Peregrine Smith: Outcroppings. See my ad in Showcase 11.

Clients have included American Airlines, Arizona Highways Magazine, Canon Cameras, Fidelity Investments, Geo Magazine, Gore-Tex, National Park Service, National Geographic Calendars and Books, Omni Magazine, Phillip Morris, Sunoco, Timberland, and US Air.

BRASSTOWN BALD, GEORGIA

SAN JUAN RIVER, UTAH

MAMMOTH CAVE NATIONAL PARK, KENTUCKY

EVERGLADES NATIONAL PARK, FLORIDA

391

Mark Tuschman
(415) 322-4157

Client list and portfolio available upon request.
Please also see American Showcase 12.

PALO ALTO MEDICAL FOUNDATION

Mark Tuschman

(415) 322-4157

UPJOHN

UPJOHN

Francisco Villaflor
(415) 921-4238

  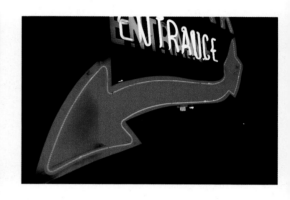

...*brings life to
pedestrian subjects...
consistently reliable...
that's the absolute truth.*
      **W. Matthews
MATTCOM**

...*determines what he can do to
make the real difference...
consummate professional.*
      **S. Kittle
Digital**

 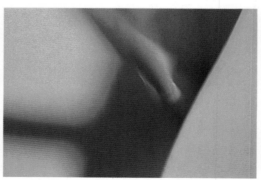 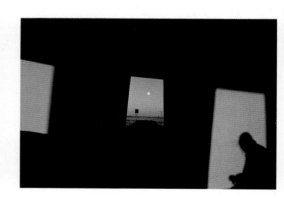

• *Apple*
• *Alamo*
• *Hewlett-Packard*
• *Pharmetrix*
• *Temple-Inland*

*Inquisitive.
Durable.
Innovative.
R. Brooks.
Miller Brooks, Inc.*

STOCK & PHOTO SERVICES

SOUTHERN STOCK PHOTOS

Our files contain images from over 100 of America's leading photographers. A collection featuring an exciting variety including unparalleled coverage of the southeastern United States and the Caribbean.

We specialize in filling your requests promptly and professionally for:
Advertising • Editorial • Calendars • Brochures • AV Shows • Annual Reports

3601 West Commercial Boulevard, Suite 33
Fort Lauderdale, Florida 33309
Phone: **(305) 486-7117** • In Miami **949-5191**
Fax: **(305) 485-5257**

Member:
American Society of Magazine Photographers
Picture Agency Council of America
American Society of Picture Professionals

DAVID MUENCH
PHOTOGRAPHY INC

805·967·4488

BOX 30500 · SANTA BARBARA · CA 93130

A CREATIVE COLLECTION OF STOCK PHOTOGRAPHY · THE AMERICAN LANDSCAPE · ORIGINAL SEEING WITH 4X5 FORMAT

PACIFIC STOCK

SPECIALIZING IN PACIFIC IMAGES Hawaii–Pacific Islands–Australia–Western U.S./Canada–Far East

© Sun Star

© David Cornwell
© Dan McSweeney

© Greg Vaughn
© Creative Focus

© Dana Edmunds

RAPHAËLE/DIGITAL TRANSPARENCIES, INC. was the first to offer image composition and digital retouching on transparencies. Now, nearly a decade later, we remain at the forefront of its development. ■ We are, first and foremost, artists. We realize there is a crucial difference between producing work and producing a work of art. ■ By designing our own equipment, we have developed a process that delivers substantial benefits to our clientele. In fact, our high-performance image processing system has no equal in the industry. ■ We provide ultra-high resolution E-6 transparencies which our clients can separate anywhere they wish. ■ Our software engineers can develop customized programs for unusually complex projects. ■ Raphaële provides client coordination and in-house direction.

RAPHAËLE / DIGITAL
TRANSPARENCIES, INC.

**616 Hawthorne
Houston, Texas 77006
(FAX 713-524-7761)**

713-524-2211

The most comprehensive collection of golf stock available.

Mike Klemme   Jeff McBride   Jim Nay

All photos © GOLFOTO, INC.

Specialists in stock and assignment photography of golf courses, resorts, real estate developments, tournaments, players, and golf equipment. Hundreds of courses, players, and events on file.

GOLFOTO.
INCORPORATED

224 N. Independence   Suite 800   Enid, Oklahoma 73701
800 338-1656 Telecopier (FAX) 405 234-8335

Shanna Hilburn, Photo Editor

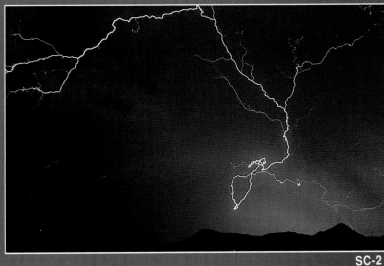

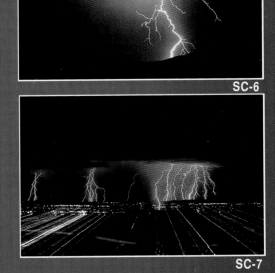

Adstock Photos
Stock & Assignment
Phoenix, Arizona
(602) 277-5903
FAX: (602) 274-9017

© 1988 Jerry Sieve

Design by Curtis Partridge/Design Studios Phoenix, Arizona

© 1988 Edward McCain

© 1988 Sue Bennett

© 1989 Mark Duran

© 1989 David Elms, Jr.

© 1989 Mike Scully

© 1988 Richard Maack

© 1989 Michael Reese Much

© 1988 Michael Fatali

Paul Ambrose Studios
PO Box 8158
Durango, Colorado 81301
(303) 259-5925
FAX: (303) 259-5968

Large format photocomposites from legend and mythology to high technology and the supernatural. From our library or custom composed to fit your needs.

For additional images, see American Showcase #12, page 363.

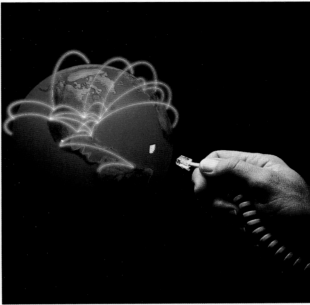

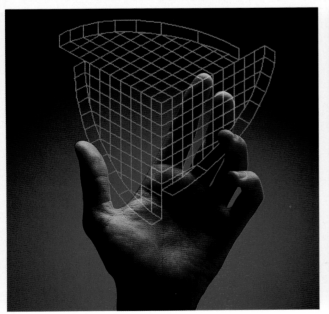

Custom Medical Stock Photo, Inc.

3819 North Southport Avenue
Chicago, Illinois 60613-2823
(800) 373-2677
(312) 248-3200
FAX: (312) 248-7427

Custom Medical Stock Photo specializes in biomedical and scientific images. CMSP is staffed by professionally trained medical photographers with advertising and research experience. Our file photographers include researchers, physicians, medical photographers and illustrators.

Images: 1. © Carr; 2. © CMSP; 3. © CMSP; 4. © CMSP; 5. © Montrose; 6. © Beebe; 7. © Carr

© 1990 CMSP

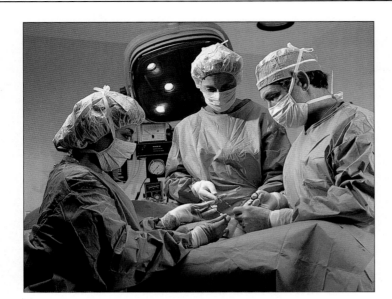

1.

2.

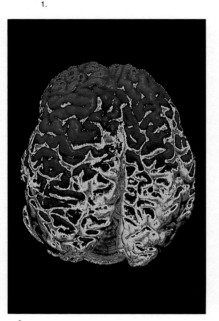

3.

4.

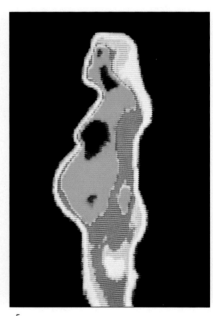

5.

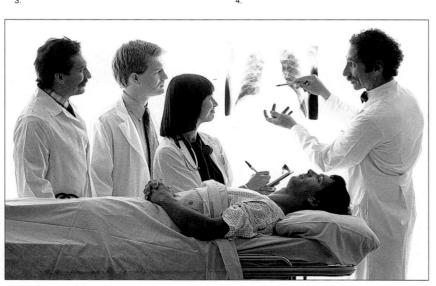

6.

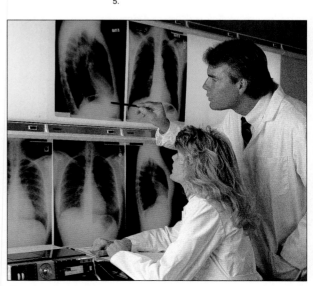

7.

Bette S. Garber
2110 Valley Drive
West Chester, Pennsylvania 19382
(215) 692-9076
FAX: (215) 692-9427

Specializing in the Trucking Industry

(215) 692-9076
West Chester, Penna.

405

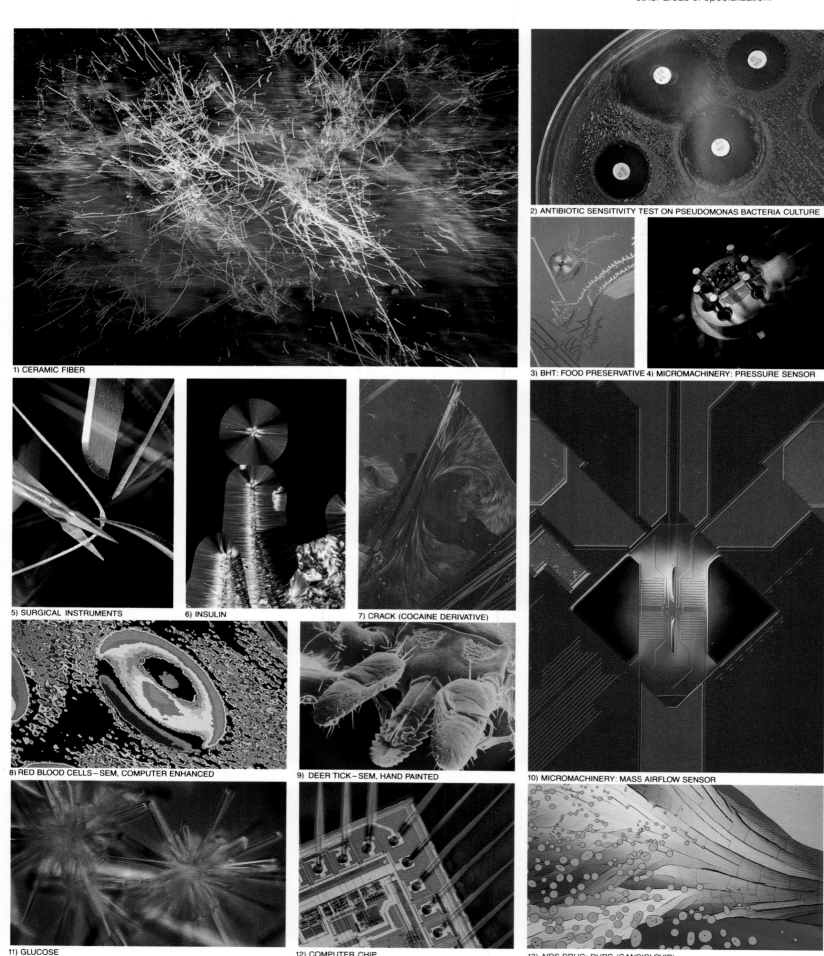

Fran Heyl Associates
230 Park Avenue
New York, New York 10169
(212) 581-6470

Assignments and Stock

Photomicrography/macrography is one of the areas in which we specialize. We provide distinctive and unusual photographs for the advertising, corporate and editorial fields, on almost any subject imaginable. Inquire about other areas of specialization.

1) CERAMIC FIBER

2) ANTIBIOTIC SENSITIVITY TEST ON PSEUDOMONAS BACTERIA CULTURE

3) BHT: FOOD PRESERVATIVE   4) MICROMACHINERY: PRESSURE SENSOR

5) SURGICAL INSTRUMENTS

6) INSULIN

7) CRACK (COCAINE DERIVATIVE)

8) RED BLOOD CELLS – SEM, COMPUTER ENHANCED

9) DEER TICK – SEM, HAND PAINTED

10) MICROMACHINERY: MASS AIRFLOW SENSOR

11) GLUCOSE

12) COMPUTER CHIP

13) AIDS DRUG: DHPG (GANCICLOVIR)

Fran Heyl Associates
230 Park Avenue
New York, New York 10169
(212) 581-6470

Representing:
Pix*Elation

Assignments and Stock

- Computer art
- Computer enhancement of photos or illustrations
- Charts and graphs from concept to finish

Show us your product, concept, photo or image, and we will create art for you- or enhance your photo or image according to your needs.

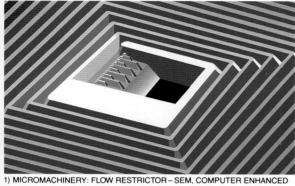

1) MICROMACHINERY: FLOW RESTRICTOR – SEM, COMPUTER ENHANCED

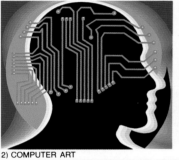

2) COMPUTER ART

3) COMPUTER ART

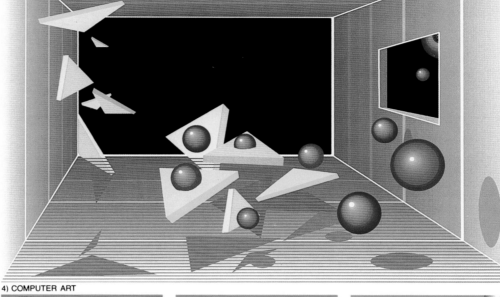

4) COMPUTER ART

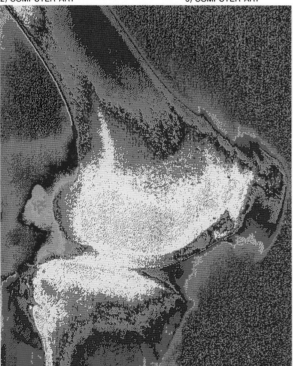

5) OSTEOARTHRITIS – COMPUTER ENHANCED X-RAY

6) COMPUTER ART (DATABASE)

7) COMPUTER ART

8) COMPUTER ART – A.I.

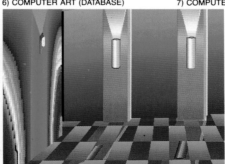

9) COMPUTER ART

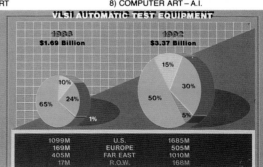

VLSI AUTOMATIC TEST EQUIPMENT

1985		1992
$1.69 Billion		$3.37 Billion
10%		15%
65%	24%	50% 30%
	1%	5%

1099M	U.S.	1685M
169M	EUROPE	505M
405M	FAR EAST	1010M
17M	R.O.W.	168M

10) CHART – CREATED ON COMPUTER

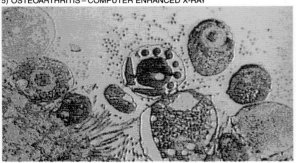

11) AIDS RELATED CRYPTOSPORIDIOSIS – TEM, COMPUTER ENHANCED

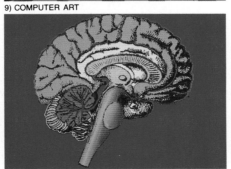

12) COMPUTER ILLUSTRATION

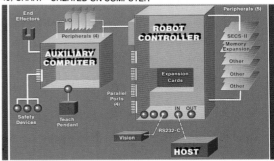

13) CHART – CREATED ON COMPUTER

407

Instock, Inc.
516 Northeast 13th Street
Fort Lauderdale, Florida 33304
(305) 527-4111
FAX: (305) 522-2562

iNSTOCK
P I C T U R E   A G E N C Y
516 Northeast 13th Street
Fort Lauderdale, Florida 33304
(305) 527-4111

Fax us your layout
Fax No. (305) 522-2562

Ron Kimball Stock
1960 Colony Street
Mountain View, California 94043
(415) 948-2939

Galloping, growling, leaping, on wing, wild, domestic, exotic, dangerous. If we don't have it we can shoot it.

Studio and location shots. Over

250,000 of the highest quality images available.

Performance cars. All formats. Studio or location.

KIMBALL

Tom & Pat Leeson
"America gone wild" Collection
PO Box 2498
Vancouver, Washington 98668
(206) 256-0436

40,000 transparencies capturing America's wildside—elk bugling, beaver building, eagles soaring, wolves howling. When it's a wilder image you need, give us a call.

Focusing on North American wildlife since 1976, this collection includes the most complete bald eagle coverage available in North America. We specialize as well in destination/ travel photography of the Northern Rocky Mountains (including Canadian Rockies), Alaska, and the Pacific Northwest.

Kent Miles Photography

465 Ninth Avenue
Salt Lake City, Utah 84103
(801) 364-5755

Evocative images in Color and in Black and White.

Assignment and Stock photography on location, emphasizing people and portraiture, travel, scenic, performance and documentary subjects. Extensive experience shooting for multi-media productions.

For Black and White samples see our page in the West section of this volume. Also see American Showcase 12 and Corporate Showcase 6, 7, 8. Portfolios and client list available on request. Member ASMP.

© 1990, Kent Miles

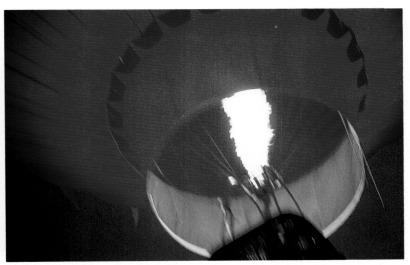

Douglas Peebles Photography

445 Iliwahi Loop
Kailua, Hawaii 96734
(808) 254-1082
FAX: (808) 254-1267

Douglas Peebles Photography is an agency of about ten photographers that specializes in Hawaii and the South Pacific. We have the people, places, sunsets, beaches, flowers, surfing, sailboarding and other sports and activities of all the Hawaiian islands as well as Tahiti, Tonga, Fiji ....These are in stock and can be delivered in 24-48 hours. The file is composed of 35mm and 2 1/4 original transparencies. Also we are, of course, available for assignment.

You can see more of our photography in Stock Workbooks 1, 2, & 3.

Stock & Assignment

VOLCANO: © LEE ALLEN THOMAS / WAVE SUNSET: © GARY HOFHEIMER / SAILBOARDER: © DARRELL WONG / FLOWERS, WATERFALL, DIAMOND HEAD: © DOUGLAS PEEBLES

Sandved & Coleman Photography

12539 North Lake Court
Fairfax, Virginia 22033
(202) 244-5711 • (703) 968-6769
FAX: (202) 966-5799

Amazon Rain Forests
Antarctica
Biological Subjects
Butterfly Alphabet
Camouflage & Mimicry
Coral Reef Animals
Designs in Nature

Habitat Destruction
Herbal Medicine
Insects
Jumping Penguins
Look-Alikes in Nature
Necking Giraffes
Orchids

Parrots & Macaws
Rice Paddies
Scenics
Secretary Birds
Smithsonian Institution
Tropical Blossoms
and Much, Much More

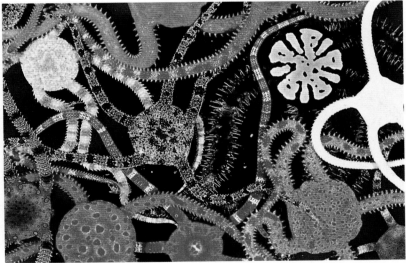

Sports File
3800 Northwest 32nd Avenue
Miami, Florida 33142
(305) 633-4666 • FAX: (305) 633-2485
MCI ID: 351-3774

How can you be sure to find the sports photograph you need, when you need it? Simple. Call Sports File.

From our outstanding library of stock photography, we can provide images of almost any kind of sport, almost anywhere in the world.

So call us at Sports File. Because you never get a second chance to make a first impression.

Visual Impact

733 Auahi Street
Honolulu, Hawaii 96813
(808) 524-8269
FAX: (808) 537-9185

Welcome to Paradise!
Sorry you can't make the trip over here!
But rest assured, we'll have your image
of Paradise on file.
Spectalcular scenics, exotic people,
incredible waterfalls, fascinating
volcanoes, snow white beaches,
tropical settings...Hawaii at its very best.

We represent several talented
photographers, both here in Honolulu
and on the outer islands. We can
provide you with excellent locations and
a top-notch crew to produce images for
advertising, corporate and editorial
assignments.

See more of our images in American
Showcase '85 through '89, the Black
Book '86 through '88, and Stock
Workbook '89, '90.

PHONE LISTINGS & ADDRESSES OF REPRESENTATIVES, VISUAL ARTISTS & SUPPLIERS

CONTENTS

REGIONS

New York City

Northeast
Connecticut
Delaware
Maine
Maryland
Massachusetts
New Hampshire
New Jersey
New York State
Pennsylvania
Rhode Island
Vermont
Washington, D.C.
West Virginia

Southeast
Alabama
Florida
Georgia
Kentucky
Louisiana
Mississippi
North Carolina
South Carolina
Tennessee
Virginia

Midwest
Illinois
Indiana
Iowa

Kansas
Michigan
Minnesota
Missouri
Nebraska
North Dakota
Ohio
South Dakota
Wisconsin

Southwest
Arizona
Arkansas
New Mexico
Oklahoma
Texas

Rocky Mountain
Colorado
Idaho
Montana
Utah
Wyoming

West Coast
Alaska
British Columbia
California
Hawaii
Nevada
Oregon
Washington

REPS

NYC

A

Altamore, Bob/237 W 54th St 4th Fl 212-977-4300
Cailor/Resnick, (P)
American Artists/353 W 53rd St #1W 212-682-2462
Don Almquist, (I), Keith Batcheller, (I), Roger Bergendorff, (I),
Dan Bridy, (I), Robert Burger, (I), Chris Butler, (I), Bob Byrd,
(I), Gary Ciccarelli, (I), Jim Deigan, (I), Bob Dorsey, (I), Lane
DuPont, (I), Michael Elins, (I), Malcolm Farley, (I), Russell
Farrell, (I), Jack Freas, (I), George Gaadt, (I), Rob Gage, (P),
Jackie Geyer, (I), John Hamagami, (I), Pam Hamilton, (I),
Karel Havileck, (I), Steve Hendricks, (I), Doug Henry, (I),
John Holm, (I), Chris Hopkins, (I), Andy Hoyos, (I), Mitch
Hyatt, (I), Richard Kriegler, (I), Alan Leiner, (I), Ned Levine,
(I), Maurice Lewis, (I), Ed Lindlof, (I), Jerry LoFaro, (I), Ron
Mahoney, (I), Mick McGinty, (I), Jean-Claude Michel, (I),
James Needham, (I), David Noyes, (I), Jim Owens, (I), Nan
Parsons, (I), Charles Passarelli, (I), Tony Randazzo, (I), Jan
Sawka, (I), Todd Schorr, (I), Michael Schumacher, (I), Victor
Scocozza, (P), Joe Scrofani, (I), Jim Starr, (I), Mike
Steirnagle, (I), Tony Ward, (P), Stan Watts, (I), Will Weston, (I),
Ron Wolin, (I), Jonathan Wright, (I), Gary Yealdhall, (I), Andy
Zito, (I)
Anthony, Ed/133 W 19th St 3rd Fl 212-924-7770
Joseph Cementi, (P)
Anton, Jerry/119 W 23rd St #203, (P 60,61) **212-633-9880**
Bobbye Cochran, (I), Abe Echevarria, (I), Norman Green, (I),
Aaron Rezny, (P), Oliver Williams, (I), Nicky Zann, (I), Chris
Vincent, (P)
Aparo, Vincent/65 W 68th St 212-877-5439
Edward Addeo, (P), Charles Baum, (P), Kevin CLarke, (P),
Anita Giraldo, (P), John Holderer, (P)
Arnold, Peter Inc/1181 Broadway 4th Fl 212-481-1190
Yann Arthus-Bertrand, (P), Fred Bavendam, (P), Dieter Blum,
(P), Herb Comess, (P), Martha Cooper, (P), Bruce Curtis, (P),
Bob Evans, (P), Helmut Gritscaher, (P), Jacques Jangoux,
(P), Manfred Kage, (P), Steve Kaufman, (P), Stephen
Krasemann, (P), Werner Muller, (P), Jim Olive, (P), Hans
Pfletschinger, (P), Jeffrey L Rotman, (P), Galen Rowell, (P),
David Scharf, (P), Erika Stone, (P), Bruno Zehnder, (P),
Dennis diCicco, (P)
Art & Commerce/108 W 18th St 212-206-0737
Artco/232 Madison Ave #600 212-889-8777
Ed Acuna, (I), George Angelini, (I), Gene Boyer, (I), Dan
Brown, (I), Alain Chang, (I), Anne Cook, (I), Jeff Cornell, (I),
Bob Dacey, (I), Beau & Alan Daniels, (I), Mort Drucker, (I),
Lisa Falkenstern, (I), Ed Gazsi, (I), Gary Glover, (I), Lisa
Henderling, (I), Lisa Henderling, (I), Kathy Jeffers, (I), Rick
McCollum, (I), John Jude Palencar, (I), Barry Phillips, (I), Al
Pisano, (I), Marcel Rozenberg, (I), Leslie Szabo, (I),
Alexander & Turner, (I), Sally Vitsky, (I)
Artists Associates/211 E 51st St #5F 212-755-1365
Norman Adams, (I), Don Brautigam, (I), Michael Deas, (I),
Michael Dudash, (I), Mark English, (I), Robert Heindel, (I),
Steve Karchin, (I), Dick Krepel, (I), Skip Liepke, (I), Fred
Otnes, (I), Daniel Schwartz, (I), Norman Walker, (I)
Arton Associates/216 E 45th St 212-661-0850
Ned Butterfield, (I), Paul Giovanopoulis, (I), Jacob Knight, (I),
Carveth Kramer, (I), Michelle Laporte, (I), Karen Laurence, (I)
Asciutto Art Reps/362 W 20th St #201 212-645-0414
Anthony Accardo, (I), Karen Beckhardt, (I), Eliot Bergman,
(I), Alex Bloch, (I), Don Bolognese, (I), John Butler, (I), Olivia
Cole, (I), Daniel Delvalle, (I), Kitty Diamantis, (I), Michael
Donato, (I), Simon Galkin, (I), Bob Giuliani, (I), Kathy
Heinemann, (I), Meryl Henderson, (I), Monica Ice, (I), Taylor
Jones, (I), Nurit Karlin, (I), Alisa Klayman, (I), Jeff Kronen, (I),
Goran Lindgren, (I), Morissa Lipstein, (I), Hal Lose, (I), Loreta
Lustig, (I), Tod Mason, (I), Savio Mizzi, (I), Sal Murdocca, (I),
James Needham, (I), Charles Peale, (I), Jan Pyk, (I), Donna
Ward, (I), Fred Winkowski, (I)

Ash, Michael/107 W 25th St 212-741-0015
Azzara, Louise/131 E 17th St 212-674-8114

B

Badd, Linda/568 Broadway #601 212-431-3377
Badin, Andy/15 W 38th St 212-532-1222
Steve Colletti, (P), Jeff Feinen, (I), Skip Kaplaw, (P), Michael
Kozmiuk, (I), Julie Lawrence, (I), Robert S Levy, (I), Harry
Pincus, (I), Bob Stuhmer, (I)
Bahm, Darwin/6 Jane St 212-989-7074
Julian Allen, (I), Harry DeZitter, (P), Gordon Kibbe, (I), Joan
Landis, (I), Rick Meyerowitz, (I), Don Ivan Punchatz, (I), Arno
Sternglass, (I), Sketch Pad Studio, (I), John Thompson, (I),
Robert Weaver, (I)
Baker, Valerie/152 W 25th St 12th Fl 212-807-7113
Barboza, Ken Assoc/853 Broadway #1603 212-505-8635
Anthony Barboza, (P), Peter Morehand, (P)
Barclay, R Francis/5 W 19th St 212-255-3440
Barnes, Fran/25 Fifth Ave #9B 212-505-2720
Barracca, Sal/381 Park Ave S #919 212-889-2400
Jeanette Adams, (I), Alan Ayers, (I), Milo Daax, (I), Robert
Evans, (I), Rick Fischer, (I), Mark Frueh, (I), Gary Gianni, (I),
Yvonne Gilbert, (I), Robert Grace, (I), Glenn Hastings, (I),
Ken Hodges, (I), Tim Jacobus, (I), Ken Laager, (I), Lina Levy,
(I), Wes Lowe, (I), David Mann, (I), Charles Moll, (I), Yan
Nascimbene, (I), Larry Noble, (I), Keith Parkinson, (I), Brad
Purse, (I), Hiram Richardson, (I), Peter Siu, (I), Jim Thiesen,
(I), Jerry Tiritilli, (I), Josie Yee, (I), Christopher Zacharow, (I),
John Zielinski, (I), Ivan Zorad, (I)
Baruch, Liz/245 E 58th St 212-752-8174
Fabrizio Gianni, (P), Anthony Gordon, (P), Neil Kirk, (P)
Becker, Erika/150 W 55th St 212-757-8987
Richard Ely, (I), Esther Larson, (I)
Becker, Noel/150 W 55th St 212-757-8987
Howard Tangye, (P), Sy Vinopoll, (P)
Beidler, Barbara/648 Broadway #506 212-979-6996
Richard Dunkley, (P)
Beilin, Frank/405 E 56th St 212-751-3074
Bernstein & Andriulli/60 E 42nd St #505 212-682-1490
Richard Anderson, (I), Tony Antonios, (I), Per Arnoldi, (I), Pat
Bailey, (I), Garin Baker, (I), Garie Blackwell, (I), Melinda
Bordelon, (I), Rick Brown, (I), Daniel Craig, (I), Everett
Davidson, (I), Craig Davis, (I), Cathy Deeter, (I), Nina Duram,
(I), Ron Fleming, (I), Lisa French, (I), Victor Gadino, (I), Joe
Genova, (I), Marika Hahn, (I), Veronika Hart, (I), John
Harwood, (I), Catherine Huerta, (I), Kevin Hulsey, (I), Tim
Jessell, (I), Cathy Johnson, (I), Mary Ann Lasher, (I), Bette
Levine, (I), Todd Lockwood, (I), Studio M, (I), Lee MacLeod,
(I), David B McMacken, (I), Michael Molkenthin, (P), Chris
Moore, (I), Bill Morse, (I), Frank Moscati, (P), Simpson/Flint,
(P), Craig Nelson, (I), Jeff Nishinaka, (I), Laura Phillips, (I),
Jake Rajs, (P), Ray Roberts, (I), Peggi Roberts, (I), Joe
Salina, (I), Marla Shega, (I), Chuck Slack, (I), Peter Stallard,
(I), J C Suares, (I), Tom Szumowski, (I), Murray Tinkelman, (I),
Clay Turner, (I), Pam Wall, (I), Brent Watkinson, (I), Chuck
Wilkinson, (I), Paul Wollman, (I), James B. Wood, (P), Matt
Zumbo, (I)
Big City Prodctns/5 E 19th St #303 212-473-3366
Bishop, Lynn/134 E 24th St 212-517-4886
Irene Stern, (P)
Black Star/450 Park Ave S 212-679-3288
John W. Alexanders, (P), Nancy Rica Schiff, (P), Arnold
Zann, (P)
Black, Fran/116 E 27th St 212-725-3806
John Alcorn, (I), Stephen Alcorn, (I), Gloria Baker, (P), Kip
Brundage, (P), Norm Clasen, (P), Michel Tcherevkoff, (P)
Black, Pamela/73 W Broadway 212-385-0667
Blum, Felice S/79 W 12th St 212-929-2166
Boghosian, Marty/201 E 21st St #10M 212-353-1313
James Salzano, (P)
Booth, Tom Inc/425 W 23rd St #17A 212-243-2750
Ann Field, (I), William Garrett, (P), John Goodman, (P),
Joshua Greene, (P), Richard Holiman, (I), Gordon Munro, (P),
Dick Nystrom, (P), Patrick Russell, (P), Geoff Spear, (P),
Alexander Vethers, (I)
Boyer, Susan/7 E 20th St 212-533-3113
Brett Froomer, (P)

Brackman, Henrietta/415 E 52nd St 212-753-6483
Brennan, Dan/568 Broadway #1005 212-925-8333
Knut Bry, (P), Vanni Burkhart, (P), Nathaniel Cramer, (P), Les
Goldberg, (P), Renato Grignaschi, (P), Anthony Horth, (P),
Tony McGee, (P), Jim Reiber, (P), Wayne Stambler, (P), Claus
Wickrath, (P)
Brigitte Inc/160 Fifth Ave #817 212-243-6811
Claus Eggers, (P), Cristina Ghergo, (P), David Stetson, (P)
Brindle, Carolyn/203 E 89th St #3D 212-534-4177
Donna Mehalko, (I), Maning Obregon, (I), Laurie Rakoff, (I),
Randall Rayon, (I), Sharon Watts, (I)
Brody, Sam/123 E 46th St 212-758-0640
Steve Heimann, (I), Fred Hilliard, (I), Carroll Seghers II, (P),
Rick Kehl, (I), Gary Kufner, (P), Allen Lieberman, (P), Rudi
Tesa, (P), Fred Ubert, (I), Woody Walkis, (I)
Brown, Doug/17 E 45th St #1008 212-953-0088
Dennis Blachut, (P), Abe Seltzer, (P)
Browne, Pema Ltd/185 E 85th St 212-369-1925
Robert Barrett, (I), Peter Catalanotto, (I), Todd Doney, (I), John
Hayes, (I), Ron Jones, (I), Kathy Krantz, (I), Karen Pritchett,
(I), John Rush, (I), John Sandford, (I), Alice deKok, (I)
Bruck, J S/322 W 57th St #40F 212-247-1130
Richard Anderson, (I), Ron Barbagallo, (I), Michael Dudash,
(I), Tom Freeman, (I), Donald Hedlin, (I), Jim Mathewuse, (I),
Richard Newton, (I), Victoria Vebell, (I), Gary Watson, (I)
Bruck, Nancy/302 W 12th St 212-645-1547
Mary Beth Farrell, (I), Gary Feinstein, (P), Warren Gerbert, (I),
Ken Goldammer, (I), Joel Peter Johnson, (I), Pamela Patrick,
(I), Scott Pollack, (I), Lionsgate, (I)
Bruml, Kathy/201 W 77th St 212-874-5659
Christopher Baker, (P), Mary Emery, (P), Grant Peterson, (P)
Buckley, Marel/165 W 20th St #4J 212-727-7422
Bush, Nan/135 Watts St 212-226-0814
Bruce Weber, (P)
Byrnes, Charles/435 W 19th St 212-627-3400
Steve Steigman, (P)

C

Cahill, Joe/135 E 50th St 212-751-0529
Shig Ikeda, (P), Brad Miller, (P), Howard Sochurek, (P)
Camp, Woodfin & Assoc/116 E 27th St 212-481-6900
Robert Azzi, (P), Kip Brundage, (P), Jason Laure, (P)
Caputo, Elise & Assoc/240 E 27th St 212-725-0503
Steve Brady, (P), James Kozyra, (P), Peter Papadopolous,
(P), Bill Robbins, (P), Becker/Bishop, (P)
Carmel/69 Mercer St 212-925-6216
Guy Powers, (P)
Carp, Stan/11 E 48th St 212-759-8880
Nick Samardge, (P), Allen Vogel, (P)
Casey, Judy/96 Fifth Ave 212-255-3252
Richard Corman, (P), Torkil Gudnason, (P), Lizzie Himmel, (P),
Andrew MacPherson, (P), Paolo Roversi, (P), Calliope, (P)
Casey, Marge/245 E 63rd St #201 212-486-9575
Geoffrey Clifford, (P), Frank Cowan, (P), Michael Cuesta, (P),
Thomas Hooper, (P), Robert Lambert, (P), Klaus Laubmayer,
(P), Michael Lupino, (P)
Celano, Nancy/345 E 80th St 212-744-7258
Chislovsky, Carol/853 Broadway #1201 212-677-9100
Randal Birkey, (I), Alex Bostic, (I), David Clemons, (I), Russell
Cobane, (I), Jon Conrad, (I), Bob Cooper, (I), Jan Evans, (I),
Bob Gleason, (I), Ignacio Gomez, (I), Ken Graning, (I), John
Gray, (I), Steve Gray, (I), Michael Haynes, (I), Mark Herman,
(I), Joe Lapinski, (I), Leon Monahan, (I), Julie Pace, (I),
Vincent Petragnani, (I), Ed Scarisbrick, (I), Chuck Schmidt,
(I), Sandra Shap, (I), Danny Smythe, (I), Randy South, (I),
Kevin Spaulding, (I), Nighthawk Studios, (I), Bob Thomas, (I),
C A Trachok, (I), Rhonda Voo, (I)
Cohen, Bruce/54 W 16th St 212-620-7839
Collignon, Daniele/200 W 15th St 212-243-4209
Dan Cosgrove, (I), Bill Frampton, (I), David Gambale, (I),
Steve Lyons, (I), Dennis Mukai, (I), Mitch O'Connell, (I), Cindy
Pardy, (I), Irena Roman, (I), Hisashi Sekine, (I), Doug Suma,
(I), Alex Tiani, (I), Don Weller, (I)
Conlon, Jean/461 Broome St 212-966-9897
Elizabeth Brady, (I), Kenro Izu, (P), Evan Polenghi, (I), David-
Carin Riley, (P), Holly Shapiro, (S)
Cornelia/448 E 37th St 212-947-5167

Cristof Gstalder, (P), Denis Malerbi, (P), Ron Nicolaysen, (P),
Jim Varriale, (P)
Craven Design/461 Park Ave S 212-696-4680
Diana Magnuson, (I), Roz Schanzer, (I)
Creative Freelancers/62 W 45th St 212-398-9540
Peter Angelo, (I), Dani Antman, (I), Harold Brooks, (I), R S
Brown, (I), Bill Brummard, (I), Tom Burasiewicz, (I), Ernest
Burden, (I), Wende Caporale, (I), Judy Clifford, (I), Donna
Corvi, (I), Rudy Cristiano, (I), Tom Daly, (I), Howard Darden,
(I), Glen Dodds, (I), Arthur Donovan, (I), John Duncan, (I),
Steve Duquette, (I), John Edens, (I), Anne Feiza, (I), Karl
Fischer, (I), Greg Fitzhugh, (I), Lynn Foster, (I), Claudia
Fouse, (I), Stephen Fritsch, (I), Peter Gallagher, (I), Ted
Glazer, (I), Julie Grau, (I), David Grove, (I), Marika Hahn, (I),
Blake Hampton, (I), Paula Havey, (I), Amy Huelsman, (I),
Peter Hunt, (I), Peter Ivanoff, (I), Chet Jezierski, (I), Dennis
Kendrick, (I), Jeff Kronen, (I), George Ladas, (I), Alice
Landry, (I), Buddy Leahy, (I), Anita Lovitt, (I), Sam Mclean, (I),
Jacqui Morgan, (I), Merideth Nemirov, (I), Michael Ng, (I),
Jan North, (I), Russ North, (I), Vilma Ortiz, (I), Masood
Parvez, (I), Robert Pasternak, (I), Elle Peek, (I), George
Poladian, (I), Mike Rodericks, (I), Meryl Rosner, (I), Barry
Ross, (I), Joanna Roy, (I), Jane Sanderson, (I), Glen
Schofield, (I), Claire Seiffert, (I), John Suchy, (I), Steve
Sullivan, (I), Steve Sweny, (I), Bill Teodecki, (I), Dana Ventura,
(I), Kurt Wallace, (I), Joanne Wanamaker, (I), Laura Westlake,
(I), Mary O'Keefe Young, (I)
Creative Talent/62 LeRoy St 212-243-7869
Marshall Cetlin, (I), Alan Henderson, (I)
Cuevas, Robert/118 E 23rd St #306 212-679-0622
Barnett Plotkin, (I)
Cullom, Ellen/55 E 9th St 212-777-1749
Robert Grant, (P)

D

Dagrosa, Terry/374 Eighth Ave 2nd Fl 212-564-8619
Rod Cook, (P)
Davies, Nora/370 E 76th St #C103 212-628-6657
Michael Pateman, (P)
Dedell, Jacqueline/58 W 15th St 6th Fl 212-741-2539
Cathie Bleck, (I), Ivan Chermayeff, (I), Teresa Fasolino, (I),
David Frampton, (I), Chermayeff and Geismar, (G), Paula
Munck, (I), Edward Parker, (I), Barry Root, (I), Kimberly B
Root, (I), Isadore Seltzer, (I), Richard Williams, (I),
Griesbach/Martucci, (I)
Des Verges, Diana/73 Fifth Ave 212-691-8674
Paccione Photography, (P)
DeVito, Kitty/43 E 30th St 14th Fl 212-889-9670
Bart DeVito, (P)
DeWan, Michael/250 Cabrini Blvd #2E 212-371-0739
Nancy Bundt, (P), Don Sparks, (P)
Dewey, Frank & Assoc/420 Lexington Ave 212-986-1249
DiBartolo/Lemkowitz/310 Madison Ave 212-297-0041
Chris Collins, (P), Steve Krongard, (P), James Porto, (P)
DiMartino, Joseph/25 W 39th St #902 212-764-5591
Mark Blanton, (I), Paul DiMartino, (I), Whistl'n Dixie, (G), Mac
Evans, (I), Graphics Group, (GD), Rudy Gutierrez, (I), Mark
Herron, (I), Steve Varnum, (I)
Dorman, Paul/430 E 57th St 212-826-6737
Studio DGM, (P)
Drexler, Sharon/451 Westminster Rd, Brooklyn 718-284-4779
Les Katz, (I)
DuCane, Alex/111 E 64th St 212-772-2840
Tony Kent, (P), Niel Kirk, (P), Cheryl Koralik, (P), Christopher
Micaud, (P), Maria Robledo, (P)
Dunn, Roark/18 College Pl, Brooklyn 718-875-2558

E

Edlitz, Ann/230 E 79th St #14F 212-744-7945
Edwards, Libby/1650 Third Ave #4A 212-867-1030
Ellis, Mirjana/176 Westminster Rd, Brooklyn 718-282-6449
Ray Ellis, (P)
Engel, Mary/65 Central Pk W 212-580-1051
Henri Dauman, (P), Peter B Kaplan, (P)
Englert, Tim/305 W 84th St #313 212-496-2074
Enright, Catherine/61 E 66th St 212-288-0249
Erika/114 E 32nd St 212-532-7897

Tony Mandarino, (P)
Erlacher, Bill/Artists Assoc/211 E 51st St #5F 212-755-1365
Norman Adams, (I), Don Brautigam, (I), Michael Deas, (I),
Michael Dudash, (I), Mark English, (I), Alex Gnidziejko, (I),
Robert Heindel, (I), Steve Karchin, (I), Dick Krepel, (I), Skip
Liepke, (I), Fred Otnes, (I), Daniel Schwartz, (I), Norman
Walker, (I)
Eyre, Susan/292 Marlboro Rd, Brooklyn 718-282-5034
Robert Phillips, (P)

F

Feldman, Robert/133 W 17th St #5A 212-741-7254
Alen MacWeeney, (P), Terry Niefield, (P)
Fischer, Bob/135 E 54th St 212-755-2131
James Moore, (P)
Fishback, Lee/350 W 21st St 212-929-2951
Folickman, Gail/399 E 72nd St 212-879-1508
Folio Reps/450 Seventh Ave #902 212-268-1788
Sid Brak, (I), David Juniper, (I), JC Knaff, (I), James Marsh,
(I), Ean Taylor, (I), George Underwood, (I), Povl Webb, (I),
Ray Winder, (I)
Foster, Pat (Ms)/6 E 36th St #1R 212-685-4580
Foster, Peter/870 UN Plaza 212-593-0793
Charles Tracey, (P)
Fraser, Gaylene/211 Thompson St 212-475-5911
Robert Cohen, (P), Rosemary Howard, (P), Yosuf Karsh, (P),
Bernard Maisner, (I), Marcus Tullis, (P)
Frazier, Victoria/40 W 27th St 212-689-4207
Friess, Susan/36 W 20th St 212-675-3021
Richard Goldman, (P)
Friscia, Salmon/20 W 10th St 212-228-4134
Daniel Sussman, (P), Masaaki Takenaka, (P)
Furst, Franz/420 E 55th St 212-684-0492
Greg Pease, (P)

G

Gargagliano, Tony/216 E 45th St 212-661-0850
Gaynin, Gail/241 Central Park West 212-580-3141
Terry Clough, (P)
Gebbia, Doreen/312 W 88th St #2R 212-496-1279
Bruce Plotkin, (P)
Giraldi, Tina/54 W 39th St 212-840-8225
Godfrey, Dennis/95 Horatio St #203 212-807-0840
Jeffrey Adams, (I), Daryl Cagle, (I), Seth Jaben, (I), Joel
Nakamura, (I), Wendy Popp, (I), David Stimson, (I)
Goldman, David/41 Union Sq W #918 212-807-6627
Norm Bendell, (I), Keith Bendis, (I), Jay Brenner, (P), Saul
Mandel, (I), Mitchell Rigie, (I), James Yang, (I)
Gomberg, Susan/145 E 22nd St 212-473-8747
Neil Brennan, (I), Jacobson/Fernandez, (I),
Sheckman/Ferguson, (I), Colin Brown, (I), Steve Carver, (I),
Robert Dale, (I), Allen Garns, (I), Ralph Giguere, (I), Franklin
Hammond, (I), Fran Hardy, (I), Jeff Leedy, (I), Dan McGowan,
(I), Enzo Messi & Urs Schmidt, (I), James Tughan, (I), Mark
Weakley, (I)
Goodman, Barbara L/50 W 34th St 212-594-9209
Goodwin, Phyllis A/10 E 81st St 212-570-6021
Carl Furuta, (P), Cosimo, (P), Howard Menken, (P), Carl
Zapp, (P)
Gordon, Barbara Assoc/165 E 32nd St 212-686-3514
Craig Bakley, (I), Ron Barry, (I), Linda Benson, (I), Judith
Cheng, (I), Bob Clarke, (I), James Dietz, (I), Glenn
Harrington, (I), Robert Hunt, (I), Nenad Jakesevic, (I), Jackie
Jasper, (I), Elizabeth Kenyon, (I), Sonja Lamut, (I), William
Maughn, (I), Roy McKie, (I), Andrew Nitzberg, (I), Jackie
Vaux, (I)
Gordon, Fran/1654 E 13th St #5A, Brooklyn 718-339-4277
Gotham Art Agency/1123 Broadway #600 212-989-2737
Grande, Carla/329 W 21st St #4R 212-691-1015
John Dugdale, (P)
Grant, Lucchi/800 West End Ave #15C 212-663-1460
Ron Bucalo, (I), Catherine Clayton-Purnell, (I), Deborah
Dudley-Max, (I), Michael Hernandez, (P), Ron Jones, (I),
Robin Lazarus, (I), Kent Neffendorf, (I), Klarie Phipps, (I),
David Purnell, (I), Pansy Sapp, (I), Marc Sasso, (I), Steven
Stipleman, (I)
Green, Anita/718 Broadway 212-674-4788

Alan Dolgins, (P), Michael Geiger, (P), Michael Molkenthin, (P)
Grien, Anita/155 E 38th St 212-697-6170
Dolores Bego, (I), Fanny Mellet Berry, (I), Julie Johnson, (I),
Julie Johnson, (I), Hal Just, (I), Jerry McDaniel, (I), Don
Morrison, (I), Alan Reingold, (I), Ellen Rixford, (I), Mangal, (I)
Gullatt, Lou/342 Madison Ave #832 212-557-8628
Michael Christian, (I), Guy Kingsberry, (I), Ken Krafchek, (I),
Dana Verkouteren, (I)

H

Hainy, Barry/82 Jane St 212-929-4313
Hajjar, Rene/240 E 27th St 212-685-0679
Chris Jones, (P)
Handelman, H Lee/77 Fifth Ave 212 645-7946
Hankins + Tegenborg Ltd/60 E 42nd St #1940 212-867-8092
Peter Attard, (I), Ralph Brillhart, (I), George Bush, (I),
Frederico Castelluccio, (I), Jamie Cavaliere, (I), Jim Cherry,
(I), Mac Conner, (I), John Dawson, (I), Guy Deel, (I), Chris
Dellorco, (I), Ron DiScensa, (I), John Dismukes, (I), Bill
Dodge, (I), Marc Ericksen, (I), George Fernandez, (I), David
Gaadt, (I), Sergio Giovine, (I), James Griffin, (I), Ray Harvey,
(I), Edwin Herder, (I), Michael Herring, (I), Kevin Hulsey, (I),
Miro, (I), Aleta Jenks, (I), Rick Johnson, (I), Uldis Klavins, (I),
Richard Lauter, (I), John Mazzini, (I), Cliff Miller, (I), Wendell
Minor, (I), Sam Montesano, (I), Jeffery Oh, (I), Greg Olanoff,
(I), Matt Peak, (I), Walter Rane, (I), Kirk Reinert, (I), Ron
Runda, (I), Peter Van Ryzin, (I), Harry Schaare, (I), Bill
Schmidt, (I), Dione Sivavec, (I), Diane Slavec, (I), Dan
Sneberger, (I), Frank Steiner, (I), Robert Travers, (I), Bob
Trondsen, (I), Victor Valla, (I), Jeff Walker, (I), John Youssi, (I)
Hansen, Wendy/126 Madison Ave 212-684-7139
Masaaki Takenaka, (P), Minh, (I)
Harmon, Rod/254 W 51st St #17E 212-245-8935
Rob Rossi, (P), Al Rubin, (P)
Head, Olive/155 Riverside Dr #10C 212-580-3323
Healy, Tim/251 W 30th St #16W 212-279-1515
Henderson, Akemi/44 W 54th St 212-581-3630
Henderson, Gayle/6 W 20th St 2nd Fl 212-689-6783
Barry Schein, (p)
Henry, John/237 E 31st St, (P 97) **212-686-6883**
Lane Berkwit (Ms), (P), Lois Greenfield, (P)
Herron, Pat/80 Madison Ave 212-753-0462
Larry Dale Gordon, (P), Malcolm Kirk, (P), Hiro, (P)
Heyl, Fran/230 Park Ave #2525, (P 406, 407) **212-581-6470**
Pix Elation, (P)
Hill, James/1026 Sixth Ave #2S 212-302-4646
Hoeye, Michael/120 W 70th St 212-222-2012
Lelo Raymond, (P)
Holmberg, Irmeli/280 Madison Ave #1402 212-545-9155
Vincent Amicosante, (I), Toyee Anderson, (I), Lee Lee
Brazeal, (I), Dan Bridy, (I), Lindy Chambers, (I), Georgan
Damore, (I), Walter Gurbo, (I), Sharmen Liao, (I), John
Martinez, (I), Barbara Maslen, (I), Lu Matthews, (I), Marilyn
Montgomery, (I), Cyd Moore, (I), Ann Neuman, (I), Jacqueline
Osborn, (I), Stephen Osborn, (I), Andrew Paquette, (I),
Deborah Pinkney, (I), Nikolai Punin, (I), Bob Radigan, (I), Bill
Rieser, (I), Lilla Rogers, (I), Randie Wasserman, (I)
Holtzberg, Diana/166 Second Ave #11K 212-829-9838
Ori Hofmekler, (I)
Hovde, Nob/1438 Third Ave 212-753-0462
Larry Dale Gordon, (P), Hiro, (P), Malcolm Kirk, (P)
Hurewitz, Gary/5 E 19th St #303 212-473-3366
Howard Berman, (P), Steve Bronstein, (P), Earl Culberson,
(P), Dan Weaks, (P)
Husak, John/236 W 26th St #805 212-463-7025
Frank Marchese, (G), William Sloan, (I)

IJ

Iglesias, Jose/1123 Broadway #1113 212-929-7962
Stan Fellerman, (P), John Uher, (P)
Italia, Mark/1501 Broadway #1606 212-354-5962
Andy Grinko, (I)
Ivy League of Artists/156 Fifth Ave #617 212-243-1333
Ernest Albanese, (I), Cheryl Chalmers, (I), William Colrus, (I),
Joseph Dawes, (I), John Dyess, (I), Paula Goodman, (I),
Mark Hannon, (I), Justin Novack, (I), Tom Powers, (I), Herb
Reed, (I), John Rice, (I), Allison Staffin, (I), Kyuzo Tsugami,

(I), Allen Welkis, (I), Debora Whitehouse, (I)
J & M Studio/107 W 25th St #3A 212-627-5460
Jedell, Joan/370 E 76th St 212-861-7861
Johnson, Bud & Evelyne/201 E 28th St 212-532-0928
Kathy Allert, (I), Betty de Araujo, (I), Irene Astrahan, (I),
Rowan Barnes-Murphy, (I), Cathy Beylon, (I), Lisa Bonforte,
(I), Carolyn Bracken, (I), Jane Chambliss-Rigie, (I), Roberta
Collier, (I), Frank Daniel, (I), Larry Daste, (I), Ted Enik, (I),
Carolyn Ewing, (I), Bill Finewood, (I), Robert Gunn, (I), Yukio
Kondo, (I), Mei-ku-Huang, (I), Tom LaPadula, (I), Turi
MacCombie, (I), Dee Malan, (I), Brookie Maxwell, (I), Darcy
May, (I), Eileen McKeating, (I), Steven Petruccio, (I),
Christopher Santoro, (I), Stan Skardinski, (I), Barbara
Steadman, (I), Pat Stewart, (I), Tom Tierney, (I), Tricia Zimic, (I)

K

Kahn, Harvey Assoc Inc/14 E 52nd St 212-752-8490
Clint Clemens, (P), Bernard Fuchs, (I), Nicholas Gaetano, (I),
Gerald Gersten, (I), Wilson McLean, (I), Bob Peak, (I)
Kane, Barney & Friends/566 Seventh Ave #603 212-221-8090
Margaret Brown, (P), Jack DeGraffenried, (I), Joe Denaro, (I),
Michael Farina, (I), Ann Fox, (I), Nat Giorgio, (I), William
Harrison, (I), David Jarvis, (I), Steven Keyes, (I), Harvey
Kurtzman, (I), Bob Lapsley, (I), Dan Lavigne, (I), Peter Lloyd,
(I), Ted Lodigensky, (I), Rich Mahon, (I), Robert Melendez, (I),
Wally Niebart, (I), Philippe Renaudin, (I), Sue Rother, (I), Gary
Ruddell, (I), Joseph Sellars, (I), Mario Stasolla, (I), Vahid, (I),
Lynn Stephens, (I), Bill Thomson, (I), Larry Winborg, (I),
Jenny Yip, (I)
Kane, Odette/236 W 27th St 212-807-8730
Maria Perez, (I), Charles Seesselberg, (P)
Kaplan, Holly/43 Crosby St 212-925-2929
Bruno, (P)
Kauss, Jean-Gabriel/235 E 40th St.............................212-370-4300
Michel Conte, (P), Roger Duncan, (P), Carel Fonteyne, (P), Jesse Gerstein, (P),
Francois Halard, (P), Mark Hispard, (P), Dominique Isserman, (P), Elizabeth
Novick, (P), John Stember, (P)
Kenney, John Assoc/145 E 49th St 212-758-4545
Gary Hanlon, (P), Elizabeth Heyert, (P)
Kent, Al/244 Madison Ave 212-687-5578
Kestner, V G/427 E 77th St #4C 212-535-4144
Kim/137 E 25th St 11 Fl...212-679-5628
Carl Shiraishi, (P)
Kimche, Tania/470 W 23rd St 212-242-6367
Paul Blakey, (I), Kirk Caldwell, (I), Richard Goldberg, (I), Hom
& Hom, (I), Rafal Olbinski, (I), Miriam Schottland, (I), E T
Steadman, (I), Christopher Zacharow, (I)
Kirchoff-Wohlberg Inc/866 UN Plaza #4014 212-644-2020
Angela Adams, (I), Bob Barner, (I), Esther Baron, (I),
Maryjane Begin Callanan, (I), Liz Callen, (I), Steve
Cieslawski, (I), Brian Cody, (I), Gwen Connelly, (I), Donald
Cook, (I), Floyd Cooper, (I), Betsy Day, (I), Rae Ecklund, (I),
Lois Ehlert, (I), Al Fiorentino, (I), Frank Fretz, (I), Jon
Friedman, (I), Dara Goldman, (I), Jeremy Guitar, (I), Konrad
Hack, (I), Ron Himler, (I), Rosekrans Hoffman, (I), Kathleen
Howell, (I), Susan Jaekel, (I), Chris Kalle, (I), Mark Kelley, (I),
Christa Kieffer, (I), Dora Leder, (I), Tom Leonard, (I), Susan
Lexa, (I), Don Madden, (I), Jane McCreary, (I), Lyle Miller, (I),
Carol Nicklaus, (I), Sharon O'Neil, (I), Robin Oz, (I), Jim
Pearson, (I), J Brian Pinkney, (I), Charles Robinson, (I),
Bronwen Ross, (I), Robert Steele, (I), Arvis Stewart, (I), Pat
Traub, (I), Lou Vaccaro, (I), Joe Veno, (I), John Wallner, (I),
Alexandra Wallner, (I), Arieh Zeldich, (I)
Klein, Leslie D/255 Sherman St, Brooklyn 718-435-6541
Klimt, Bill & Maurine/15 W 72nd St 212-799-2231
Wil Cormier, (I), Jaime DeJesus, (I), Leonid, (I), Doug Gray,
(I), Paul Henry, (I), Brian Kotzky, (I), Frank Morris, (I), Shusei
Nagaoka, (I), Alan Neider, (I), Gary Penca, (I), Leonid
Pinchevsky, (I), Mark Skolsky, (I), Carla Sormanti, (I), Susan
Tang, (I)
Knight, Harrison/1043 Lexington Ave #4.......................212-288-9777
Barbara Campbell, (P)
Kontzias, Lucy/317 Washington Ave, Brooklyn 718-857-1528
Korman, Alison/240 E 76th St 212-633-8407
David Bishop, (P), Susan Kravis, (I)
Korn, Elaine Assoc/234 Fifth Ave, new York 212-679-6739
Klaus Laubmayer, (P)

Korn, Pamela/321 E 12th St #10 212-529-6389
Brian Ajhar, (I), Wendy Braun, (I), Jeff Moores, (I), Kurt Vargo, (I)
Kramer, Ina/104 E 40th St #111.................................212-599-0435
Michael Reingold, (I)
Kramer, Joan & Assoc/720 Fifth Ave...........................212-567-5545
David Cornwell, (P), Micheal DeVecka, (P), Clark Dunbar, (P),
Stan Flint, (P), Stephen Frink, (P), John Lawlor, (P), James
McLoughlin, (P), Frank Moscati, (P), John Russell, (P), Ed
Simpson, (P), David Simpson, (P), Roger Smith, (P), Glen
Steiner, (P), Ken Whitmore, (P), Edward Young, (P)
Kreis, Ursula G/63 Adrian Ave, Bronx..........................212-562-8931
Bill Farrell, (P), George Kamper, (P), Jed Share, (P)
Krongard, Paula/210 Fifth Ave #301 212-683-1020
Douglas Foulke, (P), Bill White, (P)

L

Lada, Joe/330 E 19th St 212-254-0253
George Hausman, (P)
Lalleman, Sylvan/117 E 24th St 212-260-0112
Lamont, Mary/200 W 20th St 212-242-1087
Jim Marchese, (P)
Lander, Jane/333 E 30th St 212-679-1358
Francois Cloteaux, (I), Mel Furukawa, (I), Helen Guetary, (I),
Cathy Heck, (I), Frank Riley, (I)
Lane, Judy/444 E 82nd St 212-861-7225
Larkin, Mary/308 E 59th St 212-308-7744
Lynn St John, (P), Charles Masters, (P)
Lashua, Sonja/27 W 20th St #1003..............................212-929-5701
Rick Young, (P)
Lavaty, Frank & Jeff/509 Madison Ave 10th Fl 212-355-0910
John Berkey, (I), Jim Butcher, (I), Don Daily, (I), Bernard
D'Andrea, (I), Michael Davis, (I), Roland DesCombes, (I),
Christine Duke, (I), Bruce Emmett, (I), Gervasio Gallardo, (I),
Tim Hildebrandt, (I), Martin Hoffman, (I), Stan Hunter, (I),
Chet Jezierski, (I), David McCall Johnson, (I), Mort Kunstler,
(I), Paul Lehr, (I), Lemuel Line, (I), Robert LoGrippo, (I),
Darrel Millsap, (I), Carlos Ochagavia, (I), Ben Verkaaik, (I)
Lee, Alan/33 E 22nd St #5D 212-673-2484
Jim Barber, (P), Wayne Eastep, (P), Werner Kappes, (I)
Leff, Jerry/420 Lexington Ave #2738 212-697-8525
Franco Accornero, (I), Ken Barr, (I), Semyon Bilmes, (I), Alex
Boies, (I), Bradford Brown, (I), Mike Bryan, (I), Ron DiCianni,
(I), Richard Drayton, (I), Charles Gehm, (I), Penelope
Gottlieb, (I), Richard High, (GD), Terry Hoff, (I), Gayle
Kabaker, (I), Ron Lesser, (I), Francis Livingston, (I), Dennis
Magdich, (I), Michele Manning, (I), Frank Marciuliano, (I),
Alan Mazzetti, (I), Mercedes McDonald, (I), Gary
McLaughlin, (I), Celia Mitchell, (I), John Parsons, (I), David
Plourdes, (I), Kenn Richards, (I), Dazzeland Studios, (I), Kurt
Wallace, (I), James Woodend, (I), Judy York, (I)
Legrand, Jean Yves/41 W 84th St #4.............................212-724-5981
Leone, Mindy/381 Park Ave S #710 212-696-5674
Bill Kouirinis, (P)
Leonian, Edith/220 E 23rd St 212-989-7670
Philip Leonian, (P)
Lerman, Gary/113 E 31st St #4D 212-683-5777
John Bechtold, (P), Bruce Buyers, (P), Jan Cobb, (P)
Levin, Bruce/231 E 58th St #22B 212-832-4053
Levitt, Lee/43 W 16th St #16 718-729-1269
Levy, Leila/4523 Broadway #7G...................................212-942-8185
David Bishop, (P), Yoav Levy, (P)
Lewin, Betsy/152 Willoughby Ave, Brooklyn 718-622-3882
Ted Lewin, (I)
Lewin, Samantha/221 W 19th St 212-228-5530
LGI/241 W 36th St 7th Fl 212-736-4602
Lindgren & Smith/41 Union Sq W #1228........................212-929-5590
Barbara Banthien, (I), Bradley Clark, (I), Cam DeLeon, (I),
David Dees, (I), Regan Dunnick, (I), Cameron Eagle, (I),
Doug Fraser, (I), Lori Lohstoeter, (I), Richard Mantel, (I),
Margo Nahas, (I), Kathy O'Brien, (I), Michael Paraskevas, (I),
Charles Pyle, (I), Tim Raglin, (I), Ed Sorel, (I), Robert Gantt
Steele, (I), Cathleen Toelke, (I), Cynthia Torp, (I), Charles
White, (I), Kris Wiltse, (I), Jean Wisenbaugh, (I), Darryl
Zudeck, (I)
Locke, John Studios Inc/15 E 76th St...........................212-288-8010
John Cayea, (I), John Clift, (I), Oscar DeMejo, (I), Jean-Pierre
Desclozeaux, (I), James Endicott, (I), Richard Erdoes, (I),

Jean Michel Folon, (I), Michael Foreman, (I), Andre Francois, (I), George Giusti, (I), Edward Gorey, (I), Catherine Kanner, (I), Peter Lippman, (I), Sam Maitin, (I), Richard Oden, (I), William Bryan Park, (I), Fernando Puigrosado, (I), Hans-Georg Rauch, (I), Ronald Searle, (I), Tim, (I), Roland Topor, (I)

Longobardi, Gerard/5 W 19th St 212-255-3440
Lott, Peter & George/60 E 42nd St 212-953-7088
Juan Barberis, (I), Ted Chambers, (I), Tony Cove, (I), Jim Dickerson, (I), David Halpern, (I), Keith Hoover, (P), Ed Kurtzman, (I), Wendell McClintock, (I), Tim O'Brien, (I), Marie Peppard, (I), John Suh, (I), Barbara Tyler, (I)
Lynch, Alan/155 Ave of Americas 10th Fl 212-255-6530
Michael Armson, (I), John Dawson, (I), Stephen Hall, (I), Jim Warren, (I)

M

Macfie, Jennifer/18 Bank St 212-206-0436
Madris, Stephen/445 E 77th St 212-744-6668
Gary Perweiler, (P)
Mallory, Brooke/301 W 57th St 212-586-7594
Manasse, Michele/1974 Broadway 2nd Fl 212-873-3797
Sheldon Greenberg, (I), Narda Lebo, (I), Wallop Manyum, (I), Roger Roth, (I), John Segal, (I), Terry Widener, (I)
Mandell, Ilene/61 E 86th St 212-860-3148
Raeanne Giovanni, (I), Cheryl Rossum, (P)
Mann & Dictenberg Reps/20 W 46th St 212-944-2853
Brian Lanker, (P), Al Satterwhite, (P), Ulf Skogsbergh, (P)
Marek & Assoc Inc/160 Fifth Ave #914 212-924-6760
Walter Chin, (P), Hanns Feurer, (P), Marco Glaviano, (P), Eddy Kohli, (P), Marie Josee Lafontaine, (P), Just Loomis, (P), Deborah Turbeville, (P)
Marino, Frank/35 W 36th St 212-563-2730
Bruno Benvenuti, (I)
Mariucci, Marie A/32 W 39th St 212-944-9590
R & V Studios, (P)
Marshall, Mel & Edith/40 W 77th St 212-877-3921
Todd Haiman, (P)
Martin, Bruce Rough Riders/55 Mercer St 2nd Fl 212-219-1543
Marx, Gail/, , NJ 201-836-9087
Mason, Kathy/101 W 18th St 4th Fl 212-675-3809
Don Mason, (P)
Mayo, Vicki/425 E 86th St 212-722-7228
McKay, Colleen/229 E 5th St #2 212-598-0469
Robert Tardio, (P)
Meixler, Harriet/36 W 37th St 212-868-0078
Susanne Buckler, (P)
Mendelsohn, Richard/353 W 53rd St #1W 212-682-2462
Mendola Ltd/420 Lexington Ave #PH4,5, (P 20,21) **212-986-5680**
Peter Pioppo, (P), Stan Wan, (P), Paul Alexander, (I), Robert Berran, (I), Steve Brennan, (I), Jim Campbell, (I), Carl Cassler, (I), Deborah Chabrian, (I), Karen Chandler, (I), Garry Colby, (I), Jim Deneen, (I), Kenneth Dewey, (I), Donna Diamond, (I), John Eggert, (I), Jon Ellis, (I), Guy Fery, (I), Peter Fiore, (I), Phil Franke, (I), Antonio Gabriele, (I), Hector Garrido, (I), Ted Giavis, (I), Elaine Gigniliat, (I), Chuck Gillies, (I), Dale Gustafson, (I), Chuck Hamrick, (I), Attila Hejja, (I), Dave Henderson, (I), Mitchell Hooks, (I), Paul Jennis, (I), Bob Jones, (I), Alfons Kiefer, (I), Dave Kilmer, (I), Michael Koester, (I), Richard Leech, (I), Dennis Luzak, (I), Dennis Lyall, (I), Jeff Lynch, (I), Jeffrey Mangiat, (I), Lou Marchetti, (I), Edward Martinez, (I), Goeffrey McCormack, (I), Mark McMahon, (I), Ann Meisel, (I), Roger Metcalf, (I), Ted Michner, (I), Mike Mikos, (I), Jonathon Milne, (I), Wally Neibart, (I), Michael Noome, (I), Chris Notarile, (I), John Rosato, (I), Delro Rosco, (I), Mort Rosenfeld, (I), Brian Sauriol, (I), David Schleinkofer, (I), Mark Schuler, (I), Mike Smollin, (I), Kipp Soldwedel, (I), John Solie, (I), Cliff Spohn, (I), Jeffrey Terreson, (I), Thierry Thompson, (I), Mark Watts, (I), Richard Whitney, (I), Mike Wimmer, (I), Ben Wohlberg, (I), David Womersley, (I)
Mennemeyer, Ralph/286 Fifth Ave 4th Fl 212-279-2838
Paul Christensen, (P), Ted Morrison, (P), Katrina, (P)
Michalski, Ben/118 E 28th St 212-683-4025
Miller, Judith/20 E 35th St 212-213-1772
Miller, Susan/1641 Third Ave #29A 212-417-9604
Beth Whybrow Leeds, (I), David Shultz, (I), David Zimmerman, (P)
Mintz, Les/111 Wooster St #PH C 212-925-0491

Robert Bergin, (I), Bernard Bonhomme, (I), Mark Fisher, (I), Mark Fresh, (I), Amy Hill, (I), Shirley Kaneda, (I), Roberta Ludlow, (I), David Lui, (I), Julia McLain, (I), Jorge de Silva, (I), Kirsten Soderlind, (I), Tommy Soloski, (I), Judith Sutton, (I), Sarah Waldron, (I), Dennis Ziemienski, (I)

Moll, Jonathan/347 E 76th St #1A 212-679-9074
Monaco Reps/280 Park Ave S 212-979-5533
Charles Ford, (P), Frank Hom, (P), John Peden, (P), Danny Sit, (P), Otto Stupakoff, (P)
Moretz, Eileen P/141 Wooster St 212-254-3766
Charles Moretz, (P)
Morgan, Vicki Assoc/194 Third Ave 212-475-0440
Willardson + Assoc, (I), Nanette Biers, (I), Ray Cruz, (I), Patty Dryden, (I), Vivienne Flesher, (I), Kathy & Joe Heiner, (I), Bob Hickson, (I), Joyce Patti, (I), Ward Schumacher, (I), Joanie Schwarz, (I), Nancy Stahl, (I), Dahl Taylor, (I), Bruce Wolfe, (I), Wendy Wray, (I), Brian Zick, (I)
Morse, Lauren/78 Fifth Ave 212-807-1551
Alan Zenreich, (P)
Moscato, Lynn/118-14 83rd Ave #5B, Kew Gardens 718-805-0069
Mosel, Sue/310 E 46th St 212-599-1806
Moser, Trixie/1123 Broadway #1113 212-929-7962
Stan Fellerman, (P), John Uher, (P)
Moses, Janice/155 E 31st St #20H 212-779-7929
Moskowitz, Marion/342 Madison Ave #469 212-719-9879
Dianne Bennett, (I), Diane Teske Harris, (I), Arnie Levin, (I), Geoffrey Moss, (I)
Moss, Eileen/333 E 49th St #3J 212-980-8061
Bill Cigliano, (I), Tom Curry, (I), Deborah Denker, (P), Warren Gebert, (I), Joel Peter Johnson, (I), Pamela Patrick, (I), Robert Pizzo, (I), Scott Pollack, (I), Lionsgate, (I)
Moss, Susan/29 W 38th St 212-354-8024
Louis Mervar, (P)
Move Art Productions/117 E 24th St #6B 212-260-0112
Muth, John/37 W 26th St 212-532-3479
Pat Hill, (P)

N

Napaer, Michele/349 W Broadway 212-219-0325
Michael Abramson, (P)
Neail, Pamela R Assoc/27 Bleecker St 212-673-1600
Margaret Brown, (I), Sean Daly, (I), Gregory Dearth, (I), Dennis DiVincenzo, (I), David Guinn, (I), Celeste Henriquez, (I), Thea Kliros, (I), Michele Laporte, (I), Marina Levikova, (I), Tony Mascio, (I), Peter McCaffrey, (I), Cary McKiver, (I), Manuel Nunez, (I), Ryuji Otani, (I), Brenda Pepper, (I), Linda Richards, (I), Glenn Tunstull, (I), Jenny Vainisi, (I), Gaylord Welker, (I), Vicki Yiannias, (I), Pat Zadnik, (I)
Network Representatives/206 W 15th St 4th Fl 212-727-0044
Aaron Warkov, (P), Ross Whitaker, (P)
Newborn, Milton/135 E 54th St 212-421-0050
Braldt Bralds, (I), Carol Gillot, (I), Robert Giusti, (I), Dick Hess, (I), Mark Hess, (I), Victor Juhasz, (I), Simms Taback, (I), David Wilcox, (I)

OP

O'Rourke-Page Assoc/219 E 69th St #11G 212-772-0346
Honolulu Crtv Grp, (P), Sam Haskins, (P), Lincoln Potter, (P), Jim Raycroft, (P), Smith/Garner, (P), Eric Schweikardt, (P), William Sumner, (P), John Thornton, (P), Gert Wagner, (P), John Zimmerman, (P)
Onyx/59 W 19th St #4B 212-633-2050
Michael Abramson, (P), Josef Astor, (P), Gwendolen Cates, (P), William Coupon, (P), Terry Husebye, (P), Robb Kendrick, (P), Jonathan Levine, (P), Steve Marsell, (P), Joyce Ravid, (P), George Steinmetz, (P), Michael Tighe, (P), Bob Wagoner, (P), Barbara Walz, (P), Timothy White, (P), Tom Wolff, (P), Elizabeth Zeschin, (P)
Palmer-Smith, Glenn Assoc/104 W 70th St 212-769-3940
Jim Brill, (P), Charles Nesbitt, (P)
Penny & Stermer Group/48 W 21st St 9th Fl 212-243-4412
Manos Angelakis, (I), Ron Becker, (I), Scott Gordley, (I), Michael Hostovich, (I), Julia Noonan, (I), Thomas Payne, (I), Deborah Bazzel Pogue, (I), Gary Smith, (I), Terri Sterrett, (I), James Turgeon, (I), Terry Walsh, (I)
Petrie, Jack/28 Vesey St #2213 212-301-5196
Pierce, Jennifer/1376 York Ave 212-744-3810

Pinkstaff, Marcia/222 Central Pk S 212-246-2300
Pritchett, Tom/130 Barrow St #316 212-688-1080
Steve Durke, (I), Tom Evans, (I), George Parrish Jr, (I),
George Kanelous, (I), Mike Robins, (I), Terry Ryan, (I)
Puhalski, Ron/1133 Broadway #221 212-242-2860
Pushpin Assoc/215 Park Ave S 212-674-8080
Istvan Banyai, (I), Lou Beach, (I), Christoph Blumrich, (I),
Seymour Chwast, (I), Jose Cruz, (I), Alicia Czechowski, (I),
Dave Jonason, (I), Hiro Kimura, (I), Frank Miller, (I), R Kenton
Nelson, (I), Roy Pendleton, (I)

R

Rapp, Gerald & Cullen Inc/108 E 35th St #1C 212-889-3337
Ray Ameijide, (I), Emmanuel Amit, (I), David Brier, (I),
Michael Brown, (I), Lon Busch, (I), Ken Dallison, (I), Jack
Davis, (I), Bob Deschamps, (I), Bill Devlin, (I), Ray Domingo,
(I), Lee Duggan, (I), Randy Glass, (I), Ginnie Hoffman, (I),
Lionel Kalish, (I), Sharon Knettell, (I), Laszlo Kubinyi, (I), Lee
Lorenz, (I), Allan Mardon, (I), Elwyn Mehlman, (I), Marie
Michal, (I), Alex Murawski, (I), Lou Myers, (I), Bob Peters, (I),
Jerry Pinkney, (I), Camille Przewodek, (I), Charles Santore,
(I), Bob Tanenbaum, (I), Michael Witte, (I)
Ray, Marlys/350 Central Pk W 212-222-7680
Bill Ray, (P)
Reese, Kay Assoc/225 Central Park West 212-799-1133
Lee Balterman, (P), Gerry Cranham, (P), Ashvin Gatha, (P),
Peter Gullers, (P), Arno Hammacher, (P), Jay Leviton, (P),
George Long, (P), Jon Love, (P), Lynn Pelham, (P), Milkie
Studio, (P), T Tanuma, (P)
Reid, Pamela/66 Crosby St 212-925-5909
Andrea Blanch, (P), Madeleine Cofano, (H), Thierry des
Fontaines, (P), Laura Mercier, (MU), Bob Recine, (H), Bert
Stern, (P), Mane/Duplan, (S), Franck Thiery, (P)
Renard, Madeline/501 Fifth Ave #1407 212-490-2450
Steve Bjorkman, (I), John Collier, (I), Rob Day, (I), Glenn
Dean, (I), Carol Donner, (I), Bart Forbes, (I), Tim Girvin, (I),
Lamb & Hall, (P), Personality Inc, (I), Hideaki Kodama, (I),
John Martin, (I), Richard Newton, (I), Robert Rodriguez, (I),
Javier Romero, (I), Maso Saito, (I), Michael Schwab, (I), Goro
Shimaoka, (I), Doug Struthers, (I), Jozef Sumichrast, (I), Kim
Whitesides, (I)
Rep Rep/211 Thompson St 212-475-5911
Rob Fraser, (P), Marcus Tullis, (P)
Ridgeway, Karen/330 W 42nd St #3200NE 212-714-0130
Marilyn Jones, (I), Ron Ridgeway, (I)
Riley Illustration/81 Greene St 212-925-3053
Quentin Blake, (I), Zevi Blum, (I), CESC, (I), William Bramhall,
(I), Chris DeMarest, (I), Paul Degan, (I), Paul Hogarth, (I),
Pierre Le-Tan, (I), Paul Meisel, (I), Robert A Parker, (I), Jim
Parkinson, (I), Cheryl Peterson, (I), J J Sempe, (I), Brenda
Shahinian, (I)
Roman, Helen Assoc/140 West End Ave #9H 212-874-7074
William Cone, (I), Naiad Einsel, (I), Walter Einsel, (I), Gil
Eisner, (I), Andrea Mistretta, (I), Anna Rich, (I)
Rudoff, Stan/271 Madison Ave 212-679-8780
David Hamilton, (P), Gideon Lewin, (P)

S

S I International/43 East 19th St 212-254-4996
Karen Baumann, (I), Jack Brusca, (I), ChiChoni, (I), Richard
Corben, (I), Richard Courtney, (I), Bob Cowan, (I), Dennis
Davidson, (I), Allen Davis, (I), Walt DeRijk, (I), Fernando
Fernandez, (I), Don Gabriel, (I), Blas Gallego, (I), Devis
Grebu, (I), Enric, (I), Steve Haefele, (I), Susi Kilgore, (I),
Penalva, (I), Sergio Martinez, (I), Fred Marvin, (I), Mones-
Mateu, (I), Jose Miralles, (I), Vince Perez, (I), Martin Rigo, (I),
Doug Rosenthal, (I), Artie Ruiz, (I), Paul Tatore, (I), Kathy
Wyatt, (I)
Sacramone, Dario/302 W 12th St 212-929-0487
Tohru Nakamura, (P), Marty Umans, (P)
Samuels, Rosemary/14 Prince St #5C 212-477-3567
Beth Galton, (P)
Sander, Vicki/155 E 29th St #28G 212-683-7835
Ed Gallucci, (P), George Menda, (P)
Santa-Donato, Paul/25 W 39th St 212-921-1550
Sean Farrel, (I), John Hardie, (I), Ron Hicinbothem, (I), Check
Hom, (I), Hector Lopez, (I), John Moodie, (I), Alex Morris, (I),

Hy Rosen, (I)
Satterwhite, Joy/80 Varick St #7B 212-219-0808
Al Satterwhite, (P)
Saunders, Michele/84 Riverside Dr #5 212-496-0268
Uwe Ommer, (P)
Schecter Group, Ron Long/212 E 49th St 212-752-4400
Scher, Dotty/235 E 22nd St 212-689-7273
Harry Benson, (P), Marty Jacobs, (P), David Katzenstein, (P),
Denis Waugh, (P), Walter Wick, (P)
Schneider, Jonathan/175 Fifth Ave #2291 212-459-4325
Daniel Abraham, (I), Arthur Ackerman, (I), Joe Cole, (I),
Randy Glasbergen, (I), Peter Kuper, (I), Ned Shaw, (I), Guy
Smallwood, (I)
Schochat, Kevin R/221 W 21st St #1D 212-475-7068
Thom DeSanto, (P), Mark Ferri, (P)
Schon, Herb/1240 Lexington Ave 212-737-2945
Schub, Peter & Robert Bear/136 E 57th #1702 212-246-0679
Robert Freson, (P), Alexander Lieberman, (P), Irving Penn,
(P), Rico Puhlmann, (P), Snowdon, (P), Albert Watson, (P)
Seigel, Fran/515 Madison Ave 22nd Fl 212-486-9644
Kinuko Craft, (I), Cathy Deeter, (I), Mirko Ili'c, (I), Earl Keleny,
(I), Larry McEntire, (I), Michael Vernaglia, (I)
Shamilzadeh, Sol/214 E 24th St #3D 212-532-1977
Ryszard Horowitz, (P), The Strobe Studio, (P)
Sharlowe Assoc/275 Madison Ave 212-288-8910
Claus Eggers, (P), Nesti Mendoza, (P)
Sheer, Doug/29 John St 212-732-4216
Karen Kent, (P)
Shepherd, Judith/186 E 64th St 212-838-3214
Dennis Gottlieb, (P), Barry Seidman, (P)
Siegel, Tema/461 Park Ave S 4th Fl 212-696-4680
Sigman, Joan/336 E 54th St 212-832-7980
Robert Goldstrom, (I), John H Howard, (I), Tom Sciacca, (I),
Jeff Seaver, (I)
Sims, Jennifer/1150 Fifth Ave 212-860-3005
Clint Clemens, (P), Robert Latorre, (P)
Slome, Nancy/121 Madison Ave 212-685-8185
Joe Berger, (P), Bob Brugger, (I), Kid Kane, (I), Bill Silberts,
(I), Bonnie Timmons, (I)
Smith, Emily/30 E 21st St 212-674-8383
Jeff Smith, (P)
Solomon, Richard/121 Madison Ave 212-683-1362
Kent Barton, (I), Thomas Blackshear, (I), Steve Brodner, (I),
Rick Brown, (I), Ray-Mel Cornelius, (I), Jack Davis, (I), David
A Johnson, (I), Gary Kelley, (I), Elizabeth Koda-Callan, (I), Bill
Nelson, (I), David Palladini, (I), C F Payne, (I), Rodica Prato,
(I), Ian Ross, (I), Douglas Smith, (I), Mark Summers, (I), John
Svoboda, (I), Shelley Thornton, (I)
Sonneville, Dane/PO Box 20415 Greeley Sta 212-603-9530
Leland Bobbe, (P), Jim Kinstrey, (I), John Pemberton, (P),
Jamie Phillips, (P), Bob Shein, (I), Bill Truran, (P)
Stein, Jonathan & Assoc/353 E 77th St 212-517-3648
Mitch Epstein, (P), Burt Glinn, (P), Ernst Haas, (P), Nathaniel
Lieberman, (P), Alex McLean, (P), Gregory Murphey, (P),
Joel Sternfeld, (P), Jeffrey Zaruba, (P)
Stevens, Norma/1075 Park Ave 212-427-7235
Richard Avedon, (P)
Stockland-Martel Inc/17 E 45th St #612 212-972-4747
Joel Baldwin, (P), Walter Iooss, (P), Eric Meola, (P), Claude
Mougin, (P), Michael Pruzan, (P)
Stockwell, Jehremy/307 W 82nd St #C 212-595-5757
Stogo, Donald/310 E 46th St 212-490-1034
Tom Grill, (P), John Lawlor, (P), Tom McCarthy, (P), Manuel
Morales, (I), Peter Vaeth, (P)
Stringer, Raymond/123 W 44th St #8F 212-840-2891
Ajin, (I)

T

Taborda, Carlos/344 E 85th St #1E 212-734-1903
Tannenbaum, Dennis/286 Fifth Ave 4th Fl 212-279-2838
Terzis, Cornelia/448 W 37th St #88 212-929-5174
The Art Farm/420 Lexington Ave 212-688-4555
Bruce Aruffenbart, (I), Dick Carroll, (I), Computer Paint Group,
(I), Sururi Gumen, (I), Bob Lubbers, (I), Dick Naugler, (I), Scott
Pike, (I), Bob Walker, (I), Kong Wu, (I), Bill Zdinak, (I)
The Organisation/267 Wyckoff St, Brooklyn 718-624-1906
Zafer Baran, (I), Mark Entwisle, (I), Michael Frith, (I), Peter

Goodfellow, (I), Susan Hellard, (I), Natacha Lerwidge, (I), Ruth Rivers, (I), Nadine Wickenden, (I)
Tise, Katherine/200 E 78th St......................................212-570-9069
Raphael Boguslav, (I), John Burgoyne, (I), Bunny Carter, (I), Judy Pelikan, (I), Cheryl Roberts, (I), Cathleen Toelke, (I)
Tralongo, Katrin/144 W 27th St....................................212-255-1976
Mickey Kaufman, (P)
Turk, Melissa/145 E 49th St #5D..................................212-751-1899
Juan Barberis, (I), Barbara Bash, (I), Susan Johnston Carlson, (I), Paul Casale, (I), Robert Frank, (I), Wendy Smith-Griswold, (I)

UV

Umlas, Barbara/131 E 93rd St......................................212-534-4008
Hunter Freeman, (P), Nora Scarlett, (P)
Van Arnam, Lewis/881 7th Ave #405..........................212-541-4787
Paul Amato, (P), Mike Reinhardt, (P)
Van Orden, Yvonne/119 W 57th St..............................212-265-1223
Joe Schneider, (P)
Vitale, Marian/151 Lexington Ave #9A.........................211-683-4225
Von Schreiber, Barbara/315 Central Park West #4N......212-580-7044
Ellen Forbes Burney, (P), Nigel Dickson, (P), Oberto Gili, (P), Erica Lennard, (P), Sarah Moon, (P), Jean Pagliuso, (P), Neal Slavin, (P)

WYZ

Ward, Wendy/200 Madison Ave #2402........................212-684-0590
Mel Odom, (I)
Wasserman, Ted/51 E 42nd St....................................212-867-5360
Dick Frank, (P), Steven Green-Armytage, (P)
Wayne, Philip/66 Madison Ave #9C.............................212-696-5215
Frank Spinelli, (P), Bernard Vidal, (P)
Weber, Tricia Group/38 W 38th St...............................212-768-0481
Weissberg, Elyse/299 Pearl St #5E..............................212-406-2566
Dan Barba, (I), Jack Reznicki, (I)
Williamson, Jack/16 W 22nd St....................................212-463-8302
DiFranza Williamson, (P)
Yellen, Bert & Assoc/420 E 54th St #21E.....................212-838-3170
Bill Connors, (P), Jody Dale, (P), Harvey Edwards, (P), Robert Farber, (P), Joe Francki, (P), James Robinson, (P), Olaf Wahlund, (P)
Zitsman, Cookie/30 Magaw Pl #3A...............................212-928-6228
Calvin Redmond, (P), Ken Rosenberg, (P)
Zlotnick, Jenny/14 Prince St...212-431-7680

NORTHEAST

A

Ackermann, Marjorie/2112 Goodwin Lane, North Wales, PA..........215-646-1745
H Mark Weidman, (P)
Artco/227 Godfrey Rd, Weston, CT...............................203-222-8777
Ed Acuna, (I), George Angelini, (I), Gene Boyer, (I), Dan Brown, (I), Alain Chang, (I), Anne Cook, (I), Jeff Cornell, (I), Bob Dacey, (I), Beau & Alan Daniels, (I), Mort Drucker, (I), Lisa Falkenstern, (I), Ed Gazsi, (I), Gary Glover, (I), Lisa Henderling, (I), Lisa Henderling, (I), Kathy Jeffers, (I), Rick McCollum, (I), John Jude Palencar, (I), Barry Phillips, (I), Al Pisano, (I), Marcel Rozenberg, (I), Leslie Szabo, (I), Alexander & Turner, (I), Sally Vitsky, (I)
Artists International/7 Dublin Hill Dr, Greenwich, CT.........203-869-8010
Tony Chen, (I), Gino, (I), David Chestnut, (I), Bill Cleaver, (I), Eric D'Zenis, (I), Michael Hampshire, (I), John Nez, (I), Ed & Earl Parker, (I), Jo Sickbert, (I), Paul Vaccarello, (I)

B

Bancroft, Carol & Friends/185 Goodhill Rd, Weston, CT...............203-226-7674
Lori Anderson, (I), Yvette Banek, (I), Cal & Mary Bausman, (I), Wendy Biggins, (I), Kristine Bollinger, (I), Denise Brunkus, (I), Chi Chung, (I), Jim Cummins, (I), Susan Dodge, (I), Andrea Eberbach, (I), Joe Ewers, (I), Marla Frazee, (I), Ethel Gold, (I), Fred Harsh, (I), Ann Iosa, (I), Laurie Jordan, (I), Ketti Kupper, (I), Barbara Lanza, (I), Karen Loccisano, (I), Al Lorenz, (I), Laura Lydecker, (I), Stephen Marchesi, (I), John

Mardon, (I), Kathleen McCarthy, (I), Michael McDermott, (I), Elizabeth Miles, (I), Yoshi Miyake, (I), Stephen Moore, (I), Nancy Munger, (I), Rodney Pate, (I), Cathy Pavia, (I), Ondre Pettingill, (I), Larry Raymond, (I), Gail Roth, (I), Blanche Sims, (I), Cindy Spencer, (I), Charles Varner, (I), Linda Boehm Weller, (I), Ann Wilson, (I), Chuck Wimmer, (I)
Bassett, Lisa/291 Central Ave, Needham, MA................617-235-6012
Kathleen McNally, (I), Chris Schuh, (I)
Benser, Kendell/2313 Maryland Ave, Baltimore, MD.......301-235-5235
Beranbaum, Sheryl/115 Newbury St, Boston, MA...........617-437-9459
Kimberly Bry, (I), Michael McLaughlin, (I)
Birenbaum, Molly/7 Williamsburg Dr, Cheshire, CT.........203-272-9253
Alice Coxe, (I), W E Duke, (I), Sean Kernan, (P), Joanne Schmaltz, (P), Paul Selwyn, (I), Bill Thomson, (I)
Black Silver & Lord/66 Union St, Belfast, ME.................207-338-1113
Bogner, Fred/911 State St, Lancaster, PA......................717-393-0918
brt Photo Illustration, (P)
Bookmakers/25-Q Sylvan Rd S, Westport, CT...............203-226-4293
David Bolinsky, (I), Steve Botts, (I), George Guzzi, (I), Lydia Halverson, (I), Keith LoBue, (I), Judith Lombardi, (I), Kathy McCord, (I), Steve McIntuff, (I), David Neuhaus, (I), Marsha Serafin, (I), Dick Smolinski, (I), Sharon Steuer, (I)
Brewster, John/597 Riverside Ave, Westport, CT.............203-226-4724
Donna Almquist, (I), Mike Brent, (I), Wendy Caporale, (I), Lane Dupont, (I), Jim Herity, (P), Seth Larson, (I), Dolph LeMoult, (I), Ken Mitchell, (I), Howard Munce, (I), Alan Neider, (I), Nan Parson, (I), Nan Parsons, (I), Steven Stroud, (I), Al Weston, (I)
Breza-Collier, Susan/105 Prospect Ave, Langhorne, PA.....215-752-7216
Brown, Deborah & Assoc/7 W 22nd St.........................212-463-7732
Buscemi, Greg/2019 St Paul St, Baltimore, MD...............301-332-0767
LT Schulmeyer, (P)

C

Cadenbach, Marilyn/37 Grant St, Lexington, MA.............617-862-2506
Camp, Woodfin Inc/2025 Penn Ave NW, Washington, DC......202-223-8442
Campbell, Rita/129 Valerie Ct, Cranston, RI...................401-826-0606
Campbell, Suzi/365 Beacon St, Boston, MA..................617-266-7365
Christensen, Virgina/7 Idle Day Dr, Centerport...............516-757-6046
City Limits/360 Manville Rd, Pleasantville.....................914-747-1422
Colucci, Lou/POB 2069/86 Lachawanna Ave, W Patterson, NJ......201-890-5770
Crawford, Janice/123 Minortown Rd, Woodbury, CT........212-722-4964
Creative Advantage Inc/707 Union St, Schenectady, NY.....518-370-0312
Jack Graber, (I), Richard Siciliano, (I)
Creative Arts International/7939 Norfolk Ave, Bethesda, MD.......301-656-5722

DE

D'Angelo, Victoria/620 Centre Ave, Reading, PA............215-376-1100
Andy D'Angelo, (P)
Ella/229 Berkeley #52, Boston, MA...............................617-266-3858
Lizi Boyd, (I), Wilbur Bullock, (I), Rob Cline, (I), Richard Cowdrey, (I), Jack Crompton, (I), Susan Dodge, (I), Sharon Drinkwine, (I), Anatoly Dverin, (I), Scott Gordley, (I), Robert Gunn, (I), Kevin Hawkes, (I), Roberts & Van Heusen, (I), Eaton & Iwen, (I), Roger Leyonmark, (I), Janet Mager, (I), Bill Morrison, (I), Masato Nishimura, (I), Carol O'Malia, (I), Molly Quinn, (I), Bruce Sanders, (I), Radiomayonnaise, (I), Ron Toelke, (I), Bryan Wiggins, (I), Francine Zaslow, (P)
Erwin, Robin/54 Applecross Cir, Chalfont, PA................215-822-8258
Callahan Photography, (P)
Esto Photographics/222 Valley Pl, Mamaroneck, NY........914-698-4060
Peter Aaron, (P), Dan Cornish, (P), Jeff Goldberg, (P), Peter Mauss, (P), Jock Pottle, (P)

FG

Francisco, Carol/419 Cynwyd Rd, Bala Cynwyd, PA.......215-667-2378
Geng, Maud/25 Gray St, Boston, MA............................617-236-1920
Caroline Alterio, (I), Peter Barger, (I), Geoffrey Clifford, (P), John Curtis, (P), Sid Evans, (I), Jean-Christian Knaff, (I), Jon McIntosh, (I), Jon McIntosh, (I), Vicki Smith, (I), John Svoboda, (I)
Giandomenico, Terry (Ms)/13 Fern Ave, Collingswood, NJ.........609-854-2222
Bob Giandomenico, (P)
Giannini & Talent/1830 R St NW #61, Washington, DC.......202-328-9076
Gidley, Fenton/43 Tokeneke Rd, Darien, CT...................203-655-1321
Ginsberg, Michael/200 Croton Ave, Mt Kisco, NY...........212-628-2379

Goldstein, Gwen/91 Hundreds Rd, Wellesley Hills, MA 617-235-8658
Michael Blaser, (I), Cathy Diefendorf, (I), Steve Fuller, (I),
Lane Gregory, (I), Barbara Morse, (I), Terry Presnall, (I),
Susan Spellman, (I), Gary Torrisi, (I), Joe Veno, (I)
Gordon, Leslie/15 North Rd, Northport..................................212-772-0403

H

Haas, Ken/PO Box 86, Oley, PA.....................................215-987-3711
Rich Dunoff, (P), Carmen Console Jr, (I), Barbara Kacicek,
(I), David Reinbold, (I), Emilie Snyder, (I), Jeff Zinggeler, (I),
Randall Zwingler, (I)
Heine, Karl Promotions/327-B Heritage Village, Southbury, CT 203-853-6015
Randall Douglas, (I), Richard Olsavsky, (I), Cynthia
Piotrowicz, (I), Frank Poole, (P), Cynthia Rowland, (I), Roger
Salls, (P)
Heisey, Betsy/109 Somerstown Rd, Ossining, NY 914-762-5335
Whitney Lane, (P)
HK Portfolio/458 Newtown Trnpk, Weston, CT 203-454-4687
Randy Chewning, (I), Carolyn Croll, (I), Eldon Doty, (I), Tom
Garcia, (I), Benton Mahan, (I), Steve McInturff, (I), Jan
Palmer, (I), Suzanne Richardson, (I), Sandra Speidel, (I),
Jean & Mou-sien Tseng, (I), George Ulrich, (I), Randy
Verougstraete, (I)
Holt, Rita/920 Main St, Fords, NJ................................212-683-2002
David Burnett, (P), Chuck Ealovega, (P), Derek Gardner, (P)
Hone, Claire/859 N 28th St, Philadelphia, PA...............215-765-6900
Stephen Hone, (P)
Hopkins, Nanette/751 Conestoga Rd, Rosemont, PA.......215-649-8589
A La Carte Solution, (P)
Hubbell, Marian/99 East Elm St, Greenwich, CT.............203-629-9629
Hurewitz, Barbara, NJ..201 923-0011
William Bennett, (P)

IKL

Impress:Art/PO Box 761/15 N Main St, Williamsburg, MA 413-268-3040
Kerr, Ralph/239 Chestnut St, Philadelphia, PA...............215-592-1359
Knecht, Cliff/309 Walnut Rd, Pittsburgh, PA 412-761-5666
Jim Deigan, (I), Debbie Pinkney, (I), Lee Steadman, (I), Jim
Trusilo, (I), Phil Wilson, (I)
Kurlansky, Sharon/192 Southville Rd, Southborough, MA........508-872-4549
John Gamache, (I), Peter Harris, (I), Geoffrey Hodgkinson,
(I), Bruce Hutchison, (I), Dorthea Sierra, (I), Colleen, (I)
Labonty, Deborah/PO Box 7446, Lancaster, PA 717-872-8198
Tim Schoon, (P)
Lauren Enterprises/Box 625, West Long Branch, NJ...........201-870-8961
Leyburn, Judy/235 Haynes Rd, Sudbury, MA.................617-443-8871
Lipman, Deborah/506 Windsor Dr, Framingham, MA.........508-877-8830
Mark Fisher, (I), Richard A. Goldberg, (I), Katherine
Mahoney, (I), Susan Smith, (I), Karen Watson, (I)

M

Marcinek, Julie/409 W Broadway, Boston, MA 508-624-0464
Mattelson, Judy/37 Cary Rd, Great Neck, NY..................212-684-2974
Brian Bailey, (I), Karen Kluglein, (I), Marvin Mattelson, (I),
Gary Viskupic, (I)
Mattie, Gary/2016 Walnut St, Philadelphia, PA..............215-972-1543
McNamara, Paula B/182 Broad St, Wethersfield, CT............203-563-6159
Jack McConnell, (P)
Meara/241 A St, Boston, MA......................................617-542-6768
Metzger, Rick/5 Tsienneto Rd, Derry, NH......................
Jon Chomitz, (P), Hotshots, (P), Kevin Prieur, (P)
Montreal Crtv Consrtm/1155 Dorchester W, Montreal, QU...........514-875-5426
Morgan, Wendy/5 Logan Hill Rd, Northport, NY 516-757-5609
Scott Gordley, (I), ParaShoot, (P), Fred Labitzke, (I), Don
Landwehrle, (P), Preston Lyon, (P), Al Margolis, (I), David
Rankin, (I), Fred Schrier, (I), Art Szabo, (P), David Wilder, (P)
Murphy, Brenda/20 High Rock St, Westwood, MA.............617-329-2245
Jeanne Abboud, (I), Alan Berberian, (I), Diane Bigda, (I),
Cheryl Cicha, (I), George Courage, (I), Walter Fournier, (I),
Joe Goebel, (I), Howie Green, (I), Joshua Hayes, (I), Mark
Jenkins, (I), Loretta Krupinski, (I), Diane Kunic, (I), William
Kurt Lumpkins, (I), Stanley Roberts, (I), Valentine Sahlaenu,
(I), David Schuster, (I), Mark Seppala, (A), Mark Seppala, (I),
Catherine Severin, (I), Rich Sullivan, (C), James Taylor, (I),
Paul Wasserboehr, (I), Richard Watzulik, (I)

OP

O'Leary, Gin/1260 Boylston St, Boston, MA 617-267-9299
Oreman, Linda/22 Nelson St, Rochester, NY 716-244-6956
Nick Angello, (I), Jim & Phil Bliss, (I), Roger DeMuth, (I), Jeff
Feinen, (I), Bill Finewood, (I), Doug Gray, (I), Vicki Wehrman, (I)
Palulian, Joanne/18 McKinley St, Rowayton, CT...............203-866-3734
M John English, (I), Bonnie Hofkin, (I), David Lesh, (I), Kirk
Moldoff, (I), Dickran Palulian, (I)
Papitto, Aurelia/300 Commercial St #807, Boston, MA 617-742-3108
Pickles, Carolyn/PO Box 80370, Springfield, MA..............413-732-3522
Eric Poggenpohl, (P)
Publishers Graphics/251 Greenwood Ave, Bethel, CT............203-797-8188
Robert Alley, (I), Deborah Borgo, (I), Patti Boyd, (I), Robin
Brickman, (I), Ray Burns, (I), Eulala Conner, (I), Helen Davie,
(I), Marie DeJohn, (I), Leslie Dunlap, (I), Julie Durrell, (I),
Allan Eitzen, (I), Marlene Ekman, (I), Gioia Fiammenghi, (I),
Fuka, (I), Walter Gaffney-Kessell, (I), T.R. Garcia, (I), Joan
Goodman, (I), Dana Gustafson, (I), Susan Hall, (I), Paul
Harvey, (I), Jean Helmer, (I), Pamela Johnson, (I), John
Jones, (I), G Brian Karas, (I), Kathie Kelleher, (I), Jane
Kendall, (I), Kees de Kiefte, (I), Robin Kramer, (I), Gary
Lippincott, (I), Vikki Marshall, (I), Lisa McCue, (I), Robert A
Parker, (I), Anna Pomaska, (I), Sandy Rabinowitz, (I), David
Rickman, (I), S.D. Schindler, (I), Joel Snyder, (I), Lynn Sweat,
(I), Barbara Todd, (I), James Watling, (I), Ulises Wensell, (I)
Puleo, Donna/35 Marlborough St, Boston, MA 617-437-1413
Richard Iacovelli, (P), Steve Serio, (P)
Putscher, Tony/1214 Locust St, Philadelphia, PA 215-569-8890

R

Radxevich Standke/15 Intervale Terr, Reading, MA 617-944-3166
Christian Delbert, (P)
Redmond, Sharon/8634 Chelsea Bridge Way, Lutherville, MD.......301-823-7422
Reese-Gibson, Jean/4 Puritan Rd, N Beverly, MA..............508-927-5006
Dennis Helmar, (P), Dan Morrill, (P), Steve Rubican, (P)
Resources/511 Broadway, Saratoga Springs, NY...............518-587-4730
Russell Ley, (P), Larry Van Valkenburg, (P)
Riley, Catherine/45 Circle Dr, Hastings 0n Hudson, NY 914-478-4377
Jon Riley, (P)
Robbins, David Group/237 Hopmeadow St, Simsbury, CT...........203-658-2583
Rob Brooks, (I), Mike Eagle, (I), Kim Perkins, (I), Dan Snyder,
(I), Andy Yelenak, (I)
Roderick, Jennifer/60 Oak St, Harrison, NY...................914-835-4175
Roland, Rochel/5001 Edgemoor Lane, Bethesda, MD............301-951-0287
Rotella, Robert/88 Beacon Hill Dr, Holland, PA 215-968-3696
Ralph Giguere, (I), Abbott, Jim, (P), Michael LaRiche, (P)

S

Sandler, Cathy/641 Summer St, Stamford, CT..................212-242-9087
Aaron Rapoport, (P)
Satterthwaite, Victoria/115 Arch St, Philadelphia, PA..........215-925-4233
Michael Furman, (P)
Sequis Ltd/9 W 29th St, Baltimore, MD.......................301-467-7300
Shaner-Wasco, Sonia/PO Box 317, Lititz, PA..................717-626-0296
Grant Heilman, (P)
Sheehan, Betsy/355-3C Homeland Southway, Baltimore, MD 301-828-4020
Shulman, Carol/2 Hickory Hill Rd, Cockeysville, MD............301-561-9088
Smith, Russell/65 Washington St, S Norwalk, CT..............203-866-8871
Gordon Smith, (P)
Smith, Wayne R/22 Millbrook Rd, Wayland, MA...............617-358-4144
John Holt, (I)
Snitzel, Gary/1060 Durham Rd, Pineville, PA..................215-598-0214
Stemrich, J David/213 N 12th St, Allentown, PA...............215-776-0825
Mark Bray, (I), Bob Hahn, (P), Hub Willson, (P)
Stoller, Erica/222 Valley Pl, Mamaroneck, NY.................914-698-4060
Sweeny, Susan/425 Fairfield Ave, Stamford, CT ....

T

Tamagno, Laura/567 Tremont #1Z, Boston, MA................617-267-8177
Ternay, Louise/119 Birch Ave, Bala Cynwyd, PA..............215-667-8626
Vince Cuccinotta, (I), Don Everhart, (I), Greg Purdon, (I),
Peter Sasten, (G), Bill Ternay, (I), Victor Valla, (I)
The Art Source/444 Bedford Rd, Pleasantville, NY..............914-747-2220
James Barkley, (I), Karen Baumann, (I), Larry Bernette, (I),
Paul Birling, (I), Vince Caputo, (I), Robert Cassila, (I), Betsy

Feeney, (I), Scott Gladden, (I), Robert Lee, (I), Robert Marinelli, (I), Michael McGovern, (I), John Ramon, (I), Mary Rankin, (I), Richard Rockwell, (I), Harry Rosenbaum, (I), Jonathan Rosenbaum, (I)
The Source/2276 Mount Carmel Ave, Glenside, PA..........215-885-8227
Dimitrios Bastas, (I), Dan Fione, (I), Thomas Hamilton, (I), Jean Hein, (I), Ed Solari Jr, (I), Steve Lefkowitz, (I), Jeff Otto, (I), Susan Schiwall, (I), Tony Squadroni, (I), Drew Strawbridge, (I), Bob Vann, (I), Patrick Walsh, (I), Ray Ward, (I)
Turner, Ward/1342 Berkshire Ave, Springfield, MA..........413-543-6796
Roc Goudreau, (I), Linda Schiwall-Gallo, (I), Frederick Schneider, (I), Janet Street, (I)
TVI Creative Specialists/1325 18th St NW, Washington, DC..........292-331-7722
Don Carstens, (P), Doug Hansen, (P), Gary Iglarshi, (I), Eucalyptus Tree Studio, (I)

UVW

Unicorn/120 American Rd, Morris Plains, NJ..........201-292-6852
Greg Hildebrandt, (I)
Villoric, Phil/128 Beechtree Dr, Broomall, PA..........215-356-0362
Warner, Bob/1425 Belleview Ave, Plainfield, NJ..........201-755-7236
Lou Odor, (P), Alex Pietersen, (P)
Watterson, Libby/PO Box 1575/Lincoln City Rd, Lakeville, CT..........203-435-2064
Bill Binzen, (P)
Wayne, Lynn/99 Wilson Ave, Windsor, CT..........203-522-3143
Weisbrot, Eric/145 Claudy Ln, New Hyde Pk, NY..........212-254-5553
Wigon, Leslie/191 Plymouth Dr, Scarsdale, NY..........914-472-9459
Wolfe, Deborah Ltd/731 North 24th St, Philadelphia, PA..........215-232-6666
Skip Baker, (I), Robert Burger, (I), Rick Buterbaugh, (I), Jenny Campbell, (I), Dave Christiana, (I), Ray Dallastra, (I), Deborah Danilla, (I), Pat Duffy, (I), Jeff FitzMaurice, (I), Jim Himsworth, (I), Robin Hotchkiss, (I), Neal Hughes, (I), Eric Joyner, (I), Andy Meyer, (I), Richard Milholland, (I), Verlin Miller, (I), Steven Nau, (I), Lisa Pomerantz, (I), Scott Roberts, (I), Richard Romeo, (I), Elizabeth Strausbaugh, (I), Michael Tcherevkoff, (P), Meryl Treatner, (I), Frank Williams, (I)
Worth, Judith/131 S 22nd St #6, Philadelphia, PA..........215-557-0571

SOUTHEAST

A

Ad Artist SE/1424 N Tryon, Charlotte, NC..........704-372-6007
Gerin Choiniere, (P), Gary Crane, (I), Laura Gardner, (I), Mike McMahon, (I), Debi Merkel, (I), Gary Palmer, (I)
Aldridge Reps Inc/755 Virginia Ave NE, Atlanta, GA..........404-872-7980
Thomas Gonzalez, (I), Leslie Harris, (I), Chris Lewis, (I), Carol Norby, (I), Marcia Wetzel, (I)
And Associates/573 Hill St, Athens, GA..........404-353-8479
Elaine H Rabon, (P)
The Art Group/5856 Farington Pl, Raleigh, NC..........919-876-6765

BC

Beck, Susanne/2721 Cherokee Rd, Birmingham, AL..........205-871-6632
Charles Beck, (P)
Burnett, Yolanda/559 Dutch Vall Rd, Atlanta, GA..........404-874-0956
Jim Copland, (P), Charlie Lathem, (P)
Cary & Company/1151 W Peachtree St NW, Atlanta, GA..........404-881-0087
Mike Hodges, (I), Johnna Hogenkamp-Bandle, (I), Charlie Mitchell, (I), Greg Olsen, (I)
Comport, Allan/220 Beach Pl, Tampa, FL..........813-253-3435
Sally Wern Comport, (I)
Couch, Tom/1164 Briarcliff Rd NE #2, Atlanta, GA..........404-872-5774
Granberry/Anderson Studio, (P)

FGH

Fletcher, Robert/102 Waterford Ct, Peachtree City, GA..........404-487-2472
Forbes, Pat/11459 Waterview Cluster, Reston, VA..........703-437-7042
Kay Chernush, (P), Lautman Photography, (P), Taren Z, (P)
Gaffney, Steve/PO Box 506, Annandale, VA..........703-642-0859
Green, Cindy/280 Elizabeth St #A-105, Atlanta, GA..........404-525-1333
Hathcox, Julia/5730 Arlington Blvd, Arlington, VA..........703-845-5831
David Hathcox, (P)

J

Jernigan, Jack/4209 Canal St, New Orleans, LA..........504-486-9011
Robert Anderson, (I), Kenneth Harrison, (I), Kathleen Joffrion, (I), Wendi Schneider, (I)
Jett & Assoc/21 Theatre Square #200, Louisville, KY..........502-561-0737
Mark Cable, (I), Annette Cable, (I), John Mattos, (I), Cynthia Torp, (I), Jeff Tull, (I), David Wariner, (I), Roy Wiemann, (I), Wayne Williams, (I), Paul Wolf, (I)
Jourdan, Carolyn/520 Brickell Key Dr #1417, Miami, FL..........305-372-9425
Judge, Marie/9452 SW 77th Ave, Miami, Fl..........305-595-1700
Justice, Jim/501 N College St, Charlotte, NC..........704-377-4217
Ron Chapple, (P)

KLM

Kohler, Chris/1105 Peachtree St, Atlanta, GA..........404-876-1223
Lee, Wanda/3647 Cedar Ridge Dr, Atlanta, GA..........404-432-6309
Paul Larkin, (P), Rodger Macuch, (P)
Linden, Tamara/3565 Piedmnt/2 Piedmnt Ctr#300, Atlanta, GA..........404-262-1209
Joe Ovies, (I), Charles Passarelli, (I), Larry Tople, (I)
McGee, Linda/1816 Briarwood Ind Ct, Atlanta, GA..........404-633-1286
McLean Represents/571 Dutch Valley Rd, Atlanta, GA..........404-881-6627
Joe Isom, (I), Jack Jones, (I), Martin Pate, (I), Steve Spetseris, (I), Warren Weber, (I)

P

Perry, Sarah/968 Homewood Ct, Decatur, GA..........404-634-2349
Tom Cain, (I), John Findly, (I), Nina Laden, (I), Phil Perry, (I), Matt Spisak, (I)
Peters, Barbara/2217 Cypress Isl Dr #205, Pompano Bch, FL..........305-978-0675
Jacques Dirand, (P), Lizzie Himmel, (P)
Phelps, Catherine/2403 Dellwood Dr NW, Atlanta, GA..........404-264-0264
Tom McCarthy, (P), Tommy Thompson, (P), Bill Weems, (P)
Pitt, Karen/503 Emory Circle, Atlanta, GA..........404-378-0694
Pollard, Kiki/848 Greenwood Ave NE, Atlanta, GA..........404-875-1363
Betsy Alexander, (G), Lindy Burnett, (I), Cheryl Cooper, (I), David Guggenheim, (P), Dennis Guthrie, (I), Pat Magers, (I), Frank Saso, (I), James Soukup, (I), Mark Stanton, (I), Elizabeth Traynor, (I)
Prentice, Nancy/315-A Pharr Rd, Atlanta, GA..........404-266-9707
Arliss Day, (I), Rene Faure, (I), Doris Galloway, (I), Ed Hurlbeck, (I), George Parrish, (I), Robbie Short, (I), Morris Ward, (I), Ed Wolkis, (P), Bruce Young, (I)

RS

Reilly, J Kerry/4510-E Simsbury Rd, Charlotte, NC..........704-365-6111
Silva, Naomi/2161 Peachtree St NE #502, Atlanta, GA..........404-355-2160
Daryl Cagle, (C), Kevin Hamilton, (I), Rob Horn, (L), Mike Moore, (I), Cyd Moore, (I), Rick Paller, (I), Alan Patton, (I), Gary Penca, (I), Geo Sipp, (I), Don Sparks, (P)
Sumpter, Will/1728 N Rock Springs Rd, Atlanta, GA..........404-874-2014
Flip Chalfant, (P)

W

Wells, Susan/5134 Timber Trail, Atlanta, GA..........404-255-1430
Paul Blakey, (I), Jim Caraway, (I), Don Loehle, (I), Richard Loehle, (I), Randall McKissick, (I), Monte Varah, (I), Beth White, (I)
Wetherington, Kathleen/PO Box 8702, Atlanta, GA..........404-248-9773
Wexler, Marsha Brown/6108 Franklin Pk Rd, McLean, VA..........703-241-1776
Williams, Phillip/1270 W Peachtree St #8C, Atlanta, GA..........404-873-2287
Abe Gurvin, (I), Neal Higgins, (P), Chipp Jamison, (P), Jack Jones, (I), Rick Lovell, (I), Boris/Pittman, (G), Bill Mayer, (I), David McKelvey, (I), Pat Mollica, (I), John Robinette, (I), Danny Smythe, (I)
Wooden/Grubbs & Bate/1151 W Peachtree St NW, Atlanta, GA..........404-892-6303
Johnna Hogenkamp, (I), Kevin Hulsey, (I), Charlie Mitchell, (I), Theo Rudnak, (I)

M I D W E S T

A

Allan, Nancy/2479 W 11th St #2479, Cleveland, OH 216-621-3838
Altman, Elizabeth/820 N Franklin St, Chicago, IL............................312-266-8661
Ben Altman, (P), Don DuBroff, (P), Douglas Rothrock, (P),
Abby Sadin, (P), Russell Thurston, (I)
Art Staff Inc/1463 Premier, Troy, MI 313-649-8630
John Arvan, (I), Joy Brosious, (I), Ralph Brunke, (I), Ricardo
Capraro, (I), Larry Cory, (I), Caryl Cunningham, (I), Sheryl
DeMorris, (I), Brian Foley, (I), Dennis Goldsworthy, (I), Jim
Gutheil, (I), Vicki Hayes, (I), Jim Hodge, (I), Ben Jaroslaw, (I),
Dan Kistler, (I), Baron Lesperance, (I), John Martin, (I), Dick
Meissner, (I), Heidi Meissner, (I), Dick Miller, (I), Jerry
Monteleon, (I), Linda Nagle, (I), Colin Payne, (I), Jeff Ridky,
(I), Al Schrank, (I), Jim Slater, (I), Chris Szetela, (I), Ken
Taylor, (I), Alan Wilson, (I)

B

Ball, John/203 N Wabash, Chicago, IL 312-332-6041
Wilson-Griak Inc, (P)
Baron, Mary/2238 N Burling, Chicago, IL 312-528-5046
Bartels, Ceci Assoc/1913 Park Ave, St Louis, MO 314-241-4014
Greg Bernson, (I), Bill Bruning, (I), Bob Bullivant, (P), Justin
Carroll, (I), Gary Ciccarelli, (I), Mark Fredrickson, (I), Frank
Fruzana, (I), Stephen Grohe, (P), Jim Horne, (I), Russ Irwin,
(I), Bill Jenkins, (I), Keith Kasnot, (I), Leland Klanderman, (I),
Shannon Kriegshauser, (I), Ed Lindlof, (I), Hal Lund, (I),
Gregg MacNair, (I), Jim Olivera, (P), Kevin Pope, (C), Guy
Porfiro, (I), Jean Probert, (I), B B Sams, (C), Todd Sckorr, (I),
Jay Silverman, (P), Terry Sirrell, (I), Terry Speer, (I), Fran
Vuksanovich, (I), Tony Wade, (I), Gwyn Wahlman, (I), Wayne
Watford, (I), Ted Wright, (I)
Berendsen & Assoc/2233 Kemper Lane, Cincinnatti, OH 513-861-1400
Bernstein, Joanie/PO Box 3635, Minneapolis, MN 612-374-3169
Mark Chickinelli, (I), Lee Christiansen, (I), Eric Hanson, (I),
Jack Malloy, (I), Stan Olson, (I), Dan Picasso, (I), Bill
Reynolds, (I), Mark Wilken, (I)
Bonnen, Ed/444 Lentz Ct, Lansing, MI 517-371-3086
Darwin Dale, (P), Kim Kauffman, (P)
Bouret, Louise/208 W Kinzie St, Chicago, IL................................312-777-0271
Shanoor Photo, (P)
Brenna Associates/8716 Walton Oaks Dr, Minneapolis, MN...........612-942-9104
Don Ellwood, (I), Ron Finger, (I), Frank Miller, (P), Mike
Sobey, (I), Gary Spencer, (P), Zoe Strickler-Wilson, (P)
Brenner, Harriet/2147 W Augusta Blvd, Chicago, IL 312-384-0009
Dick Krueger, (P)
Brooks & Assoc/855 W Blackhawk St, Chicago, IL 312-642-3208
Nancy Brown, (P), VanKirk Photo, (P)
Bussler, Tom/19 E Pearson #410, Chicago, IL..............................312-642-6499
Sid Evans, (P)

C

Clift, Susan/535 N Michigan #1808, Chicago, IL...........................312-670-2150
Coleman, Woody/490 Rockside Rd, Cleveland, OH 216-661-4222
Sandy Appleoff, (I), Jeffrey Bedrick, (I), Michael Koester, (I),
Vladimir Kordic, (I), John Letostak, (I), Al Margolis, (I), David
Moses, (I), Ernest Norcia, (I), Bob Radigan, (I), James
Seward, (I), Tom Shephard, (I), Ezra Tucker, (I), Tom Utley, (I),
Monte Varah, (I)
Conishi, Angie/315 W Walton, Chicago, IL...................................312-266-8029
Richard Izui, (P)
Creative Source Inc/360 North Michigan Ave, Chicago, IL............312-649-9777

D

Daquanno, Donna/111 E Chestnut St #30 D, Chicago, IL.............312-943-2811
Hisk Prod, (F)
Demunnik, Jack/Twin Springs Farms, Durango, IA 319-588-3019
DeWalt & Assoc/210 E Michigan St #203, Milwaukee, WI...............414-276-7990
Mel Drake, (G), Tom Fritz, (P), Mary Gordon, (G), Rick
Karpinski, (I), Dennis Matz, (I), Mark Mille, (I)
Dodge, Tim/301 N Waters St 5th Fl, Milwaukee, WI 414-271-3388
Ken Hanson, (G), Dave Vander Veen, (P), Peter Wells, (I),
Matt Zumbo, (I)

Dolby, Karen/215 W Ohio 5th Fl, Chicago, IL.................................312-321-1770
Bill Floyd, (P), Charly Palmer, (I), Paul Ristau, (I)

E

Edsey, Steve/520 N Michigan Ave #706, Chicago, IL......................312-527-0351
Stuart Block, (P), Chuck Bracket, (I), Mike Carroll, (I), Bruce
Cregg, (P), Mike Dammer, (I), Tom Durfee, (I), Mike Hagel,
(I), Lou Heige, (I), Jay, (I), Nick Larson, (I), Betty Makey, (I),
Tom McKee, (I), Christian Musselman, (I), Mike Phillips, (I),
Deszo Sandy, (I), Sussan Shipley, (I), Mike Sobey, (I), Sam
Thiewe, (I)
Eldridge, Dale & Assoc/916 Olive St #300, St Louis, MO 314-231-6800
Kunio Hagio, (I), Jon Van Hamersfeld, (I), Tom Killeen, (I),
Mark Wickart, (I)
Erdos, Kitty/210 W Chicago, Chicago, IL 312-787-4976
Finished Art, (I), Jim Durish, (I), Tom Zamiar, (P)

FG

Fazio, Peter/617 W Fulton St, Chicago, IL....................................312-845-9650
Feldman, Kenneth/1821 N Dayton, Chicago, IL............................312-337-0447
Fiat, Randi/612 N Michigan Ave #408, Chicago, IL 312-784-2343
Marc Hauser, (P)
Freeman, Lisa/2507 Brewster Rd, Indianapolis, IN.........................317-872-7856
Joe LaMantia, (I), Joseph Mahler, (I), Dianne McElwain, (I),
Mark Schroeder, (I), Juana Silcox, (I)
Graphic Access/444 N Wells St, Chicago, IL.................................312-222-0087

H

Handelan-Pedersen/333 N Michigan #1005, Chicago, IL 312-782-6833
Hanson, Jim/540 N Lake Shore Dr, Chicago, IL 312-527-1114
Bob Bender, (P), Richard Fegley, (P), Bob Gelberg, (P), Rob
Johns, (P), Rick Mitchell, (P), Barry O'Rourke, (P), John
Payne, (P), Al Satterwhite, (P)
Harlib, Joel/405 N Wabash #3203, Chicago, IL.............................312-329-1370
Richard Anderson, (I), Nick Backes, (I), Michael Backus, (I),
Linda Bleck, (I), Rick Brown, (I), John Casado, (I), Russell
Cobane, (I), Esky Cook, (I), Mike Dean, (I), Lawrence Duke,
(I), Chuck Eckart, (I), Marty Evans, (P), Robert Farber, (P),
Randy Glass, (I), Abe Gurvin, (I), Scott Harris, (I), Karel
Havlicek, (I), Barbara Higgins-Bond, (I), DeWitt Jones, (P),
Gregg Keeling, (I), Vladimir Kordic, (I), John Lawlor, (P),
Richard Leech, (I), Tim Lewis, (I), Maurice Lewis, (I), Bret
Lopez, (P), David McMacken, (I), Dennis Mukai, (I), Steve
Nozicka, (P), Fred Pepera, (I), Scott Pollack, (I), Robert
Tyrrell, (I), Boris Vallejo, (I), Bill Vann, (I), Ron Villani, (I), Allan
Weitz, (P), Kim Whitesides, (I), Bruce Wolfe, (I), Jonathan
Wright, (I), Bob Ziering, (I)
Harmon, Ellen/950 W Lake St, Chicago, IL..................................312-829-8201
Harry Przekop, (P)
Hartig, Michael/3114 St Mary's Ave, Omaha, NE...........................402-345-2164
Higa, Tracy/1560 N Sandburg Terr, Chicago, IL.............................312-440-1284
Hogan, Myrna & Assoc/333 N Michigan, Chicago, IL 312-372-1616
Terry Heffernan, (P)
Holcepl, Robert/2479 W 11th St, Cleveland, OH 216-621-3838
Roman Sapecki, (P), John Watt, (P)
Horton, Nancy/939 Sanborn, Palatine, IL.....................................312-934-8966
Hull, Scott Assoc/68 E Franklin St, Dayton, OH 513-433-8383
Mark Braught, (I), Tracy Britt, (I), John Buxton, (I), Greg
Dearth, (F), David Groff, (I), Julie Hodde, (I), Bill James, (I),
Greg LaFever, (I), John Maggard, (I), Gregg Manchess, (I),
Larry Martin, (I), Ted Pitts, (I), Mark Riedy, (I), David Sheldon,
(I), Bob Thomas, (I), Don Vanderbeek, (I), Lee Woolery, (I)

K

Kamin, Vince & Assoc/111 E Chestnut, Chicago, IL......................312-787-8834
Tom Berthiaume, (P), Dave Jordano, (P), Richard Noble, (P),
Mary Anne Shea, (I), Dale Windman, (P)
Kane, Dennis/135 Rose Ave, Toronto M46 1P1, ON 416-323-3677
Kapes, Jack/233 E Wacker Dr #1412, Chicago, IL 312-565-0566
Stuart Block, (P), John Cahoon, (P), Carl Faruta, (P), Dan
Romano, (I), Nicolas Sidjakov, (G), Francine Zaslow, (P)
Keltsch, Ann/9257 Castlegate Dr, Indianapolis, IN........................317-849-7723
Kezelis, Elena/215 W Illinois, Chicago, IL 312-644-7108
William Sladcik, (P), James Wheeler, (P)
Knutson Reps/211 E Ohio, Chicago, IL ....
Koralik, Connie/900 West Jackson Blvd #7W, Chicago, IL 312-944-5680

Ron Criswell, (I), Ted Gadecki, (I), Myron Grossman, (I), Robert Keeling, (P), Chuck Ludecke, (I), Bob Scott, (I), Bill Weston, (I), Andy Zito, (I)
Kuehnel, Peter/19 E Pearson St #236, Chicago, IL 312-642-6499
Robert Cairns, (P), Ted Carr, (I), Dan Hurly, (I), Dale Stenten, (P), Phoenix Studio, (I)

LM

Lakehomer & Assoc/405 N Wabash #1402, Chicago, IL................312-644-1766
Lasko, Pat/452 N Halsted, Chicago, IL 312-243-6696
Ralph Cowan, (P)
Lawrence, Morgan/317 10th St, Toledo, OH.................................419-255-5117
Linzer, Jeff/1908 Kenwood Prkwy, Minneapolis, MN 612-377-7773
Maloney, Tom & Assoc/211 E Ohio, Chicago, IL...........................312-321-1900
McGrath, Judy/612 N Michigan Ave 4th Fl, Chicago, IL.................312-944-5116
Ray Perkins, (P), Jack Perno, (P), Tony Soluri, (P)
McNamara Associates/1250 Stephenson Hwy, Troy, MI 313-583-9200
Max Alterruse, (I), Perry Cooper, (I), Garth Glazier, (I), Rick Jacobi, (I), Hank Kolodziej, (I), Kurt Krebs, (I), Tim Paul, (I), Jack Pennington, (I), Tony Randazzo, (I), Gary Richardson, (I), Don Wieland, (I)
McNamara/Bahr/646 N Michigan Ave #325, Chicago, IL 312-266-8455
McNaughton, Toni/233 E Wacker #709, Chicago, IL.......................312-938-2148
Pam Haller, (P), Rodica Prato, (I), James B. Wood, (P)
Miller + Comstock Inc/180 Bloor St W #102, Toronto M5S 2V6, ON 416-925-4323
Miller, Richard/405 N Wabash #1204, Chicago, IL.........................312-527-0444
Geoffrey Clifford, (P), Bob Commander, (I), Ron DiCianni, (I), Michael Doret, (I), John Hull, (I), Bob Krogle, (I), Laura Smith, (I), Bill Tucker, (P)
Moore, Connie/1540 N North Park, Chicago, IL 312-787-4422
Morawski & Assoc/1550 E Nine Mile Rd, Ferndale, MI..................313-543-9440
Tim Doyle, (P)
Murphy, Sally/307 North Michigan Ave #1008, Chicago, IL 312-346-0720

NO

Neis, Judy Group/11440 Oak Drive, Shelbyville, MI......................616-672-5756
Tom Bookwater, (I), Gary Eldridge, (I), Nancy Munger, (I), Dave Schweitzer, (I)
Nicholson, Richard B/2310 Denison Ave, Cleveland, OH 216-398-1494
Mark Molesky, (P), Mike Steinberg, (P), J David Wilder, (P), Bruce Zack, (P)
Nicolini, Sandra/230 N Michigan #523, Chicago, IL 312-346-1648
Elizabeth Ernst, (P), Tom Petroff, (P)
O'Brien, Dan/444 N Michigan Ave, Chicago, IL.............................312-580-0880
O'Grady Advertising Arts/333 North Michigan Ave #2200, Chicago, IL...312-726-9833
Jerry Dunn, (P)
Ogden, Robin/3541 Burnham, Minneapolis, MN 612-374-9620
Kelly Hume, (I), Gretchen Schields, (I), Steve Umland, (P)
Ores, Kathy/17302 Hawthorne Dr, E Hazelcrest, IL.......................312-410-7139
Osler, Spike/2616 Industrial Row, Troy, MI...................................313-280-0640
Madison Ford, (P), Rob Gage, (P), Mark Preston, (P), Jim Secreto, (P), Dennis Wiand, (P)

P

Peterson, Vicki/211 E Ohio, Chicago, IL.......................................312-467-0780
Elyse Lewin, (P), Neal McPheeters, (I), Howard Menken, (P), Helmo Schmidt, (P), Charlie Westerman, (P)
Phase II/155 N Michigan Ave, Chicago, IL....................................312-565-2448
Bill Cigliano, (I), David Krainik, (I), Kathy Petrauskas, (I)
Photo Services Owens-Corning/801 Front St, Toledo, OH...........419-697-1111
Jay Langlois, (P), Joe Sharp, (P)
Pohn, Carol/2259 N Wayne, Chicago, IL.......................................312-348-0751
Ron Amis, (I), Diane O'Quinn Burke, (I), Hedwig, (I), Carl Heinz, (I), Carl Leick, (I), Roger Marchultz, (P)
Pool, Linda/7216 E 99th St, Kansas City, MO 816-761-7314
Michael Radencich, (P)
Potts, Carolyn & Assoc/4 E Ohio, Chicago, IL 312-935-1707
Mark Battrell, (I), Karen Bell, (I), Barbara Bersell, (P), John Craig, (I), Alan Dolgins, (P), Byron Gin, (I), Bob Gleason, (I), Jewell Howard, (I), Don Loehle, (I), John McCallum, (P), Rhonda Voo, (I), Leslie Wolf, (I)

R

Rabin, Bill & Assoc/666 N Lake Shore Dr, Chicago, IL..................312-944-6655
Jade Albert, (P), John Alcorn, (I), Joel Baldwin, (P), Joe

Baraban, (P), Roger Beerworth, (I), Guy Billout, (I), Howard Bjornson, (P), Thomas Blackshear, (I), R O Blechman, (I), Charles William Bush, (P), JoAnn Carney, (P), John Collier, (I), Jackie Geyer, (I), Robert Giusti, (I), Kunio Hagio, (I), Lamb & Hall, (P), Mark Hess, (I), Richard Hess, (I), Walter Ioss, (P), Art Kane, (P), Rudi Legname, (P), Daniel Maffia, (I), Jay Maisel, (P), Eric Meola, (P), Claude Mougin, (P), Robert Rodriguez, (I), Reynold Ruffins, (I), Michael Shwab, (I), Ed Sorel, (I), Simms Taback, (I), Ezra Tucker, (I), Mark Wickart, (I), David Wilcox, (I), Stephen Wilkes, (P), Bruce Wolf, (P)
Ray, Rodney/845 W Grace #1W, Chicago, IL 312-222-0337
Bruce Ayres, (P), David Beck, (I), Mort Drucker, (I), Brian Dugan, (I), Jim Endicott, (I), Marla Frazee, (I), Ken Goldammer, (I), Rick Gonnella, (I), Robert Gunn, (I), Haruo Ishioka, (I), Tom Nikosey, (I), Gary Pierazzi, (I), Bob Pryor, (I), Robin Riggs, (P), Paul Rogers, (I), Gary Ruddell, (I), Dick Sakahara, (I), Danny Smythe, (I), Mark Sparacio, (I), Greg Wray, (I)
Remien, Tami/441 E Erie #1612, Chicago, IL.................................312-222-0337
Ritchey, Deborah/920 N Franklin #202, Chicago, IL......................312-642-5763
Roche, Diann/301 E Armour Blvd #315, Kansas City, MO..............816-561-4473

S

Scarff, Signe/22 W Erie, Chicago, IL..312-359-0835
Larry Kolze, (P)
Schofield/Trenbeth Assoc/10 E Ontario Pl #1612, Chicago, IL......312-642-4599
Sell, Dan/233 E Wacker, Chicago, IL...312-565-2701
Alvin Blick, (I), Paul Bond, (I), Bob Boyd, (I), Lee Lee Brazeal, (I), Daryll Cagle, (I), Kirk Caldwell, (I), Wayne Carey, (I), Justin Carroll, (I), Mike Elins, (I), Bill Ersland, (I), Rick Farrell, (I), Dick Flood, (I), Bill Harrison, (I), Barry Jackson, (I), Dave Kilmer, (I), Dave LaFleur, (I), Tom Lochray, (I), Gregory Manchess, (I), Bill Mayer, (I), Frank Morris, (I), Stanley Olson, (I), WB Park, (I), Hank Parker, (I), Ian Ross, (I), Mark Schuler, (I), R J Shay, (I), Dale Verzaal, (I), Phil Wendy, (I), Paul Wolf, (I), John Zielinski, (I)
Sharp Shooter/387 Richmond St E, Toronto M5A 1P6, ON 416-860-0300
Shulman, Salo/215 W Ohio, Chicago, IL..312-337-3245
Stan Stansfield, (P)
Skillicorn, Roy/233 E Wacker #1209, Chicago, IL.........................312-856-1626
Tom Curry, (I), David Scanlon, (I)
Spectrum Reps/18 N 4 St, Minneapolis, MN 612-332-2361
Steiber, Doug/405 N Wabash #1503, Chicago, IL 312-222-9595

TVWZ

Timon, Clay & Assoc Inc/540 N Lake Shore Dr, Chicago, IL.........312-527-1114
Trinko, Genny/126 W Kinzie St, Chicago, IL..................................312-222-9242
Trott, David/32588 Dequiendre, Warren, MI..................................313-978-8932
Tuke, Joni/325 W Huron #310, Chicago, IL....................................312-787-6826
Dan Blanchette, (I), Chris Hopkins, (I), Susan Kindst, (P), Cyd Moore, (I), Brian Otto, (I), Gary Penca, (I), Michel Tscheveforce, (P), John Welzenbach, (P)
Vernell, Maureen/128 Fieldgate Dr, Nepan K2J 1T9, ON 613-825-4740
Viking Des/510 N Dearborn St, Chicago, IL...................................312-644-1882
Virnig, Janet/2216 e 32nd St, Minneapolis, MN.............................612-721-8832
Rick Allen, (I), Roger Boehm, (I), Don Dudley, (I), Robin Moline, (I), Kate Thomsen, (I)
Wainman, Rick & Assoc/166 E Superior #212, Chicago, IL 312-337-3960
Zann, Sheila/502 N Grove, Oak Park, IL.......................................312-386-2864
Arnold Zann, (P)
Zeitgeist/233 E Wacker Dr #209, Chicago, IL 312-938-8937

SOUTHWEST

AB

Art Rep Inc/3525 Mockingbird Lane, Dallas, TX 214-521-5156
Tom Bailey, (I), Lee Lee Brazeal, (I), Kirk Caldwell, (I), Lindy Chambers, (I), Ellis Chappell, (I), Ken Cosselt, (I), Tom Curry, (I), Tom Dolphens, (I), M John English, (I), Tim Girvin, (I), Jim Jacobs, (I), Greg King, (I), Kent Kirkley, (P), Narda Lebo, (P), Genevieve Meek, (I), Frank Morris, (I), Matthew Savins, (I), Michael Schwab, (I), Stephen Turk, (I), Andrew Vracin, (P), Terry Widener, (I)
Booster, Barbara/3910 Buena Vista #10, Dallas, TX 214-559-3640

Bozeman + Co/PO Box 140152, Dallas, TX 214-526-3317
Phil Boatwright, (I), Tim Boole, (P), Steve Brady, (P), Regan
Dunnick, (I), Stephen Durke, (I), Mike Fisher, (I), Myron
Grossman, (I), Ron Scott, (P), George Toomer, (I), Ka Yeung, (P)

C

Callahan, Joe/2733 E Flowers, Phoenix, AZ 602-954-0224
Tom Gerczynski, (P), Mike Gushock, (I), Jon Kleber, (I),
Howard Post, (I), Dan Ruiz, (I), Mark Sharpls, (I), Dan
Vermillion, (P), Balfour Walker, (P)
Campbell, Pamela/1821 W Alabama, Houston, TX..........713-523-5328
Charles Brown, (I), George Campbell, (I), Gary Faye, (P),
Benedetto Garacci, (P), Alexander Molinello, (I), Tom Nikosey,
(I), Larry Noble, (I), Jack Slattery, (I), Graham Ward, (I)
Cedeno, Lucy/PO Box 254, Cerrillos, NM 505-473-2745
David Michael Kennedy, (P)
Cobb & Friend/3232 McKinney #1260, Dallas, TX..........214-855-0055
Kent Barker, (P), Connie Connally, (I), Ray-Mel Cornelius, (I),
Michael Johnson, (P), David Kampa, (I), Margaret Kasahara,
(I), Geof Kern, (P), Mercedes McDonald, (I), Michael McGar,
(I), R Kenton Nelson, (I), Steve Pietzsch, (I), Tom Ryan, (P),
Jim Sims, (P), James N Smith, (I), James Tennison, (I),
Michele Warner, (I), Ken Westphal, (I), Neill Whitlock, (P)

DF

Davis, Brooke/2515 McKinney #900, Dallas, TX 214-969-0034
DiOrio, Diana/4614 Morningside, Houston, TX 713-266-9390
John Collier, (I), Regan Dunnick, (I), Larry Keith, (I), Bahid
Marinfar, (I), Dennis Mukai, (I), Thom Ricks, (I)
Freeman, Sandra/3333 Elm St #105, Dallas, TX 214-871-1956
Karla Tuma Cooper, (I), Jennifer Harris, (I), Mary Haverfield,
(I), Rusty Jones, (I), Ketti Kupper, (I), Lynn Rowe Reed, (I)
Frondrick, Jeff/6102 E Mockingbird Ln #192, Dallas, TX 214-324-3959
Fuller, Alyson/1322 Round Table, Dallas, TX................214-688-1322

HK

Hartman, Marsha/2622 Grist Mill Rd, Little Rock, AR 501-228-9290
Hawkins, Berry/8602 Santa Clara, Dallas, TX................214-327-7889
Matt Bowman, (P)
Holland, Mary/6638 N 13th St, Phoenix, AZ................602-275-3563
KJ Reps/2919 Welborn #101, Dallas, TX................214-559-0805
Kline, Sandra/637 Hawthorne, Houston, TX................713-522-1862
Patti Bonham, (I), Tom Bookwalter, (I), Mark Chickinelli, (I),
Stewart Cohen, (P), Keith Graves, (I), Johnna Hogenkamp,
(I), Mary Charles Kubricht, (I), Mike Robins, (I), Chris
Summers, (P), Frank White, (P)

LP

Lynch, Larry/5521 Greenville #104-338, Dallas, TX................214-369-6990
Joel Armstrong, (I), Morton Beebe, (P), Amy Bryant, (I), Mark
Busacca, (I), Denise Chapman-Crawford, (I), Bob Depew, (I),
Aaron Jones, (P), Pete Lacker, (P), Chuck Larson, (I),
Ambrose Rivera, (I), Mike Robbins, (I), Randy Rogers, (I),
Joseph Savant, (P), John Saxon, (P), Charles Varner, (I), Mike
Wimmer, (I)
Photocom Inc/2412 Converse, Dallas, TX................214-428-8781
Robb Depenport, (P), Bart Forbes, (I), Andy Post, (P), Louis
Reens, (P), Michael Steirnagle, (I), Kelly Stribling, (I), Richard
Wahlstrom, (P), Gordon Willis, (P)
Production Services/1711 Hazard, Houston, TX................713-529-7916

RST

Ryan, Linda/6438 Vickery Blvd, Dallas, TX 214-826-8118
Sands, Trudy/233 Yorktown, Dallas, TX 214-634-9538
Simpson, Elizabeth/415 N Bishop Ave, Dallas, TX................214-943-9355
Traylor Creative Resources/329 W Vernon Ave, Phoenix, AZ 602-254-8232
Allen Garns, (I), Liz Kenyon, (I), Libba Tracy, (I)

W

Washington, Dick/914 Westmoreland, San Antonio, TX................512-733-6128
Patti Bonham, (I), Guy Juke, (I), Rick Kroninger, (P), Mark
Mroz, (I), Reuben Njaa, (P), Dan Soder, (I), Mark Weakley, (I)
Whalen, Judy/2336 Farrington St, Dallas, TX................214-630-8977
Robert LaTorre, (I)
Willard, Paul Assoc/815 North First Ave #3, Phoenix, AZ 602-257-0097

Kevin Cruff, (P), Matthew Foster, (I), Rick Gayle, (P), Jack
Graham, (I), Rick Kirkman, (I), Kevin MacPherson, (I), Frank
Medeola, (I), Jim Oaks, (I), Curtis Parker, (I), Nancy
Pendleton, (I), Ray & Peggy Roberts, (I), Wayne Watford, (I),
Jean Wong, (I)

R O C K Y   M T N

BCF

Brogren-Kelly/3113 E 3rd St #220, Denver, CO 303-399-3851
Ron Sauter, (I), Elsa Warnick, (I)
Comedia/420 E 11th Ave, Denver, CO 303-832-2299
Foremark Studios/PO Box 10346, Reno, NV................702-786-3150

G

Gibson, Susan/653 Ash St, Denver, CO 303-333-8949
Goodman, Christine/1869 S Pearl St #201, Denver, CO 303-733-8722
Bill Koropp, (P), David X Tejada, (P), Geoffrey Wheeler, (P)
Guenzi, Carol/130 Pearl St #1602, Denver, CO 303-733-0128

N

No Coast Graphics/2629 18th St, Denver, CO 303-458-7086
John Cuneo, (I), Cindy Enright, (I), Tom Nikosey, (I), Chris F
Payne, (I), Jim Salvati, (I), Mike Steirnagle, (I)
Norman, Mary Lou/420 E 11th Ave, Denver, CO 303-832-2299

W E S T   C O A S T

AB

Amour, Nona/218 9th St, San Francisco, CA 415-459-0319
Arnold, Wendy/4620 Coldwater Cnyn, Studio City, CA 818-762-8850
Ayerst, Deborah/2546 Sutter St, San Francisco, CA 415-567-3570
Braun, Kathy/75 Water St, San Francisco, CA................415-775-3366
Arnold & Assoc, (F), Sandra Belce, (L), Tandy Belew, (G),
Michael Bull, (I), Anka, (I), Eldon Doty, (I), Boyington Film, (F),
Jim Fulp, (I), Stephen Osborn, (I), Jim Parkinson, (L), Allan
Rosenberg, (P), Diane Tyler, (MU)
Brenneman, Cindy/1856 Elba Cir, Costa Mesa, CA 714-641-9700
Eliot Crowley, (P), George Katzenberger, (P), Pierre Kopp,
(P), Frank Mendola, (I), Gregory Miller, (I), Jim Stefl, (I)
Brown, Dianne/732 N Highland, Los Angeles, CA 213-464-2775
David LeBon, (P), Bill Werts, (P)
Burlingham, Tricia/9538 Brighton Way #318, Beverly Hills, CA 213-271-3982
Bob Stevens, (P)
Busacca, Mary/58 Corte Madera #4, Mill Valley, CA................415-381-9047
Richard Anderson, (I), Willarson & Assocs, (I), Olden
Budwine, (I), Mark Busacca, (I), George Campbell, (I),
Ignacio Gomez, (I), Paul Hoffman, (P), Leo Monahan, (P),
Tom Nikosey, (I), Michael Pearce, (I), Jack Slattery, (I), Ed
Young, (P)
Bybee, Gerald/1811 Folsom St, San Francisco, CA................415-863-6346

C

Carriere, Lydia/PO Box 8382, Santa Cruz, CA................408-425-1090
Willis Preston Campbell, (P), Burell Dickey, (I), Don Faia,
(GD), Jeff Hicks, (P), Steve Kurtz, (I)
Church, Spencer/425 Randolph Ave, Seattle, WA................206-324-1199
Georgia Deaver, (I), John Fretz, (I), Terry Heffernan, (P), Phil
Howe, (I), Mits Katayama, (I), Tim Kilian, (I), Ed Lowe, (P),
Scott McDougall, (I), Dale Nordell, (I), Rusty Platz, (I), Ted
Rand, (I), Cheri Ryan, (I), Chuck Solway, (I), Carol Wald, (I),
Craig Walden, (I)
Collier, Jan/166 South Park, San Francisco, CA 415-552-4252
Barbara Banthien, (I), Bunny Carter, (I), Chuck Eckart, (I), Curt
Fisher, (P), Douglas Fraser, (I), Don Grimes, (I), Robert Hunt,
(I), Kathy O'Brien, (I), David Rawcliffe, (P), Steve Scott, (I),
Terry Sirrell, (I), Robert Steele, (I), Bahid, (I), Cynthia Torp, (I)
Conrad, James/2149 Lyon #5, San Francisco, CA 415-921-7140
Cook, Warren/PO Box 2159, Laguna Hills, CA 714-770-4619
Kathleen Norris Cook, (P)
Cormany, Paul/11607 Clover Ave, Los Angeles, CA 213-828-9653

Mark Busacca, (I), Dave Clemons, (I), Bob Gleason, (I),
Lamb & Hall, (P), Jim Heimann, (I), Penina Meisels, (I), Gary
Norman, (I), Kevin Spauldings, (I), Ted Swanson, (I), Stan
Watts, (I), Rob Westerberg, (I), Dick Wilson, (I), Andy Zito, (I)

Cornell, Kathleen/1042 Oakwood Ave, Venice, CA 213-399-6903
Jay Ahrens, (P), John Cuneo, (I), Nancy Duell, (I), Seith
Erlich, (P), Daniel McGowan, (I), William Thompson, (P),
Bonnie Timmons, (I)
Courtney & Natale/8800 Venice, Los Angeles, CA........................213-202-0344
Dianne Bennett, (I), Jan Evans, (I), Stan Gorman, (I), Diane
Teske Harris, (I), Ling Ta Kung, (I), Jeff Leedy, (I), Sen
Maruyama, (I), Nancy Ohanian, (P), Julie Perron, (I), Chuck
Schmidt, (I)
Cox, Linda/1129-A Folsom St, San Francisco, CA.....................415-864-5851
Creative Resource/2956 Nicada Dr, Los Angeles, CA...................213-470-2644
Gene Allison, (I), Darryl Cagle, (I), Jim Desing, (L), Carol
Etow, (I), Nick Galloway, (I), Joan Hoch, (I), Tim Huhn, (I),
Michael Humphries, (I), Steven Klipenstein, (I), Starky
LeBold, (I), John Metowan, (I), Peter Palombi, (I), Jeff
Petersen, (I), David Sarman, (P), Theona Stokes, (I), Glenn
Tarnowski, (I), Chuck Untersee, (P)

D

DeMoreta, Linda/1839 9th St, Alameda, CA 415-769-1421
DiAmbrosio, Joe/8230 Beverly Blvd #3, Los Angeles, CA.............213-655-1505
Dicker, Debbie/765 Clementina St, San Francisco, CA 415-621-0687
Keith Ovregaard, (P)
Dodge, Sharon/1017 W Armour, Seattle, WA.............................206-284-4701
Robin Bartholick, (P), Louis Bencze, (P), Rick Farrell, (I),
Steven Hunt, (P), Aaron Jones, (P), Brian Karas, (I), Frank
Renlei, (I), John Schilling, (I), Paul Schmid, (I)
Dubow, Chuck/10966 Strathmore Dr #8, Los Angeles, CA 213-208-8042
Terry Anderson, (I), Dick Ellescas, (I), David Galchutt, (I),
Richard Ikkanda, (I), Paul Kratter, (I), Bob Maile, (L)

EF

Egbert, Lydia/190 Cervantes Blvd #7, San Francisco, CA 415-921-2415
Bryon Gin, (I), Lon Goddard, (I), Nancy Haig, (I), Pamela
Hamilton, (I), Andy Zito, (I)
Epstein, Rhoni/Photo Rep/3814 Franklin Ave, Los Angeles, CA....213-663-2388
Ericson, William/1024 Mission St, South Pasadena, CA 213-461-4969
Feliciano, Terrianne/16812 Red Hill #B, Irvine, CA..................714-250-3377
Fisher, Susan/1821 Pacific Ave #16, San Francisco, CA 415-928-1816
Fleming, Laird Tyler/5820 Valley Oak Dr, Los Angeles, CA 213-469-3007
Haskell Wexler, (F), Vilmos Zsigmond, (F)
Fox & Spencer/8350 Melrose Ave #201, Los Angeles, CA..............213-653-6484
France Aline Inc/1076 S Ogden Dr, Los Angeles, CA 213-933-2500
Dan Arensault, (P), Guy Billout, (I), Thomas Blackshear, (I),
Steve Hulen, (P), Aaron Jones, (P), John Mattos, (I), Brad
Miller, (P), Manuel Nunez, (I), Jane O'Neill, (P), Michael
Schwab, (I), Steve Suston, (I), Cy Thomas, (I), Ezra Tucker,
(I), Kim Whitesides, (I), Keith Witmer, (I), Bruce Wolfe, (I)
Franco, Evelyn/328 17th St, Santa Monica, CA 213-395-5358

G

Gardner, Jean/348 N Norton Ave, Los Angeles, CA 213-464-2492
Dominic Marsden, (P), Scott Orazem, (P), Bill Robbins, (P),
Steve Smith, (P), Tim Street-Porter, (P)
George, Nancy/7811 Waring Ave, Los Angeles, CA......................213-655-0998
Robert Cooper, (I), Daniels & Daniels, (I), Bruce Dean, (I),
Dean Foster, (I), Bob Gleason, (I), Penelope Gottlieb, (I), Steve
Hendricks, (I), Bob Hickson, (I), Hank Hinton, (I), Gary Hoover,
(I), Richard Kriegler, (I), Gary Lund, (I), Jeannie Winston, (I)
Glick, Ivy/350 Townsend St #421, San Francisco, CA 415-543-6056
David Bishop, (P), Jim Blakeley, (P), Jerry Dadds, (I), Jane
Dill, (I), Don Dudley, (I), Martin French, (I), Derek Grinnell, (I),
Matthew Holmes, (I), Nobu Kaji, (I), Camille Przewodek, (I),
Mike Steirnagle, (I), Rhonda Voo, (I)
Goldman, Caren/4504 36th St, San Diego, CA 619-284-8339
John Alisi, (I), Pete Evaristo, (I), Smith, Mark GW, (I), Mark
Kessler, (I), Sparky LeBold, (I), Susie McKig, (I), Gary
Norman, (I), Gary Norman, (I), Randy Verougstaete, (I)
Graham, Corey/Pier 33 North, San Francisco, CA..........................415-956-4750
Frank Ansley, (I), Legname Berman, (F), Byron Coons, (I),
Gordon Edwards, (P), Trick Films, (F), Bob Gleason, (I),
Richard High, (L), Chuck Kuhn, (P), Rudi Legme, (P), Patricia

Mahoney, (I), Sarn, (I), Joel Nakamura, (I), Gretchen
Schields, (I), Mark Schroeder, (I), Barry Wetmore, (I)
Group West Inc/5455 Wilshire Blvd #1212, Los Angeles, CA 213-937-4472
Neil Boyle, (I), Mike Cressy, (I), Fred Hatzer, (I), Ron McKee,
(I), Bob McMahon, (I), Larry Salk, (I), Ren Wicks, (I)

H

Hackett, Pat/101 Yesler #502, Seattle, WA.............................206-447-1600
Bill Cannon, (P), Jonathan Combs, (I), Steve Coppin, (I), Bill
Evans, (I), David Hart, (I), Norman Hathaway, (I), Chris
Hopkins, (I), Gary Jacobsen, (I), Larry Lubeck, (R), Bruce
Marser, (I), Dan McGowan, (I), Leo Monahan, (I), Chuck Pyle,
(I), Jill Sabella, (P), Yutaka Sasaki, (I), Mike Schumacher, (I),
John C Smith, (I), Kelly Smith, (I), Dean Williams, (I)
Hall, Marni & Assoc/620 N Citrus Ave, Los Angeles, CA.............213-934-9420
Kevin Aguilar, (I), Dave Arkle, (I), Dave Erramouste, (I), Stan
Grant, (I), Dennis Gray, (P), Pam Hamilton, (I), Miles
Hardiman, (I), Elyse Lewin, (P), Jill Sabella, (P), Nancy
Santullo, (P), Perry Van Shelt, (I), John Turner, (P)
Hardy, Allen/1680 N Vine #1112, Los Angeles, CA 213-466-7751
Hart, Vikki/780 Bryant St, San Francisco, CA 415-495-4278
Jan Evans, (I), G K Hart, (P), Kevin Hulsey, (I), Aleta Jenks,
(I), Heather King, (I), Julie Tsuchiya, (I), Jonathan Wright, (I)
Hedge, Joanne/1838 El Cerrito Pl #3, Los Angeles, CA...............213-874-1661
Delana Bettoli, (I), Chris Dellorco, (I), Cathy Detter, (I),
Ignacio Gomez, (I), Bette Levine, (I), Rick McCollum, (I),
David McMacken, (I), Vida Pavesich, (I), Camille Przewodek,
(I), Jim Salvati, (I), Joe Saputo, (I), Steven Scott, (I), Dayal
Studio, (I), Julie Tsuchiya, (I), Brent Watkinson, (I)
Heimberg, Nancy/351 1/2 N Sycamore Ave, Los Angeles, CA 213-933-8660
Henderson, Judi/245 S Van Ness 3rd Fl, San Francisco, CA.........415-864-0516
Hillman, Betsy/Pier 33 North, San Francisco, CA........................415-391-1181
Istvan Banyai, (I), John Marriott, (P), Angel City Prod, (TV),
Randy South, (I), Greg Spalenka, (I), Kevin Spaulding, (I),
Joe Spencer, (I), Jeremy Thornton, (I), Jackson Vereen, (P)
Hjul, Diana/8696 Crescent Dr, Los Angeles, CA 213-654-9513
Neal Brisker, (P), John Reed Forsman, (P), Jim Greenberg, (P)
Hodges, Jeanette/12401 Bellwood, Los Alamitos, CA 213-431-4343
Ken Hodges, (I)
Hughes, April & Assoc/300 Ridgewood Ave, Mill Valley, CA.........415-398-6542
Dennis Dittrich, (I), Ernie Friedlander, (P), Mitch Heinze, (I),
Kim Mak, (I), Paul Matsuda, (P), Sandra Speidel, (I)
Hyatt, Nadine/PO Box 307/ 80 Wellington Ave, Ross, CA.............415-456-7711
Jeanette Adams, (I), Rebecca Archey, (I), Charles Bush, (P),
Frank Cowan, (P), Marty Evans, (P), John Hyatt, (I), Bret
Lopez, (P), K Mercedes McDonald, (I), Cristine Mortensen,
(I), Jan Schockner, (L), Liz Wheaton, (I)

JK

Jacobs, Bob/6010 Wilshire Blvd #505, Los Angeles, CA................213-931-7449
Jorgensen, Donna/609 Summit Ave, Seattle, WA..........................206-284-5080
Alice Brickner, (I), Frank Denman, (P), Fred Hilliard, (I),
Richard Kehl, (I), Doug Keith, (I), David Lund, (I), Robert
Peckham, (I), Tim Stevenson, (I)
Karpe, Michele/6671 Sunset Blvd #1592, Los Angeles, CA 213-465-0140
Mark Abrahams, (P), Stephen Danelian, (P), Claude Morigin,
(P), Victoria Pearson, (P), Mike Reinhardt, (P), Lara
Rossignol, (P), Greg Spalenka, (I), George Stavrinos, (I)
Kirsch Represents/7316 Pyramid Dr, Los Angeles, CA 213-651-3706
Bob August, (I), Kevin Hulsey, (I), David Kimble, (I), Joyce
Kitchell, (I), Royce McClure, (I), Todd Smith, (P), Jeff Wack, (I)
Knable, Ellen/1233 S La Cienega Blvd, Los Angeles, CA..............213-855-8855
Henry Bjorn, (P), Roger Chouinard, (I), Bob Commander, (I),
John Dearstyne, (I), Coppos Films, (F), Randy Glass, (I), Joe
Heiner, (I), Kathy Heiner, (I), Jeff Nadler, (P), Margo Nahas,
(I), Paul Sanders, (P), Jonathan Wright, (I), Brian Zick, (I)
Koeffler, Ann/1425 N Alta Vista Blvd #402, Los Angeles, CA.........213-850-8222
Istvan Banyai, (I), Joseph Chiodo, (I), Dick Cole, (I), Byron
Coons, (I), Marty Evans, (P), Jeremy King, (P), Chuck King,
(P), Paul Kratter, (I), Ric Olson, (I), Dan Picasso, (I), Katherine
Salentine, (I), Sandra Speidel, (I), James Stagg, (I), Pam
Wall, (I), Barry Wetmore, (I)
Kolea Reps/2815 Alaskan Way #37-A, Seattle, WA 206-443-0326
George Abe, (I), Don Baker, (I), Elaine Cohen, (I), Philip
Howe, (I), Jere Smith, (I), Kris Wiltse, (I), Glenn Yoshiyama, (I)
Kovac & Sweeney/11111 Snta Monica Blvd, Los Angeles, CA.......213-964-2429
Hank Benson, (P), Jana Taylor, (P)

L

Laycock, Louise/1351 Ocean Frt Walk #106, Santa Monica, CA 213-204-6401
Story Boards, (I), Funny Farm, (I)
Lee & Lou/1548 18th St #101, Santa Monica, CA 213-828-2259
Rob Gage, (P), Mark Laiti, (P), Lee Pisarski, (R), Tom Slatky,
(R)
Lilie, Jim/251 Kearny St #511, San Francisco, CA..........................415-441-4384
Lou Beach, (I), Ron Chan, (I), Brad Chaney, (P), Tom Foty, (I),
Nancy Freeman, (I), Ken Goldammer, (I), Robert Rodriguez,
(I), Dugald Stermer, (I), Ezra Tucker, (I), Stan Watts, (I),
Dennis Ziemienski, (I)
London, Valerie/9756 Charleville Blvd, Beverly Hills, CA 213-277-8090
Luna, Tony/45 E Walnut St, Pasadena, CA 213-681-3130

M

Marie, Rita & Friends/183 N Martell Ave #240, Los Angeles, CA ...213-934-3395
Bruce Ayres, (P), David Beck, (I), Mort Drucker, (I), Brian
Dugan, (I), Jim Endicott, (I), Rick Farrell, (I), Marla Frazee, (I),
Ken Goldammer, (I), Rick Gonnella, (I), Robert Gunn, (I),
Haruo Ishioka, (I), Hiro Kimura, (I), Tom Nikosey, (I), Gary
Pierazzi, (I), Robert Pryor, (I), Robin Riggs, (P), Paul Rogers,
(I), Gary Ruddell, (I), Dick Sakahara, (I), Danny Smythe, (I),
Mark & Erin Sparacio, (I), Greg Wray, (I)
Martha Productions/4445 Overland Ave, Culver City, CA...............213-204-1771
Bob Brugger, (I), Kirk Caldwell, (I), Brian Cronin, (I), Mike
Elins, (I), Stan Evenson, (I), Allen Garns, (I), Bryon Gin, (I),
William Harrison, (I), Jeff Hitch, (I), Dan Lavigne, (I),
Catherine Leary, (I), Ron Mazellan, (I), R Kenton Nelson, (I),
Cathy Pavia, (I), Steve Vance, (I), Wayne Watford, (I)
McBain/Sharp Reps/650 San Juan Ave, Venice, CA......................213-392-9341
Alan Dorekery, (I), Kelly Hume, (I), Duane Kuehar, (I), Bob
McMahon, (I), Greg Moraes, (I), C David Pina, (L), Judy
Reed, (I)
McCargar, Lucy/652 Bair Isl Rd, Redwood City, CA 415-363-2130
Tim Mitoma, (I), Mary Ross, (I)
McGuiness, Charlotte/2120 N 60th St, Seattle, WA 206-524-8308
Paul Ackerman, (P), Jim Mears, (P), Dave Niedopytalski, (P)
Melrose, Penny/1333 Lawrence Expwy #150, Santa Clara, CA 408-737-9494
Mix, Eva/2129 Grahn Dr, Santa Rosa, CA 707-579-1535
Moniz, Karletta/250 Newhall Ave, San Francisco, CA 415-821-6358
Anne Cook, (I)
Morgan, Michele/1100 N Main #B, Irvine, CA.................................714-474-6002
Bill Brown, (I), Rob Court, (I), Elaine DaVault, (I), Kevin
Davidson, (I), Diane Davis, (I), Dave Hudson, (I), Darlene
McElroy, (I), Morgan Pickard, (I)
Mulhauser & Young/945 Front St #206, San Francisco, CA............415-392-0542
Judy Clifford, (I), Celeste Ericsson, (I), Martin Schweitzer, (P),
Ed Taber, (I), Carlotta Tormey, (I)

NOP

Newman, Carol/1119 Colorado Ave #23, Santa Monica, CA...........213-394-5031
Ostan/Prentice/Ostan/1245 McClellan Dr #314, Los Angeles, CA .213-305-7143
Padgett, Donna/13520 Terrace Pl, Whittier, CA...............................213-945-7801
Parrish, Dave/Photopia/PO Box 2309, San Francisco, CA 415-441-5611
Curtis Degler, (P), Steve Gill, (C), Curtis Martin, (P), Jeff
Richey, (P), Pete Saloutos, (P), Vince Valdes, (P)
Partners & Artists Assoc Network/13480 Contour,
Sherman Oaks, CA...818-995-6883
Peek, Pamela/1964 N Rodney Dr #201, Los Angeles, CA...............818-760-0746
Pelkin, Christine/1962 San Pablo Ave #3, Berkeley, CA 415-841-2238
John Chui, (I), James Gayles, (I), Masami Hirokawa, (I),
Frank Remkiewicz, (I), Skrivan, (P), Nita Winter, (P)
Piscopo, Maria/2038 Calvert Ave, Costa Mesa, CA 714-556-8332
Jack Boyd, (P), Stan Sholik, (P)
Platte, Franz/3537 17th St, San Francisco, CA 415-431-0657
Pohl, Jacqueline/66 Broadway, San Francisco, CA 415-421-4220
Jon Conrad, (I), Steven Hunt, (P), Aaron Jones, (P), John
Mattos, (I), Margo Nahas, (I), Sarah Waldron, (I)
Pribble, Laurie/911 Victoria Dr, Arcadia, CA...................................818-574-0288
Warren Chang, (I), John Hull, (I), John Huxtable, (I),
Catherine Kanner, (I), Andrea Tachiera, (I)

R

Rappaport, Jodi/5410 Wilshire Blvd #206, Los Angeles, CA...........213-934-8633
Repertory/6010 Wilshire Blvd #505, Los Angeles, CA 213-931-7449

Kaz Aizawa, (I), Richard Arruda, (I), Craig Calsbeek, (I), Tom
Christopher, (I), Robert Jacobs, (R), Buena Johnson, (I), Tim
Jonke, (I), Lingta Kung, (I), Karl Parry, (P), Larry Vigon, (G)
Rosenthal, Elise/3443 Wade St, Los Angeles, CA 213-390-9595
Cary Becker, (I), Jody Eastman, (I), David English, (I),
Michael Garland, (I), Bill Hall, (I), Kyong Jalee, (I), David
Kilmer, (I), Don Kueker, (I), Roger Leyonmerk, (I), Roger
Loveless, (I), David Mann, (I), Jim McKiernan, (I), Eric Vander
Palen, (I), Tom Pansini, (I), Kim Passey, (I), Stephen Peringer,
(I), Bob Radigan, (I), Tom Reddi, (I), Bill Robles, (I), Larry
Salk, (I), Tom Tomita, (I), Chris Tuveson, (I), Ren Wicks, (I),
Larry Winborg, (I)

S

Salisbury, Sharon/116 W Blithedale, Mill Valley, CA.......................415-383-5943
Antar Dayal, (I), Cathy Deeter, (I), Jim Endicott, (I), Phil Frank,
(I), Joel Glenn, (P), Hank Hinton, (I), Tom Landecker, (P),
Michelle Manning, (I), Jock McDonald, (P), Doug Suma, (I)
Salzman, Richard W/1352 Hornblend St, San Diego, CA 619-272-8147
Tony Baker, (I), Douglas Bowles, (I), Ruben DeAnda, (I),
Kristen Funkhouser, (I), Manuel Garcia, (I), Denise Hilton-
Putnam, (I), Jewel Homad, (I), Dan Jones, (I), Bernie Lansky,
(C), Chris McAllister, (I), Dave Mollering, (I), Imagery That
Moves, (G), Dianne O'Quinn-Burke, (I), Everett Peck, (I),
Greg Shed, (I), Terry Smith, (I), James Staunton, (I), Debra
Stine, (I), Walter Stuart, (I), Jonathan Wright, (I), Daniels, (I)
Sanders, Liz/30166 Chapala Ct, Laguna Niguel, CA.......................714-641-1505
Scott, Freda/244 Ninth St, San Francisco, CA 415-621-2992
Sherry Bringham, (I), Victor Budnik, (P), David Csicsko, (I),
Robert Evans, (I), Abe Gurvin, (I), Terry Hoff, (I), Gayle
Kabaker, (I), Francis Livingston, (I), Alan Mazzetti, (I), R J
Muna, (P), Susan Schelling, (P), William Thompson, (P),
Carolyn Vibbert, (I)
Scroggy, David/2124 Froude St, San Diego, CA 619-222-2476
Ed Abrams, (I), Jodell D Abrams, (I), Rick Geary, (I), Jean
"Moevius" Giraud, (I), Jack Malloy, (I), John Pound, (I), Hal
Scroggy, (I)
Shaffer, Barry/PO Box 480888, Los Angeles, CA 213-939-2527
Slobodian, Barbara/745 N Alta Vista Blvd, Hollywood, CA 213-935-6668
Pearl Beach, (I), Bob Greisen, (I), Scott Slobodian, (P), Monte
Varah, (I)
Sobol, Lynne/4302 Melrose Ave, Los Angeles, CA 213-665-5141
Laura Manriquez, (I), Arthur Montes de Oca, (P)
Stefanski, Janice/2022 Jones St, San Francisco, CA......................415-928-0457
Adrian Day, (I), Michael Jay, (P), Barbara Kelley, (I), Steven
Lyons, (I), George Olson, (P), Katherine Salentine, (I), Cliff
Spohn, (I)
Stelling, Terry/588 Wisconsin St, San Francisco, CA 415-826-2132
Studio Artists Inc/638 S Van Ness Ave, Los Angeles, CA 213-385-4585
Chuck Coppock, (I), George Francuch, (I), Bill Franks, (I),
Duane Gordon, (I)
Sweet, Ron/716 Montgomery St, San Francisco, CA......................415-433-1222
Charles East, (D), Randy Glass, (I), John Hamagami, (I), Bob
Haydock, (I), Gregg Keeling, (I), Richard Leech, (I), Tom
Lochray, (I), Steve Mayse, (I), Will Nelson, (I), Walter
Swarthout, (P), Jack Unruh, (I), Don Weller, (I), Bruce Wolfe,
(I), James B Wood, (P)

T

The Source/Randy Pate/PO Box 687, N Hollywood, CA.................818-985-8181
Steven Chorney, (I), Chris Dellorco, (I), John Dismukes, (I),
Robert Florczak, (I), Bryan Haynes, (I), Mick McGinty, (I),
Kazuhiko Sano, (I), Mark Sokol, (I)
Thornby, Kirk/611 S Burlington, Los Angeles, CA 213-933-9883
Tos, Debbie/111 Tamarind Ave, Hollywood, CA..............................213-466-0033
Carl Furuta, (P), Michael Going, (P), David Kramer, (P),
Michael Salas, (P)
Townsend, Kris/58 Polhemus Way, Larkspur, CA 212-243-2484
David W Hamilton, (P)
Trimpe, Susan/2717 Western Ave, Seattle, WA 206-728-1300
Don Baker, (I), Patrick Chapin, (I), Wendy Edelson, (I), Liz
Kenyon, (I), Kristin Knutson, (I), Stephen Peringer, (I)

V

Valen Assocs/950 Klish Way, Del Mar, CA 203-227-7806
Chas Adams, (I), George Booth, (C), Whitney Darrow, (C),

Eldon Dedini, (I), Joe Farris, (C), William Hamilton, (C), Stan Hunt, (C), Anatol Kovarsky, (C), Henry Martin, (C), Warren Miller, (I), Frank Modell, (C), Mischa Richter, (C), Charles Saxon, (C), Jim Stevenson, (C), Henry Syverson, (C), Bob Weber, (C), Rowland Wilson, (I), Gahan Wilson, (I), Bill Woodman, (I), Bill Ziegler, (I)

Vandamme, Vicki/35 Stillman #206, San Francisco, CA..................415-543-6881
Kirk Caldwell, (I), John Collier, (I), Matthew Foster, (I), Kathy & Joe Heiner, (I), Alan Krosnick, (P), Dennis Mukai, (I), Jennie Oppenheimer, (I), Bill Rieser, (I), Michael Schwab, (I), Stuart Schwartz, (P), Kim Whitesides, (I), Nic Wilton, (I)

WY

Wagoner, Jae/654 Pier Ave #C, Santa Monica, CA..........................213-392-4877
Roger Beerworth, (I), Georgia Deaver, (I), Stephen Durke, (I), Ken Durkin, (I), Steve Jones, (I), Nobee Kanayama, (I), Leo Monahan, (I), Jeff Nishinaka, (I), Ken Rosenberg, (I), Don Weller, (I), Wills Weston, (I)

Wiley, David/1535 Green St #207, San Francisco, CA.....................415-441-1623
Steve Bjorkman, (I), Dennis Carmichael, (I), Dick Cole, (I), Ben Garvie, (I), Merilyn Moss, (L), Woody Pirtle, (G), Studio R, (R), Dave Stephenson, (I), Raden Studio, (G), Mark Tuschman, (P), Jim Wasco, (L), Keith Witmer, (I)

Winston, Bonnie/195 S Beverly Dr #400, Beverly Hills, CA.............213-275-2858
Geoffrey Barish, (P), Jake Crain, (P), Robert Elias, (P), Eshel Ezer, (P), Marco Franchina, (P), Mark Kayne, (P), Bruce Kramer, (P), Veronica Simms, (P)

Youmans, Jill/1021 1/2 N La Brea, Los Angeles, CA.......................213-469-8624
Dan Cooper, (I), Carole, Etow, (I), Jeff George, (I), Brian Leng, (P), Jeff Leung, (I), Christine Nasser, (I), Joyce Patti, (I), Bill Salada, (I)

PHOTOGRAPHERS

NYC

A

Abatelli, Gary/80 Charles St #3W, (P 54) **212-924-5887**
Abel, Jim/112 E 19th St, ...212-460-5374
Abramowitz, Ellen/166 E 35th St #4H, ...212-686-2409
Abramowitz, Jerry/680 Broadway, ...212-420-9500
Abramson, Michael/15 Renwick St, ...212-737-1890
Accornero, Franco/620 Broadway, (P 22,23) **212-674-0068**
Adamo, Jeff/50 W 93rd St #8P, ...212-866-4886
Adams, Eddie/40 W 24th St, ...212-929-1080
Adams, Jim/15 W 38th St #1203, ...212-319-1345
Addeo, Edward/151 W 19th St, ...212-206-1686
Addio, Edward/151 W 19th St 10th Fl, ...212-865-1090
Adelman, Barbara Ellen/267 Mayfair Dr, Brooklyn 718-531-8054
Adelman, Menachem Assoc/45 W 17th St 5th Fl, ...212-675-1202
Adler, Arnie/70 Park Terrace W, ...212-304-2443
Agalias, George/33 W 76th St #4A, ...212-874-7615
Aharoni, Oudi/704 Broadway, ...212-777-0847
Aich, Clara/218 E 25th St, ...212-686-4220
Albert, Jade/59 W 19th St #3B, ...212-242-0940
Alberts, Andrea/100 Fifth Ave 11th Fl, ...212-242-5794
Alcorn, Richard/160 W 95th St #7A, ...212-866-1161
Alexander, Robert/50 W 29th St, ...212-629-6049
Alexanders, John W/308 E 73rd St, ...212-734-9166
Allison, David/42 E 23rd St, ...212-460-9056
Alper, Barbara/202 W 96th St, ...212-316-6518
Alpern/Lukoski/250 W 88th St, ...212-724-5017
Altamari, Christopher/56 W 22nd St, ...212-645-8484
Amato, Paul/881 Seventh Ave #405, ...212-541-4787
Amplo, Nick/271 1/2 W 10th St, ...212-741-2799
Amrine, Jamie/30 W 22nd St, ...212-243-2178
Anik, Adam/111 Fourth Ave #1-I, ...212-228-4148
Anthony, Don/79 Prall Ave, Staten Island 718-317-6340
Antonio/Stephen Photo/45 E 20th St, ...212-674-2350
Apple, Richard/80 Varick St #4B, ...212-966-6782
Aranita, Jeffrey/60 Pineapple St, Brooklyn 718-625-7672
Ardito, Peter/108 Reade St, ...212-619-6582
Aresu, Paul/568 Broadway #608, ...212-334-9494
Arky, David/57 W 19th St #2A, ...212-242-4760
Arlak, Victoria/40 East End Ave, ...212-879-0250
Arma, Tom/38 W 26th St, ...212-243-7904
Arndt, Dianne/400 Central Park West, ...212-866-1902
Arslanian, Ovak/344 W 14th St, ...212-255-1519
Ashe, Bill/534 W 35th St, (P 62,63) **212-695-6473**
Ashley, Pat/920 Broadway, ...718-622-2583
Ashworth, Gavin/110 W 80th St, ...212-874-3879
Astor, Joseph/154 W 57th St, ...212-307-2050
Atkin, Jonathan/23 E 17th St, ...212-242-5218
Aubry, Daniel/365 First Ave, ...212-598-4191
Aurora Retouching/10 W 19th St, ...212-255-0620
Auster, Evan/215 E 68th St #3, ...212-517-9776
Auster, Walter/18 E 16th St, ...212-627-8448
Avedis/220 E 72nd St, ...212-472-8566
Avedon, Richard/407 E 75th St, ...212-879-6325
Axon, Red/17 Park Ave, ...212-532-6317
Azzato, Hank/348 W 14th St 3rd Fl, ...212-929-9455
Azzi, Robert/116 E 27th St, ...212-481-6900

B

Baasch, Diane/41 W 72nd St #11F, ...212-724-2123
Babchuck, Jacob/132 W 22nd St 3rd Fl, ...212-929-8811
Babushkin, Mark/110 W 31st St, ...212-239-6630
Bacall, Robert/1059 E 99th St, Brooklyn 718-802-1065
Back, John/15 Sheridan Sq, ...212-243-6347
Bahrt, Irv/310 E 46th St, ...212-661-5260
Baillie, Allan & Gus Francisco/220 E 23rd St 11th Fl, ...212-683-0418
Baker, Chuck/1630 York Ave, ...212-517-9060
Baker, Gloria/415 Central Park West, ...212-222-2866
Baker, Joe/35 Wooster St, ...212-925-6555
Bakerman, Nelson/220 E 4th St #2W, ...212-777-7321

Baldwin, Joel/350 E 55th St, ...212-308-5991
Bale, J R/130 W 25th St, ...212-627-1489
Baliotti, Dan/9 W 21st St #503, ...212-627-9039
Bancroft, Monty/161 W 15th St, ...212-807-8650
Barash, Howard/349 W 11th St, ...212-242-6182
Barba, Dan/305 Second Ave #322, ...212-420-8611
Barber, James/873 Broadway, ...212-598-4500
Barcellona, Marianne/175 Fifth Ave #2422, ...212-463-9717
Barclay, Bob Studios/5 W 19th St 6th Fl, ...212-255-3440
Barnett, Peggy/26 E 22nd St, ...212-673-0500
Barns, Larry/21 W 16th St, ...212-242-8833
Barr, Neal/222 Central Park South, ...212-765-5760
Barrett, John/215 W 95th St #9R, ...212-777-7309
Barrett, John E/215 W 95th St, ...212-864-6381
Barrick, Rick/12 E 18th St 4th Fl, (P 65) **212-741-2304**
Barrows, Wendy/205 E 22nd St #4H, (P 66,67) **212-685-0799**
Bartlett, Chris/21 E 37th St #2R, ...212-213-2382
Barton, Paul/111 W 19th St #2A, ...212-691-1999
Basilion, Nicholas/150 Fifth Ave #532, ...212-645-6568
Bates, Art/154 W 70th St #9L, ...212-799-3388
Batlin, Lee/37 E 28th St 8th Fl, ...212-685-9492
Baum, Charles/320 West End Ave, ...212-724-8013
Baumann, Jennifer/682 Sixth Ave, ...212-633-0160
Baumel, Ken/234 Fifth Ave #3251, ...212-929-7550
Bava, John/51 Station Ave, Staten Island 718-967-9175
Bealmear, Brad/54 Barrow St, ...212-675-8060
Bean, John/5 W 19th St, ...212-242-8106
Bechtold, John/117 E 31st St, ...212-679-7630
Beck, Arthur/119 W 22nd St, ...212-691-8331
Becker, Jonathan/451 West 24th St, ...212-929-3180
Beckhard, Robert/130 E 24th St, ...212-505-7323
Beebe, Rod/790 Amsterdam #4D, ...212-222-1242
Beechler, Greg/200 W 79th St #PH A, ...212-580-8649
Begleiter, Steven/38 Greene St, ...212-334-5262
Behl, David/13-17 Beach St 3rd fl, ...212-226-4968
Belinsky, Jon/134 W 26th St #777, ...212-627-1246
Bell-Tait, Carolyn/1123 Broadway, ...212-645-9466
Beller, Janet/568 Broadway, ...212-334-0281
Benedict, William/530 Park Ave, ...212-832-3164
Benson, Mary Anne/160 Fifth Ave #817, ...212-243-6811
Bercow, Larry/344 W 38th St, ...212-629-9000
Berenholtz, Richard/600 W 111th St #6A, ...212-222-1302
Berger, Joseph/121 Madison Ave #3B, (P 49) **212-685-7191**
Bergman, Beth/150 West End Ave, ...212-724-1867
Bergreen, John/27 W 20th St #1003, ...212-517-2463
Berkun, Phil/199 Amity St #2, Brooklyn 718-237-2648
Berkwit, Lane /262 Fifth Ave, (P 68) **212-889-5911**
Berman, Brad/295 Ecksford St, Brooklyn 718-383-8950
Berman, Howard/5 E 19th St #303, ...212-473-3366
Berman, Malcolm/446 W 25th St, ...212-727-0033
Bernson, Carol/PO Box 2244 Styvsnt Sta, ...212-473-3884
Bernstein, Alan/365 First Ave 2nd Fl, ...212-254-1355
Bernstein, Bill/38 Greene St, (P 69) **212-334-3982**
Bernstein, Steve/47-47 32nd Place, Long Island City 718-786-8100
Bessler, John/503 Broadway 5th Fl, ...212-941-6179
Bester, Roger/55 Van Dam St 11th Fl, ...212-645-5810
Betz, Charles/138 W 25th St 10th Fl, ...212-675-4760
Bevilacqua, Joe/202 E 42nd St, ...212-490-0355
Biddle, Geoffrey/5 E 3rd St, ...212-505-7713
Bies, William/21-29 41st St #1A, LI City 718-278-0236
Bijur, Hilda/190 E 72nd St, ...212-737-4458
Birdsell, Doreen/297 Third Ave, ...212-213-4141
Bisbee, Terry/290 W 12th St, ...212-242-4762
Bishop, David/251 W 19th St, ...212-929-4355
Blachut, Dennis/145 W 28th St 8th Fl, ...212-947-4270
Blackburn, Joseph M/568 Broadway #800, ...212-966-3950
Blackman, Barry/150 Fifth Ave #220, (P 70,71) **212-627-9777**
Blackman, Jeffrey/2323 E 12th St, Brooklyn 718-769-0986
Blackstock, Ann/400 W 43rd St #4E, ...212-695-2525
Blake, Rebecca/35 W 36th St, ...212-695-6438
Blakeman, Barry/150 Fifth Ave #220, ...212-627-9777
Blechman, Jeff/591 Broadway, ...212-226-0006
Blecker, Charles/350 Bleecker St #140, ...212-242-8390
Blegen, Alana/, , ...718-769-2619
Blell, Dianne/125 Cedar St, ...212-732-2990
Blinkoff, Richard/147 W 15th St 3rd Fl, ...212-620-7883
Blitz, Irvin/114 Spring St 4th Fl, ...212-219-9744
Block, Helen/385 14th St, Brooklyn 718-788-1097
Block, Ira Photography/215 W 20th St, ...212-242-2728

Block, Ray/458 W 20th St #4D, 212-691-9375
Bloom, Teri/300 Mercer St #6C, 212-475-2274
Blosser, Robert/741 West End Ave #3C, 212-662-0107
Bobbe, Leland/51 W 28th St, 212-685-5238
Bodi Studios/340 W 39th St, 212-947-7883
Bodick, Gay/11 E 80th St, 212-772-8584
Bogertman, Ralph Inc/34 W 28th St, 212-889-8871
Boisseau, Joseph/3250 Hering Ave #1, Bronx (P 72) 212-519-8672
Bolesta, Alan/11 Riverside Dr #13SE, 212-873-1932
Boljonis, Steven/555 Ft Washington Ave #4A, 212-740-0003
Bonomo, Louis/118 W 27th St #2F, 212-242-4630
Boon, Sally/108 Bowery, 212-334-9160
Bordain, Andrew/514 E 5th St, 212-995-5908
Bordnick, Barbara/39 E 19th St, 212-533-1180
Bosch, Peter/477 Broome St, 212-925-0707
Boszko, Ron/140 W 57th St, 212-541-5504
Bottomley, Jim/125 Fifth Ave, 212-677-9646
Bowditch, Richard/529 W 42nd St #4M, 212-564-5413
Bracco, Bob/43 E 19th St, 212-228-0230
Brady, Steve/1 Bond St #3B, 212-979-6322
Brakha, Moshe/77 FIfth Ave #17D, 212-645-7946
Brandt, Peter/73 Fifth Ave #6B, 212-242-4289
Braun, Yenachem/666 West End Ave, 212-873-1985
Braverman, Alan/139 Fifth Ave, 212-674-1925
Bredel, Walter/21 E 10th St, 212-228-8565
Breitrose, Howard/443 W 18th St, 212-242-7825
Brello, Ron/400 Lafayette St, 212-982-0490
Brenner, George/15 W 24th St #3E, 212-691-7436
Breskin, Michael/324 Lafayette, 212-925-2858
Brett, Clifton/51 W 14th St, 212-675-6236
Brewster, Don/235 West End Ave, 212-874-0548
Bridges, Kiki/147 W 26th St 3rd Fl, 212-807-6563
Brill Studio/270 City Island Ave, City Island 212-885-0802
Brill, James/108 Fifth Ave #17C, 212-645-9414
Britton, Peter/315 E 68th St, 212-737-1664
Brizzi, Andrea/405 W 23rd St, 212-627-2341
Brody, Bob/5 W 19th 2nd Fl, 212-741-0013
Bronstein, Steve/5 E 19th St #303, 212-473-3366
Brooke, Randy/179 E 3rd St, 212-677-2656
Brosan, Roberto/873 Broadway, 212-473-1471
Brown, Cynthia/448 W 37th St, 212-564-1625
Brown, Nancy/5 W 19th St 10th Fl, 212-924-9105
Brown, Owen Studio/224 W 29th St #PH, 212-947-9470
Bruderer, Rolf/443 Park Ave S, 212-684-4890
Bruno Burklin/873 Broadway, 212-420-0208
Bruno Photo Inc/43 Crosby St 1st Fl, (P 73) 212-925-2929
Brunswick, Cecile/127 W 96th St, 212-222-2088
Bryan-Brown, Marc/4 Jones St #4, 212-691-6045
Bryce, Sherman E/269 W 90th St #3B, 212-580-9639
Bryson, John/12 E 62nd St, 212-755-1321
Buceta, Jaime/56 W 22nd St 6th Fl, 212-807-8485
Buck, Bruce/39 W 14th St, 212-645-1022
Buckler, Susanne/344 W 38th St, 212-279-0043
Buckner, Bill/38 Greene St 2nd Fl, 212-941-1204
Buonnano, Ray/237 W 26th St, 212-675-7680
Burns, Tom/534 W 35th St, 212-927-4678
Burquez, Felizardo/22-63 38th St #1, Astoria 718-274-6139
Burrell, Fred/54 W 21st St #1207, 212-691-0808
Burridge, Derrek/299 Colony Ave, Staten Island 718-667-0805
Butler, Dennis/200 E 37th St 4th Fl, 212-686-5084
Buzoianu, Peter/32-15 41st St, Long Island City 718-278-2456
Byers, Bruce/11 W 20th St 5th Fl, 212-242-5846

C

Cadge, Jeff/341 W 47th St #1B, 212-246-6155
Cailor/Resnick/237 W 54th St 4th Fl, 212-977-4300
Cali, Deborah/333 W 86th St, 212-873-8800
Callis, Chris/91 Fifth Ave, 212-243-0231
Camera Communications/110 Greene St, 212-925-2722
Cameron Photo/78 Fifth Ave, 212-675-0089
Camp, E J (Ms)/20 E 10th St, 212-475-6267
Campbell, Barbara/138 W 17th St, 212-929-5620
Campos, John/132 W 21st St, 212-675-0601
Canady, Philip/1411 Second Ave, 212-737-3855
Cannon, Gregory/876 Broadway 2nd Fl, 212-228-3190
Cantor, Phil/75 Ninth Ave 8th Fl, 212-243-1143
Caplan, Skip/124 W 24th St, 212-463-0541
Cardacino, Michael/20 Ridge Rd, Douglaston 212-947-9307
Cargasacchi, Gianni/175 Fifth Ave, 212-254-3699
Carlson, Emerling/9 E 19th St, 212-473-5130
Carlton, Chuck/36 E 23rd St 7th Fl, 212-777-1099
Carrino, John/160 Fifth Ave #914, 212-581-4298
Carron, Les/15 W 24th St 2nd Fl, 212-255-8250
Carson, Donald/115 W 23rd St, 212-807-8987
Carter, Dwight/11 W 17th St, 212-932-1661
Casarola, Angelo/165 W 18th St 3rd Fl, 212-620-0620
Casey/10 Park Ave #3E, 212-684-1397
Cashin, Art/5 W 19th St, 212-255-3440
Castellano, Peter/314 W 53rd St, 212-206-6320
Castelli, Charles/41 Union Sq W #425, 212-620-5536
Castillo, Luis A/60 Pineapple St, Brooklyn 718-834-1380
Cattan, Robert/20 W 20th St #703, 212-243-3281
Caulfield, Patricia/115 W 86th St #2E, 212-362-1951
Caverly, Kat/414 W 49th St, 212-757-8388
Cearley, Guy/460 Grand St #10A, 212-979-2075
Celnick, Edward/36 E 12th St, 212-420-9326
Cementi, Joseph/133 W 19th St 3rd Fl, 212-924-7770
Cenicola, Tony Studio/32 Union Sq E #613, 212-420-9798
Chakmakjian, Paul/35 W 36th St 8th Fl, 212-563-3195
Chalk, David/157 Hudson St, 212-874-9042
Chalkin, Dennis/5 E 16th St, 212-929-1036
Chan, Michael/22 E 21st St, 212-460-8030
Chan, T S/174 Duane St, 212-219-0574
Chaney, Scott/11 W 20th St 6th Fl, 212-924-8440
Chanteau, Pierre/209 W 38th St, 212-221-5860
Chao, John/51 W 81st St #6B, 212-293-0014
Chapman, Mike/543 Broadway 8th Fl, 212-966-9542
Charles, Bill/265 W 37th St #PH-D, 212-719-9156
Charles, Frederick/254 Park Ave S #7F, 212-505-0686
Charles, Lisa/119 W 23rd St #500, 212-807-8600
Chauncy, Kim/123 W 13th St, 212-242-2400
Checani, Richard/1133 Broadway, 212-645-8634
Chelsea Photo/Graphics/641 Ave of Americas, 212-206-1780
Chen, Paul Inc/133 Fifth Ave, 212-674-4100
Chernin, Bruce/330 W 86th St, 212-496-0266
Chestnut, Richard/236 W 27th St, 212-255-1790
Chiba/303 Park Ave S #412, 212-674-7575
Chin, Ted/118 W 27th St 3rd Fl, 212-627-7296
Chin, Walter/160 Fifth Ave #914, 212-924-6760
Choi, Joon/10 E 18th St #5, 212-645-1248
Christensen, Paul H/286 Fifth Ave, 212-279-2838
Chrynwski, Walter/154 W 18th St, 212-675-1906
Church, Diana/31 W 31st St, 212-736-4116
Cipolla, Karen/103 Reade St 3rd Fl, 212-619-6114
Cirone, Bettina/211 W 56th St #14K, 212-262-3062
Clarke, Kevin/900 Broadway 9th Fl, 212-460-9360
Clay, Langdon/42 W 28th St, 212-689-2613
Clayton, Tom/568 Broadway #601, 212-431-3377
Clearly, Guy/460 Grant St #10A, 212-979-2075
Clementi, Joseph Assoc/133 W 19th St 3rd Fl, 212-924-7770
Clough, Terry/147 W 25th St, 212-255-3040
Cobb, Jan/5 W 19th St 3rd Fl, 212-255-1400
Cochnauer, Paul/1186 Broadway #833, 212-532-9033
Cochran, George/381 Park Ave S, 212-689-9054
Coggin, Roy/64 W 21st St, 212-929-6262
Cohen, James/36 E 20th St 4th Fl, 212-533-4400
Cohen, Lawrence Photo/247 W 30th St, 212-967-4376
Cohen, Marc David/5 W 19th, 212-741-0015
Cohen, Robert/133 W 19th St 2nd Fl, 212-529-2373
Cohn, Ric/137 W 25th St #1, 212-924-4450
Colabella, Vincent/304 E 41st St, (P 75) 212-949-7456
Colby, Ron/PO Box 839/Times Sq Station, 212-684-3084
Coleman, Bruce/381 Fifth Ave 2nd Fl, 212-683-5227
Coleman, Gene/250 W 27th St, 212-691-4752
Colen, Corrine/519 Broadway, 212-431-7425
Colletti, Steve/200 Park Ave #303E, 212-972-2218
Collins, Arlene/64 N Moore St #3E, 212-431-9117
Collins, Benton/873 Broadway, 212-254-7247
Collins, Chris/35 W 20th St, 212-633-1670
Collins, Joe J/208 Garfield Pl, Brooklyn 718-965-4836
Collins, Sheldon/27 W 24th St, 212-242-0076
Colliton, Paul/310 Greenwich St, 212-619-6102
Colton, Robert/1700 York Ave, 212-831-3953
Conn, John/1639 Plymouth Ave #2, 212-931-9051
Connelly, Hank/6 W 37th St, 212-563-9109

Cook, Irvin/534 W 43rd St, .212-925-6216
Cook, Rod/29 E 19th St, .212-995-0100
Cooke, Colin/380 Lafayette St, .212-254-5090
Cooper, Bill/118 E 28th St, .212-213-4433
Cooper, Martha/310 Riverside Dr #805, .212-222-5146
Corbett, Jane/303 Park Ave S #512, .212-505-1177
Cornish, Dan/594 Broadway #1204, .212-226-3183
Corporate Photographers Inc/45 John St, .212-964-6515
Corti, George/10 W 33rd St, .212-239-4490
Cosimo/43 W 13th St, .212-206-1818
Coupon, William/69 Murray St 8th Fl, .212-619-7473
Couzens, Larry/16 E 17th St, .212-620-9790
Cowan, Frank/5 E 16th St, .212-675-5960
Cox, David/25 Mercer St 3rd Fl, .212-925-0734
Cox, Rene/395 South End Ave, .212-321-2749
Crampton, Nancy/35 W 9th St, .212-254-1135
Crawford, Nelson/10 E 23rd #600, .212-475-7808
Crocker, Ted/42 W 24th St, .212-255-3771
Cronin, Casey/115 Wooster St, (P 76) .212-334-9253
Crum, John R Photography/124 W 24th St, .212-463-8663
Cserna, George/80 Second Ave #2, .212-477-3472
Cuington, Phyllis/36 W 25th St 11th Fl, .212-691-1901
Culberson, Earl/5 E 19th St, .212-473-3366
Cunningham, Peter/53 Gansevoort St, .212-633-1077
Curatola, Tony/18 E 17th St, .212-243-5478
Cutler, Craig/536 W 50th St, .212-966-1652
Czaplinski, Czeslaw/90 Dupont St, Brooklyn .718-389-9606

D

D'Addio, James/8 W 76th St #4A, .212-496-0777
D'Innocenzo, Paul/568 Broadway #604, .212-925-9622
Daley, James D/568 Broadway, .212-925-7192
Daly, Jack/247 W 30th St, .212-695-2726
Dantuono, Paul/433 Park Ave So, .212-683-5778
Dantzic, Jerry/910 President St, Brooklyn .718-789-7478
Datoli, Michael/121 W 17th St #4C, .212-691-8401
David, Gabrielle/4024 6th Ave, Brooklyn .718-856-2315
Davidian, Peter/58 Broadway #1203, .212-941-8077
Davidson, Bruce/79 Spring St, .212-475-7600
Davidson, Darwin K/32 Bank Street, .212-242-0095
Davis, Dick/400 E 59th St, .212-751-3276
Davis, Don/61 Horatio St, .212-989-2820
Davis, Hal/225 Lafayette St, .212-925-3001
Davis, Richard/17 E 16th St 9th Fl, .212-675-2428
Day, Lee/55 Hudson St, .212-619-4117
Day, Olita/239 Park Ave South, .212-673-9354
De Zanger, Arie/80 W 40th St, .212-354-7327
DeFever, Cyril/157 Chambers St 12th Fl,
DeFrancis, Peter/424 Broome St, .212-966-1357
DeGrado, Drew/250 W 40th St 5th Fl, .212-302-2760
Degrado, Drew/250 W 40th St, .212-302-2760
DeLeon, Katrina/286 Fifth Ave #1206, .212-714-9777
DeLeon, Martin/286 Fifth Ave #1206, .212-714-9777
DeLessio, Len/121 E 12th St #4F, .212-353-1774
DeMarchelier, Patrick/162 W 21st St, .212-924-3561
DeMelo, Antonio/126 W 22nd St, .212-929-0507
DeMilt, Ronald/873 Broadway 2nd Fl, .212-228-5321
Denker, Deborah/460 Greenwich St, .212-219-9263
Denner, Manuel/249 W 29th St 4th Fl, .212-947-6220
Dennis, Lisl/135 E 39th St, .212-532-8226
DePaul, Raymond/252 W 76th St #1A, .212-769-2550
DePra, Nancy/15 W 24th St, .212-242-0252
Dermer, Ronald/Falmouth St, Brooklyn .718-332-2464
Derr, Stephen/420 W 45th St 4th Fl, .212-246-5920
DeSanto, Thomas/116 W 29th St 2nd Fl, .212-967-1390
DeToy, Ted/511 E 78th St, .212-988-1869
Deutsch, Jack/165 W 83rd St, .212-799-7179
DeVito, Bart/43 E 30th St 14th Fl, .212-889-9670
DeVoe, Marcus E/34 E 81st St, .212-737-9073
DeWys, Leo/1170 Broadway, .212-689-5580
Diamond, Joe/915 West End Ave, .212-316-5295
Dian, Russell/432 E 88th St #201, .212-722-4348
Diaz, Jorge/142 W 24th St 12th Fl, .212-675-4783
Dibue, Robert/40 W 20th St, .212-206-0860
Dicran Studio/35 W 36th St 11th Fl, .212-695-6438
DiFranza Williamson Photography/16 W 22nd St, .212-463-8302
Dillon, Jim/39 W 38th St 12th Fl, .212-849-8158
DiMartini, Sally/1 Oyster lane, E Hampton .516-329-1236

DiMicco/Ferris Studio/40 W 17th St, .212-627-4074
DiPetto, John/245 E 54th St, .212-941-5620
Dodge, Jeff/133 Eighth Ave, .212-620-9652
Doerzbacher, Cliff/12 Cottage Ave, Staten Island .718-981-3144
Doherty, Marie/43 E 22nd St, .212-674-8767
Dole, Jody (Mr)/95 Horatio St, .212-691-9888
Dolgins, Alan/470 W 24th St, .212-741-2270
Dorf, Myron Jay/205 W 19th St 3rd Fl, (P 26,27) .212-255-2020
Dorot, Didier/48 W 21st St 9th Fl, .212-206-1608
Doubilet, David/1040 Park Ave #6J, .212-348-5011
Drabkin, Si Studios Inc/40-10 Littleneck pkwy, Littleneck .718-279-4512
Dresner, Harvey/302-46 46th Ave, Bayside .718-225-2332
Dressler, Marjory/4 E Second St, .212-254-9758
Drew, Rue Faris/177 E 77th St, .212-794-8994
Drivas, Joseph/15 Beacon Ave, Staten Island .718-667-0696
Dubler, Douglas/162 E 92nd St, .212-410-6300
Duchaine, Randy/200 W 18th St #4F, .212-243-4371
Ducote, Kimberly/445 W 19th St #7F, .212-989-3680
Dugdale, John/59 Morton St, .212-691-5264
Duke, Dana/620 Broadway, .212-260-3334
Duke, Randy/2825 Grand Concourse, Bronx .212-364-2584
Dunkley, Richard/648 Broadway #506, .212-979-6996
Dunning, Hank/50 W 22nd St, .212-675-6040
Dunning, Robert/57 W 58th St, .212-688-0788
Duomo Photo Inc/133 W 19th St, .212-243-1150

E

Eagan, Timothy/319 E 75th St, .212-517-7665
Eastep, Wayne/443 Park Ave S #1006, .212-686-8404
Eberstadt, Fred/791 Park Ave, .212-794-9471
Eckstein, Ed/234 Fifth Ave 5th Fl, .212-685-9342
Edahl, Edward/236 W 27th St, .212-929-2002
Edgeworth, Anthony/130 Madison Ave 4th Fl, .212-679-6031
Edinger, Claudio/456 Broome St, .212-219-8619
Edwards, Gregory/30 East End Ave, .212-879-4339
Edwards, Harvey/575 Madison Ave, .516-261-5239
Eggers, Claus/900 Broadway, .212-473-0064
Eguiguren, Carlos/139 E 57th St 3rd Fl, .212-888-6732
Ehrenpreis, Dave/156 Fifth Ave, .212-947-3535
Eisenberg, Steve/448 W 37th St, .212-563-2061
Eisner, Sandra/104 W 17th St, .212-727-0669
Elbers, Johan/18 E 18th St, .212-929-5783
Elgort, Arthur/136 Grand St, .212-219-8775
Elios-Zunini Studio/142 W 4th St, .212-228-6827
Elmer, Jo/200 E 87th St, .212-369-7077
Elmore, Steve/60 E 42nd St #411, .212-472-2463
Elness, Jack/236 W 26th St, .212-242-5045
Elz, Barry/13 Worth St, .212-431-7910
Emberling, David/9 E 19th St, .212-473-5130
Emil, Pamela/327 Central Park West, .212-749-4716
Emrich, Bill/45 E 25th St, .212-889-7482
Endress, John Paul Inc/254 W 31st St, (P 18,19) .212-736-7800
Engel, Mort Studio/260 Fifth Ave, .212-889-8466
Englander, Maury/43 Fifth Ave, .212-242-9777
Engle, Mort Studio Inc/260 Fifth Ave, (P 44) .212-889-8466
Englehardt, Duk/80 Varick St #4E, .212-226-6490
Englert, Michael/142 W 24th St, .212-243-3446
Ennis, Buck/331 Lafayette St, .212-966-7015
Epstein, Mitch/353 E 77th St, .212-517-3648
Epstein, Paula/146 Sullivan St #5, .212-777-5177
Essel, Robert/39 W 71st St #A, .212-877-5228
Estrada, Sigrid/902 Broadway, .212-673-4300

F

Farber, Robert/207-A 62nd St, .212-486-9090
Faria, Rui/304 Eighth Ave #3, .212-929-2993
Farrell, Bill/63 Adrian Avenue, Bronx (P 78) .212-562-8931
Farrell, John/189 Second Ave, .212-460-9001
Favero, Jean P/208 Fifth Ave #3E, .212-683-9188
Feibel, Theodor/102-10 66th Rd #15C, Forest Hills .718-897-2445
Feinstein, Gary/19 E 17th St, .212-242-3373
Feintuch, Harvey/1440 E 14th St, Brooklyn .718-339-0301
Feldman, Andy/515 10th St, Brooklyn .718-788-6585
Feller, Nora/230 West End Ave #1C, .212-580-3447
Fellerman, Stan/152 W 25th St 7th Fl, (P 50) .212-243-0027
Fellman, Sandi/548 Broadway, .212-925-5187
Ferguson, Phoebe/289 Cumberland St, Brooklyn .718-643-1675
Ferich, Lorenz/516 E 78th St #2D, (P 55) .212-517-6838

Grossman, Eugene/80 N Moore St Ste 14J,	212-962-6795
Grossman, Henry/37 Riverside Dr,	212-580-7751
Grotell, Al/170 Park Row #15D,	212-349-3165
Gruen, John/20 W 22nd St,	212-242-8415
Guatti, Albano/250 Mercer St #C403,	212-674-2230
Gudnason, Torkil/58 W 15th St,	212-929-6680
Guice, Brad Studio/31 W 31st St 6th Fl,	212-206-0966
Gurovitz, Judy/207 E 74th St,	212-988-8685
Guyaux, Jean-Marie/29 E 19th St,	212-529-5395
Guzman/31 W 31st St,	212-643-9375

H

Haar, Thomas/463 West St,	212-929-9054
Haas, Ken Photo/15 Sheridan Square,	212-255-0707
Hagen, Boyd/448 W 37th St #6A, (P 24,25)	**212-244-2436**
Haggerty, David/17 E 67th St,	212-879-4141
Hagiwara, Brian/504 La Guardia Pl,	212-674-6026
Haimann, Todd/26 W 38th St,	212-391-0810
Halaska, Jan/PO Box 6611 FDR Sta,	718-389-8923
Haling, George/231 W 29th St #302, (P 92,93)	**212-736-6822**
Hamilton, Keith/749 FDR Dr #6D,	212-982-3375
Hamilton, Mark/119 W 23rd St,	212-242-9814
Hammond, Maury/9 E 19th St,	212-460-9990
Hampton Studios/515 Broadway #4A,	212-431-4320
Hansen, Barbara/1954 Bronxdale Ave, Bronx	212-822-1676
Hansen, Constance/31 W 31st St 9th Fl,	212-643-9375
Hanson, Kent/147 Bleecker St #3R,	212-777-2399
Harbutt, Charles/1 Fifth Ave,	212-645-4274
Hardin, Ted/454 W 46th St #5A-N,	212-307-6208
Harrington, Grace/312 W 48th St,	212-246-1749
Harris, Jeff/16 W 19th St 7th Fl,	212-243-3716
Harris, Michael/18 W 21st St,	212-255-3377
Harris, Ronald G/119 W 22nd St, (P 94,95)	**212-255-2330**
Harrison, Howard/20 W 20th St 8th Fl,	212-989-9233
Hartmann, Erich/79 Spring St,	212-966-9200
Haruo/37 W 20th St #905, (P 96)	**212-505-8800**
Harvey, Ned/129 W 22nd St,	212-807-7043
Hashi Studio Inc/49 W 23rd St 3rd Fl, (P 16,17)	**212-675-6902**
Hashimoto/153 W 27th St #1202,	212-645-1221
Hathon, Elizabeth/8 Greene St,	212-219-0685
Hausman, George/1181 Broadway 6th Fl,	212-686-4810
Haviland, Brian/34 E 30th St 4th Fl,	212-481-4132
Havilland, Brian/34 E 30th St,	212-481-4132
Hayes, Kerry/35 Taft Ave, Staten Island	718-442-4804
Haynes, Richard/383 Madison Ave 2nd Fl,	305-345-2500
Hayward, Bill/596 Broadway 8th Fl,	212-966-6490
Heery, Gary/577 Broadway 2nd Fl,	212-966-6364
Hege, Laszlo/179 E 80th St,	212-737-1620
Heiberg, Milton/71 W 23rd St,	212-741-6405
Heiges, Jeff/6750 Fifth Ave, Brooklyn	718-833-3212
Heinlein, David/56 W 22nd St,	212-645-1158
Heir, Stuart/578 Broadway,	212-337-8779
Heisler, Gregory/568 Broadway #800,	212-777-8100
Hellerstein, Stephen A/56 W 22nd St 6th Fl,	212-645-0508
Helms, Bill/1175 York Ave,	212-759-2079
Hemsay, Yvonne/4520 Henry Hudson Pkwy, Riverdale	212-549-0095
Henze, Don Studio/39 W 29th St 4th Fl,	212-689-7375
Heron, Michal (Ms)/28 W 71st St,	212-787-1272
Herr, H Buff/56 W 82nd St,	212-595-4783
Hess, Brad/1201 Broadway,	212-684-3131
Heuberger, William/140 W 22nd St,	212-242-1532
Heyman, Ken Photo/37 Bank St,	212-627-2028
Hilaire, Max/218 E 27th St,	212-889-1685
Hill, Pat/37 W 26th St,	212-532-3479
Himmel, Lizzie/218 E 17th St,	212-777-6482
Hine, Skip/34 W 17th St 9th Fl,	212-691-5903
Hing/ Norton Photography/24 W 30th St 8th Fl,	212-683-4258
Hiro/50 Central Park West,	212-580-8000
Hirsch, Butch/107 W 25th St,	212-929-3024
Hirst, Michael/1150 Sixth Ave,	212-391-1215
Hitz, Brad/377 W 11th St #2B,	212-929-1432
Hochman, Allen Studio/9-11 E 19 St,	212-777-8404
Hochman, Richard/210 Fifth Ave,	212 532-7766
Hodgson, David/550 Riverside Dr,	212-864-6941
Hoffman, Ethan/95 Van Dam St,	212-645-4274
Hogan, David/352 E 91st St,	212-369-4575
Holbrooke, Andrew/50 W 29th St,	212-889-5995
Holdeier, John/37 W 20th St #606,	212-620-4260
Holderer, John/37 W 20th St #606,	212-620-4260

Holdorf, Thomas/132 W 22 St 3rd Fl,	212-727-7981
Holland, Robin/430 Greenwich St,	212-431-5351
Hollyman, Stephanie/85 South St,	212-825-1828
Hollyman, Tom/300 E 40th St #19R,	212-867-2383
Holtzman Photography/269 W 11th St,	212-242-7985
Holub, Ed/101 Stanton St #6,	212-673-9097
Holz, George/400 Lafayette,	212-505-5607
Hom, Frank/601 W 26th St #13A,	212-979-5533
Hooper, Thomas/126 Fifth Ave #5B,	212-691-0122
Hopkins, Douglas/PO Box 185,	212-243-1774
Hopkins, Stephan/475 Carlton Ave, Brooklyn	718-783-6461
Hopson, Gareth/22 E 21st St,	212-535-3800
Hori, Richard/119 W 23rd St #400,	212-645-8333
Horowitz, Ross M/206 W 15th St,	212-206-9216
Horowitz, Ryszard/137 W 25th St,	212-243-6440
Horst/188 E 64th St #1701,	212-751-4937
Horvath, Jim/95 Charles St,	212-741-0300
Houze, Philippe Louis/123 Prince St,	212-614-0435
Howard, Rosemary/902 Broadway,	212-473-5552
Howell, Josephine/127 Pacific St, Brooklyn	718-858-2451
Hower, Jennifer/18 E 64th St,	212-759-5590
Huibregtse, Jim/14 Jay St 6th Fl,	212-925-3351
Hume, Adam/231 E 76th St #6F,	212-794-1754
Huntzinger, Bob/514 W 37th St,	212-645-9035
Hurwitz, Harrison/379 Park Ave S,	212-213-4820
Huston, Larry/40 E 21st St,	212 777-7541
Huszar, Steven/377 Park Ave South,	212-532-3772
Hyatt, Morton/13 Laight St 3rd Fl,	212-226-6880
Hyman, Barry/319 E 78th St #3C,	212-879-3294
Hyman, Paul Productions/236 W 26th St, (P 99)	**212-255-1532**

I

Ianuzzi, Tom/488 W 37th St #9D,	212-563-1987
Ichi/303 Park Ave S #506,	212-254-4810
Ihara/568 Broadway #507,	212-219-9363
Ikeda, Shig/636 Sixth Ave #4C,	212-924-4744
Illography/49 Crosby St,	212-219-0244
Image Makers/310 E 23rd St #9F,	212-533-4498
Ing, Francis/112 W 31st St 5th Fl,	212-279-5022
Intrater, Roberta/1212 Beverly Rd, Brooklyn	718-462-4004
Iooss, Walter/344 W 72nd St,	212-769-1552
Irgens, O Christian/197-05 104th Ave, St Albans	718-454-3157
Irwin, William/70 Remsen St #9B, Brooklyn	718-237-2598
Isaacs, Norman/277 W 11th St,	212-243-5547
Ishimuro, Eisuke/130 W 25th St 10th Fl,	212-255-9198
Ivany, Sandra/6 W 90th St #6,	212-580-1501
Izu, Kenro/140 W 22nd St,	212-254-1002

J

Jackson, Martin/217 E 85th St #110,	215-271-5149
Jacobs, Marty/34 E 23rd St 5th Fl,	212-475-1160
Jacobsen, Paul/150 Fifth Ave,	212-243-4732
Jacobson, Alan/250 W 49th St #800,	212-265-0170
Jacobson, Jeff/230 Hamilton Ave, Staten Island	718-720-0533
Jann, Gail/352 E 85th St,	212-861-4335
Jawitz, Louis H/13 E 17th St #PH,	212-929-0008
Jeffery, Richard/119 W 22nd St, ·	212-255-2330
Jeffrey, Lance/30 E 21st St #4A,	212-674-0595
Jenkinson, Mark/142 Bleecker St Box 6,	212-529-0488
Jensen, Peter M/22 E 31st St,	212-689-5026
Jenssen, Buddy/34 E 29th St,	212-686-0865
Joel, Seth Photography/515 Broadway,	212-925-1373
Joern, James/125 Fifth Ave,	212-260-8025
Johansky, Peter/27 W 20th St,	212-242-7013
Jones, Chris/240 E 27th St,	212-685-0679
Jones, Spencer/23 Leonard St #5, (P 102)	**212-941-8165**
Jones, Steven/120 W 25th St #3E, (P 103)	**212-929-3641**
Joseph, Meryl/158 E 82nd St,	212-861-5057
Jurado, Louis/126 W 22nd St,	212-751-1894

K

Kachaturian, Armen/330 Broome St,	212-334-0986
Kahan, Eric/36 W 20th St 3rd Fl,	212-243-9727
Kahn, R T/156 E 79th St,	212-988-1423
Kahn, Steve/60 Thomas St,	212-619-7932
Kalinsky, George/4 Pennsylvania Plaza,	212-563-8095
Kalleberg, Garrett/520 E 5th St #2B,	212-674-2716

PHOTOGRAPHERS

Kamper, George Productions Ltd/63 Adrian Ave, Bronx (P 104,105)....212-562-8931
Kamsler, Leonard/140 Seventh Ave, ...212-242-4678
Kan Photography/153 W 27th St #406, ...212-645-2684
Kana, Titus/876 Broadway, ...212-473-5550
Kanakis, Michael/144 W 27th St 10th Fl, ...212-807-8232
Kane, Art/568 Broadway, ...212-925-7334
Kane, Peter T/236 W 26th St #502, ...212-924-4968
Kaniklidis, James/1270 E 18th St, Brooklyn 718-338-0931
Kaplan, Alan/7 E 20th St, ...212-982-9500
Kaplan, Michael/171 W 23d St #3A, ...212-741-3271
Kaplan, Peter B/7 E 20th St #4R, ...212-995-5000
Kaplan, Peter J/924 West End Ave, ...212-222-1193
Karales, James H/147 W 79th St, ...212-799-2483
Karia, Bhupendra/9 E 96th St #15B, ...212-860-5479
Kassabian Photography/127 E 59th St, ...212-421-1950
Kasten, Barbara/251 W 19th St #8C, ...212 627-5229
Katchian, Sonia/47 Green St, ...212-966-9641
Katrina/286 Fifth Ave #1206, ...212-279-2838
Katvan, Moshe/40 W 17th St #5B, (P 10,11)....212-242-4895
Katz, Paul/65-61 Saunders St #1L, Queens 718-275-3615
Katzenstein, David/21 E 4th St, ...718-383-8528
Kaufman, Curt/215 W 88th St, ...212-873-9841
Kaufman, Elliott/255 W 90th St, ...212-496-0860
Kaufman, Jeff/27 W 24th St, ...212-627-1878
Kaufman, Mickey/144 W 27th St, ...212-255-1976
Kaufman, Ted/121 Madison Ave #4E, ...212-685-0349
Kawachi, Yutaka/33 W 17th St 2nd Fl, ...212-929-4825
Kaye, Nancy/77 Seventh Ave #7U, ...818-886-1180
Kayser, Alex/211 W Broadway, ...212-431-8518
Keaveny, Francis/260 Fifth Ave, ...212-481-9187
Keegan, Marcia/140 E 46th St, ...212-953-9023
Keller, Tom/440 E 78th St, ...212-472-3667
Kelley, Charles W Jr/649 Second Ave #6C-30, ...212-686-3879
Kelley, David/265 W 37th St, ...212-869-7896
Kellner, Jeff/16 Waverly Pl, ...212-475-3719
Kennedy, Donald J/521 W 23rd St 10th Fl, ...212-206-7740
Kent, Karen/29 John St, ...212-962-6793
Kerbs, Ken/100 Dean St, Brooklyn 718-858-6950
Khornak, Lucille/425 E 58th St, ...212-593-0933
Kilkelly, James/784 Amsterdam Ave #3A, ...212-662-3580
Kingsford, Michael Studio/874 Broadway, ...212-475-0553
Kinmonth, Rob/3 Rutherford Pl, ...212-475-6370
Kirk, Barbara/447 E 65th St, ...212-734-3233
Kirk, Charles/276 Winchester Ave, Staten Island 212-677-3770
Kirk, Malcolm/12 E 72nd St, ...212-744-3642
Kirk, Neil/245 E 58th St, ...212-752-8174
Kirk, Russell/31 W 21st St, ...212-206-1446
Kitchen, Dennis/80 Fourth Ave 3rd fl, ...212-674-7658
Kittle, Kit/511 E 20th St, ...212-995-8866
Klauss, Cheryl/463 Broome St, ...212-431-3569
Klein, Arthur/35-42 80th St, Jackson Heights 718-278-0457
Klein, Matthew/104 W 17th St #2E, ...212-255-6400
Kligge, Robert/578 Broadway, ...212-226-7113
Klonsky, Arthur/2 W 45th St #1200, ...212-382-3939
Knowles, Robert M/2 Fordham Hill Oval #9C, Bronx 212-367-4430
Kohli, Eddy/160 Fifth Ave #914, ...212-924-6760
Kojima, Tak/25 W 23rd St, ...212-243-2243
Kolansky, Palma/291 Church St, ...212-431-5858
Kopelow, Paul/135 Madison Ave 14th Fl, ...212-689-0685
Kopitchinski, Reuben/98 Riverside Dr, ...212-724-1252
Koppelman, Jozef/1717 Ave N, Brooklyn 718-645-3548
Korsh, Ken/118 E 28th St, ...212-685-8864
Kosoff, Brian/28 W 25th St 6th Fl, ...212-243-4880
Koudis, Nick/40 E 23rd St 2nd Fl, ...212-475-2802
Kouirinis, Bill/381 Park Ave S #710, ...212-696-5674
Kovner, Richard/80 East End Ave #10A, ...212-775-7989
Kozan, Dan/32 W 22nd St, ...212-691-2288
Kozlowski, Mark/39 W 28th St, ...212-684-7487
Kozyra, James/568 Broadway, ...212-431-1911
Kramer, Daniel/110 W 86th St, ...212-873-7777
Krasner/Trebitz/PO Box 1548 Cooper Sta, ...212-777-2132
Krasowitz, Mike/330 E 76th St #4W, ...212-861-4207
Kratochvil, Antonin/448 W 37th St #6G, ...212-947-1589
Kraus, Brian/126 W 22nd St, ...212-691-1813
Krein, Jeffrey/119 W 23rd St #800, ...212-741-5207
Krementz, Jill/228 E 48th St, ...212-688-0480
Kristofik, Robert/334 E 90th St #2A, ...212-534-5541
Kroll, Eric/118 E 28th St #1005, ...212-684-2465
Kron, Dan/154 W 18th St, ...212-463-9333
Krongard, Steve/212-A E 26th St, ...212-689-5634
Kuczera, Mike/20 W 22nd St #817, ...212-620-8112
Kudo/39 Walker St, ...212-966-1856
Kuehn, Karen/49 Warren St, ...212-406-3005
Kugler, Dennis/43 Bond St, ...212-677-3826
Kuhn, Ann Spanos/1155 Broadway, ...212-685-1774
Kupinski, Steven/36 E 20th St, ...212-982-3230

L

Labar, Elizabeth/327 W 18th St, ...212-929-7463
Lachenauer, Paul/876 Broadway, ...212-529-7059
Lafontaine, Marie Josee/160 Fifth Ave, ...212-924-6760
Lambray, Maureen/120 E 75th St, ...212-879-3960
LaMoglia, Anthony/63 Eighth Ave #3B, Brooklyn 718-636-9839
LaMonica, Chuck/20 Mountain Ave, New Rochelle 212-727-7884
Lane, Morris/212-A E 26th St, ...212-696-0498
Lange, George/817 West End Ave, ...212-666-1414
Langley, David/536 W 50th St, ...212-581-3930
Lanker, Brian/20 W 46th St, ...212-944-2853
Laperruque, Scott/157 Chambers St 12th Fl, ...212-962-5200
Larrain, Gilles/95 Grand St, ...212-925-8494
Laszlo Studio/28 W 39th St, ...212-736-6690
Lategan, Barry/502 LaGuardia Pl, ...212-228-6850
Laubmayer, Klaus/234 Fifth Ave, ...212-679-6739
Laurance, Bruce Studio/253 W 28th St 5th Fl, ...212-947-3451
Laure, Jason/8 W 13th St 11th Fl, ...212-691-7466
Laurence, Mary/PO Box 1763, ...212-903-4025
Laurien Photo/9 Gramercy Park #5F, ...212-260-6177
Lavine, Arthur/1361 Madison Ave, ...212-348-2642
Lawrence, Christopher/12 E 18th St, ...212-807-8028
Lax, Ken/239 Park Ave S, ...212-228-6191
Layman, Alex/142 W 14th St 6th Fl, ...212-989-5845
LeBaube, Guy/310 E 46th St, ...212-986-6981
Lederman, Ed/166 E 34th St #12H, ...212-685-8612
Leduc, Lyle/320 E 42nd St #1014, ...212-697-9216
Lee, Jung (Ms)/132 W 21st St 3rd Fl, ...212-807-8107
Lee, Vincent/155 Wooster St #3F, ...212-254-7888
Lee, Wellington/305 Broadway 7th Fl, ...718-760-2762
Lefkowitz, Lester/370 Lexington Ave #2010, ...212-627-8088
Legrand, Michel/152 W 25th St 12th Fl, (P 110)....212-807-9754
Lehman, Amy/210 E 75th St, ...212-535-7457
Leibovitz, Annie/55 Vandam St 14th Fl, ...212-807-0220
Leicmon, John/200 W 15th St, ...212-675-3219
Leighton, Thomas/321 E 43rd St, (P 111)....212-370-1835
Lenore, Dan/249 W 29th St #2N, ...212-967-7115
Leo, Donato/866 Sixth Ave, ...212-685-5527
Leonian, Phillip/220 E 23rd St, ...212-989-7670
Lerner, Richard/20 W 20th St #501, ...212-627-2070
Lesinski, Martin/40 W 17th St #2B, ...212-463-7857
Let There Be Neon/PO Box 337/Canal St, ...212-226-4883
Leung, J Ming/60 Pineapple St #6B, Brooklyn 718-522-1894
Levin, James/1570 First Ave #3D, ...212-734-0315
Levine, Jonathan/11 W 9th St, ...212-673-4698
Levine, Nancy/41 Fifth Ave #3D, ...212-473-0015
Levinson, Ken/35 East 10th St, ...212-254-6180
Levy, Peter/119 W 22nd St, ...212-691-6600
Levy, Richard/5 W 19th St, ...212-243-4220
Lewin, Gideon/25 W 39th St, ...212-921-5558
Lewin, Ralph/156 W 74th St, ...212-580-0482
Lewis, Robert/333 Park Ave S 4th Fl, ...212-475-6564
Lewis, Ross/415 W 23rd St #1EE, ...212-691-4929
Lieberman, Allen/480 Broadway, ...212-925-8874
Liebman, Phil/315 Hudson, ...212-269-7777
Ligeti Inc/415 W 55th St, ...212-246-8949
Lindau, Dan/594 Broadway #1202, ...212-925-2020
Lindner, Steven/18 W 27th St 3rd Fl, ...212-683-1317
Lipton, Trina/60 E 8th St, ...212-533-3148
Lisi-Hoeltzell Ltd/156 Fifth Ave, ...212-255-0303
Little, Christopher/4 W 22nd St, ...212-691-1024
Lloyd, Harvey/310 E 23rd St, ...212-533-4498
Loete, Mark/33 Gold St #405, ...212-571-2235
Loew, Anthony/503 Broadway, ...212-226-1999
Logan, Kevin/119 W 23rd St #905, ...212-206-0539
Lombardi, Frederick/180 Pinehurst Ave, ...212-568-0740
Lombroso, Dorit/67 Vestry St #B, ...212-219-8722
Lomeo, Angelo/336 Central Park W, ...212-663-2122
Londoner, Hank/18 W 38th St, ...212-354-0293

Loomis, Just/160 Fifth Ave #914, ...212-924-6760
Loppacher, Peter/56 Jane St, ...212-929-1322
Lorenz, Robert/80 Fourth Ave, ...212-505-8483
Loughborough, John/169 W 85th St #4A, ...212-874-7396
Love, Robin/676 Broadway 4th Fl, ...212-777-3113
Lowe, Jacques/138 Duane St, ...212-227-3298
Lubianitsky, Leonid/1013 Ave of Americas, ...212-391-0197
Lucka, Klaus/101 Fifth Ave 2nd Fl, ...212-255-2424
Luftig, Allan/873 Broadway, (P 114,115)   212-533-4113
Lulow, William/126 W 22nd St, ...212-675-1625
Luppino, Michael/126 W 22nd St, ...212-279-9321
Luria, Dick/5 E 16th St 4th Fl, ...212-929-7575
Lusk, Frank/25 E 37th St, ...212-679-1441
Lustica, Tee/156 Fifth Ave #925, ...212-255-0303
Luttenberg, Gene/20 W 22nd St #817, ...212-620-8112
Lypides, Chris/119 W 23rd St, ...212-741-1911

M

M, Debi/225 Lafayette St, ...212-941-1180
Maass, Rob/166 E 7th St, ...212-473-5612
Macedonia, Carmine/866 Ave of Americas, ...212-889-8520
Mackiewicz, Jim/208 E 28th St, ...212-689-0766
MacLaren, Mark/430 E 20th St, ...212-674-0155
MacWeeney, Alen Inc/171 First Ave, ...212-473-2500
Madere, John/75 Spring St 5th Fl, ...212-966-4136
Maisel, Jay/190 Bowery, ...212-431-5013
Malignon, Jacques/34 W 28th St, ...212-532-7727
Maloof, Karen/110 W 94th St #4C, ...212-678-7737
Mandarino, Tony/114 E 32nd St, ...212-686-2866
Mangeim, David S/339 Hart Ave, Staten Island 718-442-4095
Mangia, Tony/11 E 32nd St #3B, ...212-889-6340
Mani, Monsor/40 E 23rd St, ...212-947-9116
Manna, Lou/20 E 30th St, ...212-683-8689
Manno, John/20 W 22nd St #802, ...212-243-7353
Marchese, Carole/91 Bedford St, ...212-627-5562
Marchese, Jim/200 W 20th St, ...212-242-1087
Marco, Phil/104 Fifth Ave 4th Fl, ...212-929-8082
Marcus, Helen/120 E 75th St, ...212-879-6903
Marcusson, Eric E/85 Barrow St #2R, ...212-924-5437
Maresca, Frank/236 W 26th St, ...212-620-0955
Margerin, Bill/41 W 25th St, ...212-645-1532
Marshall, Alec/287 Ave C #8B, ...914-779-0022
Marshall, Elizabeth/200 Central Pk S #31A, ...212-463-7884
Marshall, Jim Studio/20 Jay St, Brooklyn......................718-797-9449
Marshall, Lee/201 W 89th St, (P 116)   212-799-9717
Martin, Bard/142 W 26th St, ...212-929-6712
Martin, Gregg/169 Columbia Hts, Brooklyn...................718-522-3237
Martinez, Oscar/303 Park Ave S #408, ...212-673-0932
Marvullo Photomontage/141 W 28th St #502, ...212-564-6501
Marx, Richard/130 W 25th St, ...212-929-8880
Masca/109 W 26th St, ...212-929-4818
Mason, Donald/111 W 19th St, ...212-675-3809
Mass, Rita/119 W 23rd St 10th Fl, ...212-645-9120
Massey, Philip/475 W 186th St, ...212-928-8210
Masullo, Ralph/111 W 19th St, ...212-727-1809
Masunaga, Ryuzo/119 W 22nd St 5th Fl, ...212-807-7012
Mathews, Barbara Lynn/16 Jane St, ...212-691-0823
Mathews, Bruce Photo/95 E 7th St, ...212-529-7909
Matsuo, Toshi/105 E 29th St, ...212-532-1320
Matthews, Cynthia/200 E 78th St, ...212-288-7349
Maucher, Arnold/154 W 18th St, ...212-206-1535
Maynard, Chris/297 Church St, ...212-255-8204
Mazzeo, Michael/119 W 23rd St, ...212-927-3766
Mazzurco, Phil/150 Fifth Ave #319, ...212-823-5621
McCabe, David/39 W 67th St #1403, ...212-874-7480
McCabe, Robert/117 E 24th St, ...212-677-1910
McCarthy, Jo Anna/535 Greenwich St, ...212-255-5150
McCarthy, Margaret/31 E 31st St, ...212-696-5971
McCartney, Susan/902 Broadway #1608, ...212-533-0660
McCavera, Tom/418 W 25th St 9th Fl, ...212-675-9385
McDermott, Brian/48 W 21st St, ...212-675-7273
McGlenn, David/18-23 Astoria Blvd, LI City...................718-626-9427
McGlynn, David/18-23 Astoria Blvd, Long Island City 718-626-9427
McGoon, James/317 E 18th St, ...212-473-7680
McGrath, Norman/164 W 79th St #16, ...212-799-6422
McLaughlin, Glenn/5 W 19th St, ...212-645-7028
McLoughlin, James Inc/148 W 24th St 5th Fl, ...212-206-8207
McMullen, Mark/304 Eighth Ave #3, ...212-243-6343

McNally, Brian T/234 E 81st St #1A, ...212-744-1263
McNally, Joe/305 W 98th St #6D S, ...212-219-1014
Mead, Chris/108 Reade St, ...212-619-5616
Megna, Richard/210 Forsyth St, ...212-473-5770
Meisel, Steven/303 Park Ave S #409, ...212-777-7130
Meiselas, Susan/251 Park Ave S, ...212-475-7600
Melillo, Nicholas/118 W 27th St #3N, ...212-691-7612
Mella, Michael/217 Thompson St, ...212-777-6012
Mellon/69 Perry St, ...212-691-4166
Meltzer, Irwin & Assoc/50 W 17th St, ...212-807-7464
Memo Studio/39 W 67th St #1402, ...212-787-1658
Menashe, Abraham/306 E 5th St #27, (P 119)   212-254-2754
Menda, George/568 Broadway #403, ...212-431-7440
Menken, Howard Studios/119 W 22nd St, ...212-924-4240
Mensch, Barbara/274 Water St, ...212-349-8170
Meola, Eric/535 Greenwich St, ...212-255-5150
Merle, Michael G/54 W 16th St, ...212-741-3801
Mervar, Louis/29 W 38th St 16th Fl, ...212-354-8024
Messin, Larry/64 Carlyle Green, Staten Island 718-948-7209
Meyer, Kip/80 Madison Ave #7E, ...212-683-9039
Meyer, Rich/13 Laight St, ...212-226-7560
Meyerowitz, Joel/151 W 19th St, ...212-242-0740
Micaud, Christopher/143 Ave B, ...212-473-7266
Michals, Duane/109 E 19th St, ...212-473-1563
Michelson, Eric T/101 Lexington Ave #4B, ...212-683-6259
Mieles, Peter/20 Ave D #11I, ...212-475-6025
Milbauer, Dennis/15 W 28th St, ...212-532-3702
Miles, Ian/313 E 61st St, ...212-688-1360
Milisenda, John/424 56th St, Brooklyn.........................718-439-4571
Miller, Bert/30 Dongan Pl, ...212-567-7947
Miller, Bill Photo/130 W 25th St 4th Fl, ...212-633-2686
Miller, Donald L/295 Central Park West,
(P 120,121)   212-496-2830
Miller, Eileen/28 W 38th St, ...212-944-1507
Miller, Myron/23 E 17th St, ...212-242-3780
Miller, Sue Ann/115 W 27th St 9th Fl, ...212-645-5172
Miller, Wayne F/72 Spring Street, ...212-966-9200
Ming Studio/60 Pineapple St #6B, Brooklyn..................212-254-8570
Ming, Lung/110 E 23rd St, ...212-505-6443
Minh Studio/200 Park Ave S #1507, ...212-477-0649
Minks, Marlin/34-43 82nd St, Jackson Hts 718-507-9513
Mistretta, Martin/220 W 19th St 11th Fl, ...212-675-1547
Mitchell, Andrew/220 Berkeley Pl, Brooklyn.................718-783-6727
Mitchell, Benn/119 W 23rd St, ...212-255-8686
Mitchell, Diane/175 W 73rd St, ...212-877-7624
Mitchell, Jack/356 E 74th St, ...212-737-8940
Molkenthin, Michael/31 W 31st St, ...212-727-2788
Moon, Sarah/315 Central Park W, ...212-213-0941
Moore, Carla/11 W 19th St, ...212-633-0300
Moore, Chris/20 W 22nd St #810, ...212-242-0553
Moore, Jimmy/38 E 19th St, ...212-674-7150
Moore, Robert/11 W 25th St, ...212-691-4373
Moore, Truman/873 Broadway 4th Fl, ...212-533-3655
Moran, Nancy/568 Broadway, ...212-505-9620
Morello, Joe/40 W 28th St, (P 14,15)   212-684-2340
Moretz, Charles/141 Wooster St, ...212-245-0981
Morgan, Jeff/27 W 20th St #604, ...212-924-4000
Morris, Bill/34 E 29th St 6th Fl, ...212-685-7354
Morris, Leonard/200 Park Ave S #1410, ...212-473-8485
Morris, R Kevin/100 W 80th St, ...212-683-8160
Morris, Robert Kevin/36 E 36th St, ...212-683-8160
Morrison, Ted/286 Fifth Ave, ...212-279-2838
Morsillo, Les/13 Laight St, ...212-219-8009
Morton, Keith/39 W 29th St 11th Fl, ...212-889-6643
Moscati, Frank/5 E 16th St, ...212-255-3434
Moskowitz, Sonia/5 W 86th St #18B, ...212-877-6883
Mougin, Claude/227 W 17th St, ...212-691-7895
Mroczynski, Claus/529 W 42nd St #2L, ...212-947-2767
Mucchi, Fabio/5 W 20th St, ...212-620-0167
Mucci, Tina/568 Broadway #604, ...212-206-9402
Mullane, Fred/116 E 27th St 8th Fl, ...212-580-4045
Muller, Rick/23 W 31st St #3, ...212-967-3177
Muller, Rudy/318 E 39th St, ...212-679-8124
Munro, Gordon/381 Park Ave S, ...212-889-1610
Munson, Russell/458 Broadway 5th Fl, ...212-226-8875
Murray, Robert/149 Franklin St, ...212-226-6860
Myers, Gary/105 W 70th St #1F, ...212-787-2712
Myers, Robert J/407 E 69th St, ...212-249-8085
Myriad Communications Inc/208 W 30th St, ...212-564-4340

N

Nadelson, Jay/116 Mercer St, ...212-226-4266
Nahem, Richard/21 W 16th St, ...212-206-0039
Nahoum, Ken/260 W Broadway #4G, ...212-219-0592
Naideau, Harold/233 W 26th St, ...212-691-2942
Nakamura, Tohru/112 Greene St, ...212-334-8011
Nakano, George/8 1/2 MacDougal Alley, ...212-228-9370
Namuth, Hans/20 W 22nd St, ...212-691-3220
Nanfra, Victor/222 E 46th St, ...212-687-8920
Naples, Elizabeth/210 Fifth Ave, ...212-889-1476
Nardi, Bob/568 Broadway, ...212-219-8298
Nault, Corky/251 W 19th St, ...212-807-7310
Needham, Steven Mark/111 W 19th St 2nd Fl, ...212-206-1914
Neil, Joseph/150 Fifth Ave #319, ...212-691-1881
Neleman, Hans/348 W 14th St, ...212-645-5832
Nelken, Dan Studio Inc/43 W 27th St, (P 122,123)....212-532-7471
Nesbit, Charles/62 Greene St, ...212-925-0225
Neumann, Peter/30 E 20th St 5th Fl, ...212-420-9538
Neumann, William/119 W 23rd St #206, ...212-691-7405
Newler, Michael/135 W 29th St 4th Fl, ...212-643-0022
Newman, Arnold/39 W 67th St, ...212-877-4510
Newman, Marvin E/227 Central Park West, ...212-219-1228
Ney, Nancy/108 E 16th St 6th Fl, ...212-260-4300
Ng, Norman Kaimen/36 E 20th St, ...212-473-4999
Niccolini, Dianora/2 W 32nd St #200, ...212-564-4953
Nicholas, Peter/29 Bleecker St, ...212-529-5560
Nicholson, Nick/121 W 72nd St #2E, ...212-362-8418
Nicolaysen, Ron/448 W 37th St #12A, ...212-947-5167
Niederman, Mark/230 W 72nd St, ...212-362-3902
Niefield, Terry/12 W 27th St 13th Fl, ...212-686-8722
Nilsen, Geoffrey/463 Broome St, ...212-226-3260
Nisnevich, Lev/133 Mulberry St, ...212-219-0535
Nivelle, Serge/145 Hudson St 14th Fl, ...212-473-2802
Niwa-Ogrudek Ltd/17 W 17th St, ...212-645-8008
Nobart NY Inc/33 E 18th St, ...212-475-5522
Nons, Leonard/5 Union Sq West, ...212-741-3990
Noren, Catherine/15 Barrow St, ...212-627-7805
Norstein, Marshall/248 6th Ave, Brooklyn....718-768-0786

O

O'Connor, Michael/216 E 29th St, ...212-679-0396
O'Connor, Thom/74 Fifth Ave, ...212-620-0723
O'Neill, Michael/134 Tenth Ave, ...212-807-8777
O'Rourke, J Barry/578 Broadway #707, ...212-226-7113
Obremski, George/1200 Broadway #2A, ...212-684-2933
Ochi, Toru/109 W 27th St 6th Fl, ...212-807-7711
Oelbaum, Zeva/600 W 115th St #84L, ...212-864-7926
Ogilvy, Stephen/876 Broadway, ...212-643-9330
Ohringer, Frederick/514 Broadway, ...212-737-6487
Okada, Tom/45 W 18th St, ...212-569-0726
Olivo, John/545 W 45th St, ...212-765-8812
Olman, Bradley/15 W 24th St 11th Fl, ...212-243-0649
Ommer, Uwe/84 Riverside Dr, ...212-496-0268
Oner, Matt/231 E 14th St #4R, ...212-529-2844
Oppersdorff, Mathias/1220 Park Ave, ...212-860-4778
Oringer, Hal/568 Broadway #503, ...212-219-1588
Ort, Samuel/3323 Kings Hwy, Brooklyn....718-377-1218
Ortner, Jon/64 W 87th St, ...212-873-1950
Otfinowski, Danuta/165 W 20th St, ...212-243-6625
Otsuki, Toshi/241 W 36th St, ...212-594-1939
Oudi/704 Broadway 2nd Fl, ...212-777-0847
Outerbridge, Graeme/PO Box 182, Southampton 8,Bermda, ...809-298-0888
Owens, Sigrid/221 E 31st St, ...212-686-5190

P

Paccione/73 Fifth Ave, ...212-691-8674
Page, Lee/310 E 46th St, ...212-286-9159
Pagliuso, Jean/12 E 20th St, ...212-674-0370
Pagnano, Patrick/217 Thompson St, ...212-475-2566
Palmisano, Giorgio/309 Mott St #4A, ...212-431-7719
Palubniak, Jerry/144 W 27th St, ...212-645-2838
Palubniak, Nancy/144 W 27th St, (P 124)....212-645-2838
Papadopolous, Peter/78 Fifth Ave 9th Fl, ...212-675-8830
Pappas, Tony/110 W 31st St 3rd Fl, ...212-868-2032
Paras, Michael N/309 Fifth Ave #302, ...212-779-9135
Parks, Claudia/210 E 73rd St #1G, ...212-879-9841
Passmore, Nick/150 W 80th St, ...212-724-1401
Pastner, Robert L/166 E 63rd St, ...212-838-8335
Pastor, Mariano/20 W 22nd St, ...212-242-0553
Pateman, Michael/155 E 35th St, ...212-685-6584
Pearson, Lee/126 Fifth Ave, ...212-691-0122
Peden, John/155 W 19th St 6th Fl, ...212-255-2674
Pederson/Erwin/76 Ninth Ave 16th Fl, ...212-929-9001
Pelaez, Jose Luis/568 Broadway #103, ...212-995-2283
Peliz, Jose/172 E 7th St #4C, ...212-995-2283
Pellesier, Sam/22 W 21st St, ...212-242-7222
Pemberton, John/377 Park Ave S 2nd Fl, ...212-532-9285
Penn, Irving/89 Fifth Ave 11th Fl, ...212-880-8426
Penny, Donald Gordon/505 W 23rd St #PH, ...212-243-6453
Peoples, Joe/11 W 20th St 6th Fl, (P 125)....212-633-0026
Peress, Gilles/72 Spring St, ...212-966-9200
Perkell, Jeff/132 W 22nd St, ...212-645-1506
Perweiler, Gary/873 Broadway, ...212-254-7247
Peterson, Grant/568 Broadway #1003, ...212-475-2767
Peticolas, Kip/210 Forsyth St, ...212-473-5770
Petoe, Denes/39 E 29th St, ...212-213-3311
Pettinato, Anthony/42 Greene St, ...212-226-9380
Pfeffer, Barbara/40 W 86th St, ...212-877-9913
Pfizenmaier, Edward/42 E 23rd, ...212-475-0910
Phillips, James/82 Greene St, ...212-219-1799
Phillips, Robert/101 W 57th St, ...212-757-5190
Pich, Tom/310 E 65th St, ...212-288-3376
Piel, Denis/458 Broadway 9th Fl, ...212-925-8929
Pierce, Richard/241 W 36th St #8F, ...212-947-8241
Pilgreen, John/91 Fifth Ave #300, ...212-982-4887
Pilossof, Judd/142 W 26th St, ...212-989-8971
Pinderhugh, John/122 W 12th St 12th Fl, ...212-989-6706
Pioppo, Peter/50 W 17th St, (P 20)....212-243-0661
Pipinou, Tom/568 Broadway, ...212-431-4518
Piscioneri, Joe/333 Park Ave S, ...212-473-3345
Pite, Jonathan/244 E 21st St #7, ...212-777-5484
Pittman, Dustin/41 Union Square W #636, ...212-243-2956
Pix Elation/230 Park Ave #2525, ...212-581-6470
Pizzolorusso, Chris/381 Park Ave S, ...212-686-7175
Plotkin, Bruce/3 W 18th St 7th Fl, ...212-691-6185
Plotkin, Burt/141 Wooster St, ...212-260-5900
Pobereskin, Joseph/453 Washington Ave #4A, Brooklyn....212-619-3711
Pobiner, Bill/381 Park Ave S, ...212-679-5911
Poli, Bruce/110 Christopher St #55, ...212-242-6853
Polsky, Herb/1024 Sixth Ave, ...212-730-0508
Popper, Andrew J/330 First Ave, ...212-420-8565
Porta, Art/29 E 32nd St, ...212-353-0488
Portnoy, Neal/1 Hudson St, ...212-619-4661
Porto, James/87 Franklin St, ...212-966-4407
Poster, James Studio/210 Fifth Ave #402, ...212-206-4065
Pottle, Jock/301 W 89th St #15, ...212-874-0216
Powell, Dean/32 Union Sq East, ...212-239-9760
Powers, Guy/534 W 43rd St, (P 34,35)....212-563-3177
Pressman, Herb/137 E 30th St, ...212-945-4228
Prezant, Steve Studios/666 Greenwich St #720, ...212-727-0590
Pribula, Barry/59 First Ave, ...212-777-7612
Price, Clayton J/205 W 19th St, (P 128,129)....212-929-7721
Price, David/4 E 78th St, ...212-794-9040
Priggen, Leslie/215 E 73rd St, ...212-772-2230
Prochnow, Bob/43-40 161st St, Flushing....212-627-3244
Prozo, Marco/122 Duane St, ...212-766-4490
Pruitt, David/PO Box 832/Madison Sq Station, ...212-979-2921
Pruzan, Michael/1181 Broadway 8th Fl, ...212-686-5505
Psihoyos, Louis/521 W 23rd St, ...212-242-9090
Pugliese, Lara/354 Butler St, Brooklyn....718-636-8498
Puhlmann, Rico/530 Broadway 10th Fl, ...212-941-9433
Purvis, Charles/84 Thomas St #3, ...212-619-8028
Putnam, Quentin/1141 Brooklyn Ave, Brooklyn....718-693-7567

QR

Quat, Dan/57 Leonard St, ...212-431-7780
Raab, Michael/831 Broadway, ...212-533-0030
Rajs, Jake/252 W 30th St #10A, ...212-947-9403
Rapoport, David/55 Perry St #2D, ...212-691-5528
Rasbeck, Mark/45 E 25th St #10C, ...212-779-1796
Rattner, Robert/106-15 Jamaica Ave, Richmond Hill....718-441-0826
Ratzkin, Lawrence/392 Fifth Ave, ...212-279-1314
Ravid, Joyce/12 E 20th St, ...212-477-4233
Ray, Bill/350 Central Park West, ...212-222-7680

Raymond, Lilo/212 E 14th St, ...212-362-9546
Rea, Jimmy/151 W 19th St 10th Fl, ...212-627-1473
Reed, Robert/25-09 27th St, Astoria........................718-278-2455
Reeks, Deck/145 W 58th St, ...212-459-9816
Regan, Ken/6 W 20th St 8th Fl, ...212-989-2004
Reichert, Robert/149 W 12th St, ...212-645-9515
Reinhardt, Mike/881 Seventh Ave #405, ...212-541-4787
Reinmiller, Mary Ann/163 W 17th St, ...212-243-4302
Rentmeester, Co/4479 Douglas Ave, Riverdale 212-757-4796
Reznicki, Jack/568 Broadway #404, (P 130,131) 212-925-0771
Rezny, Aaron/119 W 23rd St #203, (P 60) 212-691-1894
Rezny, Abe/28 Cadman Plz W/Eagle Wrhse, Brooklyn Heights 212-226-7747
Rhodes, Arthur/325 E 64th St, ...212-249-3974
Ricucci, Vincent/109 W 27th St 10th Fl, ...212-807-8295
Riddle, Richard/208 E 82nd St #23, ...212-628-9370
Ries, Henry/204 E 35th St, ...212-689-3794
Ries, Stan/48 Great Jones St, ...212-533-1852
Riggs, Cole/39 W 29th St, ...212-481-6119
Riggs, Robert/502 Laguardia Pl, ...212-254-7352
Riley, David & Carin/152 W 25th St, ...212-741-3662
Riley, Jon/12 E 37th St, (P 132,133) 212-532-8326
Rivelli, William/303 Park Ave S #508, ...212-254-0990
Roberts, Grant/120 Eleventh Ave, ...212-620-7921
Robinson, CeOtis/4-6 W 101st St #49A, ...212-663-1231
Robinson, Herb/11 W 25th St, ...212-627-1478
Robinson, James/155 Riverside Dr, ...212-580-1793
Robison, Chuck/21 Stuyvesant Oval, ...212-777-4894
Rockfield, Bert/31 E 32nd St, ...212-689-3900
Rodin, Christine/38 Morton St, ...212-242-3260
Rohr, Robert/325 E 10th St #5W, ...212-674-1519
Rolo Photo/214 W 17th St, ...212-691-8355
Romanelli, Marc/244 Riverside Dr, ...212-865-5214
Rose, Uli/975 Park Ave #8A, ...212-988-8890
Rosenberg, Ken/514 West End Ave, ...212-362-3149
Rosenthal, Barry/205 W 19th St, ...212-645-0433
Rosenthal, Marshall M/231 W 18th St, ...212-807-1247
Ross, Ken/80 Madison Ave 7th Fl, ...212-213-9205
Ross, Mark/345 E 80th St, ...212-744-7258
Ross, Steve/10 Montgomery Pl, Brooklyn 718-783-6451
Rossi, Emanuel/78-29 68th Rd, Flushing 718-894-6163
Rossum, Cheryl/310 E 75th St, ...212-628-3173
Roth, Seth/137 W 25th St, ...212-620-7050
Rothaus, Ede/34 Morton St, ...212-989-8277
Roto Ad Print Studio/252 W 37th St, ...212-279-6590
Roundtree, Deborah/1316 Third St #3, Santa Monica, CA......213-394-3088
Rozsa, Nick/325 E 64th St, ...212-734-5629
Rubenstein, Raeanne/8 Thomas St, ...212-964-8426
Rubin, Al/250 Mercer St #1501, ...212-674-4535
Rubin, Daniel/126 W 22nd St 6th Fl, ...212-989-2400
Rubyan, Robert/270 Park Ave S #7C, ...212-460-9217
Rudnick, James/799 Union Street, Brooklyn 212-466-6337
Rudolph, Nancy/35 W 11th St, ...212-989-0392
Rugen-Kory/150 E 18th St, ...212-242-2772
Ruggeri, Francesco/71 St Marks Pl #9, ...212-505-8477
Rumbough, Stan/154 W 18th St #8A, ...212-206-0183
Russell, Ted/67-25 Clyde St, Forest Hills...................718-263-3725
Ryan, Will/16 E 17th St 2nd Fl, ...212-242-6270
Rysinski, Edward/109 W 27th St 2nd Fl, ...212-807-7301
Ryuzo/119 W 22nd St 5th Fl, ...212-807-7012

S

Sabal, David/20 W 20th St #501, ...212-242-8464
Sacco, Vittorio/126 Fifth Ave #602, ...212-929-9225
Sacha, Bob/370 Central Park W, ...212-749-4128
Sahaida, Michael/5 W 19th St 5th Fl, ...212-924-4545
Sailors, David/123 Prince St, ...212-505-9654
Sakas, Peter/400 Lafayette St, ...212-254-6096
Salaff, Fred/322 W 57th St, ...212-246-3699
Salaverry, Philip/133 W 22nd St, ...212-807-0896
Salvati, Jerry/206 E 26th St, ...212-696-0454
Salzano, Jim/29 W 15th St, ...212-242-4820
Samardge, Nick/568 Broadway #706, ...212-226-6770
Sanchez, Alfredo/14-23 30th Dr, L I City 718-726-0182
Sander, JT/172 E 4th St, ...212-673-0264
Sanders, Chris/130 W 23rd St #2, ...212-645-6111
Sandone, A J/132 W 21st St 9th Fl, ...212-807-6472
Sanford, Tobey/888 Eighth Ave #166, ...212-245-2736
Santos, Antonio/202 E 21st St, ...212-477-3514

Sarapochiello, Jerry/47-A Beach St, ...212-219-8545
Sartor, Vittorio/10 Bleecker St #1-D, ...212-674-2994
Sato Photo/152 W 26th St, ...212-741-0688
Satterwhite, Al/80 Varick St #7B, ...212-219-0808
Savides, Harris/648 Broadway #1009, ...212-260-6816
Saylor, H Durston/219 W 16th St #4B, ...212-620-7122
Scanlan, Richard/218 Kingsland Ave, Brooklyn 718-383-8329
Scarlett, Nora/37 W 20th St, ...212-741-2620
Scavullo, Francesco/212 E 63rd St, ...212-838-2450
Schecter, Lee/13-17 Laight St 3rd Fl, ...212-431-0088
Scheer, Stephen/261 Broadway #10E, ...212-233-7195
Schein, Barry/118-60 Metropolitan Ave, Kew Gardens......718-849-7808
Schenk, Fred/112 Fourth Ave, ...212-677-1250
Schiavone, Carmen/271 Central Park West, ...212-496-6016
Schild, Irving/34 E 23rd St, ...212-475-0090
Schillaci, Michael/320 W 30th St #3A, ...212-564-2364
Schillaci/Jones Photo/400 E 71st St #14-O, ...212-734-2798
Schinz, Marina/222 Central Park S, ...212-246-0457
Schlachter, Trudy/160 Fifth Ave, ...212-741-3128
Schneider, Josef/119 W 57th St, ...212-265-1223
Schneider, Peter/902 Broadway, ...212-982-9040
Schneider, Roy/59 W 19th St, ...212-691-9588
Schreck, Bruno/873 Broadway #304, ...212-254-3078
Schulze, Fred/38 W 21st St, ...212-242-0930
Schupf, John/568 Broadway #106, ...212-226-2250
Schurink, Yonah (Ms)/666 West End Ave, ...212-362-2860
Schwartz, Marvin/223 W 10th St, ...212-929-8916
Schwartz, Sing-Si/15 Gramercy Park S, ...212-228-4466
Schwerin, Ron/889 Broadway, ...212-228-0340
Sclight, Greg/146 W 29th St, ...212-736-2957
Scocozza, Victor/117 E 30th St, ...212-686-9440
Secunda, Sheldon/112 Fourth Ave, ...212-477-0241
Seesselberg, Charles/236 W 27th St, ...212-807-8730
Seghers, Carroll/441 Park Ave S, ...212-679-4582
Seidman, Barry/85 Fifth Ave, ...212-255-6666
Seitz, Sepp/12 E 22nd St #9F, ...212-505-9917
Selby, Richard/113 Greene St, ...212-431-1719
Seligman, Paul/163 W 17th St, ...212-242-5688
Selkirk, Neil/515 W 19th St, ...212-243-6778
Seltzer, Abe/443 W 18th St, ...212-807-0660
Seltzer, Kathleen/25 E 4th St, ...212-475-0314
Sewart, David Harry/100 Chambers St, ...212-619-7783
Sewell, Jim/720 W 181st St, ...212-923-7686
Shaffer, Stan/2211 Broadway, ...212-580-5522
Shaman, Harvey/109 81st Ave, Kew Gardens 718-793-0434
Shapiro, Pam/11 W 30th St 2nd Fl, ...212-967-2363
Share, Jed/Tokyo/63 Adrian Ave, Bronx 212-562-8931
Sharko, Greg/103-56 103rd St, Ozone Pk 718-738-9694
Shelley, George/873 Braodway 8th Fl, ...212-473-0519
Shere, Gary/217-08 75th Ave top fl, Bayside 718-776-3766
Sherman, Guy/108 E 16th St 6th Fl, ...212-675-4983
Shiki/119 W 23rd St #504, ...212-929-8847
Shipley, Christopher/18-23 Astoria Blvd, Long Island City......718-626-9427
Shiraishi, Carl/137 E 25th St 11th Fl, ...212-679-5628
Shung, Ken/236 W 27th St, ...212-807-1449
Silano, Bill/138 E 27th St, ...212-889-0505
Silbert, Layle/505 LaGuardia Pl, ...212-677-0947
Silver, Larry/236 W 26th St, ...212-807-9560
Silverman, Jeff/1 East Front St, Keyport, NJ...............201-264-3939
Simko, Robert/437 Washington St, ...212-431-6974
Simon, Peter Angelo/568 Broadway #701, ...212-925-0890
Simone, Luisa/222 E 27th St #18, ...212-679-9117
Simons, Chip/26 W 27th St, ...212-696-0259
Simpson, Coreen/599 West End Ave, ...212-877-6210
Simpson, Jerry/244 Mulberry St, ...212-941-1255
Singer, Michelle/251 W 19th St #5C, ...212-969-9522
Sint, Steven/45 W 17th St 5th Fl, Great Neck 212-463-8844
Sit, Danny/280 Park Ave S #11J, ...212-979-5533
Skalski, Ken/866 Broadway, (P 135) 212-777-6207
Skelley, Ariel/80 Varick St #6A, ...212-226-4091
Skinner, Marc/216 Van Buren St, Brooklyn 718-455-7749
Skogsbergh, Ulf/5 E 16th St, ...212-255-7536
Skolnik, Lewis/135 W 29th St, ...212-239-1455
Skott, Michael/244 Fifth Ave #PH, ...212-686-4807
Slade, Chuck/12 E 14th St #4B, ...212-807-1153
Slavin, Fred/28 W 25th St 11th Fl, ...212-627-2652
Slavin, Neal/62 Greene St, ...212-925-8167
Sleppin, Jeff/3 W 30th St, ...212-947-1433

Sloan-White, Barbara/372 Fifth Ave, ...212-760-0057
Slotnick, Jeff/115 E 34th St 10K, ...212-966-5162
Small, John/298 Fifth Ave, ...212-645-4720
Smilow, Stanford/333 E 30th St/Box 248, ...212-685-9425
Smith, Jeff/30 E 21st St, ...212-674-8383
Smith, Kevin/446 W 55th St, ...212-757-4812
Smith, Michael/140 Claremont #5A, ...212-724-2800
Smith, Rita/666 West End Ave #10N, ...212-580-4842
Smith, Sean/365 First Ave, ...212-505-5688
Smith, William E/498 West End Ave, ...212-877-8456
Snider, Lee/221 W 82nd St #9D, ...212-873-6141
Snyder, Norman/98 Riverside Dr #16C, ...212-219-0094
So Studio/34 E 23rd St, ...212-475-0090
SO Studio Inc/34 E 23rd St, ...212-475-0090
Sobel, Jane/2 W 45th St #1200, ...212-382-3939
Sochurek, Howard/680 Fifth Ave, ...212-582-1860
Solomon, Chuck/622 Greenwich St, ...212-243-4036
Solomon, Paul/440 W 34th St #13E, ...212-760-1203
Solowinski, Ray/154 W 57th St #826, ...212-757-7940
Soluri, Michael/95 Horatio St #633, ...212-645-7999
Somekh, Rick/13 Laight St, ...212-219-1613
Soot, Olaf/419 Park Ave S, ...212-686-4565
Sorce, Wayne/20 Henry St #5G, Brooklyn 718-237-0497
Sorensen, Chris/PO Box 1760, ...212-684-0551
Sotres, Craig/440 Lafayette St 6th Fl, ...212-979-6161
Spagnolo, David/144 Reade St, ...212-226-4392
Spatz, Eugene/264 Sixth Ave, ...212-777-6793
Specht, Diane/167 W 71st St #10, ...212-877-8381
Speier, Leonard/190 Riverside Dr, ...212-595-5480
Spelman, Steve/260 W 10th St, ...212-242-9381
Spielman, Les/5 W 30th St 4th Fl, ...212-947-3470
Spindel, David M/18 E 17th St, ...212-989-4984
Spinelli, Frank/12 W 21st St 12th Fl, ...212-243-8318
Spinelli, Paul/1619 Third Ave #21K, ...212-410-3320
Spreitzer, Andy/225 E 24th St, ...212-685-9669
Springston, Dan/135 Madison Ave/Penthouse So, ...212-689-0685
St John, Lynn/308 E 59th St, ...212-308-7744
Stahman, Robert/1200 Broadway #2D, ...212-679-1484
Standart, Joe/5 W 19th St 5th Fl, ...212-924-4545
Stanton, Brian/175 Fifth Ave #3086, ...212-678-7574
Stanton, William/160 W 95th St #9D, ...212-662-3571
Stark, Philip/245 W 29th St 15th Fl, ...212-868-5555
Starkoff, Robert/140 Fifth Ave, ...212-741-0669
Steadler, Lance/154 W 27th St, ...212-243-0935
Stechow, Kirsten/249 W 29th St, ...
Steedman, Richard C/214 E 26th St, ...212-684-7878
Steele, Kim/640 Broadway #7W, ...212-777-7753
Stegemeyer, Werner/377 Park Ave S, ...212-686-2247
Steigman, Steve/5 E 19th St #303, ...212-473-3366
Stein, Larry/568 Broadway #706, ...212-219-9077
Steinbrenner, Karl/225 E 24th St 3rd Fl, ...212-779-1120
Steiner, Charles/61 Second Ave, ...212-777-0813
Steiner, Christian/300 Central Park West, ...212-724-1990
Stember, John/881 Seventh Ave #1003, ...212-757-0067
Stephanie Studios/277 W 10th St #2D, ...212-929-1029
Stephens, Greg/450 W 31st St 10th Fl, ...212-239-0999
Stern, Anna/261 Broadway #3C, ...212-349-1134
Stern, Bert/66 Crosby St, ...212-925-5909
Stern, Bob/12 W 27th St, ...212-889-0860
Stern, Cynthia/515 Broadway #2B, ...212-925-2677
Stern, John/451 W Broadway, ...212-477-0656
Stern, Laszlo/57 W 19th St, (P 46) **212-691-7696**
Sternfeld, Joel/353 E 77th St, ...212-517-3648
Stetson, David/250 Eighth Ave, ...212-989-4172
Stettner, Bill/118 E 25th St, ...212-460-8180
Stevenson, Monica/130 W 25th St 4th Fl, ...212-633-0879
Stiles, James/413 W 14th St, ...212-627-1766
Stone, Erika/327 E 82nd St, ...212-737-6435
Stratos, Jim/150 W 36th St, ...212-695-5674
Strode, Mark/2026 E 29th St, Brooklyn 718-332-1241
Stroili, Elaine/416 E 85th St #3G, ...212-879-8587
Strongin, Jeanne/61 Irving Pl, (P 139) **212-473-3718**
Stuart, John/80 Varick St #4B, ...212-966-6783
Stucker, Hal/295 Washington Ave #5D, Brooklyn 718-789-1180
Studer, Lillian/305 E 24th St, ...212-683-2082
Stupakoff, Otto/80 Varick St, ...212-334-8032
Sugarman, Lynn/40 W 22nd St, ...212-691-3245
Summerline, Sam/237 Park Ave #2100, ...212-551-1446
Sun Photo/29 E 22nd St #2-N, ...212-505-9585

Sussman, Daniel/369 Seventh Ave 3rd Fl, ...212-947-5546
Sussman, David/115 E 23rd St, ...212-675-5863
Svensson, Steen/52 Grove St, ...212-242-7272
Swedowsky, Ben/381 Park Ave S, ...212-684-1454
Swick, Danille/276 First Ave #11A, ...212-777-0653
Sylvestre, Lorraine/25 W 23rd St 2nd Fl, ...212-555-1212
Symons, Abner/27 E 21st St 10th Fl, ...212-777-6660

T

Tannenbaum, Ken/16 W 21st St, ...212-675-2345
Tanous, Dorothy/652 Hudson St #3W, ...212-255-9409
Tara Universal Studios/34 E 23rd St, ...212-260-8280
Tardio, Robert/19 W 21st St, ...212-463-9085
Taufic, William/166 W 22nd St, ...212-620-8143
Taylor, Curtice/29 E 22nd St #2S, ...212-473-6886
Taylor, Jonathan/5 W 20th St 2nd Fl, ...212-741-2805
Tcherevkoff, Michel/873 Broadway, (P 140,141) **212-228-0540**
Teboul, Daniel/42 E 23rd St #7S, ...212-353-1040
Tegni, Ricardo/100 E Mosholu Pkwy S #6F, ...212-367-8972
Temogen/102-01 101st Ave, Ozone Park 718-805-1057
Terk, Neil/400 E 59th St, ...914-633-4448
Tervenski, Steve/421 E 54th St, ...212-753-6990
Tessler, Stefan/115 W 23rd St, ...212-924-9168
Testa, Michelle/200 W 16th St, ...212-627-9413
The Strobe Studio/91 Fifth Ave, ...212-532-1977
Thomas, Mark/141 W 26th St 4th Fl, ...212-741-7252
Thompson, Eleanor/147 W 25th St, ...212-675-6773
Thompson, Kenneth/220 E 95th St, ...212-348-3530
Tighe, Michael/110 E 1st St #12, ...212-254-4252
Tillinghast, Paul/20 W 20th St 7th Fl, (P 45) **212-741-3764**
Tillman, Denny/39 E 20th St, ...212-674-7160
Togashi/36 W 20th St, (P 143) **212-929-2290**
Tornberg-Coghlan Assoc/6 E 39th St, ...212-685-7333
Toto, Joe/13-17 Laight St, ...212-966-7626
Trachman, Emanuel/63 Haven Esplanade, Staten Island 718-447-1393
Truran, Bill/54 Green St, ...212-406-2440
Trzeciak, Erwin/145 E 16th St, ...212-254-4140
Tullis, Marcus/13 Laight St 3rd fl, ...212-966-8511
Tully, Roger/344 W 38th St #10D, (P 30,31) **212-947-3961**
Tung, Matthew/78 Fifth Ave 7th Fl, ...212-741-0570
Turbeville, Deborah/160 Fifth Ave #914, ...212-924-6760
Turin, Miranda/71 W 10th St #2, ...212-979-9712
Turner, Pete Photography/154 W 57th St, ...212-765-1733
Tweedy-Holmes, Karen/180 Claremont Ave #51, ...212-866-2289
Tweel, Ron/241 W 36th St, ...212-563-3452
Tyler, Mark/233 Broadway #822, ...212-962-3690

UV

Uher, John/529 W 42nd St, ...212-594-7377
Umans, Marty/29 E 19th St, ...212-995-0100
Unangst, Andrew/381 Park Ave S, ...212-889-4888
Ursillo, Catherine/1040 Park Ave, ...212-722-9297
Urwuand, Dan/250 W 40th St, ...212-921-2730
Vaeth, Peter/295 Madison Ave, ...212-685-4700
Vail, Baker /111 W 24th St, (P 48) **212-463-7560**
Valente, Jerry/193 Meserole Ave, Brooklyn 718-389-0469
Valentin, Augusto/202 E 29th St 6th Fl, ...212-888-1371
Valeska, Shonna/140 E 28th St, (P 47) **212-683-4448**
Vallini Productions/43 E 20th St 2nd Fl, ...212-674-6581
Van Der Heyden, Frans/60-66 Crosby St #4D, ...212-226-8302
Van Otteren, Juliet/568 Broadway, ...212-627-1958
Vanglintenkamp, Rik/377 Rector Pl, ...212-945-1917
Varnedoe, Sam/12 W 27th St #603, ...212-679-1230
Varon, Malcolm/125 Fifth Ave, ...212-473-5957
Vartoogian, Jack/262 W 107th St #6A, ...212-663-1341
Vega, Julio/417 Third Ave #3B, ...212-645-1867
Veldenzer, Alan/160 Bleecker St, ...212-420-8189
Vendikos, Tasso/59 W 19th St, ...212-206-6451
Veronsky, Frank/1376 York Ave, ...212-744-3810
Vest, Michael/343 E 65th St #4RE, ...212-532-8331
Vhandy Productions/401 E 57th St, ...212-759-6150
Vickers, Camille/200 W 79th St PH #A, ...212-580-8649
Vidal, Bernard/450 W 31st St #9C, ...212-629-3764
Vidol, John/37 W 26th St, ...212-889-0065
Viesti, Joe/PO Box 20424, Cherokee Sta 212-734-4890
Vincent, Chris/119 W 23rd St #203, (P 61) **212-633-9880**
Vine, David/873 Broadway 2nd Fl, ...212-505-8070
Vishniac, Roman/219 W 81st St, ...212-787-0997
Visual Impact Productions/15 W 18th St 10th Fl, ...212-243-8441

Vitale, Peter/157 E 71st St, ...212-249-8412
Vogel, Allen/348 W 14th St, ...212-675-7550
Vogel, Rich/119 W 23rd St #800, ...415-435-9207
Volchek, Boris/200 E Broadway, ...212-475-2027
Volpi, Rene/121 Madison Ave #11-I, ...212-532-7367
Von Hassell, Agostino/277 W 10th St PH-D, ...212-242-7290
Vos, Gene/440 Park Ave S, ...212-714-1155

W

Wagner Int'l Photos/216 E 45th St 14th Fl, ...212-661-6100
Wagner, Daniel/50 W 29th St, ...212-532-8255
Wagner, David A/568 Broadway #103, (P 144,145) 212-925-5149
Wahlund, Olof/7 E 17th St, ...212-929-9067
Waine, Michael/873 Broadway, ...212-533-4200
Waldo, Maje/PO Box 1156 Cooper Sta, ...212-353-9868
Waldron, William/463 Broome St, ...212-226-0356
Wallace, Randall/43 W 13th St #3F, ...212-242-2930
Wallach, Louis/417 Lafayette St, ...212-925-9553
Walsh, Bob/401 E 34th St, ...212-684-3015
Waltzer, Bill/110 Greene St #96, ...212-925-1242
Waltzer, Carl/873 Broadway #412, ...212-475-8748
Walz, Barbra/143 W 20th St, ...212-242-7175
Wan, Stan/310 East 46th St, (P 21) 212-986-5680
Wang, John Studio Inc/30 E 20th St, ...212-982-2765
Wang, Tony/118 E 28th St #908, ...212-213-4433
Warchol, Paul/133 Mulberry St, ...212-431-3461
Ward, Bob Studio/151 W 25th St, ...212-473-7584
Warinsky, Jim/38 W 26th St, ...212-206-6448
Warkov, Aaron/206 W 15th St 4th Fl, ...212-727-0044
Warsaw Photographic Assocs/36 E 31st St, ...212-725-1888
Warwick, Cyndy/144 E 22nd St, ...212-420-4760
Watanabe, Nana/130 W 25th St 10th Fl, ...212-741-3248
Watson, Albert M/80-82 Greene St, ...212-925-8552
Watson, Michael/133 W 19th St, ...212-620-3125
Watt, Elizabeth/141 W 26th St, ...212-929-8504
Watts, Cliff/360 W 36th St, ...212-629-8116
Watts, Judy/311 E 83rd St #5C, ...212-439-1851
Waxman, Dani/242 E 19th St, ...212-995-2221
Wayne, Meri/134 E 22nd St #503, ...212-979-7707
Weaks, Dan/5 E 19th St, ...212-473-3366
Webb, Alex/79 Spring St, ...212-966-9200
Weber, Bruce/135 Watts St, ...212-685-5025
Weckler, Chad/210 E 63rd St, ...212-355-1135
Weidlein, Peter/122 W 26th St, ...212-989-5498
Weinberg, Carol/40 W 17th St, ...212-206-8200
Weinberg, Michael/5 E 16th St, ...212-691-1000
Weinberg, Steve/47 E 19th St 3rd Fl, ...212-254-9571
Weinstein, Michael/508 Broadway, ...212-925-2612
Weinstein, Todd/47 Irving Pl, ...212-254-7526
Weiss, Michael Photo/10 W 18th St 2nd Fl, ...212-929-4073
Wellington, Lee/303 Broadway 7th Fl, ...718-760-2762
Werner, Perry/PO Box 3992, ...212-379-7434
West, Bonnie/156 Fifth Ave #1232, (P 147) 212-929-3338
Westheimer, Bill/167 Spring St, ...212-431-6360
Wexler, Jayne/24 Prince St, ...212-334-0229
Wexler, Mark/484 W 43rd St, ...212-564-7733
Wheatman, Truckin/251 W 30th St #4FW, ...212-239-1081
Whitaker, Ross/206 W 15th St 4th Fl, ...212-727-0044
White, Bill/34 W 17th St, ...212-243-1780
White, David/31 W 21st St, ...212-727-3454
White, John/11 W 20th St 6th Fl, ...212-691-1133
White, Timothy/448 W 37th St, ...212-971-9039
Whitehurst, William/32 W 20th St, ...212-206-8825
Whitely Presentations/60 E 42nd St #419, ...212-490-3111
Whitman, Robert/1181 Broadway 7th Fl, ...212-213-6611
Whyte, Douglas/519 Broadway, ...212-431-1667
Wick, Kevin/484 E 24th St, Brooklyn...........................718-858-6989
Wick, Walter/560 Broadway #404, (P 148,149) 212-966-8770
Wien, Jeffrey/160 Fifth Ave #912, ...212-243-7028
Wier, John Arthur/36 W 25th St 11th Fl, ...212-691-1901
Wier, Terry/20 W 20th St 2nd Fl, ...212-685-6021
Wiesehahn, Charles/249 W 29th St #2E, ...212-563-6612
Wilcox, Shorty/DPI/19 W 21st St #901, ...212-627-4060
Wilkes, Stephen/48 E 13th St, ...212-475-4010
Wilks, Harry/234 W 21st St, ...212-929-4772
Williamson, Richie/514 W 24th St, ...212-807-0816
Wills, Bret/245 W 29th St 12th Fl, (P 12,13) 212-629-4878
Wilson, Mike/441 Park Ave S, ...212-683-3557
Wing, Peter/56-08 138th St, Flushing 718-762-3617

Winstead, Jimmy/76 Charles St, ...212-929-2810
Wisenbaugh, Jean/41 Union Square W #1228, ...212-929-5590
Wohl, Marty/40 E 21st St 6th Fl, ...212-460-9269
Wojcik, James/256 Mott St, ...212-431-0108
Wolf, Bruce/123 W 28th St, ...212-695-8042
Wolf, Henry/58 W 15th St 6th Fl, ...212-741-2539
Wolff, Brian R/560 W 43rd St #5K, ...212-465-8976
Wolfson, Robert/133 W 19th St, ...212-924-1510
Wolfson, Steve and Jeff/13-17 Laight St 5th Fl, ...212-226-0077
Wong, Daniel Photography/652 Broadway #3, ...212-260-7058
Wong, Leslie/303 W 78th St, ...212-595-0434
Wood, Merrell/319 W 38th St/Twnhse, ...212-868-0262
Wood, Susan/641 Fifth Ave, ...212-371-0679
Woodward, Herbert/555 Third Ave, ...212-685-4385
Workman, Wendy/203 7th Ave, Brooklyn 718-965-0257
Wormser, Richard L/800 Riverside Dr, ...212-928-0056
Wyman, Ron/36 Riverside Dr, ...212-799-8281
Wynn, Dan/170 E 73rd St, ...212-535-1551

Y

Yamashiro, Tad/224 E 12th St, ...212-473-7177
Yee, Tom/141 W 28th St, ...212-947-5400
Yoav/4523 Broadway, ...212-942-8185
Yoshitomo Photography/37 W 20th St, ...212-505-8800
Young, Donald/166 E 61st St Box 148, ...212-593-0010
Young, James/56 W 22nd St, ...212-924-5444
Young, Ken/333 Park Ave South, ...212-475-0071
Young, Randi/223 Water St, Brooklyn..........................718-237-9018
Young, Rick/27 W 20th St #1003, (P 36,37) 212-929-5701
Young, Steve/164 W 25th St 11th Fl, ...212-691-5860
Youngblood, Lee/200 W 70th St #8F, ...212-595-7913

Z

Zager, Howard/245 W 29th St, ...212-239-8082
Zamdmer, Mona/71 E 7th St, ...212-982-7318
Zan/108 E 16th St 6th Fl, ...212-477-3333
Zander, George/141 W 28th St, ...212-971-0874
Zander, Peter/312 E 90th St #4A, ...212-348-2647
Zanetti, Gerry/36 E 20th St 3rd Fl, ...212-473-4999
Zapp, Carl/119 W 22nd St #2, ...212-924-4240
Zappa, Tony/143 Parkway Dr, Roslyn Heights 516-484-4907
Zegre, Francois/124 E 27th St, ...212-684-6517
Zehnder, Bruno/PO Box 5996, ...212-840-1234
Zeray, Peter/113 E 12th St, ...212-674-0332
Zimmerman, David/119 W 23rd St #909, ...212-268-6130
Zimmerman, Marilyn/511 W 33rd St 5th Fl, ...212-268-6130
Zingler, Joseph/18 Desbrosses St, ...212-226-3867
Zitz, Peter/PO Box 3195Ctr Station, ...212-543-7896
Zoiner, John/12 W 44th St, ...212-972-0357
Zwiebel, Michael/42 E 23rd St, ...212-477-5629

N O R T H E A S T

A

Aaron, Peter/222 Valley Pl, Mamaroneck, NY...............914-698-4060
Abarno, Richard/11 Dean Ave, Newport, RI 401-846-5820
Abbey Photographers/268 Broad Ave, Palisades Park, NJ 201-947-1221
Abbott, James/303 N 3rd St, Philadelphia, PA 215-925-9706
Abdelnour, Doug/Rt 22 PO Box 64, Bedford Village, NY 914-234-3123
Abel, Pat/23 N Wycome Ave, Landsdowne, PA 215-928-0499
Abell, Ted/51 Russell Rd, Bethany, CT 203-777-1988
Abend, Jay/18 Central St, Southborough, MA 508-624-0464
Abraham, Jack/229 Inza St, Highland Park, NJ 201-572-6093
Abrams, Larry/7 River St, Milford, CT 203-878-5090
Abramson, Dean/PO Box 610, Raymond, ME...............207-655-7386
Accame, Deborah/5161 River Rd Bldg 2B, Bethesda, MD 301-652-1303
Adamczyk, Wes/260-262 North Ave, Dunellen, NJ 201-968-4060
Adams Studio Inc/1523 22nd St NW Courtyard, Washington, DC....202-785-2188
Adams, Neill/2305 Coleridge Dr, Silver Spring, MD 301-206-5104
Addis, Kory/144 Lincoln St #4, Boston, MA 617-451-5142
Afanador, Reuven/3251 Prospect St NW, Washington, DC 202-337-3468
Agelopas, Michael/2510 N Charles St,
Baltimore, MD (P 200) 301-235-2823
Ahrens, Gene/544 Mountain Ave, Berkeley Heights, NJ.............201-464-4763
Aiello, Frank/35 S Van Brunt St, Englewood, NJ 201-894-5120

Akis, Emanuel/145 Lodi St, Hackensack, NJ 201-342-8070
Alcarez, Mark/86 Bartlett St, Charlestown, MA 617-241-8303
Alexander, Jules/9 Belmont Ave, Rye, NY 914-967-8985
Alexanian, Nubar/59 High St, Gloucester, MA 508-281-6152
Allen, C J/89 Orchard St, Boston, MA 617-524-1925
Allen, Carole/11 Crescent St, Keene, NH 603-357-1375
Allen, Tom/PO Box 518, Levittown, PA 215-945-5529
Allsopp, Jean Mitchell/16 Maple St/RR 2/PO Box 224, Shirley, MA ..617-425-2296
Alonso, Manuel/425 Fairfield Ave, Stamford, CT 203-359-2838
Althaus, Mike/5161 River Rd Bldg 2B, Bethesda, MD 301-652-1303
Altman, Steve/371 Fourth St, Jersey City, NJ 201-798-4477
Ambrose, Ken/129 Valerie Court, Cranston, RI 401-826-0606
Ames, Thomas Jr/85 Mechanic St, Lebanon, NH 603-448-6168
Amicucci, Nick/55 Fourth Ave, Garwood, NJ 201-789-1669
Amranand, Ping/4502 Saul Rd, Kensington, MD 301-564-0938
Ancker, Clint/3 Hunter Trl, Warren, NJ 201-356-4280
Ancona, George/Crickettown Rd, Stony Point, NY 914-786-3043
Andersen-Bruce, Sally/19 Old Mill Rd, New Milford, CT 203-355-1525
Anderson, Bill/27 Minkel Rd, Ossining, NY 914-762-4867
Anderson, Lee/, Washington, DC 202-547-1989
Anderson, Monica/11 Ranelegh Rd, Boston, MA 617-787-5510
Anderson, Richard Photo/2523 N Calvert St, Baltimore, MD 301-889-0585
Anderson, Ronald N/898 New mark Esplanade, Rockville, MD 301-294-3218
Anderson, Theodore/235 N Madison St, Allentown, PA 215-437-6468
Andersson, Monika L/11 Ranelegh Rd, Brighton, MA 617-787-5510
Andrews Studios/RD 3/Box 277, Pine Bush, NY 914-744-5361
Andris•Hendrickson /314 N 13th #404, Philadelphia, PA (P 58,59) 215-925-2630
Angier, Roswell/65 Pleasant St, Cambridge, MA 617-354-7784
Ankers Photo/316 F St NE, Washington, DC 202-543-2111
Ansin, Mikki/2 Ellery Square, Cambridge, MA 617-661-1640
Anthony, Greg/107 South St, Boston, MA 617-423-4983
Anyon, Benjamin/206 Spring Run Ln, Downington, PA 215-363-0744
Aperture PhotoBank/180 Lincoln St, Boston, MA 617-451-1973
Appleton, Hal/Kingston, Doug/44 Mechanic St PO Box 421, Newton, MA 617-969-5772
Arbor Studios/56 Arbor St, Hartford, CT 203-232-6543
Arce Studios/219 Henry St, Stanford, CT 203-323-1343
Aristo, Donna/80 Wheeler Ave, Pleasantville, NY ....
Armstrong, Christine/5002 Pilgrim Rd, Baltimore, MD 301-426-3069
Armstrong, James/127 Mill St, Springfield, MA 413-532-9406
Arruda, Robert/144 Lincoln St, Boston, MA 617-482-1425
Asterisk Photo/2016 Walnut St, Philadelphia, PA 215-972-1543
Atlantic Photo/Boston/669 Boylston St, Boston, MA 617-267-7480
Auerbach, Scott/32 Country Rd, Mamaroneck, NY 914-698-9073
Augenstein, Ron/509 Jenne Dr, Pittsburgh, PA 412-653-3583
Augustine, Paula/, , PA 215-455-4311
Austin, Miles/26 Sandra Cir, Westfield, NJ 201-232-1155
Avanti Studios/46 Waltham St, Boston, MA 617-574-9424
Avatar Studio/1 Grace Dr, Cohasset, MA 617-383-1099
Avics Inc/116 Washington Ave, Hawthorne, NJ 201-444-8118
Avid Productions Inc/10 Terhune Place, Hackensack, NJ 201-343-1060
Avis, Paul/300 Bedford, Manchester, NH (P 166,167) 603-627-2659
Azad/9104 Copenhaven Dr, Potomac, MD 301-340-6635

B

B & H photographics/2035 Richmond, Philadelphia, PA 215-425-0888
Baehr, Sarah/708 South Ave, New Canaan, CT 203-966-6317
Baer, Rhoda/3006 Military Rd NW, Washington, DC 202-364-8480
Baker, Bill Photo/1045 Pebble Hill Rd RD3, Doylestown, PA 215-348-9743
Baldwin, Steve/8 Eagle St, Rochester, NY 716-325-2907
Baleno, Ralph/192 Newtown Rd, Plainview, NY 516-293-3399
Banana, Joe/2479 N Jerusalem Rd, N Belmore, NY 516-783-1379
Banville, Andre/Chevalier Ave, Greenfield, MA 413-772-0606
Barber, Doug/1634 E Baltimore St, Baltimore, MD 301-276-1634
Bareish Photo/3 Briarfield Dr, Great Neck, NY 516-487-2725
Barker, Robert/1255 University Ave, Rochester, NY 716-244-6334
Barlow, Len/8 Gloucester St, Boston, MA 617-266-4030
Barnes, Christopher/122 Winnisimmet St, Chelsea, MA 617-884-2745
Barocas, Melanie Eve/78 Hart Rd, Guilford, CT 203-457-0898
Baron, Greg/35 E Stewart Ave, Lansdowne, PA 215-626-8677
Barone, Christopher/381 Wright Ave, Kingston, PA 717-287-4680
Barrett, Albert/PO Box 82, Aldelphia, NJ 201-679-5958
Barrett, Bob/323 Springtown Rd, New Paltz, NY 914-255-1591
Barrow, Pat/10 Post Office Rd, Silver Spring, MD 301-588-3131
Barrow, Scott/44 Market St, Cold Spring, NY (P 40,41) 914-265-4242

Bartlett, Linda/3316 Runnymede Pl NW, Washington, DC 202-362-4777
Basch, Richard/2627 Connecticut Ave NW, Washington, DC 202-232-3100
Baskin, Gerry/12 Union Park St, Boston, MA 617-482-3316
Bates, Carolyn/174 Battery St 2nd Fl, Burlington, VT 802-862-5386
Bavendam, Fred/PO Box 276, E Kingston, NH 603-642-3215
Beach, Jonathan/116 Townline Rd, Syracuse, NY 315-455-8261
Beall, Gordon/5106 Wehawken Rd, Bethesda, MD 301-229-0142
Bean, Jeremiah/96 North Ave, Garwood, NJ 201-789-2200
Beards, James/45 Richmond St, Providence, RI 401-273-9055
Beardsley, John/322 Summer St 5th Fl, Boston, MA 617-482-0130
Beauchesne Photo/4 Bud Way/Vantage Pt III/#2, Nashua, NH 603-880-8686
Beck, Richard/116 Manor Dr, Red Bank, NJ 201-544-4495
Becker, Art/720 Sassafras St, Erie, PA 814-459-8183
Becker, Tim/266 Burnside Ave, E Hartford, CT 203-528-7818
Bedford Photo-Graphic Studio/PO Box 64 Rt 22, Bedford, NY 914-234-3123
Beigel, Daniel/2024 Chesapeake Road, Annapolis, MD 301-974-1234
Bell, David/2705 W 17th St, Erie, PA 814-833-1657
Bell, Mike/411 Tomlinson Rd #C3, Philadelphia, PA 215-676-7393
Bender, Frank/2215 South St, Philadelphia, PA 215-985-4664
Benedetto, Angelo/825 S 7th St, Philadelphia, PA 215-627-1990
Benn, Nathan/925 1/2 F St NW, Washington, DC 202-638-5705
Bennett, William/128 W Northfield Rd, Livingston, NJ 201-992-7967
Benson, Gary/PO Box 29, Peapack, NJ 201-234-2216
Benvenuti, Judi/12 N Oak Ct, Madison, NJ 201-377-5075
Berg, Hal/67 Hilary Circle, New Rochelle, NY 914-235-9356
Bergman, LV & Assoc/East Mountain Rd S, Cold Spring, NY 914-265-3656
Berinstein, Martin/215 A St 6th Fl, Boston, MA 617-268-4117
Berndt, Jerry/41 Magnolia Ave, Cambridge, MA 617-354-2266
Berner, Curt/211 A St, Boston, MA 617-269-1698
Bernstein, Daniel/7 Fuller St, Waltham, MA 617-894-0473
Berry, Michael/838 S Broad St, Trenton, NJ 609-396-2413
Bethoney, Herb/23 Autumn Circle, Hingham, MA 617-740-2290
Bezushko, Bob/1311 Irving St, Philadelphia, PA (P 163) 215-735-7771
Bezushko, George/1311 Irving St, Philadelphia, PA (P 163) 215-735-7771
Bibikow, Walter/76 Batterymarch St, Boston, MA 617-451-3464
Biegun, Richard/56 Cherry Ave, West Sayville, NY 516-567-2645
Bilyk, I George/314 E Mt Airy Ave, Philadelphia, PA 215-242-5431
Bindas, Jan Jeffrey/205 A St, Boston, MA 617-268-3050
Bingham, Jack/66 Third St, Dover, NH 603-742-7718
Binzen, Bill/Indian Mountain Rd, Lakeville, CT 203-435-2485
Birn, Roger/150 Chestnut St, Providence, RI 401-421-4825
Bishop, Jennifer/2732 St Paul St, Baltimore, MD 301-366-6662
Blackfan Studio/286 Meetinghouse Rd, New Hope, PA (P 168,169) 215-862-3503
Blake, Mike/35 Drummer Rd, Acton, MA 617-264-9099
Blakeslee-Lane Studios/916 N Charles St, Baltimore, MD 301-727-8800
Blank, Bruce/228 Clearfield Ave, Norristown, PA 215-539-6166
Blate, Samuel R/10331 Watkins Mill Dr, Gaithersburg, MD 301-840-2248
Blevins, Burgess/601 N Eutaw St #713, Baltimore, MD 301-685-0740
Bliss, Brad/42 Audubon St, Rochester, NY 716-461-9794
Bloomberg, Robert/172 Kohanza St, Danbury, CT 203-794-1764
Bloomenfeld, Richard/200-19 E 2nd St, Huntington Sta, NY 516-424-9492
Blouin, Craig/PO Box 892, Henniker, NH 603-428-3036
Boehm, J Kenneth/96 Portland Ave, Georgetown, CT 203-544-8524
Bogacz, Mark F/11 Pondview Place, Tyngsboro, MA 617-649-3886
Bognovitz, Murray/4980 C Wyaconda Rd, Rockville, MD 301-984-7771
Bohm, Linda/7 Park St, Montclair, NJ (P 42,43) 201-746-3434
Boisvert, Paul/229 Loomis St, Burlington, VT 802-862-7249
Bolster, Mark/502 W North Ave, Pittsburgh, PA 412-231-3757
Bolton, Bea/186 Lincoln, Boston, MA 617-423-2050
Bonjour, Jon/496 Congress St, Portland, ME 207-773-5398
Bookbinder, Sigmund/Box 833, Southbury, CT 203-264-5137
Booker, David/8 Lum Lane, Newark, NJ 201-465-0944
Borg, Erik/RR #3/Drew Lane, Middlebury, VT 802-388-6302
Borkoski, Matthew/1506 Noyes Dr, Silver Spring, MD 301-589-4858
Borkovitz, Barbara/2844 Wisconsin Ave NW, Washington, DC 202-338-2533
Born, Flint/163 Summer St, Somerville, MA 617-666-3483
Borris, Daniel/126 11th St SE, Washington, DC 202-546-3193
Bova, David/731 Palisades Ave, Yonkers, NY 914-423-1942
Bowen, Dave/RD #5 Box 176, Wellsboro, PA 717-326-1212
Bowl, Greg Studio/409 W Broadway, S Boston, MA 617-268-1210
Bowman, Jo/1102 Manning St, Philadelphia, PA 215-625-0200
Bowman, Ron/PO Box 4071, Lancaster, PA 717-898-7716
Bowne, Bob/708 Cookman Ave, Asbury Park, NJ 201-988-3366
Boxer, Jeff Photography/520 Harrison Ave, Boston, MA 617-266-7755
Boyer, Beverly/17 Llanfair Rd, Ardmore, PA 215-649-0657
Bradley, Dave/840 Summer St, Boston, MA 617-268-6644

Bradley, Roy/113 S Brandywine, Schenectady, NY....518-377-9457
Bradshaw, David/107 South St, Boston, MA....617-338-0825
Branner, Phil/578 Woodbine Ave, Towson, MD....301-486-5150
Braverman, Ed/337 Summer St, Boston, MA....617-423-3373
Bravo, David/1649 Main St, Bridgeport, CT....203-384-8524
Brega, David/PO Box 13, Marshfield Mills, MA....617-555-1212
Brenner, Jay/24 S Mall St, Plainview, NY....516-752-0610
Bress, Pat/7324 Arrowood Rd, Bethesda, MD....301-469-6275
Briel, Petrisse/107 South St 2nd Fl, Boston, MA....617-338-6726
Briglia, Thomas/PO Box 487, Linwood, NJ....609-748-0864
Brignolo, Joseph B/Oxford Springs Rd, Chester, NY....914-496-4453
Brilliant, Andy/107 South St #203, Boston, MA....617-482-8938
Brittany Photo/217 N Wood Ave, Linden, NJ....201-925-0055
Britz Fotograf/2619 Lovegrove St, Baltimore, MD....301-338-1820
Broock, Howard/432 Sharr Ave, Elmira, NY....607-733-1420
Bross, Tom/, MA....617-227-4137
Brown, Christopher/, Boston, MA....617-555-1212
Brown, Dorman/POB 0700/Coach Rd #8B, Quechee, VT....802-296-6902
Brown, Martin/Cathance Lake, Grove Post Office, ME....207-454-7708
Brown, Skip/1720 21st St NW, Washington, DC....202-234-3187
Brown, Stephen R/1882 Columbia Rd NW, Washington, DC....202-667-1965
Brownell, David/PO Box 60, Andover, NH....603-735-6640
Brownell, William/1411 Saxon Ave, Bay Shore, NY....516-665-0081
Brt Photographic Illustrations/911 State St, Lancaster, PA....717-393-0918
brt Photographic Illustrations/911 State St, Lancaster, PA....717-393-0918
Bruce, Brad/101 Park Lane, Beaver Falls, PA....412-846-2776
Bruemmer, Fred/5170 Cumberland Ave, Montreal, QU....514-482-5098
Brundage, Kip/66 Union St, Belfast, ME....207-338-5210
Bubbenmoyer, Kevin/RD #2 Box 110, Orefield, PA....215-395-9167
Buchanan, Robert/56 Lafayette Ave, White Plains, NY (P 74)....914-592-1204
Buckman, Sheldon/17 Kiley Dr, Randolph, MA....617-986-4773
Bulkin, Susan/5453 Houghton Pl, Philadelphia, PA....215-483-4881
Buller, Frank/PO Box E, Ellsworth, ME....207-555-1212
Bulvony, Matt/1003 E Carson St, Pittsburgh, PA....412-431-5344
Burak, Chet/130 Taunton Ave, E Providence, RI....401-431-0625
Burdick, Gary Photography/9 Parker Hill, Brookfield, CT....203-775-2894
Burger, Oded/9 Wickford Rd, Framingham, MA....508-788-0677
Burke, Bill/6 Melville Ave, Dorchester, MA....617-265-3070
Burke, John/60 K St, Boston, MA (P 171)....617-269-6677
Burke, John & Judy/116 E Van Buren Ave, New Castle, DE....302-322-8760
Burnette, David/920 Main St, Fords, NJ....212-683-2002
Burns, Steve/PO Box 175, Westwood, NJ....201-358-1890
Burris, Ken/PO Box 592, Shelburne, VT....802-985-3263
Burwell/Burwell/6925 Willow St NW, Washington, DC....202-882-1337
Buschner & Faust/450 W Metro Pk, Rochester, NY....716-475-1170
Butler, Herbert/200 Mamaroneck Ave, White Plains, NY....914-683-1767
Butler, Jeff/317 Mortimer Ave, Rutherford, NJ....201-460-1071
Byron, Pete/75 Mill Rd, Morris Plains, NJ....201-538-7520

C

C L M Photo/272 Nassau Rd, Huntington, NY....516-423-8890
Caffee, Chris/216 Blvd of Allies, Pittsburg, PA....412-642-7734
Cafiero, Jeff/410 Church Ln, North Brunswick, NJ....201-297-8979
Cali, Guy/Layton Rd, Clarics Summit, PA....717-587-1957
Callaghan, Charles/54 Applecross Circle, Chalfont, PA....215-822-8258
Campbell, Tyler/PO Box 373, Chestertown, MD....301-778-4938
Canner, Larry/413 S Ann St, Baltimore, MD....301-276-5747
Carbone, Fred/1041 Buttonwood St, Philadelphia, PA....215-236-2266
Carol, David/12 Valentine Ave, Glencove, NY....516-674-9534
Carrino, Nick/710 S Marshall St, Philadelphia, PA....215-925-3190
Carroll, Hanson/11 New Boston Rd, Norwich, VT....802-649-1094
Carroll, Mary Claire/POB 67, Richmond, VT....802-434-2312
Carroll, Michael Photo/25 Main St, Pepperell, MA....508-433-6500
Carruthers, Alan/3605 Jeanne-Mamce, Montreal, QU....514-288-4333
Carstens, Don/2121 N Lovegrove St, Baltimore, MD....301-385-3049
Carter, J Pat/3000 Chestnut Ave #116, Baltimore, MD....301-256-2982
Carter, Philip/PO Box 479, Bedford Hills, NY....914-666-3090
Cassaday, Bruce/RD 1 Box 345 Lockwood Rd, Peekskill, NY....914-528-4343
Castalou, Nancy/RD 2/ Box 145, Valatie, NY....518-758-9565
Castle, Ed/4242 East West Highway #509, Chevy Chase, MD....301-585-9300
Cataffo, Linda/PO Box 460, Palisades Park, NJ....201-694-5047
Cavanaugh, James/On Location/PO Box 158, Tonawanda, NY....716-633-1885
Cerniglio, Tom/1115 E main St, Rochester, NY....716-654-8561
Chadbourne, Bob/595-603 Newbury St, Boston, MA....617-262-3800
Chalifour, Benoit/1030 St Alexandre #812, Montreal, QU....514-879-1869
Chandoha, Walter/RD 1 PO Box 287, Annandale, NJ....201-782-3666
Chaplin, June/230 Dunkirk Rd, Baltimore, MD....301-377-2742
Chapman, Peter/560 Harrison Ave, Boston, MA....617-357-5670
Chapple, Ross/855 Islington St, Portsmouth, NH....603-430-8899
Chase, Thomas W/PO Box 1965, Rochester, NH....603-875-2808
Chatwin, Jim/5459 Main St, Williamsville, NY....716-634-3436
Chauhan, Dilip/145 Ipswich St, Boston, MA....617-262-2359
Chauve, Karyn/75 Highland Rd, Glenn Cove, NY....516-676-0365
Chawtsky, Ann/85 Andover Rd, Rockville Centre, NY....516-766-2417
Cherin, Alan/907 Penn Ave, Pittsburgh, PA....412-261-3755
Chiusano, Michael/39 Glidden St, Beverly, MA....508-927-7067
Chomitz, Jon/3 Prescott St, Somerville, MA....617-625-6789
Choroszewski, Walter J/1310 Orchard Dr/Somerville, NJ....201-369-3555
Ciaglia, Joseph/2036 Spruce St, Philadelphia, PA....215-985-1092
Ciuccoli, Stephen/575 Broad St #219, Bridgeport, CT....203-333-5228
Clark, Conley/7713 Garland Ave, Takoma Park, MD....301-270-2375
Clark, Michael/PO Box 423, Stowe, VT....802-253-7927
Clarke, Jeff/266 Pine St, Burlington, VT....802-863-4393
Clarkson, Frank/1000 G St SE, Washington, DC....202-543-4377
Cleff, Bernie Studio/715 Pine St, Philadelphia, PA....215-922-4246
Clegg, Cheryl/107 South St, Boston, MA....617-423-6317
Clemens, Clint/345 Summer St, Boston, MA....617-482-3838
Clemens, Peter/153 Sidney St, Oyster Bay, NY....516-922-1759
Clifford, Joan/38 Hudson St, Quincy, MA....617-328-4623
Clineff, Kindra/106 S Main St, Topsfield, MA....508-887-9428
Clymer, Jonathan/180 Central Ave, Englewood, NJ....201-568-1760
Coan, Stephen/750 South 10th St, Philadelphia, PA....215-923-3183
Cobos, Lucy/PO Box 8491, Boston, MA....617-876-9537
Cohen, Daniel/744 Park Ave, Hoboken, NJ....201-659-0952
Cohen, Marc Assoc/23 Crestview Dr, Brookfield, CT....203-775-1102
Collins & Collins/PO Box 10736, State College, PA....814-234-2916
Colorworks Inc/14300 Cherry Lane Ctr, Laurel Center, MD....301-490-7909
Colucci, Joe/Box 2069/86 Lackawanna Ave, W Patterson, NJ....201-890-5770
Colwell, David/3405 Keats Terrace, Ijamsville, MD....301-865-3931
Comb, David/107 South St 2nd Fl, Boston, MA....617-426-3644
Conaty, Jim/Hanscom Fld E/Bldg #1724, Bedford, MA....617-274-8200
Conboy, John/1225 State St, Schenectady, NY....518-346-2346
Confer, Holt/2016 Franklin Pl, Wyomissing, PA....215-678-0131
Congalton, David/206 Washington St, Pembroke, MA....617-826-2788
Conner, Marian/456 Rockaway Rd #15, Dover, NJ....201-328-1823
Connor, Donna/272 Fourth Ave, Sweetwater, NJ....609-965-3396
Connors, Gail/9 Alpen Green Ct, Burtonsville, MD....301-890-9645
Contrino, Tom/22 Donaldson Ave, Rutherford, NJ....212-947-4450
Conway Photography/PO Box 165, Charlestown, MA....617-242-0064
Cooke, Doug/210 South St, Boston, MA....617-482-6154
Coolidge, Jeffrey/322 Summer St, Boston, MA....617-338-6869
Cooper, John F/One Bank Street, Summit, NJ....201-273-0368
Cooperman, Bill/126-28 S Madison, Allentown, PA....215-437-0961
Corcoran, John/310 Eighth St, New Cumberland, PA....717-774-0652
Cordingley, Ted/31 Blackburn Center, Gloucester, MA....617-283-2591
Cornell, Linc/107 South St #600, Boston, MA....617-423-1511
Cornicello, John/317 Academy Terr, Linden, NJ....201-925-6675
Corriden, Richard/373 Route 46 West, Fairfield, nj....201-227-5000
Corsiglia, Betsy/PO Box 934, Martha's Vineyard, MA....508-693-5107
Cortesi, Wendy/3034 'P' St NW, Washington, DC....202-965-1204
Cosloy, Jeff/535 Albany St, Boston, MA....617-338-6824
Coughlin, Suki/Main St, New London, NH....603-526-4645
Courtney, David M/36 Tremont St, Concord, NH....603-228-8412
Coxe, David/, Cambridge, MA....617-547-4957
CR 2/36 St Paul St, Rochester, NY....716-232-5140
Crabtree, Shirley Ann/1 Prospect St #2A, New Rochelle, NY....914-636-5494
Crane, Tom/113 Cumberland Pl, Bryn Mawr, PA....215-525-2444
Crawford, Carol/14 Fortune Dr Box 221, Billerica, MA....617-663-8662
Creative Image Photo/325 Valley Rd, West Orange, NJ....201-325-2352
Creative Images/122 Elmcroft Rd, Rochester, NY....716-482-8720
Creative Photography/Bustleton & Tyson Aves, Philadelphia, PA....215-332-8080
Croes, Larry/256 Charles St, Waltham, MA....617-894-4897
Crossley, Dorothy/Mittersill Rd, Franconia, NH....603-823-8177
Crowley, Charles/68 Phillips St, Boston, MA....617-723-5914
Cullen, Betsy/125 Kingston St, Boston, MA....617-542-0965
Cunningham, Chris/9 East St, Boston, MA....617-542-4640
Curtis, Bruce/70 Belmont Dr, Roslyn Heights, NY....516-484-2570
Curtis, Jackie/Alewives Rd, Norwalk, CT....203-866-9198
Curtis, John/50 Melcher St, Boston, MA....617-451-9117
Cushner, Susie/354 Congress St, Boston, MA....617-542-4070
Czamanske, Marty/61 Commercial St, Rochester, NY....716-546-1434
Czepiga, David/101 Fitzrandolph Ave, Hamilton, NJ....609-396-2976

D

D'Angelo, Andy/620 Centre Ave, Reading, PA....215-376-1100

Dai, Ping/30 Park St, Wakefield, MA..........617-246-4704
Daigle, James/460 Harrison Ave, Boston, MA 617-482-0939
Dalton, Douglas/236 Armington St, Cranston, RI..........401-781-4099
Danello, Peter/386 Kerrigan Blvd, Newark, NJ..........201-371-5899
Daniels, Craig/2103 St Paul St, Baltimore, MD..........301-625-9024
Daniels, Mark/8413 Piney Branch Rd,
Silver Spring, MD (P 203)..........**301-587-1727**
Dannenberg, Mitchell/261 Averill Ave, Rochester, NY 716-473-6720
Davis, Harold/299 Pavonia Ave, Jersey City, NJ..........800-759-2583
Davis, Howard/19 E 21st St, Baltimore,
MD (P 204)..........**301-625-3838**
Davis, James/159 Walnut St, Montclair, NJ..........201-747-6972
Davis, Ken/4513 MacArthur Blvd, Washington, DC 202-333-4473
Davis, Louis/572 Washington St #16, Wellesley, MA..........617-235-7625
Davis, Pat Photo/14620 Pinto Ln, Rockville, MD..........301-424-0577
Davis, Rick/210 Carter Dr #9/Matlack Ind, West Chester, PA 215-436-6050
Day, Joel/412 Walnut St, Lancaster, PA..........717-291-7228
De Lucia, Ralph/120 E Hartsdale Ave, Hartsdale, NY 914-472-2253
Dean, Floyd/2-B South Poplar St, Wilmington,
DE (P 201)..........**302-655-7193**
Dean, John/2435 Maary land Ave, Baltimore, MA..........301-243-8357
Debas, Bruno/49 Melcher St, Boston, MA..........617-451-1394
Debren, Allen/355 Pearl St, Burlington, VT..........802-864-5916
DeFilippis, Robert/70 Eighth St, Woodridge, NJ..........201-896-9241
Degginger, Phil/189 Johnson Rd, Morris Plains, NJ..........201-455-1733
Del Palazzo, Joe/122 W Church St, Philadelphia, PA..........
Delano, Jon/6 Manor Ave, Cranford, NJ..........201-276-4034
DeLellis, R A/281 Haverhill St, Lawrence, MA..........508-681-0588
Delevingne, Lionel/25 Cherry St, Northampton, MA 413-586-3424
Delmas, Didier/1 Mill St, Burlington, VT..........802-862-0120
DeMichele, Bill/40 Broadway, Albany, NY..........518-436-4927
Dempsey-Hart/241 A St, Boston, MA..........617-338-6661
Denison, Bill/302 Thornhill Rd, Baltimore, MD..........301-323-1114
Denuto, Ellen/24 Mill St, Patterson, NJ..........212-517-0296
Devenny, Joe/RFD 1/Box 147, Waldoboro, ME..........207-549-7693
Deveraux, Joanne/123 Oxford St, Cambridge, MA..........617-876-7618
DeVito, Mary/2528 Cedar Ave, Ronkonkoma, NY..........516-981-4547
DeVito, Michael Jr/40-A N Village Ave, Rockville Ctr, NY..........212-243-5267
DeWaele, John/14 Almy St, Lincoln, RI..........401-726-0084
Dibble, Warren/114 Chesham Dr, Middlebury, CT..........203-758-9233
DiBenedetto, Emilo/32 Touro Ave, Medford, MA..........617-396-0550
Dickstein, Bob/101 Hillturn Lane, Roslyn Heights, NY..........516-621-2413
Diebold, George/416 Bloomfield Ave, Montclair, NJ..........212-645-1077
Dietz, Donald/PO Box 177, Dorchester, MA..........617-265-3436
DiGiacomo, Melchior/32 Norma Rd, Harrington Park, NJ..........201-767-0870
Dillon, George/210 South St, Boston, MA..........617-482-6154
DiMaggio, Joe/512 Adams St, Centerport, NY..........516-271-6133
DiMarco, Salvatore C Jr/1002 Cobbs St, Drexel Hill, PA..........215-789-3239
DiMarzo, Bob/92 Prince St, Boston, MA..........617-720-1113
Dinn, Peter/52 Springtree Lane, S Berwick, ME..........207-384-2877
Distefano, Paul/, Hasbrouck Heights, NJ..........201-471-0368
Dittmar, Warren/217 Main St, Ossining, NY..........914-528-1673
Dixon, Mel/PO Box 468, Ossining, NY..........914-941-9336
Dodge, Brooks/PO Box 247, Jackson, NH..........603-383-6830
Dodson, George/Schoolhouse Commons, Stevensville, MD..........301-643-6202
Dolin, Penny Ann/190 Henry St, Stamford, CT..........203-359-9932
Donovan, Bill/165 Grand Blvd, Scarsdale, NY..........914-472-0938
Dorfmann, Pam/5161 River Rd Bldg 2B, Bethesda, MD..........301-652-1303
Dorman-Brown Photography/Coach Rd #8B, Quechee, VT 802-296-6902
Dorrance, Scott/131 E 23rd St, New York, NY..........212-529-4030
Douglas Associates/3 Cove of Cork Ln, Annapolis, MD..........301-266-5060
Douglass, Jim Photogroup Inc/5161 River Rd
Bldg 2A, Bethesda, MD (P 52)..........**301-652-1303**
Dovi, Sal/2935 Dahlia St, Baldwin, NY..........516-379-4273
Dow, Norman/52 Concord Ave, Cambridge, MA..........617-492-1236
Dowling, John/521 Scott Ave, Syracuse, NY..........315-446-8189
Dragan, Dan/PO Box 2, N Brunswick, NJ..........201-566-3431
Dratch, Howard/2173 Stoll Rd, Saugerties, NY..........914-246-5213
Dreyer, Peter H/916 Pleasant St #11, Norwood, MA..........617-762-8550
Dunham, Tom/335 Gordon Rd, Robinsville, NJ..........609-259-6042
Dunn, Jeffrey/32 Pearl St, Cambridge, MA..........617-864-2124
Dunn, Phoebe/20 Silvermine Rd, New Canaan,
CT (P 77)..........**203-966-9791**
Dunne, Paul/28 Southpoint Dr, S Sandwich, MA..........508-420-5511
Dunoff, Rich/1313 Delmont Ave, Havertown, PA..........215-627-3690
Dunwell, Steve/20 Winchester St, Boston, MA..........617-423-4916
Dupont, Iris/7 Bowdoin Ave, Dorchester, MA..........617-436-8474
Durrance, Dick/Dolphin Ledge, Rockport, ME..........207-236-3990
Dweck, Aboud/1238 Kallow Hill St 3206, Philadelphia, PA..........215-527-0123

Dwiggins, Gene/204 Westminster Mall, Providence, RI 401-421-6466
Dyekman, James E/14 Cherry Hill Circle, Ossining, NY 914-941-0821
Dyer, Ed/414 Brandy Lane, Mechanicsburg, PA..........717-737-6618

E

Earle, John/PO Box 63, Cambridge, MA..........617-628-1454
Eastern Light Photo/113 Arch St, Philadelphia, PA..........215-238-0655
Eastwood, Henry C/800 3rd St NE, Washington, DC..........202-543-9229
Edelman, Harry/2790 McCully Rd, Pittsburgh, PA..........412-486-8822
Edgerton, Brian/Box 364/11 Old Route 28, Whitehouse, NJ..........201-534-9400
Edson, Franz Inc/26 Watch Way, Huntington, NY..........516-692-4345
Edson, Steven/107 South St, Boston, MA..........617-357-8032
Edwards, Robert/9302 Hilltop Ct, Laurel, MD..........301-490-9659
Egan, Jim/Visualizations/150 Chestnut St, Providence, RI..........401-331-6220
Ehrlich, George/PO Box 186, New Hampton, NY..........914-355-1757
Eisenberg, Leonard J/85 Wallingford Rd, Brighton, MA..........617-787-3366
Elder, Tommy/Chapelbrook & Ashfield Rds, Williamsburg, MA 413-628-3243
Elkins, Joel/8 Minkel Rd, Ossining, NY..........914-627-4099
Elson, Paul/8200 Blvd East, North Bergen, NJ..........201-662-2882
Emmott, Bob/700 S 10th St, Philadelphia, PA..........215-925-2773
Enos, Chris/1 Fitchburg St, Somerville, MA..........617-625-8686
Epstein, Alan Photography/295 Silver St, Agawam, MA..........413-789-3320
Epstein, Robert/3813 Ingoman NW, Washington, DC..........301-320-3946
Erle, Steve/538 Beach St, Revere, MA..........617-289-3848
Esposito, Anthony Jr/48 Old Amity Rd, Bethany, CT..........203-393-2231
Esto Photo/222 Valley Pl, Mamaroneck, NY..........914-698-4060
Evans, John C/Benedum-Trees Bldg #1712, Pittsburgh, PA..........412-281-3663
Everett Studios/22 Barker Ave, White Plains, NY 914-997-2200
Everson, Martha/219 Fisher Ave, Brookline, MA..........617-232-0187
Ewing Galloway/100 Merrick Rd, Rockville Centre, NY..........516-764-8620
Eyle, Nicolas Edward/205 Onondaga Ave, Syracuse, NY 315-422-6231
Eyles, Don/249 A St, Boston, MA..........617-482-1717

F

F-90 Inc/60 Sindle Ave, Little Falls, NJ..........201-785-9090
Falkenstein, Roland/Strawberry St #4, Philadelphia, PA..........215-592-7138
Faraghan, George/940 N Delaware Ave, Philadelphia, PA..........215-928-0499
Farber, Enid/284 Barrow St, Jersey City, NJ..........201-432-3245
Farkas, Alan/114 St Paul St #2, Rochester, NY..........716-232-1124
Farrer, Herman/1305 Sheridan St NW, Washington, DC..........202-723-7979
Farris, Mark/8804 Monard Dr, Silver Spring, MD..........301-588-6637
Fatone, Bob/166 W Main St, Niantic, CT..........203-739-2427
Fatta, C Studio/25 Dry Dock Ave, Boston,
MA (P 172,173)..........**617-423-6638**
Faulkner, Robert I/52 Comstock St, New Brunswick, NJ..........201-828-6984
Fay Foto/201 South St, Boston, MA..........617-267-2000
Feil, Charles W III/36 Danforth St, Portland, ME..........207-773-3754
Feiling, David/129 E Water St, Syracuse, NY..........315-422-6215
Feingersh, Jon/18533 Split Rock Ln, Germantown, MD..........301-428-9525
Fennell, Mary/57 Maple Ave, Hastings on Hudson, NY..........914-478-3627
Feraulo, Richard/760 Plain St, Marshfield, MA..........617-837-9563
Fernando Photo/2901 James St, Syracuse, NY..........315-432-0065
Ferreira, Al/237 Naubuc Ave, East Hartford, CT..........203-569-8812
Ferrino, Paul/PO Box 3641, Milford, CT..........203-878-4785
Fetters, Paul/4916 Butterworth Place NW, Washington, DC..........202-362-2393
Ficksman, Peter/468 Fore St, Portland, ME..........207-773-3555
Fields, Tim/916 Dartmouth Glen Way, Baltimore, MD..........301-323-7831
Filipe, Tony/239 A St, Boston, MA..........617-542-8330
Findlay, Christine/Hwy 36 Airport Plaza, Hazlet, NJ..........201-264-2211
Fine, Jerome/4594 Brookhill Dr N, Manlius, NY..........315-682-7272
Fine, Ron/8600 Longacre Ct, Bethesda, MD..........301-986-5302
Fink, Mark/119 W Crooked Hill Rd #104, Pearl River, NY..........
Finlayson, Jim/PO Box 337, Locust Valley, NY..........516-676-5816
Finnegan, Michael/PO Box 901, Plandome, NY..........516-365-7942
Fischer, John/9 Shore View Rd, Port Washington, NY..........516-883-3225
Fisher, Al/601 Newbury St, Boston, MA..........617-536-7126
Fisher, Patricia/2234 Cathedral Ave NW, Washington, DC..........202-232-3781
Fiterman, Al/1415 Bayard St, Baltimore, MD..........301-625-1265
Fitton, Larry/2029 Maryland Ave, Baltimore, MD..........301-727-0092
Fitzgerald, Mark/87 Daly Rd, E Northport, NY..........516-368-6972
Fitzhugh, Susan/3406 Chestnut Ave, Baltimore, MD..........301-243-6112
Flanigan, Jim/1325 N 5th St #F4, Philadelphia, PA..........215-236-4448
Flesch, Patrice/46 McBride St, Jamaica Plains, MA..........617-522-7199
Fletcher, John C/64 Murray Hill Terrace, Bergenfield, NJ..........201-387-2171
Flint, Stan/2315 Maryland Ave, Baltimore, MD..........301-837-9923
Flowers, Morocco/520 Harrison Ave, Boston,
MA (P 174)..........**617-426-3692**
Floyd Dean Inc/2-B S Poplar St, Wilmington, DE 302-655-7193

Flynn, Bryce/14 Perry Dr Unit A, Foxboro, MA ... 508-543-3020
Foley, Paul/791 Tremont, Boston, MA ... 617-266-9336
Folti, Arthur/8 W Mineola Ave, Valley Steam, NY ... 516-872-0941
Foote, James/22 Tomac Ave, Old Greenwich, CT ... 203-637-3228
Forbes, Fred/1 South King St, Gloucester City, NJ ... 609-456-1919
Forbes, Peter/916 N Charles St, Baltimore, MD ... 301-727-8800
Ford, sandra Gould/7123 Race St, Pittsburgh, PA ... 412-731-7039
Ford, Tim/121 W Lanvale St, Baltimore, MD ... 301-383-8070
Fordham, Eric S/282 Moody St, Waltham, MA ... 617-647-7927
Forward, Jim/56 Windsor St, Rochester, NY ... 716-423-0820
Foster, Frank/PO Box 518, W Harwich, MA ... 617-536-8267
Foster, Nicholas/143 Claremont Rd, Bernardsville, NJ ... 201-766-7526
Fox, Debi/5161 River Rd Bldg 2B, Bethesda, MD ... 301-652-1303
Fox, Jon Gilbert/RR 1/Box 307G, Norwich, VT ... 802-649-2828
Fox, Peggy/701 Padonia Rd, Cockeysville, MD ... 301-252-0003
Francisco, Thomas/21 Quine St, Cranford, NJ ... 201-272-1155
Francois, Emmett W/208 Hillcrest Ave, Wycoff, NJ ... 201-652-5775
Francouer, Norm/144 Moody St, Waltham, MA ... 617-891-3830
Frank, Carol/1032 N Calvert St, Baltimore, MD ... 301-244-0092
Frank, Diane/208 North Ave West, Cranford, NJ ... 201-276-2229
Frank, Richard/48 Woodside Ave, Westport, CT ... 203-227-0496
Frank-Adise, Gale/9012 Fairview Rd, Silver Spring, MD ... 301-585-7085
Fraser, Renee/1167 Massachusetts Ave, Arlington, MA ... 617-646-4296
Frederick, Leigh/333 Robinson Lane, Wilmington, DE ... 302-428-6109
Fredericks, Michael Jr/RD 2 Box 292, Ghent, NY ... 518-672-7616
Freeman, Charles Photo/3100 St Paul St, Baltimore, MD ... 301-243-2416
Freer, Bonnie/265 S Mountain Rd, New City, NY ... 212-535-3666
Freeze Frame Studios/255 Leonia Ave, Bogota, NJ ... 201-343-1233
Freid, Joel Carl/4113 Emery Pl NW, Washington, DC ... 202-244-9073
French, Larry/162 Linden Lane, Princeton, NJ ... 609-924-2906
Freund, Bud/1425 Bedford St #9C, Stamford, CT ... 203-359-0147
Friedman, Rick/133 Beaconsfield Rd, Brookline, MA ... 617-734-8125
Fries, Janet/4439 Ellicott St NW, Washington, DC ... 202-362-4443
Frog Hollow Studio/Box 897, Bryn Mawr, PA ... 215-353-9898
Furman, Michael/115 Arch St, Philadelphia, PA (P 38,39) ... 215-925-4233
Furore, Don/49 Sugar Hollow Rd, Danbury, CT ... 203-792-9395

G

G/Q Studios/1217 Spring Garden St, Philadelphia, PA ... 215-236-7770
Gabrielsen, Ken/5 Hundley Ct, Stamford, CT ... 203-964-8254
Gale, Howard & Judy/712 Chestnut St, Philadelphia, PA ... 215-629-0506
Gale, John & Son/712 Chestnut St, Philadelphia, PA ... 215-629-0506
Gallery, Bill/86 South St, Boston, MA ... 617-542-0499
Gallo, Peter/1238 Callowhill St #301, Philadelphia, PA (P 175) ... 215-925-5230
Galvin, Kevin/1227 Broadway, Hanover, MA ... 617-826-4795
Gannon, Barbara/7 Sleepy Hollow Rd, Essex Junction, VT ...
Gans, Harriet/50 Church Lane, Scarsdale, NY ... 914-723-7017
Garaventa, John/105 Constock Rd, Manchester, CT ... 203-647-1579
Garber, Ira/150 Chestnut St, Providence, RI ... 401-274-3723
Garcia, Richard/30 Kimberly Pl, Wayne, NJ ... 201-956-0885
Gardner, Charles/12 N 4th St, Reading, PA ... 215-376-8086
Garfield, Peter/3401 K St NW, Washington, DC ... 202-333-1379
Garrett-Stow, Liliane/18 Tuthill Point Rd, East Moriches, NY ... 516-878-8587
Gates, Ralph/364 Hartshorn Dr Box 233, Short Hills, NJ ... 201-379-4456
Gawrys, Anthony P/163 Lowell St, Peabody, MA ... 508-531-5877
Gee, Elizabeth/186 Rte 24/RFD #1, Mendham, NJ ... 201-543-2447
Geer, Garry/183 St Paul St, Rochester, NY ... 716-232-2393
Gensheimer, Rich/2737 E 41st St, Erie, PA ... 814-825-5822
George, Fred/737 Canal St/Bldg #35/2nd Fl, Stamford, CT ... 203-348-7454
George, Walter Jr/20 Main St, Clinton, NJ ... 201-735-7013
Geraci, Steve/106 Keyland Ct, Bohemia, NY ... 516-567-8777
Gerardi, Marcia/64 Arch St, Piermont, NY ... 914-365-0877
Germer, Michael/27 Industrial Ave, Chelmsford, MA ... 508-250-9282
Getgen, Linda/221 North St, Hingham, MA ... 617-749-7815
Getzoff, Joseph/1 Ellis Rd, W Caldwell, NJ ... 201-226-5259
Giandomenico & Fiore/13 Fern Ave, Collingswood, NJ ... 609-854-2222
Giese, Al/RR 1/Box 302, Poundridge, NY ... 914-764-5512
Giglio, Harry/925 Penn Ave #305, Pittsburgh, PA ... 412-261-3338
Gillette, Guy/133 Mountaindale Rd, Yonkers, NY ... 914-779-4684
Gilligan Group/PO Box 29, Hackettstown, NJ ... 201-689-1343
Glasofer, David/176 Main St, Metuchen, NJ ... 201-549-1845
Glass, Mark/814 Garden St, Hoboken, NJ ... 201-798-0219
Glass, Peter/15 Oakwood St, East Hartford, CT ... 203-528-8559
Gluck, Mike/2 Bronxville Rd, Bronxville, NY ... 914-961-1677
Goell, Jon/535 Albany St, Boston, MA ... 617-423-2057
Goembl, Ponder/617 S 10th St, Philadelphia, PA ... 215-928-1797
Gold, Gary D/One Madison Pl, Albany, NY ... 518-434-4887
Goldblatt, Steven/32 S Strawberry St, Philadelphia, PA ... 215-925-3825
Goldenberg, Barry/1 Baltimore Ave , Cranford, NJ ... 201-276-1510
Goldman, Mel/329 Newbury St, Boston, MA ... 617-536-0539
Goldman, Rob/64 Division Ave, Levittown, NY ... 516-796-9327
Goldsmith, Bruce/1 Clayton Ct, Park Ridge, NJ ... 201-391-4946
Goldstein, Alan/10 Post Office Rd B-3, Silver Spring, MD ... 301-589-1690
Good, Richard/5226 Osage Ave, Philadelphia, PA ... 215-472-7659
Goodman, Howard/PO Box 433, Croton Falls, NY ... 914-277-3133
Goodman, John/337 Summer St, Boston, MA ... 617-482-8061
Goodman, John D/One Mill Street, Burlington, VT ... 802-864-0200
Goodman, Lou/322 Summer St, Boston, MA ... 617-542-8254
Goodwin, Scott/109 Broad St, Boston, MA ... 617-451-8161
Gorchev & Gorchev/11 Cabot Rd, Woburn, MA ... 617-933-8090
Gordon, David A/1413 Hertel Ave, Buffalo, NY ... 716-833-2661
Gorrill, Robert B/PO Box 206, North Quincy, MA ... 617-328-4012
Gothard, Bob/1 Music St, W Tisbury, MA ... 508-693-1060
Gottheil, Philip/1278 Lednam Ct, Merrick, NY ... 516-378-6802
Gottlieb, Steve/3601 East-West Hwy, Chevy Chase, MD ... 301-951-9648
Goudey, Blair/9 Menlo St, Brighton, MA ... 617-254-5074
Graham, Jim/720 Chestnut St, Philadelphia, PA ... 215-592-7272
Grant, Gail/7006 Valley Ave, Phildelphia, PA ... 215-482-9857
Grant, Jarvis/1650 Harvard St NW #709, Washington, DC ... 202-387-8584
Graphic Accent/446 Main St PO Box 243, Wilmington, MA ... 508-658-7602
Grassl, Jennie Lawton/5 Sycamore St, Cambridge, MA ... 617-876-1321
Gray, Daren/151 Sip Ave #51, Jersey City, NJ ... 201-792-2653
Gray, Sam/23 Westwood Rd, Wellesley, MA ... 617-237-2711
Grayson, Jay/9 Cockenoe Dr, Westport, CT ... 203-222-0072
Greco, Matt/405 Highway 18, E Brunswick, NJ ... 201-238-2272
Green, Elisabeth/52 Springtree Lane, S Berwick, ME ... 207-384-2877
Green, Jeremy/4128 Westview Rd, Baltimore, MD ... 301-366-0123
Greenberg, Andrew/313 N Albany Ave, Massapequa, NY ... 516-293-7835
Greenberg, Chip/325 High St, Metuchen, NJ ... 201-548-5612
Greenberg, Steven/560 Harrison Ave, Boston, MA ... 617-423-7646
Gregoire, Rogier/107 South St 2nd Fl, Boston, MA ... 617-574-9554
Gregory, Mark/10615 Duvall St, Glenn Dale, MD ... 301-262-8646
Greniers Commercial Photo/127 Mill St, Springfield, MA ... 413-532-9406
Griebsch, John/25 N Washington St, Rochester, NY ... 716-546-1303
Griffiths-Belt, Annie/1301 Noyes Dr, Silver Spring, MD ... 301-495-3127
Grohe, Stephen F/451 D St #809, Boston, MA ... 617-426-2290
Gruol, Dave/92 Western Ave, Morristown, NJ ... 201-267-2847
Guarinello, Greg/252 Highwood St, Teaneck, NJ ... 201-384-2172
Gude, Susann/Slip 1-A/Spruce Dr, E Patchogue, NY ... 516-654-8093
Guidera, Tom III/403 N Charles St #200, Baltimore, MD ... 301-752-7676

H

H/O Photographers Inc/PO Box 548, Hartford, CT (P 176) ... 802-295-6321
Hagerman, Ron/389 Charles St/Bldg 6/3rd Fl, Providence, RI ... 401-272-1117
Hahn, Bob/3522 Skyline Dr, Bethlehem, PA ... 215-868-0339
Hall, Gary Clayton/PO Box 838, Shelburne, VT ... 802-985-8380
Hallinan, Peter J/PO Box 183, Boston, MA ... 617-924-1539
Halsman, Irene/297 N Mountain Ave, Upper Montclair, NJ ... 201-746-9155
Halstead, Dirck/3332 P St NW, Washington, DC ... 202-338-2028
Hambourg, Serge/Box 753, Crugers, NY ... 212-866-0085
Hambright, Harlan/414 11th St SE, Washington, DC ... 202-546-1717
Hamor, Robert/2308 Columbia Cir, Merrimack, NH ... 603-424-6737
Handerhan, Jerome/113 Edgewood Ave, Pittsburgh, PA ... 412-242-6308
Handler, Lowell/147 Main St, Coldspring, NY ... 914-265-4023
Hankin, Jamie/225 Race St 3rd Fl, Philadelphia, PA ... 215-238-9076
Hansen-Mayer Photography/281 Summer St, Boston, MA ... 617-542-3080
Hansen-Sturm, Robert/334 Wall St, Kingston, NY ... 914-338-8753
Hanstein, George/389 Belmont Ave, Haledon, NJ ... 201-790-0505
Haritan, Michael/1701 Eben St, Pittsburgh, PA ... 412-343-2112
Harkey, John/90 Larch Rd, Providence, RI ... 401-831-1023
Harkins, Kevin F/219 Appleton St, Lowell, MA ... 508-452-9704
Harper, Sharon/RR #1 POB 1615, Starksboro, VT ... 802-453-4095
Harrington, Blaine III/2 Virginia Ave, Danbury, CT ... 203-798-2866
Harrington, John/455 Old Sleepy Hollow Rd, Pleasantville, NY ... 914-939-0702
Harrington, Phillip A/Wagner Ave Fleischmann's, NY ... 914-254-5227
Harris, Brownie/McGuire Lane, Croton-on-Hudson, NY ... 914-271-6426
Harrison, Jim/One Thompson Square, Charleston, MA ... 617-242-4314
Harting, Christopher/327 Summer St, Boston, MA ... 617-451-6330
Hartlove, Chris/802 Berry St, Baltimore, MD ... 301-889-7293
Harvey, Milicent/49 Melcher St, Boston, MA ... 617-482-4493
Hatos, Kathleen/3418 Keins St, Philadelphia, PA ... 215-425-3960
Hausner, Clifford/37-14 Hillside Terrace, Fairlawn, NJ ... 201-791-1170
Hayes, Barry/53 Main St, St Johnsbury, VT ... 802-748-8916

Hayes, Calvin/2125 N Charles St, Baltimore, MD..........301-685-0646
Hayes, Eric/836 LeHave St, Bridgewtr B4V 2V3, NS 902-543-0256
Hayman, James/100 Fourth Ave, North York, PA 717-843-8338
Haywood, Alan/39 Westmoreland Ave, White Plains, NY 914-946-1928
Heard, Gary/274 N Goodman St, Rochester, NY 416-271-6780
Heayn, Mark/17 W 24th St, Baltimore, MD 301-235-1608
Hecker, David/285 Aycrigg Ave, Passaic, NJ 201-471-2496
Heilman, Grant/PO Box 317, Lititz, PA 717-626-0296
Heinz, F Michael Photography/17 Rose Hill, Southport, CT 203-259-7456
Heist, Scott/616 Walnut St, Emmaus, PA 215-965-5479
Helmar, Dennis/46 Midway St, Boston, MA 617-269-7410
Henry, Benton/Rt 1/ Box 6C, Latta, SC 803-752-2097
Herity, Jim/597 Riverside Ave, Westport, CT 203-454-3979
Herko, Robert/121 Hadley St, Piscataway, NJ 201-563-1613
Herrera, Frank//318 Kentucky Ave SE, Washington, DC 301-229-7930
Hewitt, Malcolm/179 Massachusetts Ave, Boston, MA 617-262-7227
Heymann, John/76 Cedar, Somerville, MA 617-628-4791
Hickman, Louis/Box 5358, Plainfield, NJ 201-561-2696
Higgins & Ross/281 Princeton St, N Chelmsford, MA 508-454-4248
Hill, Britian (Ms)/Pleasant Pond Rd, Francestown, NH 603-547-8873
Hill, John T/388 Amity Rd, New Haven, CT 203-393-0035
Hill, Jon/159 Burlington St, Lexington, MA 617-862-6456
Hines, Harry/PO Box 10061, Newark, NJ 201-242-0214
Hinton, Ron/1 Fitchburg St C318, Somerville, MA 617-666-3565
Hirshfeld, Max/1027 33rd St NW, Washington, DC 202-333-7450
Hoachlander, Anice/1001 Sigsbee Pl NE, Washington, DC 202-269-0587
Hodges, Sue Anne/87 Gould Rd, Andover, MA 617-475-2007
Hoffman, Dave/PO Box 1299, Summit, NJ 201-277-6285
Holcomb, Kimberly/592 Columbia Rd, Boston, MA 617-436-6835
Hollander, David/147 S Maple Ave/Box 443, Springfield, NJ 201-467-0870
Holmes, Greg/2007 Hickory Hill Ln, Silver Spring, MD 301-460-3643
Holniker, Barry/400 E 25th St, Baltimore, MD 301-889-1919
Holoquist, Marcy/2820 Smallman St, Pittsburgh, PA 412-963-8021
Holt, John/25 Dry Dock Ave, Boston, MA 617-426-4658
Holt, Walter/PO Box 936, Media, PA 215-565-1977
Holz, Thomas Jay/PO Box 4, Tribes Hill, NY 518-842-7730
Homan, Mark/1916 Old Cuthbert Rd, Cherry Hill, NJ 609-795-6763
Hone, Stephen/859 N 28th St, Philadelphia, PA 215-765-6900
Honein, Elie/827 Boylston St, Boston, MA 617 437-9038
Hood, Sarah/1924 37th St NW, Washington, DC 202-337-2585
Hopkins, Tom/15 Orchard Park, Box 7A, Madison, CT 203-245-0824

Hornick/Rivlin Studio/25 Dry Dock, Boston, MA (P 161) **617-482-8614**
Horowitz, Abby/915 N 28th St, Philadelphia, PA 215-925-3600
Horowitz, Ted/214 Wilton Rd, Westport, CT 203-454-8766
Hotshots/35 Congress St/PO Box 896, Salem, MA 617-744-1557
Houck, Julie/21 Clinton St, S Portland, ME 207-767-3365
Hour Glass Photo/Latrobe 30 Plaza, Latrobe, PA 412-537-9790
Houser, Robert/PO Box 299, Litchfield, CT 203-567-4241
Houser-Tartaglia Photoworks/23 Walnut Ave, Clark, NJ 201-388-8531
Howard, Jerry/317 N Main, Natick, MA 617-653-7610
Howard, Peter/7 Bright Star Ct, Baltimore, MD 301-866-5013
Howard, Richard/45 Walnut St, Somerville, MA 617-628-5410
Hoyt, Russell/171 Westminister Ave, S Attleboro, MA 508-399-8611
Hoyt, Wolfgang/222 Valley Pl, Mamaroneck, NY 914-698-4060
Hubbell, William/99 East Elm St, Greenwich, CT 203-629-9629
Huber, William Productions/49 Melcher, Boston, MA 617-426-8205
Huet, John/107 South St, Boston, MA 617-423-6317
Hukub, Ed/145 Comac St, Ronkonhoma, NY 516-981-3100
Hulbert, Steve/PO Box 350, Lemoyne, PA 717-731-8289
Hundertmark, Charles/6264 Oakland Mills Rd, Sykesville, MD 301-242-8150
Hungaski, Andrew/Merribrook Lane, Stamford, CT 203-327-6763
Hunsberger, Douglas/115 W Fern Rd, Wildwood Crest, NJ 609-522-6849
Hunt, Barbara/5161 River Rd Bldg 2B, Bethesda, MD 301-652-1303
Hunter, Allan/56 Main St 3rd Fl, Milburn, NJ 201-467-4920
Hurwitz, Joel/PO Box 1009, Leominster, MA 617-537-6476
Huss, W John/PO Box 399, Wethersfield, CT 203-728-0545
Hutchings, Richard/24 Pinebrook Dr, Larchmont, NY 914-834-9633
Hutchinson, Clay/Viewfinder Pub/Box 41, Old Chatham, NY 518-794-7767
Hutchinson, Gardiner/239 Causeway St, Boston, MA 617-523-5180
Huyler, Willard/218 South Ave E, Cranford, NJ 201-272-8874
Hyde, Dana/PO Box 1302, South Hampton, NY 516-283-1001
Hyon, Ty/65 Drumhill Rd, Wilton, CT 203-834-0870

I

Iacovelli, Richard/560 Harrison Ave, Boston, MA 617-426-8933
Iannazzi, Robert F/450 Smith Rd, Rochester, NY 716-624-1285
Ickow, Marvin/1824 35th St NW, Washington, DC 202-342-0250

Iglarsh, Gary/2229 N Charles St, Baltimore, MD 301-235-3385
Image Photographic Svcs/96 Walnut St, Montclair, NJ 201-746-9133
Image Source Inc/PO Box 1929, Wilmington, DE 302-658-5897
Images Comm. Photo 360 Sylvan Ave, Englewood Cliffs, NJ 201-871-4406
Impact Multi Image Inc/117 W Washington, Pleasantville, NJ 609-484-8100
Impact Studios Ltd/1084 N Delaware St, Philadelphia, PA (P 100,101) **215-426-3988**
Insight Photo/55 Gill Lane, Iselin, NJ 201-283-4727
Isaacson, David/8 Garrison St, Boston, MA 617-353-0187
Iverson, Bruce/7 Tucker St #65, Pepperell, MA 617-433-8429

J

Jackson, Cappy/1034 Monkton Rd, Monkton, MD 301-343-1313
Jackson, Glenwood/3000 Chestnut Ave #10, Baltimore, MD 301-366-0049
Jackson, Martin/314 Catherine St #401, Philadelphia, PA 215-271-5149
Jackson, Reggie/135 Sheldon Terr, New Haven, CT 203-787-5191
Jagger, Warren/150 Chestnut St Box 3330, Providence, RI 401-351-7366
Jamison, Jon/247 Bly Rd, Schenectady, NY 518-869-6211
Jaramillo, Alain/613 N Eautaw St, Baltimore, MD 301-727-2220
Jarvis, Guy/109 Broad St, Boston, MA 617-482-8998
Jesudowich, Stanley/200 Henry St, Stamford, CT 203-359-8886
Joachim, Bruno/326 A Street, Boston, MA (P 152,153) **617-451-6156**
Joel, Yale/Woodybrook Ln, Croton-On-Hudson, NY 914-271-8172
Johnson, Stella/137 Langdon Ave, Watertown, MA 617-923-1263
Jones, Alexander/1243-A Maryland Ave NE, Washington, DC 301-567-2213
Jones, Isaac/19 E 22nd St, Baltimore, MD 301-659-0235
Jones, Lou/22 Randolph St, Roxbury, MA (P 177) **617-426-6335**
Jones, Peter/43 Charles St, Boston, MA 617-227-6400
Joseph, Nabil/445 St Pierre St #402, Montreal, QU 514-842-2444
Judice, Ed/83 W Main St, Orange, MA 508-544-2739
Juracka, Frank/179 Widmer Rd, Wappingers Falls, NY 914-297-9080

K

Kaetzel, Gary/PO Box 3514, Wayne, NJ 201-696-6174
Kagan, BC/43 Winter St 4th Fl, Boston, MA 617-482-0336
Kalfus, Lonny/226 Hillside Ave, Leonia, NJ 201-944-3909
Kalischer, Clemens/Main St, Stockbridge, MA 413-298-5500
Kalish, JoAnne/512 Adams St, Centerport, NY 516-271-6133
Kalisher, Simpson/North St, Roxbury, CT 203-354-8893
Kaminsky, Saul/36 Sherwood Ave, Greenwich, CT 203-531-4953
Kan, Dennis/PO Box 248, Clarksburg, MD 301-428-9417
Kane, Alice/3380 Emeric Ave, Wantagh, NY 516-781-7049
Kane, John/POB 731, New Milford, CT 203-354-7651
Kane, Martin/401 Sharpless St, West Chester, PA 215-696-0206
Kannair, Jonathan/72 Cambridge St, Worcester, MA 617-757-3417
Kaplan, Barry/5 Main St, Wickford, RI 212-254-8461
Kaplan, Carol/20 Beacon St, Boston, MA 617-720-4400
Karnow, Catherine/1707 Columbia Rd NW #518, Washington, DC (P 205) **202-332-5656**
Karosis, Rob/855 Islington St, Portsmouth, NH 603-436-8876
Karten, Roy/803 Malcolm Dr, Silver Spring, MD 301-445-0751
Kaskons, Peter/Westech Ind Park, Tyngsboro, MA 508-649-7788
Kasper, Ken/1232 Cobbs St, Drexel Hill, PA 215-789-7033
Katz, Dan/36 Aspen Rd, W Orange, NJ 201-731-8956
Katz, Geoffrey/156 Francestown Rd, New Boston, NH 603-487-3819
Katz, Philip Isaiah/286 Meetinghouse Rd, New Hope, PA (P 168,169) **215-862-3503**
Kauffman, Kenneth/915 Spring Garden St, Philadelphia, PA 215-649-4474
Kaufman, Robert/58 Roundwood Rd, Newton Upper Falls, MA 617-964-4080
Kawalerski, Ted/7 Evergreen Way, North Tarrytown, NY 212-242-0198
Keeley, Chris/4000 Tunlaw Rd NW #1119, Washington, DC 202-337-0022
Keene Studio/7170 Crystal City, Middletown, MD 301-949-4722
Keiser, Anne B/3760 39th St #f144, Washington, DC 202-966-6733
Kelley, Edward/20 White St, Red Bank, NJ 201-747-0596
Kelley, Lionel & David/560 Harrison, Boston, MA 617-482-4703
Kelley, Patsy/70 Atlantic Ave/PO Box 1147, Marblehead, MA 617-639-1147
Kelly/Mooney Photography/87 Willow Ave, North Plainfield, NJ 201-757-5924
Kenik, David Photography/9 Alaina Dr, Johnston, RI 401-934-0062
Kenneth, Victor/107 Oak Lynn Dr, Columbus, NJ 609-921-4983
Kernan, Sean/576 Leetes Island Rd, Stony Creek, CT 203-481-4478
Kerper, David/1018 E Willow Grove Ave, Philadelphia, PA 215-836-1135
Kerson, Larry/140 Huyshope Ave, Hartford, CT 203-548-9805
Kinum, Drew/Glen Avenue, Scotia, NY 518-382-7566
Kirkman, Tom/58 Carley Ave, Huntington, NY 516-549-6705
Kirschbaum, Jed/102 N Wolfe St, Baltimore, MD 301-332-6940
Kittle, James Kent/49 Brinckerhoff Ln, New Canann, CT 203-966-2442
Klapatch, David/350 Silas Deane Hwy, Wethersfield, CT 203-563-3834

Klebau, James/5806 Maiden Lane, Bethesda, MD 301-320-2666
Klein, Robert/38 E Gramercy Place, Geln Rock, NJ 201-445-6513
Kligman, Fred/4733 Elm St, Bethesda, MD 301-652-6333
Kline, Andrew/, Montpelier, VT 802-229-4924
Klinefelter, Eric/10963 Hickory Ridge Rd, Columbia, MD 301-964-0273
Knapp, Stephen/74 Commodore Rd, Worcester, MA 617-757-2507
Kobrin, Harold/187 Tamarack Trail, Otis, MA 617-527-3302
Koelsch, Chuck/4 Summer St, Hyde Park, MA 617-361-6355
Korona, Joseph/25 Foxcroft Rd, Pittsburgh, PA 412-279-9200
Kovner, Mark/14 Cindy Lane, Highland Mills, NY 914-928-6543
Kramer, Bill/, Buffalo, NY
Kramer, Phil/122 W Church St, Philadelphia, PA 215-928-9189
Kramer, Rob/409 W Broadway, Boston, MA 617-269-9269
Krasner, Stuart/7837 Muirfield Ct, Potomac, MD 301-983-1599
Krist, Bob/333 S Irving, Ridgewood, NJ 201-585-9464
Krogh, Peter Harold/4602 Davidson Dr, Chevy Chase, MD ..301-654-1339
Krohn, Lee/RR #2 Box 270, Putney, VT 802-387-4580
Krubner, Ralph/4 Juniper Court, Jackson, NJ 201-364-3640
Kruper, Alexander Jr/70 Jackson Dr Box 152, Cranford, NJ ..201-276-1510
Kucine, Cliff/100 Commercial, Portland, ME 207-773-2568
Kugielsky, Joseph/Little Brook Ln, Newtown, CT 203-426-7123

L

L I Image Works/14-20 Glenn St, Glenn Cove, NY 516-671-9661
L M Associates/20 Arlington, Newton, MA 617-232-0254
Labelle, Lise/4282 A Rue Delorimier, Montreal H2H 2B1, QU ..514-596-0010
LaBua, Frank/37 North Mountain Ave, Montclair,
NJ (P 106,107)   **201-783-6318**
Labuzetta, Steve/180 St Paul St, Rochester, NY 716-546-6825
LaCourciere, Mario/1 Rue Hamel, Quebec G1R 4J6, QU 418-694-1744
Lakin, Richard/8 Everedy Square, Frederick, MD 301-662-7778
Lamar Photographics/PO Box 470, Framingham, MA 508-881-3881
Lamb, David J/78 Hollywood Ave, Rochester, NY 716-442-2243
Lambert, Elliot/341 A Street, Boston, MA 617-482-7256
Landsman, Gary D/12115 Parklawn Dr Bay-S, Rockville, MD ..301-468-2588
Landsman, Meg/27 Industrial Ave, Chelmsford, MA 508-250-9282
Landwehrle, Don/9 Hother Ln, Bayshore,
NY (P 108)   **516-665-8221**
Lane, Rhonda/8-J Darling St, Southington, CT 203-621-6334
Lane, Whitney/109 Somerstown Rd, Ossining,
NY (P 109)   **914-762-5335**
Langlois, Mark/21 Willow St, Providence, RI 401-861-3017
Lanman, Jonathan/41 Paul Sullivan Way, Boston, MA 617-574-9420
Lapides, Susan Jane/451 Huron Ave, Cambridge, MA 617-864-7793
LaRiche, Michael/30 S Bank St, Philadelphia, PA 215-843-5574
Larrimore, Walter/916 N Charles St, Baltimore, MD 301-727-8800
Lauber, Christopher/609 Crescent Dr, Bound Brook, NJ 201-271-4077
Laurino, Don Studio/145 Pallisade St, Dobbs Ferry, NY 914-693-1199
Lautman, Robert C/4906 41 St NW, Washington, DC 202-966-2800
Lauver, David A/29 S Market St, Selinsgrove, PA 717-374-0515
Lavine, David S/4016 The Alameda, Baltimore, MD 301-467-0523
Lawfer, Larry/107 South St, Boston, MA 617-451-0628
Lawler, John/107 South St, Boston, MA 617-338-6726
Lawrence, Stefan/40 Norwood Ave, Malverne, NY 516-593-2992
Lawrence, Stephanie/3000 Chestnut Ave #220,
Baltimore, MD (P 198)   **301-574-5751**
Leach, Peter/116 S Seventh St, Philadelphia, PA 215-574-0230
Leaman, Chris/42 Old Lancaster Rd, Malvern, PA 215-647-8455
Leatherman, William/173 Massachusetts Ave, Boston, MA 617-536-5800
LeBlond, Jerry/7 Court Sq, Rutland, VT 802-773-4205
Lee, John/IBM Americas Grp/Rt 9, N Tarrytown, NY 914-332-2864
Lee, Raymond/PO Box 9743, Baltimore, MD 301-323-5764
Leeming Studios Inc/222 Richmond St, Providence, RI........401-421-1916
Lefcourt, Victoria/3207 Coquelin Terr, Chevy Chase, MD 301-652-1658
Leifer, David/251 Kelton St, Boston, MA..........................617-277-7513
Lemay, Charles J/864 Elm St, Manchester, NH 603-669-9380
Leney, Julia/PO Box 434, Wayland, MA 617-358-7229
Lennon, Jim/24 South Mall, Plainview, NY 516-752-0610
Lent, Max/24 Wellington Ave, Rochester, NY 716-328-5126
Lent, Michael/421 Madison St, Hoboken, NJ 201-798-4866
Leomporra, Greg/RTE 130 & Willow Drive, Cinnaminson, NJ ..609-829-6866
Leonard, Barney/518 Putnam Rd, Merion,
PA (P 178,179)   **215-664-2525**
Lerat, Andree/241 Perkins St #H202, Boston, MA..............617-738-9553
Leslie, Barbara/81 Grant St, Burlington, VT 802-864-0060
Leung, Jook /35 S Van Brunt St, Englewood,
NJ (P 113)   **201-894-5881**
Levart, Herb/566 Secor Rd, Hartsdale, NY 914-946-2060
Leveille, David/27-31 St Bridget's Dr, Rochester, NY 716-423-9474

Levin, Aaron M/3000 Chestnut Ave #102, Baltimore, MD 301-467-8646
Levine, Allen/B-2 Merry Lane, East Hanover, NJ................201-884-1154
Levine, Mimi/8317 Woodhaven Blvd, Bethesda, MD 301-469-6550
Levy, Seymour/10 Chestnut St, Needham, MA 617-444-4218
Lewis Studios/344 Kaplan Dr, Fairfield, NJ 201-227-1234
Lewis, Ronald/PO Box 489, East Hampton, NY 516-329-1886
Lewitt, Peter/39 Billings Park, Newton, MA 617-244-6552
Ley, Russell/103 Ardale St, Boston, MA 617-325-2500
Lidington, John/22 Industrial Park Rd, Hingham, MA 617-749-7771
Lieberman, Fred/2426 Linden Ln, Silver Spring, MD 301-565-0644
Lien, Peter/1084 N Delaware Ave, Philadelphia,
PA (P 100, 101)   **215-426-3988**
Lightstruck Studio/613 N Eutaw St, Baltimore, MD 301-727-2220
Lilley, Weaver/2107 Chancellor St, Philadelphia, PA 215-567-2881
Lillibridge, David/Rt 4 Box 1172, Burlington, CT 203-673-9786
Linck, Tony/2100 Linwood Ave, Fort Lee, NJ 201-944-5454
Lincoln, Denise/30 St John Pl, Westport, CT 203-226-3724
Lincon, James/30 St John Pl, Westport, CT 203-226-3724
Line, Craig/PO Box 11, Marshfield, VT 802-426-3592
Linehan, Clark/31 Blackburn Ctr, Gloucester, MA 808-281-3903
Lipshutz, Ellen/Buckhill Farm Rd, Arlington, VT 802-375-6316
Litoff, Walter/2919 Union St, Rochester, NY 716-232-6140
Littell, Dorothy/74 Lawn St, Boston, MA 617-739-5196
Littlehales, Breton/9520 Seminole St, Silver Spring, MD 202-291-2422
Lobell, Richard/536 West Chester St, Long Beach, NY 516-431-8899
Lokmer, John/PO Box 2782, Pittsburgh, PA 412-765-3565
Long Shots/4421 East West Hwy, Bethesda, MD 301-654-0279
Longcor, W K/Bear Pond, Andover, NJ 201-398-2225
Longley, Steven/2224 North Charles St, Baltimore, MD 301-467-4185
Lowe, Thom/1420 E Front St, Plainfield, NJ 201-769-8485
Lukowicz, Jerome/122 Arch St, Philadelphia, PA 215-922-7122

M

Macchiarulo, Tony/12 Gregory Blvd, Norwalk, CT 203-866-8414
Machalaba, Robert/4 Brentwood Dr, Livingston, NJ 201-992-4674
MacHenry, Kate/5 Colliston Rd #6, Brookline, MA 617-277-5736
Maciel, Chris/RD2 Box 176 Riley Rd, New Windsor, NY 914-564-6972
MacKenzie, Maxwell/2641 Garfield St NW, Washington, DC ..202-232-6686
Mackey, Doc/North St Church, Georgetown, MA 508-352-7055
Macomber, Peter/100 Oak St, Portland, ME 207-772-1208
MacWright, Jeff/248 East Main, Chester, NJ 201-879-4545
Macys, Sandy (Mr)/552 RR 1, Waitsfield, VT 802-496-2518
Maggio, Chris/180 St Paul St, Rochester, NY 716-454-3929
Maggio, Donald/Brook Hill Ln #5E, Rochester, NY 716-381-8053
Maglott, Larry/249 A St, Boston, MA 617-482-9347
Magnet, Jeff/Flight Source Intl/Box 1054, Cambridge, MA 617-547-8226
Magno, Thomas/19 Peters St, Cambridge, MA 617-492-5197
Magro, Benjamin/2 Mechanic St, Camden, ME 207-236-4774
Mahoney, Bob/347 Cameo Circle, Liverpool, NY 315-652-7870
Malin, Marc/221 Crafts Rd, Brookline, MA 617-734-4916
Malitsky, Ed/337 Summer St, Boston, MA 617-451-0655
Malka, Daniel/1030 St Alexandre #203, Montreal, QU 514-397-9704
Maltinsky Photo/109 Broad St, Boston, MA 617-426-2128
Malyszko, Michael/90 South St, Boston, MA 617-426-9111
Mandelkorn, Richard/309 Waltham St, W Newton, MA 617-332-3246
Manheim, Michael Philip/PO Box 35, Marblehead, MA 617-631-3560
Mann, Richard J/PO Box 2712, Dix Hills, NY 516-754-8496
Manning, Ed/875 E Broadway, Stratford, CT 203-375-3384
Marchese, Frank/56 Arbor St, Hartford, CT 203-232-4417
Mares, Manuel/185 Chestnut Hill Ave, Brighton, MA 617-782-4208
Margel, Steve/215 First St, Cambridge, MA 617-547-4445
Margolis, David/682 Howard Ave, New Haven, CT 203-777-7288
Margolis, Paul/109 Grand Ave, Englewood, NJ 201-569-2316
Marinelli, Jack/673 Willow St, Waterbury, CT 203-756-3273
Marinelli, Mary Leigh/4 Salton Stall Pkwy, Salem, MA 508-745-7035
Mark Selig/201 South St, Boston, MA..............................617-267-2000
Markel, Brad/639 'E' St NE, Washington, DC 703-920-2791
Markowitz, Joel/2 Kensington Ave, Jersey City, NJ 202-451-0413
Marsel, Steve/, Boston, MA 617-266-1181
Martin Paul Ltd/247 Newbury St, Boston, MA 617-536-1644
Martin, Bruce/266-A Pearl St, Cambridge, MA 617-492-8009
Martin, Butch/715 Hussa St, Linden, NJ 201-486-3049
Martin, Jeff/6 Industrial Way W, Eatontown, NJ 201-389-0888
Martin, Marilyn/130 Appleton St #2I, Boston, MA...............617-262-5507
Martin, Michael P/220 E Preston Ave, Wildwood Crest, NJ ...609-729-0838
Martin-Elson, Patricia/120 Crooked Hill Rd, Huntington, NY ..516-427-4799
Martine, Douglas/410 Oakwood Rd, Huntington Sta, NY.......516-423-3614
Masiello, Ralph/17 Tampa St, Worcester, MA 508-752-9871

Mason, Donald W/10 E 21st St, Baltimore, MD 301-244-0385
Mason, Lisa/516 1/2 8th St, Washington, DC 202-543-1611
Mason, Phil/15 St Mary's Ct, Brookline, MA 617-232-0908
Mason, Tom/117 Van Dyke Rd, Hopewell, NJ 609-466-0911
Massar, Ivan/296 Bedford St, Concord, MA 617-369-4090
Masser, Randy/15 Barnes Terrace, Chappaqua, NY 914-238-8167
Mastalia, Francesco/2 Midland Ave, Hawthorne, NJ 212-772-8449
Mastri, Len/1 Mill St, Burlington, VT 802-862-4009

Matt, Phil/PO Box 10406, Rochester,
NY (P 181) **716-461-5977**
Mattei, George Photography/179 Main St, Hackensack, NJ 201-342-0740
Mattingly, Brendan/4404 Independence St, Rockville, MD 301-933-3942
Maughart, Brad/13 Church St, Framingham, MA 508-875-4447
Mauro, George, Photo/211 Glenridge Ave, Montclair, NJ 201-744-7899
Mauss, Peter/222 Valley Pl, Mamaroneck, NY 914-698-4060
Mavodones, Bill/46 Waltham St #105, Boston, MA 617-423-7382
May Tell, Susan/, , NY 516-433-8244
May, Bill/PO Box 1567, Montclair, NJ 201-624-6782
Mayernik, George/41 Wolfpit Ave #2N, Norwalk, CT 203-846-1406
Maynard, Ray/149 Lynn Ave, Hampton Bay, NY 516-878-1186
Mazzone, James/1201 82nd St, N Bergen, NJ 201-861-8992
McCary, Joe/8804 Monard Dr, Silver Spring, MD 301-588-6637
McCash, Scott/10922 Pleasant Acres Dr, Adelphi, MD 301-595-8852
McConnell & McConnell/, , NY 516-883-0058
McConnell, Jack/182 Broad St, Old Wethersfield, CT 203-563-6154
McConnell, Russ/8 Adler Dr, E Syracuse, NY 315-433-1005
McCormack, Richard/459 Farimount Ave, Jersey City, NJ 201-435-8718
McCormick & Nelson, Inc/34 Piave St, Stamford, CT 203-348-5062
McCormick, Ed/55 Hancock St, Lexington, MA 617-862-2552
McCoy, Dan/Box 573, Housatonic, MA 413-274-6211
McDonald, Kevin R/319 Newtown Turnpike, Redding, CT 203-938-9276
McDowell, Bill/56 Edmonds St, Rochester, NY 716-442-8632
McFarland, Nancy & Lowell/3 Tuck Lane, Westport, CT 203-227-6178
McGovern, Michael/8205 Robin Hood Ct, Towson, MD 301-337-5044
McGrail, John/6576 Senator Ln, Bensalem, PA 215-750-6070
McKean, Thomas R/1418 Monk Rd, Gladwyne, PA 215-642-1412
McKiernan, Scott/12 Gannett Rd, Scituate, MA 617-545-0008
McLaren, Lynn/PO Box 2086, Beaufort, SC 803-524-0973
McLean, Alex/25 Bay State Rd, Boston, MA 617-536-6261
McMullin, Forest/183 St Paul St, Rochester, NY 716-262-3944
McNamara, Mr Casey/109 Broad St, Boston, MA 617-542-5337
McNeill, Brian/840 W Main St, Lansdale, PA 215-368-3326
McNiss, Chase/2 Oliver Dr, Hudson, NH 603-889-6713
McQueen, Ann/791 Tremont St #W401, Boston, MA 617-267-6258
McWilliams, Jack/15 Progress Ave, Chelmsford, MA 508-256-9615

Meacham, Joseph/601 North 3rd St, Philadelphia,
PA (P 117) **215-925-8122**
MeadowInds Photo Srvc/259 Hackensack St, E Rutherford, NJ 201-933-9121
Mecca, Jack/1508 72nd St, North Bergen, NJ 201-869-7956
Mednick, Seymour/316 S Camac, Philadelphia, PA 215-735-6100
Medvec, Emily/151 Kentucky Ave SE, Washington, DC 202-546-1220
Meech, Christopher/456 Glenbrook Rd, Stamford, CT 203-348-1158
Meehan, Joseph/RD 1/Box 39/Betwn Lakes Rd, Salisbury, CT 203-824-0866
Meek, Richard/8 Skyline Dr, Huntington, NY 516-271-0072
Mehne, Ralph/1501 Rose Terrace, Union, NJ 201-686-0668
Meiller, Henry Studios/1026 Wood St, Philadelphia, PA 215-922-1525
Melford, Michael/Petersville Farm, Mt Kisco, NY 914-241-7103
Melino, Gary/25 Bright Water Dr, Warwick, RI 508-379-0166
Melkin, Bruce/27 Tintern Lane, Scarsdale, NY 914-472-3194

Mellor, D W/1020 Mt Pleasant Rd, Bryn Mawr,
PA (P 182,183) **215-527-9040**
Melo, Michael/RR1/Box 20, Winterport, ME 207-223-8894
Melton, Janice Munnings/692 Walkhill St, Boston, MA 617-298-1443
Mendelsohn, David/Sky Farm Rd, Northwood, NH 603-942-7622
Mendez, Manny/150 Adams St, Newark, NJ 201344-4440
Mendlowitz, Benjamin/Rte 175/Box 14, Brooklin, ME 207-359-2131
Mercer, Ralph/451 D St 9th Fl, Boston, MA 617-951-4604
Merchant, Martin/22 Barker Ave, White Plains, NY 914-997-2200
Merrick, Tad/64 Main St, Middlebury, VT 802-388-9598
Merz, Laurence/215 Georgetown Rd, Weston, CT 203-222-1936
Michael's/481 Central Ave, Cedarhurst, NY 516-374-3456
Michaels, John - MediaVisions/17 May St, Clifton, NJ 201-772-0181
Milens, Sanders H/38 Mt Philo Rd POB 805, Shelburne, VT 802-388-9598
Miles, Clayton/535 Albany St, Boston, MA 617-451-0630
Millard, Howard/220 Sixth Ave, Pelham, NY 914-738-3689
Miller, David Photo/5 Lake St, Morris, NY 607-263-5060
Miller, Don/60 Sindle Ave, Little Falls, NJ 201-785-9090
Miller, Gary/PO Box 136, Bedford Hills, NY 914-666-4174
Miller, J T/12 Forest Edge Dr, Titusville, NJ 609-737-3116

Miller, John L/223 West Fell St, Summit Hill, PA 717-645-3661
Miller, Melabee/29 Beechwood Pl, Hillside, NJ 201-527-9121
Miller, Michael S/Three Clayton Rd, Morganville, NJ 201-536-9459
Miller, Roger/1411 Hollins St Union Sq, Baltimore, MD 301-566-1222
Millman, Lester Jay/PO Box 61H, Scarsdale, NY 914-946-2093
Mincey, Dale/113 Brunswick St, Jersey City, NJ 201-420-9387
Mindell, Doug/811 Boylston St, Boston, MA 617-262-3968
Mink, Mike/180 St Paul St 5th Fl, Rochester, NY 716-325-4865
Miraglia, Elizabeth/29 Drummer Ln, W Redding, CT 203-938-2261

Mirando, Gary/27 Cleveland St, Valhalla,
NY (P 160) **914-997-6588**
Mitchell, Les/RD #4/Box 93 Pittenger Pnd Rd, Freehold, NJ 201-462-2451
Mitchell, Mike/1501 14th St NW #301, Washington, DC 202-234-6400
Mogerley, Jean/1262 Pines Lake Dr W, Wayne, NJ 201-839-2355
Molinaro, Neil R/15 Walnut Ave, Clark, NJ 201-396-8980
Monroe, Robert/Kennel Rd, Cuddebackville, NY 914-754-8329
Moore, Cliff/30 Skillman Ave, Rocky Hill, NJ 609-921-3754
Moore, Marvin/5240 Blowers St, Halifax B3J 1J7, NS 902-420-1559
Mopsik, Eugene/230 Monroe St, Philadelphia, PA 215-922-3489
Moran, Richard/351 Main St, Kingston, PA 717-287-3182
Morelli, Mark/44 Roberts Rd, Cambridge, MA 617-547-0409
Morgan, Bruce/55 S Grand Ave, Baldwin, NY 516-546-3554
Morgan, Hank/14 Waterbury Ave, Stamford, CT 203-325-3120
Morley, Bob/186 Lincoln St #202, Boston, MA 617-482-7279
Morrow, Christopher W/PO Box 208, Arlington, MA 617-648-6770
Morse, Timothy/148 Rutland St, Carlisle, MA 508-369-8036
Morse/Peterson Photo/465-D Medford St, Charlestown, MA 617-241-8228
Mottau, Gary/17 Irving Place, Holliston, MA 508-429-8645
Moyer, Stephen/911 State St, Lancaster, PA 717-393-0918
Mozo Photo Design/282 Shelton Rd (Rt 110), Monroe, CT 203-261-7400
Mullen, Stephen/825 N 2nd St, Philadelphia, PA 215-574-9770
Mulligan, Bob/109 Broad St, Boston, MA 617-542-7308
Mulligan, Joseph/239 Chestnut St, Philadelphia, PA 215-592-1359
Munster, Joseph/Old Rt 28, Phoenicia, NY 914-688-5347
Murray, Chris/110 Brenner Dr, Congers, NY 914-268-5531
Murray, Matt/PO Box 53605, Philadelphia, PA 215-829-9522
Murray, Ric/232 W Exchange St, Providence, RI 401-751-8806
Murry, Peggy/1913 VWaverly St, Philadelphia, PA 215-735-4834
Muskie, Stephen O/23 Lookout Hill, Peterborough, NH 603-924-6541
Musto, Tom/225 S Main St, Wilkes-Barre, PA 717-822-5798
Mydans, Carl/212 Hommocks Rd, Larchmont, NY 212-841-2345
Myers Studios Inc/5775 Big Tree Rd, Orchard Park, NY 716-662-6002
Myers, Gene/250 N Goodman St, Rochester, NY 716-244-4420
Myers, Steve/PO Box J, Almond, NY 607-276-6400
Myron/127 Dorrance St, Providence, RI 401-421-1946

N

Nadel, Lee/10 Loveland Rd, Brookline, MA 617-451-6646
Nagler, Lanny/56 Arbor St, Hartford, CT 203-233-4040
Navin, Mr Chris/, Boston, MA 617-825-3299
Nelder, Oscar/93 Hardy St/Box 661, Presque Isle, ME 207-769-5911
Nelkin, Bruce/27 Tintern Lane, Scarsdale, NY 914-472-3194
Nelson, Janet/Finney Farm, Croton-On-Hudson, NY 914-271-5453
Nelson, Michael/5 Academy Ave, Cornwall-on-Hudson, NY 914-534-4563
Nerney, Dan/137 Rowayton Ave, Rowayton, CT 203-853-2782
Nettis, Joseph/1534 Sansom St 2nd Fl, Philadelphia, PA 215-563-5444
Neudorfer, Brien/46 Waltham St, Boston, MA 617-451-9211
Neumayer, Joseph/Chateau Rive #102, Peekskill, NY 914-739-3005

Nibauer, Scott/1084 N Delaware Ave, Philadelphia,
PA (P 100, 101) **215-426-3988**
Nible, Rick/408 Vine St 4th Fl, Philadelphia, PA 215-625-0638
Nighswander, Tim/315 Peck St, New Haven, CT 203-789-8529
Nikas, Greg/Drawer 690, Ipswich, MA 508-356-0018

Noble Inc/2313 Maryland Ave, Baltimore,
MD (P 194,195) **301-235-5235**
Nochton, Jack/1238 W Broad St, Bethlehem, PA 215-691-2223
Nodine, Dennis/PO Box 30353, Charlotte, NC 704-373-3374
Noel, Peter/18 Bartlett St, Malden, MA 617-322-7629
Nordell, John/12 Grove St, Boston, MA 617-723-5484
Norris, Robert/RFD 1 Box 4480, Pittsfield, ME 207-487-5981
North Light Photo/931 Penn Ave, Reading, PA 215-373-5553
Northlight Visual Comm Group/21-23 Quine St, Cranford, NJ 201-272-1155

O

O'Clair, Dennis/75 Stuart Ave, Amityville, NY 516-598-3546
O'Connell, Bill/791 Tremont St, Boston, MA 617-437-7556
O'Donnell, John/179 Westmoreland St, White Plains, NY 914-948-1786
O'Donoghue, Ken/8 Union Park St, Boston, MA 617-542-4898

PHOTOGRAPHERS

O'Hare, Richard/POB 273, Clifton Heights, PA 215-626-1429
O'Neill, James/1543 Kater St, Philadelphia, PA 215-545-3223
O'Neill, Martin/1914 Mt Royal Terr 1st Fl, Baltimore, MD 301-225-0522
O'Neill, Michael Photo/162 Lakefield Rd, E Northport, NY 516-754-0459
O'Shaughnessy, Bob/23 Dry Dock Ave, Boston, MA 617-542-7122
O'Toole, Terrence/104 Union Park St, Boston, MA 617-426-6357
Obermeyer, Eva/PO Box 1722, Union, NJ 201-375-3322
Odor, Lou/288 Kerrigan Blvd, Newark, NJ 201-371-2669
Ogiba, Joseph Jr/PO Box M, Somerville, NJ 201-218-8930
Olbrys, Anthony/41 Pepper Ridge Rd, Stamford, CT 203-322-9422
Oliver, Lou/8 Adler Dr, E Syracuse, NY 315-433-1005
Olivera, Bob/108 Chestnut St, Rehoboth, MA 508-252-6594
Olmstead Studio/118 South St, Boston, MA 617-542-2024
Olsen, Peter/1415 Morris St, Philadelphia, PA 215-465-9736
Orel, Mano/PO Box E, Dove Court, Croton-On-Hudson, NY 914-271-5542
Orkin, Pete/80 Washington St, S Norwalk, CT 203-866-9978
Orlando, Fran/329 Spruce St, Philadelphia, PA 215-493-8064
Orling, Alan S/Hawley Rd, North Salem, NY 914-669-5405
Orrico, Charles/72 Barry Ln, Syosset, NY 516-364-2257
Ostrowski, Waldemar/386 Brook Ave, Passaic Park, NJ 201-471-3033
Ottman, Matthew/4410 Providence Ln #8, Winston-Salem, NC 919-722-1707
Ouzer, Louis/120 East Ave, Rochester, NY 716-454-7582
Owens, John/451 D St #810, Boston, MA 617-330-1498

P

Paige, Peter/269 Parkside Rd, Harrington Park, NJ 201-767-3150
Painter, Joseph/205 Fairmont Ave, Philadelphia, PA 215-592-1612
Palmer, Gabe/Fire Hill Farm, West Redding, CT 203-938-2514
Palmiere, Jorge/316 F St NE #21, Washington, DC 202-546-7380
Pamatat, Ken/165 West Ave, Rochester, NY 716-235-1222
Panioto, Mark/95 Mohawk Ln, Weathersfield, CT 203-241-3202
Pantages, Tom/3 Raymond St, Gloucester, MA 617-525-3678
Pape, Maria/41 Magee Ave, Stamford, CT 203-348-1588
Paredes, Cesar/Lawrence Commons, Lawrenceville, NJ 609-987-8626
Parker, James/401 West Redwood St #207, Baltimore, MD 301-528-1099
Parrot Productions/3730 Zuck Rd, Erie, PA 814-833-8739
Parsons, Andrew/59 Wareham, Boston, MA 617-542-9071
Paskevich, John/1500 Locust St #3017, Philadelphia, PA 215-735-9868
Pasley, Richard/15 Bristol St, Cambridge, MA 617-864-8386
Paul, Martin/37 Winchester St, Boston, MA 617-451-1818
Paul, Richard/7525 Washington St, Pittsburgh, PA 412-271-6609
Pavlovich, James/49 Worcester St, Boston, MA 617-266-9723
Paxenos, Dennis F/2125 Maryland Ave #103, Baltimore, MD 301-837-1029
Payne, John J/43 Brookfield Pl, Pleasantville, NY (P 164) 914-747-1282
Pearson, David/158 W Clinton St, Dover, NJ 201-366-3000
Pease, Greg/23 E 22nd St, Baltimore, MD (P 206,207) 301-332-0583
Peck, Daniel/7199 Chesapeake Ave, Silver Spring, MD 301-587-1714
Peckham, Lynda/65 S Broadway, Tarrytown, NY 914-631-5050
Pehlman, Barry/701 Cadwalader Circle, Exton, PA 215-524-1404
Peirce, George E/133 Ramapo Ave, Pompton Lakes, NJ 201-831-8418
Pellegrini, Lee/381 Newtonville Ave, Newtonville, MA 617-964-7925
Peluso, Frank/15 Caspar Berger Rd, Whitehouse Station, NJ 201-534-9637
Pendergrast, Mark/RD 2/Box 1412, Stowe, VT 802-253-4159
Penn, Allan/8 Newcomb St, Boston, MA 617-442-1543
Penneys, Robert/12 E Mill Station, Newark, DE 302-733-0444
Penni, Jay/15A St Mary's Court, Brookline, MA 617-232-7281
Perez, Paul R/143 W Hoffman Ave, Lindenhurst, NY 516-226-0846
Perlman, Ilene/483 Hope St, Providence, RI 401-273-8087
Perlmutter, Steven/246 Nicoll St, New Haven, CT 203-789-8493
Perron, Robert/119 Chestnut St, Branford, CT 203-481-2004
Peterson, Brent/73 Maple Ave, Tuckahoe, NY 212-573-7195
Petrakas, George/E Berkeley, Boston, MA 617-426-8679
Petronio, Frank/74 Westchester Ave, Rochester, NY 716-288-4642
Petty, David/15 Union St/Stone Mill Bldg, Lawrence, MA 508-794-0404
Pevarnik, Gervose/180 St Paul St, Rochester, NY 716-262-3579
Philips, Jaye R/2 Crescent Hill Ave, Arlington, MA 617-646-8491
Photo Craft/50 W Gude Dr, Rockville, MD 301-424-0577
Photo Dimensions/12 S Virginia Ave, Atlantic City, NJ 609-344-1212
Photo Synthesis/216 Blvd of Allies, Pittsburgh, PA 412-642-7734
Photo-Colortura/PO Box 1749, Boston, MA 617-522-5132
Photographers & Co/113 S Brandywine Ave, Schenectady, NY 518-377-9457
Photographic House/158 W Clinton St, Dover, NJ 201-366-3000
Photographic Illustration Ltd/7th & Ranstead, Philadelphia, PA 215-925-7073
Photown Studio/190 Vandervoort St, North Tonawanda, NY 716-693-2912
Photoworks/211 Glenridge Ave, Montclair, NJ 201-509-8840
Piaget, John/155 Central Ave, New Rochelle, NY 914-235-9781
Picarello, Carmine/12 S Main St, S Norwalk, CT 203-866-8987
Pickerell, Jim H/110 Frederick Ave E Bay, Rockville, MD 301-251-0720
Pickett, John/109 Broad St, Boston, MA 617-423-4399
Pictorial/8081 Zionsville Rd, Indianapolis, IN 317-872-7220
Picture That Inc/880 Briarwood, Newtown Square, PA 215-353-8833
Picturehouse Assoc Inc/22 Elizabeth St, Norwalk, CT 203-852-1776
Picturesques Studios/1879 Old Cuthbert Rd, Cherry Hill, NJ 609-354-1903
Picturewise/10 Terhune Pl, Hackensack, NJ 201-343-1060
Pierce, Barbara/P.O. Box 196, Pittsford, VT 802-747-3070
Pietersen, Alex/29 Raynor Rd, Morristown, NJ 201-267-7003
Pinkerton, Margo Taussig/RR1/Box 81, Canaan, NH 603-523-4202
Piperno, Lauren/215 E Dean St, Freeport, NY 718-935-1550
Pivak, Kenneth/605 Pavonia Ave, Jersey City, NJ 201-656-0508
Plank, David/Cherry & Carpenter Sts, Reading, PA 215-376-3461
Platteter, George/82 Colonnade Dr, Rochester, NY 716-334-4488
Plouffe, Reid/PO Box 5142, Portsmouth, NH 603-431-2891
Pobiner, Ted Studios Inc/22 Cabriolet Lane, Melville, NY (P 127) 212-679-5911
Poggenpohl, Eric/12 Walnut St, Amherst, MA 413-256-0948
Pohuski, Michael/36 S Paca St #314, Baltimore, MD 301-962-5404
Polansky, Allen/1431 Park Ave, Baltimore, MD 301-383-9021
Polumbaum, Ted/326 Harvard St, Cambridge, MA 617-491-4947
Pope-Lance, Elton/125 Stock Farm Rd, Sudbury, MD 508-443-4393
Porcella, Phil/572 Washington St #16, Wellesley, MA 617-239-1770
Portsmouth Photography/Old Canaan Rd, Barrington, NH 603-431-3351
Potter, Anthony/509 W Fayette St, Syracuse, NY 315-428-8900
Powers, James/15 Jerome Pl, Leominster, MA 617-534-3664
Powers, Jody/135 Fifth Ave #8B, Pelham, NY 212-489-7972
Pownall, Ron/7 Ellsworth Ave, Cambridge, MA 617-354-0846
Praus, Edgar G/176 Anderson Ave, Rochester, NY 716-442-4820
Preisler, Don/8563 Greenbelt Rd #204, Greenbelt, MD 301-552-3567
Prezio, Franco/606 Allen Ln, Media, PA 215-565-6919
Price, Donald/2849 Kennedy Blvd, Jersey City, NJ 201-420-7255
Price, Greg/165 Westfield Ave, Clark, NJ 201-272-1331
Prieur, Kevin/79 Milk St #1108, Boston, MA 617-292-6411
Prince, James/329 Mercer St, Stirling, NJ 201-580-9080
Procaccini, Charles/1355 New York Ave, Huntington Sta, NY 516-549-4144
Procopio, Richard/PO Box 422, Rockport, ME 207-596-6379
Profetto, Joe Jr./566 Delsea Dr, Vineland, NJ 609-696-3771
Putnam, Sarah/8 Newell St, Cambridge, MA 617-547-3758

QR

Quin, Clark/241 A Street, Boston, MA 617-451-2686
Quindry, Richard/200 Loney St, Philadelphia, PA 215-742-6300
Raab, Timothy/163 Delaware Ave, Delmar, NY 518-439-2298
Rabdau, Yvonne/RR2 Box 590 Kelly Ct, Stormville, NY 914-221-4643
Rabinowitz, Barry/515 Willow St, Waterbury, CT 203-574-1129
Radcliffe, Tom/7002 Carroll Ave, Tokoma Park, MD 301-270-2340
Rae, John/148 Worchester St, Boston, MA 617-266-5754
Ramsdale, Jack/945 North 5th, Philadelphia, PA 215-238-1436
Ranck, Rosemary/323 W Mermaid Ln, Philadelphia, PA 215-242-3718
Rapp, Frank/327 A St, Boston, MA 617-542-4462
Rauch, Bonnie/Crane Rd, Somers, NY 914-277-3986
Rawle, Johnathan/7 Railroad Ave, Bedford, MA 617-275-3030
Ray, Dean/2900 Chestnut Ave, Baltimore, MD 301-243-3441
Raycroft, Jim/326 A Street #C, Boston, MA 617-542-7229
Rea, Mark/107 South St, Boston, MA 617-423-7053
Redding, Jim/247 Newbury St, Boston, MA 617-677-1899
Reed, Tom/9505 Adelphi Rd, Silver Spring, MD 301-439-2912
Reichel, Lorna/PO Box 63, E Greenbush, NY 518-477-7822
Reis, Jon Photography/141 The Commons, Ithaca, NY 607-272-1966
Renard, Jean/142 Berkeley St, Boston, MA 617-266-8673
Renckly, Joe/1200 Linden Pl, Pittsburgh, PA 412-323-2122
Resnick, Seth/28 Seaverns Ave #8, Boston, MA 617-983-0291
Retallack, John/207 Erie Station Rd, West Henrietta, NY 716-334-1530
Revette, David/111 Sunset Ave, Syracuse, NY (P 184) 315-422-1558
Richard, George/PO Box 392, Walker Valley, NY 914-733-4300
Richards, Christopher/737 Canal St Bldg 35A, Stamford, CT 203-964-0235
Richards, Mark/58 Falcon St, Needham, MA 617-449-7135
Richards, Toby/1 Sherbrooke Dr, Princeton Junction, NJ 609-275-1885
Richardson, Jonathan R/PO Box 617, Andover, MA 508-975-7722
Richmond, Jack/12 Farnsworth St, Boston, MA 617-482-7158
Riemer, Ken/183 St Paul St, Rochester, NY 716-232-5450
Riley, George/Sisquisic Trail PO Box 840, Yarmouth, ME 207-846-5787
Riley, Laura/Hidden Spng Fm PO Box 186, Pittstown, NJ 201-735-7707
Ritter, Frank/2414 Evergreen St, Yorktown Hts, NY 914-962-5385
Rivera, Angelo/671 Beach St, Revere, MA 617-247-6387

Rixon, Mike/1 Meadow Lane, Bow, NH 603-228-2362
Rizzi, Leonard F/5161 River Rd Bldg 2B, Bethesda, MD 301-652-1303
Rizzo, John/146 Halstead St, Rochester, NY (P 156,157) 716-288-1102
Robb, Steve/535 Albany St, Boston, MA 617-542-6565
Roberts, Mathieu/200 Henry St, Stamford, CT 203-324-3582
Roberts, Terrence/1910 Julian Rd, Wilmington, DE 302-658-8854
Robins, Susan/124 N Third St, Philadelphia, PA (P 185) 215-238-9988
Robinson, George A/4-A Stonehedge Dr, S Burlington, VT 802-862-6902
Robinson, Mike/2413 Sarah St, Pittsburgh, PA 412-431-4102
Rocheleau, Paul/Canaan Rd, Richmond, MA 413-698-2676
Rock, Dean/358R W Penn Ave, Wernersville, PA 215-678-3335
Rockhill, Morgan/204 Westminster Mall, Providence, RI 401-274-3472
Rode, Robert/2670 Arleigh Rd, East Meadow, NY 516-485-6687
Rogers, Martin/5055 MacArthur Blvd, Washington, DC 202-966-0333
Rogerson, Zebulon W/1312 18th St NW 5th Fl, Washington, DC 202-293-1687
Rolett, Robert/PO Box 7744, Lancaster, PA 717-293-8699
Romanoff, Mark/8 Wessex Rd, Silver Spring, MD 301-585-6627
Romanos, Michael/30 Stanton Rd, Brookline, MA 617-277-3504
Roos, Warren Photo Inc/135 Somerset St, Portland, ME (P 165) 207-773-3771
Roper, Bob Photo/518 Catherine St, Philadelphia, PA 215-440-9009
Roseman, Shelly/1238 Callowhill St, Philadelphia, PA 215-922-1430
Rosenblatt, Jay/360 Glenwood Ave, E Orange, NJ 201-414-8833
Rosenblum, Bruce/181 W 16th St, Bayonne, NJ 201-436-7141
Rosenthal, Stephen/59 Maple St, Auburndale, MA 617-244-2986
Rosier, Gerald/PO Box 470, Framingham, MA 617-881-2512
Rosner, Eric/314 N 13th St, Philadelphia, PA 215-629-1240
Rosner, Stu/One Thompson Sq, Charlestown, MA 617-242-2112
Ross, Alex F/1622 Chestnut St, Philadelphia, PA 215-576-7799
Ross, Doug/610 Eighth Ave, E Northport, NY 516-754-0387
Rossi, Dave/121 Central Ave, Westfield, NJ 201-232-8300
Rossotto, Frank/184 E Main St, Westfield, NY 716-326-2792
Rossow, Lee/641 Van Doren Ct, Valley Cottage, NY 914-358-6931
Roth, Eric/337 Summer St, Boston, MA (P 186,187) 617-338-5358
Rotman, Jeffrey L/14 Cottage Ave, Somerville, MA 617-666-0874
Rowan, Norm R/106 E 6th St, Clifton, NJ 201-340-2284
Rowan, Scott/1 Quail Hill Ln, Downingtown, PA 215-269-9583
Rowin, Stanley/791 Tremont St #W515, Boston, MA 617-437-0641
Rubenstein, Len/87 Pine St, Easton, MA 508-238-0744
Rubinstein, Len/, Boston, MA 617-238-0744
Ruggeri, Lawrence/10 Old Post Office Rd, Silver Spring, MD 301-588-3131
Ruggieri, Ignazio/86 Lackawanna Ave, W Paterson, NJ 201-785-2247
Ruiz, Felix/72 Smith Ave, White Plains, NY 914-949-3353
Ruiz, Robert/818 E Highland Dr, Buffalo, NY 716-837-1428
Rummel, Hal/36 S Paca St #515, Baltimore, MD 301-244-8517
Rumph, Charles/332 N St NW, Washington, DC 202-338-4431
Runyon, Paul/113 Arch St, Philadelphia, PA 215-238-0655
Russ, Clive/1311 North St, Walpole, MA 508-668-2536
Russel, Rae/75 Byram Lake Rd, Mount Kisco, NY 914-241-0057
Russell Studios/103 Ardale, Boston, MA 617-325-2500
Russo, Rich/11 Clinton St, Morristown, NJ 201-538-6954
Ryan, Michael/50 Melcher St, Boston, MA 617-236-1920

S

Sa'adah, Jonathan/PO Box 247, Hartford, VT 802-295-5327
Sabol, George Jeremy/2B Park Ave, Englishtown, NJ 201-446-4944
Sachs, John/29 Stanhope St, Boston, MA 617-497-7195
Sagala, Steve/9 Whippany RD #B-2, Whippany, NJ 201-884-9410
Sakmanoff, George/179 Massachusetts Ave, Boston, MA 617-262-7227
Salamon, Londa/2634 Parrish, Philadelphia, PA 215-765-6632
Salamone, Anthony/17 Anthol St, Brighton, MA 617-254-5427
Salant, Robin/165 Westfield Ave, Clark, NJ 201-272-1331
Salomone, Frank/296 Brick Blvd, Bricktown, NJ 201-920-1525
Salsbery, Lee/14 Seventh St NE, Washington, DC 202-543-1222
Salter, Jeff/4215 Bethel Church Rd #B12, Columbia, SC 803-787-8620
Samara, Thomas/713 Erie Blvd West, Syracuse, NY 315-476-4984
Samu, Mark/39 Erlwein Ct, Massapequa, NY 516-795-1849
Samuels Studio/8 Waltham St, PO Box 201, Maynard, MA 508-897-7901
Sanderson, John/2310 Pennsylvania Ave, Pittsburgh, PA 412-263-2121
Sanford, Eric/110 Shaw St, Manchester, NH 603-624-0122
Sansone, Nadine/7 River St, Milford, CT 203-878-5090
Santaniello, Angelo/20 Passaic St, Garfield, NJ 201-473-1141
Santos, Don/175-A Boston Post Rd, Waterford, CT 203-443-5668
Sapienza, Louis A/1344 Martine Ave, Plainfield, NJ 201-756-9200
Saraceno, Paul/Box 277, Groton, MA 508-448-2566
Sargent, William/PO Box 331, Woods Hole, MA 508-548-2673
Sasso, Ken/116 Mattabaffet Dr, Meriden, CT 203-235-1421
Sauter, Ron Photo/183 St Paul St, Rochester, NY 716-232-1361
Savage, Sally/99 Orchard Terrace, Piermont, NY 914-359-5735
Savoie, Phil/187 Lake Ave, Trumbull, CT 203-268-9917
Saydah, Gerard/PO Box 210, Demarest, NJ 201-768-2582
Sayers, Jim/325 Valley Rd, West Orange, NJ 201-325-2352
Scalera, Ron/8 Rosen Brook Dr, Lincoln Park, NJ 201-694-0234
Scarpetta, Tony/443 Albany St #305, Boston, MA 617-350-8640
Schadt, Bob/23 Ransom Rd, Brighton, MA 617-782-3734
Schaeffer, Bruce/631 N Pottstown Pike, Exton, PA 215-363-5230
Schamp, Brough/1325 18th St NW #908, Washington, DC 202-331-7722
Schenk, Andy/28 Mulberry Ln, Colts Neck, NJ 201-946-9459
Scherer, Jim/35 Kingston St, Boston, MA 617-338-5678
Scherzi, James/5818 Molloy Rd, Syracuse, NY 315-455-7961
Schlanger, Irv/946 Cherokee Rd, Huntington Valley, PA 215-663-0663
Schlegel, Robert/2 Division St #10-11, Somerville, NJ 201-231-1212
Schleipman, Russell/298-A Columbus Ave, Boston, MA (P 188) 617-267-1677
Schlowsky, Bob/73 Old Rd, Weston, MA 617-899-5110
Schmitt, Steve/33 Sleeper St, Boston, MA 617-426-0858
Schoen, Robert/241 Crescent St, Waltham, MA 617-647-5546
Schoon, Tim/PO Box 7446, Lancaster, PA 717-291-9483
Schroeder, H Robert/PO Box 7361, W Trenton, NJ 609-883-8643
Schroers, Kenneth/188 Highland Ave, Clifton, NJ 201-472-8395
Schulmeyer, LT/2019 St Paul St, Baltimore, MD 301-332-0767
Schultz, Jurgen/Rt 100 N/Box 19, Londonderry, VT 802-824-3475
Schwartz, Linda Photo/One Franklin Dr, Mays Landing, NJ 609-625-7617
Schweikardt, Eric/PO Box 56, Southport, CT 203-375-8181
Scott, Jesse/205 Broughton Ave, Bloomfield, NJ 201-338-1548
Scott, Robert Photo/Old Field Inn/Prince Frederick, MD 301-535-3741
Scully, Paula Alyce/409 W Broadway, Boston, MA 617-268-8829
Seckinger, Angela/11231 Bybee St, Silver Spring, MD 301-649-3138
Seidel, Joan/337 Summer St, Boston, MA 617-357-8674
Seng, Walt/810 Penn Ave #400, Pittsburgh, PA (P 189) 412-391-6780
Serbin, Vincent/304 Church Rd, Bricktown, NJ 201-477-5620
Serio, Steve/423 W Broadway, Boston, MA 617-269-3600
Severi, Robert/813 Richmond Ave, Silver Spring, MD 301-585-1010
Sewell, John/35 Wareham St, Boston, MA 617-338-2202
Shafer, Bob/3554 Quebec St N W, Washington, DC 202-362-0630
Shaffer, Nancy/PO Box 333, Lincroft, NJ 201-846-6304
Shaffer-Smith/56 Arbor St, Hartford, CT (P 162) 203-236-4080
Shambroom, Eric/383 Albany St, Boston, MA 617-423-0359
Shanley, James G/8 West St, Stoneham, MA 617-279-9060
Sharp, Barry/30 Tower Hill Rd, N Kingston, RI 401-295-1686
Sharp, Steve/153 N 3rd St, Philadelphia, PA (P 190) 215-925-2890
Shaw Studios/836 Richie Highway, Severne PArk, MD 301-647-1200
Shawn, John/129 Sea Girt Ave, Manasguan, NJ 201-223-1190
Shearn, Michael/214 S 12th St, Philadelphia, PA 215-232-6666
Sheldon, John/PO Box 548, Hartford, VT 802-295-6321
Shepherd, Francis/PO Box 204, Chadds Ford, PA 215-347-6799
Sher, Fred/210 Kinderkamack Rd, Oradell, NJ 201-599-1213
Sherer, Larry/5233 Eliots Oak Rd, Columbia, MD 301-235-8443
Sherman, Stephen/49 Melcher St 5th Fl, Boston, MA 617-542-1496
Sherriff, Bob/963 Humphrey St, Swampscott, MA 617-599-6955
Shields, Rob/830 Eddy St, Providence, RI 401-461-8848
Shoemake, Allan Hunter/56 Main St, Millburn, NJ 201-467-4920
Shopper, David/535 Albany St 4th fl, Boston, MA 617-350-8717
Shotwell, John/241 A Street, Boston, MA 617-357-7456
Siciliano, Richard/809 Albany St, Schenectady, NY 518-370-4417
Sidney, Rhoda/59 E Linden Ave B7, Englewood, NJ 201-568-3919
Siegel, Hyam Photography/PO Box 356, Brattleboro, VT 802-257-0691
Siegel, Marjorie/, Boston, MA 617-731-2855
Signal Stock/54 Applecross, Chalfont, PA 215-997-2311
Silk, Georgiana B/190 Godfrey Rd E, Weston, CT 203-226-0408
Silver, David/35 N Third St, Philadelphia, PA 215-925-7277
Silver, Walter S/107 South St #203, Boston, MA 617-426-4743
Silverman, Paul/49 Ronald Dr, Clifton, NJ 201-472-4339
Silverstein, Abby/3315 Woodvalley Dr, Baltimore, MD 301-486-5211
Silverstein, Roy/1604 Gary Rd, East Meadow, NY (P 134) 516-481-3218
Silvia, Peter/20 Burdick Ave, Newport, RI 401-841-5076
Simeone, J Paul/116 W Baltimore Pike, Media, PA (P 28,29) 215-566-7197
Simian, George/566 Commonwealth Ave, Boston, MA 617-267-3558

Simmons, Erik Leigh/241 A St, Boston, MA (P 158,159) **617-482-5325**
Simon, David/263 110th St, Jersey City, NJ 201-795-9326
Simons, Stuart/5 Hyde Rd, Bloomfield, NJ 201-278-5050
Sinclair, Dan/150 Preble St, Portland, ME 207-772-6161
Sinclair, Jodie/109 Broad St, Boston, MA 617-482-0328
Singer, Arthur/Sedgewood RD 12, Carmel, NY 914-225-6801
Singer, Jay/20 Russell Park Rd, Syosset, NY 516-935-8991
Siteman, Frank/136 Pond St, Winchester, MA 617-729-3747
Skalkowski, Bob/310 Eighth St, New Cumberland, PA 717-774-0652
Sklute, Kenneth/210 E Nassau St, Islip Terrace, NY 516-581-7276
Skoogford, Leif/415 Church Rd #B2, Elkins Park, PA 215-635-5186
Slezinger, Natan/1191 Chestnut St, Newton, MA 617-964-0700
Slide Graphics/262 Summer St, Boston, MA 617-542-0700
Sloan Photo/182 High St, Waltham, MA 617-542-3215
Sloan, Jim/12017 Nevel St, Rockville, MD 301-732-7940
Smith, Bill Photo/20 Newbury St, Boston, MA 617-267-4026
Smith, Brian/7 Glenley Terrace, Brighton, MA 617-782-5560
Smith, David A/PO Box 338, Lebanon, CT 203-642-6460
Smith, David K/731 Harrison Ave, Boston, MA 617-424-1555
Smith, David L/420 Goldway, Pittsburgh, PA ....
Smith, Gary & Russell/65 Washington St, S Norwalk, CT 203-866-8871
Smith, Gene/871 N Lenola Rd #1E, Moorestown, NJ 609-722-5225
Smith, Gordon E/65 Washington St, S Norwalk, CT 203-866-8871
Smith, Hugh R/2515 Burr St, Fairfield, CT 203-255-1942
Smith, Philip W/1589 Reed Rd #2A, W Trenton, NJ 609-737-3370
Smith, Stuart/68 Raymond Lane, Wilton, CT 203-762-3158
Smyth, Kevin/23 Walnut Ave, Clark, NJ 201-388-8831
Snitzer, Herb/64 Roseland St, Cambridge, MA 617-497-0251
Socolow, Carl/3642 N 3rd St, Harrisburg, PA 717-236-1906
Solaria Studio/190 Tuckerton Road, Indian Mills, NJ 609-268-0045
Soloman, Ron/PO Box 237, Glyndon, MD (P 209) **301-833-5678**
Sons, Fred/514 E St NE, Washington, DC 202-468-2588
Soorenko, Barry/5161 River Rd Bldg 2B, Bethesda, MD 301-652-1303
Sortino, Steve/2125 N Charles St, Baltimore, MD 301-625-2125
Spaulding, Matt/49 Dartmouth, Portland, ME 207-772-4725
Speedy, Richard/1 Sherbrooke Dr, Princeton Junction, NJ 609-275-1885
Spence, George A/15 Scott Ct, Ridgefield Park, NJ 201-641-3505
Spencer, Michael/735 Mt Hope Ave, Rochester, NY 716-475-6817
Sperduto, Stephen/18 Willett Ave, Port Chester, NY 914-939-0296
Spiegel, Ted/RD 2 Box 353 A, South Salem, NY 914-763-3668
Spiro, Don/137 Summit Rd, Sparta, NJ (P 136,137) **212-484-9753**
Spozarsky, Michael/5 Academy St, Newton, NJ 201-579-1385
Sprecher, Allan/1428 E Baltimore St, Baltimore, MD 301-732-7940
Staccioli, Marc/167 New Jersey Ave, Lake Hopatcong, NJ 201-663-5334
Stanley, James G/8 West St, Stoneham, MA 617-279-9060
Stapleton, John/6854 Radbourne Rd, Upper Darby, PA 215-626-0920
Starosielski, Sergei/181 Doty Circle, W Springfield, MA 413-733-3530
Stayner & Stayner/3060 Williston Rd, S Burlington, VT 802-865-3477
Stearns, Stan/1814 Glade Ct, Annapolis, MD 301-268-5777
Stein, Geoffrey R/348 Newbury St, Boston, MA 617-536-8227
Stein, Howard/200 William St, Port Chester, NY 914-939-0242
Stein, Jonathan/579 Sagamore Ave, Portsmouth, NH 603-436-6365
Stein, Marty/29 Stanhope St, Boston, MA 617-497-7195
Steiner, Peter/183 St Paul St 3rd Fl, Rochester, NY 716-454-1012
Stevenson, Jeff/496 Congress St, Portland, ME 207-773-5175
Stewart, Thomas R/Box 205 Johnson Point Rd, Penobscot, ME 207-326-9370
Stier, Kurt/451 "D" St, Boston, MA 617-330-9461
Stierer, Dennis/443 Albany St #205, Boston, MA 617-357-9488
Still, John/17 Edinboro St, Boston, MA 617-451-8178
Stillings, Jamey/87 N Clinton Ave 5th Fl, Rochester, NY 716-232-5296
Stills/1 Winthrop Sq, Boston, MA 617-482-0660
Stites, Bill/, , ... 203-655-7376
Stock, Jack/Newberg, Art/155 Myrtle St, Shelton, CT 203-735-3388
Stockfield, Bob/3000 Chestnut Av #114/Mill Ctr, Baltimore, MD 301-235-7007
Stockwell, Thomas/101 Providence St, Worcester, MA 617-755-0992
Stoller, Bob/30 Old Mill Rd, Great Neck, NY 516-829-8906
Stone, Parker II/6632 Temple Dr, E Syracuse, NY 315-463-0577
Stone, Steven/20 Rugg Rd, Boston, MA 617-782-1247
Storch, Otto/Box 712, 22 Pondview Ln, East Hampton, NY 516-324-5031
Stromberg, Bruce/PO Box 2052, Philadelphia, PA 215-735-3520
Stuart, Stephen/10 Midland Ave, Port Chester, NY 914-939-0302
Studio Assoc/30-6 Plymouth St, Fairfield, NJ 201-575-2640
Studio Tech/25 Congress St, Salem, MA 617-745-5070
Sued, Yamil R/425 Fairfield Ave Bldg 4, Stamford, CT (P 191) **203-324-0234**
Sullivan, Sharon/115 Columbia Ave, Jersey City, NJ 201-795-1930
Sunshine Photography/S Edgewood Gate, Plainview, NY 516-293-3399
Susoeff, Bill/1063 Elizabeth Dr, Bridgeville, PA 412-941-8606
Sutphen, Chazz/22 Crescent Beach Dr, Burlington, VT 802-862-5912
Sutton, Humphrey/PO Box 236, Fiskdale, MA 413-245-3733
Swann Niemann Photography/9 W 29th St, Baltimore, MD 301-467-7300
Swann/Niemann/1258 Wisconsin Ave NW, Washington, DC 202-342-6300
Sway, Fred/, Boston, MA 617-555-1212
Sweet, Ozzie/Sunnyside Acres, Francestown, NH 603-547-6611
Swertfager, Amy/343 Manville Rd, Pleasantville, NY 914-747-1900
Swett, Jennifer/PO Box 615, N Sutton, NH 603-927-4648
Swift, Dick/31 Harrison Ave, New Canaan, CT 203-966-8190
Swisher, Mark/3819 Hudson St, Baltimore, MD 301-732-7788
Swoger, Arthur/61 Savoy St, Providence, RI 401-331-0440
Szabo, Art/156-A Depot Rd, Huntington, NY 516-549-1699

T

Tadder, Morton/1010 Morton St, Baltimore, MD 301-837-7427
Taglienti, Maria/294 Whippany Rd, Whippany, NJ 201-428-4477
Tango, Rick/11 Pocconock Terrace, Ridgefield, CT 203-431-0514
Tarantola, Kathy/109 Broad St, Boston, MA 617-423-4399
Tardi, Joseph/125 Wolf Rd #108, Albany, NY 518-438-1211
Tardiff, Gary/355 Wood Rd #230, Braintree, MA 617-848-6904
Tartaglia, Vic/23 Dodd St, Bloomfield, NJ 201-429-4983
Taylor, Ed/145 Lodi St, Hackensack, NJ 201-386-8345
Tchakirides, Bill/ Photography Assoc/201 Ann St, Hartford, CT 203-525-5117
Teatum, Marc/28 Goodhue St, Salem, MA 508-745-2345
Tech Photo/37 Huyler Ct, Setauket, NY 516-751-8310
Teitelbaum, Phyliss/917 Lamberton Dr, Silver Spring, MD 301-649-1449
Tenin, Barry/PO Box 2660 Saugatuck Sta, Westport, CT 203-226-9396
Tepper, Peter/195 Tunxis Hill Rd, Fairfield, CT 203-367-6172
Tesi, Mike/12 Kulick Rd, Fairfield, NJ 201-575-7780
Thauer, Bill/542 Higgens Crowell Rd, W Yarmouth, MA 617-362-8222
Thayer, Mark/25 Dry Dock Ave, Boston, MA (P 154,155) **617-542-9532**
The Studio Inc/938 Penn Ave, Pittsburgh, PA 412-261-2022
Thiebauth, Jeffrey/57 Pine Circle, S Weymouth, MA 617-335-2686
Thomas, Edward/140-50 Huyshope Ave, Hartford, CT 203-246-3293
Thomas, Melinda L/, Boston, MA 617-628-2959
Thompson, T Stephan/333 Pemberton Browns Mills Rd, New Lisbon, NJ 609-893-2726
Titcomb, Jeffery/423 W Broadway, South Boston, MA 617-269-8777
Tkatch, James/2307 18th St NW, Washington, DC 202-462-2211
Tobey, Robert/, MA 413-584-7606
Tolbert, Brian/911 State St, Lancaster, PA 717-393-0918
Tollen, Cynthia/50 Fairmont St, Arlington, MA 617-641-4052
Tong, Darren/28 Renee Terrace, Newton, MA 617-527-3304
Tornallyay, Martin/77 Taft Ave, Stamford, CT 203-357-1777
Total Concept Photo/95-D Knickerbocker Ave, Bohemia, NY 516-567-6010
Trafidlo, James F/17 Stilling St, Boston, MA 617-338-9343
Traub, Willard/PO Box 2429, Framingham, MA 508-872-2010
Traver, Joseph/187 Hodge Ave, Buffalo, NY 716-884-8844
Treadou, Douglas/116 East Gray St, Elmira, NY 607-732-4057
Treiber, Peter/917 Highland Ave, Bethlehem, PA 215-867-3303
Tretick, Stanley/4365 Embassy Park Dr NW, Washington, DC 202-537-1445
Trian, George/PO Box 2537, Hartford, CT 203-647-1372
Tribulas, Michael/1879 Old Cuthbert Rd #14, Cherry Hill, NJ 609-354-1903
Tritsch, Joseph/507 Longstone Dr, Cherry Hill, NJ 609-424-0433
Troha, John/9030 Saunders Lane, Bethesda, MD 301-469-7440
Trola, Bob/1216 Arch St 2nd Fl, Philadelphia, PA 215-977-7078
Trueworthy, Nance/33 Bryant St, Portland, ME 207-774-6181
Truslow, Bill/855 Islington St, Portsmouth, NH 603-436-4600
Trzoniec, Stanley/58 W Main St, Northboro, MA 617-393-3800
Tsufura, Satoru/48 Bently Rd, Cedar Grove, NJ 201-239-4870
Tuemmler, Stretch/45 Casco, Portland, ME 207-871-0350
Tur, Stefan/,NY 914-557-8857
Turner, Steve/377 Main St, Westport, CT 203-454-3999
Turpan, Dennis P/25 Amsterdam Ave, Teaneck, NJ 201-837-4242

U

Ultimate Image/Photo/47 Alden St, Cranford, NJ 201-272-4455
Umstead, Dan/7475 Morgan Road 7-6, Liverpool, NY 315-457-0365
Urban, Peter/54 Lithgow St #2, Boston, MA 617-288-8635
Urbina, Walt/7208 Thomas Blvd, Pittsburgh, PA 412-242-5070
Urdang, Monroe/461-A Oldham Ct, Ridge, NY 516-744-3903
Ury, Randy/17 Dow St, Portlkand, ME 207-871-0291
Uzzle, Burk/737 N 4th St, Philadelphia, PA 215-629-1202

V

Vadnai, Peter/180 Valley Rd, Katonah, NY 914-232-5328
Valentino, Thom/25 Navaho St, Cranston, RI 401-946-3020
Valerio, Gary/278 Jay St, Rochester, NY 716-352-0163
Van Gorder, Jon/63 Unquowa Rd, Fairfield, CT 203-255-6622
Van Lockhart, Eric/145 Cross Ways Park W, Woodbury, NY 516-364-3000
Van Petten, Rob/109 Broad St, Boston, MA 617-426-8641
Van Schalkwyk, John/50 Melcher St, Boston, MA 617-542-4825
Van Valkenburgh, Larry/511 Broadway, Saratoga Springs, NY........518-583-3676
Van Zandbergen Photo/187 Riverside Dr, Binghamton, NY 607-625-3408
Vandall, D C/PO Box 515, Worchester, MA 508-852-4582
Vanden Brink, Brian/PO Box 419, Rockport, ME 207-236-4035
Vandermark, Peter/523 Medford St, Charlestown, MA 617-242-2277
Vanderwarker, Peter/28 Prince St, West Newton, MA 617-964-2728
VanderWiele, John/75 Boulevard, Pequannock, NJ 201-694-2095
Vandevanter, Jan/909 'C' St SE, Washington, DC 202-546-3520
Vangha, Ruhi/PO Box 344, Wayne, PA 215-293-1315
Vargas, John/282 4th St, Jersey City, NJ 201-795-3448
Vaughan, Ted/423 Doe Run Rd, Manheim, PA 717-665-6942
Vecchio, Dan/129 E Water St, Syracuse, NY 315-471-1064
Vecchione, Jim/1436 U St NW, Washington, DC 301-652-6333
Ventura, Michael/5016 Elm St, Bethesda, MA 301-654-6205
Verderber, Gustav/, VT 802-644-2089
Vericker, Joe/111 Cedar St 4th Fl, New Rochelle, NY 914-632-2072
Verno, Jay/101 S 16th St, Pittsburgh, PA 412-562-9880
Vicari, Jim/PO Box 134, Berryville, NY 914-557-8506
Vickery, Eric/4 Genetti Circle, Bedford, MA 617-275-0314
Vidor, Peter/48 Grist Mill Rd, Randolph, NJ 201-267-1104
Visual Productions/2121 Wisconsin Ave NW, Washington, DC 202-337-7332
Vogt, Laurie/404 Grand St, Hoboken, NJ 201-792-0485
Von Hoffmann, Bernard/2 Green Village Rd, Madison, NJ 201-377-0317
Voscar The Maine Photographer/PO Box 661, Presque Isle, ME......207-769-5911

W

Waggaman, John/2746 N 46 St, Philadelphia, PA 215-473-2827
Wagner, William/208 North Ave West, Cranford, NJ 201-276-2229
Walch, Robert/724 Cherokee St, Bethlehem, PA 215-866-3345
Walker, Robert/13 Thorne St, Jersey City, NJ 201-659-1336
Wallen, Jonathan/41 Lewis Pkwy, Yonkers, NY 914-476-8674
Walp's Photo Service/182 S 2nd St, Lehighton, PA 215-377-4370
Walsh, Dan/409 W Broadway, Boston, MA 617-268-7615
Walters, Day/PO Box 5655, Washington, DC 202-362-0022
Walther, Michael/2185 Brookside Ave, Wantagh, NY 516-783-7636
Wanamaker, Roger/PO Box 2800, Darien, CT 203-655-8383
Ward, Jack/221 Vine St, Philadelphia, PA 215-627-5311
Ward, Michael/916 N Charles St, Baltimore, MD 301-727-8800
Ward, Tony/704 South 6th St, Philadelphia, PA 215-238-1208
Warner, Laurie/205 Raymond Rd/RD 4, Princeton, NJ 201-329-3216
Warner, Lee/326 Kater St, Philadelphia, PA 215-922-5266
Warner, Roger/409 W Broadway, S Boston, MA 671-268-8333
Warniers, Randall/35 Cleveland St, Arlington, MA 617-643-0454
Warren, Murray/75B Brookside Dr, Upper Saddle River, NJ 201-327-4832
**Washnik, Andrew/145 Woodland Ave,
Westwood, NJ (P 57)** **201-664-0441**
Wasserman, Cary/Six Porter Rd, Cambridge, MA 617-492-5621
Watkins, Norman/3000 Chestnut Ave #213, Baltimore, MD 301-467-3358
Watson, H Ross/Box 897, Bryn Mawr, PA 215-353-9898
Watson, Linda M/38 Church St/Box 14, Hopkinton, MA 508-435-5671
Watson, Tom/2172 West Lake Rd, Skaneateles, NY 315-685-6033
Weber, Kevin/138 Longview Dr, Baltimore, MD 301-747-8422
Wee, John/115 Pius St, Pittsburg, PA 412-381-6826
Weese, Carl/140-150 Huyshope Ave, Hartford, CT......................203-246-6016
Weidman, H Mark/2112 Goodwin Lane, North Wales, PA 215-646-1745
Weigand, Tom/707 North 5th St, Reading, PA 215-374-4431
Weinberg, Abe/1230 Summer St, Philadelphia, PA 215-567-5454
Weiner, Jeff/168 Irving Ave, Port Chester, NY 914-939-8324
Weinrebe, Steve/, Philadelphia, PA 215-625-0333
Weinrich, Ken/21 Oriole Terrace, Newton, NJ 201-579-6784
Weisenfeld, Stanley/135 Davis St, Painted Post, NY 607-962-7314
Weisgrau, Richard/1107 Walnut St 2nd Fl, Philadelphia, PA 215-923-0348
Weiss, Michael/212 Race St, Philadelphia, PA 215-629-1685
Weitz, Allan/147 Harbinson Pl, E Windsor, NJ 609-443-5549
Weller, Bruce/3000 Chestnut Ave, Baltimore, MD 301-235-4200
Welsch, Ms Ulrike/4 Dunns Lane, Marblehead, MA 617-631-1641
Welsh, Robert/104 Brooks St, Boston, MA 617-787-3441
Wendler, Hans/RD 1 Box 191, Epsom, NH 603-736-9383

West, Judy/8 Newcomb St, Boston, MA 617-442-9343
Westphalen, James/20 Forest Ave, Brookhaven, NY 516-286-0987
Westwood Photo Productions/PO Box 859, Mansfield, MA 617-339-4141
Wexler, Ira/4911 V St NW, Washington, DC 202-337-4886
Wheat, Frank/225 W 25th St, Baltimore, MD 301-889-1780
Wheeler, Edward F/1050 King of Prussia Rd, Radnor, PA 215-964-9294
Wheeler, Nick/414 Concord Rd, Weston, MA 617-891-5525
White, Frank/18 Milton Pl, Rowayton, CT 203-866-9500
White, Sharon/107 South St, Boston, MA 617-423-0577
Whitemack, Ernie/PO Box 332, Newton, MA 617-964-3326
Whitman, Edward/613 N Eutaw St, Baltimore, MD 301-727-2220
Wierzbowski, Joe/91 Main St W, Rochester, NY 716-546-8381
Wilcox, Jed/PO Box 1271, Newport, RI 401-847-3853
Wilcox, Jed Photo/115 Ellery Ave, Middletown, RI 401-846-7212
**Wild, Terry/RD 3/Box 68 Morgan Valley Rd,
Williamsport, PA (P 212)** **717-745-3257**
Wiley, John Jay/147 Webster St, Boston, MA 617-567-0506
Wilkins, Doug/33 Church St, Canton, MA 617-828-2379
Williams, Jay/9101 W Chester Pike, Upper Darby, PA 215-789-3030
Williams, Lawrence S/9101 W Chester Pike, Upper Darby, PA 215-789-3030
Willinger, Dave/74 Pacific Blvd, Long Beach, NY 516-889-0678
Willson, Hub/113 N 17th St, Allentown, PA 215-434-2178
Wilson, John G/2416 Wynnefield Dr, Havertown, PA 215-446-4798
Wilson, Kevin/11231 Bybee St, Silver Spring, MD 301-649-3151
Wilson, Paul S/6384 Overbrook Ave, Philadelphia, PA 215-473-4455
Wilson, Robert L/PO Box 1742, Clarksburg, WV 304-623-5368
Windman, Russell/348 Congress St, Boston, MA 617-357-5140
Wise, Harriet/242 Dill Ave, Frederick, MD 301-662-6323
Wiseman, Pat/93 Prince Ave, Marstons Mills, MA 508-420-3395
Witbeck, David/77 Ives St, Providence, RI 401-274-9118
Witherell, David/171 Westminster Ave, S Attleboro, MA 617-399-8611
Wolf, Anita/49 Melcher St, Boston, MA 617-426-3929
Wolff, Tom/2102 18th St NW, Washington, DC 202-234-7130
Woloszyn, Gustav/745 McGillvray Pl, Linden, NJ 201-925-7399
Wood, Jeffrey C/309-A Barren Hill Rd, Conshohocken, PA............215-941-6632
Wood, Richard/169 Monsgnr O'Brien Hwy, Cambridge, MA 617-661-6856
Woodard, Steve/2003 Arbor Hill Ln, Bowie, MD..........................301-249-7705
Woolf, John/58 Banks St, Cambridge, MA 617-876-4074
Wrenn, Bill/200 Henry St, Stamford, CT 203-323-4409
Wright, Jeri/PO box 7, Wilmington, NY 518-946-2658
Wu, Ron/179 St Paul St, Rochester, NY 716-454-5600
Wurster, George/128 Berwick, Elizabeth, NJ 201-352-2134
Wyatt, Ronald/846 Harned St #1A, Perth Amboy, NJ 201-442-7527
Wyman, Ira/14 Crane Ave, West Peabody, MA 508-535-2880
Wyville, Mark/260 Harrison Ave, Jersey City, NJ 201-955-0836

YZ

Yablon, Ron/834 Chestnut St #PH 105, Philadelphia, PA 215-923-1744
Yamashita, Michael/25 Roxiticus Rd, Mendham, NJ 201-543-4473
Yellen, Bob/833 Second Ave, Toms River, NJ 201-341-6750
Young, Don/PO Box 249, Exton, PA 215-363-2596
Yuichi, Idaka/RR 2 Box 229D Wood Ave, Rindge, NH 603-899-6165
Z, Taran/528 F St Terrace SE, Washington, DC 202-543-5322
Zaporozec, Terry (Mr)/43 Johnson Rd, Hackettstown, NJ 201-637-6720
Zappala, John/Candlewood Echoes, Sherman, CT 203-354-6420
Zaslow, Francine/791 Tremont St, Boston, MA 617-437-0743
Zimbel, George/1538 Sherbrooke W #813, Montreal, QU 514-931-6387
Zmiejko, Tom/PO Box 126, Freeland, PA 717-636-2304
Zubkoff, Earl/2426 Linden Lane, Silver Spring, MD 301-585-7393
Zucker, Gale/PO Box 2281/Short Beach, Branford, CT 203-488-0499
Zuckerman, Robert/100 Washington St, South Norwalk, CT 203-853-2670
Zungoli, Nick/Box 5, Sugar Loaf, NY 914-469-9382
Zurich, Robert/445 Highway 35, Eatontown, NJ 201-389-9010
Zutell, Kirk/911 State St, Lancaster, PA 717-393-0918

S O U T H E A S T

A

Abel, Wilton/2609 Commonwealth Ave, Charlotte, NC 704-372-6354
Adcock, James/3108 1/2 W Leigh St #8, Richmond, VA 804-358-4399
Alexander, Rick & Assoc/212 S Graham St, Charlotte, NC 704-332-1254
Allard, William Albert/Marsh Run Farm Box 549, Somerset, VA 804-823-5951
Allen, Bob/710 W Lane St, Raleigh, NC 919-833-5991
Allen, Don/1787 Shawn Dr, Baton Rouge, LA 504-925-0251
**Allen, Erich S/602 Riverside Ave, Kingsport,
TN (P 234)** **615-246-7262**

Allen, Michael/PO Box 11510, Nashville, TN....615-754-0059
Alston, Cotten/Box 7927-Station C, Atlanta, GA....404-876-7859
Alterman, Jack/285 Meeting St, Charleston, SC....803-577-0647
Alvarez, Jorge/3105 W Granada, Tampa, FL....813-831-6765
Ames, Kevin/1324 Brainwood Ind Ct, Atlanta, GA....404-325-6736
Anderson, Suzanne Stearns/3355 Lenox Rd NE, Atlanta, GA....404-261-0439
Andrea, Michael/225 South Mint St, Charlotte, NC....704-334-3992
Atlantic Photo/319 N Main St, High Point, NC....919-884-1474
Avanti Photo/5750 Major Blvd #520, Orlando, FL....

B

Bachmann, Bill/PO Box 833, Lake Mary, FL....305-322-4444
Bady, Mary Alan/380 NW 87th Terr, Plantation, FL....305-476-1394
Baker, I Wilson/PO Box 20995, Charleston, SC (P 229)....803-577-0828
Balbuza, Joseph/25 NE 210 St, Miami, FL....305-652-1728
Ball, Roger/1402-A Winnifred, Charlotte, NC (P 227)....704-335-0479
Ballenberg, Bill/200 Cortland Ln, Virginia Beach, VA....804-463-3505
Baptie, Frank/1426 9th St N, St Petersburg, FL....813-823-7319
Barley, Bill/PO Box 280005, Columbia, SC....803-755-1554
Barnes, Billy E/313 Severin St, Chapel Hill, NC....919-942-6350
Barnes, William/8A Forrest Lake Shopping Ctr, Columbia, SC....803-782-8088
Barr, Ian/2640 SW 19th St, Fort Lauderdale, FL....305-584-6247
Barreras, Anthony/1231-C Booth St NW, Atlanta, GA (P 222)....404-352-0511
Barrs, Michael/6303 SW 69th St, Miami, FL....305-665-2047
Bartlett & Assoc/3007 Edgewater Dr, Orlando, FL....305-425-7308
Bassett, Donald/9185 Green Mdws Way, Palm Beach Grdns, FL....305-694-1109
Bateman, John H/3500 Aloma Ave W #18, Winter Park, FL....407-671-2516
Beane, Bill/PO Box 94001, Atlanta, GA....404-881-1500
Beck, Charles/2721 Cherokee Rd, Birmingham, AL....205-871-6632
Beck, G & Assoc/2135 J Deforr Hill Rd, Atlanta, GA....404-352-8385
Becker, Joel/5121 Virginia Bch Blvd #E3, Norfolk, VA....804-461-7886
Behrens, Bruce/2920 N Orange Ave, Orlando, FL....305-629-0261
Belenson, Mark/8056 NW 41st Ct, Sunrise, FL....305-749-0675
Belloise, Joe/2160 N 56th Terr, Hollywood, FL....305-966-7957
Bennett, Ken/1001 Lockwood Ave, Columbus, GA....404-324-1182
Bennett, Robert/6194 Deer Path Court, Manassas, VA....703-361-7705
Bentley, Gary/921 W Main St, Hendersonville, TN....615-822-7770
Berch, Ida/408 SE 11th Ct, Fort Lauderdale, FL....305-463-1912
Berg, Audrey & Fronk, Mark/7953-A Twist Ln, Springfield, VA....703-455-7343
Berger, Erica/One Herald Plaza, Miami, FL....305-376-3750
Bergeron, Joe/516 Natchez, New Orleans, LA....504-522-7503
Bertling, Norbert G Jr/2125 N Charles St, Baltimore, MD....301-727-8766
Beswick, Paul/4479 Westfield Dr, Mableton, GA....404-944-8579
Bewley, Glen/428 Armour Circle, Atlanta, GA....404-872-7277
Bilby, Glade/6901 Pritchard Pl, New Orleans, LA....504-866-0031
Blanchard, Gerald/325 187th St, N Miami Beach, FL....305-935-5168
Blanton, Jeff/5515 S Orange Ave, Orlando, FL....407-851-7279
Blow, Jerry/PO Box 1615, Wilmington, NC....919-763-3835
Boatman, Mike/3430 Park Ave, Memphis, TN....901-324-9337
Bollman, Brooks/1183 Virginia Ave NE, Atlanta, GA....404-876-2422
Bondarenko, Marc/212 S 41st St, Birmingham, AL....205-933-2790
Borchelt, Mark/4398-D Eisenhower Ave, Alexandria, VA....703-243-7850
Borum, Michael/625 Fogg St, Nashville, TN....615-259-9750
Bose, Patti/707 Nicolet Ave, Winter Park, FL....305-629-5650
Bostick, Rick/6959-J Stapoint Ct, Winterpark, FL....305-677-5717
Boughton, Mark/302 King Rd, Fairview, TN....615-799-2143
Boyd, Richard/PO Box 5097, Roanoke, VA....703-366-3140
Boyle, Jeffrey/8725 NW 18th Terrace #215, Miami, FL....305-592-7032
Brack, Dennis/3609 Woodhill Pl, Fairfax, VA....703-280-2285
Brasher/Rucker Photography/3373 Park Ave, Memphis, TN....901-324-7447
Braun, Bob/PO Box 7755, Orlando, FL....407-425-7921
Braun, Paulette/1500 N Orange #42, Sarasota, FL....813-366-6284
Bridges, Bob/205 Wolverine Rd, Cary, NC....919-460-0212
Brill, David/Route 4, Box 121-C, Fairbourn, GA....404-461-5488
Brinson, Rob/486 14th St, Atlanta, GA....404-874-2497
Brooks, Charles/800 Luttrell St, Knoxville, TN (P 232)....615-525-4501
Broomell, Peter/901 N Columbus St, Alexandria, VA....703-548-5767
Brown, Billy/2700 Seventh Ave S, Birmingham, AL....205-251-8327
Brown, Richard Photo/PO Box 1249, Asheville, NC....704-253-1634
Bryant, Doug/PO Box 80155, Baton Rouge, LA....504-387-1620
Bryson, Stephen/PO Box 8702, Atlanta, GA....404-248-9773
Buchman, Tim/212 S Graham St, Charlotte, NC....704-332-1254
Bumpus, Ken/1770 W Chapel Dr, Deltona, FL....305-695-0668
Burgess, Ralph/PO Box 36, Chrstnsted/St Croix, VI....809-773-6541
Burns, Jerry/331-B Elizabeth St, Atlanta, GA....404-522-9377
Busch, Scherley/4186 Pamona Ave, Coconut Grove, FL....305-661-6605
Byrd, Syndey/7932 S Clairborne #6, New Orleans, LA....504-865-7218

C

Calahan, Walter P/4656 S 34th St #B2, Arlington, VA....703-998-8380
Calamia, Ron & Assoc/8140 Forshey St, New Orleans, LA....504-482-8062
Call, Douglas/8279-A Severn Dr, Boca Raton, FL....305-977-5591
Callendrillo, Frank/2485 E Sunrise Rd, Ft Lauderdale, FL....305-566-8236
Camera Graphics/1230 Gateway Rd, Lake Park, FL....305-844-3399
Cameron, Larry/1314 Lincoln St #301, Columbia, SC....803-799-7558
Carnes, John/3730 Central Ave, Nashville, TN....615-254-5506
Carolina Photo Grp/120 W Worthington Ave, Charlotte, NC....704-334-7874
Carpenter, Michael/7704 Carrleigh Pkwy, Springfield, VA....703-644-9666
Carriker, Ronald/565 Alpine Rd, Winston Salem, NC....919-765-3852
Case, Sam/PO Box 1139, Purcellville, VA....703-338-2725
Caswell, Sylvia/807 9th Court S, Birmingham, AL....205-252-2252
Caudill, Dennis/909 Felle St, Baltimore, MD....301-563-0906
Caudle, Rod Studio/1708 Defoor Pl, Atlanta, GA....404-424-3730
Cavedo, Brent/9 W Main St, Richmond, VA....804-344-5374
Centner, Ed Productions/12950 SW 122nd Ave, Miami, FL....305-238-3338
Chalfant, Flip/1867 Windemere DR NE, Atlanta, GA....404-881-8510
Chambers, Terrell/6843 Tilton Lane, Doraville, GA....404-396-4648
Chamowitz, Mel/3931 N Glebe Rd, Arlington, VA....703-536-8356
Chapple, Ron/501 N College, Charlotte, NC....704-377-4217
Chernush, Kay/3855 N 30th St, Arlington, VA....703-528-1195
Chesler, Donna & Ken/6941 NW 12th St, Plantation, FL....305-581-6489
Choiniere, Gerin/1424 N Tryon St, Charlotte, NC....704-372-0220
Clark, Marty/1105 Peachtree St NE, Atlanta, GA....404-873-4618
Clark, Robert/1520-A Farrington Way, Columbia, SC....803-731-0418
Clay, Tommy/5820 Murray Hill Rd, Charlotte, NC....704-523-8701
Clayton, Al/141 The Prado NE, Atlanta, GA....404-577-4141
Clayton, Julie Ann/8123-B Northboro Ct, W Palm Beach, FL....407-642-4971
Cochrane, Craig/PO Box 2316, Virginia Beach, VA....804-468-1065
Cody, Dennie/5820 SW 51st Terrace, Miami, FL....305-666-0247
Colbroth, Ron/8610 Battailles Ct, Annandale, VA....703-354-2729
Collins, Michael/PO Box 608522, Orlando, FL....305-889-9242
Compton, Grant/7004 Sand Nettles Dr, Savannah, GA....912-897-3771
Contorakes, George/PO Box 430901, South Miami, FL....305-661-0731
Cook, Jamie/653 Ethel St, Atlanta, GA....404-892-1393
Cooke, Bill/7761 SW 88th St, Miami, FL....305-596-2454
Copeland, Jim/2135-F Defoor Hills Rd, Atlanta, GA....404-352-2025
Corn, Jack/27 Dahlia Dr, Brentwood, TN....615-373-3301
Cornelia, William/PO Box 5304, Hilton Head Island, SC....803-671-2576
Cornelius, John/915 W Main St, Abington, MA....703-628-1699
Cosby Bowyer Inc/209 North Foushee St, Richmond, VA (P 202)....804-643-1100
Coste, Kurt/929 Julia, New Orleans, LA....504-523-6060
Cox, Whitney/2042 W Grace St #3, Richmond, VA....804-358-3061
Cravotta, Jeff/PO Box 9487, Charlotte, NC....704-377-4912
Crawford, Dan/RT 9/ Box 546-D, Chapel Hill, NC....919-968-4290
Crocker, Will/1806 Magazine St, New Orleans, LA (P 214,215)....504-522-2651
Cromer, Peggo/1206 Andora Ave, Coral Gables, FL....305-667-3722
Crum, Lee/1536 Terpsichore St, New Orleans, LA....504-529-2156
Crum, Robert/3217 S MacDill, Tampa, FL....813-831-4595
Culpepper, Mike Studios/PO Box 1371, Columbus, GA (P 228)....404-323-5703
Cutrell, Gary/317 Draper St, Warner Robins, GA....912-929-3191

D

Dakota, Irene/2121 Lucerne Ave, Miami Beach, FL....305-674-9975
Dale, John/576 Armour Circle NE, Atlanta, GA....404-872-3203
Daniel, Ralph/1305 University Dr NE, Atlanta, GA....404-872-3946
David, Alan/416 Armour Circle NE, Atlanta, GA....404-872-2142
Davidson, Cameron/5316 Admiralty Court, Alexandria, VA (P 199)....202-328-3344
Dawson, Bill/289 Monroe, Memphis, TN....901-522-9171
Deal Bowie & Assoc/809 W University, Lafayette, LA....318-234-0576
Degast, Robert/Rt 1 Box 323, Onancock, VA....804-787-8060
DeKalb, Jed/PO Box 22884, Nashville, TN....615-331-8527
Demolina, Raul/3903 Ponce De Leon, Coral Gables, FL....305-448-8727
Design & Visual Effects/1228 Zonolite Rd, Atlanta, GA....404-872-3283
DeVault, Jim/2400 Sunset Pl, Nashville, TN....615-269-4538
Diaz, Rick/7395 SW 42nd St, Miami, FL....305-264-9761
Dickerson, John/1895 Annwicks Dr, Marietta, GA....404-977-4138
Dickinson, Dick/1781 Independence Blvd #1, Sarasota, FL (P 233)....813-355-7688

Dickinson, Rod/11450 SE 57th St, Miami, FL 305-595-6174
DiModica, James/139 Sevilla Ave, Coral Gables, FL 305-666-7710
Dix, Paul/106 W Bonito Dr, Ocean Springs, MS 601-875-7691
Dixon, Tom/3404-D W Windover Ave, Greensboro, NC 919-294-6076
Dobbs, David/812 Larry Ln, Decatur, GA 404-325-2426
Dorin, Jay/800 West Ave #345, Miami Beach, FL 305-866-3888
Doty, Gary/PO Box 23697, Ft Lauderdale, FL 305-928-0645
Douglas, Keith/405 NE 8th St, Ft Lauderdale, FL 305-763-5883
Draper, Fred/259 S Willow Ave, Cookeville, TN 615-526-1315
Dressler, Brian/300-A Huger St, Columbia, SC 803-254-7171
Duvall, Joe/1601 Philadelphia Ave, Orlando, FL 305-894-5052
Duvall, Thurman III/1021 Northside Dr NW, Atlanta, GA 404-875-0161

E

E P Productions/602 Riverside Avenue,
Kingsport, TN (P 234) **615-246-7262**
Eastmond, Peter/PO Box 856 E, Barbados,W Indies, ...809-429-7757
Easton, Steve/5937 Ravenswood Rd #H-19, Ft Lauderdale, FL 305-983-6611
Edwards, Jack/6250 Edgewater Dr #2600, Orlando, FL 305-581-6220
Edwards, Jim/416 Armour Circle NE, Atlanta, GA 404-875-1005
Eighme, Bob/1520 E Sunrise Blvd, Ft Lauderdale, FL 305-527-8445
Elliot, Tom/19756 Bel Aire Dr, Miami, FL 305-251-4315
Ellis, Bill/3410E W Andover Ave, Greensboro, NC 919-299-5074
Ellis, Gin/1203 Techwood Dr, Atlanta, GA 404-892-3204
Elmore, James/4807 5th St W, Bradenton, FL 813-755-0546
Engelman, Suzanne/1621 Woodbridge Lk Cir, W Palm Bch, FL 305-969-6666
English, Melissa Hayes/1195 Woods Circle NE, Atlanta, GA 404-261-7650
Epley, Paul/3110 Griffith St, Charlotte, NC 704-332-5466
Erickson, Jim/117 S West St, Raleigh, NC 919-833-9955
Esplinoza, Patrick/153 Patchen Dr #28, Lexington, KY 606-269-2378

F

Fedusenko, David/4200 NW 79th Ave #2A, Miami, FL................305-599-2364
Felipe, Giovanni/3465 SW 73rd Ave, Miami, FL 305-266-5308
Fernandez, Jose/1011 Valencia Ave, Coral Gables, FL 305-443-6501
Fineman, Michael/7521 SW 57th Terrace, Miami, FL 305-666-1250
Fisher, Kurt/280 Elizabeth St #A-105, Atlanta, GA 404-525-1333
Fisher, Ray/10700 SW 72nd Ct, Miami, FL 305-665-7659
Fitzgerald, Barry/808 Charlotte St, Fredericksburg, VA 703-371-3253
Foley, Roger/519 N Monroe St, Arlington, VA 703-524-6274
Forer, Dan/1970 NE 149th St, North Miami, FL 305-949-3131
Fortenberry, Mark/128 Wonderwood Dr, Charlotte, NC 704-365-4774
Fowley, Douglas/103 N Hite Ave, Louisville, KY 502-897-7222
Frazier, Jeff/1025 8th Ave S, Nashville, TN 615-242-5642
Frazier, Steve/2168 Little Brook Ln., Clearwater, FL 813-736-4235
Freeman, Tina/POB 30308, New Orleans, LA 504-523-3000
Frink, Stephen/PO Box 2720, Key Largo, FL 305-451-3737
Fulton, George/1237-F Gadsden St, Columbia, SC 803-779-8249

G

Gamand, Philippe/2636 Key Largo Lane, Fort Lauderdale, FL 305-583-7262
Gandy, Skip/302 East Davis Blvd, Tampa, FL 813-253-0340
Gardella Photography & Design/781 Miami Cr NE, Atlanta, GA 404-231-1316
Garrett, Kenneth/PO Box 208, Broad Run, VA 703-347-5848
Garrison, Gary/1052 Constance St, New Orleans, LA 504-588-9422
Gefter, Judith/1725 Clemson Rd, Jacksonville, FL 904-733-5498
Gelabert, Bill/PO Box 3231, Old San Juan, PR 809-725-4696
Gelberg, Bob/7035-E SW 47th St, Miami, FL 305-665-3200
Gemignani, Joe/13833 NW 19th Ave, Miami, FL 305-685-7636
Geniac, Ruth/13353 Sorrento Dr, Largo, FL 813-595-2275
Genser, Howard/1859 Seventh Ave, Jacksonville, FL 904-734-9688
Gentile, Arthur Sr/7335 Connan Lane, Charlotte, NC 704-541-0227
Gerlich, Fred/1220 Spring St NW, Atlanta, GA 404-872-3487
Gillian, John/10875 SW 112th Ave #218, Miami, Fl 305-251-4784
Glaser, Ken & Assoc/5270 Annunciation St,
New Orleans, LA (P 235) **504-895-7170**
Gleasner, Bill/132 Holly Ct, Denver, NC 704-483-9301
Glover, Robert/709 Second Ave, Nashville, TN 612-726-0790
Godfrey, Mark/3526 N Third St, Arlington, VA 703-527-8293
Golden, Jon/PO Box 2826, Charlottesville, VA 804-971-8100
Gomez, Rick/4950 SW 72nd Ave #114, Miami, FL 305-666-5454
Good, Jay/20901 NE 26th Ave, N Miami Beach, FL 305-935-4884
Gornto, Bill/590 Ponce De Leon Ave, Atlanta, GA 404-876-1331
Graham, Curtis/648 First Ave S, St Petersburg, FL 813-821-0444
Granberry/Anderson Studios/1211 Spring St NW, Atlanta, GA 404-874-2426
Green, Jack/1 N Pack Sq, Asheville, NC 704-274-4153
Greenberg, Bob/5277 NW 161st St, Miami, FL 305-621-8500

Griffiths, Simon/125 Woodburn Rd, Raleigh, NC.......................919-829-9109
Grigg, Roger Allen/PO Box 52851, Atlanta, GA 404-876-4748
Groendyke, Bill/6344 NW 201st Ln, Miami, FL 305-625-8293
Guggenheim, David/167 Mangum St, Atlanta,
GA (P 237) **404-577-4676**
Guider, John/517 Fairground Ct, Nashville, TN 615-255-4495
Guillermety, Edna/3133 Lakestone Dr, Tampa, Fl 813-962-1748
Gupton, Charles/5720-J North Blvd, Raleigh, NC 919-850-9441
Guravich, Dan/PO Box 891, Greenville, MS 601-335-2444

H

Haggerty, Richard/656 Ward St, High Point, NC 919-889-7744
Hall, Don/2922 Hyde Park st, Sarasota, FL 813-365-6161
Hall, Ed/7010 Citrus Point, Winter Park, FL 305-657-8182
Hamilton, Tom/2362 Strathmore Dr, Atlanta, GA 404-266-0177
Hannau, Michael/3800 NW 32nd Ave, Miami, FL 305-633-1100
Hansen, Eric/3005 7th Ave S/Box 55492, Birmingham, AL 205-251-5587
Harbison, Steve/1516 Crestwood Dr, Greeneville, TN 615-638-2535
Hardy, Frank/1003 N 12th Ave, Pensacola, FL 904-438-2712
Harkins, Lynn S/1900 Byrd Ave #101, Richmond, VA 804-285-2900
Harkness, Chris/1412 Fairway Dr, Tallahassee, FL 904-224-9805
Harrelson, Keith/4505 131st Ave N, Clearwater, FL 813-577-9812
Harris, Christopher/PO Box 2926, Covington, LA 504-893-4898
Harrison, Michael/1124-A S Mint St, Charlotte,
NC (P 224) **704-334-8008**
Hathcox, David/5730 Arlington Blvd, Arlington, VA 703-845-5831
Haviland, Patrick/323 E Kingston Ave, Charlotte, NC 701-332-7273
Hayden, Kenneth/1318 Morton Ave, Louisville, KY 502-583-5596
Heller, David/202 West Jean St, Tampa, FL 813-238-2166
Henderson, Eric/1200 Foster St NW, Atlanta, GA 404-352-3615
Henderson/Muir /6005 Chapel Hill Rd, Raleigh,
NC (P 238,239) **919-851-0458**
Hendley, Arington/454 Irwin St NE, Atlanta, GA 404-577-2300
Henley & Savage/113 S Jefferson St, Richmond,
VA (P 196,197) **804-780-1120**
Heston, Ty/4505 131st Ave N #18, Clearwater, FL 813-573-4878
Higgins, Neal/1540 Monroe Dr, Atlanta, GA 404-876-3186
Hill, Dan/9132 O'Shea Ln, W Springfield, VA 703-451-4705
Hill, Jackson/2032 Adams St, New Orleans, LA 504-861-3000
Hill, Tom/207 E Parkwood Rd, Decatur, GA 404-377-3833
Hillyer, Jonathan/450-A Bishop St, Atlanta, GA 404-351-0477
Hirsch, Alan/1259 Ponce de Leon #6C, San Juan, PR 809-723-2224
Hoflich, Richard/544 N Angier Ave NE, Atlanta, GA 404-584-9159
Hogben, Steve/6269 McDonough Dr, Norcross, GA 404-266-2894
Holland, Ralph/3706 Alliance Dr, Greensboro, NC 919-855-6422
Holland, Robert/PO Box 162099, Miami, FL 305-255-6758
Holt Group/403 Westcliff Rd/Box 35488, Greensboro, NC 919-668-2770
Hood, Robin/1101 W Main St, Franklin, TN 615-794-2041
Hope, Christina/2720 3rd St S, S Jacksonville Bch, FL 904-246-9689
Horan, Eric/PO Box 6373, Hilton Head Island, SC 803-842-3233
Hosack, Loren/2301-F Sabal Ridge Ct, Palm Bch Grdns, FL 305-627-8313
Hotvedt, Carla/5128 NW 58th Ct, Gainesville, FL 904-373-5771
Houghtaling, Jim/403 Westcliff/Box 3548, Greensboro, NC 919-668-2770
Humphries, Gordon/Boozer Shopping Ctr, Columbia, SC 803-772-3535
Humphries, Vi/Boozer Shopping Ctr, Columbia, SC 803-772-3535
Hunter, Bud/1917 1/2 Oxmoor Rd, Birmingham, AL 205-879-3153
Huntley, Robert/1210 Spring St NW, Atlanta, GA 404-892-6547

IJ

Isaacs, Lee/2321 First Ave N #105, Birmingham, AL..................205-252-2698
Isgett, Neil/4303-D South Boulevard, Charlotte,
NC (P 241) **704-376-7172**
Jamison, Chipp/2131 Liddell Dr NE, Atlanta,
GA (P 223) **404-873-3636**
Jeffcoat, Russell/1201 Hagood St, Columbia, SC 803-799-8578
Jeffcoat, Wilber L/1864 Palomino Cir, Sumter, SC 803-773-3690
Jenkins, Dave/3200 Brainerd Rd #A, Chattanooga, TN 615-629-5380
Jimison, Tom/5929 Annunciation, New Orleans, LA 504-891-8587
Johns, Douglas/2535 25th Ave N, St Petersburg, FL 813-321-7235
Johnson, Forest/7755 SW 86th St #406, Miami, FL 305-279-6074
Johnson, George L/16603 Round Oak Dr, Tampa, FL 813-963-3222
Johnson, Silvia/6110 Brook Dr, Falls Church, VA 703-532-8653
Jones, David/319-F South Westgate Dr, Greensboro,
NC (P 230) **919-294-9060**
Jones, Samuel A/131 Pineview Rd, West Columbia, SC 803-791-4896
Jordan/Rudolph Studios/1446 Mayson St NE #5L, Atlanta, GA 404-874-1829
Jureit, Robert A/916 Aguero Ave, Coral Gables, FL 305-667-1346

K

Kane, Scott/748-E Sedgefield Rd, Charlotte, NC 704-375-5033
Kaplan, Al/PO Box 611373, North Miami, FL 305-891-7595
Kaplan, Martin & Laura/PO Box 7206, McLean, VA 703-893-1660
Kappiris, Stan/PO Box 14331, Tampa, FL 813-254-4866
Katz, Arni/PO Box 724507, Atlanta, GA 404-953-1168
Kaufman, Len/5119 Arthur St, Hollywood, FL 305-920-7822
Kearney, Mitchell/301 E 7th St, Charlotte, NC 704-377-7662
Kennedy, Chuck/2745-B Hidden Lake Blvd, Sarasota, FL 813-365-5564
Kennedy, M Lewis/2700 7th Ave S, Birmingham, AL 205-252-2700
Kenner, Jack/PO Box 3269, Memphis, TN 901-527-3686
Kent, David/7515 SW 153rd Ct #201, Miami, FL 305-382-1587
Kern Photography/1243 N 17th Ave, Lake Worth, FL 305-582-2487
Kersh, Viron/PO Box 51201, New Orleans, LA 504-524-4515
Ketchum, Larry/302 Jefferson St #300, Raleigh, NC 919-856-1860
King, J Brian/1267 Coral Way, Miami, FL 305-856-6534
King, Tom/2806 Edgewater Dr, Orlando, FL 305-841-4421
Kinney, Greg/238 Burlington Pl, Nashville, TN 615-297-8084
Kinsella, Barry/1010 Andrews Rd, West Palm Beach, FL 305-832-8736
Kirkpatrick, John/351 Old Georgia Rd, Moore, SC 803-576-9643
Klass, Rubin & Erika/5200 N Federal Hwy 2, Ft Lauderdale, FL 305-565-1612
Klemens, Susan/7423 Foxleigh Way, Alexandria, VA 703-971-1226
Kling, David Photography/502 Armour Circle, Atlanta, GA 404-881-1215
Knibbs, Tom/5907 NE 27th Ave, Ft Lauderdale, FL 305-491-6263
Knight, Steve/1212 E 10th St, Charlotte, NC (P 225) 704-334-5115
Kogler, Earl/PO Box 3578, Longwood, FL 305-331-4035
Kohanim, Parish/1130 W Peachtree NW, Atlanta, GA 404-892-0099
Kollar, Robert E/1431 Cherokee Trail #52, Knoxville, TN 615-573-8191
Koplitz, William/729 N Lime St, Sarasota, FL 813-366-5905
Kralik, Scott/210 N Fillmore, Arlington, VA 703-522-8261
Kufner, Gary/2032 Harrison St, N Hollywood, FL 305-944-7740

L

LaCoe, Norm/PO Box 855, Gainesville, FL 904-466-0226
Lafayette, James/148 Windward Vill/Shipyrd, Hilton Head, SC 803-785-3201
Lair, John/1122 Roger St, Louisville, KY 502-589-7779
Langoné, Peter/516 NE 13th St, Ft Lauderdale, FL (P 242,243) 305-467-0654
Lanpher, Keith/865 Monticello Ave, Norfolk, VA 804-627-3051
Lanzone, John/10 E Madison St #1D, Baltimore, MD 301-385-0230
Larkin, Paul/710 Tenth St, Atlanta, GA 404-432-6309
Lathem, Charles & Assoc/559 Dutch Valley Rd NE, Atlanta, GA 404-873-5858
Lavenstein, Lance/4605 Pembroke Lake Cir, Virginia Bch, VA 804-499-9959
Lawrence, David/PO Box 835, Largo, FL 813-586-2112
Lawrence, John R/Box 330570, Coconut Grove, FL 305-447-8621
Lawrence, Mark/PO Box 23950, Ft Lauderdale, FL 305-565-8866
Lawson, Slick/3801 Whitland Ave, Nashville, TN 615-383-0147
Lazzo, Dino/655 SW 20th Rd, Miami, FL 305-856-1148
Lee, Carol/POB 2710/Christiansted, St Croix, VI 809-773-5412
Lee, Chung P/7820 Antiopi St, Annandale, VA 703-560-3394
Lee, George/423 S Main St, Greenville, SC 803-232-4119
Lee, Joe/PO Box 22941, Jackson, MS 601-948-5255
Leggett, Albert/1415 Story Ave, Louisville, KY 502-584-0255
Leo, Victor/121 W Main St, Louisville, KY 502-589-2423
Lex, Debra/6770 SW 101st St, Miami, FL (P 244) 305-667-0961
Lightbenders/11450 SW 57th St, Miami, FL 305-595-6174
Lightscapes Photo/7953-A Twist Lane, Springfield, VA 703-455-7343
Lipson, Stephen/15455 SW Terrace, Miami, FL 305-382-3502
Little, Chris/PO Box 467221, Atlanta, GA 404-641-9688
Llewellyn, Robert/PO Drawer L, Charlottesville, VA 804-973-8000
Long, Lewis/3130 SW 26th St, Miami, FL 305-448-7667
Loumakis, Constantinos/826 SW 13th St, Ft Lauderdale, FL 305-525-7367
Lowery Photo/Graphics Inc/409 Spears Ave, Chattanooga, TN (P 245) 615-265-4311
Lubin, Jeff/8472 Rainbow Bridge Ln, Springfield, VA 703-569-5086
Lucas, Steve/7925 SW 104th St #E-202, Miami, FL 305-238-6024
Luttrell, David/1500 Highland Dr, Knoxville, TN (P 246) 615-588-5775
Luzier, Winston/1122 Pomelo Ave, Sarasota, FL 813-952-1077
Lynch, Warren/306 Production Ct, Louisville, KY 502-491-8233

M

Macuch, Rodger/1133 Spring St, Atlanta, GA 404-876-7002
Magee, Ken/7928 Ferara Dr, New Orleans, LA 504-889-3928
Magruder, Mary & Richard/2156 Snap Finger Rd, Decatur, GA 404-289-8985
Mahen, Rich/4301 SW 10th St, Ft Lauderdale, FL 305-792-5429
Malles, Ed/1013 S Semoran Blvd, Winter Park, FL 305-679-4155
Mann, James/1007-B Norwalk, Greensboro, NC 919-288-2508
Mann, Rod/5082 Woodleigh Rd, Knotts Island, NC 919-429-3009
Maratea, Ronn/4338 Virginia Beach Blvd, Virginia Beach, VA 804-340-6464
Markatos, Jerry/Rt 2 Box 419/Rock Rest Rd, Pittsboro, NC 919-542-2139
Marquez, Toby/1709 Wainwright Dr, Reston, VA 703-471-4666
Martin, Fred/110 Country View Dr, Simpsonville, SC 803-297-0010
Mason, Chuck/8755 SW 96th St, Miami, FL 305-270-2070
Maxwell, Alan/2551 NE 195th St, Miami, FL ....
May, Clyde/1037 Monroe Dr NE, Atlanta, GA 404-873-4329
Mayo, Michael/710 Tenth St, Atlanta, GA 404-368-2883
Mayor, Randy/2007 Fifteenth Ave S, Birmingham, AL 205-933-2818
Mazey, Jon/2724 NW 30th Ave, Ft Lauderdale, FL 305-731-3300
McAuley, Mary Beth/Box 1157, Kill Devil Hill, NC 919-473-1391
McCannon, Tricia/416 Armour Cir NE, Atlanta, GA 404-873-3070
McCarthy, Tom/8960 SW 114th St, Miami, FL (P 247) 305-233-1703
McClure, Dan/320 N Milledge, Athens, GA 404-354-1234
McCord, Fred/2720 Piedmont Rd NE, Atlanta, GA 404-262-1538
McCoy, Frank T/131 Donmond Dr, Hendersonville, TN 615-822-4437
McGee, E Alan/1816-E Briarwd Ind Ct, Atlanta, GA 404-633-1286
McGurkin, Douglas/5600 Glenridge Dr #B-55, Atlanta, GA 404-252-7108
McIntyre, William/3746 Yadkinville Rd, Winston-Salem, NC 919-922-3142
McKee, Lee/1004 Ruth Jordano Ct, Ocoee, FL 305-656-9289
McKenzie & Dickerson/133 W Vermont Ave/ Sthrn Pines, NC 919-692-6131
McLaughlin, Ken/623 7th Ave S, Nashville, TN 615-256-8162
McNabb, Tommy/4015 Brownsboro Rd, Winston-Salem, NC 919-723-4640
McNeely, Burton/PO Box 338, Land O'Lakes, FL 813-996-3025
McVicker, Sam/PO Box 880, Dunedin, FL 813-734-9660
Meacham, Ralph/Rt 6 Garrison Rd, Franklin, TN 615-794-1988
Melyana Assoc/2740 Alton Rd, Miami Beach, FL 305-673-0094
Meredith, David/2900 NE 30th St #2H, Ft Lauderdale, FL 305-564-4579
Michot, Walter/1520 E Sunrise Blvd, Ft Lauderdale, FL 305-527-8445
Mikeo, Rich/2189 N Powerline Rd, Pompano Beach, FL 305-960-0485
Miller, Brad/3645 Stewart, Coconut Grove, FL 305-666-1617
Miller, Bruce/9401 61st Court SW, Miami, FL 305-666-4333
Miller, Doug Photo/2117 Westover, Roanoke, VA 703-342-2732
Miller, Randy/6666 SW 96th St, Miami, FL (P 216,217) 305-667-5765
Millington, Rod/526 N Washington Dr, Sarasota, FL 813-388-1420
Mills, Henry/5514 Starkwood Dr, Charlotte, NC 704-535-1861
Mims, Allen/107 Madison Ave, Memphis, TN (P 248,249) 901-527-4040
Minardi, Mike/PO Box 14247, Tampa, FL 813-251-1696
Mitchell, Michael/2803 Foster Ave, Nashville, TN 615-333-1008
Molony, Bernard/PO Box 15081, Atlanta, GA 404-457-6934
Montage Studio/429-A Armour Cir, Atlanta, GA 404-892-3650
Moore, George Photography/1301 Admiral St, Richmond, VA 804-355-1862
Moore, Leslie/8551 NW 47th Ct, Fort Lauderdale, FL 305-742-4074
Moore, Mark/3803 W Gray, Tampa, FL 813-874-0410
Morgan, Frank/789 Seahawk Circle #112, Virginia Beach, VA 804-422-9328
Morgan, Red/970 Hickory Trail, W Palm Beach, FL 305-793-6085
Morrah, Linda/201 E Coffee St, Greenville, SC 803-242-9108
Morris, Paul/PO Box 530894, Miami, FL 305-758-8150
Muldez, Richard/404 Investors Pl #108, Virginia Beach, VA 804-490-6640
Murphy, Lionel Jr/2311 Waldemere, Sarasota, FL 813-365-0595
Murray, Kevin/Box 212, Winston-Salem, NC 919-722-5107
Murray, Steve/1330 Mordecai, Raleigh, NC 919-828-0653
Myers, Fred/114 Regent Ln, Florence, AL 205-766-4802
Myhre, Gordon/PO Box 1226, Ind Rocks Beach, FL 813-584-3717
Mykietyn, Walt/10110 SW 133 St, Miami, FL 305-235-2342

N

Nelson, Jon/PO Box 8772, Richmond, VA 804-359-0642
Nemeth, Bruce Studio/, , NC 704-522-7782
Nemeth, Judy/930 N Poplar St, Charlotte, NC 704-375-9292
Neubauer, John/1525 S Arlington Ridge Rd, Arlington, VA 703-920-5994
Nicolay, David/4756 W Napolean #3, Metarie, LA 504-888-7510
Nilsen, Audrey/630 Fog St, Nashville, TN 615-244-0555
Noel, Rip/707 Maryville Pke, Knoxville, TN 615-573-6635
Norling Studios Inc/221 Swathmore Ave/High Point, NC 919-434-3151
Norris, Robert Photo/224 Lorna Square, Birmingham, AL 205-979-7005
North Light Studio/1803 Hendricks Ave, Jacksonville, FL 904-398-2501
Norton, Mike/4917 W Nassau, Tampa, FL 813-876-3390
Novak, Jack/PO Box 971, Alexandria, VA 703-836-4439
Novicki, Norb/6800 North West 2nd St, Margate, FL 305-971-8954
Nurnberg, Paul/810 E Sixth St, Washington, NC 617-327-3920

O

O'Boyle, Erin/7001 N Atlantic Ave #122, Cape Canaveral, FL 305-783-1923
O'Kain, Dennis/102 W Main, Lexington, GA 404-743-3140
O'Sullivan, Brian/1401 SE 8th St, Deerfield Beach, FL 305-429-0712
Oesch, James/3706 Ridge Rd, Annadale, VA 703-941-3600
Olive, Tim/754 Piedmont Ave NE, Atlanta, GA 404-872-0500
Olson, Carl/3325 Laura Way, Winston, GA 404-949-1532
Oquendo, William/4680 SW 27th Ave, Ft Lauderdale, FL (P 231) 305-981-2823
Osborne, Mitchel L/920 Frenchman St, New Orleans, LA 504-949-1366

P

Parker, Phillip M/385 S Main St, Memphis, TN 901-529-9200
Parsley, Keith/801-K Atando Ave, Charlotte, NC 704-331-0812
Patterson, Pat/1635 Old Louisburg Rd, Raleigh, NC 919-834-2223
Payne, Steve/1524 Virginia St E, Charleston, WV 304-343-7254
Peeler, Alan/2175 Madison Ave, Memphis, TN 901-272-1769
Pelosi & Chambers/684 Greenwood Ave NE, Atlanta, GA 404-872-8117
Peters, J Dirk/PO Box 15492, Tampa, FL 813-654-1573
Petrey, John/670 Clay St/Box 2401, Winter Park, FL (P 250) 407-645-1718
Phillips, David/20 Topsail Tr, New Port Richey, FL 813-849-9458
Photo-Synthesis/1239 Kensington Rd, McLean, VA 703-734-8770
Photographic Group/7407 Chancery Ln, Orlando, FL 305-855-4306
Photographic Ideas/701 E Bay St/Box 1216, Charleston, SC 803-577-7020
Photography Unlimited/3662 S West Shore Blvd, Tampa, FL 813-839-7710
Pierce, Nancy J/1715 Merry Oaks Rd, Charlotte, NC 704-535-7409
Pierson, Art/1107 Lincoln Ave, Falls Church, VA 703-237-5937
Pinckney, Jim/PO Box 22887, Lake Buena Vista, FL 407-239-8855
Pinnacle Studios/2420 Schirra Pl, Highpoint, NC 919-886-6565
Pishner, Judy/15 Waddell, Atlanta, GA 404-525-4829
Pittenger, Kerry/100 Northeast 104th St, Miami Shores, FL 305-756-8830
Plachta, Greg/721 N Mangum, Durham, NC 919-682-6873
Pocklington, Mike/9 W Main St, Richmond, VA 804-783-2731
Ponzoni, Bob/703 Westchester Dr, High Point, NC 919-885-8733
Posey, Mike/3524 Canal St, New Orleans, LA 504-488-8000
Prism Studios/1027 Elm Hill Pike, Nashville, TN 615-255-1919
Profancik, Larry/2101 Production, Louisville, KY 502-499-9220
Purin, Thomas/14190 Harbor Lane, Lake Park, FL 305-622-4131
Putnam, Don/623 7th Ave So, Nashville, TN 615-242-7325

R

Ramirez, George/303 Canals St, Santurce, PR 809-724-5727
Ramos, Victor/8390 SW 132 St, Miami, FL 305-255-3111
Randolph, Bruce/132 Alan Dr, Newport News, VA 804-877-0992
Rank, Don/2265 Lawson Way, Atlanta, GA 404-452-1658
Ratcliffe, Rodney/206 Rogers St NE #11, Atlanta, GA 404-373-2767
Rathe, Robert A/8451-A Hilltop Rd, Fairfax, VA 703-560-7222
Raymond, Tom/2608 West Market, Johnson City, TN (P 251) 615-928-2700
Reus-Breuer, Sandra/Cal Josefa Cabrera Final, Rio Pdras, PR 809-767-1568
Richards, Courtland William/PO Box 59734, Birmingham, AL 205-871-8923
Rickles, Tom/5401 Alton Rd, Miami, FL 305-866-5762
Riggall, Michael/403 8th St NE, Atlanta, GA 404-872-8242
Riggs, Benjamin/2809 Blythe Rd, Cleveland, TN 615-479-9075
Riley, Richard/34 N Ft Harrison, Clearwater, FL 813-446-2626
Rippey, Rhea/PO Box 50093, Nashville, TN 615-646-1291
Rob/Harris Productions/PO Box 15721, Tampa, FL 813-258-4061
Rodgers, Ted/544 Plasters Ave, Atlanta, GA 404-892-0967
Rogers, Brian/689 Antone St NW, Atlanta, GA 404-355-8069
Rogers, Chuck/1226-28 Spring St NW, Atlanta, GA 404-872-0062
Rosen, Olive/3415 Arnold Ln, Falls Church, VA 703-560-5557
Rossmeissl, Kirk/1921 Woodford Rd, Vienna, VA 301-899-4866
Rubio, Manny/1203 Techwood Dr, Atlanta, GA 404-892-0783
Runion, Britt/7409 Chancery Ln, Orlando, FL 305-857-0491
Russell, John Photo/PO Box 2141, High Point, NC 919-887-1163
Rutherford, Michael W/623 Sixth Ave S, Nashville, TN 615-242-5953
Rutledge, Don/13000 Edgetree Ct, Midlothian, VA 804-353-0151

S

Saenz, C M/PO Box 117, Alachua, FL 904-462-5670
Salmon, George/10325 Del Mar Circle, Tampa, FL 813-961-8687
Sambrook, Don/13 W 25th St, Baltimore, MD 301-235-0900
Sanacore, Steve/87 Westbury Close, West Palm Beach, FL 407-795-1510
Sandlin, Mark/45 Little Rd, Sharpsburg, GA 404-251-5207
Santos, Roberto/15929 NW 49th Ave, Hialeah, FL 305-621-6047
Saylor, Ted/2312 Farwell Dr, Tampa, FL 813-879-5636
Schaedler, Tim/PO Box 1081, Safety Harbor, FL 813-796-0366
Schatz, Bob/112 Second Ave N, Nashville, TN (P 252) 615-254-7197
Schenck, Gordon H/PO Box 35203, Charlotte, NC 704-332-4078
Schenker, Richard/6304 Benjamin Rd #504, Tampa, FL 813-885-5413
Schermerhorn, Tim/325 Model Farm Rd, High Point, NC 919-887-6644
Schiavone, George/355 NE 59th Terr, Miami, FL 305-662-6057
Schiff, Ken/4406 SW 74th Ave, Miami, FL 305-262-2022
Schneider, John/3702-B Alliance Dr, Greensboro, NC 919-855-0261
Schulke, Debra/6770 SW 101st St, Miami, FL 305-667-0961
Schulke, Flip/14730 SW 158th St, Miami, FL 305-251-7717
Schumacher, Karl/6254 Park Rd, McLean, VA 703-241-7424
Scott, James/210 N Fillmore St, Arlington, VA 703-522-8261
Seifried/Rt 3 Box 162, Decatur, AL (P 226) 205-355-5558
Seitelman, M D/PO Box 2477, Alexandria, VA 703-548-7217
Seitz, Arthur/1905 N Atlantic Blvd, Ft Lauderdale, FL 305-563-0060
Sharpe, David/816 N St Asaph St, Alexandria, VA 703-683-3773
Shea, David/#12 Miracle Stripe Pkwy SE, Ft Walton Bch, FL 904-244-3602
Sheffield, Scott/2707 W Broad St, Richmond, VA 804-358-3266
Sheldon, Mike/Rt 2 Box 61A, Canton, NC 704-235-8345
Sherbow, Robert/1607 Colonial Terr, Arlington, VA 202-522-3644
Sherman, Pam/103 Bonnie Brae Way, Hollywood, FL 305-652-0566
Sherman, Ron/PO Box 28656, Atlanta, GA 404-993-7197
Shone, Phil/544 Plasters Ave, Atlanta, GA 404-487-5766
Shooters Photo/1001-C W Tremont Ave, Charlotte, NC 704-334-7267
Shrout, Bill/Route 1 Box 317, Theodore, AL 205-973-1379
Silla, Jon/400 S Graham St, Charlotte, NC 704-377-8694
Sink, Richard/1225 Cedar Dr, Winston Salem, NC 919-784-8759
Sisson, Barry/6813 Bland St, Springfield, VA 703-569-6051
Smart, David/PO Box 11743, Memphis, TN 901-522-1805
Smeltzer, Robert/29 Stone Plaza Dr, Greenville, SC 803-235-2186
Smith, Clark/618 Glenwood Pl, Dalton, GA 404-226-2508
Smith, Deborah/1007-13 Norwalk St, Greensboro, NC 919-292-1190
Smith, Richard & Assoc/1007 Norwalk St #B, Greensboro, NC 919-292-1190
Smith, Richard Photo/1625 NE 3rd Ct, Ft Lauderdale, FL 305-523-8861
Smith/Garner Studios/1114 W Peachtree St, Atlanta, GA 404-875-0086
Snow, Chuck/2700 7th Ave S, Birmingham, AL 205-251-7482
Snyder, Lee/4150-D 112th Terr N, Clearwater, FL 813-578-2332
Sparkman, Clif/161 Mangum St SW #301, Atlanta, GA 404-588-9687
Sparks, Don/670 11th St NW, Atlanta, GA 404-876-7354
Spartana, Stephen/1802 E Lombard St, Baltimore, MD 301-327-1918
Speidell, Bill/1030 McConville Rd, Lynchburg, VA 804-846-2133
Spence, Christopher/6850 NW 20th Ave, Ft Lauderdale, FL 305-979-8295
St John, Chuck/2724 NW 30th Ave, Ft Lauderdale, FL 305-731-3300
St John, Michael/PO Box 1202, Oldsmar, FL 813-725-4817
Stansfield, Ross/4938-D Eisenhower Ave, Alexandria, VA 703-370-5142
Staples, Neil/5092 NE 12th Ave, Ft Lauderdale, FL 305-792-2448
Starling, Robert/PO Box 25827, Charlotte, NC 704-568-7611
Stein Photo/20240 SW 92nd Ave, Miami, FL 305-251-2868
Stein, Art/2419 Mt Vernon Ave, Alexandria, VA 703-684-0675
Stevenson, Aaron/707 Jackson Ave, Charlotte, NC 704-332-3147
Stewart, Harvey & Co Inc/836 Dorse Rd, Lewisville, NC 919-945-2101
Stoppee Photographics Group/13 W Main St, Richmond, VA 804-644-0266
Stout, Lans/2132 Kings Ave, Jacksonville, FL 904-398-3225
Stratton, Jimi/670 11th St NW, Atlanta, GA (P 220) 404-876-1876
Strode, William A/1008 Kent Rd, Goshin, KY 502-228-4446
Suraci, Carl/216 Hillsdale Dr, Sterling, VA 703-620-6645
Swann, David/776 Juniper St, Atlanta, GA 404-873-3003
Sweetman, Gary/2904 Manatee Ave W, Bradenton, FL 813-748-4004

T

Tast, Jerry/8880 Old King's Rd S #34, Jacksonville, FL 904-731-5887
Taylor, Randy/555 NE 34th St #701, Miami, FL 305-573-5200
Telesca, Chris/PO Box 51449, Raliegh, NC 919-846-0101
Tenney, Michael/PO Box 37287, Charlotte, NC 704-372-7700
Terranova, Michael/1135 Cadiz St, New Orleans, LA (P 253) 504-899-7328
Tesh, John/904-A Norwalk St, Greenboro, NC (P 221) 919-299-1400
Thomas, J Clark/2305 Elliston Place, Nashville, TN 615-327-1757
Thomas, Jay/2955 Cobb Pkwy #195, Atlanta, GA 404-432-1735
Thomas, Larry/1212 Spring St, Atlanta, GA 404-881-8850
Thomas/Bruce Studio/79-25 4th St N, St Petersburg, FL 813-577-5626
Thompson & Thompson/5180 NE 12th Ave, Ft Lauderdale, FL 305-772-4411
Thompson, Darrell/124 Rhodes Dr, Marietta, GA 404-641-2020
Thompson, Ed C/2381 Drew Valley Rd, Atlanta, GA 404-636-7258

Thompson, Michael/1579-F Monroe Dr #240, Atlanta, GA...............404-434-1011
Thompson, Rose/4338 NE 11th Ave, Oakland Park, FL.........305-563-7937
Thompson, Thomas L/2403 Dellwood Dr NW, Atlanta, GA........404-524-6929
Tilley, Arthur/1925 College Ave NE, Atlanta,
GA (P 254) **404-371-8086**
Tobias, Jerry/2117 Opa-Locka Blvd, Miami, FL.....................305-685-3003
Touchton, Ken/3011 Northeast 40th St, Ft Lauderdale, FL.............305-566-9756
Traves, Stephen/360 Elden Dr, Atlanta, GA.........................404-255-5711
Trufant, David/1902 Highland Rd, Baton Rouge, LA................504-344-9690
Truman, Gary/PO Box 7144, Charleston, WV..........................304-755-3078
Turnau, Jeffrey/7210 Red Rd #216, Miami, FL.......................305-666-5454

UV

Ustinich, Richard Photo/12 North 18th St, Richmond, VA................804-649-1477
Uzzell, Steve/1419 Trap Rd, Vienna,
VA (P 210,211) **703-938-6868**
Uzzle, Warren/5201 William & Mary Dr, Raleigh, NC.................919-266-6203
Valada, M C/204 Park Terr Ct SE, Vienna, VA........................703-938-0324
Van Calsem, Bill/824 Royal St, New Orleans, LA....................504-522-7346
Van Camp, Louis/713 San Juan Rd, New Bern, NC..................919-633-6081
Van de Zande, Doug/515 Hillsborough St, Raleigh,
NC (P 255) **919-832-2499**
Vance, David/13760 NW 19th Ave #14, Miami, FL..................305-685-2433
Vaughn, Marc/11140 Griffing Blvd, Biscayne Park, FL.............305-895-5790
Verlent, Christian/PO Box 530805, Miami,
FL (P 257) **305-751-3385**
Victor, Ira/2026 Prairie Ave, Miami Beach, FL........................305-532-4444
Vullo, Phillip Photography/565 Dutch Valley Rd NE, Atlanta, GA......404-874-0822

W

Wagoner, Mark/12-H Wendy Ct Box 18974, Greensboro, NC..........919-854-0406
Walker, Reuel Jr/PO Box 5421, Greenville, SC......................803-834-9836
Walker, Wes/301 Calvin St, Greenville, SC..........................803-242-9108
Wallace, Doyle/2408 Summit Springs Dr, Dunwoody, GA.............404-448-8300
Walpole, Gary/284 N Cleveland, Memphis, TN........................901-726-1155
Walters, Tom/3108 Airlie St, Charlotte, NC.........................704-537-7908
Wark, Mark/Rte 5 Box 239-A, Charlottesville, VA..................804-973-3370
Warren, Bob/1511 Gilford Ave, Baltimore, MD.......................301-539-2807
Watt, John/3480 Matilda, Miami, FL..................................216-621-3838
Wax, Bill/6880 Abbott Ave #201, Miami Beach, FL..................305-864-8650
Webb, Jon/2023 Kenilworth Ave, Louisville, KY.....................502-459-7081
Webster & Co/2401 Euclid Ave, Charlotte, NC.......................704-522-0647
Weinkle, Mark/PO Box 25011, Durham,
NC (P 258,259) **919-383-8449**
Weinlaub, Ralph/81 SW 6th St, Pompano Beach, FL................305-941-1368
Weithorn, Mark/13740 NW 19th Ave #6, Miami, FL.................305-688-7070
Welsh, Kelley/11450 SE 57th St, Miami, FL..........................305-595-6174
Westerman, Charlie/Cntrl Amr Bldg/Bowman Fld, Louisville, KY.....502-458-1532
Wheless, Rob/2239 Faulkner Rd NE, Atlanta, GA....................404-729-1066
White, Drake/PO Box 40090, Augusta, GA...........................404-733-4142
Whitman, Alan/724 Lakeside Dr, Mobile, AL..........................205-661-0400
Whitman, John/604 N Jackson St, Arlington, VA.....................703-524-5569
Wiener, Ray/4300 NE 5th Terrace, Oakland Park, FL................305-565-4415
Wiley, Robert Jr/1145 Washington Ave, Winter Park, FL............407-629-5823
Willard, Jean/684 Greenwood Ave, Atlanta, GA......................404-872-8117
Williams, Jimmy/3801 Beryl Rd, Raleigh, NC........................919-832-5971
Williams, Ron/105 Space Park Dr #A, Nashville, TN................615-331-2500
Williams, Sonny Photo Inc/741 Monroe Dr NE,
Atlanta, GA (P 218,219) **404-892-5551**
Willis, Joe/105 Lake Emerald Dr #314, Ft Lauderdale, FL..........305-485-7185
Wilson, Andrew/1640 Smyrna-Roswell Rd SE, Smyrna, GA.........404-436-7553
Wilson, Vickie/21 W Country Cove, Kifsimmee, FL..................305-348-4906
Wilt, Greg/PO Box 212, Clearwater, FL...............................813-442-4360
Winner, Alan/20151 NE 15th Court, Miami, FL.......................305-653-6778
Wolf, David/1770 Quail Ridge Rd, Raleigh, NC.......................919-782-8395
Wood, James/PO Box 510129, Melbourne Beach, FL................407-725-4581
Wood, Michael/470 Woods Mill Rd NW, Gainesville, GA.............404-536-9006
Woodbury & Associates/6801 NW 9th Ave #102,
Ft Lauderdale, FL (P 260) **305-977-9000**
Woodson, Richard/PO Box 12224, Raliegh, NC.....................919-833-2882
Wray, Michael/3501 Royal Palm Ave, Ft Lauderdale, FL............305-564-3433
Wright, Christopher/2001-A Dekle Ave, Tampa, FL.................813-251-5206
Wright, Timothy/PO Box 5425, Virginia Bch, VA....................804-464-6710
Wrisley, Bard/3210 Peachtree Rd NW #14, Atlanta, GA.............404-524-6929

YZ

Yankus, Dennis/223 S Howard Ave, Tampa, FL......................813-254-4156
Young, Chuck/1199-R Howell Mill Rd, Atlanta, GA..................404-351-1199

Young, Donn/3519 Live Oak St, New Orleans, LA....................514-484-6387
Zeck, Gerry/1939 S Orange Ave, Sarasota, FL........................813-953-4888
Zillioux, John/663 Woodcrest Rd, Miami,
FL (P 261) **305-361-0368**
Zimmerman, Mike/7821 Shalimar, Mira Mar, FL......................305-987-8482
Zinn, Arthur/2661 S Course Dr, Pompano Beach, FL................305-973-3851

M I D W E S T

A

Abel Photographics/7035 Ashland Dr, Cleveland, OH...................216-526-5732
Abramson, Michael L/3312 W Belle Plaine,
Chicago, IL (P 266) **312-267-9189**
Accola, Harlan J/207 E 29th St, Marshfield, WI.....................715-387-8682
Adamo, Sam/490 Parkview Dr, Seven Hills, OH......................216-447-9249
Adams Group/703 E 30th St #17, Indianapolis, IN..................317-924-2400
Adams, Steve Studio/3101 S Hanley, Brentwood, MO..............314-781-6676
Adcock, Gary/70 W Huron St #1009, Chicago, IL...................312-943-6917
AGS & R Studios/425 N Michigan Ave, Chicago, IL.................312-836-4500
Alan, Andrew/20727 Scio Church Rd, Chelsea, MI..................313-475-2310
Albiez, Scott/4144 N Clarendon, Chicago, IL........................312-327-8999
Albright, Dave/200 S Main, Northville, MI...........................313-348-2248
Alexander Glass Ingersol/3000 South Tech, Miamisburg, OH..........513-885-2008
Alexander, Gordon/1848 Porter St SW, Wyoming, MI................616-531-1204
Alexander, Mark/412 Central Ave, Cincinnati, OH...................413-651-5020
Allan-Knox Studios/450 S 92nd St, Milwaukee, WI..................414-774-7900
Allen, Carter/8081 Zionsville Rd/POB 68520, Indianapolis, IN.........317-872-7720
Altman, Ben/820 N Franklin, Chicago, IL.............................312-944-1434
Amenta/555 W Madison #3802, Chicago, IL..........................312-248-2488
Anderson Studios Inc/546 S Meridian #300, Indianapolis, IN.........317-632-9405
Anderson, Craig/105 7th St, W Des Moines, IA......................515-279-7766
Anderson, Rob/900 W Jackson, Chicago, IL..........................312-666-0417
Anderson, Whit/219 W Chicago, Chicago, IL.........................312-973-5683
Andre, Bruce/436 N Clark, Chicago, IL...............................312-661-1060
Andrew, Larry/1632 Broadway, Kansas City, MO.....................816-471-5565
Ann Arbor Photo/670 Airport Blvd, Ann Arbor, MI...................313-995-5778
Apolinski, John/735 N Oriole Ave, Park Ridge, IL...................312-696-3156
Arciero, Anthony/70 E Long Lake Rd, Bloomfield Hills, MI...........313-645-2222
Ardisson Photography/2719 N Wayne, Chicago, IL...................312-836-0464
Armour, Tony/1726 N Clybourn Ave, Chicago, IL.....................312-664-2256
Arndt, David M/4620 N Winchester, Chicago, IL......................312-334-2841
Arndt, Jim/400 First Ave N #510, Minneapolis, MN..................612-332-5050
Arpadi, Allen G/5846 Waterman Blvd, St Louis, MO.................314-863-6643
Arsenault, Bill/1244 W Chicago Ave, Chicago, IL....................312-421-2525
Ascherman, Herbert Jr/1846 Coventry Vill, Cleveland Hhts, OH......216-321-0055
Atevich, Alex/325 N Hoyne Ave, Chicago, IL.........................312-942-1453
Atkinson, David K/14 North Newstead, St Louis,
MO (P 267) **314-535-6484**
Audio Visual Impact Group/233 E Erie, Chicago, IL..................312-664-6247
Ayala/320 E 21 St, Chicago, IL.......................................312-326-0728
Azuma, Don/1335 N Wells, Chicago, IL..............................312-583-1402

B

Baer Studio/5807 Capri Ln, Morton Grove, IL........................312-966-4759
Baer, Gordon/18 E 4th St #903, Cincinnati, OH......................513-381-4466
Bagnoli, Susan/74-24 Washington Ave, Eden Prairie, MN.............612-944-5750
Bahm, Dave/711 Commercial, Belton, MO............................816-331-0257
Baker, Gregory/4630 Charles St, Rockford, IL........................815-398-1114
Baker, Jim/1632 Broadway, Kansas City, MO.........................816-471-5565
Balterman, Lee/910 N Lake Shore Dr, Chicago, IL...................312-642-9040
Baltz, Bill/3615 Superior Ave, Cleveland, OH........................216-431-0979
Banna, Kevin/617 W Fulton St, Chicago, IL..........................312-845-9650
Banner & Burns Inc/153 W Ohio, Chicago, IL........................312-644-4770
Bannister, Will/849 W Lill Ave #K, Chicago, IL.......................312-327-2143
Barge, Mike/7618 W Myrtle, Chicago, IL.............................312-762-1749
Barkan Keeling Photo/905 Vine St, Cincinnati, OH...................513-721-0700
Barlow Inc/1125 S Brentwood Blvd, Richmond Hts, MO..............314-721-2385
Barnett, Jim/5580 N Dequincy St, Indianapolis, IN..................317-257-7177
Baron, Jim/Caxton Bldg #314, Cleveland, OH........................216-781-7729
Barrett, Bob Photo/3733 Pennsylvania, Kansas City, MO.............816-753-3208
Bart, Casimir/205 Ridgemont W #703, Toronto, ON...................
Barton, Mike/5019 Nokomis Ave S, Minneapolis, MN................612-721-1349
Bartone, Tom/436 N Clark St, Chicago, 1L...........................312-836-0464
Bartz, Carl Studio Inc/321 N 22nd St, St Louis, MO.................314-231-8690
Basdeka, Pete/1254 N Wells, Chicago, IL............................312-944-3333
Bass, Alan/126 W Kinzie, Chicago, IL................................312-280-9140

Battrell, Mark/1611 N Sheffield, Chicago, IL 312-642-6650
Baver, Perry L/2923 W Touhy, Chicago, IL 312-674-1695
Bayles, Dal/4431 N 64th St, Milwaukee, WI 414-464-8917
Beasley, Michael/1210 W Webster, Chicago, IL 312-248-5769
Beaugureau Studio/704 N Sylviawood, PArk Ridge, IL 312-696-1299
Beaulieu, Allen/400 N First Ave #604, Minneapolis, MN 612-338-2327
Beck, Peter/718 Washington Ave N #605, Minneapolis, MN 612-338-5712
Beckett Photography/510 N Water St, Milwaukee, WI 414-271-2061
Beckett Studios/340 W Huron St, Chicago, IL 312-943-2648
Bednersti, Paul/5735 Bishop Rd, Detroit, MI 313-882-0427
Bellville, Cheryl Walsh/2823 8th St S, Minneapolis, MN 612-333-5788
Belter, Mark/640 N LaSalle St #555, Chicago, IL 312-337-7676
Benda, Tom/20555 LaGrange, Frankfurt, IL 815-469-3600
Bender/Bender/281 Klingel Rd, Waldo, OH 614-726-2470
Benkert, Christine/27 N 4th St #501, Minneapolis, MN 612-340-9503
Bennet, Patrick/330 E 47th St, Indianapolis, IN 317-283-7530
Benoit, Bill/1708 1/2 Washington, Wilmette, IL 312-251-7634
Bentley, David/208 West Kinzie, Chicago, IL 312-836-0242
Benyas-Kaufman Photo/8775 W 9 Mile Rd, Oak Park, MI 313-548-4400
Bergerson, Steven/3349 45th Ave S, Minneapolis, MN 612-724-0720
Berglund, Peter/718 Washington Ave N, Minneapolis, MN 612-371-9318
Bergos, Jim Studio/122 W Kinzie St, Chicago, IL 312-527-1769
Berkman, Elie/125 Hawthorn Ave, Glencoe, IL 312-835-4158
Berlin Chic Photo/1708 W School Rd 3rd Fl, Chicago, IL 312-327-2266
Berliner, Sheri/2815 N Pine Grove #1A, Chicago, IL 312-477-6692
Berlow, Marc/867 Tree Ln #105, Prospect Hts, IL 312-787-6528
Berr, Keith/1220 W 6th St #608, Cleveland, OH 216-566-7950
Berthiaume, Tom/1008 Nicollet Mall, Minneapolis, MN 612-338-1999
Bevacqua, Alberto/720 N Wabash, Chicago, IL 312-458-1760
Bidak, Lorne/827 Milwaukee Ave, Chicago, IL 312-733-3997
Bieber, Tim/3312 W Belle Plaine, Chicago, IL 312-463-3590
Biel Studios/2289-91 N Moraine Blvd, Dayton, OH 513-298-6621
Bierwagen, Ottmar/50 Woodycrest Ave, Toronto, ON 416-463-6560
Bilsley, Bill/2540 United Lane, Elk Grove Village, IL 312-860-9189
Bishop, Robert/5622 Delmar #103, St Louis, MO 314-367-8787
Bjornson, Howard/300 N Ashland, Chicago, IL 312-243-8200

Blackburn, Charles A/1100 S Lynndale,
Appleton, WI (P 276,277) **414-738-4080**
Blahut, Joseph/2400 Lakeview #906, Chicago, IL 312-525-2946
Block, Ernie/1138 Cambridge Cir Dr, Kansas City, KS 913-321-3080
Block, Stuart/1242 W Washington Blvd, Chicago, IL 312-733-3600
Bochsler, Tom/3514 Mainway, Burlington L7M 1A8, ON 416-529-9011
Bock, Edward/400 N First Ave #207, Minneapolis, MN 612-332-8504
Bodenhansen, Gary/201 Wyandotte St, Kansas City, MO 816-221-9254
Bolber Studio/6706 Northwest Hwy, Chicago, IL 312-763-5860
Bond, Paul/1421 N Dearborn #302, Chicago, IL 312-280-5488
Borde, Richard & Dawn/5328 29th Ave S, Minneapolis, MN 612-729-1913
Bornefeld, William/586 Hollywood Pl, St Louis, MO 314-962-5596
Boschke, Les/806 North Peoria, Chicago, IL 312-666-8819
Bosek, George/1301 S Wabash 2nd Fl, Chicago, IL 312-939-0777
Bosy, Peter/564 W Randolph, Chicago, IL 312-559-0042
Boucher, Joe/5765 S Melinda St, Milwaukee, WI 414-281-7653
Boulevard Photo/151 Victor Ave, Highland Park, MI 313-868-2200
Bowen, Paul/Box 3375, Wichita, KS 316-263-5537
Boyer, Dick/45W Erie #201, Chicago, IL 312-337-7211
Brackenbury, Vern/1516 N 12th St, Blue Springs, MO 816-229-6703
Braddy, Jim/PO Box 11420, Chicago, IL 312-337-5664
Bradley, Rodney/329 10th Ave SE, Cedar Rapids, IA 319-365-5071
Brandenburg, Jim/708 N 1st St, Minneapolis, MN 612-341-0166
Brandt & Assoc/Route 5 Box 148, Barrington Hills, IL 312-428-6363
Braun Photography/3966 W Bath Rd, Akron, OH 216-666-4540
Brayne, TW/326 W Kalamazoo Ave, Kalamazoo, MI 616-344-0283
Brettell, Jim/2152 Morrison Ave, Lakewood, OH 216-228-0890
Brimacombe, Gerald/7212 Mark Terrace, Minneapolis, MN 612-941-5860
Broderson, Fred/215 W Huron, Chicago, IL 312-787-1241
Brody, David & Assoc/6001 N Clark, Chicago, IL 312-761-2735
Brody, Jerry/70 W Hubbard, Chicago, IL 312-329-0660
Brookins, Carl/PO Box 80096, St Paul, MN 612-636-1733
Brosilow, Michael/480 Menomonee, Chicago, IL 312-266-1136
Brown, Alan J/815 MAin St, Cincinnati, OH 513-421-5588
Brown, James F/1349 E McMillan St, Cincinnati, OH 513-221-1144
Brown, Ron/1324 N Street, Lincoln, NE 402-476-1760
Brown, Steve/107 W Hubbard, Chicago, IL 312-467-4666
Bruno, Sam/1630 N 23rd, Melrose Park, IL 312-345-0411
Bruton, Jon/3838 W Pine Blvd, St Louis, MO 314-533-6665
Brystrom, Roy/6127 N Ravenswood, Chicago, IL 312-973-2922
Bukva, Walt/118 Anchor Rd, Michigan City, IN 219-872-9469
Bundt, Nancy/1908 Kenwood Parkway, Minneapolis, MN 612-377-7773

Burjoski, David/3524 Washington Ave 4th Fl, St Louis, MO 314-534-4060
Burress, Cliff/5420 N Sheridan, Chicago, IL 312-334-5332
Burris, Zack/445 W Erie, Chicago, IL 312-951-0131
Buschauer, Al/11416 S Harlem Ave, Worth, IL 312-448-2222
Bush, Tim/617 W Fulton St, Chicago, IL 312-337-0414
Button Down Prod. Ltd/4053 North Sheridan, Chicago, IL 312-327-6793

C

C-H Studios/517 S Jefferson 7th Fl, Chicago, IL 312-922-8880
Cabanban, Orlando/410 S Michigan Ave, Chicago, IL 312-922-1836
Cable, Wayne/2212 N Racine, Chicago, IL 312-525-2240
Cain, C C/420 N Clark, Chicago, IL 312-644-2371
Cairns, Robert/2035 W Charleston #4-SE, Chicago, IL 312-384-3114
Camacho, Mike/124 W Main St, West Dundee, IL 312-428-3135
Camera Works Inc/1260 Carnegie Ave, Cleveland, OH 216-687-1788
Camerawork, Ltd/400 S Greens St #203, Chicago, IL 312-666-8802
Campbell, Bob/722 Prestige, Joliet, IL (P 268) **815-725-1862**
Candee, Michael Studios/1212 W Jackson Blvd, Chicago, IL 312-226-3332
Caporale, Michael/6710 Madison Rd, Cincinnati, OH 513-561-4011
Carell, Lynn/3 E Ontario #25, Chicago, IL 312-935-1707
Carney, Joann/401 N Racine, Chicago, IL 312-829-2332
Carosella, Tony/4138-A Wyoming, St Louis, MO 314-664-3462
Carter, David/510 W Wellington, Chicago, IL 312-929-0306
Carter, Garry/179 Waverly, Ottawa K2P 0V5, ON 613-233-3306
Carter, Mary Ann/5954 Crestview, Indianapolis, IN 317-255-1351
Casalini, Tom/10 1/2 N Main St, Zionsville, IN 317-873-5229
Cascarano, John/657 W Ohio, Chicago, IL 312-733-1212
Caswell, George/700 Washington Ave N, Minneapolis, MN 612-332-2729
Caulfield, James/430 W Erie, Chicago, IL 312-951-7260
Cedrowski, Dwight/PO Box 5360, Northville, MI 313-455-4401
Ceolla, George/5700 Ingersoll Ave, Des Moines, IA 515-279-3508
Cephas, Donna/4703 N Malden #1, Chicago, IL 312-334-4929
Cermak Photo/96 Pine Ave, Riverside, IL 312-447-6446
Chadwick Taber Inc/617 W Fulton, Chicago, IL 312-454-0855
Chambers, Tom/153 W Ohio, Chicago, IL 312-828-9488
Chapman, Cam/126 W Kinzie, Chicago, IL 312-222-9242
Chapman, John/311 N Des Plaines, Chicago, IL 312-930-9127
Chare, Dave/1045 N Northwest Hwy, Park Ridge, IL 312-696-3188
Charlie Company/2148 Lakeside, Cleveland, OH 216-566-7464
Charlton, James/11518 N Pt Washington Rd, Mequon, WI 414-241-8634
Chauncey, Paul C/388 N Hydraulic, Wichita, KS 316-262-6733
Cherup, Thomas/PO Box 84, Dearborn Hts, MI 313-561-9376
Chicago Photographers/60 W Superior, Chicago, IL 312-944-4828
Chin, Ruth/207 N Tillotson, Muncie, IN 317-284-4582
Chobot, Dennis/2857 E Grand Blvd, Detroit, MI 313-875-6617
Christian Studios Inc/5408 N Main St, Dayton, OH 513-275-3775
Christman, Gerald/985 Ridgewood Dr, Highland Park, IL 312-433-2279
Church, Dennis/301 S Bedford St #6, Madison, WI 608-255-2726
Clark, Harold/9 Lloyd Manor, Islington M9B 5H5, ON 416-236-2958
Clark, Junebug/30419 W Twelve Mile Rd, Farmington Hills, MI 313-478-3666
Clarke, Jim/3721 Grandel Sq, St Louis, MO 314-652-6262
Clawson, David/6800 Normal Blvd, Lincoln, NE 402-489-1302
Clawson, Kent/2530 West Wilson Ave, Chicago, IL 312-583-0001
Clayton, Curt/23263 Woodward Ave, Ferndale, MI 313-548-0039
Clemens, Jim/1311 Gregory, Wilmette, IL 312-256-5413
Click/ Chicago/213 W Institute Pl #503, Chicago, IL 312-787-7880
Cloudshooters/Aerial Photo/4620 N Winchester, Chicago I, L6 12-334-2841
Clough, Jean/1446 Rosemont, Chicago, IL 312-274-7011
Coats & Greenfield Inc/2928 Fifth Ave S, Minneapolis, MN 612-827-4676
Cochrane, Jim/25 1/2 York St #1, Ottawa K1N 5S7, ON 613-234-3099
Cocose, Ellen/445 E Ohio #222, Chicago, IL 312-527-9444
Coha, Dan/9 W Hubbard, Chicago, IL 312-664-2270
Coil, Ron Studio/15 W Hubbard St, Chicago, IL 312-321-0155
Color Associates/10818 MW Industrial Blvd, St Louis, MO 800-456-SEPS
Compton, Ted/112 N Washington, Hinsdale, IL 312-654-8781
Condie, Thomas M/527 N 27th St, Milwaukee, WI 414-342-6363
Condreay, John/2501 Ottawa Dr, Lafayette, IN 317-474-8198
Conison, Joel/3201 Eastern, Cincinnati,
OH (P 265) **513-241-1887**
Copeland, Burns/6651 N Artesian, Chicago, IL 312-465-3240
Corey, Carl/222 S Morgan, Chicago, IL 312-421-3232
Coster-Mullen, John E/PO Box 1637, Appleton, WI 414-733-9001
Cote, Eaton/26 Spring Ave, Waukon, IA 319-568-2253
Cowan, Ralph/452 N Halsted St, Chicago, IL 312-243-6696
Cox, Dennis/14555 Champaign #212, Allen Park, MI 313-386-4802
CR Studio/1859 W 25th St, Cleveland, OH 216-861-5360
Cralle, Gary/83 Elm Ave #205, Toronto M4W 1P1, ON 416-923-2920
Crane, Arnold/666 N Lake Shore Dr, Chicago, IL 312-337-5544

Crane, Michael/1717 Wyandotte St, Kansas City, MO 816-221-9382
Creightney, Dorrell/1729 W Melrose, Chicago, IL 312-528-0816
Croff, Will/1100 S Lynndale, Appleton, WI (P 273) 414-738-4080
Crofoot, Ron/6140 Wayzata Blvd, Minneapolis, MN 612-546-0643
Crofton, Bill/326R Linden Ave, Wilmette, IL 312-256-7862
Cromwell, Patrick/1739 Coolidge, Berkley, MI 313-543-5610
Crosby, Paul/1083 Tenth Ave SE, Minneapolis, MN 612-378-9566
Cross, Emil/1886 Thunderbird, Troy, MI 313-362-3111
Crowther Photography/1108 Kenilworth Ave, Cleveland, OH 216-566-8066
Culbert-Aguilar, Kathleen/1338 W Carmen, Chicago, IL 312-561-1266
Culp, John L Jr/1133 E 45th St, Chicago, IL 312-285-5570
Curtis, Lucky/1540 N Park Ave, Chicago,
IL (P 269)   312-787-4422

D

D'Orio, Tony/1147 W Ohio, Chicago, IL.....................312-421-5532
Dacuisto, Todd/4455 W Bradley Rd #204, Milwaukee, WI 414-352-7527
Dale, LB/7015 Wing Lake Rd, Birmingham, MI 313-851-3296
Dali, Michael/1737 McGee, Kansas City, MO 816-931-0570
Dapkus, Jim/Westfield Photo/Rte 1 Box 247, Westfield, WI 608-296-2623
Davito, Dennis/638 Huntley Heights, Manchester, MO 314-394-0660
Day, Michael/264 Seaton St, Toronto M5A 2T4, ON 416-920-9135
Deahl, David/70 W Hubbard, Chicago, IL.....................312-644-3187
Debacker, Michael/231 Ohio, Wichita, KS 316-265-2776
Debold, Bill/1801 N Halsted, Chicago, IL.....................312-337-1177
DeBolt, Dale/120 West Kinzie St, Chicago, IL 312-644-6264
DeLaittre, Bill/1307 5th St South, Minneapolis, MN 612-936-9840
Delich, Mark/304 W 10th St #200, Kansas City, MO 816-474-6699
DeMarco Photographers/7145 W Addison, Chicago, IL 312-282-1422
DeNatale, Joe/2129 W North Ave, Chicago, IL 312-489-0089
Denning, Warren/27 Laurel, Wichita, KS 316-262-4163
Design Photography/1324 Hamilton Ave, Cleveland, OH 216-687-0099
Dieringer, Rick/19 West Court St, Cincinnati,
OH (P 271)   513-621-2544
Dinerstein, Matt/606 W 18th St, Chicago, IL 312-243-4766
Ditlove, Michel/18 W Hubbard, Chicago, IL.....................312-644-5233
Ditz, Michael/8138 W 9 Mile Rd, Oak Park, MI.....................313-546-1759
Donner, Michael/5534 S Dorchester, Chicago, IL 312-241-7896
Donofrio, Randy/6459 S Albany, Chicago, IL.....................312-737-0990
Dovey, Dean/1917 N Milwaukee, Chicago, IL 312-292-1737
Doyle, Tim/1550 E 9 Mile Rd, Ferndale, MI 313-543-9440
Drake, Brian Photo/1355 E Canton Ct, Deerfield, IL 312-446-5248
Drea, Robert/1909 S Halstead, Chicago, IL 312-472-6550
Drew, Terry-David/452 N Morgan #2E, Chicago, IL 312-829-1630
Drickey, Pat/1412 Howard St, Omaha, NE 402-344-3786
Drier, David/804 Washington St #3, Evanston, IL.....................312-475-1992
Dublin, Rick/414 Third Ave W, Minneapolis, MN 612-332-8924
DuBroff, Don/2031 W Cortez, Chicago, IL.....................312-252-7390

E

Eagle, Lin/1308 W Wrightwood, Chicago, IL.....................312-525-2170
Ebel, Bob Photography/1376 W Carroll, Chicago, IL 312-222-1123
Ebenoh, Tom/7050 Justamere Hill, Hause Springs, MO 314-671-0439
Eckhard, Kurt/1306 S 18th St, St Louis, MO.....................314-241-1116
Edwards, Bruce/930 S park Ave, Winthrop Harbor, IL 312-746-5168
Edwards, Michael/1250 Riverbed St, Cleveland, OH.....................216-281-4303
Eggebenn, Mark/1217 Center Ave, Dostburg, WI.....................414-564-2344
Eiler, Lynthia & Terry/330-B Barker Rd Rt 2, Athens, OH 614-592-1280
Einhorn, Mitchell/311 N Des Plaines #603, Chicago, IL 312-944-7028
Eisner, Scott Photography/1456 N Dayton, Chicago, IL 312-642-2217
Elinchev, Chris/1324 1/2 N Milwaukee, Chicago, IL
Elledge, Paul/1808 W Grand Ave, Chicago, IL 312-733-8021
Ellingsen/1411 Peterson, Park Ridge, IL 312-823-0192
Elliott, Peter/405 N Wabash Ave, Chicago, IL 312-329-1370
Elmore, Bob and Assoc/315 S Green St, Chicago, IL.....................312-641-2731
Englehard, J Versar/1156 West Grand, Chicago, IL 312-787-2024
Ernst, Elizabeth/1020 Elm St, Winnetka, IL 312-441-8993
ETM Studios/130 S Morgan, Chicago, IL 312-666-0660
Evans, Patricia/1153 E 56th St, Chicago, IL 312-288-2291
Ewert, Steve/17 N Elizabeth, Chicago, IL.....................312-733-5762

F

Faitage, Nick Photography/1914 W North Ave, Chicago, IL.....................312-276-9321
Farber, Gerald/445 W Erie, Chicago, IL 312-337-3324
Farmer, Jerry/620 E Adams, Springfield, IL 217-785-6102
Faverty, Richard/340 W Huron, Chicago, IL.....................312-943-2648
Fay, Mark/7301 Ohms Ln #375, Edina, MN.....................612-835-5447

Feferman, Steve/462 Fern Dr, Wheeling, IL.....................312-459-3695
Fegley, Richard/777 N Michigan #706, Chicago, IL.....................312-337-7770
Feher, Michael/1818 Chouteau, St Louis, MO.....................314-231-9200
Feher, Paul/3138 Flame Dr, Oregon, OH.....................419-698-4254
Feld, D K/675 Morningside Ct, Chicago, IL.....................312-529-2288
Feldman, Stephen L/2705 W Agatite, Chicago, IL.....................312-539-0300
Ferguson, Ken/920 N Franklin St, Chicago, IL.....................312-829-2366
Ferguson, Scott/710 North Tucker, St Louis, MO.....................314-241-3811
Fetters, Grant/8880 Water St, Montague, MI.....................616-894-5056
Ficht, Bill/244 Blue Spruce La, Aurora, IL.....................312-851-2185
Finlay & Finlay Photo/141 E Main St, Ashland, OH.....................419-289-3163
Firak Photography/11 E Hubbard, Chicago, IL.....................312-467-0208
First Light Assoc/78 Rusholme Rd, Toronto M6J 3H6, ON.....................416-532-6108
Fish Studios/17 N Elizabeth, Chicago, IL.....................312-829-0129
Fitzsimmons, J Kevin/2380 Wimbledon Rd, Columbus, OH.....................614-457-2010
Fleck, John/9257 Castlegate Dr, Indianpolis,
IN (P 285)   317-849-7723
Fleming, Larry/1029 N Wichita #3, Wichita, KS.....................316-267-0780
Fletcher, Mike/7467 Kingsbury, St Louis, MO.....................314-721-2279
Flood, Kevin/1329 Macklind St, St Louis, MO.....................314-647-2485
Floyd, Bill/215 W Ohio, Chicago, IL.....................312-321-1770
Fong, John/13 N Huron St, Toledo, OH.....................419-243-7378
Fontayne Studios Ltd/4528 W Oakton, Skokie, IL.....................312-676-9872
Foran, Bob/3930 Varsity Dr, Ann Arbor, MI.....................313-973-0960
Ford, Madison/2616 Industrial Row, Troy, MI.....................313-280-0640
Forrest, Michael/2150 Plainfield Ave NE, Grand Rapids, MI.....................616-361-2556
Forsyte, Alex/1180 Oak Ridge Dr, Glencoe, IL.....................312-835-0307
Forth, Ron/1507 Dana St, Cincinnati, OH.....................513-841-0858
Fortier, Ron/613 Main #301, Rapid City, SD.....................605-341-3739
Foster, Richard/157 W Ontario St, Chicago, IL.....................312-943-9005
Foto-Graphics/2402 N Shadeland Ave, Indianapolis, IN.....................317-353-6259
Fox Commercial Photo/119 W Hubbard, Chicago, IL.....................312-664-0162
Fox, Fred & Sons/2746 W Fullerton, Chicago, IL.....................312-342-3233
Francis, Dan/4515 Delaware St N, Indianapolis, IN.....................317-283-8244
Frantz, Ken/706 N Dearborn, Chicago, IL.....................312-951-1077
Franz, Bill/820 E Wisconsin, Delavan, WI.....................414-728-3733
Freeman, George/1061 W Balmoral, Chicago, IL.....................312-275-1122
French, Graham/387 Richmond St E, Toronto M5A 1P6, ON.....................416-860-0300
Frerck, Robert/4158 N Greenview 2nd Fl, Chicago, IL.....................312-883-1965
Frey, Jeff/405 E Superior St, Duluth, MN.....................218-722-6630
Frick, Ken/66 Northmoor Pl, Columbus, OH.....................614-263-9955
Friedman & Karant Studios/400 North May St, Chicago, IL.....................312-527-1880
Friedman, Susan J/400 North May St, Chicago, IL.....................312-527-1880
Fritz, Tom/2930 W Clybourn, Milwaukee, WI.....................414-344-8300
Futran, Eric/3454 N Bell, Chicago, IL.....................312-525-5020

G

Gabriel Photo/160 E Illinois, Chicago, IL.....................312-743-2220
Gale, Bill/3041 Aldrich Ave S, Minneapolis, MN.....................612-827-5858
Galloway, Scott/2772 Copley Rd, Akron, OH.....................216-666-4477
Gardiner, Howard/9 E Campbell #1, Arlington Hts, IL.....................312-392-0766
Gargano, Pat/3200 Coral Park Dr, Cincinnati, OH.....................513-662-2780
Garmon, Van/312 8th St #720, Des Moines, IA.....................515-247-0001
Gates, Bruce/356 1/2 S Main St, Akron, OH.....................216-375-5282
Gaymont, Gregory/1812 N Hubbard St, Chicago, IL.....................312-421-3146
Gerlach, Monte/705 S Scoville, Oak Park, IL.....................312-848-1193
Getsug, Don/1255 South Michigan Ave, Chicago, IL.....................312-939-1477
Giannetti, Joseph/127 N 7th St #402, Minneapolis, MN.....................612-339-3172
Gillette, Bill/2917 Eisenhower, Ames, IA.....................515-294-4340
Gilo, Dave/121 N Broadway, Milwaukee, WI.....................414-273-1022
Gilroy, John/2407 West Main St, Kalamazoo, MI.....................616-349-6805
Girard, Connie/609 Renolda Woods Ct, Dayton, OH.....................513-294-2095
Girard, Jennifer/1455 W Roscoe, Chicago, IL.....................312-929-3730
Glenn, Eileen/300 W Superior, Chicago, IL.....................312-944-1756
Gluth Foto Team/173 E Grand Ave, Fox LAke, IL.....................312-587-7785
Goddard, Will/PO Box 8081, St Paul, MN.....................612-645-9516
Goff, D R/66 W Wittier St, Columbus, OH.....................614-443-6530
Goldberg, Lenore/210 Park Ave, Glencoe, IL.....................312-835-4226
Goldstein, Steven/1435 Pepperdine Ct, St Louis, MO.....................314-225-4766
Goodwin, Andy/400 E Randolf St #1926, Chicago, IL.....................312-748-5426
Goss, James M/1737 McGee St, Kansas City, MO.....................816-471-8069
Goss, Michael/117 S Morgan, Chicago, IL.....................312-421-3808
Gould, Christopher/224 W Huron, Chicago, IL.....................312-944-5545
Gould, Rick Studios/#6 Benton Place, St Louis, MO.....................314-241-4862
Gould, Ron/1609 N Wolcott, Chicago, IL.....................312-235-0157
Graenicher, Kurt/112 Seventh Ave, Monroe, WI.....................608-328-8400
Graham, Stephen/1120 W Stadium #2, Ann Arbor, MI.....................313-761-6888
Graham-Henry, Diane/613 W Belden, Chicago, IL.....................312-327-4493

PHOTOGRAPHERS

Grajczyk, Chris/126 North 3rd St #405, Minneapolis, MN 612-333-6265
Gray, Walter/1035 W Lake, Chicago, IL 312-733-3800
Grayson, Dan/831 W Cornelia, Chicago, IL 312-477-8659
Greenblatt, William/20 Nantucket Ln, St Louis, MO 314-726-6151
Gremmler, Paul/221 W Walton, Chicago, IL 312-728-7723
Griffin, Maria/PO Box 14307, Chicago, IL 312-324-0732
Griffith, Sam/345 N Canal, Chicago, IL 312-648-1900
Grignon Studios/1300 W Altgeld Dr, Chicago, IL 312-975-7200
Grippentrag, Dennis/70 E Long Lake Rd, Bloomfield Hills, MI 313-645-2222
Groen, John/676 N LaSalle, Chicago, IL 312-266-2331
Grondin, Timothy/815 Main St, Cincinnati, OH 513-421-5588
Gross, Werner/465 S College, Valparaiso, IN 219-462-3453
Grubman, Steve/456 N Morgan, Chicago, IL 312-226-2272
Grunewald, Jeff/161 W Harrison St, Chicago, IL 312-663-5799
GSP/156 N Jefferson, Chicago, IL 312-944-3000
Gubin, Mark/2893 S Delaware Ave, Milwaukee, WI 414-482-0640
Guenther, Stephen/807 Church St, Evanston, IL 312-328-4837
Guerry, Tim/711 S Dearborn #304, Chicago, IL 312-294-0070
Gyssler, Glen/411 S Sangamon #5D, Chicago, IL 312-243-8482

H

Haberman, Mike/529 S 7th St #427, Minneapolis, MN 612-338-4696
Hadley, Alan/140 First Ave NW, Carmel, IN 317-846-2259
Haefner, Jim/1407 N Allen, Troy, MI 313-583-4747
Haines, W C (Bill)/3101 Mercier Ste 484, Kansas City, MO 816-531-0561
Halbe, Harrison/710 N Tucker Blvd #218, St Louis, MO 314-621-0505
Hall, Brian/900 W Jackson Blvd #8W, Chicago, IL 312-226-0853
Haller, Pam/935 W Chestnut, Chicago, IL 312-243-4462
Halsey, Daniel/13204 Freemont Ave S, Minneapolis, MN 612-890-6497
Hamill, Larry/77 Deshler, Columbus, OH 614-444-2798
Hammarlund, Vern/135 Park St, Troy, MI 313-588-5533
Handley, Robert E/1920 E Croxton, Bloomington, IL 309-828-4661
Hanselman, Linda/PO Box 8072, Cincinnati, OH 513-321-8469
Harbron, Patrick/366 Adelaide St E #331, Toronto, ON 416-462-0128
Harding Studio/727 Hudson, Chicago, IL 312-943-4010
Harlan, Bruce/52922 Camellia Dr, South Bend, IN 219-239-7350
Harquail, John/67 Mowat Ave #40, Toronto M6K 3E3, ...416-535-1620
Harrig, Rick/3316 South 66th Ave, Omaha, NE 402-397-5529
Harris, Bart/70 W Hubbard St, Chicago, IL 312-751-2977
Hart, Bob/1457 S Michigan, Chicago, IL 312-939-8888
**Hartjes, Glenn/1100 S Lynndale, Appleton,
WI (P 274)** **414-738-4080**
Hauser, Marc/1810 W Cortland, Chicago, IL 312-486-4381
Hawker, Chris/119 N Peoria, Chicago, IL 312-829-4766
Hedrich, Sandi/10-A W Hubbard, Chicago, IL 312-527-1577
Hedrich-Blessing/11 W Illinois St, Chicago, IL 312-321-1151
Helmick, William/129 Geneva, Elmhurst, IL 312-834-4798
Henebry, Jeanine/1154 Locust Rd, Wilmette, IL 312-251-8747
Henning, Paul/PO Box 92218, Milwaukee, WI 414-765-9441
Hermann, Dell/676 N LaSalle, Chicago, IL 312-664-1461
Hertzberg, Richard/436 N Clark, Chicago, IL 312-836-0464
Hill, John/4234 Howard, Western Springs, IL 312-246-3566
Hill, Roger/4040 W River Dr, Comstock Park, MI 616-784-9620
Hillery, John/PO Box 2916, Detroit, MI 313-345-9511
Hirneisen, Richard/306 S Washington St #218, Royal Oak, MI 313-399-2410
Hirschfeld, Corson/316 W Fourth St, Cincinnati, OH 513-241-0550
Hodes, Charles S/233 E Erie, Chicago, IL 312-951-1186
Hodge, Adele/465 N Wabash Ave #1211, Chicago, IL 312-828-0611
Hodges, Charles/539 W North Ave, Chicago, IL 312-664-8179
Hofer, Charles/2134 North St, Peoria, IL 309-676-6676
Holographics Design Syst/1134 W Washington, Chicago, IL 312-226-1007
Holzemer, Buck/3448 Chicago Ave, Minneapolis, MN 612-824-3874
Honor, David/415 W Superior, Chicago, IL 312-334-2030
Hooke Photography/1147 W Ohio, Chicago, IL 312-829-4568
Hoppe, Ed Photography/3057 N Kimball Ave, Chicago, IL 312-625-9466
Horstman, Mike/700 Forest Edge Dr, Vernon Hills, IL 312-634-4505
Hoskins, Sarah/1206 Isabella, Wilmette, IL 312-256-5724
Houghton, Michael/Studiohio/55 E Spring St, Columbus, OH 614-224-4885
Howrani, Armeen/2820 E Grand Blvd, Detroit, MI 313-875-3123
Hrdlicka, Mitch/4201 Levinworth, Omaha, NE 402-346-3522
Hsi, Kai/160 E Illinois, Chicago, IL 312-642-9853
Hurling, Robert/325 W Huron, Chicago, IL 312-944-2022
Hutson, David/8120 Juniper, Prairie Village, KS 913-383-1123
Hyman, Randy/7709 Carnell Ave, St Louis, MO 314-721-7489

I

Iacono, Michael/412 Central Ave, Cleveland, OH 513-621-9108

Iann-Hutchins/2044 Euclid Ave, Cleveland, OH 216-579-1570
Image Productions/115 W Church, Libertyville, IL 312-680-7100
**Image Studios/1100 S Lynndale, Appleton,
WI (P 272-277)** **414-738-4080**
Imagematrix/2 Garfield Pl, Cincinnati, OH 513-381-1380
Imagination Unlimited/1280 East Miner, Des Plaines, IL 312-803-0199
Imbrogno, James/411 N LaSalle St, Chicago, IL 312-644-7333
Ingram, Russell/1000 W Monroe St 2nd Fl, Chicago, IL 312-829-4652
Ingve, Jan & Assoc/128 Wedgewood Dr, Barrington, IL 312-381-3456
International Photo Corp/1035 Wesley, Evanston, IL 312-475-6400
Irving, Gary/PO Box 38, Wheaton, IL 312-653-0641
Isenberger, Brent/416 Armour Rd, N Kansas City, MO 816-471-0071
Itahara, Tets/676 N LaSalle, Chicago, IL 312-649-0606
Iwata, John/336 W 15th Ave, Oshkosh, WI 414-424-0317
Izquierdo, Abe/213 W Institute #208, Chicago, IL 312-787-9784
Izui, Richard/315 W Walton, Chicago, IL 312-266-8029

J

Jackson, David/1021 Hall St, Grand Rapids, MI 616-243-3325
Jackson, Jack/117-A W Walker St 4th Fl, Milwaukee, WI 414-672-7444
Jacobs, Todd/3336 N Sheffield, Chicago, IL 312-472-4401
Jacobson, Scott/3435 N County Rd #18, Plymouth, MN 612-546-9191
Jacquin Enterprise/1219 Holly Hills, St Louis, MO 314-832-4221
James, E Michael/9135 S LaSalle, Chicago, IL 312-468-9746
James, Phillip MacMillan/2300 Hazelwood Ave, St Paul, MN 612-777-2303
Jedd, Joseph/1624 S Courtland, Park Ridge, IL 312-696-1745
Jelen, Tom/2604 Windsor, Arlington Heights, IL 312-506-9479
Jenkins, David/1416 S Michigan Ave, Chicago, IL 312-922-2299
Jensen, Michael/1101 Stinson Blvd NE, Minneapolis, MN 612-379-1944
Jilling, Helmut/3420-A Cavalier Trail, Cuyahoga Falls, OH 216-928-1330
Jochim, Gary/1324 1/2 N Milwaukee, Chicago, IL 312-252-5250
Joel, David/1342 West Hood Ave, Chicago, IL 312-262-0794
Johnson, Dave/679 E Mandoline, Madison Hts, MI 313-589-0066
Johnson, Donald/2807 Brindle, Northbrook, IL 312-480-9336
Johnson, Jim/802 W Evergreen, Chicago, IL 312-943-8864
Jolly, Keith/32049 Milton Ave, Madison Hts, MI 313-588-6544
Jones, Arvell/8232 W McNichols, Detroit, MI 313-533-6313
Jones, Brent/9121 S Merrill Ave, Chicago, IL 312-933-1174
Jones, Dawson/44 E Franklin St, Dayton, OH 513-435-1121
Jones, Dick/325 W Huron St, Chicago, IL 312-642-0242
Jones, Duane/5605 Chicago Ave S, Minneapolis, MN 612-823-8173
Jones, Harrison/445 W Erie #209, Chicago, IL 312-337-4997
Jones, Mark/718 Washington Ave N, Minneapolis, MN 612-338-5712
Jons Studio/35 E Wacker, Chicago, IL 312-236-0243
Jordan, Jack/840 John St, Evansville, IN 812-423-7676
Jordano, Dave/1335 N Wells, Chicago, IL 312-280-8212
Joseph, Mark/1007 N La Salle, Chicago, IL 312-951-5333
Joyce, Todd/7815 Lake St, Cincinnati, OH 513-793-0815
Julian, Percy/2613 Waunona Way, Madison, WI 608-225-6400
Justice Patterson Studio/7609 Production Dr, Cincinnati, OH 513-761-4023

K

Kalyniuk, Jerry/4243 N Winchester, Chicago, IL 312-666-5588
Kansas City Photographic/1830 Main St, Kansas City, MO 816-221-2710
Kapal Photo/17 Ridge Rd #316, Munster, IN 219-322-6305
Kaplan, Brian/1643 N Milwaukee Ave, Chicago, IL 312-489-0676
Kaplan, Dick/708 Waukegan, Deerfield, IL 312-945-3425
Kaplan, Matthew/5452 N Glenwood, Chicago, IL 312-769-5903
Karant, Barbara/400 N May St, Chicago, IL 312-527-1880
Kaspar, Tom/1028 Curtiss, Downers Grove, IL 312-968-2442
Katz, Sue/2828 N Burling #406, Chicago, IL 312-549-5379
Kauck, Jeff/205 W 4th St #460, Cincinnati, OH 513-241-5435
Kauffman, Kim/444 Lentz Court, Lansing, MI 517-371-3036
Kavula, Ken/19 E Pearson, Chicago, IL 312-280-9060
Kazu Studio/900 West Jackson Blvd #7W, Chicago, IL 312-944-5680
Kean, Christopher/624 West Adams St, Chicago, IL 312-559-0880
Keeling, Robert/900 West Jackson Blvd #7W, Chicago, IL 312-944-5680
Keisman & Keisman/518 W 37th St, Chicago, IL 312-268-7955
Kelly, Tony/828 Colfax, Evanston, IL 312-864-0488
**Keltsch, Steve/9257 Castlegate Dr, Indianapolis,
IN (P 284)** **317-849-7723**
Ketchum, Art/812 W 33rd St #B, Chicago, IL 312-544-1222
Kimbal, Mark/23860 Miles Rd, Cleveland, OH 216-587-3555
Kinast, Susan/1035 West Lake St, Chicago, IL 312-738-0068
King, Jay Studios/1629 North Milwaukee, Chicago, IL 312-327-0011
Kingsbury, Andrew/700 N Washington #306, Minneapolis, MN 612-340-1919
Kitahara, Joe/304 W 10th St, Kansas City, MO 816-474-6699
Kleber, Gordon/525 Dearborn, Chicago, IL 312-276-4419

Klein Photography/952 W Lake, Chicago, IL 312-226-1878
Klein, Daniel/1301 E 12th St, Kansas City, MO 816-474-6491
Kloc, Howard/520 W Eleven Mile Rd, Royal Oak, MI 313-541-1704
Klutho, Dave/4617 Brookroyal Ct, St Louis, MO 314-487-3626
Knepp Studio/1742 McKinley St, Mishawaka, IN 219-259-1913
Knize, Karl/1920 N Seminary, Chicago, IL 312-243-5503
Kodama, Kiyoshi/424 N Benton, St Charles, MO 314-946-9247
Kogan, David/1242 W Washington Blvd, Chicago, IL 312-243-1929
Kolesar, Jerry /679 E Mandoline, Madison Hts, MI 313-589-0066
Kolze, Larry/22 W Erie, Chicago, IL 312-359-0835
Kompa, Jeff/25303 Lorain Rd, N Olmstead, OH 216-777-1611
Kondas, Thom Assoc/1529 N Alabama St, Indianapolis, IN 317-637-1414
Kondor, Linda/2141 West Lemoyne, Chicago, IL 312-642-7365
Korab, Balthazar/PO Box 895, Troy, MI 313-641-8881
Kransberger, Jim/2247 Boston SE, Grand Rapids, MI 616-245-0390
Krantz, Jim/5017 S 24th St, Omaha, NE 402-734-4848
Krantzen Studios/100 S Ashland, Chicago, IL 312-942-1900
Krejci, Donald/1825 E 18th St, Cleveland, OH 216-831-4730
Krinsky, Jon/9420 Saddlebrook Ln #3D, Dayton, OH 513-434-3223
Krueger, Dick/2147 W Augusta Blvd, Chicago, IL 312-384-0008
Kufrin, George/535 N Michigan #1407, Chicago, IL 312-787-2854
Kulp, Curtis/1255 S Michigan, Chicago, IL 312-786-1943
Kusel, Bob/2156 W Arthur, Chicago, IL 312-465-8283

L

Lacey, Ted/4733 S Woodlawn, Chicago, IL 312-624-2419
Lachman, Gary/1927 Grant St, Evanston, IL 312-864-0861
Lacroix, Pat/25 Brant St, Toronto M5V 2L9, ON 416-864-1858
Lallo, Ed/7329 Terrace, Kansas City, MO 816-523-6222
Lambert, Bill/2220 Hassell #308, Hoffeman Estates, IL 312-519-0189
Landau, Allan/1147 West Ohio, Chicago, IL 312-942-1382
Landis, Mike/1030 N Crooks Rd #O, Clawson, MI 313-435-5420
Lane, Jack Studio/5 W Grand Ave, Chicago, IL 312-337-2326
Lanza, Scott/3200 S 3rd St, Milwaukee, WI 414-482-4114
LaRoche, Andre/32588 Dequindre, Warren, MI 313-978-7373
Larsen, Kim/Soren Studio/114 W Kinzie, Chicago, IL 312-527-0344
LaTona, Tony/1317 E 5th, Kansas City, MO 816-474-3119
Lause, Lew/127 Prospect St, Marion, OH 614-383-1155
Lauth, Lyal/833 W Chicago Ave 6th Fl, Chicago, IL 312-829-9800
LaVoies Photo/01423 US 127, Bryan, OH 419-636-4602
Leavenworth Photo Inc/929 West St, Lansing, MI 517-482-4658
Leavitt, Debbie/2029 W Armitage, Chicago, IL 312-235-6777
Leavitt, Fred/916 Carmen, Chicago, IL 312-784-2344
Lecat, Paul/820 N Franklin, Chicago, IL 312-664-7122
Lee, Robert Photo/1512 Northlin Dr, St Louis, MO 314-965-5832
Lee, Terry/4420 N Paulina, Chicago, IL 312-561-1153
LeGrand, Peter/413 Sandburg, Park Forest, IL 312-747-4923
Lehn, John & Assoc Adv Photo/2601 E Franklin Ave, Minneapolis, MN (P 278) 612-338-0257
Leick, Jim/1709 Washington Ave, St Louis, MO 314-241-2354
Leinwohl, Stef/439 W Oakdale #3, Chicago, IL 312-975-0457
Leonard, Steve/825 W Gunnison, Chicago, IL 312-275-8833
Leslie, William F/53 Tealwood Dr, Creve Coeur, MO 314-993-8349
Levey, Don/15 W Delaware Pl, Chicago, IL 312-329-9040
Levin, Jonathan/1035 W Lake St, Chicago, IL 312-226-3898
Lewandowski, Leon/210 N Racine, Chicago, IL 312-467-9577
Lightfoot, Robert/311 Good Ave, Des Plaines, IL 312-297-5447
Linc Studio/1163 Tower, Schaumberg, IL 312-882-1311
Lindblade, George R/PO Box 1342, Sioux City, IA 712-255-4346
Lindwall, Martin/1269 Briarwood Ln, Libertyville, IL 312-680-1578
Lipschis, Helmut Photography/2053 N Sheffield, Chicago, IL 312-935-7886
Liss, Leroy/6243 N Ridgeway Ave, Chicago, IL 312-539-4540
Little, Scott/4331 Woodland, Des Moines, IA 515-286-1150
Lohbeck, Stephen/710 North Tucker, St Louis, MO 314-231-6038
Lord, David/1449 N Pennsylvania, Indianapolis, IN 317-634-1244
Love, Ken/6911 N Mcalpin Ave, Chicago, IL 312-775-5779
Lowenthal, Jeff/PO Box 1345, Fairfield, IA 515-472-5124
Lowry, Miles/222 S Morgan #3B, Chicago, IL 312-666-0882
Loynd, Mel/208 Queen St S, Streetsville L5M1L5, ON 416-821-0477
Lubeck, Larry/405 N Wabash Ave, Chicago, IL 312-726-5580
Lucas, John V/4100 W 40th St, Chicago, IL 312-927-4500
Lucas, Joseph/20 N Wacker Dr #1425, Chicago, IL 312-782-6905
Ludwigs, David/3600 Troost St, Kansas City, MO 816-531-1363
Luke, John/1100 S Lynndale, Appleton, WI (P 275) 414-738-4080
Lutynski, Dennis/5517 Odana Rd, Madison, WI 608-274-9838
Lyles, David/401 W Superior 5th Fl, Chicago, IL 312-642-1223

M

Maas, Curt/5860 Merle Hay Rd/Box 127, Johnston, IA 515-270-3732
MacDonald, Al/32 Martin Lane, Elk Grove, IL 312-437-8850
MacDonald, Neil/1515 W Cornelia, Chicago, IL 312-525-5401
Mack, Richard/2119 Lincoln, Evanston, IL 312-869-7794
Mactavish, Arndt/4620 N Winchester, Chicago, IL 312-334-2841
Magin, Betty/412 Spring Valley Ct, Chesterfield, MO 314-878-5388
Maguire, Jim/144 Lownsdale, Akron, OH 216-630-9050
Maki & Smith Photo/6156 Olson Mem Hwy, Golden Valley, MN 612-541-4722
Malinowski, Stan/1150 N State #312, Chicago, IL 312-951-6715
Mally Assoc/20 W Hubbard #3E, Chicago, IL 312-644-4367
Manarchy, Dennis/229 W Illinois, Chicago, IL 312-828-9117
Mandel, Avis/40 E Cedar, Chicago, IL 312-642-4776
Mankus, Gary/156 W Huron #4D, Chicago, IL 312-787-5438
Mann, Milton & Joan/PO Box 413, Evanston, IL 312-777-5656
Mar, Jan/343 Harrison St, Oak Park, IL 312-524-1898
Marden Photo/4515 N Delaware, Indianapolis, IN 317-251-8373
Marianne Studio/117 S Jefferson, Mt Pleasant, IA 319-986-6573
Marienthal, Michael/1832 S Halsted, Chicago, IL 312-226-5505
Mark, Roger/14849 W 95th St, Lenexa, KS 913-362-7800
Marovitz, Bob/3450 N Lake Shore Dr, Chicago, IL 312-975-1265
Marshall, Don Photography/415 W Huron, Chicago, IL 312-944-0720
Marshall, Paul/623 W Randolph 1st Fl, Chicago, IL 312-559-1270
Marshall, Simeon/1043 W Randolph, Chicago, IL 312-243-9500
Martin, Barbara E/46 Washington Terrace, St Louis, MO 314-361-0838
Marvy, Jim/41 Twelfth Ave N, Minneapolis, MN 612-935-0307
Masheris, R Assoc Inc/1338 Hazel Ave, Deerfield, IL 312-945-2055
Mathews, Bruce/16520 Ellison Way, Independence, MO 816-373-2920
Matlow, Linda/300 N State St #3926, Chicago, IL 312-321-9071
Matusik, Jim/3714 N Racine, Chicago, IL 312-327-5615
Mauney, Michael/1405 Judson Ave, Evanston, IL 312-869-7720
May, Ron/PO Box 8359, Ft Wayne, IN 219-483-7872
May, Sandy/18 N 4th St #506, Minneapolis, MN 612-332-0272
McAlpine, Scott/110 S Elm St, N Manchester, IN 219-982-8822
McCabe, Mark/1301 E 12th St, Kansas City, MO 816-474-6491
McCaffery, Randy/3309 Industrial Pkwy, Jeffersonville, NY 812-284-3456
McCall, Paul/1844 Rutherford, Chicago, IL 312-622-4880
McCann, Larry/666 W Hubbard, Chicago, IL 312-942-1924
McCann, Michael/15416 Village Woods Dr, Eden Prairie, MN 612-949-2407
McCay, Larry Inc/3926 N Fir Rd #12, Mishawaka, IN 219-259-1414
McClelan, Thompson/206 S First St, Champaign, IL 217-356-2767
McDunn, James/PO Box 8053, Rolling Meadows, IL 312-934-4288
McGee, Alan/3050 Edgewood St, Portage, IN 219-762-2805
McGleam, Patrick/, Chicago, IL 312-691-2847
McHale Studios Inc/2827 Gilbert Ave, Cincinnati, OH 513-961-1454
McKay, Doug/512 S Hamley, St Louis, MO (P 279) 314-863-7167
McKellar, William/1200 W Webster, Chicago, IL 312-935-5511
McKinley, William/113 N May, Chicago, IL 312-666-5400
McMahon, David/800 Washington Ave N, Minneapolis, MN 612-339-9709
McMahon, Franklin/1319 Chestnut, Wilmette, IL 312-256-5528
McNichol, Greg/1638 W Greenleaf Ave, Chicago, IL 312-973-1032
Mead, Robert/711 Hillgrove Ave, La Grange, IL 312-354-8300
Meier, Lori/9100 Guthrie, St Louis, MO 314-428-0120
Melkus, Larry/679-E Mandoline, Madison Hts, MI 313-589-0066
Meoli, Rick/710 N Tucker #306, St Louis, MO 314-231-6038
Meredith, Paul/737 W Randolph, Chicago, IL 312-559-9209
Merrithew, Jim/PO Box 1510, Almonte K0A 1A0, ON 613-729-3862
Meyer, Aaron/1302 W Randolph, Chicago, IL 312-243-1458
Meyer, Fred/415 N Dearborn, Chicago, IL 312-527-4873
Meyer, Gordon/216 W Ohio, Chicago, IL 312-642-9303
Meyer, Robert/208 W Kinzie St, Chicago, IL 312-467-1430
Michael, William/225 W Hubbard, Chicago, IL 312-644-6137
Micus Photo/PO Box 38, Lombard, IL 312-941-8945
Mignard Associates/1950-R S. Glenstone, Springfield, MO 417-881-7422
Mihalevich, Mike/9235 Somerset Dr, Overland Park, KS 913-642-6466
Miller Photo/7237 W Devon, Chicago, IL 312-631-1255
Miller, Buck/PO Box 33, Milwaukee, WI 414-273-0985
Miller, Daniel D/1551 North Orleans, Chicago, IL 312-944-7192
Miller, Frank/6016 Blue Circle Dr, Minnetonka, MN 612-935-8888
Miller, Jon/11 W Illinois, Chicago, IL 312-738-1816
Miller, Pat/1101 Stinson Blvd NE, Minneapolis, MN 612-378-9043
Miller, Spider/833 North Orleans, Chicago, IL 312-944-2880
Mills, Gary/PO Box 260, Granger, IN 219-232-4221
Milne, Brian/78 Rusholme Rd, Toronto M6J 3H6, ON 416-532-6108
Mitchell, John Sr/2617 Greenleaf, Elk Grove, IL 312-956-8230
Mitchell, Rick/652 W Grand, Chicago, IL 312-829-1700

Mitzit, Bruce/331 S Peoria/Box 6638, Chicago, IL 312-508-1937
Mooney, Kevin/511 N Noble, Chicago, IL 312-738-1816
Moore, Bob c/o Mofoto Grphcs/1615 S 9th St, St Louis, MO 314-231-1430
Moore, Dan/1029 N Wichita #9, Wichita, KS 316-264-4168
Morrill, Dan/1811 N Sedgewick, Chicago, IL 312-787-5095
Morton & White/7440 Pingue Dr, Worthington, OH.............614-885-8687
Mortone Inc/209 S Main St 5th Fl, Akron, OH.............216-434-8200
Moshman Photo/401 W Superior, Chicago, IL.............312-869-6770
Moss, Jean/1255 S Michigan Ave, Chicago, IL.............312-786-9110
Mottel, Ray/760 Burr Oak Dr, Westmont, IL.............312-323-3616
Moustakas, Dan/1255 Rankin, Troy, MI (P 280) **313-589-0100**
Moy, Clinton Photography/4815 W Winnemar, Chicago, IL.............312-666-5577
Moy, Willie/364 W Erie, Chicago, IL.............312-943-1863
Mueller, Linda/1900 Delmar, St Louis, MO 314-621-2400
Muresan, Jon/4713 Horger St, Dearborne, MI 313-581-5445
Murphey, Gregory/1134 W Wrightwood, Chicago, IL.............312-327-4856
Musich, Jack/325 W Huron, Chicago, IL.............312-644-5000
Mutrux, John L/5217 England, Shawnee Missn, KS.............913-722-4343

N

Nagler, Monte/38881 Lancaster Dr, Farmington Hills, MI.............313-661-0826
Najdychor, Elvira/441 E Erie #2213, Chicago, IL.............312-943-7670
Nathanson, Neal/7531 Cromwell, St Louis, MO.............314-727-7244
Nawrocki, William S/332 S Michigan Ave, Chicago, IL.............312-427-8625
Neal, Les/319 N Albany, Chicago, IL.............312-508-5299
Nelson, Tom/800 Washington Ave N #301, Minneapolis, MN.............612-339-3579
Nelson-Curry, Loring/420 N Clark, Chicago, IL.............312-644-2371
Neumann, Robert/101 S Mason St, Saginaw, MI.............616-784-7111
New View Photo/5275 Michigan Ave, Rosemont, IL.............312-671-0300
Nexus Productions/10-A Ashdale Ave, Toronto, ON.............416-463-5078
Niedorf, Steve/700 Washington Ave N, Minneapolis, MN.............612-332-7124
Nielsen, Ron/1313 W Randolph #326, Chicago, IL.............312-226-2661
Nienhuis, John/3623 N 62nd St, Milwaukee, WI.............414-442-9199
Njaa, Reuben/5929 Portland Ave S, Minneapolis, MN.............612-371-0731
Nobart Inc/1133 S Wabash Ave, Chicago, IL.............312-427-9800
Nolan, Tim/2548 Shirley, St Louis, MO.............314-388-4125
Norman, Rick/1353 E Grand St, Springfield, MO.............417-865-0772
Norris, James/2301 N Lowell, Chicago, IL.............312-342-1050
Northlight Studio/1539 E 22nd St, Cleveland, OH.............216-621-3111
Norton, Ron/2609 Vine St, Cincinnati, OH.............513-281-5002
Novak, Ken/2483 N Bartlett Ave, Milwaukee, WI.............414-962-6953
Novak, Sam/230 W Huron, Chicago, IL.............312-664-6733
Nozicka, Steve/405 N Wabash #3203, Chicago, IL.............312-329-1370
Nugent Wenckus Inc/110 Northwest Hwy, Des Plaines, IL.............312-694-4151

O

O'Barski, Don/17239 Parkside Ave, S Holland, IL.............312-596-0606
O'Keefe, JoAnne/2963 Pacific, Omaha, NE.............402-341-4128
Oakes, Kenneth Ltd/902 Yale Ln, Highland Park, IL.............312-432-4809
Oberle, Frank/6633 Delmar, St Louis, MO.............314-721-5838
Oberreich, S/1930 N Alabama St, Indianapolis, IN.............317-923-1980
Officer, Hollis/905 E 5th St, Kansas City, MO.............816-474-5501
Ogden, Sam/, Boston, MA.............617-547-5422
Olausen, Judy/213 1/2 N Washington Ave, Minneapolis, MN.............612-332-5009
Ollis, Karen/1231 Superior Ave E, Cleveland, OH.............216-781-8646
Olsson, Russ/215 W Illinois, Chicago, IL.............312-329-9358
Ontiveros, Don/1378 N Wolcott 2nd Fl, Chicago, IL.............312-342-0900
Oscar & Assoc/63 E Adams, Chicago, IL.............312-922-0056
Oxendorf, Eric/1442 N Franklin Pl Box 92337, Milwaukee, WI.............414-273-0654
Oyd, Tim/12470 Pineneedle Dr, Indianapolis, IN.............317-823-6310

P

Pacific Studio/632 Krenz Ave, Cary, IL.............312-639-5654
Palmisano, Vito/1147 W Ohio St, Chicago, IL.............312-565-0524
Panama, David/1100 N Dearborn, Chicago, IL.............312-642-7095
Panich, Wil/20 W Hubbard, Chicago, IL.............312-828-0742
Parker, Norman/710 N 2nd St #300N, St Louis, MO.............314-621-8100
Parks, Jim/210 W Chicago, Chicago, IL.............312-321-1193
Passman, Roger/2202 N Clark St, Chicago, IL.............312-472-4085
Paszkowski, Rick/7529 N Claremont #1, Chicago, IL.............312-761-3018
Paternite, David/1245 S Clevelnd-Massilon Rd #3, Akron, OH.............216-666-7720
Paulson, Bill/5358 Golla Rd, Stevens Point, WI.............715-341-6100
Payne-Garrett Photo/5301 Michigan Ave, Chicago, IL.............312-671-0300
Pazovski, Kazik/2340 Laredo Ave, Cincinnati, OH.............513-281-0030
Pech, Ted/10818 Midwest Industrial Blvd, St Louis, MO.............800-456-7377
Perkins, Ray/222 S Morgan St, Chicago, IL.............312-421-3438
Perman, Craig/1645 Hennepin #311, Minneapolis, MN.............612-338-7727

Perno, Jack/1956 W Grand, Chicago, IL.............312-829-5292
Perraud, Gene/Box 2025, Northbrook, IL.............312-564-5278
**Perry, Eric W/617 East Lincoln, Royal Oak,
MI (P 281)** **313-548-1152**
Perspective Inc/2322 Pennsylvania St, Fort Wayne, IN.............219-424-8136
Peterson, Jan/325 16th St, Bettendorf, IA.............319-355-5032
Peterson, Richard Photo/529 S 7th St #315, Minneapolis, MN.............612-341-0480
Petroff, Tom/19 W Hubbard, Chicago, IL.............312-836-0411
Petrovich, Steve/679-E Mandoline, Madison Hts, MI.............313-589-0066
Phelps Photo/1057 W Dakin, Chicago, IL.............312-248-2536
Phillips, David R/1230 W Washington Blvd, Chicago, IL.............312-733-3277
Philpott, Keith/13736 W 82nd St, Lenexa, KS.............913-492-0715
Photo by Robert K/17 Ridge Rd, Munster, IN.............219-922-8756
Photo Concepts/23042 Commerce Dr, Farmington Hills, MI.............313-477-4301
Photo Enterprises/2134 North St, Peoria, IL.............309-676-6676
Photo Group/1945 Techny Rd, Northbrook, IL.............312-564-9220
Photo Ideas Inc/804 W Washington Blvd, Chicago, IL.............312-666-3100
Photo Images/1945 Techny #9, Northbrook, IL.............312-272-3500
Photo Reserve/2924 N Racine St, Chicago, IL.............312-871-7371
Photocraft/220 N Walnut St, Muncie, IN.............317-288-1454
Photographic Arts/624 W Adams, Chicago, IL.............312-876-0818
Photographic Illustration/404 Enterprise Dr, Westerville, OH.............614-888-8682
Pier Photo/16120 Robbin Rd, Grand Haven, MI.............616-842-8893
Pierce, Rod/917 N Fifth St, Minneapolis, MN.............612-332-2670
Pieroni, Frank/2432 Oak Industrial Dr NE, Grand Rapids, MI.............616-459-8325
Pintozzi, Peter/42 E Chicago, Chicago, IL.............312-266-7775
Pioneer Hi-Bred Intrn'ti/5860 Merle Hay Rd, Johnston, IA.............515-270-3732
Pitt, Tom/1201 W Webster, Chicago, IL.............312-281-5662
Pohlman Studios Inc/535 N 27th St, Milwaukee, WI.............414-342-6363
Pokempner, Marc/1453 W Addison, Chicago, IL.............312-525-4567
Polaski, James/9 W Hubbard, Chicago, IL.............312-944-6577
Poli, Frank/158 W Huron, Chicago, IL.............312-944-3924
Polin, Jack Photography/7306 Crawford, Lincolnwood, IL.............312-676-4312
Pomerantz, Ron/325 W Huron #406, Chicago, IL.............312-787-6407
Poon On Wong, Peter/516 First Ave #305, Minneapolis, MN.............612-340-0798
Pope, Kerig/414 N Orleans, Chicago, IL.............312-222-8999
**Poplis, Paul/3599 Refugee Rd Bldg B,
Columbus, OH (P 282)** **614-231-2942**
Portney, Michael/4975 Gateshead, Detroit, MI.............313-881-0378
Portnoy, Lewis/5 Carole Lane, St Louis, MO.............314-567-5700
Powell, Jim/326 W Kalamazoo, Kalamazoo, MI.............616-381-2302
Price, Paul/8138 W Nine Mile Rd, Oak Park, MI.............313-546-1759
Proctor & Proctor Photo/1146 W Kinzie, Chicago, IL.............312-798-6849
**Przekop, Harry J Jr/950 W Lake St, Chicago,
IL (P 283)** **312-829-8201**
Puffer, David/213 W Institute, Chicago, IL.............312-266-7540
Puza, Greg/PO Box 1986, Milwaukee, WI.............414-444-9882
Pyrzynski, Larry/2241 S Michigan, Chicago, IL.............312-472-6550

QR

Quinn, James/518 S Euclid, Oak Park, IL.............312-383-0654
Quist, Bruce/1370 N Milwaukee, Chicago, IL.............312-252-3921
Rack, Ron/215 E Ninth St, Cincinnati, OH.............513-421-6267
Radencich, Michael/3016 Cherry, Kansas City, MO.............816-756-1992
Radlund & Associates/4704 Pflaum Rd, Madison, WI.............608-222-8177
Randall, Bob/2340 W Huron, Chicago, IL.............312-235-4613
Randolph, Jon/1434 W Addison, Chicago, IL.............312-248-9406
Rawls, Ray/, MN.............612-895-9717
Reames-Hanusin /3306 Commercial Ave, Northbrook, IL.............312-564-2706
Reed, Dick/1330 Coolidge, Troy, MI.............313-280-0090
Reeve, Catherine/822 Madison St, Evanston, IL.............312-327-3734
Reffner, Wayne/4178 Dayton-Xenia Rd, Dayton, OH.............513-429-2760
Reid, Ken/800 W Huron #3S, Chicago, IL.............312-733-2121
Reiss, Ray/2144 N Leavitt, Chicago, IL.............312-384-3245
Remington, George/1455 W 29th St, Cleveland, OH.............216-241-1440
Renerts, Peter Studio/633 Huron Rd, Cleveland, OH.............216-781-2440
Renken, Roger/PO Box 11010, St Louis, MO.............314-394-5055
Reuben, Martin/1231 Superior Ave, Cleveland, OH.............216-781-8644
Ricco, Ron/117 W Walker St 4th Fl, Milwaukee, WI.............414-645-6450
Rice, Ted/2599 N 4th St, Columbus, OH.............614-263-8656
Rich, Larry/29731 Everett, Southfield, MI.............313-557-7676
Richland, Kathy/839 W Wrightwood, Chicago, IL.............312-935-9634
Ritter, Gene/2440 W 14th St, Cleveland, OH.............216-521-5494
River, Milissa/2500 Lakeview, Chicago, IL.............312-929-5031
Robert, Francois/740 N Wells, Chicago, IL.............312-787-0777
Robinson, David/1147 W Ohio, Chicago, IL.............312-942-1650
Roessler, Ryan/401 W Superior, Chicago, IL.............312-951-8702
Rogowski, Tom/214 E 8th St, Cincinnati, OH.............513-621-3826

Rohman, Jim/2254 Marengo, Toledo, OH 419-865-0234
Rollo, Jim/1830 Main St, Kansas City, MO 816-221-2710
Rosmis, Bruce/118 W Ohio, Chicago, IL..............................312-787-9046
Ross, Allan/430 W Erie St #3W, Chicago, IL.......................312-642-2288
Rossi Studio/4555 Emery Ind Pkwy #105, Cleveland, OH 216-831-0688
Rostron, Philip/489 Wellington St W, Toronto M5V 1E9, ON 416-596-6587
Rothrock, Douglas/368 West Huron, Chicago, IL..................312-951-9045
Rottinger, Ed/5409 N Avers, Chicago, IL.............................312-583-2917
Rovtar, Ron/49 Walhalla Rd, Columbus, OH........................614-261-6083
Rowley, Joe/368 W Huron, Chicago, IL...............................312-266-7620
Rubin, Laurie/1111 W Armitage, Chicago, IL.......................312-348-6644
Rush, Michael/415 Delaware, Kansas City, MO.....................816-471-1200
Russetti, Andy/1260 Carnegie St, Cleveland, OH.................216-687-1788
Rustin, Barry/934 Glenwood Rd, Glenview, IL......................312-724-7600
Rutt, Don/324 Munson St, Traverse City, MI.........................616-946-2727
Rutten, Bonnie/414 Sherburne Ave, St Paul, MN..................612-224-5777
Ryan, Gary/23245 Woodward, Ferndale, MI.........................313-861-8199

S

S T Studio/362 W Erie, Chicago, IL......................................312-943-2565
Sacco Photography Ltd/2035 W Grand Ave, Chicago, IL.........312-243-5757
Sacks, Andrew/20727 Scio Church Rd, Chelsea, MI.............313-475-2310
Sacks, Ed/Box 7237, Chicago, IL..312-871-4700
Sadin, Abby/820 N Franklin, Chicago, IL.............................312-944-1434
Saks Photography Inc /9257 Castlegate Dr,
Indianapolis, IN (P 284,285) **317-849-7723**
Sala, Don/950 W Willow, Chicago, IL...................................312-751-2858
Salisbury, Mark/161 W Harrison 12th Fl, Chicago, IL............312-922-7599
Salter, Tom/685 Pallister, Detroit, MI...................................313-874-1155
Saltzman, Ben/700 N Washington, Minneapolis, MN.............612-332-5112
Sanders, Kathy/411 South Sangamon, Chicago, IL...............312-829-3100
Sanderson, Glenn/1002 Pine St, Green Bay, WI...................414-336-6500
Sandoz Studios/118 W Kinzie, Chicago, IL..........................312-527-1800
Santow, Loren/3057 N racine, Chicago, IL...........................312-929-1993
Sapecki, Roman/56 E Oakland Ave, Columbus, OH...............614-262-7497
Sarnacki, Michael/18101 Oakwood Blvd, Dearborn, MI.........313-548-1149
Sauer, Neil W/2844 Arsenal, St Louis, MO...........................314-664-4646
Schabes, Charles/1220 W Grace St, Chicago, IL...................312-787-2629
Schanuel, Anthony/10901 Oasis Dr, St Louis, MO................314-849-3495
Schaugnessy, Abe/32 Martin Ln, Elk Grove Village, IL...........312-437-8850
Schewe, Jeff/624 West Willow, Chicago, IL..........................312-951-6334
Schmidt, Jerry/Rt 4/Box 882W, Warrensburg, MO.................816-429-2305
Schnaible, Gary/651 Morse Ave #4, Schaumberg, IL.............312-351-4464
Schnepf, James/4518 W Dean Rd, Milwaukee, WI.................414-354-1331
Schoenbach, Glenn/329 Enterprise Ct, Bloomfield Hills, MI......313-335-5100
Scholtes, Marc/726 Central Ave NE, Minneapolis, MN...........612-378-1888
Schrempp, Erich/723 W Randolph, Chicago, IL.....................312-454-3237
Schridde, Charles Photo Inc/600 Ajax Dr,
Madison Hts, MI (P 287) **313-589-0111**
Schube-Soucek/1735 Carmen Dr, Elk Grove Village, IL.........312-439-0640
Schuemann, Bill/1591 S Belvoir Blvd, South Euclid, OH.........216-382-4409
Schuessler, Dave/40 E Delaware, Chicago, IL......................312-787-6868
Schuette, Bob/207 E Buffalo #645, Milwaukee, WI................414-347-1113
Schulman, Bruce/1102 W Columbia, Chicago, IL..................312-917-6420
Schulman, Lee/669 College Ave/Box 09506, Columbus, OH......614-235-5307
Schultz Assoc, Carl/740 W Washington, Chicago, IL.............312-454-0303
Schultz, Tim/215 W Huron, Chicago, IL...............................312-943-3318
Schwartz, Linda/2033 N Orleans, Chicago, IL......................312-327-7755
Scott, Denis/216 W Ohio St, Chicago, IL.............................312-467-5663
Secreto, Jim/2626 Industrial Row, Troy, MI..........................313-280-0640
Seed, Brian/213 W Institute Pl #503, Chicago, IL..................312-787-7880
Segal, Doug Panorama/230 N Michigan Ave, Chicago, IL........312-236-8545
Segal, Mark/230 N Michigan Ave, Chicago, IL......................312-236-8545
Segielski, Tony/1886 Thunderbird, Troy, MI.........................313-362-3111
Semeniuk, Robert/78 Rusholme Rd, Toronto M6J 3H6, ON......416-532-6108
Sereta, Greg/2108 Payne Ave #400, Cleveland, OH..............216-861-7227
Severson, Kent/529 S 7th St #637, Minneapolis, MN.............612-375-1870
Sexton, Ken/118 W Kinzie, Chicago, IL................................312-854-0180
Seymour, Ronald/314 W Superior, Chicago, IL.....................312-642-4030
Shafer, Ronald/4428 N Malden, Chicago, IL.........................312-878-1346
Shaffer, Mac/526 E Dunedin Rd, Columbus, OH...................614-268-2249
Shafman, Frank/466 Bathurst St #4, Toronto M5T 2S6, ON......
Shambroom, Paul/1607 Dupont Ave N, Minneapolis, MN.........612-521-5835
Shanoor Photo/116 W Illinois, Chicago, IL...........................312-266-0465
Shapiro, Terry/1147 W Ohio St, Chicago, IL.........................312-226-3384
Sharp, Joe/PO Box 1494, Toledo, OH.................................419-243-1450
Shaughnessy & MacDonald/32 Martin Ln, Elk Grove Vill, IL......312-437-8850
Shay, Arthur/618 Indian Hill Rd, Deerfield, IL.......................312-945-4636

Shelli, Bob/PO Box 2062, St Louis, MO..............................314-772-8540
Shepherd, Clark/461 E College St, Oberlin, OH....................216-775-4825
Sheppard, Richard/421 N Main St, Mt Prospect, IL...............312-259-4375
Shigeta-Wright Assoc/1546 N Orleans St, Chicago, IL..........312-642-8715
Shippert, Philip/1049 N Paulina, Chicago, IL.......................312-235-1500
Shirmer, Bob/11 W Illinois St, Chicago, IL...........................312-321-1151
Shotwell, Chuck/2111 N Clifton, Chicago, IL........................312-929-0168
Shoulders, Terry/676 N LaSalle, Chicago, IL........................312-642-6622
Siede/Preis Photo/1526 N Halsted, Chicago, IL....................312-787-2725
Sieracki, John/676 N LaSalle, Chicago, IL...........................312-664-7824
Sigman, Gary/2229 W Melrose St, Chicago, IL.....................312-871-8756
Silber, Gary Craig/300 Main St, Racine, WI.........................414-637-5097
Silker, Glenn/5249 W 73rd St #A, Edina, MN.......................612-835-1811
Sills, Anne Margaret/411 N LaSalle St, Chicago, IL..............312-670-3660
Sills, Casey/411 N Lasalle, Chicago, IL...............................312-670-3660
Silver, Jared N/660 La Salle Pl, Chicago, IL.........................312-433-3866
Simeon, Marshall/1043 W Randolph St, Chicago, IL.............312-243-9500
Simmons Photography Inc/326 Chicago Ave, Chicago, IL.......312-944-0326
Simpson, Paul/2530 Superior Ave, Cleveland, OH................216-579-0618
Sindelar, Dan/2517 Grove Springs Ct, St Louis, MO..............314-846-4775
Singer, Beth/25741 River Dr, Franklin, MI............................313-626-4860
Sinkler, Paul/510 N First Ave #307, Minneapolis, MN............612-343-0325
Sinklier, Scott/5860 Merle Hay Rd/Box 127, Johnston, IA......515-270-3732
Skalak, Carl/47-46 Grayton Rd, Cleveland, OH....................216-676-6508
Skrebneski, Victor/1350 N LaSalle St, Chicago, IL................312-944-1339
Skutas, Joe/17 N Elizabeth, Chicago, IL..............................312-733-1266
Sladcik, William/215 W Illinois, Chicago, IL.........................312-644-7108
Smetzer, Donald/2534 N Burling St, Chicago, IL...................312-327-1716
Smith, Bill/600 N McClurgh Ct #802, Chicago, IL.................312-787-4686
Smith, Crain/POB 30043, Cleveland, OH............................216-661-0636
Smith, Doug Photo/2911 Sutton, St Louis, MO.....................314-645-1359
Smith, Mike/PO Box 493, Westmont, IL...............................312-759-0262
Smith, Richard/PO Box 455, Round Lake, IL.........................312-546-0977
Smith, Richard Hamilton/PO Box 14208,
St Paul, MN (P 288,289) **612-645-5070**
Smith, Robert/496 W Wrightwood Ave, Elmhurst, IL..............312-941-7755
Snook, Allen/1433 W Fullerton, Addison, IL.........................312-495-3939
Snook, J J/118 W Ohio, Chicago, IL...................................312-495-3939
Snow, Andy/701 N Union Rd #164, Clayton, OH...................513-836-0294
Snyder, Don/1452 Davenport Ave, Cleveland, OH................216-771-6811
Snyder, John/368 W Huron, Chicago, IL..............................312-440-1053
Soluri, Tony/1147 W Ohio, Chicago, IL................................312-243-6580
Sorokowski, Rick/1051 N Halsted, Chicago, IL......................312-280-1256
Spahr, Dick/1133 E 61st St, Indianapolis, IN........................317-255-2400
Spectra Studios/213 W Institute #512, Chicago, IL...............312-787-0667
Spencer, Gary/3546 Dakota Ave S, Minneapolis, MN............612-929-7803
Spingola, Laurel/1233 W Eddy, Chicago, IL.........................312-883-0020
Spitz, Robert/804 Milford St, Evanston, IL...........................312-869-4992
Stansfield, Stan/215 W Ohio, Chicago, IL............................312-337-3245
Starkey, John/551 W 72nd St, Indianapolis, IN.....................317-254-0700
Starmark Photo/706 N Dearborn, Chicago, IL......................312-944-6700
Stealey, Jonathan/PO Box 611, Findlay, OH.........................419-423-1149
Steele, Charles/531 S Plymouth Ct #22, Chicago, IL.............312-922-0201
Stegbauer, Jim/421 Transit, Roseville, MN...........................612-333-1982
Stegel, Mark/9 Davis Ave #300, Toronto M4M 2A6, ON..........416-462-3244
Stein, Frederic/955 West Lake St, Chicago, IL......................312-226-7447
Steinberg, Mike/633 Huron Rd, Cleveland, OH....................216-589-9953
Steinhart Photography/625 W Dening Pl #5A, Chicago, IL......312-944-0226
Stenberg, Pete Photography/225 W Hubbard, Chicago, IL......312-644-6137
Stenbroten, Scott/107 W Van Buren #211, Chicago, IL..........312-929-4677
Sterling, Joseph/2216 N Cleveland, Chicago, IL...................312-348-4333
Stewart, Ron/314 E Downer Pl, Aurora, IL............................312-897-4317
Stone, Tony Worldwide/233 East Ontario, Chicago, IL...........312-787-7880
Stornello, Joe/4319 Campbell St, Kansas City, MO...............816-756-0419
Straus, Jerry/247 E Ontario, Chicago, IL.............................312-787-2628
Strauss, Sara/134 Upland Ave, Youngstown, OH..................216-794-5881
Strouss, Sarah/134 Upland Ave, Youngstown, OH................216-744-2774
Struse, Perry L Jr/232 Sixth St, West Des Moines, IA.............515-279-9761
Stump Studio/1920 N Dayton, Chicago, IL...........................312-477-5569
Summers Studio/153 W Ohio, Chicago, IL...........................312-527-0908
Sundlof, John/1324 Isabella St, Wilmette, IL........................312-256-8877
Sutter, Greg/6621-B Century Ave, Middleton, WI..................608-836-5744
Swan, Tom/2417 N Burling, Chicago, IL..............................312-871-8370
Swanson, Michael/215 W Ohio, Chicago, IL.........................312-337-3245
Sykaluk, John/2416 Harlem Blvd, Rockford, IL......................815-968-3819

T

Taback, Sidney/415 Eastern Ave, Toronto M4M1B7, ON........416-463-5718

Taber, Gary/305 S Green St, Chicago, IL 312-726-0374
Talbot, Mark/1725 North Ave, Chicago, IL 312-276-1777
Tappin, Mike/4410 N Hermitage, Chicago, IL 312-275-7735
Taxel, Barney/4614 Prospect Ave, Cleveland, OH 216-431-2400
Taylor, Dale E/2665-A Scott Ave, St Louis, MO 314-652-9665
Technigraph Studio/1212 Jarvis, Elk Grove Village, IL 312-437-3334
Tepporton, Earl/8701 Harriet Ave S, Minneapolis, MN 612-887-7852
Teschl, Josef/31 Brock Ave #203, Toronto, ON 416-743-5146
Teufen, Al/600 E Smith Rd, Medina, OH (P 264) 216-723-3237
The Photo Place/4739 Butterfield, Hillside, IL 312-544-1222
The Picture Place/3721 Grandel Sq, St Louis, MO 314-652-6262
The Studio, Inc/4239 N Lincoln, Chicago, IL 312-348-3556
Thien, Alex/2754 N Prospect Ave, Milwaukee, WI 414-964-4349
Thill, Nancy/124 W Polk #307, Chicago, IL 312-939-7770
Thoen, Greg/14940 Minnetonka Indust Rd, Minnetonka, MN 612-938-2433
Thomas, Bill/Rt 4 Box 387, Nashville, IN 812-988-7865
Thomas, Tony/676 N Lasalle St 6th Fl, Chicago, IL 312-337-2274
Thornberg, Russell/PO Box 101, Akron, OH 216-724-2852
Tillis, Harvey S/1050 W Kinzie, Chicago, IL 312-733-7336
Tirotta, John/420 W Sample St, South Bend, IN 219-234-4244
Tolchin, Robert/1057 Kenton Rd, Deerfield, IL 312-729-2522
Tower Photo/4327 N Elston, Chicago, IL 312-478-8494
Townsend, Wesley/, Lombard, IL 312-620-7118
TPS Studio/4016 S California, Chicago, IL 312-847-1221
Tracy, Janis/213 W Institute Pl, Chicago, IL 312-787-7166
Trantafil, Gary/222 S Morgan, Chicago, IL 312-666-1029
Trotter, Jim/12342 Conway Rd, St Louis, MO 314-878-0777
Trujillo, Edward/345 N Canal St #1604, Chicago, IL 312-454-9798
Tucker, Bill/114 W Illinois, Chicago, IL 312-321-1570
Tushas, Leo/111 N Fifth Ave #309, Minneapolis, MN 612-333-5774
Tweton, Roch/524 Hill Ave, Grafton, ND 701-352-1513
Tyson, Joye/PO Box 778, Normal, IL 309-454-2922
Tytel, Jeff/59 W Hubbard, Chicago, IL 312-329-0222

UV

Uhlmann, Gina/1611 N Sheffield, Chicago, IL 312-642-6650
Umland, Steve/600 Washington Ave N, Minneapolis, MN 612-332-1590
Upitis, Alvis/620 Morgan Ave S, Minneapolis, MN 612-374-9375
Urba, Alexis/148 W Illinois, Chicago, IL 312-644-4466
Van Allen, John/U of Iowa Fndtn/Alumni Ctr, Iowa City, IA ...319-354-9512
Van Antwerp, Jack/1220 W Sixth St #704, Cleveland, OH ...216-621-0515
Van Marter, Robert/1209 Alstott Dr S, Howell, MI 517-546-1923
Vandenberg, Greg/161 W Harrison 12th Fl, Chicago, IL 312-939-2969
Vander Lende, Craig/129 S Division St, Grand Rapids, MI ...616-235-3233
Vander Veen, David/5151 N 35th St, Milwaukee, WI 414-527-0450
VanKirk, Deborah/855 W Blackhawk St, Chicago, IL 312-642-3208
Variakojis, Danguole/5743 S Campbell, Chicago, IL 312-776-4668
Vaughan, Jim/321 S Jefferson, Chicago, IL 312-663-0369
Vedros, Nick/215 W 19th St, Kansas City, MO 816-471-5488
Ventola, Giorgio/230 W Huron, Chicago, IL 312-951-0880
Vergos Studio/122 W Kinzie 3rd Fl, Chicago, IL 312-527-1769
Viernum, Bill/1629 Mandel Ave, Westchester, IL 312-562-4143
Villa, Armando/1872 N Clybourne, Chicago, IL 312-472-7003
Visser, James/4274 Shenandoah Ave, St Louis, MO 314-771-6857
Visual Data Systems Inc/5617 63rd Pl, Chicago, IL 312-585-3060
Vizanko Adv. Photo/11511 K-Tel Drive, Minnetonka, MN 612-933-1314
Vollan, Michael/175 S Morgan, Chicago, IL 312-644-1792
Von Baich, Paul/78 Rusholme Rd, Toronto M6J 3H6, ON 416-532-6108
Von Photography/685 W Ohio, Chicago, IL 312-243-8578
Voyles, Dick/2822 Breckenridge Ind Ctr, St Louis, MO 314-968-3851
Vuksanovich/401 W Superior St, Chicago, IL 312-664-7523
Vyskocil, Debbie/PO Box 395, Summit, IL 312-496-8057

W

Wagenaar, David/1035 W Lake St, Chicago, IL 312-942-0943
Waite, Tim/717 S Sixth St, Milwaukee, WI 414-643-1500
Wakefield, John/5122 Grand Ave, Kansas City, MO 816-531-8448
Walker, Jessie Assoc/241 Fairview, Glencoe, IL 312-835-0522
**Wallace, David/1100 S Lynndale, Appleton,
WI (P 272) 414-738-4080**
Wans, Glen/325 W 40th, Kansas City, MO 816-931-8905
Ward, Les/21477 Bridge St #C & D, Southfield, MI 313-350-8666
Warkenthien, Dan/117 South Morgan, Chicago, IL 312-666-6056
Warren, Lennie/401 W Superior, Chicago, IL 312-664-5392
Watts, Dan/245 Plymouth, Grand Rapids, MI 616-451-4693
Watts, Ron/78 Rusholme Rd, Toronto M6J 3H6, ON 416-532-6108
Weber, J Andrew/303 S Donald Ave, Arlington Hts, IL 312-255-2738
Wedlake, James/750 Jossman Rd, Ortonville, MI 313-627-2711

Wehlage, John/325 16th St, Bettendorf, IA 319-355-5032
Weidemann, Skot/6621-B Century Ave, Middleton, WI 608-836-5744
Weiland, Jim/1100 S Lynndale Dr, Appleton, WI 414-739-7824
Weiner, Jim/540 N Lakeshore Dr, Chicago, IL 312-644-0040
Weinstein, John/2413 N Clybourn Ave, Chicago, IL 312-327-8184
Weinstein, Phillip/343 S Dearborn, Chicago, IL 312-922-1945
Weispfenning, Donna/815 W 53rd St, Minneapolis, MN 612-333-1453
Welzenbach, John/368 W Huron St, Chicago, IL 312-337-3611
Wengroff, Sam/2052 N Dayton, Chicago, IL 312-248-6623
West, Mike/300 Howard Ave, Des Plaines, IL 312-699-7886
West, Stu/430 First Ave #210, Minneapolis, MN 612-375-0404
Westerman, Charlie/630 W Oakdale, Chicago, IL 312-248-5709
Whitford, T R/1900 Delmar #2, St Louis, MO 314-621-2400
Whitmer, Jim/125 Wakeman, Wheaton, IL 312-653-1344
Wicks, L Photography/1235 W Winnemac Ave, Chicago, IL ...312-878-4925
Wiegand, Eric/2339 Ferndale, Sylvan Lake, MI 313-682-8746
Wilcox, Anthony/PO Box 148191, Chicago, IL 312-935-4050
Wilder, J David/411 W St Clair Ave, Cleveland, OH 216-771-7687
Wilker, Clarence/2021 Washington Ave, Lorain, OH 216-244-5497
Wilkes, Mike/2530 Superior, Cleveland, OH 216-781-0605
Willette, Brady T/1030 Nicollett Mall #203, Minneapolis, MN ..612-338-6727
Williams, Alfred G/Box 10288, Chicago, IL 312-947-0991
Williams, Barry/18 W Northwood Ave, Columbus, OH 614-291-9774
Williams, Basil/4068 Tanglefoot Terrace, Bettendorf, IA 319-355-7142
Williams, Bob/32049 Milton Ave, Madison Heights, MI 313-588-6544
Williams, David/3064 Reed Dr, Toledo, OH 419-476-0295
Williams, James/510 First Ave N #301, Minneapolis, MN 612-332-3095
Williamson, John/224 Palmerston Ave, Toronto, ON 416-530-4511
Wilson, Jack/212 Morgan St, St Louis, MO 314-241-1149
Wilson, Tim/1020 W Roscoe #1E, Chicago, IL 312-486-0500
Wirthlin, Walter/PO Box 660, Osage Beach, MO 314-348-3058
Witte, Scott J/3025 W Highland Blvd, Milwaukee, WI 414-933-3223
Woburn/4715 N Ronald St, Harwood Heights, IL 312-867-5445
Woehrle, Mark/1709 Washington Ave, St Louis, MO 314-231-9949
Wojcik, Richard R/151 Victor Ave, Highland Park, MI 313-868-2200
Wojnowski, Tom/6990 Nightingale, Dearborn Hts, MI 313-561-4192
Wolf, Bobbe/1101 W Armitage, Chicago, IL 312-472-9503
Wolff, Ed/11357 S Second St, Schoolcraft, MI 616-679-4702
Wolford, Rick/2300 E Douglas, Wichita, KS 316-264-3013
Wooden, John/219 N 2nd St J#306, Minneapolis, MN 612-339-3032
Woodward, Greg/811 W Evergreen #204, Chicago, IL 312-337-5838
Worzala, Lyle/8164 W Forest Preserve #1, Chicago, IL 312-434-7156
Wright, James/5740 S Kenwood #1, Chicago, IL 312-856-1838

YZ

Yamashiro, Paul Studio/1500 N Halstead, Chicago, IL 312-321-1009
Yapp, Charles/723 Randolph, Chicago, IL 312-558-9338
Yarrington, Todd/897 Ingleside Ave, Columbus, GA 614-297-0498
Yates, Peter/515 Spring St, Ann Arbor, MI 313-995-0839
Yaworski, Don/600 White Oak Ln, Kansas City, MO 816-455-4814
Zaitz, Dan/1643 N Milwaukee Ave, Chicago, IL 312-276-3565
Zake, Bruce/633 Huron Rd 3rd Fl, Cleveland, OH 216-694-3686
Zamiar, Thomas/210 W Chicago, Chicago, IL 312-787-4976
Zann, Arnold/502 N Grove Ave, Oak Park, IL 312-386-2864
Zarlengo, Joseph/419 Melrose Ave, Boardman, OH 216-782-7797
Zena Photography/633 Huron Rd SE 5th Fl, Cleveland, OH ..216-621-6366
Zimion/Marshall Studio/1043 W Randolph, Chicago, IL 312-243-9500
Zoom Photo/427 Queen St West, Toronto M5V 2A5, ON 416-593-0690
Zorn, Jim/1880 Holste Rd, Northbrook, IL 312-498-4844
Zukas, R/311 N Desplaines #500, Chicago, IL 312-648-0100

S O U T H W E S T

A

**Abraham, Joe/11944 Hempstead Rd #C,
Houston, TX (P 303) 713-460-4948**
Aker/Burnette Studio/4710 Lillian, Houston, TX 713-862-6343
Alexander, Laury/516 111th St NW #3, Albuquerque, NM ...505-843-9163
Alford, Jess/1800 Lear St #3, Dallas, TX 214-421-3107
Allen, Jim Photo/5600 Lovers Ln #212, Dallas, TX 214-351-3200
Anderson, Derek Studio/3959 Speedway Blvd E, Tucson, AZ ..602-881-1205
Anderson, Randy/1606 Lewis Trail, Grand Prairie, TX 214-660-1071
Angle, Lee/1900 Montgomery, Fort Worth, TX 817-737-6469
Ashe, Gil/Box 686, Bellaire, TX 713-668-8766
Ashley, Constance/2024 Farrington St, Dallas, TX 214-747-2501

Associated Photo/2344 Irving Blvd, Dallas, TX 214-630-8730
Austin, David/2412 Fifth Ave, Fort Worth, TX 817-335-1881

B

Badger, Bobby/1355 Chemical, Dallas, TX 214-634-0222
Bagshaw, Cradoc/PO Box 25706, Albuquerque, NM 505-243-1096
Baker, Bobbe C/1119 Ashburn, College Station, TX 409-696-7185
Baker, Jeff/2401 S Ervay #302, Dallas, TX 214-720-0178
Baker, Lane/1429 W Elna Rae #103, Tempe, AZ 602-829-7455
Baldwin/Watriss Assoc/1405 Branard St, Houston, TX 713-524-9199
Baraban, Joe/2426 Bartlett #2, Houston, TX 713-526-0317
Bardin, Keith Jr/PO Box 191241, Dallas, TX 214-686-0611
Barker, Kent/2039 Farrington, Dallas, TX 214-760-7470
Baxter, Scott/PO Box 25041, Phoenix, AZ 602-254-5879
Bayanduryan, Rubik/PO Box 1791, Austin, TX 512-469-0958
Beebe, Kevin/2460 Eliot St, Denver, CO 303-455-3627
Beebower Brothers/9995 Monroe #209, Dallas, TX 214-358-1219
Bennett, Sue/PO Box 1574, Flagstaff, AZ 602-774-2544
Bennett, Tony R/PO Box 568366, Dallas, TX 214-747-0107
Benoist, John/PO Box 20825, Dallas, TX 214-692-8813
Berman, Bruce/140 N Stevens #301, El Paso, TX 915-544-0352
Berrett, Patrick L/2425-C NE Monroe, Albuquerque, NM 505-881-0935
Berry, George S Photo/Rt 2 Box 325B, San Marcos, TX 512-396-4805
Bissell, Gary/120 Paragon #217, El Paso, TX 915-833-1942
Bland, Ron/2424 S Carver Pkwy #107, Grand Prairie, TX 214-660-6600
Blue, Janice/1708 Rosewood, Houston, TX 713-522-6899
Bondy, Roger/309 NW 23rd St, Oklahoma City, OK 405-521-1616
Booth, Greg/1322 Round Table, Dallas, TX 214-688-1855
Bowman, Matt/8602 Santa Clara, Dallas,
TX (P 304,305) **214-637-0211**
Bradley, Matt/15 Butterfield Ln, Little Rock, AR 501-224-0692
Bradshaw, Reagan/4101 Guadalupe, Austin, TX 512-458-6101
Brady, Steve/5250 Gulfton #2G, Houston, TX 713-660-6663
Britt, Ben/8602 Santa Clara, Dallas, TX (P 298)........**214-327-7889**
Brousseau, Jay/415 North Bishop Ave,
Dallas, TX (P 307) **214-638-1248**
Brown, David Photo/280 Edgewood Ct, Prescott, AZ 602-445-2485
Buffington, David/2401 S Ervay #105, Dallas, TX 214-428-8221
Bumpass, R O/1222 N Winnetka, Dallas, TX 214-742-3414
Burger, Steven/3102 W Lewis #10, Phoenix, AZ 602-272-9950
Burkey, J W/2739 Irving Blvd, Dallas, TX 214-630-1369

C

Cabluck, Jerry/Box 9601, Fort Worth, TX 817-336-1431
Caldwell, Jim/101 W Drew, Houston,
TX (P 308,309) **713-527-9121**
Campbell, Doug/5617 Matalee, Dallas, TX 214-823-9151
Cannedy, Carl/2408 Farrington, Dallas, TX 214-638-1247
Captured Image Photography/5131 E Lancaster, Ft Worth, TX 817-457-2302
Cardellino, Robert/315 Ninth St #2, San Antonio, TX 512-224-9606
Carr, Fred/3346 Walnut Bend, Houston, TX 713-266-2872
Chehabi, Saad/5028 Airline, Dallas, TX 214-526-4989
Chenn, Steve/6301 Ashcroft, Houston, TX 713-271-0631
Chisholm, Rich & Assoc/6813 Northampton Way, Houston, TX 713-957-1250
Clair, Andre/11415 Chatten Way, Houston, TX 713-465-5507
Clark, H Dean/18405 FM 149, Houston, TX 713-469-7021
Clifford, Geoffrey C/4719 Brisa Del Norte, Tucson, AZ 602-577-6439
Clintsman, Dick/3001 Quebec #102, Dallas,
TX (P 311) **214-630-1531**
Cobb, Lynn/2708 Rincon Port, Santa Fe, NM 505-473-3094
Cohen, Stewart Charles/2401 S Ervay #206, Dallas, TX 214-421-2186
Cole, Alan Michael/Route A Box 197, Flippin, AR 501-425-9107
Cole, Ralph/PO Box 2803, Tulsa, OK 918-585-9119
Colombo, Michel/3311 Oaklawn #200, Dallas, TX 214-522-1238
Connolly, Danny F/PO Box 1290, Houston, TX 713-862-8146
Cooke, Richard & Mary/209 E Ben White Blvd #110, Austin, TX 512-444-6100
Cotter, Austin/1350 Manufacturing #211, Dallas, TX 214-742-3633
Countryman, Mike/1925 Crooked Lane, Fort Worth, TX 817-654-4018
Cowlin, James/PO Box 34205, Phoenix, AZ 602-264-9689
Craig, George/314 E 13th St, Houston, TX 713-862-6008
Crittendon, James/5914 Lake Crest, Garland, TX 214-226-2196
Crossley, Dave/1412 W Alabama, Houston, TX 713-523-5757
Cruff, Kevin/2318 E Roosevelt, Phoenix, AZ 602-225-0273
Crump, Bill/1357 Chemical, Dallas, TX 214-630-7745
Cutter, Stephen/1535 E Dolphin Ave, Mesa, AZ 602-962-4359

D

Davey, Robert/PO Box 2421, Prescott, AZ 602-445-1160

Davidson, Josiah/PO Box 607, Cloudcroft, NM 800-537-7810
Davis, Mark/8718 Boundbrook Ave, Dallas, TX 214-348-7679
Dawson, Greg/2211 Beall St, Houston, TX 713-862-8301
Debenport, Robb/2412 Converse, Dallas, TX 214-631-7606
Drews, Buzzy/1555 W Mockingbird #202, Dallas, TX 214-351-9968
Driscoll, W M/PO Box 8463, Dallas, TX 214-363-8429
DuBose, Bill/5627 Richard Ave, Dallas, TX 214-781-6147
Duncan, Nena/306 Shady Wood, Houston, TX 713-782-3130
Duran, Mark/66 East Vernon, Phoenix, AZ 602-279-1141
Durham, Thomas/PO Box 4665, Witchita Falls, TX 817-691-2202
Durke, Vernon W/5250 Gulfton #4A, Houston,
TX (P 368) **713-457-7101**
Dyer, John/107 Blue Star, San Antonio, TX 512-223-1891
Dykinga, Jack/3808 Calle Barcelona, Tucson, AZ 602-326-6094

E

Easley, Ken/2810 S 24th St #109, Phoenix, AZ 602-244-9727
Eclipse/2727 E 21st St #600, Tulsa, OK 918-747-1991
Edens, Swain/110 N Leona, San Antonio, TX 512-226-2210
EDS Photography Services/4817 Iberia,
Dallas, TX (P 312,313) **214-790-5075**
Edwards, Bill/3820 Brown, Dallas, TX 214-521-8630
Eglin, Tom/3950 W Mais St, Tucson, AZ 602-748-1299
Enger, Linda/915 South 52nd St #5, Tempe,
AZ (P 314) **602-966-5776**
Ewasko, Tommy/5645 Hillcroft #202, Houston, TX 713-784-1777

F

Fantich, Barry/PO Box 70103, Houston, TX 713-520-5434
Farris, Neal/500 Exposition #104, Dallas, TX 214-821-5612
Faye, Gary/2421 Bartlett, Houston, TX (P 315).........**713-529-9548**
Findysz, Mary/3550 E Grant, Tucson, AZ 602-325-0260
Fontenot, Dallas/6002 Burning Tree Dr, Houston, TX 713-988-2183
Ford, Bill/202 S Center Valley, Irving, TX 214-255-5312
Foxall, Steve/3417 Main St, Dallas, TX 214-824-1977
Frady, Connie/2808 Fifth Ave, Fort Worth, TX 817-927-7589
Freeman, Charlie/3333-A Elm St, Dallas, TX 214-742-1446
Fry, John/5909 Goliad, Dallas, TX 214-821-1689
Fuller, Timothy Woodbridge/135 1/2 S Sixth Ave, Tucson, AZ 602-622-3900

G

Gaber, Brad/4946 Glen Meadow, Houston, TX 713-723-0030
Galloway, Jim/2335 Valdina St, Dallas, TX 214-954-0355
Garacci, Benedetto/1821 W Alabama, Houston, TX 713-526-5278
Gary & Clark Photographic Studio/2702 Main, Dallas, TX 214-939-9070
Gatz, Larry/5250 Gulfton #3B, Houston, TX 713-666-5203
Gayle, Rick/2318 E Roosevelt, Phoenix, AZ 602-267-8845
Geffs, Dale/15715 Amapola, Houston, TX 713-777-2228
Gerczynski, Tom/2211 N 7th Ave, Phoenix, AZ 602-252-9229
Germany, Robert/3102 Commerce St, Dallas, TX 214-747-4548
Gilbert, Bruce/12335 Braesridge, Houston, TX 713-723-1486
Gilmore, Dwight/2437 Hillview, Fort Worth, TX 817-536-4825
Gilstrap, L C/132 Booth Calloway, Hurst, TX 817-284-7701
Giordano, Michael/PO Box 15497, San Antonio, TX 512-734-5552
Glentzer, Don Photography/3814 S Shepherd Dr, Houston, TX 713-529-9686
Gomel, Bob/10831 Valley Hills, Houston, TX 713-988-6390
Goodman, Robert/2025 Levee, Dallas, TX 214-653-1120
Graham, Boyce/2809 Canton St, Dallas, TX 214-644-1280
Grass, Jon/3141 Irving #209, Dallas, TX 214-634-1455
Green, Mark/2406 Taft St, Houston, TX (P 316).........**713-523-6146**
Grider, James/732 Schilder, Fort Worth, TX 817-732-7472
Guerrero, Charles/2207 Comal St, Austin, TX 512-477-6642

H

Hagler, Skeeter/PO Box 628, Red Oak, TX 214-576-5620
Hale, Butch Photography/1319 Conant, Dallas, TX 214-637-3987
Halpern, David/7420 E 70th St, Tulsa, OK 918-252-4973
Ham, Dan/1350 Manufacturing #212, Dallas, TX 214-742-8700
Hamblin, Steve/4718 Iberia, Dallas, TX 214-630-2848
Hamburger, Jay/1817 State St, Houston, TX 713-869-0869
Hamilton, Jeffrey Muir/6719 Quartzite Canyon Pl, Tucson, AZ 602-299-3624
Hand, Ray/10921 Shady Trail #100, Dallas, TX 214-351-2488
Handel, Doug/1001 3rd St, Carrollton, TX 214-446-2236
Harness, Brian/1402 S Montreal Ave, Dallas, TX 214-330-4419
Hart, Len/2100 Wilcrest #102, Houston, TX 713-974-3265
Hart, Michael/7320 Ashcroft #105, Houston, TX 713-271-8250
Hartman, Gary/911 South St Marys St, San Antonio, TX 512-225-2404

Hatcok, Tom/113 W 12th St, Deer Park, TX 713-479-2603
Hawks, Bob/1345 E 15th St, Tulsa, OK 918-584-3351
Hawn, Gray Photography/PO Box 16425, Austin, TX.....................512-328-1321
Haynes, Mike/10343 Best Dr, Dallas, TX......................................214-352-1314
Hedrich, David/4006 South 23rd St #10, Phoenix, AZ...................602-220-0090
Heiner, Gary/2039 Farrington, Dallas, TX.....................................214-760-7471
Heinsohn, Bill/5455 Dashwood #200, Bellaire, TX.........................713-666-6515
Heit, Don/8502 Eustis Ave, Dallas, TX...214-324-0305
Henry, Steve/7403 Pierrepont Dr, Houston, TX.............................713-937-4514
Hollenbeck, Phil/2833 Duval, Dallas, TX.......................................214-331-8328
Hollingsworth, Jack/3141 Irving Blvd #209, Dallas, TX..................214-620-1285
Hood, Bob/2312 Grand, Dallas, TX..214-428-6080
Hubbard, Tim/Box 44971/Los Olivos Sta, Phoenix, AZ..................602-274-6985
Huber, Phil/13562 Braemar Dr, Dallas, TX...................................214-243-4011
Hulsey, Jim Photo/8117 NW 80th St, Oklahoma City, OK..............405-720-2767

J

Jacoby, Doris/1317 Conant, Dallas, TX...214-526-5026
Jenkins, Gary/4817 Iberia, Dallas, TX (P 313)   **214-790-5075**
Jennings, Steve/PO Box 33203, Tulsa, OK...................................918-745-0836
Jew, Kim/1518 Girard NE, Albuquerque, NM...................................505-255-6424
Johnson, Michael/830 Exposition #215, Dallas, TX........................214-828-9550
Jones, C Bryan/2900 N Loop W #1130, Houston, TX.....................713-956-4166
Jones, Jerry/5250 Gulfton #4A, Houston, TX................................713-668-4328
Jones, Will/4602 E Elwood St #13, Phoenix, AZ.............................602-968-7664

K

Kaluzny, Zigy/4700 Strass Dr, Austin, TX (P 317) **512-452-4463**
Kasie Photos/2123 Avignon, Carrollton, TX..................................214-492-7837
Katz, John/5222 Red Field, Dallas, TX...214-637-0844
Kellis, Shawn/3433 W earll Dr, Phoenox, AZ.................................602-272-7777
Kendrick, Robb/2700 Albany #303, Houston, TX...........................713-528-4334
Kennedy, David Michael/PO Box 254, Cerrillos, NM.......................505-473-2745
Kenny, Gill/3220 E Calle de la Punta, Tucson, AZ.........................602-577-1232
Kern, Geof/1337 Crampton, Dallas, TX...214-630-0856
Kirkland, Bill/5423 Peterson Ln #209, Dallas, TX..........................214-741-7673
Kirkley, Kent/4906 Don Drive, Dallas, TX (P 299)   **214-688-1841**
Klemme, Mike/PO Box 3045, Enid, OK...405-234-8284
Klumpp, Don/804 Colquitt, Houston, TX..713-521-2090
Knowles, Jim/6102 E Mockingbird Ln #499, Dallas, TX...................214-699-5335
Knudson, Kent/PO Box 10397, Phoenix,
AZ (P 294,295)   **602-277-7701**
Korab, Jeanette/9000 Directors Row, Dallas, TX............................214-337-0114
Kretchmar, Phil Photography/233 Yorktown, Dallas, TX...................214-744-2039
Kroninger, Rick/PO Box 15913, San Antonio, TX...........................512-733-9931
Kuntz, Bryan/7700 Renwick #5A, Houston,
TX (P 319)   **713-667-4200**
Kuper, Holly/5522 Anita St, Dallas, TX...214-827-4494

L

Lacker, Pete/235 Yorktown, Dallas, TX...214-748-7488
Larsen, Peter/1350 Manufacturing #206, Dallas, TX......................214-478-1776
Latorre, Robert/2336 Farrington St, Dallas, TX.............................214-630-8977
Lawrence, David/2720 Stemmons #1206, Dallas, TX....................214-637-4686
Lawrie, Bill/3030 Sundial Dr, Dallas, TX..214-991-2604
Laybourn, Richard/4657 Westgrove, Dallas, TX............................214-931-9984
Lettner, Hans/830 North 4th Ave, Phoenix, AZ..............................602-258-3506
Lorfing, Greg/1900 W Alabama, Houston, TX.................................713-529-5968
Loven, Paul/1405 E Marshall, Phoenix, AZ....................................602-253-0335
Luker, Tom/PO Box 6112, Coweta, OK..918-486-5264

M

Mack, Rick/3102 W Lewis St #8, Phoenix, AZ...............................602-264-6718
Mader, Bob/2570 Promenade Center N, Richardson, TX................214-690-5511
Magee, Mike/1325 Conant St, Dallas, TX......................................214-638-6868
Mageors & Rice Photo/240 Turnpike Ave, Dallas, TX....................214-941-3777
Major, Bert/11056 Shady Trail #119, Dallas, TX............................214-956-9338
Maloney, John W/170 Leslie, Dallas, TX.......................................214-521-9958
Manley, Dan/1350 Manufacturing #213, Dallas, TX.......................214-748-8377
Manning, John/1240 Hanna Circle, DeSoto, TX..............................214-224-6787
Manske, Thaine/7313 Ashcroft #216, Houston, TX........................713-771-2220
Maples, Carl/1811 Cohn, Houston, TX..713-868-1289
Mark, Richard/3102 W Lewis St #8, Phoenix, AZ...........................602-272-6610
Markham, Jim/2739 S E Loop 410, San Antonio, TX......................512-648-0403
Markow Southwest Inc/2222 E McDowell Rd,
Phoenix, AZ (P 320,321)   **602-273-7985**
Marks, Stephen/4704-C Prospect NE, Albuquerque, NM.................505-884-6100

Marshall, Jim/7451 Long Rifle Rd/Box 2421, Carefree, AZ..............602-488-3373
Matthews, Michael/2727 Cancun, Dallas, TX.................................214-306-8000
Maxham, Robert/223 Howard St, San Antonio,
TX (P 322)   **512-223-6000**
Mayer, George H/933 Stonetrail, Plano (Dallas), TX.......................214-424-4409
McAlister, Steve/4817 Iberia, Dallas, TX (P 312).....**214-790-5075**
McClain, Edward/756 N Palo Verde, Tucson, AZ............................602-326-1873
McCormick, Mike/5950 Westward Ave, Houston, TX.......................713-988-0775
McCoy, Gary/2700 Commerce St, Dallas, TX.................................214-320-0002
McIntosh, W S/605 Stillmeadow, Richardson, TX...........................214-783-1711
McNee, Jim/PO Box 741008, Houston, TX.....................................713-796-2633
McPherson, Rocky/3744 E Speedway, Tucson, AZ.........................602-326-2550
Meredith, Diane/2425 Bartlett, Houston, TX..................................713-527-8677
Messina, John/4440 Lawnview, Dallas, TX.....................................214-388-8525
Meyerson, Arthur/4215 Bellaire Blvd, Houston, TX.........................713-660-0405
Meyler, Dennis/1903 Portsmouth #25, Houston, TX.......................713-520-1800
Mills, Jack R/PO Box 32583, Oklahoma City, OK...........................405-787-7271
Moberley, Connie/215 Asbury, Houston, TX..................................713-864-3638
Molen, Roy/3302 N 47 Pl, Phoenix, AZ..602-840-5439
Monteaux, Michele/223 Ojo De La Vaca, Santa Fe, NM.................505-982-5598
Moore, Terrence/PO Box 41536, Tucson, AZ.................................602-623-9381
Moot, Kelly/2331-D Wirtcrest Ln, Houston, TX...............................713-683-6400
Morgan, Roger/828 Birdsong, Bedford, TX...................................817-282-2170
Morris, Garry/9281 E 27th St, Tucson, AZ.....................................602-795-2334
Morris, Mike/4003 Gilbert #6, Dallas, TX.......................................214-528-3600
Morrison, Chet Photography/2917 Canton, Dallas, TX....................214-939-0903
Morrow, James R/PO Box 2718, Grapevine, TX.............................214-402-9960
Muir, Robert/Box 42809 Dept 404, Houston, TX.............................713-784-7420
Murdoch, Lane/1350 Manufacturing #205, Dallas, TX....................214-651-0200
Murphy, Dennis/101 Howell St, Dallas, TX (P 302)...**214-651-7516**
Myers, Jim/165 Cole, Dallas, TX (P 297)   **214-698-0500**

N

Neely, David/412 Briarcliff Lane, Bedford, TX.................................817-498-6741
Netzer, Don/1345 Conant, Dallas, TX...214-869-0826
Newby, Steve/4501 Swiss, Dallas, TX...214-821-0231
Noble, Jeff/688 West 1st St #5, Tempe, AZ..................................602-968-1434
Norrell, J B/7315 Ashcroft #110, Houston, TX...............................713-981-6409
Norton, Michael/4810 S 40th St #3, Phoenix, AZ...........................602-840-9463

OP

O'Dell, Dale/2040 Bissonet, Houston, TX (P 323)......**713-521-2611**
Olvera, Jim/235 Yorktown St, Dallas,
TX (P 324,325)   **214-760-0025**
Pantin, Tomas/1601 E 7th St #100, Austin, TX...............................512-474-9968
Parrish, John/1218 Manufacturing, Dallas,
TX (P 326,327)   **214-742-9457**
Parsons, Bill/518 W 9th St, Little Rock, AR...................................501-372-5892
Patrick, Richard/215 W 4th St #B, Austin, TX................................512-472-9092
Payne, A F/830 North 4th Ave, Phoenix, AZ...................................602-258-3506
Payne, C Ray/2643 Manana, Dallas, TX..214-350-1055
Payne, Richard/1701 Hermann Dr #2304, Houston, TX...................713-524-7525
Payne, Tom/2425 Bartlett, Houston, TX...713-527-8670
Perlstein, Mark/1844 Place One Ln, Garland, TX............................214-690-0168
Peterson, Bruce/2430 S 20th St, Phoenix, AZ...............................602-252-6088
Pettit, Steve/206 Weeks, Arlington, TX...817-265-8776
Pfuhl, Chris/PO Box 542, Phoenix, AZ...602-253-0525
Phelps, Greg/2360 Central Blvd, Brownsville, TX............................512-541-4909
Photo Media, Inc/2805 Crockett, Fort Worth, TX............................817-332-4172
Pogue, Bill/1412 W Alabama, Houston, TX....................................713-523-5757
Post, Andy/4748 Algiers #300, Dallas, TX.....................................214-634-4490
Poulides, Peter/PO Box 202505, Dallas, TX...................................214-902-8800
Probst, Kenneth/3527 Oak Lawn Blvd #375, Dallas, TX.................214-522-2031

QR

The Quest Group/3007 Paseo, Oklahoma City, OK.........................405-525-6591
Quilia, Jim/3125 Ross, Dallas, TX...214-276-9956
Ralph, Michael/10948 Pelham, El Paso, TX....................................915-595-3787
Raphaele Inc/616 Hawthorne, Houston, TX....................................713-524-2211
Rascona, Donna & Rodney/4232 S 36th Place, Phoenix, AZ...........602-437-0866
Raymond, Rick/1244 E Utopia, Phoenix, AZ...................................602-581-8160
Records, Bill/505 W 38, Austin, TX...512-458-1017
Redd, True/2328 Farrington, Dallas, TX...214-638-0602
Reens, Louis/4814 Sycamore, Dallas, TX......................................214-827-3388
Reese, Donovan/3007 Canton, Dallas, TX.....................................214-357-6615
Reisch, Jim/235 Yorktown St, Dallas, TX.......................................214-748-0456
Robbins Jr, Joe D/7700 Renwick #5, Houston, TX.........................713-667-5050
Robbins, Joe/7700 Renwick #5A, Houston,

TX (P 328) **713-667-5050**
Robson, Howard/3807 E 64th Pl, Tulsa, OK 918-492-3079
Roe, Cliff/47 Woodelves Pl, The Woodlands, TX 713-363-5661
Rogers, John/PO Box 35753, Dallas, TX 214-351-1751
Rubin, Janice/705 E 16th St, Houston, TX 713-868-6060
Running, John/PO Box 1237, Flagstaff, AZ 602-774-2923
Rusing, Rick/1555 W University #106, Tempe, AZ 602-967-1864
Russell, Gail/PO Box 241, Taos, NM 505-776-8474
Russell, Nicholas/849-F Harvard, Houston, TX 713-864-7664
Ryan, Tom/1821 Levee, Dallas, TX 214-651-7085

S

Samaha, Sam/2739 Irving Blvd, Dallas, TX 214-630-1369
Savant, Joseph/4756 Algiers St, Dallas, TX (P 329).....**214-951-0111**
Savins, Matthew/101 Howell St, Dallas, TX (P 296).....**214-651-7516**
Saxon, John/1337 Crampton, Dallas, TX 214-630-5160
Scheer, Tim/1521 Centerville Rd, Dallas, TX 214-328-1016
Scheyer, Mark/3317 Montrose #A1003, Houston, TX 713-861-0847
Schlesinger, Terrence/PO Box 32877, Phoenix, AZ 602-957-7474
Schmidt, David/382 North First Ave, Phoenix,
AZ (P 300) **602-258-2592**
Schneps, Michael/700 Renwick #5A, Houston,
TX (P 330) **713-668-4600**
Schultz, Dave/111 N Gilbert #2048, Mesa, AZ 602-834-8920
Schuster, Ellen/3719 Gilbert, Dallas, TX 214-526-6712
Scott, Ron/1000 Jackson Blvd, Houston, TX 713-529-5868
Seeger, Stephen/2931 Irving Blvd #101, Dallas, TX 214-634-1309
Segrest, Jerry Photography/1707 S Arvay, Dallas, TX 214-426-6360
Segroves, Jim/170 Leslie, Dallas, TX 214-827-5482
Sellers, Dan/1317 Conant, Dallas, TX 214-631-4705
Shands, Nathan/1107 Bryan, Mesquite, TX 214-285-5382
Shaw, Robert/1723 Kelly SE, Dallas, TX 214-428-1757
Shepherd, Michael/3702 E Roeser Rd #13, Phoenix, AZ........602-437-1511
Siegel, Dave/224 N 5th Ave, Phoenix, AZ 602-257-9509
Sieve, Jerry/PO Box 1777, Cave Creek, AZ 602-488-9561
Simon, Frank/4030 N 27th Ave #B, Phoenix,
AZ (P 331) **602-279-4635**
Simpson, Micheal/1415 Slocun St. #105, Dallas,
TX (P 332,333) **214761-0000**
Sims, Jim/2811 McKinney #224, Dallas, TX 214-855-0055
Sims, John/336 Melrose #14A, Richardson, TX 214-231-6065
Smith, Ralph/2211 Beall, Houston, TX 713-862-8301
Smith/Garza Photography/PO Box 10046, Dallas, TX 214-941-4611
Smothers, Brian/834 W 43rd St, Houston, TX 713-695-0873
Snedeker, Katherine/, Dallas, TX 214-745-1250
Sperry, Bill/3300 E Stanford, Paradise Valley, AZ 602-955-5626
St Angelo, Ron/3630 Harry Hines Blvd, Dallas, TX 817-481-1833
St Gil & Associates/PO Box 820568, Houston, TX 713-870-9458
Staartjes, Hans/34Lana Ln, Houston, TX (P 334)......**713-621-8503**
Stewart, Craig/1900 W Alabama, Houston, TX......................713-529-5059
Stiller, Rick/1311 E 35th St, Tulsa, OK 918-749-0297
Studio 3 Photography/2804 Lubbock, Fort Worth, TX 817-923-9931
Suddarth, Robert/3402 73rd St, Lubbock, TX 806-795-4553
Summers, Chris/2437 Bartlett St, Houston, TX 713-524-7371
Sumner, Bill/122 Parkhouse, Dallas, TX 214-948-6860
Swindler, Mark/206 Santa Rita, Odessa, TX 915-332-3515

T

Talley, Paul/4756 Algiers St, Dallas, TX 214-951-0039
Thatcher, Charles/2401 Farrington St, Dallas, TX.................214-823-4356
Thompson, Dennis/15 E Brady, Tulsa, OK.............................918-582-8850
Thompson, Wesley/800 W Airport Frwy #301, Irving, TX 214-438-7762
Timmerman, Bill/844 S Edward Dr #1, Tempe, AZ 602-968-9474
Tomlinson, Doug/9307 Mercer Dr, Dallas, TX 214-321-0600
Trent, Rusty/1121 Bomar St, Houston, TX 713-526-3651
Tunison, Richard/7829 E Foxmore Lane, Scottsdale, AZ 602-998-4708
Turner, Danny/4228 Main St, Dallas, TX 214-760-7472

UV

Urban, Linda/2931 Irving Blvd #101, Dallas, TX 214-634-9009
Vandivier, Kevin/904 E 44th St, Austin, TX...........................512-450-1506
VanOverbeek, Will/305 E Sky View, Austin, TX.....................512-454-1501
Vantage Point Studio/1109 Arizona Ave, El Paso, TX 915-533-9688
Vener, Ellis/3601 Allen Pkwy #123, Houston, TX 713-523-0456
Viewpoint Photographers/217 McKinley, Phoenix, AZ 602-245-0013
Vine, Terry/5455 Dashwood #200, Houston,
TX (P 292,293) **713-664-2920**
Vracin, Andy/4609 Don Drive, Dallas, TX (P 301) **214-688-1841**

WYZ

Walker, Balfour/1838 E 6th St, Tucson, AZ 602-624-1121
Webb, Drayton/5455 Dashwood, Belaire, TX 713-660-7497
Weeks, Christopher/1260 E 31st Pl, Tulsa, OK 918-749-8289
Wells, Craig/537 W Granada, Phoenix, AZ 602-252-8166
Welsch, Diana/PO Box 1791, Austin, TX 512-451-8960
Werre, Bob/2437 Bartlett St, Houston, TX (P 335).....**713-529-4841**
Wheeler, Don/4928 E 26th Pl, Tulsa, OK...............................918-747-7114
White, Frank Photo/2702 Sackett, Houston, TX 713-524-9250
Whitlock, Neill/122 E 5th St, Dallas, TX 214-948-3117
Wilke, Darrell/2608 Irving Blvd, Dallas, TX 214-631-6459
Williams, Laura/223 Howard, San Antonio, TX 512-223-6000
Williams, Oscar/8535 Fairhaven, San Antonio, TX 512-690-8807
Williamson, Thomas A/10830 N Central Expy #201, Dallas, TX....214-373-4999
Willis, Gordon/3910 Buena Vista #11, Dallas, TX 214-520-7035
Wolenski, Stan/2919 Canton, Dallas, TX 214-749-0749
Wolfhagen, Vilhelm/4916 Kelvin, Houston, TX 713-522-2787
Wollam, Les/5215 Goodwin Ave, Dallas, TX 214-760-7721
Wood, Keith Photo Inc/1308 Conant St, Dallas,
TX (P 336) **214-634-7344**
Wristen, Don/2025 Levee St, Dallas, TX 214-748-5317
Yeung, Ka Chuen/4901 W Lovers Lane, Dallas, TX 214-350-8716
Zabel, Ed/PO Box 58601, Dallas, TX....................................214-748-2910

R O C K Y   M T N

A

Adams, Butch/1414 South 700 West,
Salt Lake City, UT (P 338,339).................................**801-973-0939**
Aiuppy, Larry/PO Box 26, Livingston, MT 406-222-7308
Alaxandar/1201 18th St #240, Denver, CO 303-298-7711
Allen, Lincoln/1705 Woodbridge Dr, Salt Lake City, UT 801-277-1848
Alston, Bruce/PO Box 2480, Steamboat Springs, CO............303-879-1675
Appleton, Roger/3106 Pennslyvania, Colorado Springs, CO 719-635-0393
Archer, Mark/228 S Madison St, Denver, CO 303-399-5272

B

Bailey, Brent P/PO Box 70681, Reno, NV.............................702-826-4104
Bako, Andrew/3047 4th St SW, Calgary T2S 1X9, AB 403-243-9789
Barry, Dave/6669 S Kit CArson St, Littleton, CO 303-798-9995
Bartek, Patrick/PO Box 26994, Las Vegas, NV 702-368-2901
Bator, Joe/2011 Washington Ave, Golden, CO 303-279-4163
Bauer, Erwin A/Box 543, Teton Village, WY 307-733-4023
Beery, Gale/150 W Byers, Denver, CO 303-777-0458
Berchert, James H/2886 W 119th Ave, Denver, CO...............303-466-7414
Berge, Melinda/1280 Ute Ave, Aspen, CO............................303-925-2317
Biggs, Deborah/8335 E Fairmont #11-207, Denver, CO 719-388-5846
Birnbach, Allen/3600 Tejon St, Denver, CO..........................303-455-7800
Blake, John/4132 20th St, Greeley, CO 303-330-0980
Bluebaugh, David Studio/1594 S Acoma St, Denver, CO.......303-778-7214
Bosworth/Graves Photo Inc/1055 S 700 W, Salt Lake City, UT........801-972-6128
Brock, Sidney/3377 Blake St #102, Denver, CO 303-296-9462
Burggraf, Chuck/2941 W 23rd Ave, Denver, CO....................303-480-9053
Busath, Drake/701 East South Temple St, Salt Lake City, UT..........801-364-6645
Bush, Michael/2555 Walnut St, Denver, CO 303-292-2874

C

Cambon, Jim/216 Racquette Dr, Ft Collins,
CO (P 365)...**303-221-4545**
Cassaro, Vince/PO Box 11612, Aspen, CO 303-963-9384
Chesley, Paul/Box 94, Aspen, CO 303-925-1148
Christensen, Barry/4505 South 2300 West, Roy, UT.............801-731-3521
Clasen, Norm/PO Box 4230, Aspen, CO...............................303-925-4418
Coca, Joe/213 1/2 Jefferson St, Ft Collins, CO 303-482-0858
Collector, Stephen/1836 Mapleton Ave, Boulder, CO............303-442-1386
Cook, James/PO Box 11608, Denver, CO.............................303-433-4874
Coppock, Ron/1764 Platte St, Denver, CO............................303-477-3343
Cronin, Bill/2543 Xavier, Denver, CO 303-458-0883

D

DeHoff, RD/632 N Sheridan, Colorado Springs, CO..............303-635-0263
DeLespinasse, Hank/2300 E Patrick Ln #21, Las Vegas, NV 702-798-6693
DeMancznk, Phillip/1625 Wilber Pl, Reno, NV 702-329-0339

DeSciose, Nick/2700 Arapahoe St #2, Denver, CO 303-296-6386
DeVore, Nicholas III/1280 Ute, Aspen, CO..........................303-925-2317
Dickey, Marc/PO Box 4705, Denver, CO 303-449-6310
Dimond, Craig/831 S Richards St, Salt Lake City, UT 801-363-7158
Douglass, Dirk/2755 S 300 W #D, Salt Lake City, UT 801-485-5691
Dowbenko, Uri/PO Box 207, Emigrant, MT 406-333-4322
Downs, Jerry/1315 Oak Ct, Boulder, CO 303-444-8910

EFG

Elder, Jim/PO Box 1600, Jackson Hole, WY 307-733-3555
Fader, Bob/14 Pearl St, Denver, CO 303-744-0711
Farace, Joe Photo/14 Inverness #B100, Englewood, CO ...303-799-6606
Feld, Stephen/9480 Union Sq #208, Sandy, UT 801-571-1752
Ford, David/954 S Emerson, Denver, CO 303-778-7044
Frazier, Van/2770 S Maryland Pkwy, Las Vegas, NV 702-735-1165
Gallian, Dirk/PO Box 4573, Aspen, CO 303-925-8268
Gerke, Randy/PO Box 2327, Grand Junction, CO 303-243-8994
Goetze, David/3215 Zuni, Denver, CO 303-458-5026
Gorfkle, Gregory D/6901 E Baker Pl, Denver, CO 303-759-2737
Graf, Gary/1870 S Ogden St, Denver, CO 303-722-0547

H

H B R Studios/3310 South Knox Court, Denver, CO 303-789-4307
Harris, Richard/935 South High, Denver, CO 303-778-6433
Havey, James/1836 Blake St #203, Denver, CO 303-296-7448
Hazen, Ryne/172 West 36th St, Ogden, UT 801-621-6400
Heaton, Grant/982 South 400 West, Salt Lake City, UT 801-532-2456
Henderson, Gordon/182 Gariepy Crescent, Edmonton , AB 403-483-8049
Herridge, Brent/736 South 3rd West, Salt Lake City, UT 801-363-0337
Hiser, David C/1280 Ute Ave, Aspen, CO 303-925-2317
Holdman, Floyd/1908 Main St, Orem, UT 801-224-9966
Hooper, Robert Scott/4330 W Desert Inn Rd, Las Vegas, NV 702-873-5823
Hunt, Steven/1139 W Shepard Ln, Farmington, UT 801-451-6552
Huntress, Diane/3337 W 23rd Ave, Denver, CO 303-480-0219

JK

Johnson, Jim Photo/16231 E Princeton Circle, Denver, CO 303-680-0522
Johnson, Ron/2460 Eliot St, Denver, CO 303-458-0288
Kay, James W/PO Box 81042, Salt Lake City, UT 801-583-7558
Kelly, John P/PO Box 1550, Basalt, CO (P 378) **303-927-4197**
King, Jennifer/9810 E Colorado #107, Denver, CO 303-337-3137
Kitzman, John/3060 22nd St, Boulder, CO 303-440-7623
Koropp, Robert/901 E 17th Ave, Denver, CO 303-830-6000
Krause, Ann/PO Box 4165, Boulder, CO 303-444-6798

L

Laidman, Allan/110 Free Circle Ct A102, Aspen, CO 303-925-4791
Laszlo, Larry/420 E 11th Ave, Denver, CO 303-832-2299
Lee, Jess/6799 N Derek Ln, Idaho Falls, ID 208-529-4535
LeGoy, James M/PO Box 21004, Reno, NV 702-322-0116
Levy, Patricia Barry/3389 W 29th Ave, Denver, CO 303-458-6692
Lichter, Michael/3300 14th St, Boulder, CO 303-443-9198
Lissy, David/14472 Applewood Ridge Rd, Golden, CO 303-277-0232
Lokey, David/PO Box 7, Vail, CO 303-949-5750
Lonczyna, Longin/257-R S Rio Grande St, Salt Lake City, UT 801-355-7513
Lotz, Fred/4220 W 82nd Ave, Westminster, CO 303-427-2875

M

Mahaffey, Marcia/283 Columbine #135, Denver, CO 303-778-6316
Mangelsen, Tom/PO Box 2935, Jackson Hole, WY 307-733-6179
Markus, Kurt/237 1/2 Main St, Kalispell, MT 406-756-9191
Marlow, David/111-R Atlantic Ave, Aspen, CO 303-925-8882
Masamori, Ron/5051 Garrison St, Wheatridge, CO 303-423-8120
McDonald, Kirk/350 Bannock, Denver, CO 303-733-2958
McDowell, Pat/PO Box 283, Park City, UT 801-649-3403
McManemin, Jack/662 S State St, Salt Lake City, UT 801-359-3100
Meleski, Mike/3151A Larimer St, Denver, CO 303-623-1965
Melick, Jordan/1250 W Cedar St, Denver, CO 303-744-1414
Messineo, John/PO Box 1636, Fort Collins, CO 303-482-9349
Miles, Kent/465 Ninth Avenue, Salt Lake City,
UT (P 379,411) **801-364-5755**
Milmoe, James O/14900 Cactus Cr, Golden, CO 303-279-4364
Milne, Lee/3615 W 49th Ave, Denver, CO 303-458-1520
Mitchell, Paul/1517 S Grant, Denver, CO 303-722-8852
Mullen, Kevin/71 Sunhurst Crescent SE, Calgary, AB 403-256-5749
Munro, Harry/2355 W 27th Ave, Denver, CO 303-355-5612

NOP

Neligh, Dave/PO Box 811, Denver, CO 303-534-9005
Ordway, Robert/105 N Edison #17, Reno, NV 702-322-4889
Oswald, Jan/921 Santa Fe, Denver, CO 303-893-8038
Outlaw, Rob/PO Box 1275, Bozeman, MT 406-587-1482
Patryas, David/504 Main St, Longmont, CO 303-678-0959
Paul, Ken/1523 E Montane Dr E, Genesee, CO 303-526-1162
Payne, Brian/2685 Forest, Denver, CO 303-355-5373
Peck, Michael/2046 Arapahoe St, Denver,
CO (P 382) **303-296-9427**
Peregrine Studio/1541 Platte St, Denver, CO 303-455-6944
Perkin, Jan/428 L St, Salt Lake City, UT 801-355-0112
Phillips, Ron/12201 E Arapahoe #B2, Englewood, CO 303-790-8114
Powell, Todd/PO Box 2279, Breckenridge, CO 303-453-0469
Proctor, Keith/, Park City, UT

QR

Quinney, David Jr/423 East Broadway,
Salt Lake City, UT (P 384) **801-363-0434**
Radstone, Richard/3480 Spring Mt Rd, Las Vegas, NV 702-364-2004
Rafkind, Andrew/1702 Fairview Ave, Boise, ID 208-344-9918
Ramsey, Steve/4800 N Washington St, Denver, CO 303-295-2135
Ranson Photographers Ltd/26 Airport Rd, Edmonton, AB 403-454-9674
Redding, Ken/PO Box 717, Vail, CO 303-476-2446
Rehn, Gary/860 Toedtli Dr, Boulder, CO 303-499-9550
Reynolds, Roger/3310 S Knox Ct, Englewood, CO 303-789-4307
Rosen, Barry/1 Middle Rd, Englewood, CO 303-758-0648
Rosenberg, David/1545 Julian SE, Denver, CO 303-893-0893
Rosenberger, Edward/2248 Emerson Ave, Salt Lake City, UT 801-355-9007
Russell, John/PO Box 4739, Aspen, CO 303-920-1431

S

Saehlenou, Kevin/3478 W 32nd Ave, Denver, CO 303-455-1611
Sallaz, William/PO Box 6050, Helena, MT 406-442-0522
Saviers, Trent/2606 Rayma Ct, Reno, NV 702-747-2591
Schlack, Greg/1510 Lehigh St, Boulder, CO 303-499-3860
Schmiett, Skip/740 W 1700 S #10, Salt Lake City, UT 801-973-0642
Schoenfeld, Michael/PO Box 876, Salt Lake City, UT 801-532-2006
Shupe, John R/4090 Edgehill Dr, Ogden, UT 801-627-1157
Smith, David Scott/1437 Ave E, Billings, MT 406-259-5656
Smith, Derek/925 SW Temple, Salt Lake City, UT 801-363-1061
Smith, Dorn/1201-A Santa Fe, Denver, CO 303-825-3588
Sokol, Howard/3006 Zuni St, Denver, CO 303-433-3353
St John, Charles/1760 Lafayette St, Denver, CO 303-860-7300
Staver, Barry/5122 S Iris Way, Littleton, CO 303-973-4414
Stearns, Doug/1738 Wynkoop St #102, Denver, CO 303-296-1133
Stewert, Sandy/18230 W 4th Ave, Golden, CO 303-278-8039
Stoecklein, David/PO Box, Ketchum, ID 208-726-5191
Sunlit Ltd/1523 E Montane Dr, Genesse, CO 303-526-1162
Swartz, Bill/5992 S Eudora Ct, Littleton, CO 303-773-2776
Sweitzer, David/4800 Washington, Denver, CO 303-295-0703

TVWY

Tanner, Scott/2755 South 300 West #D, Salt Lake City, UT 801-466-6884
Tejada, David X/1553 Platte St #205, Denver, CO 303-458-1220
Tharp, Brenda/PO Box 4412, Denver, CO 303-980-0639
Till, Tom/3160 Rimrock Lane, Moab, UT (P 391) **801-259-5327**
Tobias, Philip/3614 Morrison Rd, Denver, CO 303-936-1267
Travis, Tom/1219 South Pearl St, Denver,
CO (P 352) **303-722-2040**
Tregeagle, Steve/2994 S Richards St #C, Salt Lake City, UT 801-484-1673
Van Hemert, Martin/5481 Cyclamen Ct, Salt Lake City, UT 801-969-3569
Viggio Studio/3819 N 26 St, Boulder, CO 303-444-3342
Walker, Rod/PO Box 2418, Vail, CO 303-926-3210
Wayda, Steve/5725 Immigration Canyon, Salt Lake City, UT 801-582-1787
Weeks, Michael/PO Box 6965, Colorado Springs, CO 719-632-2996
Wellisch, Bill/2325 Clay St, Denver, CO 303-455-8766
Welsh, Steve Photo/1191 Grove St, Boise,
ID (P 358) **208-336-5541**
Wheeler, Geoffrey/721 Pearl St, Boulder, CO 303-449-2137
White, Stuart/4229 Clark Ave, Great Falls, MT 406-761-6666
Yarborough, Carl/PO Box 4739, Aspen, CO 303-920-1431

WEST COAST

A

Abecassis, Andree L/756 Neilson St, Berkeley, CA 415-526-5099

Abraham, Russell/60 Federal St #303,
San Francisco, CA (P 362,363) **415-896-6400**
Abramowitz, Alan/PO Box 45121, Seattle, WA 206-621-0710
Ackroyd, Hugh S/Box 10101, Portland, OR 503-227-5694
Adams, Michael/25875 Via Pera, Mission Viejo, CA 714-472-4559
Adamstein, Jerome/2601 Broadmoor Dr., Palm Springs, CA 619-321-2260
Addor, Jean-Michel/1456 63rd St, Emeryville, CA 415-653-1745

Adler,Robert/33 Ellert St, San Francisco,
CA (P 355) **415-695-2867**
Agee, Bill & Assoc/715 Larkspur, Corona Del Mar, CA 714-760-6700
Ahrend, Jay/1046 N Orange Dr, Hollywood, CA 213-462-5256
All Sports Photo USA/6160 Fairmont Ave #H, San Diego, CA 319-280-3595
Allan, Larry/3503 Argonne St, San Diego, CA 619-270-1850
Allen, Charles/537 S Raymond Ave, Pasadena, CA 818-795-1053
Allen, Judson Photo/654 Gilman St, Palo Alto, CA 415-324-8177
Allison, Glen/1910 Griffith Park Blvd, Los Angeles, CA 213-666-0883
Ambrosio, Joe/8230 Beverly Blvd #3, Los Angeles, CA 213-655-1505
Amdal, Philip/916 W Raye, Seattle, WA 206-282-8666
Andelotte, John/15747 East Valley Blvd, City of Industry, CA 818-961-2118
Andersen, Kurt/250 Newhall, San Francisco, CA 415-641-4276
Anderson, Karen/1170 N Western Ave, Los Angeles, CA 213-461-9100
Anderson, Rick/8871-B Balboa Ave, San Diego, CA 619-268-1957
Ansa, Brian/2605 N Lake Ave, Altadena, CA 818-797-2233
Apton, Bill/1060 Folsom St, San Francisco, CA 415-861-1840
Arend, Christopher/5401 Cordova St, Anchorage, AK 907-562-3173
Armas, Richard/6913 Melrose Ave, Los Angeles, CA 213-931-7889
Arnold, Robert Photo/1379 Natoma, San Francisco, CA 415-621-6161
Arnone, Ken/3886 Ampudia St, San Diego, CA 619-298-3141
Aron, Jeffrey/17801 Sky Park Cir #H, Irvine, CA 714-250-1555
Aronovsky, James/POB 83579, San Diego, CA 619-232-5855
Arzola, Frank/4903 Morena Blvd #1201, San Diego, CA 619-483-3810
Atiee, James/922 N Formosa Ave, Hollywood, CA 213-850-6112
Atkinson Photo/4320 Viewridge Ave #C, San Diego, CA 619-565-0672
Avery, Franklin/800 Duboce #201, San Francisco, CA 415 986-3701
Avery, Ron/11821 Mississippi Ave, Los Angeles, CA 213-477-1632
Ayres, Robert Bruce/8609 Venice Blvd, Los Angeles, CA 213-837-8190

B

Bacon, Garth/18576 Bucknall Rd, Saratoga, CA 408-866-5858
Bagley, John/730 Clemintina, San Francisco, CA 415-861-1062
Baker, Bill/265 29th St, Oakland, CA 415-832-7685
Baker, Frank/15031-B Parkway Loop, Tustin, CA 714-259-1462
Balderas, Michael/5837-B Mission Gorge Rd, San Diego, CA 619-563-7077
Baldwin, Doug/216 S Central Ave, Glendale, CA 818-547-9268
Banko, Phil/1249 First Ave S, Seattle, WA 206-621-7008
Banks, Ken/135 N Harper Ave, Los Angeles, CA 213-930-2831
Bardin, James/111 Villa View Dr, Pacific Palisades, CA 213-689-4566
Bare, John/3001 Red Hill Ave #4-102, Costa Mesa, CA 714-979-8712
Barkentin, Pamela/1218 N LaCienga, Los Angeles, CA 213-854-1941
Barnes, John/301 Parnassus #209, San Francisco, CA 415-431-5264
Barnhurst, Noel/34 Mountain Spring Ave, San Francisco, CA 415-731-9979
Barros, Robert/1813 E Sprague Ave, Spokane, WA 509-535-6455
Barta, Patrick/1274 Folsom, San Francisco, CA 415-626-6085
Bartay Studio/66 Retiro Way, San Francisco, CA 415-563-0551
Bartholick, Robin/89 Yesler Way 4th Fl, Seattle, WA 206-467-1001
Barton, Hugh G/33464 Bloomberg Rd, Eugene, OR 503-747-8184
Bartone, Laurence/335 Fifth St, San Francisco, CA 415-974-6010
Bartruff, Dave/PO Box 800, San Anselmo, CA 415-457-1482
Basse, Cary Photographers/6927 Forbes Ave, Van Nuys, CA 818-781-4856
Bates, Frank/5158 Highland View Ave, Los Angeles, CA 213-258-5272
Batista-Moon Studio/1620 Montgomery, San Francisco, CA 415-777-5566
Bayer, Dennis/130 Ninth St, San Francisco, CA 415-255-9467
Bear, Brent/8659 Hayden Pl, Culver City, CA 213-558-4471
Becker Bishop Studios/1830 17th St, San Francisco, CA 415-552-4254
Beebe, Morton/150 Lombard St #808, San Francisco, CA ...415-362-3530
Behrman, C H/8036 Kentwood, Los Angeles, CA 213-216-6611
Belcher, Richard/2565 Third St #206, San Francisco, CA 415-641-8912
Bell, Robert/1360 Logan Ave #105, Costa Mesa, CA 714-957-0772
Benchmark Photo/1442 N Hundley, Anaheim, CA 714-630-7965
Bencze, Louis/2442 NW Market St #86, Seattle, WA 206-283-6314
Benet, Ben/333 Fifth St #A, San Francisco, CA 415-974-5433
Bennion, Chris/5234 36th Ave NE, Seattle, WA 206-526-9981

Benson, Gary Photo/11110 34th Pl SW, Seattle, WA 206-242-3232
Benson, Hank/653 Bryant St, San Francisco, CA 415-543-8153
Benson, John/130 Ninth St #302, San Francisco, CA 415-621-5247
Benton, Richard/4810 Pescadero, San Diego, CA 619-224-0278
Bergman, Alan/8241 W 4th St, Los Angeles, CA 213-852-1408
Berman, Steve/7955 W 3rd, Los Angeles, CA 213-933-9185
Bernstein, Andrew/1450 N Chester, Pasadena, CA 818-797-3430
Bernstein, Gary/8735 Washington Blvd, Culver City, CA 213-550-6891
Bertholomey, John/17962 Sky Park Cir #J, Irvine, CA 714-261-0575
Betz, Ted R/527 Howard Top Fl, San Francisco, CA 415-777-1260
Bez, Frank/71 Zaca Lane, San Luis Obispo, CA 805-541-2878
Bielenberg, Paul/2447 Lanterman Terr, Los Angeles, CA 213-669-1085
Big City Visual Prdctn/1039 Seventh Ave , San Diego, CA ...619-232-3366
Biggs, Ken/1147 N Hudson Ave, Los Angeles, CA 213-462-7739
Bilecky, John/5047 W Pico Blvd, Los Angeles, CA 213-931-1610
Bilyell, Martin/600 NE Couch St, Portland, OR 503-238-0349
Bishop, David Photo/320 D Street, San Rafael, CA 415-
Bjoin, Henry/146 N La Brea Ave, Los Angeles, CA 213-937-4097
Black, Laurie/540 Seventh Ave, San Francisco, CA 503-665-5939
Blair, Richard/2207 Fourth St, Berkeley, CA 415-548-8350
Blakeley, Jim/1061 Folsom St, San Francisco, CA 415-558-9300
Blakeman, Bob/710 S Santa Fe, Los Angeles, CA 213-624-6662
Blattel, David/19730 Observation Dr, Topanga, CA 818-848-1166
Blaustein, Alan/885 Autumn Ln, Mill Valley, CA 415-383-1511
Blaustein, John/911 Euclid Ave, Berkeley, CA 415-525-8133
Bleyer, Pete/807 N Sierra Bonita Ave, Los Angeles, CA 213-653-6567
Blumensaadt, Mike/306 Edna, San Francisco, CA 415-333-6178
Bolanos, Edgar/PO Box 16328, San Francisco, CA 415-585-7805
Boonisar, Peter/PO Box 2274, Atascadero, CA 805-466-5577
Boudreau, Bernard/1015 N Cahuenga Blvd, Hollywood, CA 213-467-2602
Boulger & Kanuit/503 S Catalina, Redondo Beach, CA 213-540-6300
Bowen, John E/PO Box 1115, Hilo, HI 808-959-9460
Bowles, Bruce/526 Lombard, San Francisco, CA 415-362-8381
Boyd, Bill/201 E Haley St, Santa Barbara, CA 805-962-9193
Boyd, Jack/2038 Calvert Ave, Costa Mesa, CA 714-556-8332
Boyer, Dale/PO Box 391535, Mountainview, CA 415-968-9656
Boyer, Neil/1416 Aviation Blvd, Redondo Beach, CA 213-374-0443
Brabant, Patricia/245 S Van Ness 3rd Fl, San Francisco, CA 415-864-0591
Bracke, Vic/912 E 3rd St #106, Los Angeles, CA 213-625-1531
Bradley, Glenn/4618 W Jefferson, Los Angeles, CA 213-737-5156
Bradley, Leverett/Box 1793, Santa Monica, CA 213-394-0908
Bragstad, Jeremiah O/1041 Folsom St, San Francisco, CA ...415-776-2740
Brandon, Randy/PO Box 1010, Girdwood, AK 907-563-3351
Brazil, Larry/41841 Albrae St, Freemont, CA 415-657-1311
Brenneis, Jon/2576 Shattuck, Berkeley, CA 415-845-3377
Brewer, Art/27324 Camino Capistrano , Laguna Nigel, CA ...714-582-9085
Brewer, Bill/620 Moulton Ave #213, Los Angeles, CA 213-227-6861
Brewer, James/4649 Beverly Blvd #103, Los Angeles, CA ...213-461-6241
Brian, Rick/555 S Alexandria Ave, Los Angeles, CA 213-387-3017
Britt, Jim/140 N LaBrea, Los Angeles, CA 213-836-6317
Broaddus, Steve/6442 Santa Monica Blvd, Los Angeles, CA 213-466-9866
Brod, Garry/6502 Santa Monica Blvd, Hollywood, CA 213-463-7887
Brookhause, Win/2316 Porter St #11, Los Angeles, CA 213-488-9143
Brown, George/1417 15th St, San Francisco, CA 415-621-3543
Brown, Matt/PO Box 956, Anacortes, WA 206-293-3540
Brown, Michael/PO Box 45969, Los Angeles, CA 213-379-7254
Browne, Rick/145 Shake Tree Ln, Scotts Valley, CA 408-438-3919
Browne, Turner/10546 Greenwood Ave N, Seattle, WA 206-367-3782
Brubaker, Craig/11739 SW Beaverton Hwy, Beaverton, OR 503-647-9904
Brun, Kim/5555-L Santa Fe St, San Diego, CA 619-483-2124
Bubar, Julie/12559 Palero Rd, San Diego, CA 619-234-4020

Buchanan, Craig/1026 Folsom St #207,
San Francisco, CA (P 364) **415-861-5566**
Buckley, Jim/1310 Kawaihao St, Honolulu, HI 808-538-6128
Budnik, Victor/125 King St, San Francisco, CA 415-541-9050
Burke, Kevin/1015 N Cahuenga Blvd, Los Angeles, CA 213-467-0266
Burke, Leslie/947 La Cienega, Los Angeles, CA 213-652-7011

Burke/Triolo/940 East 2nd St #2, Los Angeles,
CA (P 350) **213-687-4730**
Burkhart, Howard/1783 S Holt Ave, Los Angeles, CA 213-836-9654
Burkholder, Jeff/3984 Park Circle Lane, Carmichael, CA 916-944-2128
Burman & Steinheimer/2648 Fifth Ave, Sacramento, CA 916-457-1908
Burr, Bruce/2867 1/2 W 7th St, Los Angeles, CA 213-388-3361
Burr, Lawrence/76 Manzanita Rd, Fairfax, CA 415-456-9158
Burroughs, Robert/6713 Bardonia St, San Diego, CA 619-469-6922
Burry, D L/PO Box 1611, Los Gatos, CA 408-354-1922
Burt, Pat/1412 SE Stark, Portland, OR 503-284-9989
Burton, Steve/PO Box 52092, Pacific Grove, CA 408-372-1610
Bush, Chan/PO Box 819, Montrose, CA 818-957-6558

Bush, Charles/940 N Highland Ave, Los Angeles, CA......................213-466-6630
Bush, Dave/2 St George Alley, San Francisco, CA 415-981-2874
Busher, Dick/7042 20th Place NE, Seattle, WA 206-523-1426
Butler, Erik/655 Bryant St, San Francisco, CA 415-777-1656

C

C & I Photography/3523 Ryder St, Santa Clara, CA 408-733-5855
Cable, Ron/17835 Skypark Cir #N, Irvine, CA......................714-261-8910
Caccavo, James/1000 S Crescent Hts Blvd, Los Angeles, CA 213-939-9594
Cacitti, Stanley R/589 Howard, San Francisco, CA......................415-974-5668
Campbell Comm Photo/8586 Miramar Pl, San Diego, CA......................619-587-0336
Campbell, Tom + Assoc/PO Box 1409, Topanga Canyon, CA 213-473-6054
Campbell, Willis Preston/1015 Cedar St, Santa Cruz, CA......................408-425-5700
Campos, Michael/705 13th St, San Diego, CA......................619-233-9914
Cannon, Bill/516 Yale Ave North, Seattle, WA......................206-682-7031
Caplan, Stan/7014 Santa Monica Blvd, Los Angeles, CA......................213-462-1271
Capps, Alan/137 S La Peer Dr, Los Angeles, CA......................213-276-3724
Capra, Robert/1256 Lindell Dr, Walnut Creek, CA......................415-947-0323
Caputo, Tony/6636 Santa Monica Blvd, Hollywood, CA......................213-464-6636
Carey, Ed/438 Treat Ave, San Francisco, CA......................415-621-2349
Carlson, Craig/266 J Street, Chula Vista, CA......................619-422-4937
Carlson, Joe/901 El Centro, S Pasadena, CA......................213-682-1020
Carofano, Ray/1011 1/4 W 190th St, Gardena, CA......................213-515-0310
Carpenter, Mert/2020 Granada Wy, Los Gatos, CA......................408-370-1663
Carroll, Bruce/517 Dexter Ave N, Seattle, WA......................206-623-2119
Carroll, Tom/26712 Calle Los Alamos, Capistrano Beach, CA.........714-493-2665
Carroon, Chip/PO Box 590451, San Francisco, CA......................415-864-1082
Carruth, Kerry/9428 Eton Ave #H, Chatsworth, CA......................818-718-4014
Carry, Mark/3375 Forest Ave, Santa Clara, CA......................408-248-7872
Cartwright, Casey/434 9th St, San Francisco, CA......................415-621-7393
Casilli, Mario/2366 N Lake Ave, Altadena, CA......................213-681-4476
Casler, Christopher/1600 Viewmont Dr, Los Angeles, CA......................213-854-7733
Cato, Eric/7224 Hillside Ave #38, Los Angeles, CA......................213-851-5606
Caulfield, Andy/PO Box 41131, Los Angeles, CA......................213-258-3070
Chamberlain, Paul/319 1/2 S Robertson Blvd, Beverly Hills, CA 213-659-4647
Chaney, Brad/1750 Army St #H, San Francisco, CA......................415-826-2030
Charles, Cindy/1040 Noe St, San Francisco, CA......................415-821-4457
Chase, Julie/400 Treat Ave #E, San Francisco, CA......................415-863-4749
Chen, James/1917 Anacapa St, Santa Barbara, CA......................805-569-1849
Chen, Ken/11622 Idaho Ave #6, Los Angeles, CA......................213-826-8272
Chernus, Ken/9531 Washington Blvd, Culver City, CA......................213-838-3116
Chesser, Mike/5290 W Washington Blvd, Los Angeles, CA......................213-934-5211
Chester, Mark/PO Box 99501, San Francisco, CA......................415-922-7512
Chin, Albert/1150 Homer St, Vancouver V6B 2X6, BC......................604-685-2000
Chin, K P/PO Box 421737, San Francisco, CA......................415-282-3041
Chmielewski, David/230-C Polaris, Mountain View, CA......................415-969-6639
Christensen, David/321 Collingwood #2, San Francisco, CA 415-647-7442
Chubb, Ralph/340 Tesconi Cicle #B, Santa Rosa, CA......................707-579-9995
Chung, Ken-Lei/5200 Venice Blvd, Los Angeles, CA......................213-938-9117
Ciskowski, Jim/2444 Wilshire Blvd #B100, Santa Monica, CA 213-829-7375
Clark, Richard/334 S LaBrea, Los Angeles, CA......................213-933-7407
Clark, Tom/2042 1/2 N Highland, Hollywood, CA......................213-851-1650
Clayton, John/160 South Park, San Francisco, CA......................415-495-4562
Clement, Michele/221 11th St, San Francisco, CA......................415-558-9540
Cobb, Bruce/1537-A 4th St #102, San Rafael, CA......................415-454-0619
Cobb, Rick/10 Liberty Ship Way, Sausalito, CA......................415-332-8739
Coccia, Jim/PO Box 81313, Fairbanks, AK......................907-479-4707
Cocco, Dan/2283 Lincoln Ave, San Jose, CA......................408-978-7300
Cogen, Melinda/1112 N Beachwood Dr, Hollywood, CA......................213-467-9414
Cohen, Hilda/637 N Harper Ave, Los Angeles, CA......................213-655-4004
Coit, Jim/1205 J St #A, San Diego, CA......................619-234-2874
Cole, Steve/16710 Orange Ave #A-4, Paramount, CA......................213-408-1008
Coleman, Arthur/303 N Indian Ave, Palm Springs, CA......................619-325-7015
Colladay, Charles/705 13th Ave, San Diego, CA......................619-231-2920
Collison, James/6950 Havenurst, Van Nuys, CA......................818-995-3171
Coluzzi, Tony/897 Independence Ave #2B, Mt View, CA......................415-969-2955
Connell, John/4120 Birch St #108, Newport Beach, CA......................714-995-3212
Connors, William/, Los Angeles, CA
Conrad, Chris/719 East Pike, Seattle, WA......................206-324-2208
Cook, Kathleen Norris/PO Box 2159, Laguna Hills, CA......................714-770-4619
Corell, Volker/3797 Lavell Dr, Los Angeles, CA......................213-255-3336
Cormier, Glenn/828 K St #305, San Diego, CA......................619-237-5006
Cornfield, Jim/8609 Venice Blvd, Los Angeles, CA......................213-204-5747
Cornwell, David/1311 Kalakaua Ave, Honolulu, HI......................808-949-7000
Corwin, Jeff/CPC Assoc/1910 Weepah Way, Los Angeles, CA 213-656-7449
Courbet, Yves/6516 W 6th St, Los Angeles, CA......................213-655-2181
Courtney, William/4524 Rutgers Way, Sacramento, CA......................916-487-8501
Cowin, Morgin/5 Windsor Ave, San Rafael, CA......................415-459-7722

Crane, Wally/PO Box 81, Los Altos, CA 415-960-1990
Crepea, Nick/12137 Kristy Lane, Saratoga, CA......................408-257-5704
Crowley, Eliot/3221 Benda Place, Los Angeles,
CA (P 348) **213-851-5110**
Cummings, Ian/2400 Kettner Blvd, San Diego, CA......................619-231-1270
Cummins, Jim/1527 13th Ave, Seattle, WA......................206-322-4944
Curtis, MP/2400 E Lynn St, Seattle, WA 206-323-1230

D

Dahlstrom Photography Inc/2312 NW Savier St, Portland, OR.........503-222-4910
Dajani, Haas/405 Eldridge Ave, Mill Valley, CA......................415-383-3291
Dancs, Andras/518 Beatty St #603, Vancouver V6B 2L3, BC.........604-684-6760
Daniel, Jay/517 Jacoby St #11, San Rafael, CA......................415-459-1495
Daniels, Charles/905 N Cole Ave #2120, Hollywood,
CA (P 366,367) **213-463-7513**
Dannehl, Dennis/3303 Beverly Blvd, Los Angeles, CA......................213-388-3888
Davenport, Jim/PO Box 296, Chula Vista, CA......................619-549-8733
David/Gayle Photo/911 Western Ave #510, Seattle, WA......................206-624-5207
Davidson, Dave/25003 S Beeson Rd, Beavercreek, OR......................503-632-7650
Davidson, Jerry/3923 W Jefferson Blvd, Los Angeles, CA 213-735-1552
Davis, Tim/PO Box 1278, Palo Alto, CA 415-327-4192
Day, Bob/1922 Leavenworth St, San Francisco, CA......................415-387-0191
Dayton, Ted/1112 N Beachwood, Los Angeles, CA......................213-462-0712
DeCastro, Mike/2415 De La Cruz, Santa Clara, CA......................408-988-8696
DeCruyenaere, Howard/1825 E Albion Ave, Santa Ana, CA......................714-997-4446
DeGabriele, Dale/900 1st Ave S #305, Seattle, WA......................206-624-9928
deGennaro Associates/902 South Norton Ave,
Los Angeles, CA (P 344,345) **213-935-5179**
Degler, Curtis/1050 Carolan Ave #311, Burlingame, CA......................415-342-7381
Del Re, Sal/211-E East Columbine Ave, Santa Ana, CA......................714-432-1333
Delancie, Steve/790 Church St #202, San Francisco, CA......................415-864-2640
Delzell, Bill/2325 3rd St #409, San Francisco, CA......................415-626-3467
Demerdjian, Jacob/3331 W Beverly Blvd, Montebello, CA......................213-724-9630
Denman, Frank B/1201 First Ave S, Seattle, WA......................206-325-9260
Denny, Michael/2631 Ariane Dr, San Diego, CA......................619-272-9104
Denson, Walt/3792 N Ranchford Ct, Concord, CA......................212-496-7305
DePaola, Mark/1560 Benedict Cnyn Dr, Beverly Hills, CA......................213-550-5910
Der Cruyenaere, Howard/1825 E Albion Ave, Santa Ana, CA 714-997-4446
Der, Rick Photography/50 Mandell St, San Francisco, CA......................415-824-8580
Deras, Frank/342 N Ferndale Ave, Mill Valley, CA......................415-381-2324
Derhacopian, Ronald/3109 Beverly Blvd, Los Angeles, CA......................213-388-6724
DeSilva, Dennis/3449 San Pablo Dam Rd, El Sobrante, CA......................415-222-0385
Devol, Thomas/236 W First Ave, Chico, CA......................916-894-8277
DeVries, Nancy/11740 Sunset Blvd, Los Angeles, CA......................213-874-2200
DeWilde, Roc/953 Mt View Dr #119, Lafayette, CA......................415-934-1119
DeYoung, Skip/1112 N Beachwood, Los Angeles, CA......................213-462-0712
Diaz, Armando/19 S Park, San Francisco, CA......................415-495-3552
Digital Art/3000 S Robertson Blvd #260, Los Angeles, CA......................213-836-7631
Dockery, Alan/4679 Hollywood Blvd, Los Angeles, CA......................213-662-8153
Dominick/833 N LaBrea Ave, Los Angeles, CA......................213-934-3033
Donaldson, Peter/118 King St, San Francisco, CA......................415-957-1102
Dorr, Ken/1 Grand View Ave, San Francisco, CA......................415-647-1087
Dow, Larry/1537 W 8th St, Los Angeles, CA......................213-483-7970
Drake, Brian/407 Southwest 11th Ave, Portland, OR......................503-241-4532
Dreiwitz, Herb/3906 Franklin Ave, Los Angeles, CA......................213-662-0622
Dresser, Rod/1620 Montgomery St, San Francisco, CA......................415-781-2726
Dressler, Rick/1322 Bell Ave #M, Tustin, CA......................714-730-9113
Driver, Wallace/2540 Clairemont Dr #305, San Diego, CA......................619-275-3159
Drobek, Carol/1260 Broadway #106, San Francisco, CA......................415-776-6188
Duff, Rodney/4901 Morena Blvd #323, San Diego, CA......................619-270-4082
Duffey, Robert/9691 Campus Dr, Anaheim, CA......................714-956-4731
Duka, Lonnie/919 Oriole Dr, Laguna Beach, CA......................714-494-7057
Dull, Ed/1745 NW Marshall, Portland, OR......................503-224-3754
Dumentz, Barbara/39 E Walnut St, Pasadena, CA......................213-467-6397
Dunbar, Clark/1260-B Pear Ave, Mountain View, CA......................415-964-4225
Dunmire, Larry/PO Box 338, Balboa Island, CA......................714-673-4058
Dunn, Roger/544 Weddell Dr #3, Sunnyvale, CA......................408-730-1630
Durke, Vernon W/842 Folsom #128, San Francisco,
CA (P 368) **415-648-1262**
Dyer, Larry/1659 Waller St, San Francisco, CA......................415-668-8049

E

Ealy, Dwayne/2 McLaren #B, Irvine, Ca......................714-951-5089
Earnest, Robert G/1407 Buena Vista #6,
San Clemente, CA (P 353) **714-498-6488**
Edmunds, Dana/188 N King St, Honolulu, HI......................808-521-7711
Edwards, Grant P/1470 Rancho Encinitas Dr, Olivenhain, CA.........619-458-1999
Ehrlich, Seth/1046 N Orange Dr, Hollywood, CA 213-462-5256

Elgin, John-Paul/20812 Vose St, Canoga Park, CA....818-347-7719
Elias, Robert Studio/959 N Cole, Los Angeles, CA....213-460-2988
Elk, John III/3163 Wisconsin, Oakland, CA....415-531-7469
Emanuel, Manny/2257 Hollyridge Dr, Hollywood, CA....213-465-0259
Emberly, Gordon/1479 Folsom, San Francisco, CA....415-621-9714
English, Rick/639 High St, Palo Alto, CA....415-328-1155
Enkelis, Liane/764 Sutter Ave, Palo Alto, CA....415-326-3253
Epstein, Rachel/PO Box 772, Ukiah, CA....707-468-0514
Ergenbright, Ric/PO Box 1067, Bend, OR (P 369)....503-389-7662
Erickson, Susan/17791 Fjord Dr NE, Poulsbo, WA....206-697-1994
Esgro, Dan/PO Box 38536, Los Angeles, CA....213-932-1919
Eskenazy, Marcel/1231 24th St #4, Santa Monica, CA....213-828-4464
Estel, Suzanne/2325 3rd St, San Francisco, CA....415-864-3661
Evans, Marty/6850-K Vineland Ave, N Hollywood, CA....818-762-5400

F

Fabrick, Ken/1320 Venice Blvd #308, Venice, CA....213-822-1030
Fahey, Michael/608 3rd St, San Raphael, CA....415-459-8777
Falconer, Michael/610 22nd St, San Francisco, CA....415-626-7774
Falk, Randolph/123 16th Ave, San Francisco, CA....415-751-8800
Faries, Tom/8520 Ostrich Circle, Fountain Valley, CA....714-775-5767
Farruggio, Matthew J/3239 Kempton, Oakland, CA....415-444-0665
Faubel, Warren/627 S Highland Ave, Los Angeles, CA....213-939-8822
Feldman, Marc/6442 Santa Monica Blvd, Hollywood, CA....213-463-4829
Feller, Bob/Worldway Ctr #91435, Los Angeles, CA....213-670-1177
Felt, Jim/1316 SE 12th Ave, Portland, OR....503-238-1748
Felzman, Joe/4504 SW Corbett Ave #120, Portland, OR....503-224-7983
Ferro, Daniel/559 Matadero Ave #6, Palo Alto, CA....415-424-9681
Finnegan, Kristin/3045 NW Thurman St, Portland, OR....503-241-2701
Firebaugh, Steve/6750 55th Ave South, Seattle, WA (P 370,371)....206-721-5151
Fischer, Curt/51 Stillman St, San Francisco, CA....415-974-5568
Fisher, Arthur Vining/271 Missouri St, San Francisco, CA....415-626-5483
Fitch, Wanelle/1142 Manhattan Ave , Manhattan Beach, CA....213-546-2490
Flavin, Frank/901 W 54th St, Anchorage, AK....907-561-1606
Flood, Alan/206 14th Ave, San Mateo, CA....415-572-0439
Fogg, Don/400 Treat St #E, San Francisco, CA....415-974-5244
Foothorap, Robert/426 Bryant St, San Francisco, CA....415-957-1447
Forsman, John/8696 Crescent Dr, Los Angeles, CA....213-933-9339
Forster, Bruce/431 NW Flanders, Portland, OR....503-222-5222
Fort, Daniel/PO Box 11324, Costa Mesa, CA....714-546-5709
Fowler, Bradford/1522 SAnborn Ave, Los Angeles, CA....213-464-5708
Frankel, Tracy/641 Bay St, Santa Monica, CA....213-396-2766
Franklin, Charly/3352 20th St, San Francisco, CA (P 372)....415-824-4000
Franz-Moore, Paul/855 Folsom St #204, San Francisco, CA....415-495-6183
Franzen, David/746 Ilaniwai St #200, Honolulu, HI....808-537-9921
Fraser, Peter/863 S Winchester Blvd #274, San Jose, CA....408-985-9280
Frazier, Kim Andrew/PO Box 6132, Hayward, CA....415-889-7050
Freed, Jack/749 N La Brea, Los Angeles, CA....213-931-1015
Freeman, Hunter/1123 S Park, San Francisco, CA....415-495-1900
Freis, Jay/416 Richardson St, Sausalito, CA....415-332-6709
French, Peter/PO Box 100, Kamuela, HI....808-889-6488
Friedlander, Ernie/275 Sixth St, San Francisco, CA....415-777-3373
Friedman, Todd/PO Box 3737, Beverly Hills, CA....213-474-6715
Friend, David/3886 Ampudia St, San Diego, CA....619-260-1603
Frigge, Eric/, ,....714-854-2985
Frisch, Stephen/ICB - Gate 5 Rd, Sausalito, CA....415-332-4545
Frisella, Josef/340 S Clark Dr, Beverly Hills, CA....213-659-7676
Fritz, Michael/PO Box 4386, San Diego, CA (P 373)....619-281-3297
Fritz, Steve/3201 San Gabriel Ave, Glendale, CA....213-629-8052
Fritze, Jack/2106 S Grand, Santa Ana, CA....714-545-6466
Fruchtman, Jerry/8735 Washington Blvd, Culver City, CA....213-839-7891
Fry, George B III/PO Box 2465, Menlo Park, CA....415-323-7663
Fujioka, Robert/715 Stierlin Rd, Mt View, CA....415-960-3010
Fukuda, Steve/454 Natoma, San Francisco, CA....415-543-9339
Fukuhara, Richard Yutaka/1032-2 Taft Ave, Orange, CA....714-998-8790
Fuller, George/4091 Lincoln Ave, Oakland, CA....415-530-3814
Furon, Daniel/1456 63rd St, Emeryville, CA....415-655-0504
Furuta, Carl/7360 Melrose Ave, Los Angeles, CA....213-655-1911
Fusco, Paul/7 Melody Ln, Mill Valley, CA....415-388-8940

G

Gage, Rob/789 Pearl St, Laguna Beach, CA....714-494-7265
Gallagher, John/PO Box 4070, Seattle, WA....206-937-2422
Galvan, Gary/4626 1/2 Hollywood Blvd, Los Angeles, CA....213-667-1457
Garcia, Elma/2565 Third St #308, San Francisco, CA....415-641-9992
Gardner, Robert/800 S Citrus Ave, Los Angeles, CA....213-931-1108
Gasperini, Robert/PO Box 954, Folsom, CA....916-985-6474
Gelineau, Val/1265 S Cochran, Los Angeles, CA....213-465-6149
Gendreau, Raymond/303-B Belmont Ave East, Seattle, WA (P 374,375)....206-527-1999
Gerretsen, Charles/1714 N Wilton Pl, Los Angeles, CA....213-462-6342
Gersten, Paul/1021 1/2 N La Brea, Los Angeles, CA....213-850-6045
Gervais, Lois/923 E 3rd St, Los Angeles, CA....213-617-3338
Gervase, Mark/PO Box 38573, Los Angeles, CA....213-877-0928
Ghelerter, Michael/1020 41st St, Emeryville, CA....415-547-8456
Giannetti Photo730 Clementina St, San Francisco, CA....415-864-0270
Gibbs, Christopher/700-B W 58th St, Anchorage, AK....907-563-6112
Gick, Peter/659 W Dryden St #5, Glendale, CA....818-500-0880
Giefer, Sebastian/3132 Hollyridge Dr, Hollywood, CA....213-461-1122
Gilbert, Elliot/311 N Curson Ave, Los Angeles, CA....213-939-1846
Gillman, Mitchell/610 22nd St #307, San Francisco, CA....415-621-5334
Gilmore, Ed/54 Palm Ave, San Francisco, CA....415-861-7882
Giraud, Steve/2960 Airway Ave #B-103, Costa Mesa, CA....714-751-8191
Gleis, Nick/4040 Del Rey #7, Marina Del Rey, CA....213-823-4229
Glendinning, Edward/1001 East 1st St, Los Angeles, CA....213-617-1630
Glenn, Joel/439 Bryant St, San Francisco, CA....415-957-1273
Gnass, Jeff/PO Box 2196, Oroville, CA....916-533-6788
Goavec, Pierre/1464 La Playa #303, San Francisco, CA....415-564-2252
Goble, James/620 Moulton Ave #205, Los Angeles, CA....213-222-7661
Goble, Jeff/300 Second Ave W, Seattle, WA....206-285-8765
Godwin, Bob/1427 E 4th St #1, Los Angeles, CA....213-269-8001
Going, Michael/1117 N Wilcox Pl, Los Angeles, CA....213-465-6853
Goldman, Larry/23674 Stagg, West Hills, CA....818-347-6865
Goldner, David/833 Traction Ave, Los Angeles, CA....212-617-0761
Goldstein, Larry/21 E 5th St, Vancouver V6H 1N5, BC....604-877-1117
Goodman, Todd/1417 26th #E, Santa Monica, CA....213-453-3621
Gordon, Jon/2052 Los Feliz Dr, Thousand Oaks, CA....805-496-1485
Gordon, Larry Dale/225 Crossroads #410, Carmel, CA....408-624-1313
Gorman, Greg/1351 Miller Dr, Los Angeles, CA....213-650-5540
Gottlieb, Mark/1915 University Ave, Palo Alto, CA....415-321-8761
Gowans, Edward/10316 NW Thompson Rd, Portland, OR....503-223-4573
Grady, Noel/277 Rodney Ave, Encinitas, CA....619-753-8630
Graham, Don/1545 Marlay Dr, Los Angeles, CA....213-656-7117
Graham, Ellen/614 N Hillcrest Rd, Beverly Hills, CA....213-275-6195
Graves, Robert/30 NW 1st Ave #202, Portland, OR....503-226-0099
Gray, Dennis/8705 W Washington Blvd, Culver City, CA....213-559-1711
Gray, Marion/42 Orben Pl, San Francisco, CA....415-821-7079
Gray, Todd/1962 N Wilcox, Los Angeles, CA....213-466-6088
Greene, Jim Photo/PO Box 2150, Del Mar, CA....619-270-8121
Greenleigh, John/756 Natoma, San Francisco, CA....415-864-4147
Grigg, Robert/1050 N Wilcox Ave, Hollywood, CA....213-469-6316
Grimm, Tom & Michelle/PO Box 83, Laguna Beach, CA....714-494-1336
Grodske, Kirk/19235-7 Hamlin St, Reseda, CA....818-344-5966
Groenekamp, Greg/2922 Oakhurst Ave, Los Angeles, CA....213-838-2466
Groutoge, Monty/2214 S Fairview Rd, Santa Ana, CA....714-751-8734
Gunn, Lorenzo/POB 13352, San Diego, CA....619-280-6010

H

Hagopian, Jim/915 N Mansfield Ave, Hollywood, CA....213-856-0018
Hagyard, Dave/1205 E Pike, Seattle, WA....206-322-8419
Haislip, Kevin/PO Box 1862, Portland, OR....503-254-8859
Hale, Bruce H/421 Bryant St, San Francisco, CA....415-882-9695
Hall, Bill Photo/917 20th St, Sacramento, CA....916-443-3330
Hall, George/601 Minnesota St, San Francisco, CA....415-821-7373
Hall, Norman/55 New Montgomery St, San Francisco, CA....415-543-8070
Hall, Steven/645 N Eckhoff St #P, Orange, CA....714-634-1132
Hall, William/19881 Bushard St, Huntington Bch, CA....714-968-2473
Halle, Kevin/8165 Commerce Ave, San Diego, CA....619-549-8881
Hamilton, David W/725 S Eliseo Dr #4, Greenbrea, CA....415-461-5901
Hamman, Rich/3015 Shipway Ave, Long Beach, CA....213-421-5708
Hammid, Tino/6305 Yucca St #500, Los Angeles, CA....213-461-8017
Hammond, Paul/1200 Carlisle, San Mateo, CA....415-574-9192
Hampton, Wally/4190 Rockaway Beach, Bainbridge Isl, WA....206-842-9900
Hanauer, Mark/2228 21st St, Santa Monica, CA....213-462-2421
Hands, Bruce/PO Box 16186, Seattle, WA....206-938-8620
Hansen, Jim/2800 S Main St #1, Santa Ana, CA....714-545-1343
Hara/265 Prado Rd #4, San Luis Obispo, CA....805-543-6907
Harding, C B/660 N Thompson St, Portland, OR....503-281-9907
Harmel, Mark/714 North Westbourne Dr, West Hollywood, CA (P 354)....213-659-1633
Harrington, Kim/1420 45th St 326, Emeryville, CA....415-653-6554
Harrington, Marshall/2775 Kurtz St #2, San Diego, CA....619-291-2775
Harris, Paul/4601 Larkwood Ave, Woodland Hills, CA....818-347-8294

Hart, G K/780 Bryant St, San Francisco, CA 415-495-4278
Hart, Jerome/4612 NE Alameda, Portland, OR 503-224-3003
Hartman, Raiko/1060 N Lillian Way, Los Angeles, CA 213-278-4700
Harvey, Stephen/7801 West Beverly Blvd, Los Angeles, CA (P 376) 213-934-5817
Hastings, Ryan/309 S Cloverdale, Seattle, WA 206-762-8691
Hathaway, Steve/400 Treat Ave #F, San Francisco, CA....415-255-2100
Hawkes, William/5757 Venice Blvd, Los Angeles, CA 213-931-7777
Hawley, Larry/6502 Santa Monica Blvd, Hollywood, CA....213-466-5864
Healy, Brian/333-A 7th St, San Francisco, CA....415-861-1008
Heffernan, Terry/352 6th St, San Francisco, CA....415-626-1999
Hellerman, Robert/920 N Citrus Ave, Los Angeles, CA 213-466-6030
Henderson, Tom/11722 Sorrento Vly Rd #A, San Diego, CA 619-481-7743
Hendrick, Howard/839 Bridge Rd, San Leandro, CA....415-483-1483
Herrin, Kelly/1623 South Boyd, Santa Ana, ca 714-261-1102
Herrmann, Karl/3165 S Barrington Ave #F, Los Angeles, CA....213-397-5917
Herron, Matt/PO Box 1860, Sausalito, CA 415-479-6994
Hess, Geri/134 S Roxbury Dr, Beverly Hills, CA....213-276-3638
Hewett, Richard/5725 Buena Vista Terr, Los Angeles, CA 213-254-4577
Hicks, Alan/333 N W Park, Portland, OR 503-226-6741
Hicks, Jeff/41 E Main St, Los Gatos, CA 408-395-2277
Higgins, Donald/201 San Vincente Blvd, Santa Monica, CA 213-393-8858
Hildreth, James/2374 25th Ave, San Francisco, CA 415-821-7398
Hill, Dennis/20 N Raymond Ave #14, Pasadena, CA 818-795-2589
Hiller, Geoff/44 Jersey St, San Francisco, CA 415-824-7020
Hines, Richard/734 E 3rd St, Los Angeles, CA 213-625-2333
Hirshew, Lloyd/750 Natoma, San Francisco, CA 415-861-3902
Hishi, James/612 S Victory Blvd, Burbank, CA 213-849-4871
Hixson, Richard/1261 Howard St, San Francisco, CA 415-621-0246
Hodes, Brian Black/812 S Robertson Blvd, Los Angeles, CA....213-282-0500
Hodges, Rose/2325 3rd St #401, San Francisco, CA 415-550-7612
Hodges, Walter/1605 Twelfth Ave #25, Seattle, WA 206-325-9550
Hoffman, Davy/1923 Colorado Ave, Santa Monica, CA 213-453-4661
Hoffman, Paul/4500 19th St, San Francisco, CA....415-863-3575
Hofmann, Mark/827 N Fairfax Ave, Los Angeles, CA 213-450-4236
Hogg, Peter/1221 S La Brea, Los Angeles, CA....213-937-0642
Holden, Andrew/17944-M Sky Park Circle, Irvine, CA 714-553-9455
Hollenbeck, Cliff/Box 4247 Pioneer Sq, Seattle, WA 206-682-6300
Holmes, Mark/PO Box 556, Mill Valley, CA....415-383-6783
Holmes, Robert/PO Box 556, Mill Valley, CA....415-383-6783
Holt, David/1624 Cotner Ave #B, Los Angeles, CA (P 340,341) 213-478-1188
Honolulu Creative Group/424 Nahua St, Honolulu, HI 808-926-6188
Honowitz, Ed/39 E Walnut St, Pasadena, CA....818-584-4050
Hopkins, Stew/414 Rose Ave, Venice, CA....213-935-3527
Horikawa, Michael/508 Kamakee St, Honolulu, HI....808-538-7378
Housel, James F/84 University Pl #409, Seattle, WA....206-682-6181
Howe, Christina/17202 NE *5th Pl #J119, Redmond, WA 206-869-9348
Hudetz, Larry/11135 SE Yamhill, Portland, OR 503-245-6001
Hunt, Phillip/3435 Army St #206, San Francisco, CA....415-821-9879
Hunter, Jeff/4626 1/2 Hollywood Blvd, Los Angeles, CA 213-669-0468
Hussey, Ron/229 Argonne #2, Long Beach, CA 213-439-4438
Hylen, Bo/1640 S LaCienega, Los Angeles, CA 213-271-6543
Hyun, Douglass/13601 Ventura Blvd, Sherman Oaks, CA....818-789-4729

I

Illusion Factory/4657 Abargo St, Woodland Hills, CA....818-883-4501
Imstepf, Charles/620 Moulton Ave #216, Los Angeles, CA 213-222-8773
Ingham, Stephen/2717 NW St Helens Rd, Portland, OR....503-274-9788
Ingham, Steven/2717 NW St Helens Rd, Portland, OR 503-274-9788
Iri, Carl/5745 Scrivener, Long Beach, CA....213-658-5822
Irwin, Dennis/164 Park Ave, Palo Alto, CA 415-321-7959
Isaacs, Robert/1646 Mary Ave, Sunnyvale, CA 408-245-1690
Iverson, Michele/1527 Princeton #2, Santa Monica, CA 213-829-5717

J

Jacobs, Michael/646 N Cahuenga Blvd, Los Angeles, CA....213-461-0240
James, Patrick/1412 Santa Cruz, San Pedro, CA....213-519-1357
Jarnell, Kirk/PO Box 3653, Chico, CA 916-345-1903
Jarrett, Michael/16812 Red Hill, Irvine, CA....714-250-3377
Jay, Michael/1 Zeno Pl Folsom Cmplx, San Francisco, CA....415-543-7101
Jenkin, Bruce/1305 E St/Gertrude Pl #D, Santa Ana, CA....714-546-2949
Jenner, Steve/5950 Grizzly Peak Blvd, Oakland, CA 415-547-3300
Jensen, John/449 Bryant St, San Francisco, CA....415-957-9449
Johannesson Photography/1162 E Valencia Dr, Fullerton, CA....714-738-1152
Johnson, Charles/2124 3rd Ave W, Seattle, WA....206-284-6223
Johnson, Conrad/350 Sunset Ave, Venice, CA 213-392-0541
Johnson, Edward/11823 Blythe St, N Hollywood, CA 818-765-2890
Johnson, Payne B/4650 Harvey Rd, San Diego, CA....619-299-4567
Johnson, Ron Photo/2104 Valley Glen, Orange, CA 714-637-1145
Johnson, Stuart/688 S Santa Fe Ave #301, Los Angeles, CA 213-488-1675
Jones, Aaron/608 Folsom St, San Francisco, CA....415-495-6333
Jones, William B/2171 India St #B, San Diego, CA....619-235-8892

K

Kaake, Phillip/47 Lusk, San Francisco, CA 415-546-4079
Kaestner, Reed/2120 J Durante Blvd #4, Del Mar, CA....619-755-1200
Kahoon, John/1419-C Elliott Ave West, Seattle, WA....206-282-6111
Kaldor, Kurt/1011 Grandview Dr, S San Francisco, CA....415-583-8704
Kallewaard, Susan/PO Box 7808, Fremont, CA 415-792-3147
Kam, Henrick/2325 3rd St #408, San Francisco, CA 415-861-7093
Kamens, Les/333-A 7th St, San Francisco, CA....415-621-1888
Kamin, Bonnie/PO Box 745, Fairfax, CA 415-456-5913
Kaplan, Fred/5618 Berkshire Dr, Los Angeles, CA 213-227-8858
Karageorge, Jim/610 22nd St #309, San Francisco, CA 415-648-3444
Karau, Timothy/4213 Collis Ave, Los Angeles, CA....213-221-9749
Kasmier, Richard/441 E Columbine #I, Santa Ana, CA 714-545-4022
Kasparowitz, Josef/PO Box 14408, San Luis Obispo, CA....805-544-8209
Katano, Nicole/112 N Harper, Los Angeles, CA....213-655-1717
Katzenberger, George/211-D E Columbine St, Santa Ana, CA....714-545-3055
Kauffman, Helen/9017 Rangeley Ave, Los Angeles, CA....213-275-3569
Kaufman, Mitch/2244 Walnut Grove Ave, Rosemead, CA 818-302-7983
Kaufman, Robert/259 Ridge Rd, San Carlos, CA....415-369-5908
Kauschke, Hans-Gerhard/13 Oak St, Sausalito, CA 415-383-4230
Kearney, Ken/8048 Soquel Dr, Aptos, CA 408-688-4546
Keenan, Elaine Faris/421 Bryan St, San Francisco, CA 415-546-9246
Keenan, Larry/421 Bryant Street, San Francisco, CA (P 377)....415-495-6474
Kehl, Robert/769 22nd St, Oakland, CA....415-452-0501
Keller, Greg/769 22nd St, Oakland, CA....415-452-0501
Kelley, Tom/8525 Santa Monica Blvd, Los Angeles, CA 213-657-1780
Kermani, Shahn/109 Minna St #210, San Francisco, CA 415-567-6073
Kerns, Ben/1201 First Ave S, Seattle, WA 206-621-7636
Kilberg, James/3371 Cahuenga Blvd W, Los Angeles, CA....213-874-9514
Killian, Glen/1270 Rio Vista, Los Angeles, CA....213-263-6567
Kim, James/5765 Thorwood Dr, Santa Barbara, CA 805-964-1400
Kimball, Ron/1960 Colony, Mt View, CA 415-948-2939
Kimball-Nanessence/PO Box 2408, Julian, CA....619-762-0765
Kimura, Margaret/940 N Highland Ave, Los Angeles, CA 213-467-1923
King, CR/2420 24th St, San Francisco, CA 415-652-5112
King, Kathleen/1932 1st Ave, Seattle, WA....206-443-2800
King, Nicholas/3102 Moore St, San Diego, CA 619-296-8200
King, Taylor/620 Moulton Ave #210, Los Angeles, CA 213-225-9722
Kious, Gary/9800 Sepulvada Blvd #304, Los Angeles, CA 213-536-4880
Kirkland, Douglas/9060 Wonderland Pk Ave, Los Angeles, CA 213-656-8511
Kirkpatrick, Mike/1115 Forest Way, Brookdale, CA....408-395-1447
Kleinman, Kathryn/3020 Bridgeway #315, Sausalito, CA 415-331-5070
Knox, Karl/2440 16th St #205, San Francisco, CA....415-898-7632
Kobayashi, Ken/1750-H Army St, San Francisco, CA....415-826-4382
Koch, Jim/1360 Logan Ave #106, Costa Mesa, CA 714-957-5719
Kodama & Moriarty/4081 Glencoe Ave, Marina Del Rey, CA....213-306-7574
Koehler, Rick/1622 Edinger #A, Tustin, CA 714-259-8787
Kohler, Heinz/163 W Colorado Blvd, Pasadena, CA 213-681-9195
Kolodny, Jeff/20335 Arminta, Canoga Park, CA....818-718-9010
Koosh, Dan/PO Box 6038, Westlake Village, CA 818-991-2105
Kopp, Pierre/PO Box 8337, Long Beach, CA....213-430-8534
Kosta, Jeffrey/2565 Third St #306, San Francisco, CA 415-285-7001
Kramer, David/3109 1/2 Beverly Blvd, Los Angeles, CA....213-388-6747
Krasner, Carin/3239 Helms Ave, Los Angeles, CA 213-280-0082
Kredenser, Peter/2551 Angelo Dr, Los Angeles, CA 213-278-6356
Krisel, Ron/1925 Pontius Ave, Los Angeles, CA 213-477-5519
Krosnick, Alan/2800 20th St, San Francisco, CA 415-285-1819
Krueger, Gary/PO Box 543, Montrose, CA 818-249-1051
Krupp, Carl/PO Box 910, Merlin, OR 503-479-6699
Kubly, Jon/604 Moulton, Los Angeles, CA 213-224-8947
Kuhn, Chuck/206 Third Ave S, Seattle, WA....206-624-4706
Kuhn, Robert/3022 Valevista Tr, Los Angeles, CA....213-461-3656
Kunkel, Larry/729 Minna Alley, San Francisco, CA 415-621-0729
Kupersmith, Dan/PO Box 7401, Studio City, CA 213-935-6232
Kurihara, Ted/601 22nd St, San Francisco, CA....415-285-3200
Kurisu, Kaz/819 1/2 N Fairfax Ave, Los Angeles, CA (P 356)....213-655-7287
Kurtz, Steve/PO Box 625, Soquel, CA....408-425-1090
Kurzweil, Gordon M/211 15th St, Santa Monica, CA....213-395-0624
Kuslich, Lawrence J/3386 SE 20th Ave, Portland, OR 503-236-3454

L

Lamb & Hall/7318 Melrose, Los Angeles, CA 213-931-1775
Lammers, Bud/211-A East Columbine, Santa Ana, CA 714-546-4441
Lamont, Dan/2227 13th Ave E, Seattle, WA 206-324-7757
Lamotte, Michael/828 Mission St, San Francisco, CA 415-777-1443
Lan, Graham/PO Box 211, San Anselmo, CA 415-492-0308
Landau, Robert/7274 Sunset Blvd #3, Los Angeles, CA 213-851-2995
Landecker, Tom/288 7th St, San Francisco, CA 415-864-8888
Landreth, Doug/1940 124th Ave NE #A-108, Bellevue, WA.........206-453-0466
Lane, Bobbi/7213 Santa Monica Blvd, Los Angeles, CA 213-874-0557
Langdon, Harry/8275 Beverly Blvd, Los Angeles, CA 213-651-3212
LaRocca, Jerry/3734 SE 21st Ave, Portland, OR 503-232-5005
Larson, Dean/7668 Hollywood Blvd, Los Angeles, CA 213-876-1033
LaTona, Kevin/159 Western Ave W #454, Seattle, WA 206-285-5779
Lauderborn, Lawrence/301 8th St #213, San Francisco, CA 415-863-1132
Law, Graham/PO Box 211, San Anselmo, CA 415-492-0308
Lawder, John/2672 S Grand, Santa Ana, CA 714-557-3657
Lawlor, John/6101 Melrose, Hollywood, CA 213-468-9050
Lawne, Judith/6863 Sunnycove, Hollywood, CA 213-874-3095
Lawson, Greg/PO Box 1680, Ramona, CA...............................619-789-8878
Lea, Thomas/181 Alpine, San Francisco, CA 415-864-5941
Leatart, Brian/520 N Western, Los Angeles, CA 213-856-0121
LeBon, David/23870 Madison St, Torrance, CA 213-375-4877
LeCoq, John Land/2527 Fillmore St, San Francisco, CA 415-563-4724
Lee, Larry/PO Box 4688, North Hollywood, CA.........................805-259-1226
Lee, Roger Allyn/1628 Folsom St, San Francisco, CA 415-861-1147
Lee, Sherwood/632 Alta Vista Circle, Pasadena, CA 213-255-1338
Legname, Rudi/389 Clementina St, San Francisco, CA 415-777-9569
Lehman, Danny/6643 W 6th St, Los Angeles, CA......................213-652-1930
Leighton, Ron/1360 Logan #105, Costa Mesa, CA 714-641-5122
Leng, Brian/1021 1/2 N La Brea, Los Angeles, CA 213-469-8624
LeNoue, Wayne/1441 Kearny St, San Francisco, CA..................415-981-1776
Levasheff, Michael/1112 N Beachwood, Los Angeles, CA...........213-946-2511
Levenson, Alan/1402 N Sierra Bonita Ave, Los Angeles, CA.........213-851-8837
Levy, Paul/2830 S Robertson Blvd, Los Angeles, CA 213-838-2252
Levy, Richard J/1015 N Kings Rd #115, Los Angeles, CA............213-654-0335
Levy, Ronald/PO Box 3416, Soldotna, AK 907-262-1383
Lewin, Elyse/820 N Fairfax, Los Angeles, CA 213-655-4214
Lewine, Rob/8929 Holly Pl, Los Angeles, CA 213-654-0830
Lewis, Cindy/2554 Lincoln Blvd #1090, Marina Del Rey, CA 213-301-1977
Lewis, Don/2350 Stanley Hills Dr, Los Angeles, CA 213-656-2138
Li, Jeff/8954 Ellis Ave, Los Angeles, CA..................................213-837-5377
Lidz, Jane/33 Nordhoff St, San Francisco, CA 415-587-3377
Liles, Harry/1060 N Lillian Way, Hollywood, CA 213-466-1612
Lindsey, Gordon/2311 Kettner Blvd, San Diego, CA 619-234-4432
Lindstrom, Mel/2510 Old Middlefield Way, Mt View, CA 415-962-1313
Linn, Alan/5121 Santa Fe St #B, San Diego, CA 619-483-2122
Livzey, John/1510 N Las Palmas, Hollywood, CA 213-469-2992
London, Matthew/15326 Calle Juanito, San Diego, CA 619-457-3251
Longwood, Marc/3045 65th St #6, Sacramento, CA 916-731-5373
Lopez, Bret/533 Moreno Ave, Los Angeles, CA 213-393-8841
Louie, Ming/14 Otis St, San Francisco, CA 415-558-8663
Lovell, Buck/2145 W La Palma, Anaheim, ca 714-635-9040
Lovell, Craig/80 Laurel Dr, Carmel Valley, CA...........................408-659-4445
Lund, John M/860 Second St, San Francisco, CA 415-957-1775
Lund, John William/741 Natoma St, San Francisco, CA 415-552-7764
Lyon, Fred/237 Clara St, San Francisco, CA 415-974-5645
Lyons, Marv/2865 W 7th St, Los Angeles, CA...........................213-384-0732

M

Madden, Daniel J/PO Box 965, Los Alamitos, CA 213-429-3621
Madison, David/2330 Old Middlefield Rd, Mt View, CA 415-961-6297
Maharat, Chester/15622 California St, Tustin, CA 714-832-6203
Maher, John/1425 SE Main St #3, Portland, OR.........................503-238-3645
Mahieu, Ted/PO Box 42578, San Francisco, CA 415-641-4747
Maloney, Jeff/265 Sobrante Way #D, Sunnyvale, CA 408-739-4030
Malphettes, Benoit/816 S Grand St, Los Angeles, CA 213-629-9054
Manchee, Doug/2343 3rd St #297, San Francisco, CA 415-552-2422
Mangold, Steve/PO Box 1001, Palo Alto, CA 415-969-9897
Mar, Tim/PO Box 3488, Seattle, WA 206-583-0093
Marcus, Ken/6916 Melrose Ave, Los Angeles, CA 213-937-7214
Marenda, Frank/721 Hill St #105, Santa Monica, CA 213-399-5206
Mareschal, Tom/5816 182nd Pl SW, Lynnwood, WA...................206-771-6932
Margolies, Paul/22 Rosemont Pl, San Francisco, CA..................415-621-3306
Marks, Michael/, Los Angeles, CA...
Marley, Stephen/1160 Industrial Way, San Carlos, CA................415-966-8301

Marriott, John/1830 McAllister, San Francisco, CA 415-922-2920
Marsden, Dominic/3783 W Cahuenga Blvd, Studio City, CA 818-508-5222
Marshall, Jim/3622 16th St, San Francisco, CA 415-864-3622
Marshall, John Lewis/2210 Wilshire Blvd, Santa Monica, CA 213-478-7464
Marshall, Kent/899 Pine St #1912, San Francisco, CA 415-641-0932
Marshutz, Roger/1649 S La Cienega Blvd, Los Angeles, CA 213-273-1610
Martin, John F/118 King St, San Francisco, CA 415-957-1355
Martinelli, Bill/1118 Cyprus Ave, San Mateo, CA 415-347-3589
Mason, Pablo/3026 North Park Way, San Diego, CA 619-298-2200
Mastandrea, Michael/PO Box 68944, Seattle, WA.....................206-244-6756
Masterson, Ed/11211-S Sorrento Val Rd, San Diego, CA 619-457-3251
Matsuda, Paul/920 Natoma St, San Francisco, CA 415-626-6146
Mauskopf, Norman/615 W California Blvd, Pasadena, CA 818-578-1878
Maxwell, Craig/725 Clementina, San Francisco, CA 415-861-4131
May, P Warwick/PO Box 19308, Oakland, CA 415-530-7319
McAfee, Lynn/12745 Moorpark #10, Studio City, CA 818-761-1317
McCall, Stuart/518 Beatty St #603, Vancouver V6B 2L3, BC 604-684-6760
McClain, Stan/39 E Walnut St, Pasadena, CA 818-795-8828
McCrary, Jim/211 S LaBrea Ave, Los Angeles, CA 213-936-5115
McCumsey, Robert/3535 E Coast Hwy, Corona Del Mar, CA........714-720-1624
McDermott, John/31 Genoa Place, San Francisco, CA 415-982-2010
McEvilley, John/1428 Havenhurst, Los Angeles, CA 213-656-7476
McGuire, Gary/1248 S Fairfax Ave, Los Angeles, CA 213-938-2481
McKinney, Andrew/1628 Folsom St, San Francisco, CA 415-621-8415
McMahon, Steve/1164 S LaBrea, Los Angeles, CA 213-937-3345
McNally, Brian/9937 Durant Dr, Beverly Hills, CA......................213-462-6565
McRae, Colin/1063 Folsom, San Francisco, CA 415-863-0119
McVay, Matt/PO Box 1103, Mercer Island, WA 206-236-1343
Mears, Jim/1471 Elliot Ave W, Seattle, WA 206-284-0929
Mejia, Michael/244 9th St, San Francisco, CA 415-621-7670
Melgar Photographers Inc/2971 Corvin Dr, Santa Clara, CA 408-733-4500
Mendenhall, Jim/PO Box 4114, Fullerton, CA 714-447-8555
Menuez, Doug/PO Box 2284, Sausalito, CA 415-332-8154
Menzel, Peter J/136 N Deer Run Lane, Napa, CA 707-255-3528
Menzie, W Gordon/2311 Kettner Blvd, San Diego, CA 619-234-4431
Merfeld, Ken/3951 Higuera St, Culver City, CA 213-837-5300
Merken, Stefan/900 N Citrus Ave, Los Angeles, CA 213-466-4533
Mihulka, Chris/PO Box 1515, Springfield, OR 503-741-2289
Miles, Reid/1136 N Las Palmas, Hollywood, CA 213-462-6106
Milholland, Richard/911 N Kings Rd #113, Los Angeles, CA 213-650-5458
Miller, Bill/12429 Ventura Court, Studio City, CA 818-506-5112

Miller, D/1467 12th St #C, Manhattan Beach,
CA (P 380) **213-546-3205**

Miller, Donald/447 S Hewitt, Los Angeles, CA..........................213-680-1896
Miller, Earl/3212 Bonnie Hill Dr, Los Angeles, CA 213-851-4947
Miller, Ed/705 32nd Ave, San Francisco, CA 415-221-5687
Miller, Jeff/300 Second Ave West, Seattle, WA.........................206-285-5975
Miller, Jim/1122 N Citrus Ave, Los Angeles, CA 213-466-9515
Miller, Jordan/506 S San Vicente Blvd, Los Angeles, CA 213-655-0408
Miller, Martin/5039 September St, San Diego, CA 619-276-4208
Miller, Peter Read/3413 Pine Ave, Manhattan Beach, CA 213-545-7511
Miller, Ray/PO Box 450, Balboa, CA 714-646-5748
Miller, Wynn/4083 Glencoe Ave, Marina Del Rey, CA 213-821-4948
Milliken, Brad/3341 Bryant St, Palo Alto, CA............................415-424-8211
Milne, Robbie/400 E Pine St, Seattle, WA 206-329-3757
Milroy/McAleer/711 W 17th St #G-7, Costa Mesa, CA 714-722-6402
Mineau, Joe/8921 National Blvd, Los Angeles, CA 213-558-3878
Mishler, Clark/1238 G St, Anchorage, AK 907-279-0892
Mitchell, David Paul/564 Deodar lane, Bradbury, CA 415-540-6518
Mitchell, Josh/1984 N Main St #501, Los Angeles, CA 818-398-8422
Mitchell, Margaretta K/280 Hillcrest Rd, Berkeley, CA 415-655-4920
Mizono, Robert/650 Alabama St, San Francisco, CA 415-648-3993
Mock, Dennis/13715 Sparren Ave, San Diego, CA 619-693-3201
Molenhouse, Craig/PO Box 7678, VAn Nuys, CA......................818-901-9306
Montague, Chuck/18005 Skypark Cir #E, Irvine, CA 714-250-0254
Montes de Oca, Arthur/4302 Melrose Ave, Los Angeles, CA 213-665-5141
Moore, Gary/1125 E Orange Ave, Monrovia, CA 818-359-9414
Moran, Edward/5264 Mount Alifan Dr, San Diego, CA 619-693-1041
Morduchowicz, Daniel/600 Moulton Ave, Los Angeles, CA 213-223-1867
Morfit, Mason/897 Independence Ave #D, Mt View, CA 415-969-2209
Morgan, Jay P/618 Moulton Ave #D, Los Angeles, CA 213-224-8288
Morgan, Mike/16252 E Construction, Irvine, CA 714-551-3391
Morgan, Scott/612-C Hampton Dr, Venice, CA 213-392-1863
Morrell, Paul/300 Brannan St #207, San Francisco, CA 415-543-5887
Morris, Steve/PO Box 40261, Santa Barbara, CA 805-965-4859
Mosgrove, Will/250 Newhall, San Francisco, CA 415-282-7080
Motil, Guy/253 W Canada, San Clemente, CA 714-492-1350
Muckley, Mike /8057 Raytheon Rd #3, San Diego, CA 619-565-6033

Mudford, Grant/5619 W 4th St #2, Los Angeles, CA 213-936-9145
Muench, David/PO Box 30500, Santa Barbara, CA 805-967-4488
Muna, R J/63 Encina Ave, Palo Alto, CA 415-328-1131
Murphy, Suzanne/2442 Third St, Santa Monica, CA 213-399-6652
Murray, Derik/1128 Homer St, Vancouver V6B 2X6, BC 604-669-7468
Murray, Michael/15431 Redhill Ave #E, Tustin, CA 714-259-9222
Murray, William III/15454 NE 182nd Pl, Woodinville, WA 206-485-4011
Musilek, Stan/2141 3rd St, San Francisco, CA 415-621-5336
Myers, Jeffry W Photo/1218 3rd Ave #510, Seattle, WA 206-527-1853

N

Nadler, Jeff/520 N Western Ave, Los Angeles, CA 213-467-2135
Nakashima, Les/600 Moulton Ave #101A, Los Angeles, CA (P 346,347) 213-226-0506
Nance, Ancil/600 SW 10th #509, Portland, OR 503-223-9534
Narciso, Mike/600 Moulton Ave #101-A, Los Angeles, CA (P 346,347) 213-226-0506
Nation, Bill/937 N Cole #7, Los Angeles, CA 213-937-4888
Nease, Robert/441 E Columbine #E, Santa Ana, CA 714-545-6557
Nebeux, Michael/13450 S Western Ave, Gardena, CA 213-532-0949
Neill, William/PO Box 162, Yosemite Nat Park, CA 209-379-2841
Nels/311 Avery St, Los Angeles, CA 213-680-2414
Nese, Robert/1215 E Colorado St #204, Glendale, CA 818-247-2149
Newman, Greg/1356 Brampton Rd, Pasadena, CA 213-257-6247
Nishihira, Robert/6150 Yarrow Dr #G, Carlsbad, CA 619-438-0366
Nissing, Neil B/711 South Flower St, Burbank, CA (P 357) 213-849-1811
Noble, Richard/7618 Melrose Ave, Los Angeles, CA 213-655-4711
Nolton, Gary/107 NW Fifth Ave, Portland, OR (P 351) 503-228-0844
Normark, Don/1622 Taylor Ave N, Seattle, WA 206-284-9393
Northlight Photo/123 Lake St S, Kirkland, WA 206-881-9306
Norwood, David/9023 Washington Blvd, Culver City, CA 213-204-3323
Noyle, Ric/733 Auahi St, Honolulu, HI 808-524-8269
NTA/600 Moulton Ave #101-A, Los Angeles, CA (P 346,347) 213-226-0506
Nuding, Peter/2423 Old Middlefield Way #K, Mt View, CA 415-967-4854
Nyerges, Suzanne/413 S Fairfax, Los Angeles, CA 213-938-0151

O

O'Brien, Tom/450 S La Brea, Los Angeles, CA 213-938-2008
O'Connor, Kelly/PO Box 2151, Los Gatos, CA 408-378-5600
O'Hara, Yoshi/6341 Yucca St, Hollywood, CA 213-466-8031
O'Rear, Chuck/PO Box 361, St Helena, CA 707-963-2663
Odgers, Jayme/703 S Union, Los Angeles, CA 213-461-8173
Ogilvie, Peter/20 Millard Rd, Larkspur, CA 415-924-5507
Ohno, Aki/940 E 2nd St #3, Los Angeles, CA 213-617-1685
Oldenkamp, John/3331 Adams Ave, San Diego, CA 619-283-0711
Olson, George/451 Vermont, San Francisco, CA 415-864-8686
Olson, Jon/4045 32nd Ave SW, Seattle, WA 206-932-7074
Olson, Rosanne/5200 Latona Ave NE, Seattle, WA (P 381) 206-633-3775
Orazem, Scott/1150 1/2 Elm Dr, Los Angeles, CA 213-277-7447
Osbornem Bill/3118 196th Ave, Sumner, WA 206-862-1977
Oshiro, Jeff/2534 W 7th St, Los Angeles, CA 213-383-2774
Otto, Glenn/10625 Magnolia Blvd, North Hollywood, CA 818-762-5724
Ounjian, Michael/612 N Myers St, Burbank, CA 818-842-0880
Ovregaard, Keith/765 Clementina St, San Francisco, CA 415-621-0687
Oyama, Rick/1265 S Cochran, Los Angeles, CA 213-465-6149

P

Pacheco, Robert/11152 3/4 Morrison, N Hollywood, CA 818-761-1320
Pacific Image/930 Alabama, San Francisco, CA 415-282-2525
Pack, Ross/2375 North Ave, Chico, CA 916-891-3442
Pacura, Tim/756 Natoma St, San Francisco, CA 415-552-3512
Padys, Diane/PO Box 77307, San Francisco, CA 415-285-6443
Pagos, Terry/3622 Albion Pl N, Seattle, WA 206-633-4616
Pan, Richard/722 N Hoover St, Los Angeles, CA 213-661-6638
Panography/1514 Fruitvale, Oakland, CA 415-261-3327
Pape, Ross/1369 Lansing Ave, San Jose, CA 415-595-4242
Parker, Douglas/3279 Lowry Rd, Los Angeles, CA 213-660-6145
Parker, Suzanne/601 Minnesota, San Francisco, CA 415-821-7373
Parks, Jeff/12936 133rd Pl NE, Kirkland, WA 206-821-5450
Parks, Peggy/21 Broadview Dr, San Rafael, CA 415-457-5300
Parrish, Al/3501 Buena Vista Ave, Glendale, CA 818-957-3726
Parry, Karl/8800 Venice Blvd, Los Angeles, CA 213-558-4446
Pasquali, Art/1061 Sunset Blvd, Los Angeles, CA 213-250-0134
Patterson, Robert/915 N Mansfield Ave, Hollywood, CA 213-462-4401
Paullus, Bill/PO Box 432, Pacific Grove, CA 408-679-1624
Pavloff, Nick/PO Box 2339, San Francisco, CA 415-452-2468
Pazderka, Franti/1830 Clay St #501, San Francisco, CA 415-775-3282
Peacock, Christian/930 Alabama St, San Francisco, CA 415-641-8088
Pearlman, Andy/1920 Main St #2, Santa Monica, CA 213-550-4505
Pedrick, Frank/2690 Union st, Oakland, CA 415-465-5080
Peebles, Doug/445 Ilwahi Loop, Kailua, HI 808-533-6686
Penoyar, Barbara/911 E Pike St #211, Seattle, WA 206-324-5632
Percey, Roland/626 N Hoover, Los Angeles, CA 213-660-7305
Perla, Dario/18 LaJacque Ct, Sacramento, CA 916-555-1212
Perry, David/837 Traction Ave #104, Los Angeles, CA 213-625-3567
Perry, David E/Box 4165 Pioneer Sq Sta, Seattle, WA 206-932-6614
Peterson, Bryan/PO Box 892, Hillsboro, OR 503-985-3276
Peterson, Darrell/84 University #306, Seattle, WA 206-624-1762
Peterson, Richard/733 Auahi St, Honolulu, HI 808-536-8222
Peterson, Richard Studio/711 8th Ave #A, San Diego, CA 619-236-0284
Peterson, Scott/301 8th St #212, San Francisco, CA 415-285-5112
Petrucelli, Tony/169 Rockwood Ln, Irvine, CA 714-458-6914
Pett, Laurence J/5907 Cahill Ave, Tarzana, CA 818-344-9453
Petzke, Karl/610 22 St #305, San Francisco, CA 415-626-5979
Pfleger, Mickey/PO Box 280727, San Francisco, CA 415-355-1772
Pharoah, Rick/2830 Shoreview Circle, Westlake Village, CA 805-496-7196
Phase Infinity/R Jones/10225 Barns Cany Rd, San Diego, CA 619-546-0551
Phillips, Lee/4964 Norwich Place, Newark, CA 415-794-7447
Photo File/110 Pacific Ave #102, San Francisco, CA 415-397-3040
Photography Northwest/1415 Elliot Ave W, Seattle, WA 206-285-5249
Pinckney, Jim/PO Box 1149, Carmel Valley, CA 408-659-3002
Piper, Jim/922 SE Ankeny, Portland, OR 503-231-9622
Piscitello, Chuck/11440 Chandler Blvd, N Hollywood, CA 213-460-6397
Pizur, Joe/194 Ohukai Rd, Kihie, Maui, HI 808-879-6633
Place, Chuck/2940 Lomita Rd, Santa Barbara, CA 805-682-6089
Pleasant, Ralph B/8755 W Washington Blvd, Culver City, CA 213-202-8997
Ploch, Thomas/30 S Salinas, Santa Barbara, CA 805-965-1312
Plummer, Bill/963 Yorkshire Ct, Lafayette, CA 415-284-1535
Poppleton, Eric/1755 Correa Way, Los Angeles, CA 213-471-2845
Porter, James/3955 Birch St #F, Newport Beach, CA 714-852-8756
Poulsen, Chriss/104-A Industrial Center, Sausalito, CA 415-331-3495
Powers, David/17 Brosnan St, San Francisco, CA 415-864-7974
Powers, Lisa/1112 Beachwood, Los Angeles, CA 213-465-5546
Powers, Michael/3045 65th St #7, Sacramento, CA 916-451-5606
Prater, Yvonne/Box 940 Rt 1, Ellensburg, WA 509-925-1774
Preuss, Karen/369 Eleventh Ave, San Francisco, CA 415-752-7545
Pribble, Paul/911 Victoria Dr, Arcadia, CA 213-262-8305
Price, Tony/PO Box 5216, Portland, OR 503-239-4228
Pritchett, Bill/1771 Yale St, Chula Vista, CA 619-421-6005
Pritzker, Burton/456 Denton Way, Santa Rosa, CA (P 383) 415-626-3471
Proehl, Steve/916 Rodney Dr, San Leandro, CA 415-483-3683
Professional Photo Srvc/1011 Buenos Ave , San Diego, CA 619-299-4410
Pruitt, Brett/720 Iwilei Rd #260, Honolulu, HI 808-521-1929

R

Rahn, Stephen/259 Clara St, San Francisco, CA 415-495-3556
Ramey, Michael/2905 W Thurman, Seattle, WA 206-329-6936
Rampy, Tom/PO Box 3980, Laguna Hills, CA 714-850-4048
Ramsey, Gary/1412 Ritchey #A, Santa Ana, CA 714-547-0782
Rand, Marvin/1310 W Washington Blvd, Venice, CA 213-306-9779
Randall, Bob/1118 Mission St, S Pasadena, CA 818-441-1003
Randlett, Mary/Box 10536, Bainbridge Island, WA 206-842-3935
Randolph, Tom/324 Sunset Ave, Venice, CA 213-399-7058
Rapoport, Aaron/3119 Beverly Blvd, Los Angeles, CA 213-738-7277
Rappaport, Rick/2725 NE 49th St, Portland, OR 503-249-0705
Rausin, Chuck/1020 Woodcrest Ave, La Habra, CA 213-697-0408
Rawcliffe, David/7609 Beverly Blvd, Los Angeles, CA 213-938-6287
Rayniak, J Bart/3510 N Arden Rd, Otis Orchards, WA 509-924-0004
Reed, Bob/1816 N Vermont Ave, Los Angeles, CA 213-662-9703
Reiff, Robert/1920 Main St #2, Santa Monica, CA 213-938-3064
Reitzel, Bill/1001 Bridgeway #537, Sausalito, CA 415-457-7385
Ressmeyer, Roger/2269 Chestnut #400, San Francisco, CA 415-921-1675
Rhoney, Ann/2264 Green St, San Francisco, CA 415-922-4775
Rich, Bill/109 Minna #459, San Francisco, CA 415-775-8214
Ricketts, Mark/2809 NE 55th St, Seattle, WA 206-526-1911
Riggs, Robin/3785 Cahuenga W, N Hollywood, CA 818-506-7753
Ripley, John/281 Green St, San Francisco, CA 415-781-4940
Ritts, Herb/7927 Hillside Ave, Los Angeles, CA 213-876-6366
Robbins, Bill/7016 Santa Monica Blvd, Los Angeles, CA 213-930-1382
Robin, David/818 Brannan, San Francisco, CA 415-863-8900
Rodal, Arney A/395 Winslow Way E, Bainbridge Island, WA 206-842-4989

Rodney, Andrew/501 N Detroit St, Los Angeles, CA...................213-939-7427
Rogers, Art/The Old Creamery/Route 1, Point Reyes, CA............415-663-8345
Rogers, Ken/PO Box 3187, Beverly Hills, CA.............................213-553-5532
Rogers, Peter/15621 Obsidian Ct, Chino Hills, CA 714-597-4394
Rojas, Art/2465 N Batavia, Orange, CA....................................714-921-1710
Rokeach, Barrie/32 Windsor, Kensington, CA............................415-527-5376
Rolston, Matthew/8259 Melrose Ave, Los Angeles, CA................213-658-1151
Rorke, Lorraine/146 Shrader St, San Francisco, CA...................415-386-2121
Rose, Peter/651 N Russell, Portland, OR 503-249-5864
Rosenberg, Alan/3024 Scott Blvd, Santa Clara, CA....................408-986-8484
Ross, Alan C/202 Culper Ct, Hermosa Beach, CA.......................213-379-2015
Ross, Dave/1619 Tustin Ave, Costa Mesa, CA...........................714-642-0315
Ross, James Studio/2565 3rd St #220, San Francisco, CA...........415-821-5710
Rothman, Michael/1816 N Vermont Ave, Los Angeles, CA.............213-662-9703
Rowan, Bob/209 Los Banos Ave, Walnut Creek, CA.....................415-930-8687
Rowe, Wayne/567 North Beverly Glen, Los Angeles, CA...............213-475-7810
Rowell, Galen/1483-A Solano Ave, Albany, CA...........................415-524-9343
Rubin, Ken/4140 Arch Dr #209, Studio City, CA.........................818-508-9028
Rubins, Richard/3268 Motor Ave, Los Angeles, CA.....................213-287-0350
Ruppert, Michael/5086 W Pico, Los Angeles, CA........................213-938-3779
Ruscha, Paul/940 N Highland Ave, Los Angeles, CA....................213-465-3516
Ruthsatz, Richard/8735 Washington Blvd, Culver City, CA............213-838-6312
Ryder Photo/136 14th St Apt B, Seal Beach, CA.........................315-622-3499

S

Sabransky, Cynthia/3331 Adams Ave, San Diego, CA...................619-283-0711
Sacks, Ron/PO Box 5532, Portland, OR....................................503-641-4051
Sadlon, Jim/118 King St #530, San Francisco, CA.......................415-541-0977

Safron, Marshal Studios Inc/1041 N McCadden Pl,
Los Angeles, CA (P 385-387).................................**213-461-5676**
Sakai, Steve/724 S Stanley Ave #2, Los Angeles, CA..................213-460-4811
Saks, Stephen/807 Laurelwood Dr, San Mateo, CA......................415-574-4534
Salas, Michael/398 Flower St, Costa Mesa, CA...........................714-722-9908
Saloutos, Pete/11225 Huntley Pl, Culver City, CA.......................213-397-5509
Samerjan, Peter/743 N Fairfax, Los Angeles, CA........................213-653-2940
Sanchez, Kevin/1200 Indiana, San Francisco, CA........................415-285-1770
Sanders, Paul/7378 Beverly Blvd, Los Angeles, CA.....................213-933-5791
Sanderson, Mark/2307 Laguna Cny Rd, Laguna Beach, CA............714-497-4615
Sandison, Teri/1545 N Wilcox #102, Hollywood, CA....................213-461-3529
Santos, Bill/5711 Florin Perkins Rd#1, Sacramento, CA...............916-383-7969
Santullo, Nancy/7213 Santa Monica Blvd, Los Angeles, CA..........213-874-1940
Sarpa, Jeff/11821 Mississippi Ave, Los Angeles, CA...................213-479-4988
Sasso, Gene/1285 Laurel Ave, Pomona, CA...............................714-623-7424
Saunders, Paul/9272 Geronimo #111, Irvine, CA.........................714-768-4624
Scharf, David/2100 Loma Vista Pl, Los Angeles, CA....................213-666-8657
Schelling, Susan/244 Ninth St, San Francisco, CA......................415-621-2992
Schenck, Rocky/2210 N Beachwood Dr, Los Angeles, CA.............213-465-1547
Schenker, Larry/2830 S Robertson Blvd, Los Angeles, CA...........213-837-2020
Scherl, Ron/1301 Guerrero, San Francisco, CA..........................415-285-8865
Schermeister, Phil/472 22nd Ave, San Francisco, CA..................415-386-0218
Schiff, Darryll/8153 W Blackburn Ave, Los Angeles, CA 213-658-6179
Schiff, Nancy Rica/, Los Angeles, CA.......................................
Schubert, John/11478 Burbank Blvd, N Hollywood, CA...............213-935-6044
Schultz, Jeff/PO Box 241452, Anchorage, AK............................907-561-5636
Schwager, Ron/PO Box 6157, Chico, CA....................................916-891-6682
Schwartz, Stuart/301 8th St #204, San Francisco, CA.................415-863-8393
Schwob, Bill/5675-B Landragan, Emeryville, CA.........................415-547-2232
Scoffone, Craig/1169 Husted Ave, San Jose, CA.........................408-723-7011
Scott, Mark/1208 S Genesee, Hollywood, CA.............................213-931-9319
Sebastian Studios/5161-A Santa Fe St, San Diego, CA...............619-581-9111
Sedam, Mike/PO Box 1679, Bothell, WA....................................206-488-9375
Segal, Susan/11738 Moor Pk #B, Studio City, CA........................818-763-7612
Seidemann, Bob/1183 S Tremaine Ave, Los Angeles, CA.............213-938-2786
Selig, Jonathan/29206 Heathercliff Rd, Malibu, CA.....................213-457-5856
Selland Photography/461 Bryant St, San Francisco, CA..............415-495-3633
Sessions, David/2210 Wilshire Blvd #205, Santa Monica, CA.......213-394-8379
Sexton, Richard/128 Laidley St, San Francisco, CA.....................415-550-8345
Shaneff, Carl/1100 Alakea St #224, Honolulu, HI........................808-533-3010
Sharpe, Dick/2475 Park Oak Dr, Los Angeles, CA.......................213-462-4597
Shelton, Randy/10925 SW 108th St, Tigard, OR.........................503-226-4117
Shirley, Ron/8755 W Washington, Culver City, CA......................213-204-2177
Sholik, Stan/1946 E Blair Ave, Santa Ana, CA...........................714-250-9275
Short, Glenn/14641 La Maida, Sherman Oaks, CA.......................818-990-5599
Shorten, Chris/60 Federal St, San Francisco, CA........................415-543-4883
Shrum, Steve/PO Box 6360, Ketchikan, AK................................907-225-5453
Shuman, Ronald/1 Menlo Pl, Berkeley, CA.................................415-527-7241
Shvartzman, Ed/31210 La Vaya Dr, Westlake Village, CA.............818-707-3227
Sibley, Scott/764 Bay, San Francisco, CA.................................415-673-7468

Silk, Gary Photography/4164 Wanda Dr, Los Angeles, CA............213-664-9639
Silva, Keith/771 Clementina Alley, San Francisco, CA.................415-863-5655
Silverek, Don/914 Ripley St, Santa Rosa, CA............................707-525-1155
Silverman, Jay Inc/920 N Citrus Ave, Hollywood, CA..................213-466-6030
Sim, Veronica/4961 W Sunset Blvd, Los Angeles, CA..................213-656-4816
Simon, Wolfgang/PO Box 807, La Canada, CA............................818-790-1605
Simpson, Stephen/701 Kettner Blvd #124, San Diego, CA............619-239-6638
Sinick, Gary/3246 Ettie St, Oakland, CA...................................415-655-4538
Sirota, Peggy/4391 Vanalden Ave, Tarzana, CA.........................818-344-2020
Sjef's Fotographie/2311 NW Johnson St, Portland, OR 503-223-1089
Sjoberg/742 N LaCienega, Los Angeles, CA...............................213-659-7158
Skrivan, Tom/1081 Beach Park Blvd #205, Foster City, CA..........415-574-4847
Slabeck, Bernard/2565 Third St #316, San Francisco, CA...........415-282-8202
Slatery, Chad/11627 Ayres Ave, Los Angeles, CA.......................213-434-4525
Slaughter, Paul D/771 El Medio Ave, Pacific Palisades, CA..........213-454-3694
Slenzak, Ron/7106 Waring Ave, Los Angeles, CA........................213-934-9088
Sloben, Marvin/3026 N Park Way, San Diego, CA........................619-239-2828
Slobin, Marvin/1065 15th St, San Diego, CA..............................619-239-2828
Slobodian, Scott/6519 Fountain Ave, Los Angeles, CA...............213-464-2341
Smith, Charles J/7163 Construction Crt, San Diego, CA..............619-271-6525
Smith, Don/1527 Belmont #1, Seattle, WA 206-324-5748
Smith, Elliott Varner/PO Box 5268, Berkeley, CA.......................415-654-9235
Smith, Gary Photos/75 South Main #303, Seattle, WA................206-343-7105
Smith, Gil/2865 W 7th St, Los Angeles, CA...............................213-384-1016
Smith, Steve/228 Main St #E, Venice, CA..................................213-392-4982
Smith, Todd/7316 Pyramid Dr, Hollywood, CA............................213-651-3706
Snook, Randy/4220 Frida Maria Ct, Carmichael, CA....................916-944-8419
Snyder, Mark/2415 Third St #265, San Francisco, CA.................415-861-7514
Sokol, Mark/6518 Wilkinson Ave, North Hollywood,
CA (P 388,389)..**818-506-4910**
Sollecito, Tony/1120-B W Evelyn Ave, Sunnyvale, CA................408-773-8118
Solomon, Marc/PO Box 480574, Los Angeles,
CA (P 342,343)..**213-935-1771**
Spahn, Brian/2565 3rd St #339, San Francisco, CA....................415-282-6630
Spahn, David/920 Natoma St, San Francisco, CA........................212-689-6120
Speier, Brooks/6022 Haviland Ave, Whittier, CA.........................213-695-3552
Spradling, David/2515 Patricia Ave, Los Angeles, CA..................213-559-9870
Spring, Bob & Ira/18819 Olympic View Dr, Edmonds, WA............206-776-4685
Springmann, Christopher/PO Box 745, Point Reyes, CA.............415-663-8428
St Jivago Desanges/PO Box 24AA2, Los Angeles, CA.................213-931-1984
Stahn, David/920 Natoma, San Francisco, CA............................415-864-1453
Staley, Bill/1160 21st St, W Vancouver V7V 4B1, BC.................604-922-6695
Stampfli, Eric/50 Mendell #10, San Francisco, CA......................415-824-2305
Stanley, Maria/2170 Chatsworth, San Diego, CA........................619-224-2848
Stanley, Paul/3911 Pacific Hwy #100, San Diego, CA.................619-293-3535
Starkman, Rick/544 N Rios Ave, Solana Beach, CA.....................619-943-1468
Starr, Ron/PO Box 339, Santa Cruz, CA (P 361).........**408-426-6634**
Steele, Melissa/PO Box 280727, San Francisco, CA...................415-355-1772
Stein, Robert/319 1/2 S Robertson Blvd, Beverly Hills, CA.........213-652-2030
Steinberg, Bruce/2128 18th St, San Francisco, CA....................415-864-0739
Steiner, Glenn Rakowsky/3102 Moore St, San Diego, CA............619-299-0197
Steinke, Paula/783 9th Ave, San Francisco, CA.........................415-387-9426
Stevens, Bob/608 Moulton Ave, Los Angeles, CA.......................213-224-8082
Stillman, Richard/10 Old Creek Ct, Danville, CA.........................415-838-2222
Stinson, John/376 W 14th St, San Pedro, CA............................213-831-8495
Stoaks, Charles/PO Box 6417, Portland, OR..............................503-243-2635
Stock, Richard/1205 Raintree Circle, Culver City, CA.................213-559-3344
Stockton, Michael/10660 Olive Grove Ave, Sunland, CA.............818-352-3607
Stone, Pete/1410 NW Johnson, Portland, OR.............................503-224-7125
Stormont, Bill/28279 Rainbow Valley Rd, Eugene, OR................503-485-1684
Strandoo, Paul/1318 10th Ave, San Francisco, CA.....................415-661-1650
Strauss, Andrew/6442 Santa Monica Blvd, Los Angeles, CA........213-464-5394
Streano, Vince/PO Box 662, Laguna Beach, CA..........................714-497-1908
Street-Porter, Tim/6938 Camrose Dr, Los Angeles, CA...............213-874-4278
Streshinsky, Ted/PO Box 674, Berkeley, CA..............................415-526-1976
Strickland, Steve/Box 3486, San Bernardino, CA.......................714-883-4792
Stromberg, Tony/PO Box 2334, Los Gatos, CA..........................408-354-5355
Stryker, Ray/900 First Ave S, Seattle, WA................................206-623-9653
Studio AV/1227 First Ave S, Seattle, WA..................................206-292-9931
Studio B/5121-B Santa Fe St, San Diego, CA............................619-483-2122
Su, Andrew/5733 Benner St, Los Angeles, CA...........................213-256-0598
Sugar, James/45 Midway Ave, Mill Valley, CA............................415-388-3344
Sullivan, Jeremiah S/PO Box 7870, San Diego, CA.....................619-236-0711
Sund, Harald/PO Box 16466, Seattle, WA..................................206-938-1080
Sutton, John/333 Fifth St, San Francisco, CA............................415-974-5452
Svendsen, Linda/3915 Bayview Circle, Concord, CA....................415-676-8299
Swank & Newell/1551 Third Ave, Walnut Creek, CA....................415-930-9229
Swarthout, Walter & Assoc/370 Fourth St, San Francisco, CA......415-543-2525
Swartz, Fred/135 S LaBrea, Los Angeles, CA............................213-939-2789

Swenson, John/4353 W 5th St #D, Los Angeles, CA 213-384-1782

T

Tachibana, Kenji/1067 26th Ave East, Seattle, WA 206-325-2121
Taggart, Fritz/1117 N Wilcox Pl, Los Angeles, CA 213-469-8227
Tankersley, Todd/91 Eldora Dr, Mountain View, CA 415-964-5346
Tapp, Carlan/820 Industry Dr, Seattle, WA 206-575-1775
Tarleton, Gary/2589 NW 29th, Corvalis, OR 503-752-3759
Taub, Doug/5800 Fox View Dr, Malibu, CA 213-457-8600
Tauber, Richard/4221 24th St, San Francisco, CA 415-824-6837
Teeter, Jeff/2205 Dixon St, Chico, CA.....................916-895-3255
Teke/4338 Shady Glade Ave, Studio City, CA 818-985-9066
Theis, Rocky/1457 Ridgeview Dr, San Diego, CA 619-527-0776
Thimmes, Timothy/8749 Washington Blvd, Culver City, CA 213-204-6851
Thomas, Neil/7622 Jayseel St, Sunland, CA 213-202-0051
Thompson, Michael/7811 Alabama Ave, Canoga Park, CA 818-883-7870
Thompson, William/PO Box 4460, Seattle, WA.....................206-621-9069
Thomson, Sydney (Ms)/PO Box 1032, Keaau, HI 808-966-8587
Thornton, Tyler/4706 Oakwood Ave, Los Angeles, CA 213-465-0425
Tilger, Stewart/71 Columbia #206, Seattle, WA.....................206-682-7818
Tise, David/975 Folsom St, San Francisco, CA 415-777-0669
Tomsett, Rafe/5380 Carol Way, Riverside, CA 714-686-6638
Tracy, Tom/1 Maritime Plaza #1300, San Francisco, CA 415-340-9811
Trafficanda, Gerald/1111 N Beachwood Dr, Los Angeles, CA.....................213-466-1111
Trailer, Martin/8615 Commerce Ave, San Diego, CA 619-549-8881
Trindl, Gene/3950 Vantage Ave, Studio City, CA 213-877-4848
Trousdale, Mark/2849-A Fillmore St, San Francisco, CA.....................415-391-0564
Tschoegl, Chris/600 Moulton Ave #101-A,
Los Angeles, CA (P 346,347) **213-226-0506**
Tucker, Kim/2428 Canyon Dr, Los Angeles, CA 213-465-9233
Turk, Roger/123 Lake St S, Kirkland, WA 206-881-9306
Turner & DeVries/1200 College Walk #212, Honolulu, HI.....................808-537-3115
Turner, John Terence/173 37th Ave E, Seattle, WA.....................206-325-9073
Turner, Richard/Box 64205 Rancho Pk Sta, Los Angeles, CA.....................213-279-2127
Tuschman, Mark/300 Santa Monica, Menlo Park,
CA (P 392,393) **415-322-4157**
Tussey, Ron/57 Sunshine Ave, Sausalito, CA 415-331-1427

UV

Ueda, Richard/618 Moulton Ave St E, Los Angeles, CA 213-224-8709
Undheim, Timothy/1039 Seventh Ave, San Diego, CA 619-232-3366
Unger, Trudy/PO Box 536, Mill Valley, CA 415-381-5683
Uniack/8933 National Blvd, Los Angeles, CA 213-938-0287
Upton, Tom/1879 Woodland Ave, Palo Alto, CA.....................415-325-8120
Urie, Walter Photography/1810 E Carnegie, Santa Ana, CA.....................714-261-6302
Vallely, Dwight/2027 Charleen Circle, Carlsbad, CA 619-434-3828
VanderHeiden, Terry/563 E Lewelling Blvd, San Lorenzo, CA.....................415-278-2411
Vanderpoel, Fred/1118 Harrison, San Francisco, CA 415-621-4405
Vanderschuit, Carl & Joan/627 8th Ave, San Diego, CA 619-232-4332
VanSciver, Diane/3500 SE 22nd Ave, Portland, OR 503-239-7817
Varie, Bill/923 E 3rd St #403, Los Angeles, CA 213-620-6257
Vega, Raul/3511 W 6th Tower Suite, Los Angeles, CA 213-387-2058
Veitch, Julie/5757 Venice Blvd, Los Angeles, CA 213-936-4231
Venera, Michael/527 Howard St, San Francisco, CA 415-543-3562
Venezia, Jay/1373 Edgecliffe Dr, Los Angeles, CA 213-665-7382
Vereen, Jackson/570 Bryant St, San Francisco, CA 415-777-5272
Viarnes, Alex/Studio 33/Clementina, San Francisco, CA 415-543-1195
Vignes, Michelle/654 28th St, San Francisco, CA 415-550-8039
Villaflor, Francisco/PO Box 883274, San Francisco,
CA (P 394) **415-921-4238**
Visually Speaking/3609 E Olympic Blvd, Los Angeles, CA.....................213-269-9141
Vogt, Jurgen/936 E 28th Ave, Vancouver V5V 2P2, BC 604-876-5817
Vollenweider, Thom/3430 El Cajon Blvd, San Diego, CA 619-280-3070
Vollick, Tom/5245 Melrose, Los Angeles, CA 213-464-4415

W

Wade, William/5608 E 2nd St, Long Beach, CA.....................213-439-6826
Wahlstrom, Richard/650 Alabama St 3rd Fl, San Francsico, CA.....................415-550-1400
Wallace, Marlene/1624 S Cotner, Los Angeles, CA 213-826-1027
Warden, John/9201 Shorecrest Dr, Anchorage, AK 907-243-1667
Warren Aerial Photography/1585 E Locust, Pasadena, CA 213-681-1006
Wasserman, David/252 Caselli, San Francisco, CA 415-552-4428
Watanabe, David/14355 132nd Ave NE, Kirkland, WA 206-823-0692
Waterfall, William/1160-A Nuuanu, Honolulu, HI 808-521-6863
Waters, Don/4886 Woodthrugh Rd, Pleasanton, CA.....................415-462-1305
Watson, Alan/710 13th St #300, San Diego, CA 619-239-5555
Watson, Joe/1110 Putney Dr, Santa Rosa, CA 408-296-2900

Watson, Stuart/620 Moulton Ave, Los Angeles, CA 213-221-3886
Waz, Anthony/1115 S Trotwood Ave, San Pedro, CA.....................213-548-3758
Weaver, James/PO Box 2091, Manteca, CA.....................209-823-6368
Weibel, Joyce/10050 N Foothill Blvd, Cupertino, CA.....................408-973-1564
Werner, Jeffery R/4910 1/4 McConnell, Los Angeles, CA 213-821-2384
Werts, Bill/732 N Highland, Los Angeles, CA 213-464-2775
West, Charles/3951 Duncan Pl, Palo Alto, CA.....................415-856-4003
Wexler, Glen/736 N Highland, Los Angeles, CA 213-465-0268
Wheeler, Richard/PO Box 3739, San Rafael, CA.....................415-457-6914
Whetstone, Wayne/149 W Seventh Ave, Vancouver, BC.....................604-873-8471
White, Lee/1172 S LaBrea Ave, Los ANgeles, CA 213-934-5993
White, Randall/1514 Fruitvale, Oakland, CA 415-261-3327
Whitfeld, Brent Studio/816 S Grand Ave #202,
Los Angeles, CA (P 349) **213-624-7511**
Whitmore, Ken/1038 N Kenter, Los Angeles, CA 213-472-4337
Whittaker, Steve/111 Glen Way #8, Belmont, CA 415-595-4242
Wiener, Leigh/2600 Carman Crest Dr, Los Angeles, CA.....................213-876-0990
Wietstock, Wilfried/877 Valencia St, San Francisco, CA 415-285-4221
Wildschut, Sjef/2311 NW Johnson, Portland, OR 503-223-1089
Wilhelm, Dave/2565 Third St #303, San Francisco, CA 415-826-9399
Wilkings, Steve/Box 22810, Honolulu, HI 808-732-6288
Williams, Bill/9601 Owensmouth #13, Chatsworth, CA 818-341-9833
Williams, David Jordan/6122 W Colgate, Los Angeles, CA 213-936-3170
Williams, Harold/705 Bayswater Ave, Burlingame, CA 415-340-7017
Williams, Keith/PO Box 17891, Irvine, CA 714-259-9165
Williams, Sandra/PO Box 16130, San Diego, CA 619-283-3100
Williams, Steven Burr/8260 Grandview, Los Angeles, CA 213-469-5749
Williams, Waldon/258 Redondo Ave, Long Beach, CA 213-434-1782
Williams, Wayne/7623 Beverly Blvd, Los Angeles, CA 213-937-2882
Williamson, Scott/1901 E Carnegie #1G, Santa Ana, CA 714-261-2550
Wilson, Don/10754 2nd Ave NW, Seattle, WA 206-367-4075
Wilson, Douglas M/10133 NE 113th Pl, Kirkland, WA 206-822-8604
Wimberg, Mercier/8751 W Washington Blvd, Culver City, CA 213-839-7521
Wimpey, Christopher/627 Eighth Ave, San Diego, CA 619-232-3222
Windus, Scott/928 N Formosa Ave, Los Angeles, CA 213-874-3160
Wing, Frank/2325 Third, San Francisco, CA 415-626-8066
Winholt, Bryan/PO Box 331, Sacramento, CA 916-969-1112
Winter, Nita/176 Caselli Ave, San Francisco, CA 415-626-6588
Witbeck, Sandra/581 Seaver Dr, Mill Valley, CA 415-383-6834
Witmer, Keith/16203 George St, Los Gatos, CA 408-395-9618
Wittner, Dale/507 Third Ave #209, Seattle, WA 206-623-4545
Wolf, Bernard/2520 3rd St #18, Santa Monica, CA 213-399-6803
Wolfe, Dan E/45 E Walnut, Pasadena, CA 213-681-3130
Wolman, Baron/PO Box 1000, Mill Valley, CA 415-388-0181
Wong, Darrell/PO Box 90157, Honolulu, HI 808-737-5269
Wong, Ken/3431 Wesley St, Culver City, CA 213-836-3118
Wood, Darrell/517 Aloha St, Seattle, WA 206-283-7900
Woodward, Jonathan/5121 Santa Fe St #A, San Diego, CA 619-270-5501
Woolslair, James/17229 Newhope St #H, Fountain Valley, CA.....................714-957-0349
Wortham, Robert/521 State St, Glendale, CA 818-243-6400
Wright, Armand/4026 Blairmore Ct, San Jose, CA 408-629-0559
Wyatt, Tom Photography/585 Mission St, San Francisco, CA.....................415-543-2813

YZ

Yellin, Jan/PO Box 81, N Hollywood, CA 818-508-5669
Young, Bill/PO Box 27344, Honolulu, HI 808-595-7324
Young, Edward/860 2nd St, San Francisco, CA 415-543-6633
Young, Irene/888 44th St, Oakland, CA 415-654-3846
Yudelman, Dale/1833 9th St, Santa Monica, CA 213-452-5482
Yudelson, Jim/33 Clementina, San Francisco, CA 415-543-3325
Zaboroskie, K Gypsy/5584 Mission, San Francisco, CA.....................415-239-4230
Zajack, Greg/1517 W Alton Ave, Santa Ana, CA 714-432-8400
Zak, Ed/80 Tehama St, San Francisco, CA 415-781-1611
Zanzinger, David/2411 Main St, Santa Monica, CA 213-399-8802
Zens, Michael/84 University St, Seattle, WA.....................206-623-5249
Zenuk, Alan/POB 3531, Vancouver BC, Canada V6B 3Y6, ...604-733-8271
Zimberoff, Tom/31 Wolfback Ridge Rd, Sausalito, CA 415-331-3100
Zimmerman, Dick Studio/8743 W Washington Blvd,
Los Angeles, CA (P 359) **213-204-2911**
Zimmerman, John/9135 Hazen Dr, Beverly Hills, CA 213-273-2642
Zippel, Arthur/2110 E McFadden #D, Santa Ana, CA 714-835-8400
Zurek, Nikolay/276 Shipley St, San Francisco, CA.....................415-777-9210
Zwart, Jeffrey R/1900-E East Warner, Santa Ana, CA 714-261-5844
Zyber, Tom/1305 E St/Gertrude Pl #D, Santa Ana, CA.....................714-546-2949

S T O C K

N Y C

American Heritage Picture Library/60 Fifth Ave,	212-206-5500
American Library Color Slide Co/121 W 27th St 8th Fl,	212-255-5356
Animals Animals/65 Bleecker St 9th Fl,	212-982-4442
Animals Unlimited/10 W 20th St,	212-633-1004
Argent and Aurum/470 W 24th St,	203-355-9875
Arnold, Peter Stock/1181 Broadway 4th Fl,	212-481-1190
Art Resource Inc/65 Bleecker St 9th Fl,	212-505-8700
Beck's Studio/37-44 82nd St, Jackson Heights	718-424-8751
The Bethel Agency/513 W 54th St #1,	212-664-0455
Bettmann Archive/902 Broadway,	212-777-6200
Black Star/Stock/450 Park Ave South,	212-679-3288
Camera Five Inc/6 W 20th St,	212-989-2004
Camera Press/275 Seventh Ave 5th Fl,	212-689-1340
Camerique Stock Photography/1181 Broadway 2nd Fl,	212-685-3870
Camp, Woodfin Assoc/116 E 27th St,	212-481-6900
Coleman, Bruce Inc/381 Fifth Ave 2nd Fl,	212-683-5227
Comstock/30 Irving Pl,	212-889-9700
Contact Press Images/116 E 27th St 8th Fl,	212-481-6910
Contact Stock Images/415 Madison Ave,	212-750-1020
Cooke, Jerry/161 E 82nd St,	212-288-2045
Culver Pictures Inc/150 W 22nd St 3rd Fl,	212-645-1672
Design Conceptions/Elaine Abrams/112 Fourth Ave,	212-254-1688
DeWys, Leo Inc/1170 Broadway,	212-689-5580
DMI Inc/341 First Ave,	212-777-8135
DPI Inc/19 W 21st St #901,	212-627-4060
Ellis Wildlife Collection/69 Cranberry St, Brooklyn Hts	718-935-9600
Ewing Galloway/, New York,	212-719-4720
Flying Camera Inc/114 Fulton St,	212-619-0808
Focus on Sports/222 E 46th St,	212-661-6860
Four by Five Inc/11 W 19th St 6th Fl,	212-633-0300
FPG International/251 Park Ave S,	212-777-4210
Fundamental Photographs/210 Forsythe St,	212-473-5770
Gabriel Graphic News Service/38 Madison Sq Sta,	212-254-8863
Galloway, Ewing/100 Merrick Road, Rockville Center	516-764-8620
Gamma-Liaison Photo Agency/11 E 26th St,	212-888-7272
Globe Photos Inc/275 Seventh Ave 21st Fl,	212-689-1340
The Granger Collection/1841 Broadway,	212-586-0971
Gross, Lee Assoc/366 Madison Ave,	212-682-5240

**Heyl, Fran Assoc/230 Park Ave #2525,
(P 406,407)** **212-581-6470**

Heyman, Ken/37 Bank St,	212-627-2028

The Image Bank/111 Fifth Ave, (P Back Cover) **212-529-6700**

Image Resources/224 W 29th St,	212-736-2523
Images Press Service/22 E 17th St #226,	212-675-3707
Index Stock International Inc/126 Fifth Ave,	212-929-4644
International Stock Photos/113 E 31st St #1A,	212-696-4666
Keystone Press Agency Inc/202 E 42nd St,	212-924-8123
The Kobal Collection/10 W 20th St,	212-633-1005
Lewis, Frederick Inc/134 W 29th St #1003,	212-594-8816
Life Picture Service/Rm 28-58 Time-Life Bldg,	212-522-4800
London Features Int'l USA Ltd/215 W 84th St #406,	212-724-8780
Magnum Photos Inc/251 Park Ave S,	212-475-7600
Maisel, Jay/190 Bowery,	212-431-5013
MediChrome/232 Madison Ave,	212-679-8480
Memory Shop Inc/109 E 12th St,	212-473-2404
Monkmeyer Press Photo Agency/118 E 28th St #615,	212-689-2242
Nance Lee/215 W 84th St #406,	212-724-8780
NBA Entertainment/38 E 32nd St,	212-532-6223
Omni Photo Communication/5 E 22nd St #6N,	212-995-0805
Onyx Enterprises/59 W 19th St,	212-633-2050
Photo Files/1235 E 40th St, Brooklyn	718-338-2245
Photo Researchers Inc/60 E 56th St,	212-758-3420
Photofest/47 W 13th St 2nd Fl,	212-633-6330
Photography for Industry/1697 Broadway,	212-757-9255
Photoreporters/875 Ave of Americas #1003,	212-736-7602
Phototake/4523 Broadway #7G,	212-942-8185
Pictorial Parade/130 W 42nd St,	212-840-2026
Plessner Internt'l/95 Madison Ave,	212-686-2444
Rangefinder Corp/275 Seventh Ave,	212-689-1340
RDR Productions/351 W 54th St,	212-586-4432
Reese, Kay/225 Central Park West,	212-799-1133
Reference Pictures/900 Broadway #802,	212-254-0008
Retna Ltd/36 W 56th St #3A,	212-489-1230

Roberts, H Armstrong/1181 Broadway,	212-685-3870
Roberts, John/433 W 21st St #5A,	503-227-0051
Science Photo Library Int'l/118 E 28th St #715,	212-683-4028
Shashinka Photo/501 Fifth Ave #2108,	212-490-2180
Shostal Assoc/10 W 20th St,	212-633-0101
Sochurek, Howard Inc/680 Fifth Ave,	212-582-1860
Sovfoto-Eastphoto Agency/225 W 34th St #1505,	212-564-5485
Spano/Roccanova/16 W 46th St,	212-840-7450
Sports Illustrated Pictures/Time-Life Bldg 20th Fl,	212-522-2803
Steinhauser, Art Ent/305 E 40th St,	212-953-1722

The Stock Market/1181 Broadway 3rd Fl, (P 401) **212-684-7878**

The Stock Shop/232 Madison Ave,	212-679-8480
Stockphotos Inc/373 Park Ave S 6th Fl,	212-686-1196
The Strobe Studio Inc/91 Fifth Ave,	212-532-1977
Superstock/10 W 20th St,	212-633-0200
Sygma Photo News/225 W 57th St 7th Fl,	212-765-1820
Tamin Productions/440 West End Ave #4E,	212-807-6691
Taurus Photos/118 E 28th St,	212-683-4025
Telephoto/8 Thomas St,	212-406-2440
Time Picture Synd/Time & Life Bldg,	212-522-3866
Uncommon Stock/1181 Broadway 4th Fl,	212-481-1190
UPI/Bettmann Newsphotos/902 Broadway 5th Fl,	212-777-6200
Vierheller, Shirley/11 W 19th St 6th Fl,	212-633-0300
Visions & Images/57-59 W 19th St #6D,	212-627-9040
Wheeler Pictures/Comstock/30 Irving Place,	212-564-5430
Wide World Photos Inc/50 Rockefeller Plaza,	212-621-1930
Winiker, Barry M/173 W 78th St,	212-580-0841

N O R T H E A S T

Allen, John Inc/116 North Ave, Park Ridge, NJ	201-391-3299
Anthro-Photo/33 Hurlbut St, Cambridge, MA	617-497-7227
Authenticated News Int'l/29 Katonah Ave, Katonah, NY	914-232-7726
Bergman, LV & Assoc/East Mountain Rd S, Cold Spring, NY	914-265-3656
Blizzard, William C/PO Box 1696, Beckley, WV	304-755-0094
Camerique Stock Photo/45 Newbury St, Boston, MA	617-267-6450
Camerique Stock Photo/1701 Skippack Pike, Blue Bell, PA	215-272-4000
Cape Scapes/542 Higgins Crowell Rd, West Yarmouth, MA	508-362-8222
Chandoha, Walter/RD 1 PO Box 287, Annandale, NJ	201-782-3666
Chimera Productions/PO Box 1742, Clarksburg, WV	304-623-5368
Consolidated News Pictures/209 Penn Ave SE, Washingtn, DC	202-543-3203
Cyr Color Photo/PO Box 2148, Norwalk, CT	203-838-8230
DCS Enterprises/12806 Gaffney Rd, Silver Spring, MD	301-622-2323
Devaney Stock Photos/755 New York Ave, Huntington, NY	516-673-4477
Dunn, Phoebe/20 Silvermine Rd, New Canaan, CT	203-966-9791
Earth Scenes/Animals Animals/17 Railroad Ave, Chatham, NY	518-392-5500
Educational Dimension Stock/PO Box 126, Stamford, CT	203-327-4612
Ewing Galloway/100 Merrick Rd, Rockville Centre, NY	516-764-8620
F/Stop Pictures Inc/PO Box 359, Springfield, VT	802-885-5261
Folio/3417 1/2 M St NW, Washington, DC	202-965-2410

**Garber, Bette S/2110 Valley Dr, West Chester,
PA (P 405)** **215-692-9076**

Headhunters/2619 Lovegrove St, Baltimore, MD	301-338-1820
Heilman, Grant/506 W Lincoln Ave, Lititz, PA	717-626-0296

The Image Bank/, Boston, MA (P Back Cover) **617-267-8866**

Image Photos/Main St, Stockbridge, MA	413-298-5500
Image Specialists/12 Sharon St, Medford, MA	617-483-1422
The Image Works Inc/PO Box 443, Woodstock, NY	914-679-5603
Jones, G P - Stock/45 Newbury St, Boston, MA	617-267-6450
Lambert, Harold M/2801 W Cheltenham Ave, Phila, PA	215-224-1400
Light, Paul/1430 Massachusetts Ave, Cambridge, MA	617-628-1052
Lumiere/512 Adams St, Centerport, NY	516-271-6133
Mercier, Louis/15 Long Lots Rd, Westport, CT	203-227-1620
Morons, Bill/Box 4166/Molyneaux Rd, Camden, ME	207-236-3130
Myers Studios/5575 Big Tree Rd, Orchard Park, NY	716-662-6002
Natural Selection/177 St Paul St, Rochester, NY	716-232-1502
North Wind Picture Archives/RR 1 Box 172, Alfred, ME	207-490-1940
Philiba, Allan A/3408 Bertha Dr, Baldwin, NY	516-623-7841
Photo Resources Stock/511 Broadway, Saratoga Springs, NY	518-587-4730
The Picture Cube/89 Broad St, Boston, MA	617-367-1532
Picture Group/5 Steeple St, Providence, RI	401-273-5473
Positive Images/317 N Main St, Natick, MA	508-653-7610
Rainbow/PO Box 573, Housatonic, MA	413-274-6211
Roberts, H Armstrong/4203 Locust St, Philadelphia, PA	215-386-6300
Rotman, Jeff/14 Cottage Ave, Somerville, MA	617-666-0874
Sandak Inc/180 Harvard Ave, Stamford, CT	203-348-4721
Seitz & Seitz/1006 N Second Ave #1A, Harrisburg, PA	717-232-7944
Sequis Stock Photo/9 W 29th St, Baltimore, MD	301-467-7300
Sickles Photo Reporting/PO Box 98, Maplewood, NJ	201-763-6355
Sportschrome/10 Brynkerhoff Ave 2nd Fl, Palisades Park, NJ	201-568-1412

Starwood/PO Box 40503, Washington, DC 202-362-7404
Stock Boston Inc/36 Gloucester St, Boston, MA 617-266-2300
Stock Option/213 N 12th St, Allentown, PA 215-776-7381
Sutton, Bug/6 Carpenter St, Salem, MA 508-741-0806
Undersea Systems/PO Box 29M, Bay Shore, NY 516-666-3127
Uniphoto Picture Agency/3205 Grace St SW, Washington, DC........202-333-0500
Vermont Stock Photo/22 Crescent Beach Dr, Burlington, VT 802-862-5912
View Finder Stock Photo/2310 Penn Ave, Pittsburgh, PA...............412-391-8720
Weidman, H Mark/2112 Goodwin Lane, North Wales, PA...............215-646-1745
Woppel, Carl/PO Box 199, Islip, NY 516-581-7762

SOUTHEAST

Camera MD Studios/8290 NW 26 Pl, Ft Lauderdale, FL 305-741-5560
Florida Image File/222 2nd St N, St Petersburg, FL......................813-894-8433
Focus/Virginia/PO Box 5778, Richmond, VA.................................804-783-1703
Fotoconcept/408 SE 11th Ct, Ft Lauderdale, FL............................305-463-1912
The Image Bank/, Naples, FL (P Back Cover)..............**813-566-3444**
**The Image Bank/3490 Piedmont Rd NE #1106,
Atlanta, GA (P Back Cover)**..**404-233-9920**
**Instock Inc/516 NE 13th St, Ft Lauderdale,
FL (P 408)**...**305-527-4111**
National Stock Network/8960 SW 114th St, Miami, FL 305-233-1703
Phelps Agency/3210 Peachtree St NW, Atlanta, GA.....................404-264-0264
Photo Options/1432 Linda Vista Dr, Birmingham, AL....................205-979-8412
Photri(Photo Research Int'l)/505 W Windsor/Alexandria, VA 703-836-4439
Picturesque/1520 Brookside Dr #3, Raleigh, NC 919-828-0023
Pinckney, Jim Photo/PO Box 22887, Lake Buena Vista, FL 407-239-8855
**Sandved & Coleman/12539 North Lake Court,
Fairfax, VA (P 413)**..**703-968-6769**
Sharp Shooters/4950 SW 72nd Ave #114, Miami, FL...................305-666-1266
Sherman, Ron/PO Box 28656, Atlanta, GA..................................404-993-7197
**Southern Stock Photos/3601 W Commercial Blvd
#33, Ft Lauderdale, FL (P 396)**..**305-486-7117**
Sports File/3800 NW 32nd Ave, Miami, FL (P 414).......**305-633-4666**
Stills Inc/3210 Peachtree Rd NE #14, Atlanta, GA.......................404-233-0022
Stock Options/851 French St, New Orleans, LA............................504-486-7700
Stockfile/2107 Park Ave, Richmond, VA.......................................804-358-6364
The Waterhouse/PO Box 2487, Key Largo, FL..............................305-451-3737

MIDWEST

A-Stock Photo Finder/230 N Michigan #1100, Chicago, IL.............312-645-0611
Artstreet/111 E Chestnut St, Chicago, IL 312-664-3049
Blasdel, John/2815 W 89th St, Leawood, KS 913-648-5973
Brooks & VanKirk/855 W Blackhawk St, Chicago, IL....................312-642-7766
Bundt, Nancy/1908 Kenwood Pkw, Minneapolis, MN.....................612-377-7773
Camerique Stock Photo/233 E Wacker Dr, Chicago, IL.................312-938-4466
Camerique Stock Photo/180 Bloor St W, Toronto 416-925-4323
Campbell Stock/28000 Middlebelt Rd, Farmington Hills, MI 313-626-5233
Click/ Chicago Ltd/213 W Institute Pl #503, Chicago, IL...............312-787-7880
Collectors Series/161 W Harrison, Chicago, IL.............................312-427-5311
**Custom Medical Stock Photo Inc/3819 North
Southport Ave, Chicago, IL (P 404)**.....................................**312-248-3200**
Focus Stock Photo/950 Yonge St, Toronto M4W 2J4, ON 416-968-6619
Frozen Images/400 First Ave N #626, Minneapolis, MN................612-339-3191
Gartman, Marilyn/510 N Dearborn, Chicago, IL............................312-661-1656
Gibler, Mike/2716 Pestalozzi, St Louis, MO 314-776-5885
Hedrich-Blessing/11 W Illinois St, Chicago, IL.............................312-321-1151
Historical Picture Service/921 W Van Buren #201, Chicago, IL 312-346-0599
Hot Shots Stock/309 Lesmill Rd, Toronto M3B 2V1, ON...............416-441-3281
Ibid Inc/935 West Chestnut, Chicago, IL......................................312-733-8000
**The Image Bank/550 Queen St E #300, Toronto,
ON (P Back Cover)**..**416-362-6931**
**The Image Bank/822 Marquette Ave, Minneapolis,
MN (P Back Cover)**...**612-332-8935**
**The Image Bank/510 N Dearborn #930, Chicago,
IL (P Back Cover)**...**312-329-1817**
Journalism Services Stock/118 E 2nd St, Lockport, IL..................312-951-0269
Masterfile/2 Carlton St #617, Toronto M5B 1J3, ON ....
Miller + Comstock/180 Bloor St W #102, Toronto, ON..................416-925-4323
Nawrocki Stock Photo/332 S Michigan Ave #1630, Chicago, IL.....312-427-8625
Northern Light/5517 Odana Rd, Madison, WI 608-274-2765
Panoramic Stock Images/230 N Michigan Ave, Chicago, IL 312-236-8545
Photographic Resources/6633 Delmar St, St Louis, MO...............314-721-5838
The Photoletter/Pine Lake Farm, Osceola, WI..............................715-248-3800
Pix International/300 N State #3926, Chicago, IL..........................312-321-9071
Schroeder, Loranelle/400 First Ave N #626, Minneapolis, MN 612-339-3191
Stone, Tony Worldwd/233 East Ontario, Chicago, IL....................312-787-7880
Studio B Stock/107 W Van Buren #211, Chicago, IL.....................312-939-4677
Thill, Nancy/124 E Wpolk #307, Chicago, IL 312-939-7770

Third Coast Stock/PO Box 92397, Milwaukee, WI.......................414-765-9442
Zehrt, Jack/PO Box 122A Rt5, Pacific, MO..................................314-458-3600

SOUTHWEST

**Adstock Photos/6219 North 9th Place, Phoenix,
AZ (P 402)**...**602-437-8772**
Condroy, Scott/4810 S 40th St #3A, Phoenix, AZ.......................602-437-8772
Gilbert, Wayne/PO Box 66615, Houston, TX...............................714-521-9582
**Golfoto Inc/224 N Independence #800, Enid,
OK (P 400)**...**800-338-1656**
The Image Bank/, Houston, TX (P Back Cover)..........**713-668-0066**
**The Image Bank/1336 Conant St, Dallas,
TX (P Back Cover)**..**214-631-3808**
Image Venders/1222 N Winnetka, Dallas, TX..............................214-742-3414
**Ives, Tom/2250 North El Moraga, Tucson,
AZ (P 401)**...**602-743-0750**
McLaughlin, Herb & Dorothy/2344 W Holly, Phoenix, AZ............602-258-6551
Photo Assoc of Texas/PO Box 887, Tomball, TX 713-351-5740
Photobank/313 E Thomas Rd #102, Phoenix, AZ........................602-265-5591
**Raphaele/Digital Transparencies Inc/616 Hawthorne,
Houston, TX (P 399)**...**713-524-2211**
Running Productions/PO Box 1237, Flagstaff, AZ........................602-774-2923
The Stock House Inc/9261 Kirby, Houston, TX.............................713-796-8400
Visual Images West/600 E Baseline Rd #B-6, Tempe, AZ............602-820-5403

ROCKY MTN

**Ambrose, Paul Studios/PO Box 8158, Durango,
CO (P 403)**...**303-259-5925**
Aspen Stock Photo/PO Box 4063, Aspen, CO.............................303-925-8280
Bair, Royce & Assoc/6640 South 2200 West, Salt Lake City, UT....801-569-1155
Dannen, Kent & Donna/851 Peak View/MEstes Park, CO............303-586-5794
Hill, Judy/205 South Mill St, Aspen, CO......................................303-925-1836
Images of Nature/PO Box 2935, Jackson Hole, WY.....................307-733-6179
International Photo File/PO Box 343, Magna, UT..........................801-250-3447
**Miles, Kent/465 Ninth Avenue, Salt Lake City,
UT (P 379,411)**..**801-364-5755**
The Photo Bank/271 Second Ave N Box 3069, Ketchum, ID.........208-726-5731
Stack, Tom/1322 N Academy Blvd, Colorado Springs, CO 303-570-1000
The Stock Broker/450 Lincoln St #110, Denver, CO.....................303-698-1734
Stock Imagery/711 Kalamath St, Denver, CO..............................303-592-1091
The Stock Solution/6640 South, 2200 West, Salt Lake City, UT....801-569-1155
Wild Pic/1818 16th St, Boulder, CO...
Williams, Hal/PO Box 10436, Aspen, CO....................................303-920-2802

WEST COAST

Adventure Photo/3750 W Pacific Coast Hwy, Ventura, CA............805-643-7751
After Image Inc/6100 Wilshire Blvd #240, Los Angeles, CA..........213-938-1700
Alaska Pictorial Service/Drawer 6144, Anchorage, AK.................907-344-1370
All Sports Photo USA/320 Wilshire Blvd Santa Monica, CA..........213-395-2955
Beebe, Morton & Assoc/150 Lombard St, San Francisco, CA.......415-362-3530
Big City Visual Prdctns/1039 Seventh Ave , San Diego, CA 619-232-3366
Burr, Lawrence/76 Manzanita Rd, Fairfax, CA.............................415-456-9158
Camerique Stock Photo/6640 Sunset Blvd, Hollywood, CA..........213-469-3900
Catalyst/PO Box 689, Haines, AK..907-766-2670
Dae Flights/PO Box 1086, Newport Beach, CA 714-676-3902
Dritsas, George/207 Miller Ave, Mill Valley, CA...........................415-381-5485
Earth Images/PO Box 10352, Bainbridge Isl, WA 206-842-7793
Ergenbright, Ric Photo/PO Box 1067, Bend, OR.........................503-389-7662
Focus West/4112 Adams Ave, San Diego, CA.............................619-280-3595
Four by Five Inc/99 Osgood Place, San Francisco, CA.................415-781-4433
French, Peter/PO Box 100, Kamuela, HI......................................808-889-6488
Gibson, Mark/PO Box 14542, San Francisco, CA........................415-524-8118
Great American Stock/7566 Trade St, San Diego, CA..................619-297-2205
Grubb, T D/5806 Deerhead Rd, Malibu, CA.................................213-457-5539
Havens, Carol/POB 662, Laguna Beach, CA...............................714-497-1908
**The Image Bank/, San Francisco,
CA (P Back Cover)**..**415-788-2208**
**The Image Bank/8228 Sunset Blvd #310,
Los Angeles, CA (P Back Cover)**...**213-656-9003**
Jeton/513 Harrington Ave NE, Renton, WA.................................206-226-1408
**Kimball, Ron Stock/1960 Colony, Mt View,
CA (P 409)**...**415-948-2939**
**Leeson, Tom & Pat/PO Box 2498, Vancouver,
WA (P 410)**...**206-256-0436**
Live Stock Photo/190 Parnassus Ave #5, San Francisco, CA.......415-753-6261
Long Photo Inc/57865 Rickenbacher Rd, Los Angeles, CA..........213-888-9944
Madison, David/2330 Old Middlefield Rd, Mt View, CA.................415-961-6297
**Muench, David Photo Inc/PO Box 30500,
Santa Barbara, CA (P 397)**...**805-967-4488**
The New Image Inc/38 Quail Ct 200, Walnut Creek, CA...............415-934-2405

NFL Photos/6701 Center Dr W #1111, Los Angeles, CA 213-215-3813
O'Hara, Pat/PO Box 955, Port Angeles, WA......................................206-457-4212
Pacific Stock/PO Box 90517, Honolulu,
HI (P 398) **808-922-0975**
Peebles, Douglas /445 Iliwahi Loop, Kailua,
HI (P 412) **808-533-6686**
Photo Network/1541 Parkway Loop #J, Tustin, CA 714-259-1244
Photo Vault/1045 17th St, San Francisco, CA 415-552-9682
Photobank/CA/17952-B Skypark Circle, Irvine, CA..........................714-250-4480
Photophile/2311 Kettner Blvd, San Diego, CA 619-234-4431
Shooting Star/PO Box 93368, Hollywood, CA 213-876-2000
Simpson, Ed/PO Box 397, S Pasadena, CA....................................213-682-3131
Terraphotographics/BPS/PO Box 490, Moss Beach, CA 415-726-6244
TRW/9841 Airport Blvd #1414, Los Angeles, CA 213-536-4880
Visual Impact/733 Auahi St, Honolulu,
HI (P 415) **808-524-8269**
West Light/2223 S Carmelina Ave, Los Angeles, CA......................213-477-0421
West Stock/83 S King St #520, Seattle, WA 206-621-1611
Zephyr Pictures/2120 Jimmy Durante Blvd, Del Mar, CA.................619-755-1200

LABS & RETOUCHERS

NYC

Accu-Color Group Inc/103 Fifth Ave,	212-989-8235
ACS Studios/2 West 46th St,	212-575-9250
Adams Photoprint Co Inc/60 E 42nd St,	212-697-4980
Alchemy Color Ltd/125 W 45th St,	212-997-1944
American Blue Print Co Inc/7 E 47th St,	212-751-2240
American Photo Print Co/285 Madison Ave,	212-532-2424
American Photo Print Co/350 Fifth Ave,	212-736-2885
Andy's Place/17 E 48th St,	212-371-1362
Apco-Apeda Photo Co/250 W 54th St,	212-586-5755
Appel, Albert/119 W 23rd St,	212-989-6585
Arkin-Medo/30 E 33rd St,	212-685-1969
ASAP Photolab/40 E 49th St,	212-832-1223
AT & S Retouching/230 E 44th St,	212-986-0977
Atlantic Blue Print Co/575 Madison Ave,	212-755-3388
Authenticolor Labs Inc/227 E 45th St,	212-867-7905
Avekta Productions Inc/164 Madison Ave,	212-686-4550
AZO Color Labs/149 Madison Ave,	212-982-6610
Bebell Color Labs/416 W 45th St,	212-245-8900
Bellis, Dave/15 E 55th St,	212-753-3740
Bellis, Dave Studios/155 E 55th St,	212-753-3740
Benjamin, Bernard/1763 Second Ave,	212-722-7773
Berger, Jack/41 W 53rd St,	212-245-5705
Berkey K & L/222 E 44th St,	212-661-5600
Bishop Retouching/236 E 36th St,	212-889-3525
Blae, Ken Studios/1501 Broadway,	212-869-3488
Bluestone Photoprint Co Inc/19 W 34th St,	212-564-1516
Bonaventura Studio/307 E 44th St #1612,	212-687-9208
Broderson, Charles Backdrops/873 Broadway #612,	212-925-9392
Brunel, Jean Inc/11 Jay St,	212-226-3009
C & C Productions/445 E 80th St,	212-472-3700
Cacchione & Sheehan/1 West 37th St,	212-869-2233
Carlson & Forino Studios/230 E 44th St,	212-697-7044
Cavalluzzo, Dan/49 W 45th St,	212-921-5954
Certified Color Service/2812 41st Ave, Long Island City	212-392-6065
Chapman, Edwin W/20 E 46th St,	212-697-0872
Chroma Copy/423 West 55th St,	212-399-2420
Chrome Print/104 E 25th St,	212-228-0840
CitiChrome Lab/158 W 29th St,	212-695-0935
Clayman, Andrew/334 Bowery #6F,	212-674-4906
Colmer, Brian-The Final touch/310 E 46th St,	212-682-3012
Coln, Stewart/563 Eleventh Ave,	212-868-1440
Color Design Studio/19 W 21st St,	212-255-8103
Color Masters Inc/143 E 27th St,	212-889-7464
Color Perfect Inc/200 Park Ave S,	212-777-1210
Color Pro Labs/40 W 37th St,	212-563-5599
Color Unlimited Inc/443 Park Ave S,	212-889-2440
Color Vision Photo Finishers/642 9th Avenue,	212-757-2787
Color Wheel Inc/227 E 45th St,	212-697-2434
Colorama Labs/40 W 37th St,	212-279-1950
Colorite Film Processing/115 E 31st St,	212-532-2116
Colotone Seperator/555 Fifth Ave,	212-557-5564
Columbia Blue & Photoprint Co/14 E 39th St,	212-532-9424
Commerce Photo Print Co/415 Lexington Ave,	212-986-2068
Compo Photocolor/18 E 48th St,	212-758-1690
Copy-Line Corp/40 W 37th St,	212-563-3535
Copycolor/8 W 30th St,	212-725-8252
Copytone Inc/8 W 45th St,	212-575-0235
Cordero, Felix/159 E 104th St,	212-289-2861
Corona Color Studios Inc/10 W 33rd St,	212-239-4990
Cortese, Phyllis/306 E 52nd St,	212-421-4664
Crandall, Robert Assoc/306 E 45th St,	212-661-4710
Creative Color Inc/25 W 45th St,	212-582-3841
Crowell, Joyce/333 E 30th St,	212-683-3055
Crown Photo/370 W 35th St,	212-279-1950
Dai Nippon Printing/1633 Broadway,	212-397-1880
Davis-Ganes/15 E 40th St,	212-687-6537
Diamond Art Studio/11 E 36th St,	212-685-6622
Diamond, Richard/50 E 42nd St,	212-697-4720

Diana Studio/301 W 53rd St,	212-757-0445
Dimension Color Labs Inc/1040 Ave of Amer,	212-354-5918
DiPierro-Turiel/210 E 47th St,	212-752-2260
Drop Everything/20 W 20th St,	212-242-2735
Duggal Color Projects Inc/9 W 20th St,	212-924-6363
Dzurella, Paul Studio/15 W 38th St,	212-840-8623
Ecay, Thom/49 W 45th St,	212-840-6277
Edstan Productions/240 Madison Ave,	212-686-3666
Egelston Retouching Services/333 Fifth Ave 3rd Fl,	212-213-9095
Evans-Avedisian DiStefano Inc/29 W 38th St,	212-697-4240
Exact Photo/247 W 30th St,	212-564-2568
Farmakis, Andreas/835 Third Ave,	212-758-5280
Filmstat/520 Fifth Ave,	212-840-1676
Fine-Art Color Lab Inc/221 Park Ave S,	212-674-7640
Finley Photographics Inc/488 Madison Ave,	212-688-3025
Flax, Sam Inc/111 Eighth Ave,	212-620-3000
Flushing Photo Center/36-33 Main St, Flushing	718-658-6033
Fodale Studio/247 E 50th St,	212-755-0150
Forway Studios Inc/441 Lexington Ave,	212-661-0260
Four Colors Photo Lab Inc/10 E 39th St,	212-889-3399
Foursome Color Litho/30 E Irving Pl,	212-475-9219
Frenchys Color Lab/10 E 38th St,	212-889-7787
Frey, Louis Co Inc/90 West St,	212-791-0500
Friedlob, Herbert/1810 Ave N #3C, Brooklyn	718-375-4857
Friedman, Estelle Retouchers/160 E 38th St,	212-532-0084
Fromia, John A/799 Broadway,	212-473-7930
Fuji Film/350 Fifth Ave,	INSIDE BACK
Gads Color/135 W 41st St,	212-221-0923
Gayde, Richard Assoc Inc/515 Madison Ave,	212-421-4088
Gilbert Studio/210 E 36th St,	212-683-3472
Giraldi, Bob Prodctns/581 Sixth Ave,	212-691-9200
Goodman, Irwin Inc/1156 Avenue of the Americas,	212-944-6337
Graphic Images Ltd/151 W 46th St,	212-869-8370
Gray, George Studios/230 E 44th St,	212-661-0276
Greller, Fred/325 E 64th St,	212-535-6240
Grubb, Louis D/155 Riverside Dr,	212-873-2561
GW Color Lab/36 E 23rd St,	212-677-3800
H-Y Photo Service/16 E 52nd St,	212-371-3018
Hadar, Eric Studio/10 E 39th St,	212-889-2092
Hudson Reproductions Inc/76 Ninth Ave,	212-989-3400
J & R Color Lab/29 W 38th St,	212-869-9870
J M W Studio Inc/230 E 44th St,	212-986-9155
Jaeger, Elliot/49 W 45th St,	212-840-6278
Jellybean Photographics Inc/99 Madison Ave 14th Fl,	212-679-4888
JFC Color Labs Inc/443 Park Ave S,	212-889-0727
Katz, David Studio/6 E 39th St,	212-889-5038
Kaye Graphics Inc/151 Lexington Ave,	212-889-8240
KG Studios Inc/56 W 45th St,	212-840-7930
Kurahara, Joan/611 Broadway,	212-505-8589
LaFerla, Sandro/108 W 25th St,	212-620-0693
Langen & Wind Color Lab/265 Madison Ave,	212-686-1818
Larson Color Lab/123 Fifth Ave,	212-674-0610
Laumont Color Labs/333 W 52nd St,	212-245-2113
Lawrence Color Systems/250 W 40th St,	212-944-7039
Lieberman, Ken Laboratories/118 W 22nd St 4th Fl,	212-633-0500
Loy-Taubman Inc/34 E 30th St,	212-685-6871
Lucas, Bob/10 E 38th St,	212-725-2090
Lukon Art Service Ltd/56 W 45th St 3rd Fl,	212-575-0474
Mann & Greene Color Inc/320 E 39th St,	212-481-6868
Manna Color Labs Inc/42 W 15th St,	212-691-8360
Marshall, Henry/6 E 39th St,	212-686-1060
Martin, Tulio G Studio/140 W 57th St,	212-245-6489
Martin/Arnold Color Systems/150 Fifth Ave #429,	212-675-7270
Mayer, Kurt Color Labs Inc/1170 Broadway,	212-532-3738
McCurdy & Cardinale Color Lab/65 W 36th St,	212-695-5140
McWilliams, Clyde/151 West 46th St,	212-221-3644
Media Universal Inc/116 W 32nd St,	212-695-7454
Medina Studios Inc/141 E 44th St,	212-867-3113
Miller, Norm & Steve/17 E 48th St,	212-752-4830
Modernage Photo Services/312 E 46th St,	212-661-9190
Moser, Klaus T Ltd/127 E 15th St,	212-475-0038
Motal Custom Darkrooms/25 W 45th St 3rd Fl,	212-757-7874
Murray Hill Photo Print Inc/32 W 39th St,	212-921-4175
My Lab Inc/117 E 30th St,	212-686-8684
My Own Color Lab/45 W 45th St,	212-391-8638
National Reprographics Co/110 W 32nd St,	212-736-5674
New York Camera/131 W 35th St,	212-564-4398
New York Film Works Inc/928 Broadway,	212-475-5700

New York Flash Rental/156 Fifth Ave, ...212-741-1165
Olden Camera/1265 Broadway, ...212-725-1234
Ornaal Color Photos/24 W 25th St, ...212-675-3850
Paccione, E S Inc/150 E 56th St, ...212-755-0965
Palevitz, Bob/333 E 30th St, ...212-684-6026
Pastore dePamphilis Rampone/145 E 32nd St, ...212-889-2221
Pergament Color/305 E 47th St, ...212-751-5367
Photo Retouch Inc/160 E 38th St, ...212-532-0084
Photographic Color Specialists /10-36 47th Rd, L I City, ...718-786-4770
Photographics Unlimited/43 W 22nd St, ...212-255-9678
Photorama/239 W 39th St, ...212-354-5280
PIC Color Corp/25 W 45th St, ...212-575-5600
Portogallo Photo Services/72 W 45th St, ...212-840-2636
Positive Color Inc/405 Lexington, ...212-687-9600
Precision Chromes Inc/310 Madison Ave, ...212-687-5990
Preferred Photographic Co/165 W 46th St, ...212-757-0237
Procil Adstat Co Inc/7 W 45th St, ...212-819-0155
Prussack, Phil/155 E 55th St, ...212-755-2470
Quality Color Lab/305 E 46th St, ...212-753-2200
R & V Studio/32 W 39th St, ...212-944-9590
Rahum Supply Co/1165 Broadway, ...212-685-4784
Rainbow Graphics & Chrome Services/49 W 45th St, ...212-869-3232
Ram Retouching/380 Madison Ave, ...212-599-0985
Ramer, Joe Assoc/509 Madison Ave, ...212-751-0894
Rasulo Graphics Service/36 E 31st St, ...212-686-2861
Regal Velox/25 W 43rd St, ...212-840-0330
Reiter Dulberg/157 W 54th St, ...212-582-6871
Renaissance Retouching/136 W 46th St, ...212-575-5618
Reproduction Color Specialists/9 E 38th St, ...212-683-0833
Retouchers Gallery/211 E 53rd St, ...212-751-9203
Retouching Inc/9 E 38th St, ...212-683-4188
Retouching Plus/125 W 45th St, ...212-764-5959
Rio Enterprises/240 E 58th St, ...212-758-9300
Rivera and Schiff Assoc Inc/21 W 38th St, ...212-354-2977
Robotti, Thomas/5 W 46th St, ...212-840-0215
Rogers Color Lab Corp/165 Madison Ave, ...212-683-6400
Russo Photo Service/432 W 45th St, ...212-247-3817
Sa-Kura Retouching/123 W 44th St, ...212-764-5944
San Photo-Art Service/165 W 29th St, ...212-594-0850
Sang Color Inc/19 W 34th St, ...212-594-4205
Scala Fine Arts Publishers Inc/65 Bleecker St, ...212-673-4988
Schiavone, Joe/301 W 53rd St #4E, ...212-757-0660
Scope Assoc/11 E 22nd St, ...212-674-4190
Scott Screen Prints/228 E 45th St, ...212-697-8923
Scott, Diane Assoc/339 E 58th St, ...212-355-4616
Sharkey, Dick The Studio/301 W 53rd St, ...212-265-1036
Sharron Photographic Labs/260 W 36th St, ...212-239-4980
Simmons-Beal Inc/3 E 40th St, ...212-532-6261
Skeehan Black & White/61 W 23rd St, ...212-675-5454
Slide by Slide/445 E 80th St, ...212-879-5091
Slide Shop Inc/220 E 23rd St, ...212-725-5200
Spano/Roccanova Retouching Inc/16 W 46th St, ...212-840-7450
Spector, Hy Studios/56 W 45th St, ...212-221-3656
Spectrum Creative Retouchers Inc/230 E 44th St, ...212-687-3359
Stanley, Joseph/211 W 58th St, ...212-246-1258
Steinhauser, Art Retouching/305 E 40th St, ...212-953-1722
Stewart Color Labs Inc/563 Eleventh Ave, ...212-868-1440
Studio 55/39 W 38th St, ...212-840-0920
Studio Chrome Lab Inc/36 W 25th St, ...212-989-6767
Studio Macbeth Inc/130 W 42nd St, ...212-921-8922
Studio X/20 W 20th St, ...212-989-9233
Sunlight Graphics/401 5th Ave, ...212-683-4452
Super Photo Color Services/165 Madison Ave, ...212-686-9510
Sutton Studio/112 E 17th St, ...212-777-0301
T R P Slavin Colour Services/920 Broadway, ...212-674-5700
Tanksley, John Studios Inc/210 E 47th St, ...212-752-1150
Tartaro Color Lab/29 W 38th St, ...212-840-1640
The Creative Color Print Lab Inc/25 W 45th St, ...212-582-6237
The Darkroom Inc/222 E 46th St, ...212-687-8920
Todd Photoprint Inc/1600 Broadway, ...212-245-2440
Trio Studio/18 E 48th St, ...212-752-4875
Truglio, Frank & Assoc/835 Third Ave, ...212-371-7635
Twenty/Twenty Photographers Place/20 W 20th St, ...212-675-2020
Ultimate Image/443 Park Ave S 7th Fl, ...212-683-4838
Van Chromes Corp/311 W 43rd St, ...212-582-0505
Venezia, Don Retouching/488 Madison Ave, ...212-688-7649
Verilen Reproductions/3 E 40th St, ...212-686-7774
Vidachrome Inc/25 W 39th St 6th Fl, ...212-391-8124

Vogue Wright Studios/423 West 55th St, ...212-977-3400
Wagner Photoprint Co/121 W 50th St, ...212-245-4796
Ward, Jack Color Service/220 E 23rd St, ...212-725-5200
Way Color Inc/420 Lexington Ave, ...212-687-5610
Weber, Martin J Studio/171 Madison Ave, ...212-532-2695
Weiman & Lester Inc/21 E 40th St, ...212-679-1180
Welbeck Studios Inc/39 W 38th St, ...212-869-1660
Wind, Gerry & Assoc/265 Madison Ave, ...212-686-1818
Winter, Jerry Studio/333 E 45th St, ...212-490-0876
Wolf, Bill/212 E 47th St, ...212-697-6215
Wolsk, Bernard/509 Madison Ave, ...212-751-7727
Zazula, Hy Assoc/2 W 46th St, ...212-819-0444

N O R T H E A S T

Able Art Service/8 Winter St, Boston, MA.....................617-482-4558
Adams & Abbott Inc/46 Summer St, Boston, MA............617-542-1621
Alfie Custom Color/155 N Dean St, Englewood, NJ..........201-569-2028
Alves Photo Service/14 Storrs Ave, Braintree, MA...........617-843-5555
Artography Labs/2419 St Paul St, Baltimore, MD.............301-467-5575
Asman Custom Photo/926 Penn Ave SE, Washington, DC ...202-547-7713
Assoc Photo Labs/1820 Gilford, Montreal, QU................514-523-1139
Blakeslee Lane Studio/916 N Charles St, Baltimore, MD 301-727-8800
Blow-Up/2441 Maryland Ave, Baltimore, MD 301-467-3636
Bonaventure Color Labs/425 Guy St, Montreal, QU..........514-989-1919
Boris Color Lab/35 Landsdowne St, Boston, MA 617-437-1152
Boston Photo Service/112 State St, Boston, MA..............617-523-0508
Calverts Inc/938 Highland Ave, Needham Hts, MA 617-444-8000
Campbell Photo & Printing/1328 'I' St NW, Washington, DC ...202-347-9800
Central Color/1 Prospect Ave, White Plains, NY..............914-681-0218
Chester Photo/398 Centrl Pk Ave/Grnvl Plz, Scarsdale. NY ...914-472-8088
Cinema Services/116 North Ave, Parkridge, NJ...............201-391-3463
Color Film Corp/440 Summer St, Boston, MA................617-426-5655
Color Services/120 Hampton Ave, Needham, MA 617-444-5101
Colorama/420 Valley Brook Ave, Lyndhurst, NJ..............201-933-5660
Colorlab/5708 Arundel Ave, Rockville, MD....................301-770-2128
Colortek/111 Beach St, Boston, MA...........................617-451-0894
Colotone Litho Seperator/260 Branford 97, N Branford, CT....203-481-6190
Complete Photo Service/703 Mt Auburn St, Cambridge, MA ...617-864-5954
Dimension Systems/680 Rhd Islnd Ave NE/Washington, DC....202-832-5401
Dunigan, John V/62 Minnehaha Blvd, Oakland, NJ............201-337-6656
Dunlop Custom Photolab/2321 4th St NE, Washington, DC ...202-526-5000
Durkin, Joseph/25 Huntington, Boston, MA...................617-267-0437
Eastman Kodak/343 State St, Rochester, NY..................716-724-4688
EPD Photo Service/67 Fulton St, Hempstead, NY.............516-486-5300
Five-Thousand K/281 Summer St, Boston, MA................617-542-5995
Foto Fidelity Inc/35 Leon St, Boston, MA......................617-267-6487
G F I Printing & Photo Co/2 Highland St, Port Chester, NY 914-937-2823
Gould, David/76 Coronado St, Atlantic Beach, NY 516-371-2413
Gourdon, Claude Photo Lab/60 Sir Louis VI, St Lambert, QU ...514-671-4604
Graphic Accent/446 Main St PO Box 243, Wilmington, MA 508-658-7602
Iderstine, Van/148 State Hwy 10, E Hanover, NJ..............201-887-7879
Image Inc/1919 Pennsylvania Ave, Washington, DC 202-833-1550
Industrial Color Lab/P O Box 563, Framingham, MA 617-872-3280
JTM Photo Labs Inc/125 Rt 110, Huntington Station, NY 516-549-0010
K E W Color Labs/112 Main St, Norwalk, CT..................203-853-7888
Leonardo Printing Corp/529 E 3rd St, Mount Vernon, NY 914-664-7890
Light-Works Inc/77 College St, Burlington, VT.................802-658-6815
Lighthaus/109 Broad St, Boston, MA..........................617-426-5643
Meyers, Tony/W 70 Century Rd, Paramus, NJ................201-265-6000
Modern Mass Media/Box 950, Chatham, NJ..................201-635-6000
Moore's Photo Laboratory/1107 Main St, Charleston, WV 304-357-4541
Muggeo, Sam/63 Hedgebrook Lane, Stamford, CT..........212-972-0398
Musy, Mark/PO Box 755, Buckingham, PA....................215-794-8851
National Color Labs Inc/306 W 1st Ave, Roselle, NJ..........201-241-1010
National Photo Service/1475 Bergen Blvd, Fort Lee, NJ.......212-860-2324
Noll, Chris/Photo Hand-Tinting, , NJ............................201-775-6825
Northeast Color Research/40 Cameron Ave, Somerville, MA 617-666-1161
Ogunquit Photo School/PO Box 568, Ogunquit, ME..........207-646-7055
Photo Dynamics/PO Box 731, 70 Jackson Dr, Cranford, NJ....201-272-8880
Photo Publishers/1899 'L' St NW, Washington, DC 202-833-1234
Photo-Colortura/PO Box 1749, Boston, MA..................617-522-5102
Regester Photo Service/50 Kane St, Baltimore, MD...........301-633-7600
Retouching Graphics/205 Roosevelt Ave, Massapequa Pk, NY....516-541-2960
Riter, Warren/2291 Penfield, Pittsford, NY.....................716-381-4368
Rothman, Henry/6927 N 19th St, Philadelphia, PA............215-424-6927
Select Photo Service/881 Montee de Liesse, Montreal, QU....514-735-2509
Snyder, Jeffrey/915 E Street NW, Washington, DC 202-347-5777
Spaulding Co Inc/301 Columbus, Boston, MA................617-262-1935

Starlab Photo/4727 Miller Ave, Washington, DC 301-986-5300
Sterling Photo Processing/345 Main Ave, Norwalk, CT 203-847-9145
STI Group/606 W Houstatonic St, Pittsfield, MA.................413-443-7900
Stone Reprographics/44 Brattle St, Cambridge, MA 617-495-0200
Subtractive Technology/338-B Newbury St, Boston, MA.............617-437-1887
Superior Retouching/1955 Mass Ave, Cambridge, MA 617-661-9094
Technical Photography/1275 Bloomfield Ave, Fairfield, NJ 201-227-4646
The Darkroom/443 Broadway, Saratoga Springs, NY 518-587-6465
The Darkroom Inc/232 First Ave, Pittsburgh, PA 412-261-6056
Trama, Gene/571 South Ave, Rochester, NY 716-232-6122
Universal Color Lab/810 Salaberry, Chomeday, QU 514-384-2251
Van Vort, Donald D/71 Capital Hts Rd, Oyster Bay, NY 516-922-5234
Visual Horizons/180 Metropark, Rochester, NY 716-424-5300
Weinstock, Bernie/162 Boylston, Boston, MA 617-423-4481
Wilson, Paul/25 Huntington Ave, Boston, MA 617-437-1236
Zoom Photo Lab/45 St Jacques, Montreal, QU 514-288-5444

SOUTHEAST

A Printers Film Service/904-D Norwalk, Greensboro, NC 919-852-1275
AAA Blue Print Co/3649 Piedmont Rd, Atlanta, GA 404-261-1580
Advance Color Proc/1807 Ponce de Leon Blvd, Miami, FL 305-443-7323
Allen Photo/3808 Wilson Blvd, Arlington, VA 703-524-7121
Associated Photographers/19 SW 6th St, Miami, FL 305-373-4774
Atlanta Blue Print/1052 W Peachtree St N E, Atlanta, GA 404-873-5911
B & W Processing/6808 Hanging Moss, Orlando, FL 305-677-8078
Barral, Yolanda/100 Florida Blvd, Miami, FL 305-261-4767
Berkey Film Processing/1200 N Dixie Hwy, Hollywood, FL.........305-927-8411
Bristow Photo Service/2018 Wilson St, Hollywood, FL 305-920-1377
Chromatics/625 Fogg St, Nashville, TN 615-254-0063
Clark Studio/6700 Sharon Rd, Charlotte, NC 704-552-1021
Color Copy Center/5745 Columbia Cir, W Palm Beach, FL 305-842-9500
Color Copy Inc/925 Gervais St, Columbia, SC 803-256-0225
Color Image-Atlanta/478 Armour Circle, Atlanta, GA 404-876-0209
Color Retouching/1715 Kirby Pkwy, Memphis, TN 901-754-2411
Colorcraft/331 Sunset Shopping Center, Columbia, SC 803-252-0600
Customlab/508 Armour Cr, Atlanta, GA......................404-875-0289
Dixie Color Lab/520 Highland S, Memphis, TN 901-458-1818
E-Six Lab/53 14th St NE, Atlanta, GA 404-885-1293
Eagle Photographics/3612 Swann Ave, Tampa, FL 813-870-2495
Florida Color Lab/PO Box 10907, Tampa, FL 813-877-8658
Florida Photo Inc/781 NE 125th St, N Miami, FL 305-891-6616
Fordyce, R B Photography/4873 NW 36th St, Miami, FL...........305-885-3406
Gables Blueprint/4075 Ponce De Leone Blvd, Coral Gbls, FL 305-443-7146
General Color Corp/604 Brevard Ave, Cocoa Beach, FL 305-631-1602
Infinite Color/2 East Glebe Rd, Alexandria, VA 703-549-2242
Inter-American Photo/8157 NW 60th St, Miami, FL 305-592-3833
Janousek & Kuehl/3300 NE Expressway #1-I, Atlanta, GA 404-458-8989
Klickovich, Robert/1638 Eastern Pkwy, Louisville, KY............502-459-0295
Laser Color Labs/Fairfield Dr, W Palm Beach, FL 305-848-2000
Litho Color Plate/7887 N W 55th St, Miami, FL 305-592-1605
Mid-South Color Laboratories/496 Emmet, Jackson, TN 901-422-6691
Northside Blueprint/5141 New Peachtree Rd, Atlanta, GA 404-458-8411
Par Excellence/2900 Youree Dr, Shreveport, LA 318-869-2533
Photo-Pros/635 A Pressley Rd, Charlotte, NC 704-525-0551
Plunkett Graphics/1052 W Peachtree St, Atlanta, GA 404-873-5976
Reynolds, Charles/1715 Kirby Pkwy, Memphis, TN 901-754-2411
Rich, Bob Photo/12495 NE 6th Ave, Miami, FL 305-893-6137
Rothor Color Labs/1251 King St, Jacksonville, FL 904-388-7717
S & S Pro Color Inc/2801 S MacDill Ave, Tampa, FL............813-831-1811
Sheffield & Board/18 E Main St, Richmond, VA 804-649-8870
Smith's Studio/2420 Wake Forest Rd, Raleigh, NC 919-834-6491
Spectrum Custom Color Lab/302 E Davis Blvd, Tampa, FL 813-251-0338
Studio Masters Inc/1398 NE 125th St, N Miami, FL 305-893-3500
Supreme Color Inc/71 NW 29th St, Miami, FL 305-573-2934
Taffae, Syd/3550 N Bayhomes Dr, Miami, FL 305-667-5252
The Color Lab/111 NE 21st St, Miami, FL 305-576-3207
Thomson Photo Lab/4210 Ponce De Leon Blvd, Coral Gbls, FL 305-443-0669
Viva-Color Labs/121 Linden Ave NE, Atlanta, GA 404-881-1313
Williamson Photography Inc/9511 Colonial Dr, Miami, FL 305-255-6400
World Color Inc/1281 US #1 North, Ormond Beach, FL 904-677-1332

MIDWEST

A-1 Photo Service/105 W Madison St #907, Chicago, IL 312-346-2248
Absolute Color Slides/197 Dundas E, Toronto 15A 124, ON..........416-868-0413
AC Color Lab Inc/2160 Payne Ave, Cleveland, OH 216-621-4575
Ad Photo/2056 E 4th St, Cleveland, OH.....................216-621-9360
Advantage Printers/1307 S Wabash, Chicago, IL...............312-663-0933
Airbrush Arts/1235 Glenview Rd, Glenview, IL.................312-998-8345

Amato Photo Color/818 S 75th St, Omaha, NE 402-393-8380
Anderson Graphics/521 N 8th St, Milwaukee, WI 414-276-4445
Anro Color/1819 9th St, Rockford, IL.......................815-962-0884
Arrow Photo Copy/523 S Plymouth St, Chicago, IL 312-427-9515
Artstreet/111 E Chestnut St, Chicago, IL 312-664-3049
Astra Photo Service/6 E Lake, Chicago, IL 312-372-4366
Astro Color Labs/61 W Erie St, Chicago, IL 312-280-5500
Benjamin Film Labs/287 Richmond St, Toronto, ON 416-863-1166
BGM Color Labs/497 King St E, Toronto, ON 416-947-1325
Boulevard Photo/333 N Michigan Ave, Chicago, IL 312-263-3508
Brookfield Photo Service/9146 Broadway, Brookfield, IL 312-485-1718
Buffalo Photo Co/60 W Superior, Chicago, IL 312-787-6476
Carriage Barn Studio/2360 Riverside Dr, Beloit, WI 608-365-2405
Chroma Studios/2300 Maryland Ln, Columbus, OH 614-471-1191
Chromatics Ltd/4507 N Kedzie Ave, Chicago, IL 312-478-3850
Cockrell, Ray/1737 McGee, Kansas City, MO 816-471-5959
Color Central/612 N Michigan Ave, Chicago, IL 312-321-1696
Color Corp of Canada/1198 Eglinton W, Toronto, ON 416-783-0320
Color Darkroom Corp/3320 W Vliet St, Milwaukee, WI 414-344-3377
Color Detroit Inc/310 Livernois, Ferndale, MI 313-546-1800
Color Graphics Inc/5809 W Divison St, Chicago, IL 312-261-4143
Color International Labs/593 N York St, Elmhurst, IL 312-279-6632
Color Perfect Inc/24 Custer St, Detroit, MI 313-872-5115
Color Service Inc/325 W Huron St, Chicago, IL 312-664-5225
Color Studio Labs/1553 Dupont, Toronto, ON 416-531-1177
Color Systems/5719 N Milwaukee Ave, Chicago, IL 312-763-6664
Color Technique Inc/57 W Grand Ave, Chicago, IL 312-337-5051
Color West Ltd/1901 W Cermak Rd, Broadview, IL 312-345-1110
Coloron Corp/360 E Grand Ave, Chicago, IL 312-265-6766
Colorprints Inc/410 N Michigan Ave, Chicago, IL 312-467-6930
Commercial Colorlab Service/41 So Stolp, Aurora, IL 312-892-9330
Copy-Matics/6324 W Fond du Lac Ave, Milwaukee, WI 414-462-2250
Corley D & S Ltd/3610 Nashua Dr #7, Mississaugua, ON 416-675-3511
Custom Color Processing Lab/1300 Rand Rd, Des Plaines, IL 312-297-6333
Cutler-Graves/535 N Michigan Ave, Chicago, IL 312-828-9310
D-Max Colorgraphics/1662 Headlands Dr, Fenton, MO 314-343-3570
Diamond Graphics/6324 W Fond du Lac Ave, Milwaukee, WI 414-462-2250
Drake, Brady Copy Center/413 N 10th St, St Louis, MO 314-421-1311
Draper St Photolab/1300 W Draper St, Chicago, IL 312-975-7200
Duncan, Virgil Studios/4725 E State Blvd, Ft Wayne, IN 219-483-6011
Dzuroff Studios/1020 Huron Rd E, Cleveland, OH 216-696-0120
Eastman Kodak Co/1712 S Prairie Ave, Chicago, IL 312-922-9691
Emulsion Stripping Ltd/4 N Eighth Ave, Maywood, IL 312-344-8100
Fotis Photo/25 E Hubbard St, Chicago, IL 312-337-7300
Foto-Comm Corporation/215 W Superior, Chicago, IL 312-943-0450
Fromex/188 W Washington, Chicago, IL 312-853-0067
Gallery Color Lab/620 W Richmond St, Toronto, ON 416-367-9770
Gamma Photo Lab Inc/314 W Superior St, Chicago, IL 312-337-0022
Graphic Lab Inc/124 E Third St, Dayton, OH 513-461-3774
Graphic Spectrum/523 S Plymouth Ct, Chicago, IL 312-427-9515
Greenhow, Ralph/333 N Michigan Ave, Chicago, IL 312-782-6833
Grignon Studios/1300 W Altgeld, Chicago, IL 312-975-7200
Grossman Knowling Co/7350 John C Lodge, Detroit, MI 313-832-2360
Harlem Photo Service/6706 Northwest Hwy, Chicago, IL 312-763-5860
Hill, Vince Studio/119 W Hubbard, Chicago, IL 312-644-6690
Imperial Color Inc/618 W Jackson Blvd, Chicago, IL 312-454-1570
J D H Inc/1729 Superior Ave, Cleveland, OH 216-771-0346
Jahn & Ollier Engrvng/817 W Washington Blvd, Chicago, IL..........312-666-7080
Janusz, Robert E Studios/1020 Huron Rd, Cleveland, OH 216-621-9845
John, Harvey Studio/823 N 2nd St, Milwaukee, WI 414-271-7170
Jones & Morris Ltd/24 Carlaw Ave, Toronto, ON 416-465-5466
K & S Photo/1155 Handley Industrial Ct, St Louis, MO...........314-962-7050
K & S Photographics/180 N Wabash Ave, Chicago, IL 312-207-1212
Kai-Hsi Studio/160 E Illinois St, Chicago, IL 312-642-9853
Kier Photo Service/1627 E 40th St, Cleveland, OH 216-431-4670
Kitzerow Studios/203 N Wabash, Chicago, IL 312-332-1224
Kluegel, Art/630 Fieldston Ter, St Louis, MO 314-961-2023
Kolorstat Studios/415 N Dearborn St, Chicago, IL 312-644-3729
Kremer Photo Print/228 S Wabash, Chicago, IL 312-922-3297
LaDriere Studios/1565 W Woodward Ave, Bloomfield Hills, MI 313-644-3932
Lagasca, Dick & Others/203 N Wabash Ave, Chicago, IL 312-263-1389
Langen & Wind Color/2871 E Grand Blvd, Detroit, MI 313-871-5722
Lim, Luis Retouching/405 N Wabash, Chicago, IL 312-645-0746
Lubeck, Larry & Assoc/405 N Wabash Ave, Chicago, IL 312-726-5580
Merrill-David Inc/3420 Prospect Ave, Cleveland, OH 216-391-0988
Meteor Photo Company/1099 Chicago Rd, Troy, MI 313-583-3090
Midwest Litho Arts/5300 B McDermott Dr, Berkeley, IL 312-449-2442
Multiprint Co Inc/153 W Ohio St, Chicago, IL 312-644-7910

Munder Color/2771 Galilee Ave, Zion, IL 312-764-4435
National Photo Service/114 W Illinois St, Chicago, IL 312-644-5211
NCL Graphics/575 Bennett Rd, Elk Grove Village, IL 312-593-2610
Noral Color Corp/5560 N Northwest Hwy, Chicago, IL 312-775-0991
Norman Sigele Studios/270 Merchandise Mart, Chicago, IL 312-642-1757
NVK Image Systems/110 W Beaver Cr, Richmond Hill,ON 416-764-8196
O'Brien, Tom & Assoc/924 Terminal Rd, Lansing, MI...........517-321-0188
O'Connor-Roe Inc/111 E Wacker, Chicago, IL 312-856-1668
O'Donnell Studio Inc/333 W Lake St, Chicago, IL 312-346-2470
P-A Photocenter Inc/310 W Washington St, Chicago, IL......312-641-6343
Pallas Photo Labs/207 E Buffalo, Milwaulkee, WI...............414-272-2525
Pallas Photo Labs/319 W Erie St, Chicago, IL.....................312-787-4600
Parkway Photo Lab/57 W Grand Ave, Chicago, IL...............312-467-1711
Photocopy Inc/104 E Mason St, Milwaukee, WI...................414-272-1255
Photographic Specialties/225 Border Ave N, Minn, MN........612-332-6303
Photomatic Corp/59 E Illinois St, Chicago, IL.....................312-527-2929
Precision Photo Lab/5787 N Webster St, Dayton, OH..........513-898-7450
Procolor/909 Hennepin Ave, Minneapolis, MN....................612-332-7721
Proctor, Jack/2050 Dain Tower, Minneapolis, MN 612-338-7777
Professional Photo Colour Service/126 W Kinzie, Chicago, IL..........312-644-0888
Quantity Photo Co/119 W Hubbard St, Chicago, IL 312-644-8288
Race Frog Stats/207 E Michigan Ave, Milwaukee, WI.........414-276-7828
Rahe, Bob/220 Findlay St, Cincinnati, OH 513-241-9060
Rees, John/640 N LaSalle, Chicago, IL................................312-337-5785
Reichart, Jim Studio/2301 W Mill Rd, Milwaukee, WI 414-228-9089
Reliable Photo Service/415 N Dearborn, Chicago, IL...........312-644-3723
Repro Inc/912 W Washington Blvd, Chicago, IL 312-666-3800
Rhoden Photo/7833 S Cottage Grove, Chicago, IL...............312-488-4815
Robb Ltd/362 W Erie, Chicago, IL.......................................312-943-2664
Robin Color Lab/2106 Central Parkway, Cincinnati, OH 513-381-5116
Ross-Ehlert/225 W Illinois, Chicago, IL...............................312-644-0244
Schellhorn Photo Techniques/3916 N Elston Ave, Chicago, IL........312-267-5141
Scott Studio & Labs/26 N Hillside Ave, Hillsdale, IL............312-449-3800
SE Graphics Ltd/795 E Kings St, Hamilton, ON 416-545-8484
Sladek, Dean/8748 Hollyspring Trail, Chagrin Falls, OH......216-543-5420
Speedy Stat Service/566 W Adams, Chicago, IL.................312-939-3397
Standard Studios Inc/3270 Merchandise Mart, Chicago, IL ...312-944-5300
Superior Bulk Film/442 N Wells St, Chicago, IL..................312-644-4448
The Color Market/3177 MacArthur Blvd, Northbrook, IL 312-564-3770
The Foto Lab Inc/160 E Illinois St, Chicago, IL 312-321-0900
The Retouching Co/360 N Michigan Ave, Chicago, IL..........312-263-7445
The Stat Center/666 Euclid Ave #817, Clevland, OH 216-861-5467
Thorstad,Retouching/119 No 4th St #311, Minneapolis, MN 612-338-2597
Transparency Duplicating/847 W Jackson Blvd, Chicago, IL...312-733-4464
Transparency Processing/324 W Richmond St, Toronto, ON 416-593-0434
UC Color Lab/3936 N Pulaski Rd, Chicago, IL.....................312-545-9641
Uhlir, Louis J/2509 Kingston Rd, Cleveland Hts, OH 216-932-4837
Wichita Color Lab/231 Ohio, Wichita, KS.............................316-265-2598
Williams, Warren E & Assoc/233 E Wacker Dr, Chicago, IL...312-565-2689
Winnipeg Photo Ltd/1468 Victoria Park Ave, Toronto, ON......416-755-7779
Witkowski Art Studio/52098 N Central Ave, South Bend, IN 219-272-9771
Wood, Bruce/185 N Wabash, Chicago, IL 312-782-4287
Yancy, Helen/421 Valentine St, Dearborn Heights, MI 312-278-9345

S O U T H W E S T

A-1 Blue Print Co Inc/2220 W Alabama, Houston, TX..........713-526-3111
Alamo Photolabs/3814 Broadway, San Antonio, TX 512-828-9079
Alied & WBS/6305 N O'Connor #111, Irving, TX..................214-869-0100
Baster, Ray Enterprises/246 E Watkins, Phoenix, AZ 602-258-6850
Burns Floyd & Lloyd Indu/3223 Alabama Crt, Houston, TX 713-622-8255
Casey Color Inc/2115 S Harvard Ave, Tulsa, OK................918-744-5004
Century Copi-Technics Inc/710 N St Paul St, Dallas, TX......214-741-3191
Collins Color Lab/2714 McKinney Ave, Dallas, TX...............214-824-5333
Color Mark Laboratories/2202 E McDowell Rd, Phoenix, AZ.........602-273-1253
Commercial Color Corporation/1621 Oaklawn St, Dallas, TX 214-744-2610
Custom Photographic Labs/601 W ML King Blvd, Austin, TX........512-474-1177
Dallas Photolab/3942 Irving Blvd, Dallas, TX......................214-630-4351
Dallas Printing Co/3103 Greenwood St, Dallas, TX..............214-826-3331
Darkroom B&W Lab/897-2B Independence Ave, Mt View, CA......415-969-2955
Five-P Photographic Proc/2122 E Gvnr's Cir, Houston, TX 713-688-4488
Gilbert Retouching/PO Box 66615, Houston, TX...................714-521-9582
H & H Blueprint & Supply Co/5042 N 8th St, Phoenix, AZ......602-279-5701
Hall Photo/6 Greenway Plaza, Houston, TX.........................713-961-3454
Hot Flash Photographics/5933 Bellaire Blvd #114, Houston, TX......713-666-9510
Hunter, Marilyn Art Svc/8415 Gladwood, Dallas, TX............214-341-4664
Kolor Print Inc/PO Box 747, Little Rock, AR 501-375-5581
Magna Professional Color Lab/2601 N 32nd St, Phoenix, AZ.........602-955-0700
Master Printing Co Inc/220 Creath St, Jonesboro, AR 501-932-4491

Meisel Photochrome Corp/9645 Wedge Chapel, Dallas, TX...........214-350-6666
NPL/1926 W Gray, Houston, TX..713-527-9300
Optifab Inc/1550 W Van Buren St, Phoenix, AZ...................602-254-7171
Photographic Works Lab/3550 E Grant Rd, Tucson, AZ 602-327-7291
PhotoGraphics/1700 S Congress, Austin, TX.......................512-447-0963
Pounds/909 Congress, Austin, TX..512-472-6926
Pounds Photo Lab Inc/2507 Manor Way, Dallas, TX 214-350-5671
Pro Photo Lab Inc/2700 N Portland, Oklahoma City, OK.......405-942-3743
PSI Film Lab Inc/3011 Diamond Park Dr, Dallas, TX 214-631-5670
Raphaele/Digital Transparencies Inc/616 Hawthorne,
Houston, TX (P 399)   **713-524-2211**
River City Silver/906 Basse Rd, San Antonio, TX 512-734-2020
Spectro Photo Labs Inc/4519 Maple, Dallas, TX..................214-522-1981
Steffan Studio/1905 Skillman, Dallas, TX.............................214-827-6128
Texas World Entrtnmnt/8133 Chadbourne Rd, Dallas, TX......214-351-6103
The Black & White Lab/4930 Maple Ave, Dallas, TX.............214-528-4200
The Color Place/4201 San Felipe, Houston, TX....................713-629-7080
The Color Place/2927 Morton St, Fort Worth, TX.................817-335-3515
The Color Place/1330 Conant St, Dallas, TX........................214-631-7174
The Photo Company/124 W McDowell Rd, Phoenix, AZ 602-254-5138
Total Color Inc/1324 Inwood Rd, Dallas, TX........................214-634-1484
True Color Photo /710 W Sheridan Ave, Oklahoma City, OK.........405-232-6441

R O C K Y   M T N

Cies/Sexton Photo Lab/275 S Hazel Ct, Denver, CO 303-935-3535
Pallas Photo Labs/700 Kalamath, Denver, CO 303-893-0101
Rezac, R Retouching/7832 Sundance Trail, Parker, CO........303-841-0222

W E S T   C O A S T

A & I Color Lab/933 N Highland, Los Angeles, CA...............213-464-8361
ABC Color Corp/3020 Glendale Blvd, Los Angeles, CA.........213-662-2125
Action Photo Service/251 Keany, San Francisco, CA............415-543-1777
Alan's Custom Lab/1545 Wilcox, Hollywood, CA 213-461-1975
Aristo Art Studio/636 N La Brea, Los Angeles, CA..............213-939-0101
Art Craft Custom Lab/1900 Westwood Blvd, Los Angeles, CA........213-475-2986
ASA Prod/Rental Darkrooms/905 N Cole Ave , Hollywood, CA 213-463-7513
Atkinson-Stedco Color Film /7610 Melrose, Los Angeles, CA 213-655-1255
Bakes, Bill Inc/265 29th St, Oakland, CA............................415-832-7685
Black & White Color Repro/38 Mason, San Francisco, CA.....415-989-3070
Bogle Graphic Photo/1117 S Olive, Los Angeles, CA............213-749-7461
Boston Media Prod/330 Townsend St, San Francisco, CA......415-495-6662
Chrome Graphics/449 N Huntley Dr, Los Angeles, CA..........213-657-5055
Chromeworks Color Proc/425 Bryant St, San Francisco, CA 415-957-9481
Coletti, John/333 Kearny #703, San Francisco, CA 415-421-3848
Color Lab Inc/742 Cahuenga Blvd, Los Angeles, CA............213-466-3551
Colorscope/250 Glendale Blvd, Los Angeles, CA.................213-250-5555
Colortek/10425 Venice Blvd, Los angeles, CA......................213-870-5579
Complete Negative Service/6007 Waring Ave, Hollywood, CA 213-463-7753
CPS Lab/1759 Las Palmas, Los Angeles, CA......................213-464-0215
Cre-Art Photo Labs Inc/6920 Melrose Ave, Hollywood, CA......213-937-3390
Croxton, Stewart Inc/8736 Melrose, Los Angeles, CA...........213-652-9720
Custom Graphics/15162 Goldenwest Circle, Westminster, CA........714-893-7517
Custom Photo Lab/123 Powell St, San Francisco, CA...........415-956-2374
Faulkner Color Lab/1200 Folsom St, San Francisco, CA........415-861-2800
Focus Foto Finishers/138 S La Brea Ave, Los Angeles, CA......213-934-0013
Frosh, R L & Sons/4114 Sunset Blvd, Los Angeles, CA........213-662-1134
G P Color Lab/215 S Oxford Ave, Los Angeles, CA..............213-386-7901
Gamma Photo Labs/555 Howard St, San Francisco, CA........415-495-8833
Gibbons Color Lab/606 N Almont Dr, Los Angeles, CA.........213-275-6806
Giese, Axel Assoc/544 Starlight Crest Dr, La Canada, CA......213-790-8768
Glusha, Laura/1053 Colorado Blvd #F, Los Angeles, CA.......213-255-1997
Good Stats Inc/1616 N Cahuenga Blvd, Hollywood, CA.........213-469-3501
Gornick Film Production/4200 Camino Real, Los Angeles, CA 213-223-8914
Graphic Center/7386 Beverly, Los Angeles, CA 213-938-3773
Graphic Process Co/979 N LaBrea, Los Angeles, CA...........213-850-6222
Graphicolor/8134 W Third, Los Angeles, CA........................213-653-1768
Hecht Photo/Graphics/1711 N Orange Dr, Hollywood, CA......213-466-7106
Hollywood Photo Repro/6413 Willoughby Ave, Hollywood, CA......213-469-5421
Imperial Color Lab/365 Howard St, San Francisco, CA..........415-777-4020
Ivey-Seright/424 8th Ave North, Seattle, WA.......................206-623-8113
Jacobs, Ed/937 S Spaulding, Los Angeles, CA....................213-935-1064
Jacobs, Robert/6010 Wilshire Blvd, Los Angeles, CA............213-931-3751
Johnston, Chuck/1111 Wilshire, Los Angeles, CA................213-482-3362
Kawahara, George/250 Columbus, San Francisco, CA..........415-543-1637
Kimbo Color Laboratory Inc/179 Stewart, San Francisco, CA 415-288-4100
Kinney, Paul Productions/818 19th St, Sacramento, CA 916-447-8868
Landry, Carol/8148-L Ronson Rd, San Diego, CA................619-560-1778
Laursen Color Lab/1641 Reynolds, Irvine, CA 714-261-1500

Lee Film Processing/8584 Venice Blvd, Los Angeles, CA 213-559-0296
M PS Photo Srvc/17406 Mt Cliffwood Cir, Fountain Valley, CA..........714-540-9515
M S Color Labs/740 Cahuenga Blvd, Los Angeles, CA..................213-461-4591
Maddocks, J H/4766 Melrose Ave, Los Angeles, CA....................213-660-1321
Marin Color Lab/41 Belvedere St, San Rafael, CA.....................415-456-8093
Mark III Colorprints/7401 Melrose Ave, Los Angeles, CA..............213-653-0433
MC Photographics/PO Box 1515, Springfield, OR.......................503-741-2289
Metz Air Art/2817 E Lincoln Ave, Anaheim, CA........................714-630-3071
Modern Photo Studio/5625 N Figueroa, Los Angeles, CA................213-255-1527
Modernage/470 E Third St, Los Angeles, CA...........................213-628-8194
Newell Color Lab/630 Third St, San Francisco, CA....................415-974-6870
Olson, Bob/7775 Beverly Blvd, Los Angeles, CA.......................213-931-6643
Ostoin, Larry/22943 B Nadine Cr, Torrance, CA.......................213-530-1121
Production & Location/424 Nahua St, Honolulu, HI....................808-924-2513
Paragon Photo/7301 Melrose Ave, Los Angeles, CA.....................213-933-5865
Personal Color Lab/1552 Gower, Los Angeles, CA......................213-467-0721
Petron Corp/5443 Fountain Ave, Los Angeles, CA......................213-461-4626
Pevehouse, Jerry Studio/3409 Tweedy Blvd, South Gate, CA...........213-564-1336
Photoking Lab/6612 W Sunset Blvd, Los Angeles, CA...................213-466-2977
Prisma Color Inc/5619 Washington Blvd, Los Angeles, CA.............213-728-7151
Professional Color Labs/96 Jessie, San Francisco, CA...............415-397-5057
Quantity Photos Inc/5432 Hollywood Blvd, Los Angeles, CA...........213-467-6178
Rapid Color Inc/1236 S Central Ave, Glendale, CA....................213-245-9211
Remos, Nona/4053 Eighth Ave, San Diego, CA..........................619-692-4044
Repro Color Inc/3100 Riverside Dr, Los Angeles, CA..................213-664-1951
Retouching Chemicals/5478 Wilshire Blvd, Los Angeles, CA...........213-935-9452
Revilo Color/4650 W Washington Blvd, Los Angeles, CA................213-936-8681
Reynolds, Carol Retouching/1428 N Fuller Ave, Hollywood, CA........213-874-7083
RGB Lab Inc/816 N Highland, Los Angeles, CA.........................213-469-1959
Ro-Ed Color Lab/707 N Stanley Ave, Los Angeles, CA.................213-651-5050
Roller, S J/6881 Alta Loma Terrace, Los Angeles, CA.................213-876-5654
Ross, Deborah Design/10806 Ventura Blvd #3, Studio City, CA........818-985-5205
Rudy Jo Color Lab Inc/130 N La Brea, Los Angeles, CA...............213-937-3804
Schaeffer Photo Rapid Lab/6677 Sunset Blvd, Hollywood, CA..........213-466-3343
Snyder, Len/238 Hall Dr, Orinda, CA.................................415-254-8687
Staidle, Ted & Assocs/544 N Larchmont Blvd, Los Angeles, CA........213-462-7433
Stat House/8126 Beverly Blvd, Los Angeles, CA.......................213-653-8200
Still Photo Lab/1216 N LaBrea, Los Angeles, CA......................213-465-6106
Studio Photo Service/733 N LaBrea Ave, Hollywood, CA................213-935-1223
Technicolor Inc/1738 No Neville, Orange, CA.........................714-998-3424
Thomas Reproductions/1147 Mission St, San Francisco, CA............415-431-8900
Timars/918 N Formosa, Los Angeles, CA...............................213-876-0175
Tom's Chroma Lab/514 No LaBrea, Los Angeles, CA.....................213-933-5637
Trans Tesseract/715 N San Antonio Rd, Los Altos, CA.................415-949-2185
Tri Color Camera/1761 N Vermont Ave, Los Angeles, CA................213-664-2952
Universal Color Labs/1076 S La Cienega Blvd, Los Angeles, CA.......213-652-2863
Vloeberghs, Jerome/333 Kearny St, San Francisco, CA.................415-982-1287
Waters Art Studio/1820 E Garry St #207, Santa Ana, CA ....
Wild Studio/1311 N Wilcox Ave, Hollywood, CA........................213-463-8369
Williams, Alan & Assoc Inc/8032 W Third St, Los Angeles, CA........213-653-2243
Wolf Color Lab/6416 Selma, Los Angeles, CA..........................213-463-0766
Zammit, Paul/5478 Wilshire Blvd #300, Los Angeles, CA...............213-933-8563
Ziba Photographics/591 Howard St, San Francisco, CA................415-543-6221

L I G H T I N G

N Y C

Altman Stage Lighting Co Inc/57 Alexander, Yonkers....................212-569-7777
Artistic Neon by Gasper/75-49 61st St, Glendale, ...718-821-1550
Balcar Lighting Systems/15 E 30th St, ...212-889-5080
Barbizon Electric Co Inc/426 W 55th St, ...212-586-1620
Bernhard Link Theatrical Inc/104 W 17th St, ...212-929-6786
Big Apple Cine Service/49-01 25th Ave, Woodside, ...718-626-5210
Big Apple Lights Corp/533 Canal St, ...212-226-0925
Camera Mart/456 W 55th St, ...212-757-6977
Electra Displays/122 W 27th St, ...212-924-1022
F&B/Ceco Lighting & Grip Rental/315 W 43rd St, ...212-974-4640
Feature Systems Inc/512 W 36th St, ...212-736-0447
Ferco/707 11th Ave, ...212-245-4800
Filmtrucks, Inc/450 W 37th St, ...212-868-7065
Fiorentino, Imero Assoc Inc/44 West 63rd St, ...212-246-0600
Four Star Stage Lighting Inc/585 Gerard Ave, Bronx, ...212-993-0471

Kliegl Bros Universal/32-32 48th Ave, Long Island City, ...718-786-7474
Lee Lighting America Ltd/534 W 25th St, ...212-924-5476
Litelab Theatrical & Disco Equip/76 Ninth Ave, ...212-675-4357
Lowel Light Mfg Inc/475 10th St, ...212-949-0950
Luminere/160 W 86th St, ...212-724-0583
Metro-Lites Inc/750 Tenth Ave, ...212-757-1220
Movie Light Ltd/460 W 24th St, ...212-989-2318
New York Flash/156 Fifth Ave, ...212-741-1165
Paris Film Productions/213-23 99th Ave, Queens Village, ...718-740-2020
Photo-Tekniques/119 Fifth Ave, ...212-254-2545
Production Arts Lighting/636 Eleventh Ave, ...212-489-0312
Ross, Charles Inc/333 W 52nd St, ...212-246-5470
Stage Lighting Discount Corp/346 W 44th St, ...212-489-1370
Stroblite Co Inc/10 E 23rd St, ...212-677-9220
Tekno Inc/15 E 30th St, ...212-887-5080
Times Square Stage Lighting Co/318 W 47th St, ...212-541-5045
Vadar Ltd/150 Fifth Ave, ...212-989-9120

N O R T H E A S T

Barbizon Light of New England/3 Draper St, Woburn, MA 617-935-3920
Blake, Ben Films/104 W Concord St, Boston, MA......................617-266-8181
Bogen/PO Box 448, Engelwood, NJ....................................201-568-7771
Capron Lighting & Sound/278 West St, Needham, MA...................617-444-8850
Cestare, Thomas Inc/188 Herricks Rd, Mineola, NY...................516-742-5550
Cody, Stuart Inc/300 Putnam Ave, Cambridge, MA.....................617-661-4540
Dyna-Lite Inc/140 Market St, Kenilworth, NJ........................201-245-7222
Film Associates/419 Boylston St ((n))209, Boston, MA...............617-266-0892
Filmarts/38 Newbury St, Boston, MA.................................617-266-7468
Heller, Brian/200 Olney St, Providence, RI.........................401-751-1381
Lighting Products, GTE Sylvania/Lighting Center, Danvers, MA.......617-777-1900
Limelight Productions/Yale Hill, Stockbridge, MA...................413-298-3771
Lycian Stage Lighting/P O Box 68, Sugar Loaf, NY...................914-469-2285
Martorano, Salvatore Inc/9 West First St, Freeport, NY.............516-379-8097
McManus Enterprises/111 Union Ave, Bala Cynwyd, PA.................215-664-8600
Norton Assoc/53 Henry St, Cambridge, MA............................617-876-3771
Packaged Lighting Systems/29-41 Grant, Walden, NY..................914-778-3515
Penrose Productions/4 Sandalwood Dr, Livingston, NJ................201-992-4264
R & R Lighting Co/813 Silver Spring Ave, Silver Spring, MD.........301-589-4997
Reinhard, Charles/39 Ocean Ave, Massapequa, NY.....................516-799-1615

S O U T H E A S T

Kupersmith, Tony/320 N Highland Ave NE, Atlanta, GA 404-577-5319

M I D W E S T

Duncan, Victor Inc/32380 Howard St, Madison Heights, MI 313-589-1900
Film Corps/3101 Hennepin Ave, Minneapolis, MN......................612-338-2522
Frost, Jack/234 Piquette, Detroit, MI..............................313-873-8030
Grand Stage Lighting Co/630 W Lake, Chicago, IL....................312-332-5611
Midwest Cine Service/304 W 79th Terr, Kansas City, MO..............816-333-0022
Midwest Stage Lighting/2104 Central, Evanston, IL..................312-328-3966
Studio Lighting/1345 W Argyle St, Chicago, IL......................312-989-8808

S O U T H W E S T

ABC Theatrical Rental & Sales/825 N 7th St, Phoenix, AZ............602-258-5265
Astro Audio-Visual/1336 W Clay, Houston, TX........................713-528-7119
Chase Lights/1942 Beech St, Amarillo, TX...........................806-381-0575
Dallas Stage Lighting Co/2813 Florence, Dallas, TX.................214-827-9380
Duncan, Victor Inc/2659 Fondren Dr, Dallas, TX.....................214-369-1165
FPS Inc/11250 Pagemill Rd, Dallas, TX..............................214-340-8545
Gable, Pee Wee Inc/PO Box 11264, Phoenix, AZ.......................602-242-7660
MFC-The Texas Outfit/5915 Star Ln, Houston, TX.....................713-781-7703
Southwest Film & TV Lighting/904 Koerner Ln, Austin, TX............512-385-3483

R O C K Y   M T N

Rocky Mountain Cine Support/1332 S Cherokee, Denver, CO 303-795-9713

W E S T   C O A S T

Aguilar Lighting/3230 Laurel Canyon Blvd, Studio City, CA..........213-766-6564
American Mobile Power/3218 W Burbank Blvd, Burbank, CA..............213-845-5474
Astro Generator Rentals/2835 Bedford St, Los Angeles, CA...........213-838-3958
B S Rental Co/1082 La Cresta Dr, Thousand Oaks, CA.................805-495-8606
B S Rental Co/18857 Addison St, North Hollywood, CA................213-761-1733
Backstage Studio Equipment/5554 Fairview Pl, Agoura, CA............213-889-9816
Casper's Camera Cars/8415 Lankershim Blvd, Sun Valley, CA..........213-767-5207
Castex Rentals/591 N Bronson Ave, Los Angeles, CA..................213-462-1468
Ceco, F&B of CA Inc/7051 Santa Monica Blvd, Hollywood, CA..........213-466-9361
Cine Turkey/2624 Reppert Ct, Los Angeles, CA.......................213-654-6495
Cine-Dyne Inc/9401 Wilshire Blvd #830, Beverly Hills, CA...........213-622-7016

Cine-Pro/1037 N Sycamore Ave, Hollywood, CA 213-461-4794
Cinemobile Systems Inc/11166 Gault St, North Hollywood, CA 213-764-9900
Cineworks-Cinerents/5724 Santa Monica Blvd, Hollywood, CA 213-464-0296
Cool Light Co Inc/5723 Auckland Ave, North Hollywood, CA..........213-761-6116
Denker, Foster Co/1605 Las Flores Ave, San Marino, CA 213-799-8656
Fiorentino, Imero Assoc Inc/6430 Sunset Blvd, Hollywood, CA.......213-467-4020
Great American Market/PO Box 178, Woodlands Hill, CA 213-883-8182
Grosso & Grosso/7502 Wheatland Ave, Sun Valley, CA.................213-875-1160
Hollywood Mobile Systems/7021 Hayvenhurst St, Van Nuys, CA ..213-782-6558
Independent Studio Services/11907 Wicks St, Sun Valley, CA.........213-764-0840
Kalani Studio Lighting/129-49 Killion St, Van Nuys, CA.................213-762-5991
Key Lite/333 S Front St, Burbank, CA 213-848-5483
Leoinetti Cine Rentals/5609 Sunset Blvd, Hollywood, CA..............213-469-2987
Mobile Power House/3820 Rhodes Ave, Studio City, CA 213-766-2163
Mole Richardson/937 N Sycamore Ave, Hollywood, CA.................213-851-0111
Pattim Service/10625 Chandler, Hollywood, CA 213-766-5266
Picture Package Inc/22236 Cass Ave, Woodland Hills, CA............213-703-7168
Producer's Studio/650 N Bronson St, Los Angeles, CA.................213-466-3111
Production Syst Inc/5759 Santa Monica Blvd, Hollywood, CA........213-469-2704
RNI Equipment Co/7272 Bellaire Ave, North Hollywood, CA..........213-875-2656
Skirpan Lighting Control Co/1100 W Chestnut St, Burbank, CA......213-840-7000
Tech Camera/6370 Santa Monica Blvd, Hollywood, CA 213-466-3238
Wallace Lighting/6970 Varna Ave, Van Nuys, CA 213-764-1047
Young Generations/8517 Geyser Ave, Northridge, CA...................213-873-5135

STUDIOS

NYC

3G Stages Inc/236 W 61st St, ...212-247-3130
Amer Museum of the Moving Image/31-12 36th St, Astoria.............718-784-4520
Antonio/Stephen Ad Photo/45 E 20th St, ...212-674-2350
Boken Inc/513 W 54th St, ...212-581-5507
C & C Visual/12 W 27th St 7th Fl, ...212-684-3830
Camera Mart Inc/456 W 55th St, ...212-757-6977
Cine Studio/241 W 54th St, ...212-581-1916
Codalight Rental Studios/151 W 19th St, ...212-206-9333
Contact Studios/165 W 47th St, ...212-354-6400
Control Film Service/321 W 44th St, ...212-245-1574
DeFilippo/207 E 37th St, ...212-986-5444
Duggal Color Projects/9 W 20th St, ...212-242-7000
Farkas Films Inc/385 Third Ave, ...212-679-8212
Gruszczynski Studio/821 Broadway, ...212-673-1243
Horvath & Assoc Studios/95 Charles St, ...212-741-0300
Matrix Studios Inc/727 Eleventh Ave, ...212-265-8500
Mothers Sound Stages/210 E 5th St, ...212-260-2050
National Video Industries/15 W 17th St, ...212-691-1300
New York Flash Rental/156 Fifth Ave, ...212-741-1165
Ninth Floor Studio/1200 Broadway, ...212-679-5537
North American Video/423 E 90th St, ...212-369-2552
North Light Studios/122 W 26th St, ...212-989-5498
Osonitsch, Robert/112 Fourth Ave, ...212-533-1920
PDN Studio/167 Third Ave, ...212-677-8418
Phoenix State Ltd/537 W 59th St, ...212-581-7721
Photo-Tekniques/119 Fifth Ave, ...212-254-2545
Production Center/221 W 26th St, ...212-675-2211
Professional Photo Supply/141 W 20th St, ...212-924-1200
Reeves Teletape Corp/304 E 44th St, ...212-573-8888
Rotem Studio/259 W 30th St, ...212-947-9455
Schnoodle Studios/54 Bleecker St, ...212-431-7788
Silva-Cone Studios/260 W 36th St, ...212-279-0900
Stage 54 West/429 W 54th St, ...212-757-6977
Stages 1&2 West/460 W 54th St, ...212-757-6977
Studio 35/35 W 31st St, ...212-947-0898
Studio 39/144 E 39th St, ...212-685-1771
Studio Twenty/6 W 20th St, ...212-675-8067
The 95th St Studio/206 E 95th St, ...212-831-1946
Vagnoni, A Devlin Productions/150 W 55th St, ...212-582-5572
Yellowbox/47 E 34th St, ...212-532-4010

NORTHEAST

Allscope Inc/PO Box 4060, Princeton, NJ 609-799-4200
Bay State Film Productions/35 Springfield St, Agawam, MA 413-786-4454

Century III/651 Beacon St, Boston, MA...617-267-6400
Color Leasing Studio/330 Rt 46 East, Fairfield, NJ 201-575-1118
D4 Film Studios Inc/109 Highland Ave, Needham, MA....................617-444-0226
Impact Studios/1084 N Delaware Ave, Philadelphia, PA 215-426-3988
Penrose Productions/4 Sandalwood Dr, Livingston, NJ 201-992-4264
Pike Productions Inc/47 Galen St, Watertown, MA.........................617-924-5000
September Productions Inc/171 Newbury St, Boston, MA................617-262-6090
Television Productions & Services/55 Chapel St, Newton, MA 617-965-1626
Ultra Photo Works/468 Commercial Ave, Palisades Pk, NJ 201-592-7730
Videocom Inc/502 Sprague St, Dedham, MA.................................617-329-4080
WGGB-TV/PO Box 3633, Springfield, MA 413-785-1911
WLNE-TV/430 County St, New Bedford, MA 617-993-2651

SOUTHEAST

Enter Space/20 14th St NW, Atlanta, GA.......................................404-885-1139
Great Southern Stage/15221 NE 21st Ave, NMiami Bch, FL............305-947-0430
Williamson Photography Inc/9511 Colonial Dr, Miami, FL...............305-255-6400

MIDWEST

Emerich Style & Design/PO Box 14523, Chicago, IL 312-871-4659
Gard, Ron/2600 N Racine, Chicago, IL..312-975-6523
Hanes, Jim/1930 N Orchard, Chicago, IL.......................................312-944-6554
Lewis, Tom/2511 Brumley Dr, Flossmoor, IL..................................312-799-1156
Rainey, Pat/4031 N Hamlin Ave, Chicago, IL 312-463-0281
Sosin, Bill/415 W Superior St, Chicago, IL.....................................312-751-0974
Stratford Studios Inc/2857 E Grand Blvd, Detroit, MI....................313-875-6617
The Production Center/151 Victor Ave, Highland Park, MI 313-868-6600
Zawaki, Andy & Jake/1830 W Cermak, Chicago, IL.......................312-422-1546

SOUTHWEST

AIE Studios/3905 Braxton, Houston, TX 713-781-2110
Arizona Cine Equipment/2125 E 20th St, Tucson, AZ 602-623-8268
Hayes Productions Inc/710 S Bowie, San Antonio, TX....................512-224-9565
MFC Film Productions Inc/5915 Star Ln, Houston, TX.....................713-781-7703
Pearlman Productions Inc/2506 South Blvd, Houston, TX................713-523-3601
Stokes, Bill Assoc/5642 Dyer, Dallas, TX.......................................214-363-0161
Tecfilms Inc/2856 Fort Worth Ave, Dallas, TX.................................214-339-2217

WEST COAST

39 East Walnut/39 E Walnut St, Pasadena, CA 818-584-4090
ASA Productions/Studio/905 Cole Ave #2100, Hollywood, CA.........213-463-7513
Blakeman, Bob Studios/710 S Santa Fe, Los Angeles, CA..............213-624-6662
Carthay Studio/5907 W Pico Blvd, Los Angeles, CA 213-938-2101
Chris-Craft Video Tape/915 N LaBrea, Los Angeles, CA 213-850-2236
Cine-Rent West Inc/991 Tennessee St, San Francisco, CA..............415-864-4644
Cine-Video/948 N Cahuenga Blvd, Los Angeles, CA.......................213-464-6200
Columbia Pictures/Columbia Plaza, Burbank, CA...........................818-954-6000
Design Arts Studios/1128 N Las Palmas, Hollywood, CA................213-464-9118
Disney, Walt Productions/500 S Buena Vista St, Burbank, CA..........818-840-1000
Dominick/833 N LaBrea Ave, Los Angeles, CA 213-934-3033
Eliot, Josh Studio/706 W Pico Blvd, Los Angeles, CA.....................213-742-0367
Goldwyn, Samuel Stds/1041 N Formosa Ave, Los Angeles, CA 213-650-2500
Great Amer Cinema/10711 Wellworth Ave, Los Angeles, CA...........213-475-0937
Hill, Dennis Studio/20 N Raymond Ave #14, Pasadena, CA.............818-795-2589
Hollywood National Studios/6605 Eleanor Ave, Hollywood, CA........213-467-6272
Hollywood Stage/6650 Santa Monica Blvd, Los Angeles, CA 213-466-4393
Inner Vision/1417 15th St, San Francisco, CA.................................415-864-4959
Kelley, Tom Studios/8525 Santa Monica Blvd, Los Angeles, CA 213-657-1780
Kings Point Corporation/9336 W Washington, Culver City, CA 213-836-5537
Lewin, Elyse/820 N Fairfax Ave, Los Angeles, CA...........................213-655-4214
Liles, Harry Prod/1060 N Lillian Way, Los Angeles, CA...................213-466-1612
MGM Studios/10202 W Washington, Culver City, CA.......................213-836-3000
MPI Studios/1714 N Wilton Pl, Los Angeles, CA 213-462-6342
Norwood, David/9023 Washington Blvd, Culver City, CA 213-204-3323
Paramount/5555 Melrose, Los Angeles, CA....................................213-468-5000
Raleigh Studio/650 N Bronson Ave, Los Angeles, CA......................213-466-7778
Solaris T V Studios/2525 Ocean Park Blvd, Santa Monica, CA 213-450-6227
Studio AV/1227 First Ave S, Seattle, WA..206-292-9931
Studio Center CBS/4024 Radford Ave, Studio City, CA 818-760-5000
Studio Resources/1915 University Ave, Palo Alto, CA 415-321-8763
Sunset/Gower Studio/1438 N Gower, Los Angeles, CA 213-467-1001
Superstage/5724 Santa Monica Blvd, Los Angeles, CA...................213-464-0296
Team Prod/4133 Lankershim Blvd, North Hollywood, CA................818-506-5700
Television Ctr Studios/846 N Cahuenga Blvd, Los Angeles, CA........213-462-5111
Trans-American Video/1541 Vine St, Los Angeles, CA.....................213-466-2141
Twentieth Century Fox/10201 W Pico Blvd, Los Angeles, CA...........213-277-2211
Universal City Studios/Universal Studios, Universal City, CA............213-985-4321
UPA Pictures/4440 Lakeside Dr, Burbank, CA 213-842-7171

Videography Studios/8471 Universal Plz, Universal City, CA 213-204-2000
Vine Street Video Center/1224 Vine St, Pasadena, CA 213-462-1099
Warner Brothers/4000 Warner Blvd, Burbank, CA 213-843-6000
Wolin/Semple Studio/520 N Western Ave, Los Angeles, CA...........213-463-2109

A N I M A L S

N Y C

A P A/230 W 10th St, ...212-929-9436
Abacus Productions Inc/475 Fifth Ave, ...212-532-6677
ALZ Productions/11 Waverly Pl, ...212-473-7620
Ani-Live Film Service Inc/45 W 45th St, ...212-819-0700
Animated Productions Inc/1600 Broadway, ...212-265-2942
Animation Camera Workshop/49 W 24th St, ...212-807-6450
Animation Center Inc/15 W 46th St, ...212-869-0123
Animation Service Center/293 W 4th St, ...212-924-3937
Animation Services Inc/221 W 57th St 11th Fl, ...212-333-5656
Animex Inc/1540 Broadway, ...212-575-9494
Animus Films/15 W 44th St, ...212-391-8716
Avekta Productions Inc/164 Madison Ave, ...212-686-4550
Backle, RJ Prod/321 W 44th St, ...212-582-8270
Bakst, Edward/160 W 96th St, ...212-666-2579
Beckerman, Howard/45 W 45th St #300, ...212-869-0595
Blechman, R O/2 W 47th St, ...212-869-1630
Broadcast Arts Inc/632 Broadway, ...212-254-5910
Cel-Art Productions Inc/20 E 49th St, ...212-751-7515
Charisma Communications/32 E 57th St, ...212-832-3020
Charlex Inc/2 W 45th St, ...212-719-4600
Cinema Concepts/321 W 44th St, ...212-541-9220
Clark, Ian/229 E 96th St, ...212-289-0998
Computer Graphics Lab/405 Lexington Ave, ...212-557-5130
D & R Productions Inc/6 E 39th St, ...212-532-5303
Dale Cameragraphics Inc/12 W 27th St, ...212-696-9440
Darino Films/222 Park Ave S, ...212-228-4024
DaSilva, Raul/137 E 38th St, ...212-696-1657
Devlin Productions Inc/150 W 55th St, ...212-582-5572
Diamond & Diaferia/12 E 44th St, ...212-986-8500
Digital Effects Inc/321 W 44 St, ...212-581-7760
Dolphin Computer Animation/140 E 80th St, ...212-628-5930
Doros Animation Inc/475 Fifth Ave, ...212-684-5043
Elinor Bunin Productions Inc/30 E 60th St, ...212-688-0759
Fandango Productions Inc/15 W 38th St, ...212-382-1813
Feigenbaum Productions Inc/25 W 43rd St # 220, ...212-840-3744
Film Opticals/144 E 44th St, ...212-697-4744
Film Planning Assoc/38 E 20th, ...212-260-7140
Gati, John/881 Seventh Ave #832, ...212-582-9060
Granato Animation Photography/15 W 46th St, ...212-869-3231
Graphic Motion Group Ltd/16 W 46th St, ...212-354-4343
Grossman, Robert/19 Crosby St, ...212-925-1965
High-Res Solutions Inc/10 Park Ave #3E, ...212-684-1397
Howard Graphics/36 W 25th St, ...212-929-2121
I F Studios/15 W 38th St, ...212-697-6805
ICON Communications/717 Lexington Ave, ...212-688-5155
Image Factory Inc/18 E 53rd St, ...212-759-9363
International Production Center/514 W 57th St, ...212-582-6530
J C Productions/16 W 46th St, ...212-575-9611
Kim & Gifford Productions Inc/548 E 87th St, ...212-986-2826
Kimmelman, Phil & Assoc Inc/50 W 40th St, ...212-944-7766
Kurtz & Friends/130 E 18th St, ...212-777-3258
Leo Animation Camera Service/25 W 43rd St, ...212-997-1840
Lieberman, Jerry/76 Laight St, ...212-431-3452
Locomo Productions/875 West End Ave, ...212-222-4833
Marz Productions Inc/118 E 25th St, ...212-477-3900
Metropolis Graphics/28 E 4th St, ...212-677-0630
Motion Picker Studio/416 Ocean Ave, Brooklyn...................718-856-2763
Murphy, Neil/208 W 23rd St, ...212-691-5730
Musicvision, Inc/185 E 85th St, ...212-860-4420
New York Siggraph/451 W 54th St, ...212-582-9223
Ovation Films/49 W 24th St, ...212-675-4700
Paganelli, Albert/21 W 46th St, ...212-719-4105
Perpetual Animation/17 W 45th St, ...212-840-2888
Polestar Films & Assoc Arts/870 Seventh Ave, ...212-586-6333

Rankin/Bass Productions/1 E 53rd St, ...212-759-7721
Rembrandt Films/59 E 54th St, ...212-758-1024
Robinson, Keith Prod Inc/200 E 21st St, ·......................212-533-9078
Seeger, Hal/45 W 45th St, ...212-575-8900
Shadow Light Prod, Inc/12 W 27th St 7th Fl, ...212-689-7511
Singer, Rebecca Studio Inc/111 W 57th St, ...212-944-0466
Stanart Studios/1650 Broadway, ...212-586-0445
Stark, Philip/245 W 29th St 15th Fl, ...212-868-5555
Sunflower Films/15 W 46th St, ...212-869-0123
Telemated Motion Pictures/PO Box 176, ...212-475-8050
The Fantastic Animation Machine/12 E 46th St, ...212-697-2525
Today Video, Inc/45 W 45th St, ...212-391-1020
Triology Design/25 W 45th St, ...212-382-3592
Videart Inc/39 W 38th St, ...212-840-2163
Video Works/24 W 40th St, ...212-869-2500
Weiss, Frank Studio/66 E 7th St, ...212-477-1032
World Effects Inc/20 E 46th St, ...212-687-7070
Zanders Animation Parlour/18 E 41st St, ...212-725-1331

N O R T H E A S T

Aviation Simulations International Inc/Box 358, Huntington, NY 516-271-6476
Comm Corps Inc/711 4th St NW, Washington, DC 202-638-6550
Consolidated Visual Center/2529 Kenilworth Ave, Tuxedo, MD........301-772-7300
Felix, Luisa/180 12th St, Jersey City, NJ 201-653-1500
Hughes, Gary Inc/PO Box, Cabin John, MD 301-229-1100
Penpoint Prod Svc/331 Newbury St, Boston, MA 617-266-1331
Pilgrim Film Service/2504 50th Ave, Hyattsville, MD 301-773-7072
Symmetry T/A/13813 Willoughby Road, Upper Marlboro, MD.........301-627-5050
Synthavision-Magi/3 Westchester Plaza, Elmsford, NY 212-733-1300
The Animators/247 Ft Pitt Blvd, Pittsburgh, PA.................412-391-2550
West End Film Inc/2121 Newport Pl NW, Washington, DC 202-331-8078

S O U T H E A S T

Bajus-Jones Film Corp/401 W Peachtree St, Atlanta, GA 404-221-0700
Cinetron Computer Systems/6700 IH 85 N, Norcross, GA.............404-448-9463

M I D W E S T

AGS & R Studios/425 N Michigan Ave, Chicago, IL 312-836-4500
Associated Audio-Visual Corp/2821 Central St, Evanston, IL.........312-866-6780
Bajus-Jones Film Corp/203 N Wabash, Chicago, IL 312-332-6041
Boyer Studio/1324 Greenleaf, Evanston, IL......................312-491-6363
Coast Prod/505 N Lake Shore Dr, Chicago, IL 312-222-1857
Filmack Studios Inc/1327 S Wabash, Chicago, IL 312-427-3395
Freese & Friends Inc/1429 N Wells, Chicago, IL.................312-642-4475
Goldsholl Assoc/420 Frontage Rd, Northfield, IL 312-446-8300
Goodrich Animation/405 N Wabash, Chicago, IL 312-329-1344
Kayem Animation Services/100 E Ohio, Chicago, IL 312-664-7733
Kinetics/444 N Wabash, Chicago, IL.............................312-644-2767
Optimation Inc/9055 N 51st St, Brown Deer, WI..................414-355-4500
Pilot Prod/1819 Ridge Ave, Evanston, IL 312-328-3700
Quicksilver Assoc Inc/16 W Ontario, Chicago, IL 312-943-7622
Ritter Waxberg & Assoc/200 E Ontario, Chicago, IL 312-664-3934
Simott & Associates/676 N La Salle, Chicago, IL................312-440-1875
The Beach Productions Ltd/1960 N Seminary, Chicago, IL.........312-281-4500

S O U T H W E S T

Graphic Art Studio/5550 S Lewis Ave, Tulsa, OK.................918-743-3915
Media Visions Inc/2716 Bissonnet #408, Houston, TX.............713-521-0626

R O C K Y   M T N

Phillips, Stan & Assoc/865 Delaware, Denver, CO.................303-595-9911

W E S T   C O A S T

Abel, Bob & Assoc/953 N Highland Ave, Los Angeles, CA...........213-462-8100
Animation Filmakers Corp/7000 Romaine St, Hollywood, CA.........213-851-5526
Animedia Prod/10200 Riverside Dr, N Hollywood, CA..............213-851-4777
Bass, Saul/Herb Yeager/7039 Sunset Blvd, Hollywood, CA 213-466-9701
Bosustow Entertainment/1649 11th St, Santa Monica, CA..........213-394-0218
Cinema Research Corp/6860 Lexington Ave, Hollywood, CA 213-461-3235
Clampett, Bob Prod/729 Seward St, Hollywood, CA 213-466-0264
Cornerstone Productions/5915 Cantelope Ave, Van Nuys, CA 213-994-0007
Court Productions/1030 N Cole, Hollywood, CA...................213-467-5900
Craig, Fred Productions/932 S Pine, San Gabriel, CA 213-287-6479
Creative Film Arts/7026 Santa Monica Blvd, Hollywood, CA 213-466-5111
DePatie-Freleng Ent/16400 Ventura Blvd, Encino, CA.............818-906-3375
Duck Soup Prod/1026 Montana Ave, Santa Monica, CA 213-451-0771
Energy Productions/846 N Cahuenga Blvd, Los Angeles, CA.........213-462-3310
Excelsior Animated Mvng Picts/749 N LaBrea, Hollywood, CA.......213-938-2335

Filmcore/849 N Seward, Hollywood, CA 213-464-7303
Filmfair/10900 Ventura Blvd, Studio City, CA........................213-877-3191
Gallerie Int'l Films/11320 W Magnolia Blvd, Hollywood, CA 213-760-2040
Hanna-Barbera/3400 W Cahuenga, Hollywood, CA 213-466-1371
Jacques, Jean-Guy/633 N LaBrea Ave, Hollywood, CA 213-936-7177
Kurtz & Friends/2312 W Olive Ave, Burbank, CA.....................213-461-8188
Littlejohn, William Prod/23425 Malibu Colony Dr, Malibu, CA.........213-456-8620
Lumeni Productions/1727 N Ivar, Hollywood, CA 213-462-2110
Marks Communication/5550 Wilshire Blvd, Los Angeles, CA...........213-464-6302
Melendez, Bill Prod/439 N Larchmont Blvd, Los Angeles, CA..........213-463-4101
Murakami Wolf Swenson/1463 Tamarind Ave, Hollywood, CA 213-462-6474
New Hollywood Inc/1302 N Cahuenga Blvd, Hollywood, CA............213-466-3686
Pantomime Picts/12144 Riverside Dr, North Hollywood, CA...........818-980-5555
Pegboard Prod/1310 N Cahuenga Blvd, Hollywood, CA...............818-353-4991
Quartet Films Inc/5631 Hollywood Blvd, Hollywood, CA 213-464-9225
R & B EFX/1802 Victory Blvd, Glendale, CA..........................818-956-8406
Raintree Produ/666 N Robertson Blvd, Hollywood, CA 213-652-8330
S & A Graphics/3350 Barham Blvd, Los Angeles, CA 213-874-2301
Spungbuggy Works Inc/8506 Sunset Blvd, Hollywood, CA 213-657-8070
Sullivan & Associates/3377 Barham Blvd, Los Angeles, CA 213-874-2301
Sunwest Productions Inc/1021 N McCadden Pl, Hollywood, CA.....213-461-2957
Title House/738 Cahuenga Blvd, Los Angeles, CA....................213-469-8171
Triplane Film/328 1/2 N Sycamore Ave, Los Angeles, CA.............213-937-1320
U P A Pictures Inc/875 Century Park East, Los Angeles, CA..........213-556-3800

MODELS & TALENT

NYC

Abrams Artists/420 Madison Ave, ...212-935-8980
Act 48 Mgt Inc/1501 Broadway #1713, ...212-354-4250
Adams, Bret/448 W 44th St, ...212-246-0428
Agency for Performing Arts/888 Seventh Ave, ...212-582-1500
Agents for the Arts/1650 Broadway, ...212-247-3220
Alexander, Willard/660 Madison Ave, ...212-751-7070
Amato, Michael Theatrical Entrps/1650 Broadway, ...212-247-4456
Ambrose Co/1466 Broadway, ...212-921-0230
American Intl Talent/166 W 125th St, ...212-663-4626
American Talent Inc/888 Seventh Ave, ...212-977-2300
Anderson, Beverly/1472 Broadway, ...212-944-7773
Associated Booking/1995 Broadway, ...212-874-2400
Associated Talent Agency/41 E 11th St, ...212-674-4242
Astor, Richard/1697 Broadway, ...212-581-1970
Avantege Model Management/205 E 42nd St #1303, ...212-687-9890
Baldwin Scully Inc/501 Fifth Ave, ...212-922-1330
Barbizon Agency/3 E 54th St, ...212-371-3617
Barbizon Agency of Rego Park/95-20 63rd, ...718-275-2100
Barry Agency/165 W 46th St, ...212-869-9310
Bauman & Hiller/250 W 57th St, ...212-757-0098
Beilin, Peter/230 Park Ave, ...212-949-9119
Big Beauties Unlimited/159 Madison Ave, ...212-685-1270
Bloom, J Michael/400 Madison Ave, ...212-832-6900
Brifit Models/236 E 46th St 4th Fl, ...212-949-6262
Buchwald, Don & Assoc Inc/10 E 44th St, ...212-867-1070
Cataldi, Richard Agency/180 Seventh Ave, ...212-741-7450
Celebrity Lookalikes/235 E 31st St, ...212-532-7676
Click Model Management/881 Seventh Ave #1013, ...212-245-4306
Coleman-Rosenberg/667 Madison Ave, ...212-838-0734
Columbia Artists/165 W 57th St, ...212-397-6900
Cunningham, W D/919 Third Ave, ...212-832-2700
Deacy, Jane Inc/300 E 75th St, ...212-752-4865
DeVore, Ophelia/1697 Broadway, ...212-586-2144
Diamond Artists/119 W 57th St, ...212-247-3025
DMI Talent Assoc/250 W 57th St, ...212-246-4650
Dolan, Gloria Management Ltd/850 Seventh Ave, ...212-696-1850
Draper, Stephen Agency/37 W 57th St, ...212-421-5780
Eisen, Dulcina Assoc/154 E 61st St, ...212-355-6617
Elite Model Management Corp/150 E 58th St, ...212-935-4500
Faces Model Management/567 Third Ave, ...212-661-1515
Fields, Marje/165 W 46th St, ...212-764-5740
Ford Models Inc/344 E 59th St, ...212-753-6500

Foster Fell Agency/26 W 38th St, ...212-944-8520
Funny Face/440 E 62nd St, ...212-752-6090
Gage Group Inc/1650 Broadway, ...212-541-5250
Greco, Maria & Assoc/888 Eighth Ave, ...212-757-0681
Hadley, Peggy Ent/250 W 57th St, ...212-246-2166
Harth, Ellen Inc/149 Madison Ave, ...212-686-5600
Hartig, Michael Agency Ltd/114 E 28th St, ...212-684-0010
Henderson-Hogan/200 W 57th St, ...212-765-5190
Henry, June/175 Fifth Ave, ...212-475-5130
Hesseltine Baker Assocs/165 W 46th St, ...212-921-4460
Hunt, Diana Management/44 W 44th St, ...212-391-4971
Hutto Management Inc/405 W 23rd St, ...212-807-1234
HV Models/305 Madison Ave, ...212-751-3005
International Creative Management/40 W 57th St, ...212-556-5600
International Legends/40 E 34th St, ...212-684-4600
International Model Agency/232 Madison Ave, ...212-686-9053
Jacobsen-Wilder Inc/419 Park Ave So, ...212-686-6100
Jan J Agency/224 E 46th St, ...212-490-1875
Jordan, Joe Talent Agency/200 W 57th St, ...212-582-9003
Kahn, Jerry Inc/853 Seventh Ave, ...212-245-7317
Kay Models/328 E 61st St, ...212-308-9560
Kennedy Artists/237 W 11th St, ...212-675-3944
Kid, Bonnie Agency/25 W 36th St, ...212-563-2141
King, Archer/1440 Broadway, ...212-764-3905
Kirk, Roseanne/161 W 54th St, ...212-888-6711
KMA Associates/303 W 42nd St #606, ...212-581-4610
Kolmar-Luth Entertainment Inc/1501 Broadway #201, ...212-730-9500
Kroll, Lucy/390 West End Ave, ...212-877-0556
L B H Assoc/1 Lincoln Plaza, ...212-787-2609
L'Image Model Management Inc/114 E 32nd St, ...212-725-2424
Larner, Lionel Ltd/850 Seventh Ave, ...212-246-3105
Leach, Dennis/160 Fifth Ave, ...212-691-3450
Leaverton, Gary Inc/1650 Broadway, ...212-541-9640
Leigh, Sanford Entrprs Ltd/440 E 62nd St, ...212-752-4450
Leighton, Jan/205 W 57th St, ...212-757-5242
Lenny, Jack Assoc/140 W 58th St #1B, ...212-582-0270
Lewis, Lester Assoc/110 W 40th St, ...212-921-8370
M E W Company/370 Lexington Ave, ...212-889-7272
Mannequin Fashion Models Inc/40 E 34th St, ...212-684-5432
Martinelli Attractions/888 Eighth Ave, ...212-586-0963
Matama Talent & Models/30 W 90th St, ...212-580-2236
McDearmon, Harold/45 W 139th St, ...212-283-1005
McDermott, Marge/216 E 39th St, ...212-889-1583
McDonald/ Richards/235 Park Ave S, ...212-475-5401
MMG Ent/Marcia's Kids/250 W 57th St, ...212-246-4360
Models Models Inc/37 E 28th St #506, ...212-889-8233
Models Service Agency/1457 Broadway, ...212-944-8896
Models Talent Int'l/1140 Broadway, ...212-684-3343
Morris, William Agency/1350 Sixth Ave, ...212-586-5100
New York Production Studio/250 W 57th St, ...212-765-3433
Nolan, Philip/184 Fifth Ave, ...212-243-8900
Oppenheim-Christie/565 Fifth Ave, ...212-661-4330
Oscard, Fifi/19 W 44th St #1500, ...212-764-1100
Ostertag, Barna Agency/501 Fifth Ave, ...212-697-6339
Our Agency/19 W 34th St #700, ...212-736-9582
Packwood, Harry Talent Ltd/250 W 57th St, ...212-586-8900
Palmer, Dorothy/250 W 57th St, ...212-765-4280
Perkins Models/1697 Broadway, ...212-582-9511
Petite Model Management/123 E 54th St #9A, ...212-759-9304
Pfeffer & Roelfs Inc/850 Seventh Ave, ...212-315-2230
Plus Models/49 W 37th St, ...212-997-1785
PlusModel Model Management Ltd/49 W 37th St, ...212-997-1785
Powers, James Inc/12 E 41st St, ...212-686-9066
Prelly People & Co/296 Fifth Ave, ...212-714-2060
Premier Talent Assoc/3 E 54th St, ...212-758-4900
Prestige Models/80 W 40th St, ...212-382-1700
Rogers, Wallace Inc/160 E 56th St, ...212-755-1464
Roos, Gilla Ltd/555 Madison Ave, ...212-758-5480
Rosen, Lewis Maxwell/1650 Broadway, ...212-582-6762
Rubenstein, Bernard/215 Park Ave So, ...212-460-9800
Ryan, Charles Agency/200 W 57th St, ...212-245-2225
Sanders, Honey Agency Ltd/229 W 42nd St, ...212-947-5555
Schuller, William Agency/1276 Fifth Ave, ...212-532-6005
Silver, Monty Agency/200 W 57th St, ...212-765-4040
Smith, Friedman/850 Seventh Ave, ...212-581-4490
Stars/360 E 65th St #17H, ...212-988-1400
STE Representation/888 Seventh Ave, ...212-246-1030
Stein, Lillian/1501 Broadway, ...212-840-8299

Stewart Artists Corp/215 E 81st St, ...212-249-5540
Stroud Management/119 W 57th St, ...212-688-0226
Summa/38 W 32nd St, ...212-947-6155
Szold Models/644 Broadway, ...212-777-4998
Talent Reps Inc/20 E 53rd St, ...212-752-1835
Tatinas Models & Fitters Assoc/1328 Broadway, ...212-947-5797
The Lantz Office/888 Seventh Ave, ...212-586-0200
The Starkman Agency/1501 Broadway, ...212-921-9191
Theater Now Inc/1515 Broadway, ...212-840-4400
Thomas, Michael Agency/22 E 60th St, ...212-755-2616
Total Look/404 Riverside Dr, ...212-662-1029
Tranum Robertson Hughes Inc/2 Dag Hammarskjold Plaza, ...212-371-7500
Triad Artists/888 Seventh Ave, ...212-489-8100
Troy, Gloria/1790 Broadway, ...212-582-0260
Universal Attractions/218 W 57th St, ...212-582-7575
Universal Talent/505 5th Ave, ...212-661-3896
Van Der Veer People Inc/225 E 59th St #A, ...212-688-2880
Waters, Bob Agency/510 Madison Ave, ...212-593-0543
Wilhelmina Models/9 E 37th St, ...212-532-6800
Witt, Peter Assoc Inc/215 E 79th St, ...212-861-3120
Wright, Ann Assoc/136 E 57th St, ...212-832-0110
Zoli/146 E 56th St, ...212-758-5959

NORTHEAST

Cameo Models/392 Boylston St, Boston, MA................617-536-6004
Carnegie Talent Agency/300 Northern Blvd, Great Neck, NY..........516-487-2260
Conover, Joyce Agency/33 Gallowae, Westfield, NJ......201-232-0908
Copley 7 Models & Talent/29 Newbury St, Boston, MA....617-267-4444
Hart Model Agency/137 Newbury St, Boston, MA...........617-262-1740
Johnston Model Agency/32 Field Point Rd, Greenwich, CT......203-622-1137
National Talent Assoc/40 Railroad Ave, Valley Stream, NY.....516-825-8707
Rocco, Joseph Agency/Public Ledger Bldg, Philadelphia, PA........215-923-8790
Somers, Jo/29 Newbury St, Boston, MA 617-267-4444
The Ford Model Shop/176 Newbury St, Boston, MA.......617-266-6939
Trone, Larry/19-A Dean St, New Castle, DE 302-328-8399

SOUTHEAST

Adel Corral Models/5830 Argonne Blvd, New Orleans, LA 504-482-8963
Act 1 Casting Agency/1460 Brickell Ave, Miami, FL......305-371-1371
Amaro Agency/1617 Smith St, Orange Park, FL............904-264-0771
Atlanta Models & Talent/3030 Peachtree Rd NW, Atlanta, GA.........404-261-9627
Birmingham Models & Talent/1023 20th St, Birmingham, AL..........205-252-8533
Brown, Bob Marionettes/1415 S Queen St, Arlington, VA......703-920-1040
Brown, Jay Theatrical Agency/221 W Waters Ave, Tampa, FL......813-933-2456
Bruce Enterprises/1022 16th Ave S, Nashville, TN 615-255-5711
Burns, Dot Model & Talent Agcy/478 Severn St, Tampa, FL......813-251-5882
Byrd, Russ Assoc/9450 Koger Blvd, St Petersburg, FL......813-586-1504
Carolina Talent/1347 Harding Pl, Charlotte, NC 704-332-3218
Cassandra Models Agency/635 N Hyer St, Orlando, FL......305-423-7872
Central Casting of FL/PO Box 7154, Ft Lauderdale, FL......305-379-7526
Chez Agency/922 W Peachtree St, Atlanta, GA............404-873-1215
Dassinger, Peter Inter'l/1018 Royal, New Orleans, LA 504-525-8382
Directions Talent/400-C State St Station, Greensboro, NC......919-373-0955
Dodd, Barbara Studios/3508 Central Ave, Nashville, TN......615-385-0740
Faces, Ltd/2915 Frankfort Ave, Louisville, KY..............502-893-8840
Falcon, Travis Modeling Agency/17070 Collins Ave, Miami, FL......305-947-7957
Flair Models/PO Box 373, Nashville, TN.......................615-361-3737
Florida Talent Agency/2631 E Oakland Pk, Ft Lauderdale, FL.........305-565-3552
House of Talent/996 Lindridge Dr NE, Atlanta, GA 404-261-5543
Irene Marie Models/3212 S Federal Hwy, Ft Lauderdale, FL......305-522-3262
Jo-Susan Modeling/3415 West End Ave, Nashville, TN......615-383-5850
Lewis, Millie Modelingl/880 S Pleasantburg Dr, Greenville, SC 803-271-4402
Lewis, Millie Modeling/10 Calendar Ct #A, Forest Acres, SC 803-782-7338
Mar Bea Talent Agency/923 Crandon Blvd, Key Biscayne, FL........305-361-1144
Marilyns Modeling Agency/3800 W Wendover, Greensboro, NC 919-292-5950
McQuerter, James/4518 S Cortez, Tampa, FL...............813-839-8335
Parker, Sarah/425 S Olive Ave, West Palm Beach, FL......305-659-2833
Polan, Marian Talent Agency/PO Box 7154, Ft Lauderdale, FL......305-525-8351
Pommier, Michele/7520 Red Rd, Miami, FL..................305-667-8710
Powers, John Robert School/828 SE 4th St, Fort Lauderdale, FL.....305-467-2838
Professional Models Guild/210 Providence Rd, Charlotte, NC 704-377-9299
Rose, Sheila/8218 NW 8th St, Plantation, FL...............305-473-9747
Serendipity/3130 Maples Dr NE #19, Atlanta, GA..........404-237-4040
Signature Talent Inc/PO Box 221086, Charlotte, NC 704-542-0034
Sovereign Model & Talent/11111 Biscayne Blvd, Miami, FL 305-899-0280
Spivia, Ed/PO Box 38097, Atlanta, GA.........................404-292-6240
Stevens, Patricia Modeling/3312 Piedmont Rd, Atlanta, GA..........404-261-3330
Talent & Model Land, Inc/1501 12th Ave S, Nashville, TN 615-385-2723

Talent Enterprises Inc/3338 N Federal Way, Ft Lauderdale, FL 305-949-6099
Talent Management/2940 N Lynnhaven Rd, Virginia Bch, VA......804-486-5550
The Agency South/1501 Sunset Dr, Coral Gables, FL......305-667-6746
The Casting Directors Inc/1524 NE 147th St, North Miami, FL......305-944-8559
The Talent Shop Inc/3210 Peachtree Rd NE, Atlanta, GA......404-261-0770
Theatrics Etcetera/PO Box 11862, Memphis, TN............901-278-7454
Thompson, Jan Agency/1708 Scott Ave, Charlotte, NC......704-377-5987
Top Billing Inc/PO Box 121089, Nashville, TN...............615-327-1133
Tracey Agency Inc/PO Box 12405, Richmond, VA...........804-358-4004
Wellington Models/823 E Las Olas Blvd, Ft Lauderdale, FL 305-728-8003

MIDWEST

A-Plus Talent Agency Corp/666 N Lakeshore Dr, Chicago, IL 312-642-8151
Advertisers Casting/15 Kercheval Ave, Grosse Pt Farms, MI..........313-881-1135
Affiliated Talent/28860 Southfield Rd #100, Southfield, MI......313-559-3110
Arlene Willson Agency/9205 W Center St, Milwaukee, WI......414-259-1611
Creative Casting Inc/430 Oak Grove, Minneapolis, MN......612-871-7866
David & Lee Model Management/70 W Hubbard, Chicago, IL......312-661-0500
Gem Enterprises/5100 Eden Ave, Minneapolis, MN........612-927-8000
Hamilton, Shirley Inc/620 N Michigan Ave, Chicago, IL......312-644-0300
Lee, David Models/70 W Hubbard, Chicago, IL.............312-661-0500
Limelight Assoc Inc/3460 Davis Lane, Cincinnati, OH......513-631-8276
Marx, Dick & Assoc Inc/101 E Ontario St, Chicago, IL......312-440-7300
Monza Talent Agency/1001 Westport Rd, Kansas City, MO 816-931-0222
Moore, Eleanor Agency/1610 W Lake St, Minneapolis, MN......612-827-3823
National Talent Assoc/3525 Patterson Ave, Chicago, IL......312-539-8575
New Faces Models/310 Groveland Ave, Minneapolis, MN......612-871-6000
Pastiche Models Inc/161 Ottawa NW #300K, Grand Rapids, MI......616-451-2181
Powers, John Robert/5900 Roche Dr, Columbus, OH......614-846-1047
Schucart, Norman Ent/1417 Green Bay Rd, Highland Park, IL......312-433-1113
SR Talent Pool/206 S 44th St, Omaha, NE....................402-553-1164
Stat 12-Producers Exp/1759 Woodgrove Ln, Bloomfid Hills, MI 313-855-1188
Talent & Residuals Inc/303 E Ohio St, Chicago, IL..........312-943-7500
Talent Phone Productions/612 N Michagan Ave, Chicago, IL......312-664-5757
The Model Shop/415 N State St, Chicago, IL.................312-822-9663
Verblen, Carol Casting Svc/2408 N Burling, Chicago, IL......312-348-0047
White House Studios/9167 Robinson, Kansas City, MO 913-341-8036

SOUTHWEST

Aaron, Vicki/2017 Butterfield, Grand Prairie, TX...........214-641-8539
Accent Inc/6051 N Brookline, Oklahoma City, OK..........405-843-1303
Actors Clearinghouse/501 N IH 35, Austin, TX.............512-476-3412
ARCA/ Freelance Talent/PO Box 5686, Little Rock, AR......501-224-1111
Ball, Bobby Agency/808 E Osborn, Phoenix, AZ............602-264-5007
Barbizon Agency/1647-A W Bethany Home Rd, Phoenix, AZ......602-249-2950
Bennett, Don Agency/4630 Deepdale, Corpus Christi, TX......512-854-4871
Blair, Tanya Agency/3000 Carlisle St, Dallas, TX...........214-748-8353
Creme de la Creme/5643 N Pennsylvania, Oklahoma City, OK......405-721-5316
Dawson, Kim Agency/PO Box 585060, Dallas, TX..........214-638-2414
Ferguson Modeling Agency/1100 W 34th St, Little Rock, AR......501-375-3519
Flair Modeling/11200 Menaul Rd, Albuquerque, NM.......505-296-5571
Fosi's Talent Agency/2777 N Campbell Ave #209, Tucson, AZ......602-795-3534
Fullerton, Jo Ann/923 W Britton Rd, Oklahoma City, OK......405-848-4839
Hall, K Agency/503 W 15th St, Austin, TX....................512-476-7523
Harrison-Gers Modeling/1707 Wilshire Blvd NW, Okla City, OK......405-840-4515
Layman, Linda Agency/3546 E 51st St, Tulsa, OK..........918-744-0888
Mannequin Modeling Agency/204 E Oakview, San Antonio, TX......512-231-4540
Melancon, Joseph Studios/2934 Elm, Dallas, TX...........214-742-2982
Models and Talent of Tulsa/4528 S Sheridan Rd, Tulsa, OK......918-664-5340
Models of HoustonAgency/7676 Woodway, Houston, TX......713-789-4973
New Faces Inc/5108-B N 7th St, Phoenix, AZ...............602-279-3200
Norton Agency/3900 Lemon Ave, Dallas, TX.................214-528-9960
Parks, Page Model Reps/2915 Vine St 3300, Dallas, TX......214-891-9003
Plaza Three Talent Agency/4343 N 16th St, Phoenix, AZ......602-264-9703
Powers, John Robert/3005 S University Dr, Fort Worth, TX......817-923-7305
Shaw, Ben Modeling Studios/4801 Woodway, Houston, TX......713-850-0413
Southern AZ Casting/2777 N Campbell Ave, Tucson, AZ......602-795-3534
Strawn, Libby/3612 Foxcroft Rd, Little Rock, AR...........501-227-5874
The Mad Hatter/7349 Ashcroft Rd, Houston, TX............713-995-9090
The Texas Cowgirls Inc/4300 N Central #109C, Dallas, TX......214-696-4176
Wyse, Joy Agency/2600 Stemmons, Dallas, TX............214-638-8999

ROCKY MTN

Aspen/Vannoy Talent/PO Box 8124, Aspen, CO...........303-771-7500
Denver/ Vannoy Talent/7400 E Caley Ave, Engelwood, CO......303-771-6555
Illinois Talent/2664 S Krameria, Denver, CO................303-757-8675
Mack, Jess Agency/111 Las Vegas Blvd S, Las Vegas, NV......702-382-2193
Morris, Bobby Agency/1629 E Sahara Ave, Las Vegas, NV 702-733-7575
Universal Models/953 E Sahara Ave, Las Vegas, NV......702-732-2499

WEST COAST

Adrian, William Agency/520 S Lake Ave, Pasadena, CA 213-681-5750
Anthony's, Tom Precision Driving/1231 N Harper, Hollywood, CA 213-462-2301
Artists Management Agency/2232 Fifth Ave, San Diego, CA 619-233-6655
Barbizon Modeling/15477 Ventura Blvd, Sherman Oaks, CA 213-995-8238
Barbizon Modeling/452 Fashion Valley E, San Diego, CA 714-296-6366
Blanchard, Nina/1717 N Highland Ave, Hollywood, CA 213-462-7274
Brebner Agency/185 Berry St, San Francisco, CA 415-495-6700
Celebrity Look-Alikes/9000 Sunset Blvd, W Hollywood, CA 213-273-5566
Character Actors/935 NW 19th Ave, Portland, OR 503-223-1931
Commercials Unlimited/7461 Beverly Blvd, Los Angeles, CA 213-937-2220
Crosby, Mary Talent Agency/2130 Fourth Ave, San Diego, CA 714-234-7911
Cunningham, William D/261 S Robertson, Beverly Hills, CA 213-855-0200
Demeter and Reed Ltd/70 Zoe #200, San Francisco, CA 415-777-1337
Drake, Bob/3878-A Fredonia Dr, Hollywood, CA 213-851-4404
Franklin, Bob Talent/10325 NE Hancock, Portland, OR 503-253-1655
Frazer-Nicklin/4300 Stevens Creek Blvd, San Jose, CA 408-554-1055
Garrick, Dale Agency/8831 Sunset Blvd, Los Angeles, CA 213-657-2661
Grimme Agency/207 Powell St, San Francisco, CA 415-392-9175
Hansen, Carolyn Agency/1516 6th Ave, Seattle, WA 206-622-4700
Intern'l Creative Mngmnt/8899 Beverly Blvd, Los Angeles, CA 213-550-4000
Kelman, Toni Agency/8961 Sunset Blvd, Los Angeles, CA 213-851-8822
L'Agence Models/100 N Winchester Blvd #370, San Jose, CA 408-985-2993
Leonetti, Ltd/6526 Sunset Blvd, Los Angeles, CA 213-462-2345
Liebes School of Modeling Inc/45 Willow Lane, Sausalito, CA 415-331-5383
Longenecker, Robert/11500 Olympic Blvd, Los Angeles, CA 213-477-0039
Media Talent Center/4315 NE Tillamook, Portland, OR 503-281-2020
Model Management Inc/1400 Castro St, San Francisco, CA 415-282-8855
Neuman, Allan/825 W 16th St, Newport Beach, CA 714-548-8800
Pacific Artists, Ltd/515 N La Cienaga, Los Angeles, CA 213-657-5990
Playboy Model Agency/8560 Sunset Blvd, Los Angeles, CA 213-659-4080
Powers, John Robert/1610 6th Ave, Seattle, WA 206-624-2495
Remington Models/924 Westwood Blvd, Los Angeles, CA 213-552-3012
Schwartz, Don Agency/8721 Sunset Blvd, Los Angeles, CA 213-657-8910
Seattle Models Guild/1610 6th Ave, Seattle, WA 206-622-1406
Shaw, Glen Agency/3330 Barham Blvd, Los Angeles, CA 213-851-6262
Smith, Ron's Look-Alikes/9000 Sunset Blvd, Hollywood, CA 213-273-5566
Sohbi's Talent Agency/1750 Kalakaua Ave #116, Honolulu, HI 808-946-6614
Stern, Charles Agency/9220 Sunset Blvd, Los Angeles, CA 213-273-6890
Studio Seven/261 E Rowland Ave, Covina, CA 213-331-6351
Stunts Unlimited/3518 Cahuenga Blvd W, Los Angeles, CA 213-874-0050
Tanner, Herb & Assoc/6640 W Sunset Blvd, Los Angeles, CA 213-466-6191
TOPS Talent Agency/404 Piikoi St, Honolulu, HI 808-537-6647
Wormser Heldford & Joseph/1717 N Highlnd, Los Angeles, CA 213-466-9111

CASTING

NYC

BCI Casting/1500 Broadway, ...212-221-1583
Brinker, Jane/51 W 16th St, ...212-924-3322
Brown, Deborah Casting/250 W 57th St, ...212-581-0404
Burton, Kate/271 Madison Ave, ...212-243-6114
C & C Productions/445 E 80th St, ...212-472-3700
Carter, Kit & Assoc/160 W 95th St, ...212-864-3147
Cast Away Casting Service/14 Sutton Pl S, ...212-755-0960
Central Casting Corp of NY/200 W 54th St, ...212-582-4933
Cereghetti Casting/119 W 57th St, ...212-307-6081
Claire Casting/118 E 28th St, ...212-889-8844
Complete Casting/240 W 44th St, ...212-382-3835
Contemporary Casting Ltd/41 E 57th St, ...212-838-1818
Davidson/Frank Photo-Stylists/209 W 86th St #701, ...212-799-2651
Deron, Johnny/30-42 32nd St, Astoria........................718-728-5326
DeSeta, Donna Casting/424 W 33rd St, ...212-239-0988
Digiaimo, Lou/PO Box 5296 FDR Sta, ...212-691-6073
Fay, Sylvia/71 Park Ave, ...212-889-2626
Feuer & Ritzer Casting Assoc/1650 Broadway, ...212-765-5580
Greco, Maria Casting/888 Eighth Ave, ...212-757-0681
Herman & Lipson Casting, Inc/114 E 25th St, ...212-777-7070
Howard, Stewart Assoc/215 Park Ave So, ...212-477-2323
Hughes/Moss Assoc/311 W 42nd St, ...212-307-6690
Iredale/ Burton Ltd/271 Madison Ave, ...212-889-7722
Jacobs, Judith/336 E 81st St, ...212-744-3758

Johnson/Liff/1501 Broadway, ...212-391-2680
Kressel, Lynn Casting/111 W 57th St, ...212-581-6990
L 2 Casting, Inc/4 W 83rd St, ...212-496-9444
McCorkle-Sturtevant Casting Ltd/240 W 44th St, ...212-888-9160
Navarro-Bertoni Casting Ltd/25 Central Park West, ...212-765-4251
Reed/Sweeney/Reed Inc/1780 Broadway, ...212-265-8541
Reiner, Mark Contemporary Casting/16 W 46th St, ...212-838-1818
Schneider Studio/119 W 57th St, ...212-265-1223
Shapiro, Barbara Casting/111 W 57th St, ...212-582-8228
Shulman/Pasciuto, Inc/1457 Broadway #308, ...212-944-6420
Silver, Stan/108 E 16th St, ...212-477-5900
Todd, Joy/250 W 57th St, ...212-765-1212
Weber, Joy Casting/250 W 57th St #1925, ...212-245-5220
Wollin, Marji/233 E 69th St, ...212-472-2528
Woodman, Elizabeth Roberts/222 E 44th St, ...212-972-1900

NORTHEAST

Baker, Ann Casting/6 Wheeler Rd, Newton, MA 617-964-3038
Booking Agent Lic/860 Floral Ave, Union, NJ 201-353-1595
Central Casting/623 Pennsylvania Ave SE, Washington, DC 202-547-6300
Dilworth, Francis/496 Kinderkamack Rd, Oradell, NJ 201-265-4020
Holt/Belajac & Assoc Inc/The Bigelow #1924, Pittsburgh, PA ..412-391-1005
Lawrence, Joanna Agency/82 Patrick Rd, Westport, CT 203-226-7239
Panache/3214 N St NW, Washington, DC 202-333-4240
Producers Audition Hotline/18156 Darnell Dr, Olney, MD 301-924-4327
Taylor Royal Casting/2308 South Rd, Baltimore, MD 301-466-5959

SOUTHEAST

Central Casting/PO Box 7154, Ft Lauderdale, FL 305-379-7526
DiPrima, Barbara/2951 So Bayshore Dr, Coconut Grove, FL 305-445-7630
Elite Artists, Inc/785 Crossover, Memphis, TN 901-761-1046
Manning, Maureen/1283 Cedar Hts Dr, Stone Mt, GA 404-296-1520

MIDWEST

Sta 12 Producers Exp/1759 Woodgrove Ln, Bloomfield Hills, MI 313-855-1188

SOUTHWEST

Abramson, Shirley/321 Valley Cove, Garland, TX 214-272-3400
Austin Actors Clearinghouse/501 North 1H 35, Austin, TX 512-476-3412
Blair, Tanya Agency/3000 Carlisle #101, Dallas, TX.........214-748-8353
Chason, Gary & Assoc/5645 Hillcroft St, Houston, TX 713-789-4003
Greer, Lucy/600 Shadywood Ln, Richardson, TX...............214-231-2086
KD Studio/2600 Stemons #147, Dallas, TX 214-638-0484
Kegley, Liz/Shari Rhodes/5737 Everglade, Dallas, TX 214-475-2353
Kegley, Liz/Shari Rhodes/2021 Southgate, Houston, TX 713-522-5066
Kent, Rody/5338 Vanderbilt Ave, Dallas, TX 214-827-3418
New Visions/Box 14 Whipple Station, Prescott, AZ...........602-445-3382
Schermerhorn, Jo Ann/PO Box 2672, Conroe, TX 409-273-2569

ROCKY MTN

Aspen/Vannoy Talent/PO Box 8124, Aspen, CO 303-771-7500
Denver/ Vannoy Talent/7400 E Caley Ave, Engelwood, CO 303-771-6555

WEST COAST

Abrams-Rubaloff/9012 Beverly Blvd, Los Angeles, CA 213-273-5711
Assoc Talent Intern'l/9744 Wilshire Blvd, Los Angeles, CA 213-271-4662
BCI Casting/5134 Valley, Los Angeles, CA 213-222-0366
C H N International/7428 Santa Monica Blvd, Los Angeles, CA ..213-874-8252
Celebrity Look-Alikes/9000 Sunset Blvd, W Hollywood, CA 213-273-5566
Commercials Unlimited/7461 Beverly Blvd, Los Angeles, CA ...213-937-2220
Creative Artists/1888 Century Park E, Los Angeles, CA 213-277-4545
Cunningham, William/261 S Robertson Blvd, Beverly Hills, CA 213-855-0200
Davis, Mary Webb/515 N LaCienega, Los Angeles, CA 213-652-6850
Garrick, Dale Internat'l/8831 Sunset Blvd, Los Angeles, CA 213-657-2661
Hecht, Beverly/8949 Sunset Blvd, Los Angeles, CA 213-278-3544
Kelman, Toni Agency/8961 Sunset Blvd, Los Angeles, CA 213-851-8822
Leonetti, Caroline Ltd/6526 Sunset Blvd, Los Angeles, CA ...213-462-2345
Lien, Michael Casting/7461 Beverly Blvd, Los Angeles, CA ...213-550-7381
Loo, Bessi Agency/8235 Santa Monica, W Hollywood, CA 213-650-1300
Mangum, John Agency/8831 Sunset Blvd, Los Angeles, CA 213-659-7230
Morris, William Agency/151 El Camino Dr, Beverly Hills, CA 213-274-7451
Pacific Artists/515 N LaCienega Blvd, Los Angeles, CA 213-657-5990
REB-Sunset Intern'l/6912 Hollywood Blvd, Hollywood, CA 213-464-4440
Rose, Jack/6430 Sunset Blvd #1203, Los Angeles, CA 213-463-7300
Schaeffer, Peggy/10850 Riverside Dr, N Hollywood, CA 818-985-5547
Schwartz, Don & Assoc/8721 Sunset Blvd, Los Angeles, CA ...213-657-8910
Stern, Charles H Agency/9220 Sunset Blvd, Los Angeles, CA....213-273-6890
Sutton Barth & Venari/8322 Beverly Blvd, Los Angeles, CA ...213-653-8322

Tannen, Herb & Assoc/6640 Sunset Blvd, Los Angeles, CA 213-466-6191
Wilhelmina/West/1800 Centry Park E #504, Century City, CA........213-553-9525
Wormser Heldford & Joseph/1717 N Highland, Hollywood, CA 213-466-9111
Wright, Ann Assoc/8422 Melrose Place, Los Angeles, CA 213-655-5040

A N I M A T O R S

N Y C

All Tame Animals/37 W 57th St, ...212-752-5885
Animals for Advertising/310 W 55th St, ...212-245-2590
Berloni Theatrical Animals/314 W 57th St Box 37, ...212-974-0922
Canine Academy of Ivan Kovach/3725 Lyme Ave, Brooklyn, ...718-682-6770
Captain Haggertys Theatrical Dogs/1748 First Ave, ...212-410-7400
Chateau Theatrical Animals/608 W 48th St, ...212-246-0520
Claremont Riding Academy/175 W 89th St, ...212-724-5100
Dawn Animal Agency/160 W 46th St, ...212-575-9396
Mr Lucky Dog Training School Inc/27 Crescent St, Brooklyn, ...718-827-2792

N O R T H E A S T

American Driving Society/PO Box 1852, Lakeville, CT 203-435-0307
Animal Actors Inc/Box 221, RD 3, Washington, NJ......................201-689-7539
Davis, Greg/Box 159T, RD 2, Greenville, NY..............................518-966-8229
Long Island Game Farm & Zoo/Chapman Blvd, Manorville, NY......516-727-7443
Parrots of the World/239 Sunrise Hwy, Rockville Center, NY.............212-343-4141

S O U T H E A S T

Maida,Bob/Dog Trng/7605 Old Centerville Rd, Manassas, VA........713-631-2125
Studio Animal Rentals/170 W 64th St, Hialeah, FL.....................305-558-4160

M I D W E S T

Olthuis, Stan/387 Richmond St E, Toronto M5A 1P6, ON................416-860-0300
Plainsmen Zoo/Rt 4, Box 151, Elgin, IL.....................................312-697-0062

S O U T H W E S T

Bettis, Ann J/Rt 1-A Box 21-B, Dripping Springs, TX 512-264-1952
Dallas Zoo in Marsalis Park/621 E Clarendon, Dallas, TX 214-946-5155
Estes, Bob Rodeos/PO Box 962, Baird, TX.................................915-854-1037
Fort Worth Zoo Park/2727 Zoological Park Dr., Fort Worth, TX 817-870-7050
Intern'l Wildlife Park/601 Wildlife Pkwy, Grand Prairie, TX..........214-263-2203
Newsom's Varmints N' Things/13015 Kaltenbrun, Houston, TX........713-931-0676
Scott, Kelly Buggy & Wagon Rentals/Box 442, Bandera, TX 512-796-3737
Taylor, Peggy/6311 N O'Connor 3 Dallas Comm, Irving, TX 214-869-1515
Y O Ranch/Dept AS, Mountain Home, TX....................................512-640-3222

R O C K Y   M T N

Denver/ Vannoy Talent/7400 E Caley Ave, Engelwood, CO.............303-771-6555

W E S T   C O A S T

American Animal Enterprises/PO Box 337, Littlerock, CA 805-944-3011
Animal Action/PO Box 824, Arleta, CA 818-767-3003
Animal Actors/864 Carlisle Rd, Thousand Oaks, CA 805-495-2122
Birds and Animals/25191 Riverdell Dr, El Toro, CA 714-830-7845
Casa De Pets/11814 Ventura Blvd, Studio City, CA 818-761-3651
Di Sesso's, Trained Wildlife/24233 Old Rd, Newhall, CA 805-255-7969
Frank Inn Inc/12265 Branford St, Sun Valley, CA 818-896-8188
Gentle Jungle/3815 W Olive Ave, Burbank, CA 818-841-5300
Griffin, Gus/11281 Sheldon St, Sun Valley, CA........................818-767-6647
Martin, Steve Working Wildlife/PO Box 65, Acton, CA 805-268-0788
Pyramid Bird/1407 W Magnolia, Burbank, CA 818-843-5505
Schumacher Animal Rentals/14453 Cavette Pl, Baldwin Pk, CA 818-338-4614
Stansbury Co/9304 Santa Monica Blvd, Beverly Hills, CA............213-273-1138
The American Mongrel/PO Box 2406, Lancaster, CA 805-942-7550
The Blair Bunch/7561 Woodman Pl, Van Nuys, CA.....................213-994-1136
Weatherwax, Rob/16133 Soledad Cnyn Rd, Cnyn Country, CA 805-252-6907

H A I R   &   M A K E - U P

N Y C

Abrams, Ron/126 W 75th St, ...212-580-0705
Baeder, D & Sehven, A/135 E 26th St, ...212-532-4571
Barba, Olga/201 E 16th St, ...212-420-8611
Barron, Lynn/135 E 26th St, ...212-532-4571
Beauty Booking/130 W 57th St, ...212-977-7157
Blake, Marion/130 W 57th St, ...212-977-7157
Boles, Brad/, ...212-724-2800
Boushelle/444 E 82nd St, ...212-861-7225
Braithwaite, Jordan/130 W 57th St, ...212-977-7157
Hammond, Claire/440 E 57th St, ...212-838-0712
Imre, Edith Beauty Salon/8 W 56th St, ...212-758-0233
Jenrette, Pamela/300 Mercer St, ...212-673-4748
Keller, Bruce Clyde/422 E 58th St, ...212-593-3816
Multiple Artists/42 E 23 St, ...212-473-8020
Narvaez, Robin/360 E 55th St, ...212-371-6378
Richardson, John Ltd/119 E 64th St, ...212-772-1874
Stessin, Warren Scott/, ...212-243-3319
Tamblyn, Thom Inc/240 E 27th St, ...212-683-4514
Weithorn, Rochelle/431 E 73rd St, ...212-472-8668

N O R T H E A S T

E-Fex/623 Pennsylvania Ave SE, Washington, DC......................202-543-1241
Rothman, Ginger/1915 Lyttonsville Rd, Silver Spring, MD 301-565-2020

S O U T H E A S T

Irene Marie Models/3212 S Federal Hwy, Ft Lauderdale, FL 305-522-3262
Parker, Julie Hill/PO Box 19033, Jacksonville, FL 904-724-8483

M I D W E S T

Adams, Jerry Hair Salon/1123 W Webster, Chicago, IL 312-327-1130
Alderman, Frederic/Rt 2 Box 205, Mundelein, IL........................312-438-2925
Bobak, Ilona/300 N State, Chicago, IL....................................312-321-1679
Camylle/112 E Oak, Chicago, IL 312-943-1120
Cheveux/908 W Armitage, Chicago, IL 312-935-5212
Collins Chicago, Inc/67 E Oak, Chicago, IL 312-266-6662
Emerich, Bill/PO Box 14523, Chicago, IL.................................312-871-4659
International Guild of Make-Up/6970 N Sheridan, Chicago, IL.........312-761-8500
Okains Costume & Theater/2713 W Jefferson, Joliet, IL................815-741-9303
Sguardo, Che/716 N Wells St, Chicago, IL 312-440-1616
Simmons, Sid Inc/2 E Oak, Chicago, IL 312-943-2333
Wawiorka, Karen/, Chicago, IL 312-642-4219

S O U T H W E S T

Dawson, Kim Agency/PO Box 585060, Dallas, TX.......................214-638-2414

W E S T   C O A S T

Andre, Maurice/9426 Santa Monica Blvd, Beverly Hills, CA.............213-274-4562
Antovniov/11908 Ventura Blvd, Studio City, CA........................818-763-0671
Armando's/607 No Huntley Dr, W Hollywood, CA.......................213-657-5160
Bourget, Lorraine/559 Muskingum Pl, Pacific Palisades, CA...........213-454-3739
Cassandre 2000/18386 Ventura Blvd, Tarzana, CA.....................818-881-8400
Cloutier Inc/704 N Gardner, Los Angeles, CA...........................213-655-1263
Craig, Kenneth/13211 Ventura Blvd, Studio City, CA..................818-995-8717
Design Pool/11936 Darlington Ave #303, Los Angeles, CA.............213-826-1551
Francisco/PO Box 49995, Los Angeles, CA...............................213-826-3591
Frier, George/, CA...213-393-0576
Gavilan/139 S Kings Rd, Los Angeles, CA 213-655-4452
Geiger, Pamela/, CA...213-274-5737
Hamilton, Bryan J/909 N Westbourne Dr, Los Angeles, CA.............213-654-9006
Hirst, William/15130 Ventura Blvd, Sherman Oaks, CA................818-501-0993
HMS/1541 Harvard St #A, Santa Monica, CA.............................213-828-2080
Johns, Arthur/8661 Sunset Blvd, Hollywood, CA.......................213-855-9306
Ray, David Frank/15 Wave Crest, Venice, CA............................213-392-5640
Samuel, Martin/6138 W 6th, Los Angeles, CA...........................213-930-0794
Serena, Eric/840 N Larabee, Bldg 4, W Hollywood, CA.................213-652-4267
Studio Seven/261 E Rowland Ave, Covina, CA...........................213-331-6351
Total You Salon/1647 Los Angeles Ave, Simi, CA 805-526-4189
Towsend, Jeanne/433 N Camden Dr, Beverly Hills, CA.................213-851-7044
Welsh, Franklyn/704 N LaCienega Blvd, Los Angeles, CA.............213-656-8195

HAIR

NYC

Albert-Carter/Hotel St Moritz, ...212-688-2045
Benjamin Salon/104 Washington Pl, ...212-255-3330
Caruso, Julius/22 E 62nd St, ...212-751-6240
Daines, David Salon Hair Styling/833 Madison Ave, ...212-535-1563
George V Hair Stylist/501 Fifth Ave, ...212-687-9097
Moda 700/700 Madison Ave, ...212-935-9188
Monsieur Marc Inc/22 E 65th St, ...212-861-0700
Peter's Beauty Home/149 W 57th St, ...212-247-2934
Pierro, John/130 W 57th St, ...212-977-7157

NORTHEAST

Brocklebank, Tom/249 Emily Ave, Elmont, NY 516-775-5356

SOUTHEAST

Yellow Strawberry/107 E Las Olas Blvd, Ft Lauderdale, FL 305-463-4343

MIDWEST

Rodriguez, Ann/1123 W Webster, Chicago, IL..........................312-327-1130

SOUTHWEST

Southern Hair Designs/3563 Far West Blvd, Austin, TX...........512-346-1734

ROCKY MTN

City Lights Hair Designs/2845 Wyandote, Denver, CO.............303-458-0131
Zee for Hair/316 E Hopkins, Aspen, CO.................................303-925-4434

WEST COAST

Anatra, M Haircutters/530 No LaCienega, Los Angeles, CA 213-657-1495
Barronson Hair/11908 Ventura, Studio City, CA 818-763-4337
Beck, Shirley/, CA...213-763-2930
Edwards, Allen/455 N Rodeo Dr, Beverly Hills, CA 213-274-8575
Ely, Shannon/616 Victoria, Venice, CA 213-392-5832
Fisher, Jim/c/o Rumours, 9014 Melrose, Los Angeles, CA.......213-550-5946
Francisco/PO Box 49995, Los Angeles, CA.............................213-826-3591
Grieve, Ginger/, CA..818-347-2947
Gurasich, Lynda/, CA..818-981-6719
Hjerpe, Warren/9018 Beverly Blvd, Los Angeles, CA..............213-550-5946
HMS/1541 Harvard St #A, Santa Monica, CA 213-828-2080
Iverson, Betty/, CA...213-462-2301
John, Michael Salon/414 N Camden Dr, Beverly Hills, CA.......213-278-8333
Kemp, Lola/, CA...213-293-8710
Lorenz, Barbara/, CA..213-657-0028
Malone, John/, CA..213-246-1649
Menage a Trois/8822 Burton Way, Beverly Hills, CA...............213-278-4431
Miller, Patty/, CA..818-843-5208
Morrissey, Jimie/, CA..213-657-4318
Payne, Allen/, CA...213-395-5259
Phillips, Marilyn/, CA..213-923-6996
Sami/1230 N Horn Ave #525, Los Angeles, CA......................213-652-5816
Sassoon, Vidal/2049 Century Park E, Los Angeles, CA...........213-553-6100
The Hair Conspiracy/11923 Ventura Blvd, Studio City, CA.......818-985-1126
Trainoff, Linda/, CA..818-769-0373
Vecchio, Faith/, CA..818-345-6152

MAKE-UP

NYC

Adams, Richard/130 W 57th St, ...212-977-7157
Armand/147 W 35th St, ...212-947-2186
Bertoli, Michele/264 Fifth Ave, ...212-684-2480
Bonzignor's Cosmetics/110 Fulton, ...212-267-1108
Lawrence, Rose/444 E 82nd St, ...212-861-7225
Make-Up Center Ltd/150 W 55th St, ...212-977-9494
Oakley, Sara/, ...212-749-5912
Richardson, John Ltd/119 E 64th St, ...212-772-1874
Ross, Rose Cosmetics/16 W 55th St, ...212-586-2590

Sartin, Janet of Park Ave Ltd/480 Park Ave, ...212-751-5858
Stage Light Cosmetics Ltd/630 Ninth Ave, ...212-757-4851
Suzanne de Paris/509 Madison Ave, ...212-838-4024

NORTHEAST

Damaskos-Zilber, Zoe/78 Waltham St #4, Boston, MA............617-628-6583
Douglas, Rodney N/473 Avon Ave #3, Newark, NJ 201-375-2979
Fiorina, Frank/2400 Hudson Terr #5A, Fort Lee, NJ 212-242-3900
Gilmore, Robert Assoc Inc/990 Washington St, Dedham, MA......617-329-6633
Meth, Miriam/96 Greenwood Ln, White Plains, NY 212-787-5400
Minassian, Amie/62-75 Austin St, Rego Park, NY 212-446-8048
Phillipe, Louise Miller/22 Chestnut Pl, Brookline, MA 617-566-3608
Phillipe, Robert/22 Chestnut Pl, Brookline, MA 617-566-3608
Something Special/1601 Walter Reed Dr S, Arlington, VA 703-892-0551
Tyson, Karen/344 E 85th St #6D, ...212-517-3508
Zack, Sandra/94 Orient Ave, East Boston, MA........................617-567-7581

SOUTHEAST

Star Styled of Miami/475 NW 42nd Ave, Miami, FL.................305-541-2424
Star Styled of Tampa/4235 Henderson Blvd, Tampa, FL...........813-872-8706

SOUTHWEST

ABC Theatrical Rental & Sales/825 N 7th St, Phoenix, AZ.......602-258-5265
Chelsea Cutters/One Chelsea Pl, Houston, TX 713-529-4813
Copeland, Tom/502 West Grady, Austin, TX 512-835-0208
Corey, Irene/4147 Herschel Ave, Dallas, TX...........................214-528-4836
Dobes, Pat/1826 Nocturne, Houston, TX 713-465-8102
Ingram, Marilyn Wyrick/10545 Chesterton Drive, Dallas, TX...........214-349-2113
Schakosky, Laurie/, Dallas, TX..214-458-6941
Stamm, Louis M/721 Edgehill Dr, Hurst, TX............................817-268-5037

ROCKY MTN

Moen, Brenda/, CO...303-871-9506
Moon Sun Emporium/2019 Broadway, Boulder, CO.................303-443-6851

WEST COAST

Astier, Guy/11936 Darlington Ave #303, Los Angeles, CA.......213-826-1551
Blackman, Charles F/12751 Addison, N Hollywood, CA...........818-761-2177
Blackman, Gloria/12751 Addison, N Hollywood, CA...............818-761-2177
Case, Tom/5150 Woodley, Encino, CA 818-788-5268
Cooper, David/3616 Effie, Los Angeles, CA............................213-660-7326
Cosmetic Connection/9484 Dayton Way, Beverly Hills, CA......213-550-6242
D'Ifray, T J/468 N Bedford Dr, Beverly Hills, CA......................213-274-6776
Dawn, Wes/11113 Hortense St, N Hollywood, CA...................818-761-7517
Fradkin, Joanne c/o Pigments/8822 Burton Way, Beverly Hills, CA..213-858-7038
Francisco/PO Box 49995, Los Angeles, CA.............................213-826-3591
Freed, Gordon/, CA...818-360-9473
Geike, Ziggy/, CA...818-789-1465
Henrriksen, Ole/8601 W Sunset Blvd, Los Angeles, CA...........213-854-7700
Howell, Deborah/291 S Martel Ave, Los Angeles, CA.............213-655-1263
Koelle, c/o Pigments/8822 Burton Way, Beverly Hills, CA.......213-668-1690
Kruse, Lee C/, CA...818-894-5408
Laurent, c/o Menage a Trois/8822 Burton Way, Beverly Hills, CA.....213-278-4430
Logan, Kathryn/, CA...818-988-7038
Malone, John E/, CA...818-247-5160
Manges, Delanie (Dee)/, CA..818-763-3311
Maniscalco, Ann S/, CA...818-894-5408
Menage a Trois/8822 Burton Way, Beverly Hills, CA...............213-278-4431
Minch, Michelle/339 S Detroit St, Los Angeles, CA.................213-484-9648
Natasha/4221 1/2 Avocado St, Los Angeles, CA....................213-663-1477
Nielsen, Jim/, CA..213-461-2168
Nye, Dana/, CA...213-477-0443
Odessa/1448 1/2 N Fuller Ave, W Hollywood, CA..................213-876-5779
Palmieri, Dante/, CA...213-396-6020
Penelope/, ...213-654-6747
Pigments/8822 Burton Way, Beverly Hills, CA........................213-858-7038
Romero, Bob/5030 Stern Ave, Sherman Oaks, CA..................818-891-3338
Rumours/9014 Melrose, W Hollywood, CA.............................213-550-5946
Sanders, Nadia/, CA..213-465-2009
Shulman, Sheryl Leigh/, CA...818-760-0101
Sidell, Bob/, ...818-360-0794
Striepke, Danny/4800 #C Villa Marina, Marina Del Rey, CA.......213-823-5957
Tuttle, William/, ...213-454-2355
Tyler, Diane/, ...415-381-5067
Warren, Dodie/, ...818-763-3172
Westmore, Michael/, ...818-763-3158
Westmore, Monty/, ...818-762-2094
Winston, Stan/, ...818-886-0630
Wolf, Barbara/, CA..213-466-4660

STYLISTS

NYC

Baldassano, Irene/16 W 16th St,	212-255-8567
Bandiero, Paul/PO Box 121 FDR Station,	212-586-3700
Barritt, Randi Stylist/240 W 15th St,	212-255-5333
Batteau, Sharon/130 W 57th St,	212-977-7157
Beauty Bookings/130 W 57th St,	212-977-7157
Benner, Dyne (Food)/311 E 60th St,	212-688-7571
Berman, Benicia/399 E 72nd St,	212-737-9627
Bromberg, Florence/350 Third Ave,	212-255-4033
Cheverton, Linda/150 9th Avenue,	212-691-0881
Chin, Fay/67 Vestry St,	212-219-8770
Cohen, Susan/233 E 54th St,	212-755-3157
D'Arcy, Timothy/43 W 85th St,	212-580-8804
Davidson/Frank Photo-Stylists/209 W 86th St #701,	212-799-2651
DeJesu, Joanna (Food)/101 W 23rd St,	212-255-3895
Eller, Ann/7816 Third Ave, Brooklyn	718-238-5454
Final Touch/55-11 13th Ave, Brooklyn	718-435-6800
Galante, Kathy/9 W 31st St,	212-239-0412
George, Georgia A/404 E 55th St,	212-759-4131
Goldberg, Hal/11 Fifth Ave,	212-982-7588
Greene, Jan/200 E 17th St,	212-233-8989
Haynie, Cecille/105 W 13th St #7C,	212-929-3690
Herman, Joan/15 W 84th St,	212-724-3287
Joffe, Carole Reiff/233 E 34th St,	212-725-4928
Klein, Mary Ellen/330 E 33rd St,	212-683-6351
Lakin, Gaye/345 E 81st St,	212-861-1892
Levin, Laurie/55 Perry St,	212-242-2611
Lopes, Sandra/444 E 82nd St,	212-249-8706
Magidson, Peggy/182 Amity St, Brooklyn	212-508-7604
Manetti, Palmer/336 E 53rd St,	212-758-3859
McCabe, Christine/200 W 79th St,	212-799-4121
Meshejian, Zabel/125 Washington Pl,	212-242-2459
Meyers, Pat/436 W 20th St,	212-620-0069
Minch, Deborah Lee/175 W 87th St,	212-873-7915
Nagle, Patsy/242 E 38th St,	212-682-0364
Orefice, Jeanette/, Brooklyn	718-643-8266
Ouellette, Dawn/336 E 30th St,	212-799-9190
Peacock, Linda/118 W 88th St,	212-580-1422
Reilly, Veronica/60 Gramercy Park N,	212-840-1234
Sampson, Linda/431 W Broadway,	212-925-6821
Scherman, Joan/450 W 24th St,	212-620-0475
Schoenberg, Marv/878 West End Ave #10A,	212-663-1418
Seymour, Celeste/130 E 75th St,	212-744-3545
Sheffy, Nina/838 West End Ave,	212-662-0709
Slote, Ina/7 Park Ave,	212-679-4584
Smith, Rose/400 E 56th St #19D,	212-758-8711
Specht, Meredith/166 E 61st St,	212-832-0750
Weithorn, Rochelle/431 E 73rd St,	212-472-8668
West, Susan/59 E 7th St,	212-982-8228

NORTHEAST

Bailey Designs/110 Williams St, Malden, MA	617-321-4448
Baldwin, Katherine/109 Commonwealth Ave, Boston, MA	617-267-0508
Carafoli, John (Food)/1 Hawes Rd, Sagamore Beach, MA	617-888-1557
E-Fex/623 Pennsylvania Ave SE, Washington, DC	202-543-1241
Gold, Judy/40 Sulgrave Rd, Scarsdale, NY	914-723-5036
Maggio, Marlene/Brook Hill Ln Ste 5E, Rochester, NY	716-381-8053
Onesti, Jacqueline/266 Meetinghouse Rd, New Hope, PA	215-862-3503
Rosemary's Cakes Inc/299 Rutland Ave, Teaneck, NJ	201-833-2417
Rothman, Ginger/1915 Lyttonsville Rd, Silver Spring, MD	301-565-2020
Rubin, L A/359 Harvard St #2, Cambridge, MA	617-576-1808

SOUTHEAST

Foodworks/1541 Colonial Ter, Arlington, VA	703-524-2606
Gaffney, Janet D/464 W Wesley N W, Atlanta, GA	404-355-7556
Kupersmith, Tony/320 N Highland Ave NE, Atlanta, GA	404-577-5319
Parker, Julie Hill/PO Box 19033, Jacksonville, FL	904-724-8483
Polvay, Marina Assoc/9250 NE 10th Ct, Miami Shores, FL	305-759-4375
Ramos, Robyn & Harris, Jody/, Orlando, FL	407-896-4028
Reelistic Productions/6467 SW 48th St, Miami, FL	305-284-9989
Stern, Ellen (Food)/13501 S Biscane River Dr, Miami, FL	305-681-0090
Torres, Martha/927 Third St, New Orleans, LA	504-895-6570

MIDWEST

Alan, Jean/1032 W Altgeld, Chicago, IL	312-929-9768
Carlson, Susan/255 Linden Park Pl, Highland Park, IL	312-433-2466
Carter, Karen/3323 N Kenmore, Chicago, IL	312-935-2901
Chevaux Ltd/908 W Armitage, Chicago, IL	312-935-5212
Ellison, Faye/3406 Harriet Ave S, Minneapolis, MN	612-822-7954
Emruh Style Design/714 W Fullerton, Chicago, IL	312-871-4659
Erickson, Emily/2954 No Racine, Chicago, IL	312-281-4899
Heller, Nancy/1142 W Diversey, Chicago, IL	312-549-4486
Lapin, Kathy Santis/925 Spring Hill Dr, Northbrook, IL	312-272-7487
Mary, Wendy/719 W Wrightwood, Chicago, IL	312-871-5476
Pace, Leslie/6342 N Sheridan, Chicago, IL	312-761-2480
Perry, Lee Ann/1615 No Clybourne, Chicago, IL	312-649-1815
Rabert, Bonnie/2230 W Pratt, Chicago, IL	312-743-7755
Sager, Sue/875 N Michigan, Chicago, IL	312-642-3789
Seeker, Christopher/100 E Walton #21D, Chicago, IL	312-944-4311
Shaver, Betsy/3714 N Racine, Chicago, IL	312-327-5615
Style Vasilak and Nebel/314 W Institute Pl, Chicago, IL	312-280-8516
The Set-up & Co/1049 E Michigan St, Indianapolis, IN	317-635-2323
Weber-Mack, Kathleen/2119 Lincoln, Evanston, IL	312-869-7794

SOUTHWEST

Bishop, Cindy/6101 Charlotte, Houston, TX	713-666-7224
Janet-Nelson/PO Box 143, Tempe, AZ	602-968-3771
Riley, Kim Manske/1858 Lexington, Houston, TX	713-529-6104
Taylor, John Michael/2 Dallas Commun Complex, Irving, TX	214-823-1333
Thomas, Jan/5651 East Side Ave, Dallas, TX	214-823-1955

WEST COAST

Akimbo Prod/801 Westbourne, W Hollywood, CA	213-657-4657
Alaimo, Doris/8800 Wonderland Ave, Los Angeles, CA	213-851-7044
Allen, Jamie R/, Los Angeles, CA	213-655-9351
Altbaum, Patti/244-CS Lasky Dr, Beverly Hills, CA	213-553-6269
Azzara, Marilyn/3165 Ellington Drive, Los Angeles, CA	213-851-0531
Castaldi, Debbie/10518 Wilshire Blvd #25, Los Angeles, CA	213-475-4312
Chinamoon/642 S Burnside Ave #6, Los Angeles, CA	213-937-8251
Corwin-Hankin, Aleka/1936 Cerro Gordo, Los Angeles, CA	213-665-7953
Craig, Kenneth/13211 Ventura Blvd, Studio City, CA	818-995-8717
Davis, Rommie/4414 La Venta Dr, West Lake Village, CA	818-906-1455
Design Pool/11936 Darlington Ave #303, Los Angeles, CA	213-826-1551
Evonne/, CA	213-275-1658
Flating, Janice/8113 1/2 Melrose Ave, Los Angeles, CA	213-653-1800
Frank, Tobi/1269 N Hayworth, Los Angeles, CA	213-552-7921
Gaffin, Lauri/1123-12th St, Santa Monica, CA	213-451-2045
Governor, Judy/963 North Point, San Francisco, CA	415-861-5733
Graham, Victory/24 Ave 26, Venice, CA	213-934-0990
Granas, Marilyn/200 N Almont Dr, Beverly Hills, CA	213-278-3773
Griswald, Sandra/963 North Point, San Francisco, CA	415-775-4272
Hamilton, Bryan J/1269 N Hayworth, Los Angeles, CA	213-654-9006
Hewett, Julie/7551 Melrose Ave, Los Angeles, CA	213-651-5172
Hirsch, Lauren/858 Devon, Los Angeles, CA	213-271-7052
HMS/1541 Harvard St #A, Santa Monica, CA	213-828-2080
Howell, Deborah/219 S Martel Ave, Los Angeles, CA	213-655-1263
James, Elizabeth/5320 Bellingham Ave, N Hollywood, CA	213-761-5718
Kimball, Lynnda/133 S Peck Dr, Beverly Hills, CA	213-461-6303
King, Max/308 N Sycamore Ave, Los Angeles, CA	213-938-0108
Lawson, Karen/6836 Lexington Ave, Hollywood, CA	213-464-5770
Lynch, Jody/19130 Pacific Coast Hwy, Malibu, CA	213-456-2383
Material Eyes/501 Pacific Ave, San Francisco, CA	415-362-8143
Miller, Freyda/1412 Warner Ave, Los Angeles, CA	213-474-5034
Minot, Abby/53 Canyon Rd, Berkeley, CA	415-841-9600
Moore, Francie/842 1/2 N Orange Dr, Los Angeles, CA	213-462-5404
Morrow, Suzanne/26333 Silver Spur, Palos Verdes, CA	213-378-2909
Neal, Robin Lynn/3105 Durand, Hollywood, CA	213-465-6037
Olsen, Eileen/1619 N Beverly Dr, Beverly Hills, CA	213-273-4496
Parshall, Mary Ann/19850 Pacific Coast Hwy, Malibu, CA	213-456-8303
Prindle, Judy Peck/6057 Melrose Ave, Los Angeles, CA	213-650-0962
Russo, Leslie/377 10th, Santa Monica, CA	213-395-8461
Shatsy/9008 Harratt St, Hollywood, CA	213-275-2413
Skinner, Jeanette/1622 Moulton Pkwy #A, Tustin, CA	714-730-5793
Skinner, Randy/920 S Wooster St, Los Angeles, CA	213-659-2936
Skuro, Bryna/134-B San Vicente Blvd, Santa Monica, CA	213-394-2430
Sloane, Hilary/6351 Ranchito, Van Nuys, CA	213-855-1010
Stillman, Denise/PO Box 7692, Laguna Niguel, CA	714-496-4841
Surkin, Helen/2100 N Beachwood Dr, Los Angeles, CA	213-464-6847
Thomas, Lisa/9029 Rangely Ave, W Hollywood, CA	213-858-6903
Townsend, Jeanne/433 N Camden Dr, Beverly Hills, CA	213-851-7044
Tucker, Joan/1402 N Fuller St, Los Angeles, CA	213-876-3417

Tyre, Susan/, CA 213-877-3884
Valade/, CA 213-659-7621
Weinberg & James Foodstyle/3888 Woodcliff Rd,
Sherman Oaks, CA 213-274-2383
Weiss, Sheri/2170 N Beverly Glen, Los Angeles, CA....................213-470-1650

COSTUMES

NYC

Academy Clothes Inc/1703 Broadway, ...212-765-1440
AM Costume Wear/135-18 Northern Blvd, Flushing 718-358-8108
Austin Ltd/140 E 55th St, ...212-752-7903
Capezio Dance Theater Shop/755 Seventh Ave, ...212-245-2130
Chenko Studio/167 W 46th St, ...212-944-0215
David's Outfitters Inc/36 W 20th St, ...212-691-7388
Eaves-Brookes Costume/21-07 41st Ave, L I City, ...718-729-1010
G Bank's Theatrical & Custom/320 W 48th St, ...212-586-6476
Grace Costumes Inc/254 W 54th St, ...212-586-0260
Herbert Danceware Co/902 Broadway, ...212-677-7606
Huey, Camilla/145 W 58th St #2C, ...212-459-9716
Ian's Boutique Inc/1151-A Second Ave, ...212-838-3969
Karinska/16 W 61st St, ...212-247-3341
Kulyk/72 E 7th St, ...212-674-0414
Lane Costume Co/234 Fifth Ave, ...212-684-4721
Martin, Alice Manougian/239 E 58th St, ...212-688-0117
Meyer, Jimmy & Co/428 W 44th St, ...212-765-8079
Michael-Jon Costumes Inc/39 W 19th St, ...212-741-3440
Mincou, Christine/405 E 63rd St, ...212-838-3881
Purcell, Elizabeth/105 Sullivan St, ...212-925-1962
Rubie's Costume Co/1 Rubie Plaza, Richmond Hill, ...718-846-1008
Sampler Vintage Clothes/455 W 43rd St, ...212-757-8168
Stivanello Costume Inc/66-38 Clinton Ave, Maspeth, ...718-651-7715
Tint, Francine/1 University Pl, ...212-475-3366
Universal Costume Co Inc/1540 Broadway, ...212-575-8570
Weiss & Mahoney Inc/142 Fifth Ave, ...212-675-1915
Winston, Mary Ellen/11 E 68th St, ...212-879-0766
Ynocencio, Jo/302 E 88th St, ...212-348-5332

NORTHEAST

At-A-Glance Rentals/712 Main, Boonton, NJ 201-335-1488
Baldwin, Katharine/109 Commonwealth Ave, Boston, MA...............617-267-0508
Barris, Alfred Wig Maker/10 E Sirtsink Dr, Pt Washington, NY 516-883-9061
Costume Armour/Shore Rd Box 325, Cornwall on Hudson, NY..........914-534-9120
Douglas, Rodney N/473 Avon Ave #3, Newark, NJ 201-375-2979
House of Costumes Ltd/166 Jericho Tpk, Mineola, NY...............516-294-0170
Penrose Productions/4 Sandalwood Dr, Livingston, NJ 201-992-4264
Strutters/11 Paul Sullivan Way, Boston, MA.......................617-423-9299
Westchester Costume Rental/540 Nepperhan Ave, Yonkers, NY 914-963-1333

SOUTHEAST

ABC Costume/185 NE 59th St, Miami, FL 305-757-3492
Atlantic Costume Co/2089 Monroe Dr, Atlanta, GA..................404-874-7511
Carol, Lee Inc/2145 NW 2nd Ave, Miami, FL 305-573-1759
Fun Stop Shop/1601 Biscyne Blvd Omni Int F27, Miami, FL..........305-358-2003
Goddard, Lynn Prod Svcs/712 Pelican Ave, New Orleans, LA 504-367-0348
Poinciana Sales/2252 W Flagler St, Miami, FL 305-642-3441
Star Styled/475 NW 42nd Ave, Miami, FL...........................305-649-3030

MIDWEST

Advance Theatrical Co/1900 N Narragansett, Chicago, IL...........312-889-7700
Backstage Enterprises/1525 Ellinwood, Des Plaines, IL...........312-692-6159
Be Something Studio/5533 N Forest Glen, Chicago, IL 312-685-6717
Broadway Costumes Inc/932 W Washington, Chicago, IL.............312-829-6400
Brune, Paul/6330 N Indian Rd, Chicago, IL 312-763-1117
Center Stage/Fox Valley Shopping Cntr, Aurora, IL 312-851-9191
Chicago Costume Co Inc/1120 W Fullerton, Chicago, IL 312-528-1264
Ennis, Susan/2961 N Lincoln Ave, Chicago, IL 312-525-7483
Kaufman Costumes/5117 N Western, Chicago, IL 312-561-7529
Magical Mystery Tour, Ltd/6010 Dempster, Morton Grove, IL 312-966-5090
Okains Costume & Theater/2713 W Jefferson, Joliet, IL 815-741-9303
Stechman's Creations/1920 Koehler, Des Plaines, IL 312-827-9045
Taylor, Corinna/1700B W Granville, Chicago, IL...................312-472-6550

The Set-up & Co/1049 E Michigan St, Indianapolis, IN...............317-635-2323
Toy Gallery/1640 N Wells, Chicago, IL.............................312-944-4323

SOUTHWEST

A & J Costume Rental/304 White Oaks Dr, Austin, TX 512-836-2733
ABC Theatrical Rental & Sales/825 N 7th St, Phoenix, AZ..........602-258-5265
Abel, Joyce/Rt 1 Box 165, San Marcos, TX.........................512-392-5659
Campioni, Frederick/1920 Broken Oak, San Antonio, TX............512-342-7780
Corey, Irene/4147 Herschel Ave, Dallas, TX.......................214-528-4836
Incredible Productions/3327 Wylie Dr, Dallas, TX.................214-350-3633
Lucy Greer & Assoc/600 Shadywood Ln, Richardson, TX.............214-231-2086
Moreau, Suzanne/1007-B West 22nd St, Austin, TX 512-477-1532
Nicholson, Christine/c/o Lola Sprouse, Carrollton, TX............214-245-0926
Old Time Teenies Vintage Clothing/1126 W 6th St, Austin, TX........512-477-2022
Second Childhood/900 W 18th St, Austin, TX.......................512-472-9696
Starline Costume Products/1286 Bandera Rd, San Antonio, TX......512-435-3535
Thomas, Joan S/6904 Spanky Branch Court, Dallas, TX..............214-931-1900
Welch, Virginia/3707 Manchaca Rd #138, Austin, TX................512-447-1240

ROCKY MTN

And Sew On-Jila/2017 Broadway, Boulder, CO.......................303-442-0130
Raggedy Ann Costume/1213 E Evans Ave, Denver, CO 303-733-7937

WEST COAST

Aardvark/7579 Melrose Ave, Los Angeles, CA 213-655-6769
Adele's of Hollywood/5059 Hollywood Blvd, Hollywood, CA..........213-663-2231
American Costume Corp/12980 Raymer, N Hollywood, CA..............818-764-2239
Auntie Mame/1102 S La Cienaga Blvd, Los Angeles, CA 213-652-8430
Burbank Studios Wardrobe/4000 Warner Blvd, Burbank, CA 818-954-1218
CA Surplus Mart/6263 Santa Monica Blvd, Los Angeles, CA 213-465-5525
Capezio Dancewear/1777 Vine St, Hollywood, CA 213-465-3744
CBS Wardrobe Dept/7800 Beverly Blvd, Los Angeles, CA............213-852-2345
Courtney, Elizabeth/8636 Melrose Ave, Los Angeles, CA...........213-657-4361
Crystal Palace (Sales)/8457 Melrose Ave, Hollywood, CA..........818-761-1870
Design Studio/6685-7 Sunset Blvd, Hollywood, CA.................213-469-3661
E C 2 Costumes/431 S Fairfax, Los Angeles, CA...................213-934-1131
Fantasy Costume/4310 San Fernando Rd, Glendale, CA..............213-245-7367
International Costume Co/1269 Sartori, Torrance, CA..............213-320-6392
Kings Western Wear/6455 Van Nuys Blvd, Van Nuys, CA.............818-785-2586
Krofft Entertainment/7200 Vineland Ave, Sun Valley, CA..........213-875-0324
LA Uniform Exchange/5239 Melrose Ave, Los Angeles, CA...........213-469-3965
MGM/UA Studios Wardrobe Dept/10202 W Washington Blvd,
Culver City, CA 213-558-5600
Military Antiques & War Museum/208 Santa Monica Ave,
Santa Monica, CA..213-393-1180
Minot, Abby/53 Canyon Rd, Berkeley, CA..........................415-841-9600
Nudies Rodeo Tailor/5015 Lanskershim Blvd, N Hollywood, CA 818-762-3105
Palace Costume/835 N Fairfax, Los Angeles, CA...................213-651-5458
Paramount Studios Wardrobe/5555 Melrose Ave, Hollywood, CA....213-468-5288
Peabodys/1102 1/2 S La Cienaga Blvd, Los Angeles, CA............213-352-3810
Piller's, Jerry/8163 Santa Monica Blvd, Hollywood, CA...........213-654-3038
Tuxedo Center/7360 Sunset Blvd, Los Angeles, CA.................213-874-4200
Valu Shoe Mart/5637 Santa Monica Blvd, Los Angeles, CA..........213-469-8560
Western Costume Co/5335 Melrose Ave, Los Angeles, CA............213-469-1451

PROPS

NYC

Abet Rent-A-Fur/307 Seventh Ave, ...212-989-5757
Abstracta Structures Inc/347 Fifth Ave, ...212-532-3710
Ace Galleries/91 University Pl, ...212-991-4536
Adirondack Direct/219 E 42nd St, ...212-687-8555
Alice's Antiques/552 Columbus Ave, ...212-874-3400
Alpha-Pavia Bookbinding Co Inc/55 W 21st St, ...212-929-5430
Archer Surgical Supplies Inc/544 W 27th St, ...212-695-5553
Artisan's Studio/232 Atlantic Ave, Brooklyn......................718-855-2796
Artistic Neon by Gasper/75-49 61st St, Glendale 718-821-1550
Arts & Crafters/175 Johnson St, Brooklyn 718-875-8151
Arts & Flowers/234 W 56th St, ...212-247-7610
Associated Theatrical Designer/220 W 71st St, ...212-362-2648
Austin Display/139 W 19th St, ...212-924-6261
Baird, Bill Marionettes/41 Union Square, ...212-989-9840

Baker, Alex/30 W 69th St, ...212-799-2069
Bill's Flower Mart/816 Ave of the Americas, ...212-889-8154
Brandon Memorabilia/222 E 51st St, ...212-691-9776
Breitrose, Mark/156 Fifth Ave, ...212-242-7825
Brooklyn Model Works/60 Washington Ave, Brooklyn 718-834-1944
California Artificial Flower Co/225 Fifth Ave, ...212-679-7774
Carroll Musical Instrument Svc/351 W 41st St, ...212-868-4120
Chateau Stables Inc/608 W 48th St, ...212-246-0520
Churchill/Winchester Furn Rental/44 E 32nd St, ...212-535-3400
Constructive Display/142 W 26th St, ...212-675-7320
Cooper Film Cars/132 Perry St, ...212-929-3909
Cycle Service Center Inc/74 Sixth Ave, ...212-925-5900
Doherty Studios/252 W 46th St, ...212-840-6219
Eclectic Properties Inc/204 W 84th St, ...212-799-8963
Encore Studio/410 W 47th St, ...212-246-5237
Florenco Foliage/30-28 Starr Ave, L I C 718-729-6600
Furs, Valerie/150 W 30th St, ...212-947-2020
Golden Equipment Co Inc/422 Madison Ave, ...212-838-3776
Gordon Novelty Co/933 Broadway, ...212-254-8616
Gossard & Assocs Inc/801 E 134th St, Bronx, ...212-665-9194
Gothic Color Co Inc/727 Washington St, ...212-929-7493
Guccione/333 W 39th St, ...212-279-3602
Harra, John Wood & Supply Co/39 W 19th St, 11th Fl, ...212-741-0290
Harrison/Erickson/95 Fifth Ave, ...212-929-5700
Jeffers, Kathy-Modelmaking/106 E 19th St 12th Fl, ...212-475-1756
Joyce, Robert Studio Ltd/321 W 44th St #404, ...212-586-5041
Kaplan, Howard/35 E 10th St, ...212-674-1000
Karpen, Ben/212 E 51st St, ...212-755-3450
Kempler, George J/160 Fifth Ave, ...212-989-1180
Kenmore Furniture Co Inc/156 E 33rd St, ...212-683-1888
Mallie, Dale & Co/35-30 38th St, Astoria 718-706-1234
Manhattan Model Shop/40 Great Jones St, ...212-473-6312
Maniatis, Michael Inc/48 W 22nd St, ...212-620-0398
Manwaring Studio/232 Atlantic Ave, Brooklyn, ...718-855-2796
Marc Modell Associates/430 W 54th St, ...212-541-9676
Mason's Tennis Mart/911 Seventh Ave, ...212-757-5374
Matty's Studio Sales/543 W 35th St, ...212-757-6246
McConnell & Borow Inc/10 E 23rd St, ...212-254-1486
Mendez, Raymond A/220 W 98th St #12B, ...212-864-4689
Messmore & Damon Inc/530 W 28th St, ...212-594-8070
Metro Scenery Studio Inc/215-31 99th Ave, Queens Village, ...718-464-6328
Modern Miltex Corp/280 E 134th St, Bronx, ...212-585-6000
Movie Cars/825 Madison Ave, ...212-288-6000
Nazz, James/159 Second Ave #12, ...212-228-9713
Newell Art Galleries Inc/425 E 53rd St, ...212-758-1970
Nostalgia Alley Antiques/547 W 27th St, ...212-695-6578
Novel Pinball Co/593 Tenth Ave, ...212-736-3868
Plant Specialists Inc/524 W 34th St, ...212-279-1500
Plastic Works!/2107 Broadway @ 73rd, ...212-362-1000
Plexability Ltd/200 Lexington Ave, ...212-679-7826
Porter-Rayvid/155 Attorney, ...212-460-5050
Portobello Road Antiques Ltd/370 Columbus Ave, ...212-724-2300
Props and Displays/132 W 18th St, ...212-620-3840
Props for Today/15 W 20th St, ...212-206-0330
Ray Beauty Supply Co Inc/721 Eighth Ave, ...212-757-0175
Ridge, John Russell/531 Hudson St, ...212-929-3410
Say It In Neon/434 Hudson St, ...212-691-7977
Simon's Dir of Theatrical Mat/27 W 24th St, ...212-255-2872
Smith & Watson/305 E 63rd St, ...212-355-5615
Smith, David/, ...212-730-1188
Solco Plumbing & Baths/209 W 18th St, ...212-243-2569
Special Effects/40 W 39th St, ...212-869-8636
Starbuck Studio - Acrylic props/162 W 21st St, ...212-807-7299
State Supply Equipment Co Inc/68 Thomas St, ...212-233-0474
The Manhattan Model Shop/40 Great Jones St, ...212-473-6312
The Place for Antiques/993 Second Ave, ...212-475-6696
The Prop House Inc/76 Ninth Ave, ...212-691-9099
The Prop Shop/26 College Pl, Brooklyn Heights, ...718-522-4606
Theater Technology Inc/37 W 20th St, ...212-929-5380
Times Square Theatrical & Studio/318 W 47th St, ...212-245-4155
Uncle Sam's Umbrella/161 W 57th St, ...212-582-1976
Whole Art Inc/259 W 30th St, ...212-868-0978
Wizardworks/67 Atlantic Ave, Brooklyn, ...718-349-5252
Zakarian, Robert Prop Shop/26 College Pl, Brooklyn Hts, ...718-522-4606
Zeller, Gary & Assoc/Special Effects/40 W 39th St, ...212-869-8636

N O R T H E A S T

Antique Bicycle Props/113 Woodland Ave, Montvale, NJ...............201-391-8780
Atlas Scenic Studios Ltd/46 Brokfield Ave, Bridgeport, CT 203-334-2130
Baily Designs/110 Williams St, Malden, MA 617-321-4448
Baldwin, Katherine/109 Commonwealth Ave, Boston, MA.............617-267-0508
Bestek Theatrical Productions/218 Hoffman, Babylon, NY 516-225-0707
Cadillac Convertible Owners/, Thiells, NY 914-947-1109
Dewart, Tim Assoc/83 Old Standley St, Beverly, MA.............617-922-9229
Geiger, Ed/12 Church St, Middletown, NJ 201-671-1707
Hart Scenic Studio/35-41 Dempsey Ave, Edgewater, NJ 212-947-7264
L I Auto Museum/Museum Square, South Hampton, NY 516-283-1880
Master & Talent Inc/1139 Foam Place, Far Rockaway, NY........516-239-7719
Model Sonics/272 Ave F, Bayonne, NJ 201-436-6721
Morozko, Bruce/653 Jersey Ave, Jersey City, NJ...............201-798-9269
Newbery, Tomas/Ridge Rd, Glen Cove, NY 516-759-0880
Pennington Inc/72 Edmund St, Edison, NJ 201-985-9090
Rindner, Jack N Assoc/112 Water St, Tinton Falls, NJ.........201-542-3548
Stewart, Chas H Co/6 Clarendon Ave, Sommerville, MA 617-625-2407
Strutters/11 Paul Sullivan Way, Boston, MA....................617-423-9299

S O U T H E A S T

Alderman Company/325 Model Farm Rd, High Point, NC...........919-889-6121
Arawak Marine/PO Box 7362, St Thomas, VI 809-775-1858
Charisma Prod Services/PO Box 19033, Jacksonville, FL 904-724-8483
Crigler, MB/Smooth As Glass/607 Bass St, Nashville, TN 615-254-6061
Dangar, Jack/3640 Ridge Rd, Smyrna, GA 404-434-3640
Dunwright Productions/15281 NE 21st Ave, N Miami Beach, FL......305-944-2464
Enter Space/20 14th St NW, Atlanta, GA........................404-885-1139
Kupersmith, Tony/320 N Highland Ave NE, Atlanta, GA 404-577-5319
Manning, Maureen/1283 Cedar Heights Dr, Stone Mt, GA 404-296-1520
Miller, Lee/Rte 1, Box 98, Lumpkin, GA 912-838-4959
Player, Joanne/3403 Orchard St, Hapeville, GA 404-767-5542
Reelistic Productions/6467 SW 48th St, Miami, FL 305-284-9989
S C Educational TV/2712 Millwood Ave, Columbia, SC 803-758-7284
Smith, Roscoe/15 Baltimore Pl NW, Atlanta, GA 404-252-3540
Sugar Creek Studio Inc/16 Young St, Atlanta, GA 404-522-3270
Sunshine Scenic Studios/1370 4th St, Sarasota, FL 813-366-8848
Winslow, Geoffrey C/1027 North Ave, Atlanta, GA 404-522-1669

M I D W E S T

Advance Theatrical/125 N Wabash, Chicago, IL 312-889-7700
Becker Studios Inc/2824 W Taylor, Chicago, IL 312-722-4040
Bregstone Assoc/440 S Wabash, Chicago, IL 312-939-5130
Cadillac Plastic/1924 N Paulina, Chicago, IL 312-342-9200
Carpenter, Brent Studio/314 W Institute Pl, Chicago, IL 312-787-1774
Center Stage/Fox Valley Shopping Cntr, Aurora, IL 312-851-9191
Chanco Ltd/3131 West Grand Ave, Chicago, IL 312-638-0363
Chicago Scenic Studios Inc/2217 W Belmont Ave, Chicago, IL 312-477-8362
Hartman Furniture & Carpet Co/220 W Kinzie, Chicago, IL 312-664-2800
Hollywood Stage Lighting/5850 N Broadway, Chicago, IL 312-869-3340
House of Drane/410 N Ashland Ave, Chicago, IL 312-829-8686
Merrick Models Ltd/1426 W Fullerton, Chicago, IL 312-281-7787
Okains Costume & Theater/2713 W Jefferson, Joliet, IL 815-741-9303
Scroungers Inc/351 Lyndale Ave S, Minneapolis, MN 612-823-2340
Starr, Steve Studios/2654 N Clark St, Chicago, IL 312-525-6530
Studio Specialties/409 W Huron, Chicago, IL 312-337-5131
The Emporium/1551 N Wells, Chicago, IL 312-337-7126
The Model Shop/415 N State St, Chicago, IL 312-822-9663
The Set-up & Co/1049 E Michigan St, Indianapolis, IN 317-635-2323
White House Studios/9167 Robinson, Kansas City, MO 913-341-8036

S O U T H W E S T

Creative Video Prod/5933 Bellaire Blvd, Houston, TX...........713-661-0478
Desert Wren Designs,/7340 Scottsdale Mall, Scottsdale, AZ 602-941-5056
Doerr, Dean/11321 Greystone, Oklahoma City, OK 405-751-0313
Eats/PO Box 52, Tempe, AZ 602-966-7459
Janet-Nelson/PO Box 143, Tempe, AZ...........................602-968-3771
Marty, Jack/2225 South First, Garland, TX 214-840-8708
Melancon, Joseph Studios/2934 Elm, Dallas, TX 214-742-2982
Riley, Kim Manske/1858 Lexington, Houston, TX 713-529-6104
Southern Importers/4825 San Jacinto, Houston, TX 713-524-8236
Young Film Productions/PO Box 50105, Tucson, AZ..............602-623-5961

W E S T   C O A S T

A & A Special Effects/7021 Havenhurst St, Van Nuys, CA........818-782-6558
Abbe Rents/600 S Normandie, Los Angeles, CA..................213-384-5292
Aldik Artificial Flowers Co/7651 Sepulveda Blvd, Van Nuys, CA 213-988-5970
Allen, Walter Plant Rentals/5500 Melrose Ave, Hollywood, CA.........213-469-3621

Altbaum, Patti/244-CS Lasky Dr, Beverly Hills, CA..............213-553-6269
Anabel's Diversified Srvc/PO Box 532, Pacific Palisades, CA.........213-454-1566
Antiquarian Traders/8483 Melrose Ave, Los Angeles, CA 213-658-6394
Arnelle Sales Co/7926 Beverly Blvd, Los Angeles, CA...............213-930-2900
Asia Plant Rentals/1215 225th St, Torrance, CA 818-775-1811
Astrovision, Inc/7240 Valjean Ave, Van Nuys, CA...................818-989-5222
Backings,20th Cent Fox/10201 W Pico Blvd, Los Angeles, CA.......213-277-0522
Baronian Manufacturing/1865 Farm Bureau Rd, Concord, CA........415-671-7199
Barris Kustom Inc/10811 Riverside Dr, N Hollywood, CA 213-877-2352
Barton Surrey Svc/518 Fairview Ave, Arcadia, CA...................818-447-6693
Bischoff's/449 S San Fernando Blvd, Burbank, CA...................213-843-7561
Boserup House of Canes/1636 Westwood Blvd, L A, CA.............213-474-2577
Brown, Mel Furniture/5840 S Figueroa St, Los Angeles, CA..............213-778-4444
Buccaneer Cruises/Berth 76W-33 Ports O'Call, San Pedro, CA......213-548-1085
Burbank Studios Prop Dept/4000 Warner Blvd, Burbank, CA 818-954-6000
Cinema Float/447 N Newport Blvd, Newport Beach, CA..............714-675-8888
Cinema Mercantile Co/5857 Santa Monica Blvd, Hollywood, CA....213-466-8201
Cinema Props Co/5840 Santa Monica Blvd, Hollywood, CA 213-466-8201
City Lights/404 S Figueroa, Los Angeles, CA 213-680-9876
Colors of the Wind/2900 Main St, Santa Monica, CA...............213-399-8044
Corham Artifical Flowers/11800 Olympic Blvd, Los Angeles, CA....213-479-1166
Custom Neon/3804 Beverly Blvd, Los Angeles, CA 213-386-7945
D'Andrea Glass Etchings/3671 Tacoma Ave, Los Angeles, CA.......213-223-7940
Decorative Paper Productions/1818 W 6th St, Los Angeles, CA 213-484-1080
Deutsch Inc/426 S Robertson Blvd, Los Angeles, CA 213-273-4949
Ellis Mercantile Co/169 N LaBrea Ave, Los Angeles, CA 213-933-7334
Featherock Inc/20219 Bohama St, Chatsworth, CA 818-882-3888
First Street Furniture/1123 N Bronson Ave, Los Angeles, CA 213-462-6306
Flower Fashions/9960 Santa Monica Blvd, Beverly Hills, CA...........213-272-6063
Games Unlimited/8924 Lindblade, Los Angeles, CA.................213-836-8920
Golden West Billiard Sply/21260 Deering Ct, Canoga Pk, CA........213-877-4100
Grand American Fare/3008 Main St, Santa Monica, CA 213-450-4900
Haltzman Office Furniture/1417 S Figueroa, Los Angeles, CA 213-749-7021
Hawaii Design Create/1750 Kalakaua Ave #116, Honolulu, HI........808-235-2262
Hollywood Toys/6562 Hollywood Blvd, Los Angeles, CA.............213-465-3119
House of Props Inc/1117 N Gower St, Hollywood, CA...............213-463-3166
Hume, Alex R/1527 W Magnolia, Burbank, CA 213-849-1614
Independent Studio Svcs/11907 Wicks St, Sun Valley, CA...........213-764-0840
Iwasaki Images/19330 Van Ness Ave, Torrance, CA................213-533-5986
Jackson Shrub Supply/9500 Columbus Ave, Sepulveda, CA.........213-893-6939
Johnson, Ray M Studio/5555 Sunset Blvd, Hollywood, CA...............213-465-4108
Krofft Enterprise/1040 Las Palmas, Hollywood, CA 213-467-3125
Living Interiors/7273 Santa Monica Blvd, Los Angeles, CA..........213-874-7815
Macduff Flying Circus/5527 Saigon St, Lancaster, CA..............805-942-5406
Malibu Florists/21337 Pacific Coast Hwy, Malibu, CA...............213-456-2014
Marvin, Lennie/1105 N Hollywood Way, Burbank, CA...............818-841-5882
McDermott, Kate/1114 S Point View, Los Angeles, CA..............213-935-4101
MGM Studios Prop Dept/10202 W Washington Blvd,
Culver City, CA 213-836-3000
Modelmakers/216 Townsend St, San Francisco, CA................415-495-5111
Mole-Richardson/937 N Sycamore Ave, Hollywood, CA............213-851-0111
Moskatels/733 S San Julian St, Los Angeles, CA 213-627-1631
Motion Picture Marine/616 Venice Blvd, Marina del Rey, CA........213-822-1100
Music Center/5616 Santa Monica Blvd, Hollywood, CA............213-469-8143
Omega Cinema Props/5857 Santa Monica Blvd, L A, CA............213-466-8201
Pacific Palisds Florists/15244 Sunset Blvd, Pacific Palisds,CA.......213-454-0337
Paramount Studios Prop/5555 Melrose Ave, Los Angeles, CA.........213-468-5000
Photo Productions/400 Montgomery St, San Francisco, CA............415-392-5985
Post, Don Studios/8211 Lankershim Blvd, N Hollywood, CA...........818-768-0811
Producers Studio/650 N Bronson Ave, Los Angeles, CA............213-466-7778
Professional Scenery Inc/7311 Radford Ave, N Hollywood, CA.......213-875-1910
Prop City/9336 W Washington, Culver City, CA.....................213-559-7022
Prop Service West/918 N Orange Dr, Los Angeles, CA 213-461-3371
Rent-A-Mink/6738 Sunset Blvd, Hollywood, CA....................213-467-7879
Roschu/6514 Santa Monica Blvd, Hollywood, CA 213-469-2749
Rouzer, Danny Studio/7022 Melrose Ave, Hollywood, CA 213-936-2494
Scale Model Co/4613 W Rosecrans Ave, Los Angeles, CA...........213-679-1436
School Days Equipment Co/973 N Main St, Los Angeles, CA.........213-223-3474
Silvestri Studios/1733 W Cordova St, Los Angeles, CA..............213-735-1481
Snakes/6100 Laurel Canyon Blvd, North Hollywood, CA.............213-985-7777
Special Effects Unlltd/752 N Cahuenga Blvd, Hollywood, CA...........213-466-3361
Spellman Desk Co/6159 Santa Monica Blvd, Hollywood, CA.........213-467-0628
Stage Right/Box 2265, Canyon Country, CA........................805-251-4342
Star Sporting Goods/1645 N Highland Ave, Hollywood, CA..........213-469-3531
Stembridge Gun Rentals/431 Magnolia, Glendale, CA..............818-246-4833
Studio Specialties/3013 Gilroy St, Los Angeles, CA.................213-480-3101
Stunts Unlimited/3518 Cahuenga Blvd W, Los Angeles, CA.........213-874-0050
Surf, Val/4807 Whitsett, N Hollywood, CA 818-769-6977

The Hand Prop Room/5700 Venice Blvd, Los Angeles, CA 213-931-1534
The High Wheelers Inc/109 S Hidalgo, Alhambra, CA...............213-576-8648
The Plantation/38 Arena St, El Segundo, CA........................213-322-7877
Transparent Prod/3410 S Lacienaga Blvd, Los Angeles, CA.........213-938-3821
Tri-Tronex Inc/2921 W Alameda Ave, Burbank, CA..................213-849-6115
Tropizon Plant Rentals/1401 Pebble Vale, Monterey Park, CA........213-269-2010
Western Costume Company/5335 Melrose Ave, Hollywood, CA.....213-469-1451
Wizards Inc/8333 Lahui, Northridge, CA............................818-368-8974

LOCATIONS

NYC

A Perfect Space/PO Box 1669, ...212-941-0262
Act Travel/310 Madison Ave, ...212-697-9550
Ayoub, Jimmy/132 E 16th St, ...212-598-4467
C & C Productions/445 E 80th St, ...212-472-3700
Carmichael-Moore, Bob Inc/PO Box 5, ...212-255-0465
Cinema Galleries/517 W 35th St 1st Fl, ...212-627-1222
Dancerschool/400 Lafayette St, ...212-260-0453
Davidson/Frank Photo-Stylists/209 W 86th St #701, ...212-799-2651
Howell, T J Interiors/301 E 38th St, ...212-532-6267
Juckes, Geoff/295 Bennett Ave, ...212-567-5676
Kopro, Ken/206 E 6th St, ...212-677-1798
Leach, Ed Inc/160 Fifth Ave, ...212-691-3450
Location Connection/31 E 31st St, ...212-684-1888
Location Locators/225 E 63rd St, ...212-832-1866
Loft Locations/50 White St, ...212-966-6408
Marks, Arthur/140 E 40th St, ...212-685-2761
Myriad Communications, Inc/208 W 30th St, ...212-564-4340
NY State Film Commission/230 Park Ave #834, ...212-309-0540
Ruekberg, Brad/3211 Ave I #5H, Brooklyn 718-377-3506
Terrestris/409 E 60th St, ...212-758-8181
The Perfect Place Ltd/182 Amity St, Brooklyn...................718-570-6252
This Must Be The Place/2119 Albermarle Terrace, Brooklyn 718-282-3454
Unger, Captain Howard/80 Beach Rd, Great Neck................718-639-3578
Wolfson, Paula/227 W 10th St, ...212-741-3048

NORTHEAST

C-M Associates/268 New Mark, Rockville, MD 301-340-7070
Cinemagraphics/100 Massachusetts Ave, Boston, MA 617-266-2200
Connecticut State Travel Office/210 Washington St, Hartford, CT 203-566-3383
Cooper Productions/175 Walnut St, Brookline, MA 617-738-7278
Delaware State Travel Service/99 Kings Highway, Dover, DE...........302-736-4254
Dobush, Jim/148 W Mountain, Ridgefield, CT 203-431-3718
E-Fex/623 Pennsylvania Ave SE, Washington, DC.................202-543-1241
Film Services of WV Library Comm/1900 Washington St E,
Charleston, WV..304-348-3977
Florentine Films, Inc/25 Main St, Northampton, MA..............413-584-0816
Forma, Belle/433 Claflin Ave, Mamaroneck, NY..................914-698-2598
Gilmore, Robert Assoc Inc/990 Washington St, Dedham, MA 617-329-6633
Girl/Scout Locations/One Hillside Ave, Port Washington, NY 516-883-8409
Great Locations/97 Windsor Road, Tenafly, NJ 201-567-1455
Hackerman, Nancy Prod Inc/6 East Eager St, Baltimore, MD...........301-685-2727
Hampton Locations/109 Hill Street, South Hampton, NY 516-283-2160
Jurgielewicz, Annie/PO Box 422, Cambridge, MA................617-628-1141
Krause, Janet L/43 Linnaean St #26, Cambridge, MA.............617-492-3223
Lewis, Jay/87 Ripley St, Newton Center, MA.....................617-332-1516
Location Scouting Service/153 Sidney St, Oyster Bay, NY 516-922-1759
Location Services/30 Rockledge Rd, W Redding l, CT..............203-938-3227
Location Unlimited/24 Briarcliff, Tenafly, NJ 201-567-2809
Locations-Productions/, Boston, MA.............................617-423-9793
Maine State Development Office/193 State St, Augusta, ME...........207-289-2656
Maryland Film Commission/45 Talvert, Annapolis, MD 301-269-3577
Mass State Film Bureau/100 Cambridge St, Boston, MA...........617-727-3330
McGlynn, Jack/34 Buffum St, Salem, MA........................617-745-8764
Nassau Farmer's Market/600 Hicksville Rd, Bethpage, NY 516-931-2046
New Hampshire Vacation Travel/PO Box 856, Concord, NH 603-271-2666
NJ State Motion Pic Dev/Gateway One, Newark, NJ 201-648-6279
Nozik, Michael/9 Cutler Ave, Cambridge, MA....................617-783-4315
Pennington Inc/72 Edmund St, Edison, NJ 201-985-9090
Pennsylvania Film Bureau/461 Forum Bldg, Harrisburg, PA 717-787-5333
Penrose Productions/4 Sandalwood Dr, Livingston, NJ 201-992-4264

PhotoSonics/1116 N Hudson St, Arlington, VA.................703-522-1116
Proteus Location/9217 Baltimore Blvd, College Pk, MD 301-441-2928
RenRose Locations, Ltd/4 Sandalwood Dr, Livingston, NJ..............201-992-4264
Rhode Island State Tourist Div/7 Jackson Wlkwy, Providence, RI.....401-277-2601
Strawberries Finders Service/Buck County, Reigelsville, PA.........215-346-8000
Terry, Karen/131 Boxwood Dr, Kings Park, NY.................516-724-3964
The Hermitage/PO Box 4, Yorktown Heights, NY.................914-632-5315
The Location Hunter/16 Iselin Terr, Larchmont, NY.................914-834-2181
Upstate Production/277 Alexander St, Rochester, NY.........716-546-5417
Verange, Joe - Century III/545 Boylston St, Boston, MA.........617-267-9800
Vermont State Travel Division/134 State, Montpelier, VT.........802-828-3236
Washington Public Space Comm/415 12th St, NW Washngtn, DC...202-629-4084

SOUTHEAST
Alabama State Film Comm/340 North Hull St, Montgomery, AL 800-633-5898
Baker, Sherry/1823 Indiana Ave, Atlanta, GA.................404-373-6666
Bruns, Ken & Gayle/7810 SW 48th Court, Miami, FL.........305-666-2928
Charisma Prod Services/PO Box 19033, Jacksonville, FL.........904-724-8483
Dangar, Jack/3640 Ridge Rd, Smyrna, GA.................404-434-3640
Darracott, David/1324 Briarcliff Rd #5, Atlanta, GA.........404-872-0219
Fl State Motion Picture/TV/107 W Gaines St, Tallahassee, FL.........904-487-1100
Georgia State Film Office/PO Box 1776, Atlanta, GA.........404-656-3591
Harris, George/2875 Mabry Lane NE, Atlanta, GA 404-231-0116
Irene Marie/3212 S Federal Hwy, Ft Lauderdale, FL.........305-522-3262
KY Film Comm/Berry Hill Mansion/Louisville, Frankfort, KY 502-564-3456
Kupersmith, Tony/320 N Highland Ave NE, Atlanta, GA.........404-577-5319
Locations Extraordinaire/6794 Giralda Cir, Boca Raton, FL.........305-487-5050
McDonald, Stew/6905 N Coolidge Ave, Tampa, FL.........813-886-3773
Miller, Lee/Rte 1, Box 98, Lumpkin, GA 912-838-4959
Mississippi State Film Commission/PO Box 849, Jackson, MS 601-359-3449
Natchez Film Comm/Liberty Pk Hwy, Hwy 16, Natchez, MS.........601-446-6345
North Carolina Film Comm/430 N Salisbury St, Raleigh, NC 919-733-9900
Player, Joanne/3403 Orchard St, Hapeville, GA 404-767-5542
Reel Wheels/2267 NE 164th St, Miami, FL.................305-947-9304
Rose, Sheila/8218 NW 8th St, Plantation, FL.................305-473-9747
S Florida Location Finders/7621 SW 59th Court, S Miami, FL.........305-445-0739
Tennessee Film Comm/James Polk Off Bldg, Nashville, TN 615-741-3456
TN State Econ & Comm Dev/1007 Andrew Jackson Bldg,
Nashville, TN.................615-741-1888
USVI Film Promotion Office/, St Thomas, VI.................809-774-1331
Virginia Division of Tourism/202 North 9th St, Richmond, VA 804-786-2051

MIDWEST
A-Stock Photo Finder/230 N Michigan #1100, Chicago, IL.................312-645-0611
Illinois State Film Office/100 W Randolph #3-400, Chicago, IL.........312-793-3600
Indiana State Tourism Development/1 N Capital, Indianapolis, IN ...317-232-8860
Iowa State Development Comm/600 E Ct Ave, Des Moines, IA.......515-281-3251
Kansas State Dept-Econ Div/503 Kansas Ave, Topeka, KS.........913-296-3481
Location Services Film & Video/417 S 3rd St, Minneapolis, MN 612-338-3359
Manya Nogg Co/9773 Lafayette Plaza, Omaha, NB.........402-397-8887
Michigan State Travel Bureau/PO Box 30226, Lansing, MI.........517-373-0670
Minnesota State Tourism Division/419 N Robert, St Paul, MN 612-296-5029
MO State Tourism Comm/301 W High St, Jefferson City, MO.........314-751-3051
ND State Business & Industrial/Liberty Memorial Bldg,
Bismarck, ND.................701-224-2810
Ohio Film Bureau/30 E Broad St, Columbus, OH 614-466-2284
Stock Market/4211 Flora Place, St Louis, MO 314-773-2298

SOUTHWEST
Alamo Village/PO Box 528, Brackettville, TX.................512-563-2580
Arizona Land Co/PO Box 63441, Phoenix, AZ.................602-956-5552
Arkansas State Dept of Eco/#1 Capital Mall, Little Rock, AR.........501-371-1121
Blair, Tanya Agency/3000 Carlisle, Dallas, TX.................214-748-8353
Cinema America/Box 56566, Houston, TX.................713-780-8819
Dawson, Kim Agency/PO Box 585060, Dallas, TX.................214-638-2414
Duncan, S Wade/PO Box 140273, Dallas, TX 214-828-1367
El Paso Film Liaison/5 Civic Center Plaza, El Paso, TX.................915-544-3650
Epic Film Productions/1203 W 44th St, Austin, TX.................512-452-9461
Fashion Consultants/262 Camelot Center, Richardson, TX.........214-234-4006
Flach, Bob/3513 Norma, Garland, TX.................214-272-8431
Fowlkes, Rebecca W/412 Canterbury Hill, San Antonio, TX.........512-826-4142
Grapevine Productions/3214-A Hemlock Avenue, Austin, TX.........512-472-0894
Greenblatt, Linda/6722 Waggoner, Dallas, TX.................214-691-6552
Griffin, Gary Productions/12667 Memorial Dr #4, Houston, TX.........713-465-9017
Kessel, Mark/3631 Granada, Dallas, TX.................214-526-0415
MacLean, John/10017 Woodgrove, Dallas, TX.................214-343-0181
Maloy, Buz/Rt 1 Box 155, Kyle, TX.................512-398-3148
Maloy, John W/718 W 35th St, Austin, TX.................512-453-9660

McLaughlin, Ed M/3512 Rashti Court, Ft Worth, TX.................817-927-2310
Murray Getz Commer & Indust/2310 Genessee, Houston, TX.........713-526-4451
Nichols, & Richardson/6043 Vanderbilt Ave, Dallas, TX.................214-349-3171
OK State Tourism-Rec Dept/500 Will Rogers Bldg,
Oklahoma City, OK.................405-521-3981
Oklahoma Film Comm/500 Will Rogers Bldg, Okla City, OK.........405-521-3525
Putman, Eva M/202 Dover, Richardson, TX.................214-783-9616
Ranchland - Circle R/Rt 3, Box 229, Roanoke, TX.................817-430-1561
Ray, Al/2304 Houston Street, San Angelo, TX.................915-949-2716
Ray, Rudolph/2231 Freeland Avenue, San Angelo, TX.................915-949-6784
Reinninger, Laurence H/501 North IH 35, Austin, TX.................512-478-8593
San Antonio Zoo & Aquar/3903 N St Marys, San Antonio, TX.........512-734-7184
Senn, Loyd C/PO Box 6060, Lubbock, TX 806-792-2000
Summers, Judy/1504 Harvard, Houston, TX.................713-661-1440
Taylor, Peggy/6311 N O'Connor 3 Dallas Comm, Irving, TX.........214-869-1515
TBK Talent Enterprises/5255 McCullough, San Antonio, TX.........512-822-0508
Texas Film Comm/PO Box 12428 Capitol Station, Austin, TX.........512-475-3785
Texas Pacific Film Video, Inc/501 North IH 35, Austin, TX.........512-478-8585
Texas World Entrtnmnt/8133 Chadbourne Road, Dallas, TX.........214-358-0857
Tucson Film Comm/Ofc of Mayor Box 27370, Tucson, AZ.........602-791-4000
Wild West Stunt Company/Box T-789, Stephenville, TX.........817-965-4342
Young Film Productions/PO Box 50105, Tucson, AZ.................602-623-5961
Zimmerman & Associates, Inc/411 Bonham, San Antonio, TX.........512-225-6708
Zuniga, Tony/2616 North Flores #2, San Antonio, TX.................512-227-9660

ROCKY MTN
Montana Film Office/1424 Ninth Ave, Helena, MT.................406-449-2654
Wyoming Film Comm/IH 25 & College Dr #51, Cheyenne, WY 307-777-7851

WEST COAST
California Film Office/6922 Hollywood Blvd, Hollywood, CA 213-736-2465
Daniels, Karil,/2477 Folsom St, San Francisco, CA.................415-821-0435
Design Art Studios/1128 N Las Palmas, Hollywood, CA.................213-464-9118
Excor Travel/1750 Kalakaua Ave #116, Honolulu, HI.................808-946-6614
Film Permits Unlimited/8058 Allott Ave, Van Nuys, CA.................213-997-6197
Herod, Thomas Jr/PO Box 2534, Hollywood, CA.................213-353-0911
Juckes, Geoff/3185 Durand Dr, Hollywood, CA.................213-465-6604
Location Enterprises Inc/6725 Sunset Blvd, Los Angeles, CA 213-469-3141
Mindseye/767 Northpoint, San Francisco, CA.................415-441-4578
Minot, Abby/53 Canyon Rd, Berkeley, CA.................415-841-9600
Newhall Ranch/23823 Valencia, Valencia, CA.................818-362-1515
Pacific Production & Location Svc/424 Nahua St, Honolulu, HI.........808-926-6188
S F Conv/Visitors Bur/1390 Market St #260, San Francisco, CA.......415-626-5500
The Location Co/8646 Wilshire Blvd, Beverly Hills. CA.................213-855-7075

SETS

NYC
Abstracta Structures/347 Fifth Ave,.................212-532-3710
Alcamo Marble Works/541 W 22nd St,.................212-255-5224
Baker, Alex/30 W 69th St,.................212-799-2069
Coulson, Len/717 Lexington Ave,.................212-688-5155
Dynamic Interiors/760 McDonald Ave, Brooklyn,.................718-435-6326
Golden Office Interiors/574 Fifth Ave, ...212-719-5150
LaFerla, Sandro/108 W 25th St,.................212-620-0693
Lincoln Scenic Studio/560 W 34th St,.................212-244-2700
Nelson, Jane/21 Howard St,.................212-431-4642
Oliphant, Sarah/38 Cooper Square,.................212-741-1233
Plexability Ltd/200 Lexington Ave,.................212-679-7826
Set Shop/3 W 20 St,.................212-929-4845
Siciliano, Frank/125 Fifth Ave,.................212-620-4075
Stage Scenery/155 Attorney St,.................212-460-5050
Theater Technology Inc/37 W 20th St,.................212-929-5380
Unique Surfaces/28 W 27th St,.................212-696-9229
Variety Scenic Studio/25-19 Borden Ave, L I C.................718-392-4747
Yurkiw, Mark/568 Broadway,.................212-243-0928

NORTHEAST
Davidson, Peter/144 Moody St, Waltham, MA.................617-899-3239
Foothills Theater Company/PO Box 236, Worcester, MA 617-754-0546
Morozko, Bruce/653 Jersey Ave, Jersey City, NJ.................201-798-9269
Penrose Productions/4 Sandalwood Dr, Livingston, NJ.................201-992-4264

The Focarino Studio/31 Deep Six Dr, East Hampton, NY 516-324-7637
Trapp, Patricia/42 Stanton Rd, Brookline, MA 617-734-9321
Videocom, Inc/502 Sprague St, Dedham, MA 617-329-4080
White Oak Design/PO Box 1164, Marblehead, MA.........................617-426-7171

S O U T H E A S T

Crigler, MB/607 Bass St, Nashville, TN 615-254-6061
Enter Space/20 14th St NW, Atlanta, GA...404-885-1139
Great Southern Stage/15221 NE 21 Ave, N Miami Beach, FL 305-947-0430
Kupersmith, Tony/320 N Highland Ave NE, Atlanta, GA 404-577-5319
Sugar Creek Scenic Studio, Inc/465 Bishop St, Atlanta, GA............404-351-9404

M I D W E S T

Backdrop Solution/311 N Desplaines Ave #607, Chicago, IL...........312-993-0494
Becker Studio/2824 W Taylor, Chicago, IL 312-722-4040
Centerwood Cabinets/3700 Main St NE, Blaine, MN 612-786-2094
Chicago Scenic Studios Inc/213 N Morgan, Chicago, IL 312-942-1483
Dimension Works/4130 W Belmont, Chicago, IL................................312-545-2233
Douglas Design/2165 Lakeside Ave, Cleveland, OH.........................216-621-2558
Grand Stage Lighting Co/630 W Lake, Chicago, IL..........................312-332-5611
Morrison, Tamara/1225 Morse, Chicago, IL 312-864-0954
The Set-up & Co/1049 E Michigan St, Indianapolis, IN....................317-635-2323

S O U T H W E S T

Country Roads/701 Ave B, Del Rio, TX 512-775-7991
Crabb, Ken/3066 Ponder Pl, Dallas, TX 214-352-0581
Dallas Stage Lighting & Equipment/1818 Chestnut, Dallas, TX........214-428-1818
Dallas Stage Scenery Co, Inc/3917 Willow St, Dallas, TX................214-821-0002
Dunn, Glenn E/7412 Sherwood Rd, Austin, TX 512-441-0377
Edleson, Louis/6568 Lake Circle, Dallas, TX.....................................214-823-7180
Eschberger, Jerry/6401 South Meadows, Austin, TX 512-447-4795
Freeman Design & Display Co/2233 Irving Blvd, Dallas, TX.............214-638-8800
H & H Special Effects/2919 Chisholm Trail, San Antonio, TX 512-826-8214
Houston Stage Equipment/2301 Dumble, Houston, TX 713-926-4441
Reed, Bill Decorations/333 First Ave, Dallas, TX...............................214-823-3154
Texas Scenic Co Inc/5423 Jackwood Dr, San Antonio, TX 512-684-0091
Texas Set Design/3103 Oak Lane, Dallas, TX 214-426-5511

R O C K Y   M T N

Love, Elisa/1035 Walnut, Boulder, CO...303-442-4877

W E S T   C O A S T

Act Design & Execution/PO Box 5054, Sherman Oaks, CA.............818-788-4219
American Scenery/18555 Eddy St, Northridge, CA 818-886-1585
Backings, J C/10201 W Pico Blvd, Los Angeles, CA.......................213-277-0522
Carthay Set Services/5176 Santa Monica Blvd, Hollywood, CA 213-469-5618
Carthay Studio/5907 W Pico, Los Angeles, CA................................213-938-2101
CBS Special Effects/7800 Beverly Blvd, Los Angeles, CA 213-852-2345
Cloutier Inc/704 N Gardner, Los Angeles, CA..................................213-655-1263
Erecter Set Inc/1150 S LaBrea, Hollywood, CA 213-938-4762
Grosh, R L & Sons/4144 Sunset Blvd, Los Angeles, CA.................213-662-1134
Grosh, RL & Sons/4144 Sunset Blvd, Los Angeles, CA..................213-662-1134
Hawaii Design Create/1750 Kalakaua Ave #116, Honolulu, HI........808-235-2262
Hollywood Scenery/6605 Elenor Ave, Hollywood, CA 213-467-6272
Hollywood Stage/6650 Santa Monica Blvd, Los Angeles, CA 213-466-4393
Krofft Entrprs/1040 Las Palmas, Hollywood, CA 213-467-3125
Pacific Studios/8315 Melrose Ave, Los Angeles, CA.......................213-653-3093
Producers Studio/650 N Bronson Ave, Los Angeles, CA.................213-466-3111
RJ Show Time/1011 Gower St, Hollywood, CA 213-467-2127
Shafton Inc/5500 Cleon Ave, N Hollywood, CA...............................818-985-5025